*Fashion Drive.*
*Extreme Clothing in the Visual Arts*

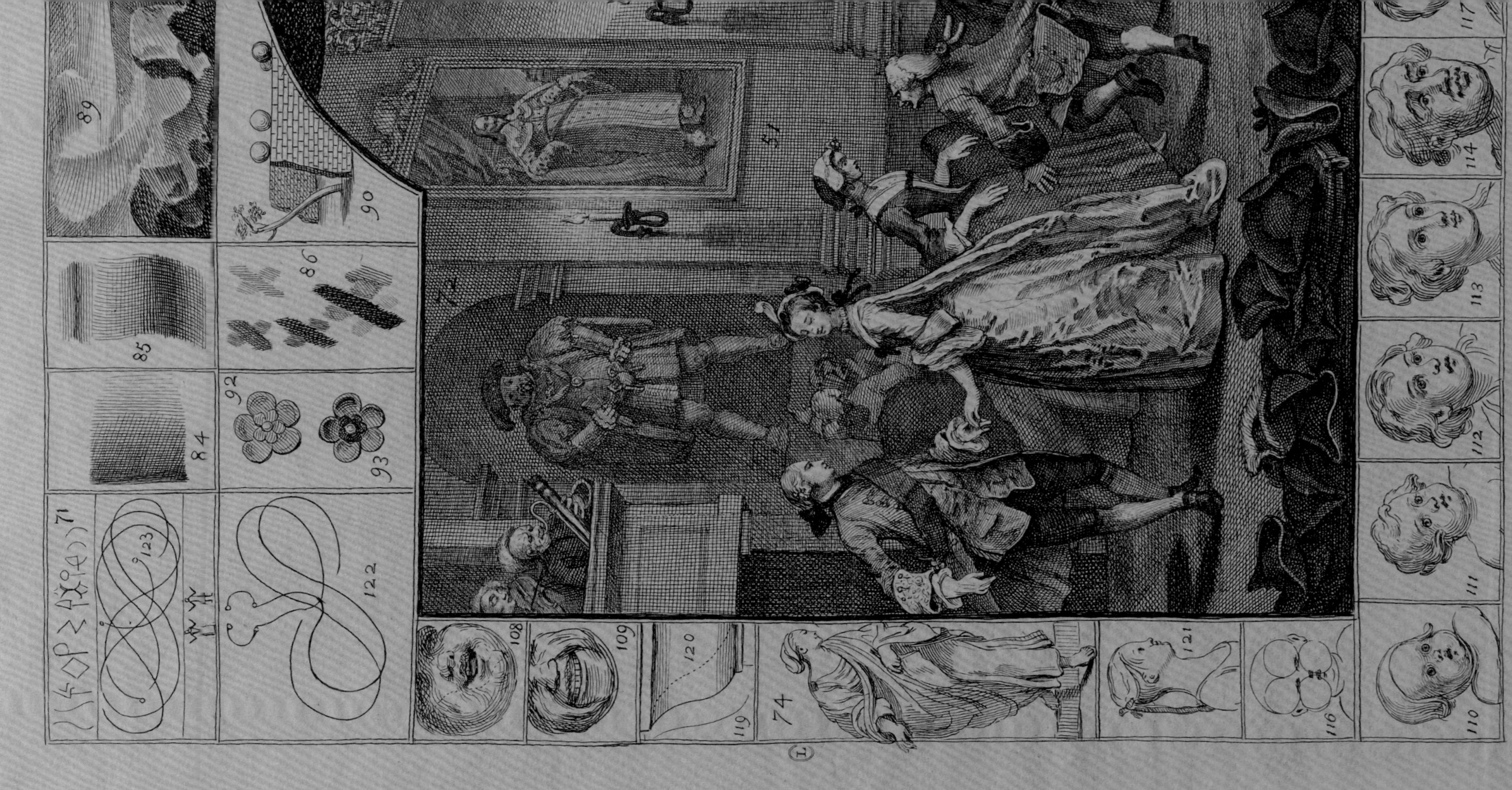

178 William Hogarth (1697–1764)
*The dance*, sheet 2 from the series *The Analysis of Beauty*, March 1753
Etching and copper engraving, sheet: 47.9 × 64.4 cm
Kunsthaus Zürich,
Department of Prints and Drawings

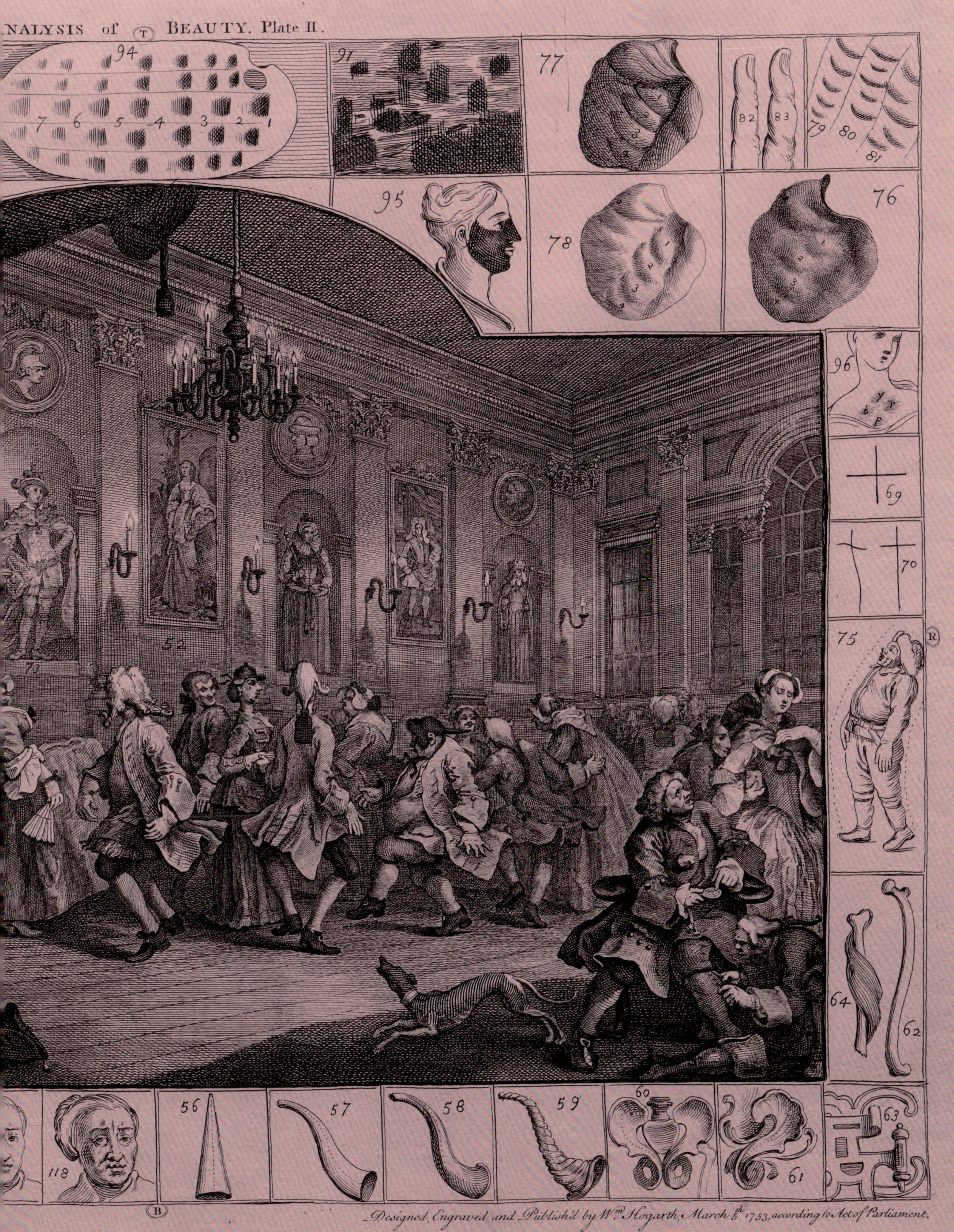

ANALYSIS of BEAUTY. Plate II.
Designed, Engraved, and Publish'd by Wm. Hogarth, March 5th 1753, according to Act of Parliament.

# *Fashion Drive.*

## *Extreme in the*


***Cathérine Hug and Christoph Becker***

*Sonja Eismann / Nora Gomringer / Janine Jakob / Elfriede Jelinek*
*Monica Kurzel-Runtscheiner / Inessa Kouteinikova*
*Peter McNeil / Aileen Ribeiro / Franz Schuh / Werner Telesko*
*Katharina Tietze / Barbara Vinken / Philipp Zitzlsperger*

# *Clothing Visual Arts*

KERBER CULTURE

*Kunsthaus Zürich*

### Catalogue

#### Slashes and Codpieces during the Renaissance



#### Pleats during the Baroque Era



#### Rococo and Revolution



#### First French Empire and Congress of Vienna

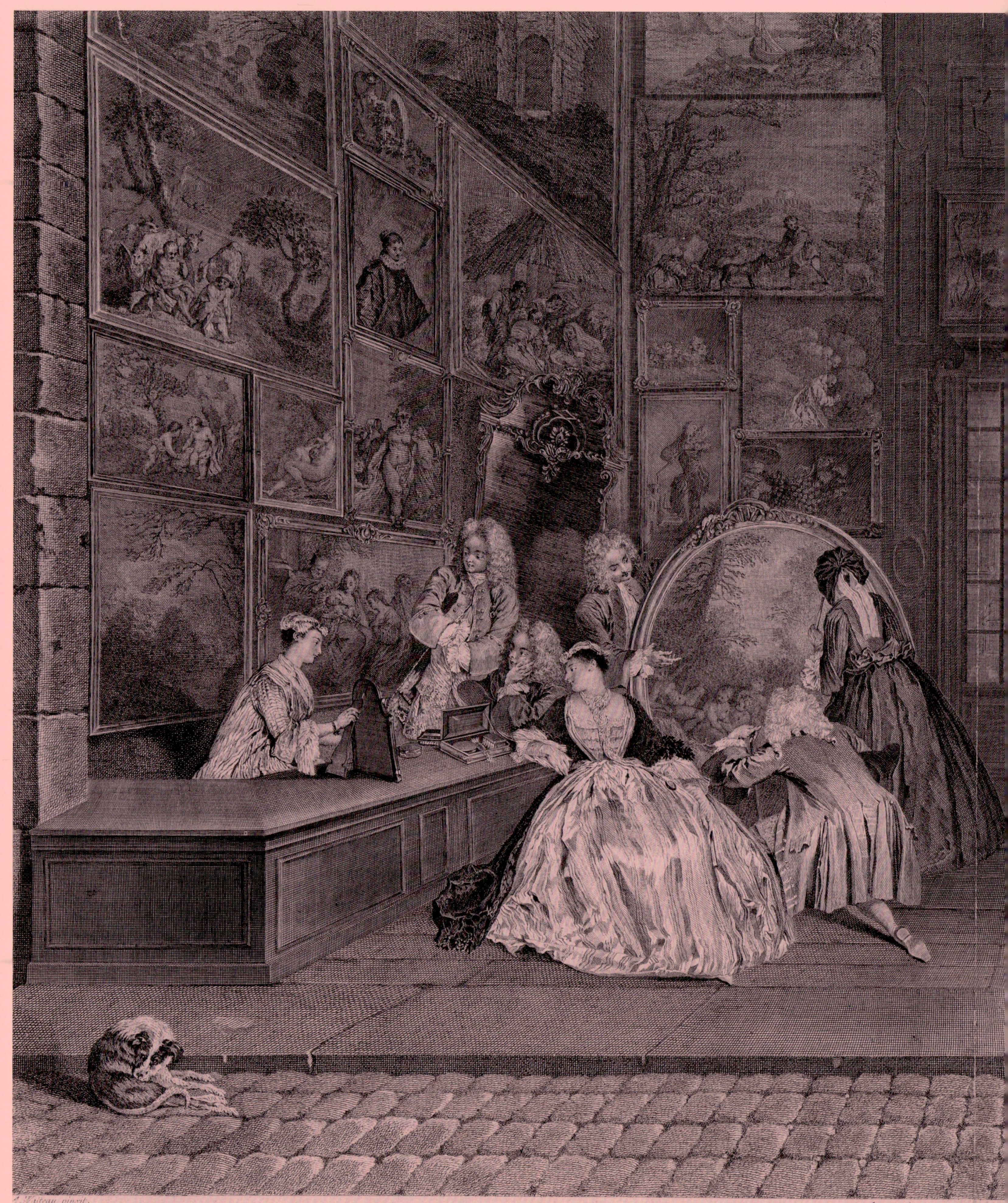


A. Watteau pinxit.
Watteau, dans cette enseigne, à la fleur de ses ans,
Des Maistres de son Art Imite la maniere ;
Leurs caracteres differens,
Leurs touches et leur goût Composent la matiere
L'ENSEIG
Gravée d'apres le Tableau en Plat-fond peint par Wat
sur le Pont Nôtre Dame. haut de 5. pieds sur 9.
dans le Cabinet de M.r De

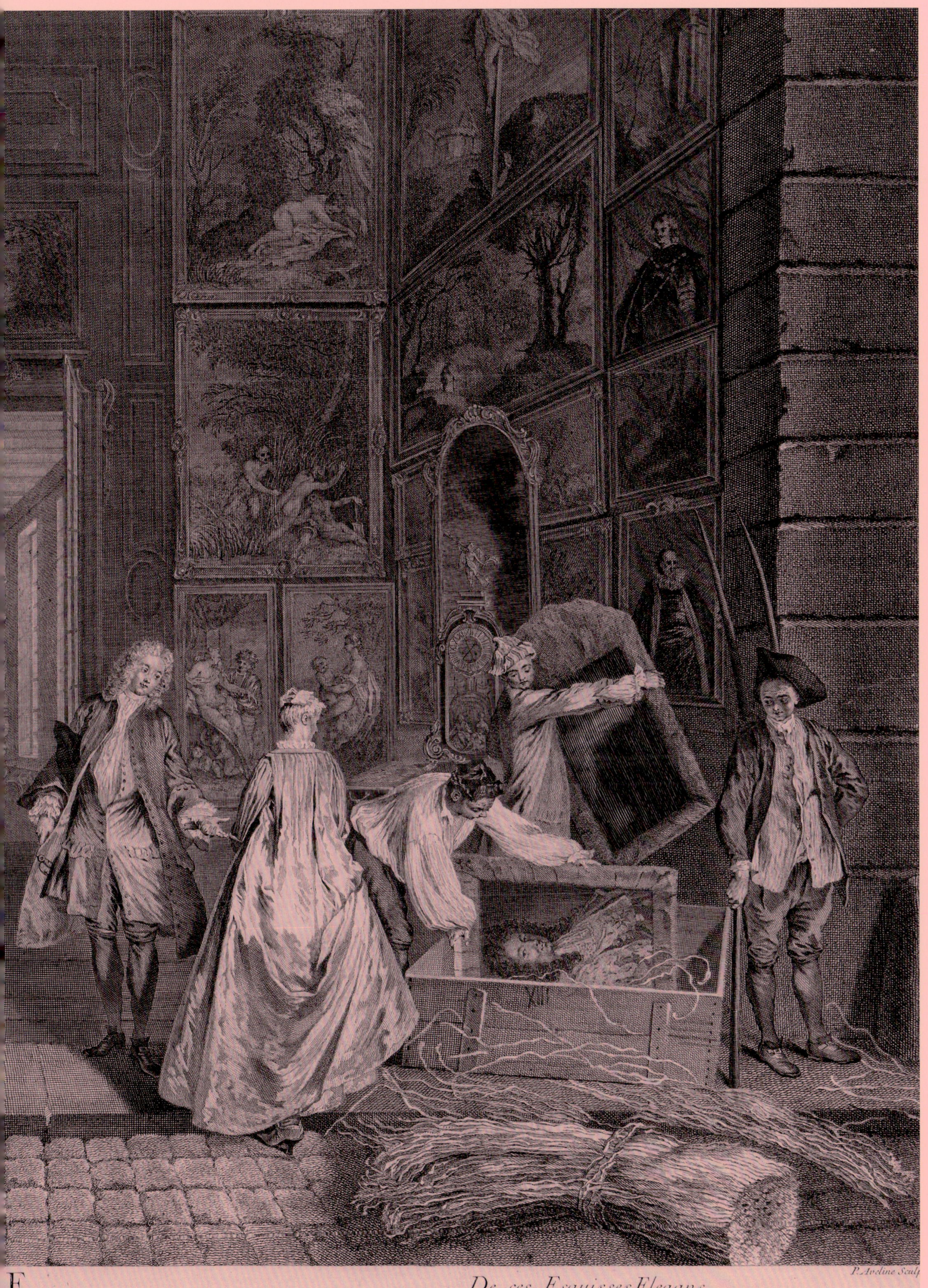


**298** after Jean-Antoine Watteau (1684–1721)
Pierre-Alexandre Aveline (1702–1760), etcher
Marguerite Chéreau, publisher
*L'Enseigne*, 1732
Etching and etching needle, sheet: 57.2 × 84.3 cm
Ville de Genève, Musées d'art et d'histoire

*We would like to thank the lenders for their generous support of our exhibition:*

Gewerbemuseum Basel, Museum für Gestaltung
HMB – Historisches Museum Basel
Spielzeug Welten Museum Basel
Stampa Galerie, Basel
KOW, Berlin
Staatliche Museen zu Berlin, Nationalgalerie
Staatliche Museen zu Berlin, Gemäldegalerie
Staatliche Museen zu Berlin, Kunstbibliothek
Biagiotti Cigna Foundation
Collection Udo and Anette Brandhorst
Museum of Fine Arts, Szépművészeti Múzeum, Budapest
Feldbusch Wiesner Rudolph Galerie
Ville de Genève, Musées d'art et d'histoire
Musei di strada nuova, Genua
Collection of Kim Jones
Martin Kamer
Collection Kamer-Ruf
Staatliche Kunsthalle Karlsruhe
Kaskanian, Vartanian GbR
Hessische Hausstiftung, Kronberg im Taunus
Young Kim, Estate of Malcolm McLaren
Collection Ph. Konzett, Vienna
Le Havre, Musée d'art moderne André Malraux
English Heritage, The Iveagh Bequest (Kenwood, London)
The National Gallery, London
National Portrait Gallery, London
Tate, London
Victoria and Albert Museum, London
Matthew Marks Gallery
Musée d'Arts de Nantes
Marian Goodman Gallery, New York
Oehmen Collection
Musée des Arts décoratifs, Paris
Paris, Musée du Louvre
Paris, Musée d'Orsay
Collection Pictet
Rennes, Musée des beaux-arts
Galleria Continua, San Gimignano/Bejing/Les Moulins/Habana
Collection Nicola von Senger, Switzerland
Liechtenstein. The Princely Collections, Vaduz–Vienna
Établissement public du château, du musée et du domaine national de Versailles
Paintings Gallery, Academy of Fine Arts Vienna
KHM-Museumsverband, Gemäldegalerie, Vienna
KHM-Museumsverband, Hofjagd- und Rüstkammer, Vienna
KHM-Museumsverband, Kaiserliche Wagenburg, Monturdepot, Vienna
Vienna, Österreichische Nationalbibliothek, Picture Archives and Graphics Department
Vienna, Österreichische Nationalbibliothek, Map Department and Globe Museum
Wien Museum
Hahnloser/Jaeggli-Stiftung, Winterthur
Karma International, Zurich and Los Angeles
Galerie Peter Kilchmann, Zurich
Galerie Francesca Pia, Zurich
Schweizerisches Nationalmuseum, Zurich
Galerie Gregor Staiger, Zurich
Zürcher Hochschule der Künste ZHdK, Medien- und Informationszentrum
Zürcher Hochschule der Künste ZHdK, Museum für Gestaltung Zürich, Grafiksammlung

Numerous private collections in Switzerland and abroad

*We would sincerely like to thank our sponsors for making this exhibition possible:*

Main sponsor:
Zürcherische Seidenindustrie-Gesellschaft

Further sponsors:
Swiss Re, Partner für zeitgenössische Kunst

We also thank
the Roswitha Haftmann Foundation, Zurich
and the Bundeskanzleramt für Kunst und Kultur, Vienna

A cooperation with the Festspiele Zürich



Acknowledgements

*We are particularly grateful to the following persons who contributed to the success of the exhibition:*

Larry Abrahamson, Tel Aviv
Patrizia Baldi and Barbara Junod, Museum für Gestaltung Zürich, Zurich
Katja Borlein and Martha Gutschi, Studio Erwin Wurm
Thomas Boyd-Bowman, Benjamin Doller, Andrea Jungmann, Sotheby's London, New York, Vienna
Martin A. Bühler, Basel
Bénédicte Burrus, Galerie Thaddaeus Ropac, Paris
Laurence des Cars and Claire Bernardi, Musée d'Orsay, Paris
Karolina Dankow and Marina Olson, Karma International, Zurich and Los Angeles
Mathieu da Vinha, Centre de recherche du Château de Versailles, Versailles
Christoph Doswald, Zurich
Alexander Eiling, Staatliche Kunsthalle Karlsruhe
Florence Evans, The Weiss Gallery, London
Lorenzo Fiaschi, Galleria Continua, San Gimignano/Bejing/Les Moulins/Habana
Monica Germann and Daniel Lorenzi, Zurich
Sandra Gianfreda, Kunsthaus Zürich
Karen van Godtsenhoven, Modemuseum Provincie Antwerpen, Antwerp
Leo Haidar, Paris
Annette Haudiquet and Clémence Ducroix, Le Havre, Musée d'art moderne André Malraux
Elisabeth Hipp, Bayerische Staatsgemäldesammlungen, Alte Pinakothek, Munich
Claudine Hug, Montreal
Kazu Huggler, Zurich
Batsheva Ida-Goldman, Tel Aviv Museum
Joya Indermühle, Schweizerisches Nationalmuseum, Zurich
Kathryn Johnson, Rachel Murphy and Liz Wilkinson, Victoria and Albert Museum, London
Katrin Käding, loans, Staatliche Museen zu Berlin, Kunstbibliothek
Romuald Karmakar, Berlin
Jerzy J. Kierkuc-Bielinsky, English Heritage, The Iveagh Bequest (Kenwood, London)
Emily-Jane Kirwan, Marian Goodman Gallery, New York
Alexander Klee, Österreichische Galerie Belvedere, Vienna
Carlo Knoell, Basel
Mario Kramer, MMK Museum für Moderne Kunst, Frankfurt am Main
Stefan Krause, Kunsthistorisches Museum Wien, Vienna
Frédéric Lacaille, Musée national des châteaux de Versailles et de Trianon
Pierre Leguillon, Brussels
Michèle Lorin, France
Benjamin Lindbergh, Paris
Hélène Mariéthoz, Geneva
Corinna Matter, Zurich
Karl McCool, Electronic Arts Intermix, New York
Robert Menasse, Vienna
Sigrid Mittersteiner, Kunsthalle Wien, Vienna
Yandi Morgado Martinez, Montreal
Sacha Nacinovic, Zurich
Véronique Nichanian, Paris
Raphael Oberhuber, Berlin
Dragos and Erika Olea, Apparatus 22, Bucharest
Loredana Pessa, Museo di Strada Nuova, Genoa
Katia Poletti, Fondation Félix Vallotton, Lausanne
Marlene Poeckh, central registrar, KHM-Museumsverband, Vienna
Adelheid Rasche, Germanisches Nationalmuseum, Nuremberg
Csilla Regős, Museum of Fine Arts/Szépművészeti Múzeum, Budapest
Isabel Reiss, Zurich
Christian Rümelin, Ville de Genève, Musées d'art et d'histoire
Anita Rufer, Zurich
Michelle Sapori
Gesa Schneider, Literaturhaus Zürich, Zurich
Michaela Reichel, Thessy Schönholzer Nichols and Barbara Karl, Textilmuseum, St. Gall
Michael Schweller, Fürstliche Sammlungen Art Service GmbH & Co OG, Vienna
Laura Sinanovitch, Spielzeug Welten Museum Basel
Erik Steinbrecher, Berlin
Angela Stief, Vienna
Alain Tarica, Geneva
Ilya Umanskiy
Barbara Vernocchi, Biagiotti Cigna Foundation
Filippo Weck und Lenz Zimmermann, Galerie Buchholz, Berlin and Cologne
Stefan Weppelmann, Kunsthistorisches Museum Wien, Vienna
Lisa Wenger, Carona
Nives Widauer, Vienna
Sarah Wilson, The Courtauld Institute, London
Kelso Wyeth, Gagosian Gallery, London
Peter Zarth, Dusseldorf
Mara Züst, Zurich
Stefan Zweifel, Zurich



---

Acknowledgements

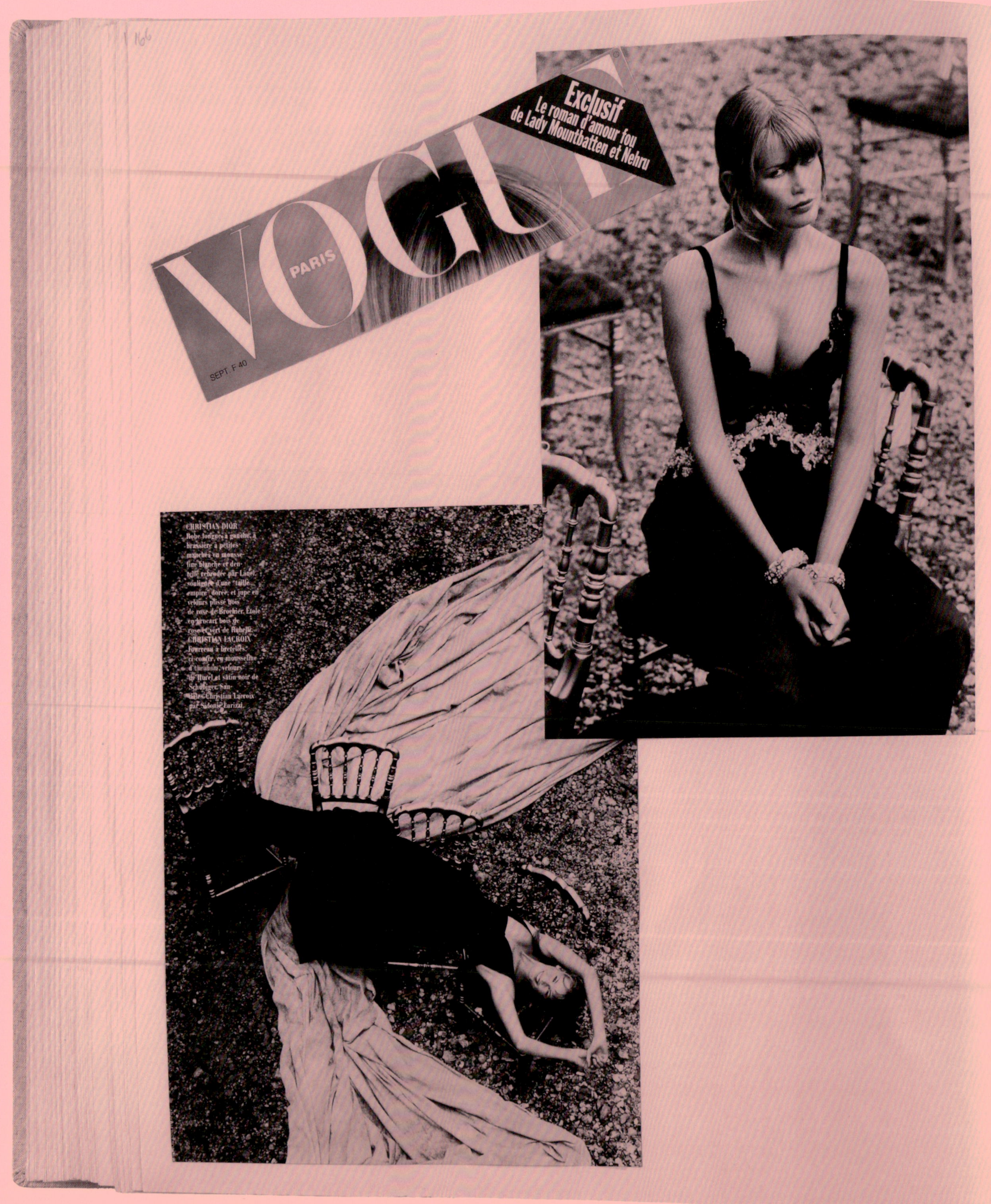


**32** Abraham AG (1941–2002)
Scrapbook, 1991–1996
Collected press cuttings about topics related to the Abraham company
from autumn 1991 to winter 1995/96
231 pages; paper, hardcover, pasted, binding: linen, 51 × 43 × 6.5 cm
Schweizerisches Nationalmuseum, Zurich

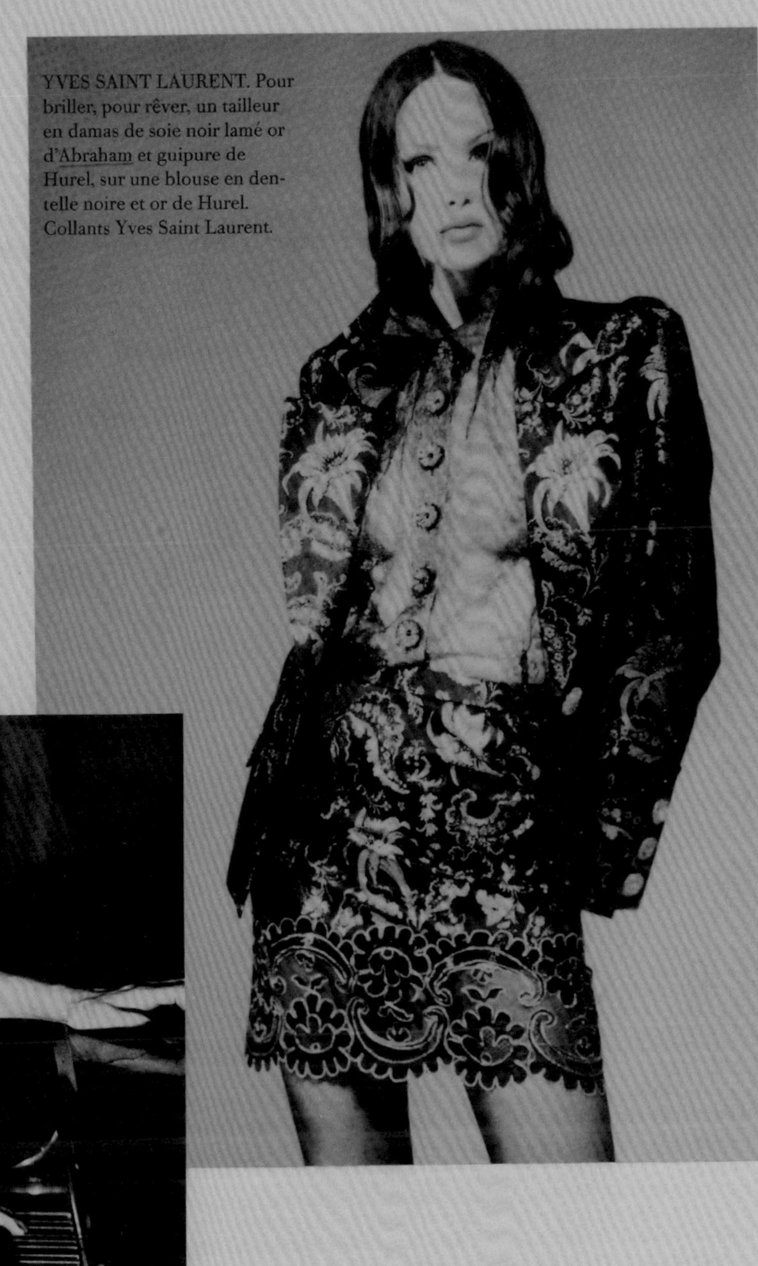

YVES SAINT LAURENT. Pour briller, pour rêver, un tailleur en damas de soie noir lamé or d'Abraham et guipure de Hurel, sur une blouse en dentelle noire et or de Hurel. Collants Yves Saint Laurent.

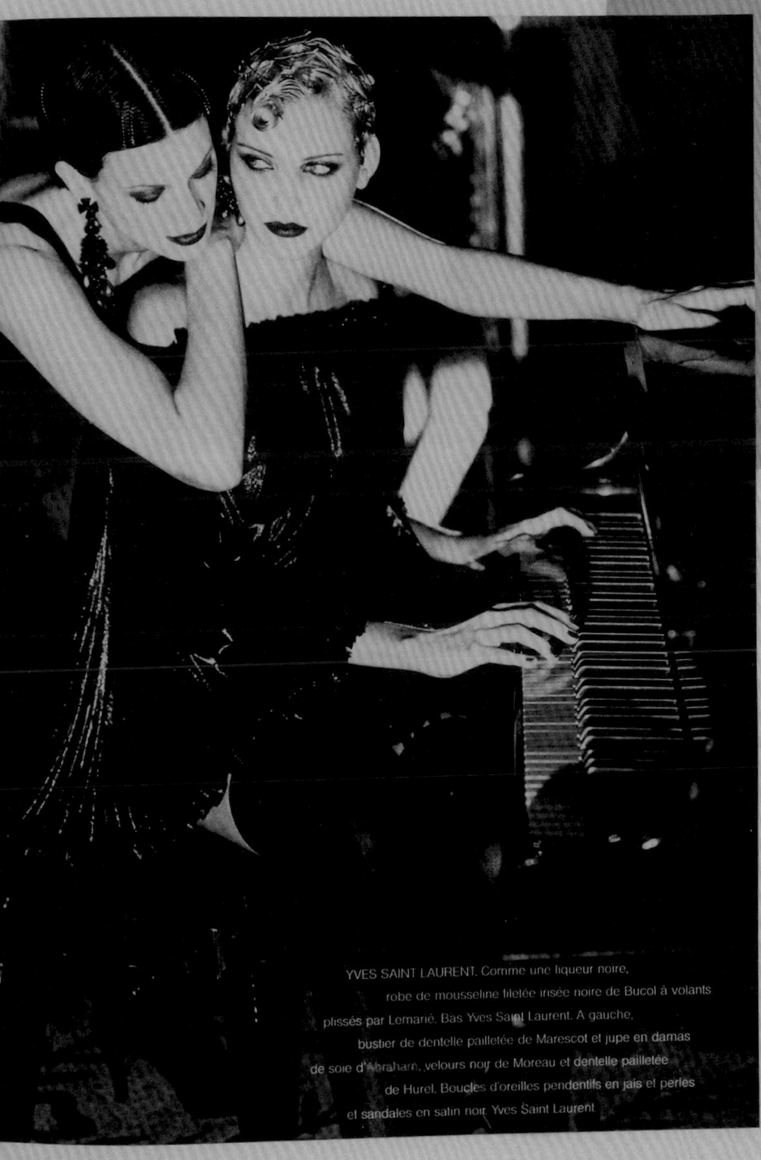

YVES SAINT LAURENT. Comme une liqueur noire, robe de mousseline filetée insée noire de Bucol à volants plissés par Lemarié. Bas Yves Saint Laurent. A gauche, bustier de dentelle pailletée de Marescot et jupe en damas de soie d'Abraham, velours noy de Moreau et dentelle pailletée de Hurel. Boucles d'oreilles pendentifs en jais et perles et sandales en satin noir Yves Saint Laurent.

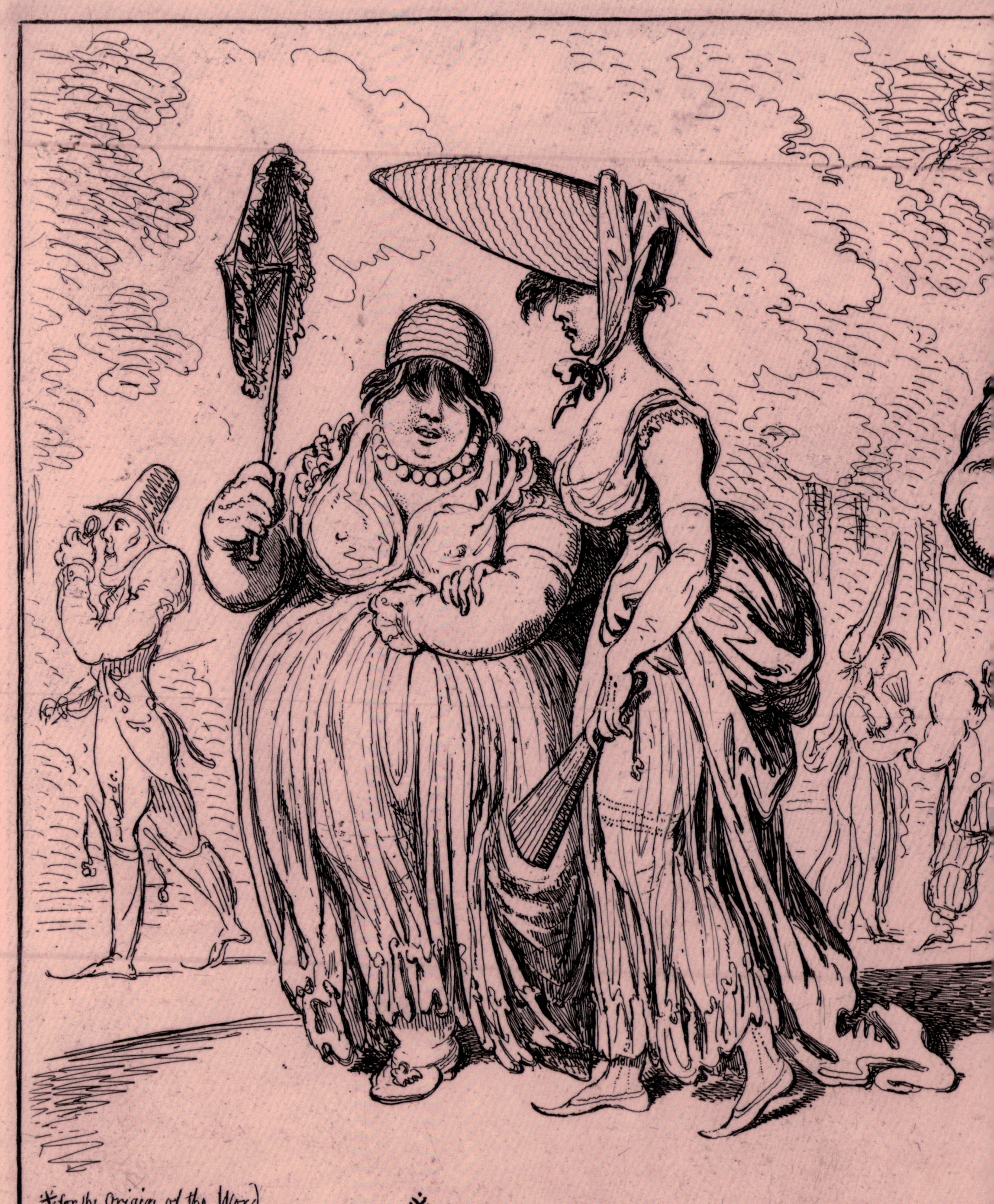
* for the Origin of the Word
consult the Johnssonian Dictionary..
Edition of 1799
* "MONSTROSITIES" of 1799

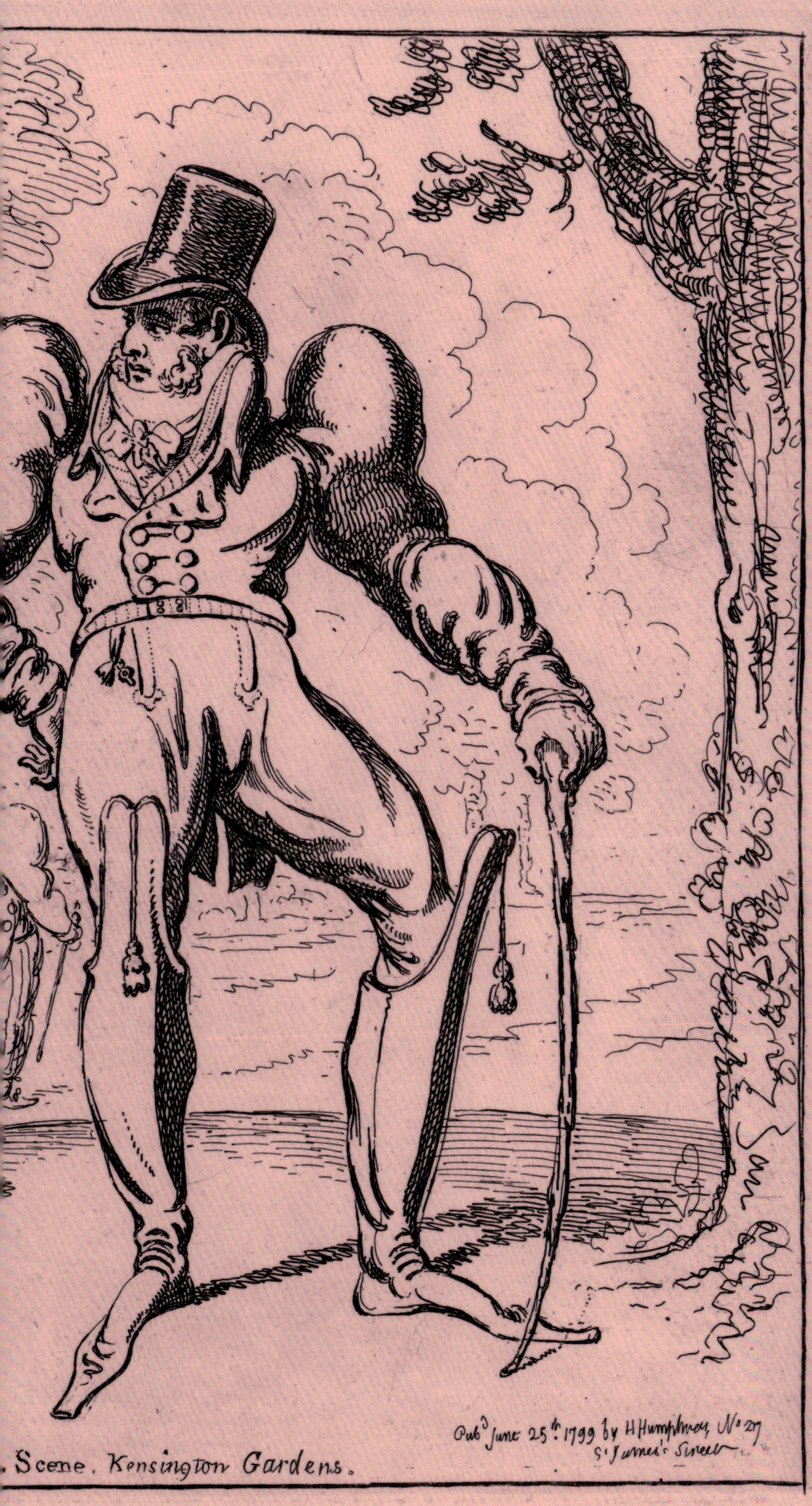



**153** after James Gillray (1756–1815)
*Monstrosities of 1799*
Plate 159, in *The genuine works of James Gillray*, engraved by himself, 1830
Etching, sheet: 58.8 × 42.7 cm
Staatliche Museen zu Berlin, Kunstbibliothek

# Foreword

*This book accompanies the exhibition* Fashion Drive, *and we are pleased to thank
the many people who made our ambitious project a reality. Innumerable talks
and discussions with international experts, with our authors and with colleagues
at the Kunsthaus provided a wide variety of ideas for the realisation of our vision
for an exhibition that explored and presented the interaction between art and fashion
in its extreme manifestations through five centuries of art and cultural history.*

*Our project received generous support from the Zürcherische Seidenindustrie Gesell-
schaft, and we sincerely thank its president, Thomas Isler, the board and the managing
director, Alexis Schwarzenbach, for their very pleasant and inspiring cooperation.
Swiss Re, our partner for contemporary art, has given the project additional impetus
with a substantial donation, for which we are especially grateful. With its commitment,
Swiss Re continuously creates space for new opportunities in the field of contemporary
art that benefit the public and our institution. Our colleague Monique Spaeti who,
for more than 15 years, has been responsible for sponsoring, has done an extraordinary
service for the Kunsthaus; her persistent and successful work helped make our ideas
a reality. We all thank her warmly for her pleasant and enduring cooperation!*

*Under the title 'Beauty/Mania', the Festspiele Zürich takes place in June 2018, and the
exhibition is the official contribution of the Kunsthaus to the diverse cultural programme.
We thank the Foundation Board, chaired by Mrs. Ursula Gut-Winterberger, as well
as the managing director, Alexander Keil, for the generous financial support. Thanks to
numerous sponsors, we can, after the now legendary Dada Ball, once again have
another big celebration, and look forward to the first Fashion Ball at the Kunsthaus
Zürich in May 2018.*

*The entire complex organisation of about 200 loans an the catalogue was in the
hands of Carlotta Graedel Matthäi, who was efficiently accompanied and supported
by Franziska Lentzsch. The cooperation with our lenders includes many personal
encounters that we remember with pleasure. We were able to draw from the fabulous
private costume collection that Martin Kamer and Wolfgang Ruf have assembled.
The Kunsthistorisches Museum Wien provided us with valuable and sometimes
spectaular loans from the Imperial Armory, the Department of Court Uniforms and*

**1** Kolman Helmschmid (1471–1532), armourer
Daniel Hopfer (1470–1536), etched decoration
Landsknecht armour of Baron of
the Empire Wilhelm von Rogendorf (1481–1541),
Augsburg 1523
Uncoated iron (with traces of old blueing),
etched ornamentation: filled with black
(traces of former fire gilding), leather
KHM-Museumsverband, Imperial Armoury

*the Picture Gallery, for which we are very grateful to Sabine Haag, Stefan Krause, Monica Kurzel-Runtscheiner and Stefan Weppelmann. The rector of the Academy of Fine Arts Vienna, Eva Blimlinger, and Julia Nauhaus, the director of the Paintings Gallery, also had an open ear to our requests and provided fascinating masterpieces. Special thanks go to the seemingly inexhaustible Lipperheidesche Kostümbibliothek in the Kunstbibliothek of the Staatliche Museen zu Berlin, to Adelheid Rasche and the director Moritz Wullen.*

*We are also proud that Laurent Salomé and Frédéric Lacaille have allowed us to select some treasures from the Château de Versailles. Thanks to the numerous private lenders and the colleagues at about three dozen museums and foundations who helped us greatly, as well as the many artists who have realised some elaborate projects for the large exhibition hall. Together with the exhibition architect Ulrich Zickler, the team of the Kunsthaus has created something special, an exploration of 500 years of art and fashion history that turned our idea into a sensual event.*

*Thanks to the in-depth contributions of the authors, this book is much more than a souvenir. It shows the diverse facets of our theme in the equally precise and memorable design by Lena Huber. Accompanied by Sonja Eismann, Janine Jakob, Nora Gomringer, Elfriede Jelinek, Inessa Kouteinikova, Monica Kurzel-Runtscheiner, Peter McNeil, Aileen Ribeiro, Franz Schuh, Werner Telesko, Katharina Tietze, Barbara Vinken and Philipp Zitzlsperger, you can now immerse yourself in the wondrous world of fashion in art – in its extreme appearances. We would like you to share in our pleasure with* Fashion Drive *and we wish you lots of inspiration!*

*Cathérine Hug and Christoph Becker*

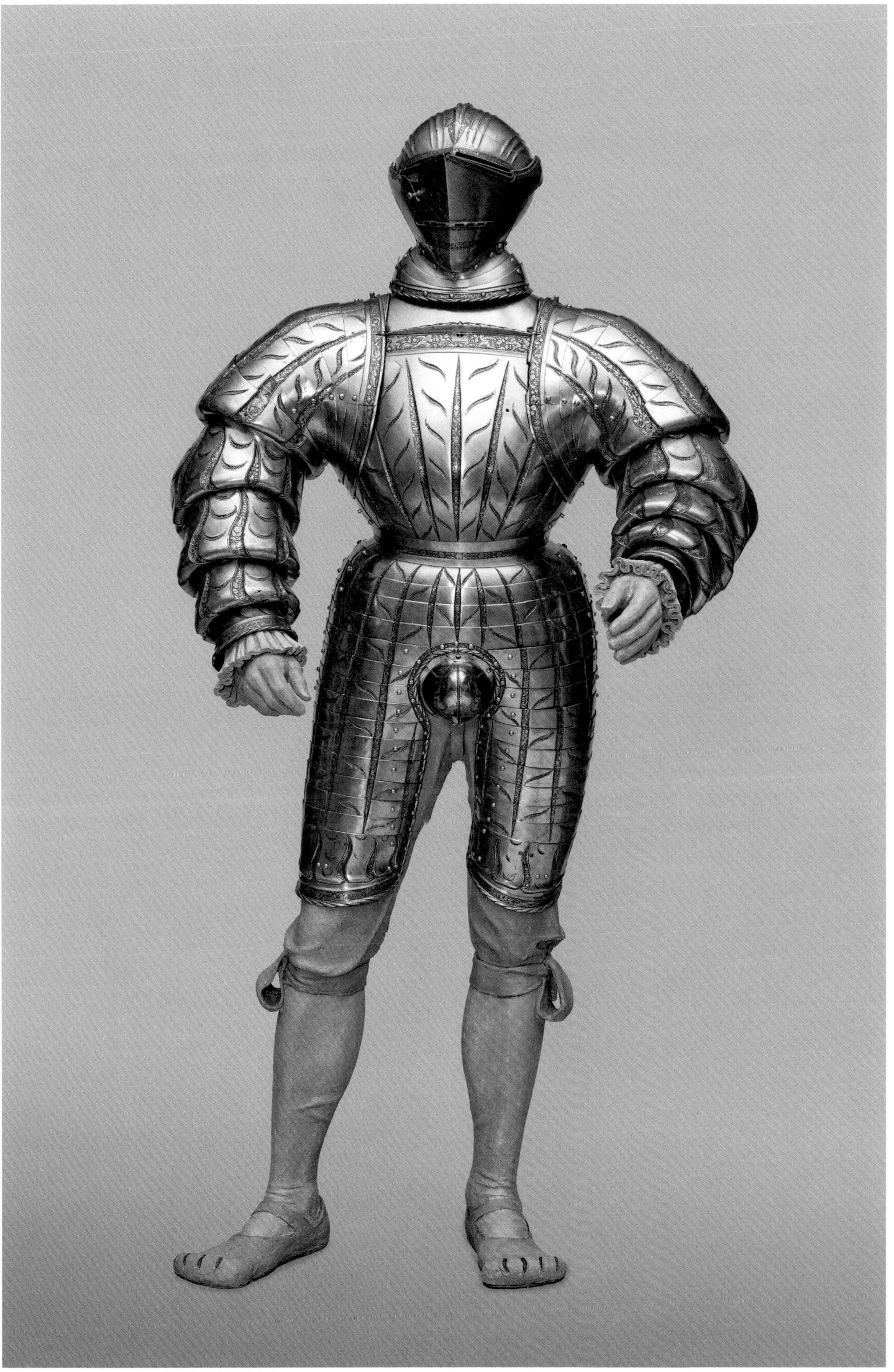

# Made of Steel

## Christoph Becker

No doubt, whoever dressed in the doublet, leggings and gloves, was assured of a grandiose appearance: chest and back in an elegant contour, the shoulders wide, the hips narrow, the thighs muscularly shaped, and the codpiece between padded breeches literally left room for speculation. The outfit shone and glittered. Everything was made-to-measure, down to the smallest detail, and the tailor, a genius, had done a great job. The comfort, however, left something to be desired, for it could not be put on or taken off without someone's help, and movements were determined by hooks, eyes and hinges that made peculiar noises. Despite its beauty and tremendous robustness, it had one major drawback, it rusted. | <sup>Page</sup> 19 | This extraordinary male outfit was one-of-a-kind, and there is no doubt that it was worn, if not in warlike battle, then during parades and ceremonial events. Although the helmet hid the face, it made the wearer, in a crowd of similarly dressed or dressed up contemporaries, a prominent figure. It represented visualised distinction, effective only in public. We know little about the reasons for commissioning this desirable object from one of the most famous and expensive blacksmiths, but the fact that the wearer chose this particular form of armour to attract attention reveals much about the subject, even 500 years later, which is our focus here: the extreme phenomena of fashion.

The shape and details of the armour were unusual for a craft that served, first and foremost, war and its requirements for survival. Obviously, the protagonist had benefitted from the tailoring of textile role models, certain phenotypic appearances of a marauding soldiery, which attracted attention, not by a uniform, but by special identifying features such as the extra-wide padded shoulders, puffy sleeves and wide padded breeches. All was not well with the landsknechts', or lansquenets', reputation, but their bellicose courage, their unsettled way of life and their special way of dressing had made them famous throughout Europe within a few years. Despite the good pay, their outfits consisted of cheap raw materials: hemp, linen and coarsely spun wool because the expenses for clothing were high. Disconcertingly extravagant were the idiosyncratic cuts, the monstrous padding, the gathering of enormous quantities of fabric on the arms and legs, the crude emphasis on secondary and primary sexual features, the shrill contrasts, and the coarse openings from which the lining oozed out. Whether these slashes, the obligatory mark of the landsknechts' costume, were due to coincidence or purpose is uncertain, but within a few years the phenomenon spread throughout Europe almost epidemically and beyond class borders; the soldier, burgher, nobleman, men and women, and even the emperor wore slashed clothing, and for a few decades the banal hole in a piece of fabric did not limit refinement.

The armour was adapted to this clothing reserved for a different social class, by means of a highly sophisticated technical change of material transposing their genuine characteristics to a higher, if not even unattainable level, emphasising their strongest characteristic, the obligatory slashes. The master armourer imitated them by means of indentations, chiselling and blackening, even though holes in armour made no sense, just as the bulkily dressed-up landsknechts did not do justice to their formidable reputation on the battlefield. Clothing is, in principle, utilitarian, but this outfit followed other criteria. It was only partially practical because the process of adaptation brought other aspects into the foreground. The steel garment was not a copy of the ordinary clothes of the landsknechts, but referred back to the costly costumes of the courtly class. In an affirmative process, certain costume parameters underwent a kind of aesthetic extraction process through selection and exaggeration. This required experts, masters of cutting and combining techniques, who created a harmonious whole from ambivalent parts. The metalworker worked much like a tailor, who shaped his material in such a way that the result contained more than the essential parameters. Here and there, aesthetic distinction arose from high-standing craftsmanship, which ultimately turned the item of clothing into an object of fashion, as in a metamorphosis born of an exact knowledge of conventions, of social norms and role models, of deviations and interpretations, of an opportunistic play of circumstances and change. There is no need to search far to find numerous, sometimes extremely fashionable phenomena in art of the sixteenth, seventeenth or eighteenth centuries –

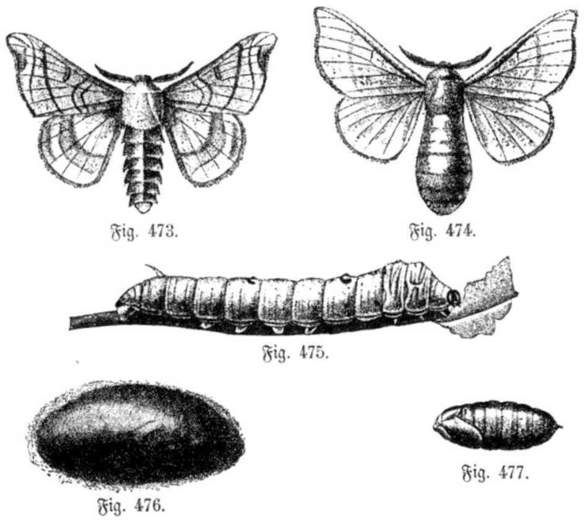



and discover the coloured reflection of a material that led textile art to extraordinary achievements, with garments that gave their wearers the aura of distinctiveness and exquisiteness.

Reserved for the highest clergy and secular majesties, silk made its first triumphal march through Europe in the Middle Ages at the beginning of the sixteenth century, thanks to better trade routes and increased production. The courtly model for the peculiar armour *à la mode* could only have been made of this material.

With some skill, the start of the almost invisible, endless thread can be found on the dirty-yellow cocoon which is barely three centimetres in size. Carefully uncoiling three to eight of the cocoons creates a stable, yarn-like structure of 800 to 3000 metres in length. From 3000 cocoons about 200 grams of a matt-glossy thread can be obtained, which is washed, re-twisted, dyed and woven on narrow looms into ribbons or panels of a fabric in different, but always robust quality, to become – through further processing to the highest Ideal – the raw material for the power and beauty of fashion. What remains is a small animal, an inconspicuous caterpillar, which spins a cocoon around itself with reflex movements of its head, without reaching the last stage of its existence in its simple housing because fashion cannot use the inconspicuous moths of the genus Bombyx, the silk moth.

For centuries and right up to the present day, objects, situations and persons have been depicted in works of art that cannot be adequately described with the Latin word *modus*, which means measured or grasped, since fashion is a complex, very versatile term: Fashion is at the same time virtually contagious, present and comprehensible in paintings, sculptures, graphics, photographs and films. Thus, one has to search for its extreme phenomena in art to come closer to this dazzling phenomenon of our culture. This is an attempt, nothing more, nothing less.

**123** Albrecht Dürer (1471–1528)
*Der Fahnenschwinger/Der Fähnrich,* c. 1501
The standard bearer
Copper engraving, image: 11.4 × 7 cm
Kunsthaus Zürich,
Department of Prints and Drawings,
Sammlung Landammann Dietrich Schindler, 2000

**2** Armour with pleated skirt of the
Margrave Albrecht von Brandenburg-
Ansbach (1490–1568),
Low German (Brunswick) c. 1526
Uncoated iron, partly etched:
with black fillings, leather
KHM-Museumsverband, Imperial Armoury

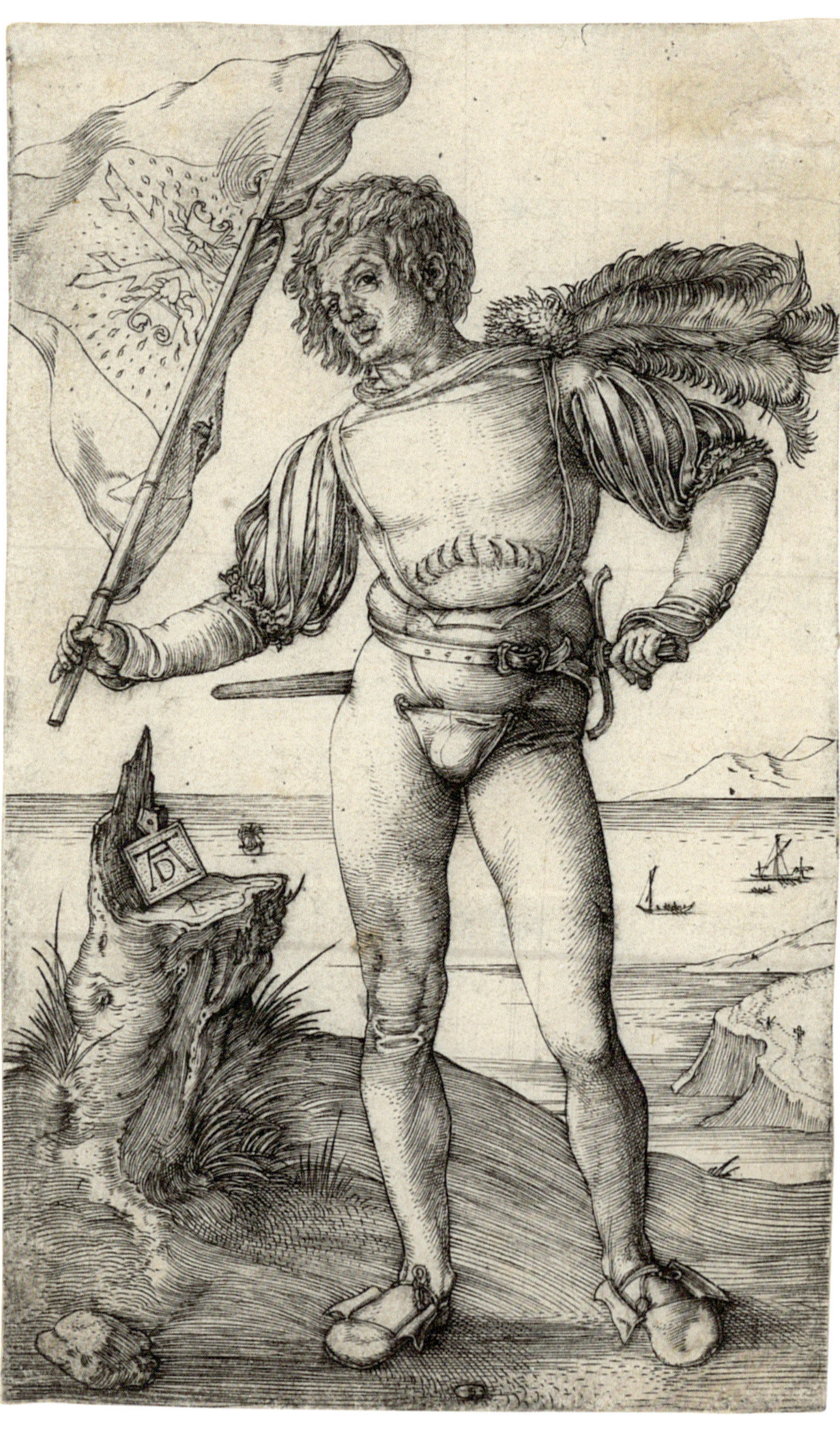

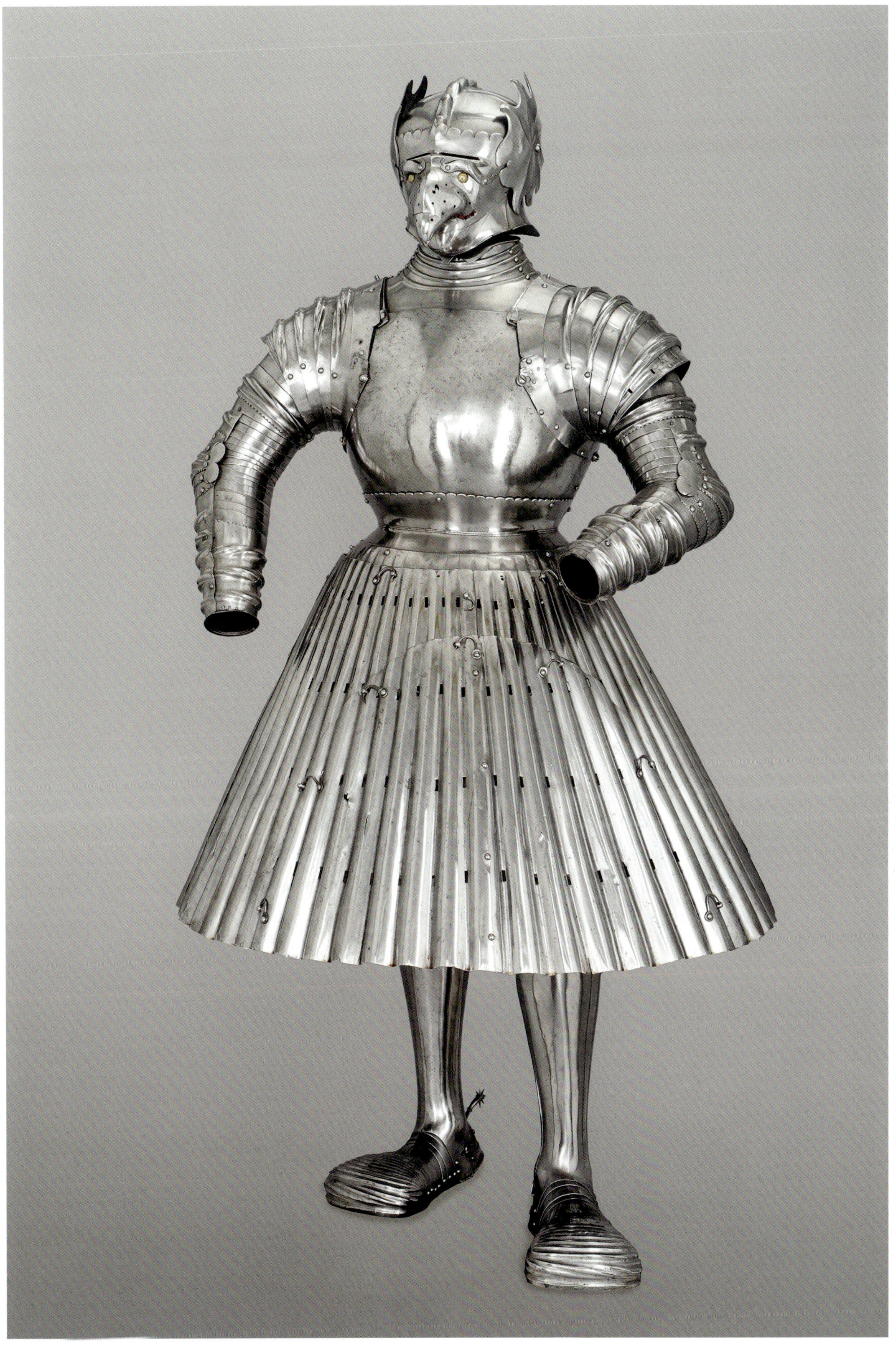

# Fashion Drive

Cathérine Hug

# *An Introduction*



Why 'Fashion Drive'? Fashion is both a driving force and a dilemma; it can be unbearably superficial and at the same time a serious indicator of social change. As early as 1905, Georg Simmel drew attention, in *The Philosophy of Fashion,* to the destructive effect of the consequential dichotomy between distinction and imitation: 'The essence of fashion consists in the fact that it should always be exercised by only a part of a given group, the great majority of whom are merely on the road to adopting it [...] life according to fashion consists of a mixture of destruction and construction; its content acquires its characteristics by destruction of an earlier form....'[1] Furthermore, Simmel notes, with a surprisingly emancipated attitude for that time, why fashion had been particularly important for women in their social development: 'If fashion both gives expression to the impulse towards equalisation and individualisation, as well as to the allure of imitation and conspicuousness, this perhaps explains why it is that women, broadly speaking, adhere especially strongly to fashion. Out of the weakness of the social position to which women were condemned throughout the greatest part of history there arises their close relationship to all that is "custom", to that which is "right and proper".'[2]

Fashion is therefore more than just an economic factor: it is a seismograph that registers sensitivities and desires and, likewise, an instrument of the explicit mechanisms of inclusion and exclusion. The question of who triggers the corresponding waves remains fascinating and unanswered at the same time: sometimes it was the nobility or a political elite, then rebels, sometimes pop and movie stars à la Madonna or James Dean, then again youth and subcultures, from zazous[3] and punks to hip hop and techno culture. Clothing and the resulting fashions allow us to detect certain signals and read group affiliations. In short, fashion is a form of communication, a universal and yet not so easy to understand aesthetic language that lets all people – and not just women – talk to each other. Or, to put it in the words of Roland Barthes, who coined 'fashion as a language': 'Any preoccupation with authored clothing first confronts us with an infinite stream of messages from which we know neither their units nor their functions, since their structure is also that of a speech, but does not coincide exactly with the language.'[4]

---

1     Georg Simmel, 'Philosophie der Mode' (1905), in Georg Simmel, *Gesamtausgabe,* Otthein Rammstedt (ed.), vol. 10, Frankfurt am Main 1995, pp. 16, 20. English taken from *The Consumption Reader,* David B. Clarke et al. (eds), London and New York 2003, pp. 238–39.

2     Simmel quoted in Clarke et al. 2003, p. 240.

3     The zazous were an Americano-Anglophile fashion movement surrounding personalities (such as Boris Vian) during the time of the Nazi occupation in France, with a fondness for swing, curled hair and chequered, strongly tapered jackets. In protest against the collaboration politics of head of state Philippe Pétain and the discriminating Star of David, some wore the star voluntarily with the modified inscription 'Zazou' or 'Swing' and paid with their life for this courageous gesture of solidarity. See here Jean-Claude Loiseau, *Les zazous,* Paris 1977.

4     Roland Barthes, *The Language of Fashion,* London and New York 2006 (first ed. in French, 2004). A richly illustrated overview on the cultural history of clothing is offered in the standard reference by Alison Lurie, *The Language of Clothes: The Definitive Guide to People Watching through the Ages,* Middlesex 1981.

**5** Elaborately commentated, interdisciplinary anthologies with basic texts have been published, among them to be recommended: Barbara Vinken (ed.), *Die Blumen der Mode: Klassische & neue Texte zur Mode,* Stuttgart 2016; Gertrud Lehnert, Alicia Kühl, Katja Weise (eds), *Modetheorie: Klassische Texte aus vier Jahrhunderten,* Bielefeld 2014; Sonja Eismann (ed.), *absolute Fashion,* Freiburg im Breisgau 2012; Peter McNeil (ed.), *Fashion: Critical and Primary Sources,* 4 vols, Oxford 2009.

**6** Gottfried Keller, *Der grüne Heinrich,* vol. 1, Brunswick 1854, p. 315. See also Gottfried Keller, *Kleider machen Leute,* Leipzig 1874.

**7** Cf. pp. 40ff.

**8** Orderic Vitalis's citation excerpted from the *Historia Ecclesiastica* (1123–1131) is Latin in the original. See Sarah-Grace Heller, 'The Birth of Fashion', in Giorgio Riello/Peter McNeil (eds), *The Fashion History Reader: Global Perspectives*, London and New York 2010, pp. 31–32, here footnote 33, p. 36.

**9** Among the many standard references dedicated to the chronology of fashion, the following three titles are particularly outstanding: Anne Hollander, *Seeing through Clothes,* New York 1978; Aileen Ribeiro, *Clothing Art: The Visual Culture of Fashion 1600–1914,* Yale 2017. Excellent but limited to the twentieth century is Jan Brand/José Teunissen/ Catelijne de Muijnck, *Fashion and Imagination: About Clothes and Art,* Arnheim 2009.

Clerics, writers, philosophers, sociologists: They all dealt with the fads of their time. The most famous among them (in chronological order of their publications) include: William Shakespeare, Jean-Jacques Rousseau, G.W.F. Hegel, Honoré de Balzac, Gottfried Keller, Charles Baudelaire, Stéphane Mallarmé, Émile Zola, Virginia Woolf, Walter Benjamin, Theodor W. Adorno, Simone de Beauvoir, Pierre Bourdieu, Elfriede Jelinek and Michel Onfray.[5] Keller, for example, described the fashion of the coloured frockcoat, which contrasted sharply in colour with its successor, the simple suit: 'We were dressed in a green uniform, and I already thought that I would mingle with my particular green in the general green and be saved from my nickname; but far from it, my mother took it upon herself to give the seemingly never-ending green coats of my father to the tailor, and so my uniform never lacked to be a shade darker or brighter than all the rest and it perpetually distinguished me.'[6]

And what about the artists? When did their exploration of fashion begin? Is it even possible to isolate this engagement chronologically? In a brief history of fashion in this volume, Peter McNeil outlines the genealogy of fashion and how historical clothing, for lack of realia, is closely linked to its depiction by artists.[7] In general, the birth of fashion occurs at the court of Burgundy in 1100, where men, after six centuries of short tunics, relatively abruptly turned to the long robe, full beard, blowing hair and the endlessly tapered shoe tips, as the Benedictine monk Orderic Vitalis (1075–c. 1142) warily observed: 'At the time great evils appeared and increased rapidly all over the world. Men of knightly rank abandoned the customs of their fathers in the style of dress and cut of hair; in a little while townsmen and peasants and all the lower ranks followed their example.'[8] What is striking about these statements is that fashion evidently originated from an emancipatory act and law enforcers such as the church perceived it as a threat. Initially it was predominantly a literary subject for chroniclers, but gradually moved into art with the flourishing of portrait painting in the Renaissance. This is where our exhibition begins.[9]

One can say that visual artists began to deal with reality and its sartorial expression at an early stage, that is, after their renunciation of ecclesiastical patrons during the Renaissance. Fashion has always fascinated or irritated, but, above all, has provided an identity-creating moment for both those who wear and those who look at it. Thus, Honoré de Balzac observed that the French Revolution was also a fashion issue when one considers the distinctive appearance of the sans-culottes – as they also called themselves a political group.[10] Or one can consider the Congress of Vienna that not only redrew the map of Europe but also increased awareness of the participating countries' codes of conduct and the associated guidelines for dressing, as Monica Kurzel-Runtscheiner, and Werner Telesko explain in this volume.[11] Up to the nineteenth century, Zurich, Basel or Paris had different mandates – hardly imaginable today – that regulated the clothing of citizens and prohibited immoderateness and false portrayal of status. However, these norms were also imaginatively undermined



Cathérine Hug

in the art of self-representation, as Janine Jakob explains to us in this volume.[12] Clothing is the second protective skin of humans. When it becomes fashion, it expresses something about the intentions of the wearer. If it is adopted by all, it becomes mainstream, the uniform of the respective zeitgeist. Our epoch-spanning exhibition, divided into eleven sections, focuses on the late eighteenth to early twentieth centuries and extends into the Renaissance and the present. It is interested in the manifestations of fashion shortly before or exactly at the tipping point when it was still extreme, shrill, loud, camouflaged or frowned upon. In a *tour d'horizon,* the subversive moments of fashion history are reflected in the mirror of art that reveals how fashions manifest themselves in painting, drawing, sculpture, installation and in new media and what they can say about the sensitivities of their time.

With Cecil Beaton's legendary exhibition *Fashion: An Anthology* in London, fashion as art first appeared in the museum sphere about 45 years ago.[13] Since then, numerous exhibitions have taken place, predominantly, of course, in fashion nations of the Anglo-Saxon and French regions with their fashion museums. In most cases, they had two fundamental questions: was fashion art and how could fashion and art enrich each other? Fashion historians, but now also curators, also considered the question of how art – both affirmatively and critically – reflects fads or so-called sartorial expressions. This question is also our starting point. A series of exhibitions in various countries have provided essential inspiration for this, and they will be listed briefly in chronological order: the exhibition *Tenue correcte exigée: Quand le vêtement fait scandale,* curated by Denis Bruna in Paris, is the most recent show that sheds light on the scandalous moments of fashion's history from the fourteenth century to the present day; the exhibition depicts the bridge between specific events, real costumes and their artistic reception in a way that is both unusual and sensuous, and sometimes a bit confusing.[14] Then, the exhibition *Reflecting Fashion: Kunst und Mode seit der Moderne,* organised by Susanne Neuburger and Barbara Rüdiger in Vienna, had an unprecedented focus on the exciting and plausible thesis that fashion plays a decisive role in modern art.[15]

**10**  Honoré de Balzac, *Le Dernier Chouan ou La Bretagne en 1800,* Paris 1829.

**11**  Cf. pp. 150ff. and 128ff.

**12**  Cf. pp. 80ff.

**13**  *Fashion: An Anthology,* Madeleine Ginsburg (ed.), exh. cat. Victoria and Albert Museum, London 1971.

**14**  *Tenue correcte exigée. Quand le vêtement fait scandale,* Denis Bruna (ed.), exh. cat. Musée des Arts décoratifs, Paris 2016.

**15**  *Reflecting Fashion: Kunst und Mode seit der Moderne,* Susanne Neuburger/Barbara Rüdiger (eds), exh. cat. Museum moderner Kunst Stiftung Ludwig Wien 2012.

16    *Impressionism, Fashion and Modernity,* Guy Cogeval, Gloria Groom, Susan A. Stein and Philippe Thiébaut (eds), exh. cat. Musée d'Orsay, Paris; The Art Institute of Chicago; The Metropolitan Museum of Art, New York 2012.

17    *Double-Face: The Story about Fashion and Art from Mohammed to Warhol,* Christoph Doswald (ed.), exh. cat. Kunstmuseum, Historisches Museum, Textilmuseum and Neue Kunst Halle, St. Gallen, Zurich 2006.

18    *Zweite Haut – Kunst und Kleidung,* Valerio Dehó/Elisabeth Hartung (eds), exh. cat. Frauenmuseum Evelyn Ortner, Meran; Museum Bellerive, Zurich, Meran 2001; *Gegen den Strich: Kleider von Künstlern,* Radu Stern (ed.), exh. cat. Museum Bellerive, Zurich; Musée des arts décoratifs, Lausanne, Bern 1992.

The groundbreaking show *Impressionism, Fashion & Modernity* in Paris, Chicago and New York, curated by Guy Cogeval and Gloria Groom, had an unrivalled precision in its critical examination of realia and their sartorial expressions in the second half of the nineteenth century, namely during the birth of the fashion industry. At the exhibition, numerous original costumes were displayed for the first time alongside high-quality paintings.[16] In 2006, in Switzerland, Christoph Doswald approached the complex topic with the exhibition *Double-Face.* With an exploratory and exemplary overview of the history of ideas, he retraced the fruitful attempts to advance art and fashion from the eighteenth century to the present.[17] In Zurich, the Museum Bellerive has repeatedly devoted itself to the utopian character of these intersections in the twentieth century, for example, with the unconventional exhibition *Zweite Haut: Kunst und Kleidung* by Valerio Dehó and Elisabeth Hartung in 2002 as well as the reference exhibition *Gegen den Strich: Kleider von Künstlern 1900–1940,* curated by Radu Stern ten years earlier.[18] Stern represents the thesis, interesting in our context, that fashion was not merely an invention of industrialisation, but also emerged from rejecting the mercantile logic and was thus able to develop a utopian character with artistic aspirations.[19] Already at an early stage in the artist-run *(Offspace)* sector, artists also explored the question of how artists and designers could inspire each other and work together without commercial coercion, as was highlighted by the exhibition *Creatures Comfort* in 1997, curated by the artists Monica Germann and Daniel Lorenzi in the Kombirama in Zurich.[20] Last but not least, one should mention Michèle Lachowsky's exhibition *Mode & Art 1960–1990,* which dealt with idiosyncratic themes such as 'New Spatiality', 'Punk', 'Zapping', 'Transience' and 'Role-Playing' from the perspective of the up-and-coming, fashion-nation Belgium (Keyword 'Antwerp Six') and cast a whole new light on the difficult relationship between art and fashion.[21]

This volume has eleven chapters, which also mirror the setting of the layout of the exhibition *Fashion Drive: Extreme Clothing in the Visual Arts:* Renaissance, Baroque, Rococo and French Revolution, Empire and Vienna Congress, dandies, the return of the hoop skirt and the first couturiers, fashion and the public, artists designing clothes, post-war period, self-staging and the birth of the top model and, finally, the posthuman and holistic. In this volume, the fourteen authors engage with these chronologically structured sections sometimes with scholarly analyses, other times with essays or poetry. The chronology of fashion in the visual arts will be presented in the following manner, with a fast-forward through selected examples.



Cathérine Hug

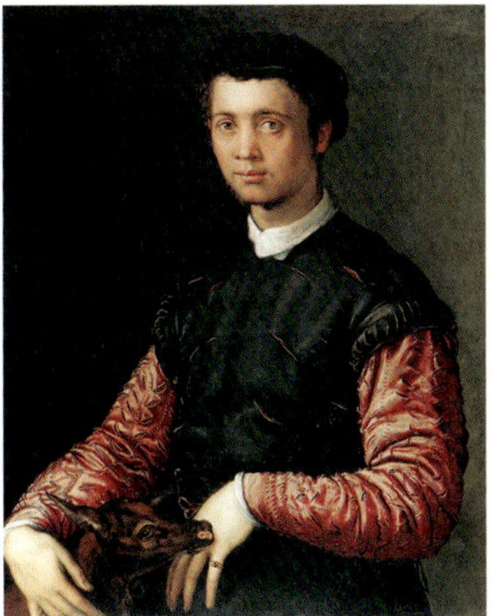

**239** Francesco Salviati | Page 53 |
*Portrait of a young man,* after 1548

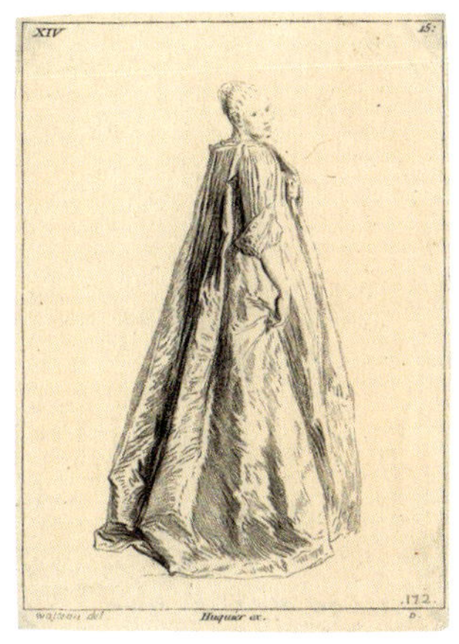

**296** after Jean-Antoine Watteau | Page 107 |
*Jeune femme debout avec la tête tournée
vers le spectateur,* 1717–28

## Slashes and Codpieces during the Renaissance

The so-called slashed fashion was in demand in Europe in the sixteenth century until its prohibition in 1633. It symbolises prosperity through waste, since one had to let an additional textile layer swell up through the slashed or torn fabric. This fashion was even incorporated into timeless biblical depictions, such as Joos van Cleve's *Lucretia* (1515/18), | <sup>Page</sup> **50** | thus providing an informative anachronism that transcends the style of the original times. As examples from the entire continent reveal, the slashes and tears could have very different shapes, from the orderly stylised and the arbitrarily realistic to the excruciatingly detailed engrailing, such as in William Larkin's *Portrait of Diana Cecil, later Countess of Oxford (c. 1614–18),* | <sup>Page</sup> **54** | in the portrait of *Infant Don Carlos (1564)* by Alonso Sánchez Coello | <sup>Page</sup> **59** | and in Francesco Salviati's *Portrait of a young man* (after 1548).[22] | <sup>Page</sup> **53** | Contrary to some assumptions, the fashion of slashed clothes is much older than their current rebirth, triggered by the punk movement with Malcolm McLaren and Vivienne Westwood. | <sup>Pages</sup> **68, 260** | Another notable feature of the Renaissance was the codpiece: it was located at the level of the male genitalia and it spread across the continent, even to small, relatively remote places such as Solothurn. | <sup>Page</sup> **58** | Named *brayette* in French or *Schamkapsel* in German-speaking countries, it served to highlight male virility and potency; the codpiece found its high point with Henry VIII (1491–1547).[23]

## Pleats during the Baroque Era

During Elizabeth I's reign from 1558 to 1603, fashion's focus on the male genitalia was gradually displaced. As an example of the new era, Catherine Carey, the 'Gentlewoman of the Privy Chamber to Queen Elizabeth I', was one of the most influential figures in the monarch's entourage. The large, full-length portrait *Catherine Carey, Countess of Nottingham* (c. 1597) | <sup>Page</sup> **69** | is one of the most technically demanding and thematically richest representations of a dress from that time. Since Carey was also 'mistress of the robes', it may well be that this precious silk dress originally belonged to Elizabeth I. Today, the Stowe Inventory (1600,

**19** Radu Stern, *Against Fashion: Clothing as Art,* 1850–1930, Cambridge 2004, p. 3.

**20** Exhibition without catalogue. Katja Alves, 'Kunst und Mode für Leib und Seele', in *Tages-Anzeiger,* 24 February 1997, p. 21.

**21** *Mode & Art 1960–1990,* Michèle Lachowsky (ed.), exh. cat. Palais des Beaux-Arts de Bruxelles, Brussels; Musée d'Art Contemporain de Montréal, Montréal, Brussels 1996. The 'Antwerp Six' consisted of the independent and, in some cases, still active fashion designers today Walter Van Beirendonck, Ann Demeulemeester, Dries Van Noten, Dirk Van Saene, Dirk Bikkembergs, Marina Yee, and temporarily Martin Margiela.

**22** A good introduction to slashed fashion is César Imbert, 'Le vêtement déchiré. De l'interdit biblique aux jeans lacérés', in Bruna 2016 (as in note 14), pp. 186–91.

**23** One of the most fascinating articles on the topic is Will Fischer, 'Codpieces and Masculinity in Early Modern England', in Riello/McNeil 2010 (as in note 8), pp. 62–80.

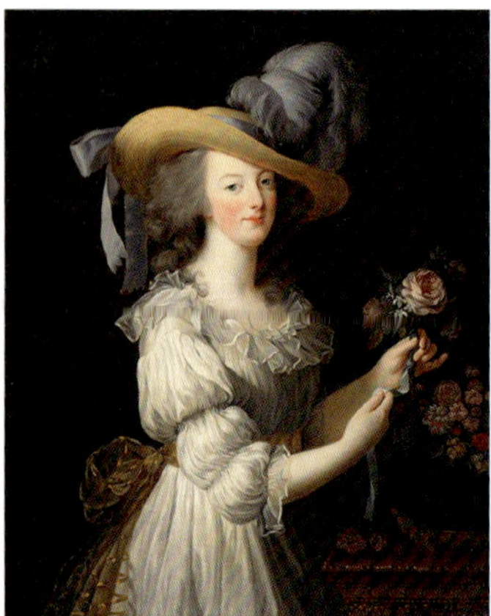

**292** Marie Louise Élisabeth Vigée-Lebrun | Page 103 |
*Marie-Antoinette en chemise,* 1783

British Library, London) indicates that Elizabeth I owned around 1,200 individual pieces of clothing. The recurring motif of the back view, especially of female figures, is a topos coined by Jean-Antoine Watteau to help the viewer enter into the picture (comparable to objects in the foreground or edge of a painting called the *repoussoir*). The type of *fête galante* comes from the pastoral, as Titian in *Fête champêtre* (c. 1509, Musée du Louvre, Paris) showed for the first time. Watteau, however, dressed the women depicted in fashionably flowing, coloured silk. The dresses are thus less static and the aleatory aspect of the folds seem to enter into a dialogue with nature. | ᴾᵃᵍᵉ **8, 106, 107** | The nonchalance with which wealth was demonstrated this way and was even downright rubbed in the noses of the underclass – not depicted here – on the street or in an outside space had both a potential to inspire admiration, but also to fuel latent rebellion: a source of conflict discharged 70 years later in the French Revolution. Watteau's typical back view had once again influenced a fashion concept, namely the *plis à la Watteau* (fold à la Watteau), which is an unmistakable characteristic in the *robe volante* (c. 1725) and its successor *robe à la française* (from 1740 to c. 1765). The earliest surviving costumes also date from this period as realia. | ᴾᵃᵍᵉ **101** |

### Rococo and Revolution

The portrait *Marie-Antoinette en chemise ou en gaulle* (1783), | **292** | painted by one of the first successful women painters Marie Louise Élisabeth Vigée-Lebrun, belongs to the most controversial and, at the same time, one of the last courtly representations before the Revolution's break of the epoch. In this scandalous picture, the Queen of the French dared for the first time in history to be depicted below her status – contra court etiquette. Here, we encounter Marie-Antoinette in a simple, translucent cotton blouse in a naive idealisation of an agrarian-pastoral life. What's more, Vigée-Lebrun presented the painting when she first participated in the renowned Salon, which customarily excluded women artists. In a kind of 'palace revolution', as Stefan Zweig aptly described it, the last queen of the Ancien Régime initiated a change to which she herself

24   Stefan Zweig, *Marie Antoinette: Bildnis eines mittleren Charakters,* Frankfurt am Main 1981 (first published in 1932), p. 122.

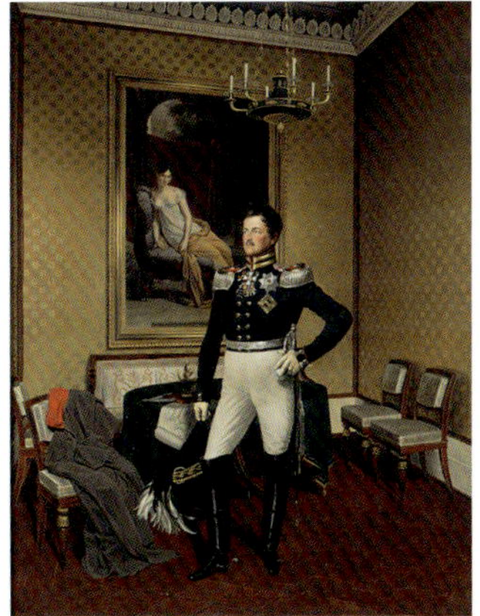

**188** Franz Krüger | Page 141 |
*Prinz August von Preussen*, c. 1828

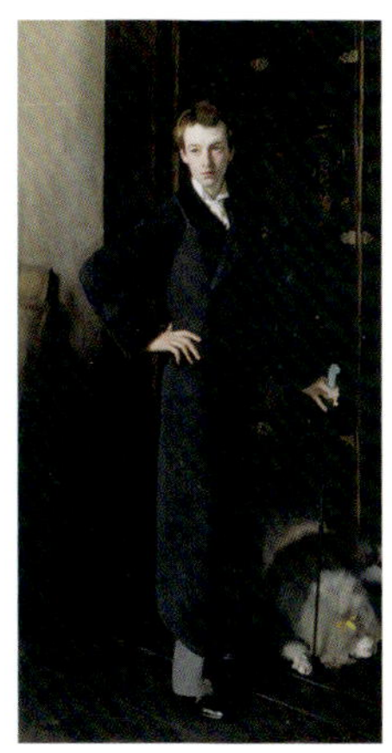

**240** John Singer Sargent | Page 175 |
*W. Graham Robertson*, 1894

would later fall victim and be executed on the guillotine.[24] The Revolution of 1789 and the Declaration of Human Rights were accompanied by the right to choose freely one's own clothing. After the Jacobin reign of terror, the aristocrats, who had fled to Koblenz, returned to Paris and developed an extravagant dress style that has inspired the imagination of couturiers to this day and which was known then under the names *Merveilleuses* (for the *marvellous* women) and *Incroyables* (for the *incredible* men). | Pages 113, 114, 139 |

## First French Empire and Congress of Vienna

The medium-formatted, full-length portrait *Prinz August von Preussen* (c. 1828) | Page 141 | shows the statesman in the uniform of the Artillery Guards and brings him in a dialogue with the portrait in the background. This is François Gérard's painted portrait of 1805 of the highly idolised Madame Récamier and today is the most famous work of the First French Empire (now in the Musée Carnavalet in Paris). Récamier was considered an intelligent, fashionable beauty and maintained a salon in Paris where the Napoleon-critical elite met, including Madame de Staël. Because of Récamier's refusal to become the lady-in-waiting of the Empress Joséphine and because she was suspected of entertaining subversive contacts, Napoleon I had her salon shut down in 1803 and even banished her from France in 1811. Prince August von Preussen met her in the parlour of Madame de Staël in Coppet, near Geneva, and he deeply adored her from then on, as shown by their exchange of letters and the unusual constellation of this painting within a painting. As a token of her affection, Récamier gave the prince her portrait by Gérard in 1808. Along with Empress Joséphine, Récamier is regarded as the female icon of the Empire, and it can be considered an irony of history that she, as Napoleon's opponent, paradigmatically symbolises fashion of the Empire, with its high waistline, translucent fabric and great freedom for the body. Prince August was also regarded as a strong, less intellectual-cultural but rather military, opponent of Napoleon, and after winning battles, he played an important role in the Congress of Vienna in 1814/15. The tense relationship between the private and the public person which cannot always be reconciled, can be recognised in this double portrait, and in the formal similarity between the coat, nonchalantly thrown over the chair of the prince, and the orange wrap, prudishly held over the lap of his beloved.

## Macaroni, Incroyables and Dandies

No history of fashion can be meaningful without the history of the dandy, among which George Brummell (1778–1840), Oscar Wilde (1854–1900) and Robert de Montesquiou (1855–1921) are among the most popular protagonists. | Pages 173, 174, 166 | Contemporaries considered their taste subversive; with their love of fine detail, they contributed significantly to the restrained elegance that prevails in men's fashion today. The focus is still on a simple taste that avoids any distraction from the face and hands, the precision of a strict and self-controlled silhouette and a subtle penchant for expensive materials and their perfect finishing. Giovanni Boldini, John Singer Sargent and

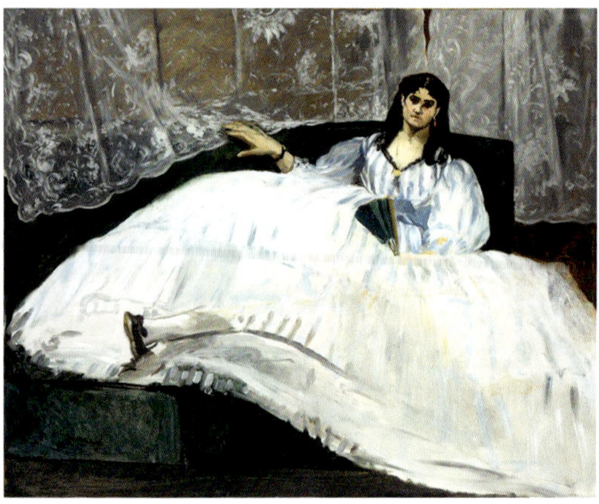

**211** Édouard Manet | Page 191 |
*Jeanne Duval, la maîtresse de Baudelaire (La Dame à l'éventail),* 1862

James Tissot belong to the most accurate observers of their time in terms of changing fashion and, at the same time, as 'fashionable' portraitists they received valuable commissions from the wealthy social classes. Baron Aimé de la Seillière, portrayed by Tissot in 1866, is depicted in this kind of self-conception. He presents himself confidently as head and owner of the Vosges textile company 'Manufacture Saint-Maurice de Senones'. | Page 174 | Tissot paid much attention to the fabrics, and he evoked the tactile quality of the material with meticulous care, which must have been entirely in the interest of the textile manufacturer.

### Return to the Hoop Skirt and First Fashion Designers

During the Second Empire under the reign of Napoleon III, the hoop skirt, already believed extinct, was suddenly fashionable again. In his full-length portrait of Jeanne Duval (1862) | Page 191 | Édouard Manet clearly emphasises the extremely cumbersome characteristics of this garment. He depicts a woman jauntily revealing her foot from under the mountain of clothes. This woman's lover, Charles Baudelaire (1821–1867), was an enthusiastic but not an uncritical commentator of his time, and in 1863, wrote about fashion as having to be 'variable', that is, surprising in its variations, to be beautiful.[25] The painter and conceptual artist John Baldessari responded to Manet's iconic painting in 2012 by contrasting the crinoline in the upper part of the picture with a similarly sluggish passenger steamship, whose technological advance after the 1850s coincides with the reversion to crinoline fashion. | Page 190 | In spite of the politically conservative mood, the 1850s gave birth, as a product of the industrial revolution, the first couturier in demand throughout Europe, Charles Frederick Worth (1825–1895). His clients included celebrities such as Empress Eugénie, Queen Victoria and actress Sarah Bernhardt. Incidentally, Worth developed the concept of the clothing label on the inside of the collar for marking a brand.[26] | Fig. 1 | Through new achievements in mobility and architecture and the meteoric rise of department store culture, as stated in the corresponding essay in this volume, a new form of public life developed in the second half of the nineteenth century that greatly benefited and influenced fashion.[27]

25　Charles Baudelaire, *Das Schöne, die Mode und das Glück,* Berlin (West) 1988, p. 10.

26　From the rich literature on Charles F. Worth, the following essay should be especially mentioned: Aileen Ribeiro, 'Worth and the Founding of Haute Couture', in Ribeiro 2017 (as in note 9), pp. 330–38.

27　Cf. pp. 194–203.

28　See here: Christine Bard, *Les Garçonnes: Modes et fantasmes des Années folles,* Paris 1998. Christian Mothes/ Dominik Bartmann (eds), *Tanz auf dem Vulkan: Das Berlin der Zwanziger Jahre im Spiegel der Künste,* Berlin 2015; *Glanz und Elend in der Weimarer Republik,* Ingrid Pfeiffer (ed.), exh. cat. Schirn Kunsthalle Frankfurt 2017.



Cathérine Hug

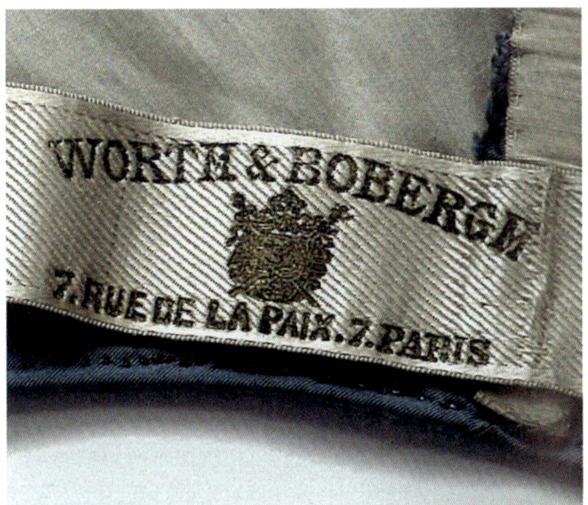

**Fig. 1** Worth & Bobergh label on
an evening gown, 1866/67

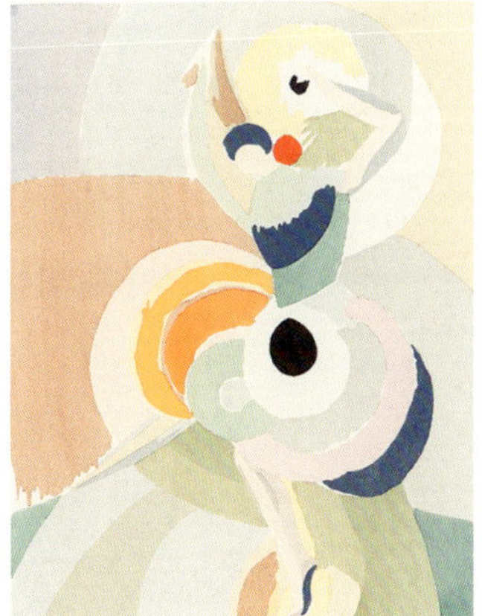

**113** Sonia Delaunay | Page 236 |
Clothing designs, 1924



## Artists Design Clothes

In a manifesto on futuristic menswear, Filippo Marinetti and Giacomo Balla pleaded in 1914 for the death of dark, symmetrical and small-minded fashion in order to counter the dreary appearance of the masses on the street. | Page **222** | Balla created corresponding designs in the same year, and a few years later he had the colourfully daring pieces of clothing partially realised. | Pages **223**ff. | This all had to do with the understanding of art as a *Gesamtkunstwerk,* which had evolved during the fin de siècle and which manifested itself in all spheres of life. The social potential of fashion fascinated the former Dadaist and later Surrealist Max Ernst and many of his colleagues such as Erwin Blumenfeld, | Page **227** | George Grosz | Page **176** | or Hannah Höch. | Page **232** | In 1919, Ernst published, for example, the provocative, schematic fashion sketches *Fiat modes, pereat ars* ('Let there be fashion, down with art') | Page **230** | long before the fashion of designers such as Jean-Paul Gaultier and Karl Lagerfeld was declared art.

The 1920s were characterised by global upheavals and were therefore also known as the 'Roaring Twenties' or 'Années folles' as reflected in, among other things, fashion. After the gradual introduction of women's suffrage began to fundamentally change the political landscape, women also became more self-conscious in terms of fashion, as shown by the short hair and skirts.[28] | Page **234** | Practising sports played an important role and hence the social acceptance of the casual look created by couturiers like Elsa Schiaparelli. | Page **235** | At the same time, with the primacy of the healthy body, youthfulness became increasingly more important, and it is still prevalent today. Mai-Thu Perret's sculpture *Flow My Tears I* (2011) | Page **238** | combines fashion design, art history and the current interaction between the two disciplines. The Swiss concept artist thus pays homage to the congenial collaboration between Elsa Schiaparelli and Salvador Dalí, who produced the revolutionary skeleton evening dress before the beginning of the war, in anticipation of the morbid and gloomy political times to come. This collaboration between a fashion designer and an artist is one of the earliest examples of this kind. | Page **239** |

## Subcultures during the Post-War Era

The European art world saw Andy Warhol (1928–1987) as the counterpart to Joseph Beuys (1921–1986); both today are among the most famous and influential artists of the post-war era. They are distinctive phenomena in their own way, and although, at least in Beuys, the individual persons are not the primary objects of their art, in both cases, work and artist are inextricably linked. With their cleverly devised self-staging, including their carefully considered clothing, they shaped a new image of artists that anticipated the trend toward self-advancement and self-marketing in the twenty-first century. Both Beuys and Warhol knew very well how to use mass media to convey their art and were often the subject of this mediatisation (especially television). Unlike today, the military look alluded by the pattern in Warhol's *Camouflage. Joseph Beuys* (1986) | Page **258** | did not affirm the military,

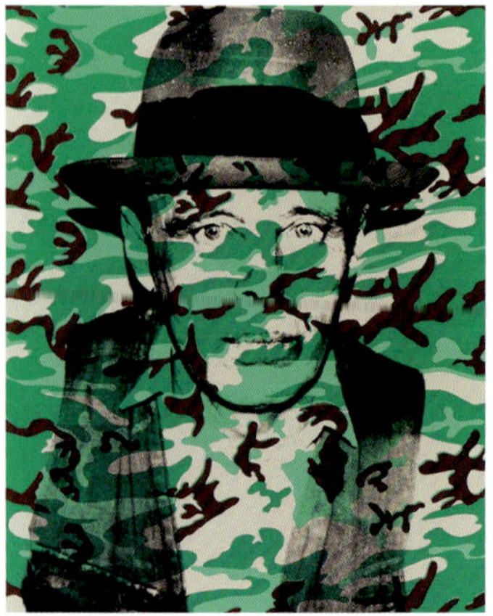

**294** Andy Warhol | Page 258 |
*Camouflage. Joseph Beuys,* 1986

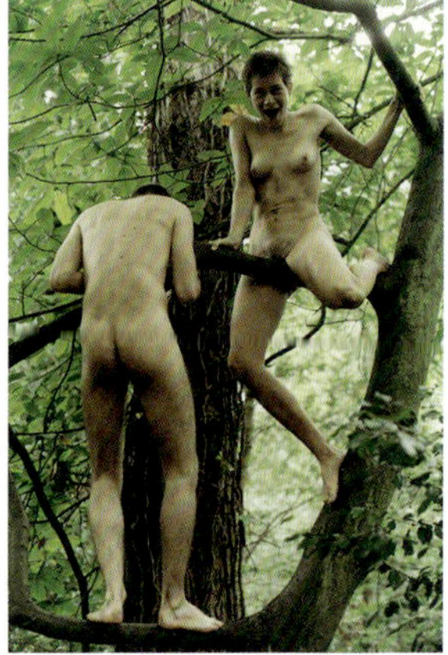

**252** Wolfgang Tillmans | Page 277
*Lutz & Alex, climbing tree,* 1992

but was part a critical trend of the hippie and punk movements against the Vietnam War and later against the offensive Thatcher-Reagan policy. Franz Schuh discusses the explosive-constructive potential of the infiltration principle of subcultures in more detail in this volume.[29] Warhol also refers, however, to Beuys's ambivalently transfigured history as a soldier during World War II and to the role Constructivist and Cubist artists had already played in designing army camouflage patterns during World War I. This monumental painting originated in the year of Beuys's death, and thus the overlay of camouflage patterns and artist portrait can also be interpreted as a metaphor for transience and the associated disappearance.

## Supermodels and Self-Staging

In the 1980s, fashion photography and its key figure, Peter Lindbergh, made a significant contribution to the establishment of the top model – who, with exceptions such as Twiggy, were hardly mentioned previously by name. The photograph *Linda Evangelista, Christy Turlington & Naomi Campbell, Brooklyn* (1990) | Page 272 | is especially meaningful here because it portrays women of diverse ethnic backgrounds with masculine hairstyles and posing in unusually colourful and 'bad' fitting men's suits: a visionary breach of the taboo in many ways. In the post-war period, and especially with the triumph of youth movements, subcultures have become the decisive driving force behind new fashion trends.[30] Fashion is no longer simply dictated by a single couturier, but draws its inspiration directly from the street, in blogs and from ordinary people, as Wolfgang Tillmans has been examining artistically since the mid-1990s and thus influencing the history of fashion. | Pages 248, 277 | The achievement of artists such as Lindbergh, Juergen Teller and Tillmans lies, above all, in the fact that they do not treat models in their work as a pure silhouette, but leave space for their individual personalities – to bring their respective characters to light, to tell stories. The interaction between the author and the protagonists is not one-sided, the models do not simply accept instructions, but become self-determined performers. However, performative self-staging appeared earlier in the visual arts as a strategy of self-empowerment – as in Beuys and Warhol – and in the 1980s with Manon and Leigh Bowery, | Pages 279, 263 | in the 1970s with Lady Shiva, General Idea and Urs Lüthi, | Pages 254, 255, 275, 67 | in the 1960s with Meret Oppenheim and James Rosenquist, | Pages 242, 241 | or in the 1920s with Marcel Duchamp and Elsa von Freytag-Loringhoven, | Page 228 | to name but a few. A much earlier phenomenon is the Contessa di Castiglione (1837–1899): the Italian aristocrat was photographed by Pierre-Louis Pierson (1822–1913) from the 1860s to the 1890s and left behind, thanks to this unusual collaboration, more than 450 portraits, which were as idiosyncratic then as they are now. | Page 278 | Apart from rumours about her liaison with Napoleon III, the Contessa was already a legend during her lifetime, and she portrayed herself on dazzling social occasions as the Queen of Hearts, Queen Etruria, Madame du Bary, and Madame Récamier or as a victim or a disabled person. It has been reported

Cathérine Hug

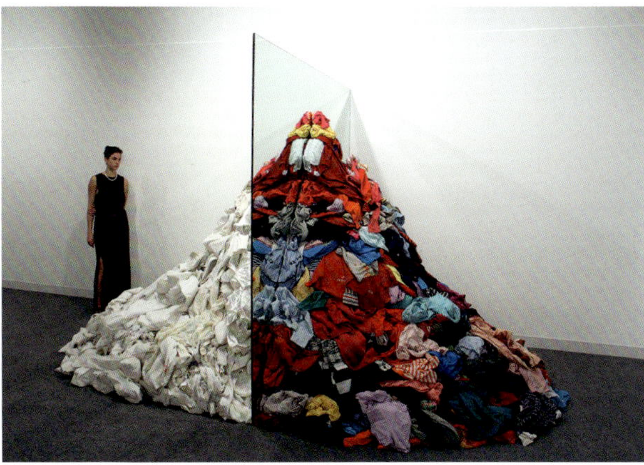

**230** Michelangelo Pistoletto | Page 302 |
*Metamorfosi,* 1976–2016


**29**  Cf. pp. 246ff.

**30**  *Energy Flash – The Rave
Movement,* Nav Haq (ed.),
exh. cat. M HKA, Antwerp 2016.

**31**  Alain Decaux, *La Castiglione,
Dame de Cœur de l'Europe,*
Paris 1953, p. 3.

**32**  The art world rediscovered
La Castiglione at the end of the
1990s and her artistic achievement
was honoured. See here: *'La Divine
Comtesse': Photographs of the
Countess de Castiglione,* Emily
Walter/Judith Wardmann (eds),
exh. cat. Musée d'Orsay, Paris;
The Metropolitan Museum of Art,
New York, New Haven, Conn. 1999.

**33**  For more on this topic,
please see Sonja Eismann's essay
in this volume, cf. pp. 264ff.

**34**  https://www.theguardian.
com/membership/video/2014/
oct/29/vivienne-westwood-
capitalism-clothing-video
www.viviennewestwood.com/
en-gb/blog/love-story-vivienne-
westwood-fashion-revolution
(accessed on 10 December 2017).


that sophisticated Parisian personalities such as the dandy Robert de Montesquiou, | [Page] **176** | with his 434 gelatine silver prints, possessed practically all portraits of the Contessa.[31] La Castiglione had planned to present her collection to the public at the Exposition Universelle (world's fair) of 1900 in Paris under the title, 'La plus belle femme de son siècle' (the most beautiful woman of her century), but because of her death it did not happen at that time.[32]

### Posthuman and Holistic

Michelangelo Pistoletto's installation *Metamorfosi* (1976–2016) | [Pages] **302**[f.] | reveals our current approach to clothing: although the eco-movement had already warned of the humanitarian and environmental consequences of the fashion industry in the 1970s, the capitalist 'fast fashion' logic of fashion companies has developed to a catastrophic extent. The collapse of the Rana Plaza textile processing plant in Bangladesh, where workers were forced to work in inhumane conditions and 1,134 of them were killed in May 2013, shocked the world's public opinion, leading to radical reconsiderations, and compelling industry stakeholders to take urgent action.[33] But the promise of the 'clean clothes' industry alone is not enough: there should be less overall consumption and more sustainable quality. In April 2017, Vivienne Westwood, the fashion designer and activist, who appears in our context as an artist, loudly demanded, 'Buy less, choose well and make it last!'[34]

But what role does fashion play today – in contrast to clothing, which naturally can never be declared dead and constantly dies? Does it exist in its singularity or do we find it in much more elusive polymorphic forms everywhere, in fleeting appearances bound by communities of interest?[35] 'It is becoming routine for people to try to alter their appearance, their behaviour, and their consciousness beyond what was once thought possible. The new construction of the self is conceptual rather than natural' was emphatically announced in 1992 in a foreshadowing exhibition.[36] Certainly fashion has lost its predominant status in favour of alternative beautification and life improvement measures such as plastic surgery and Botox, bodybuilding and fitness, yoga and meditation, slow food and the digital diet. Furthermore, the red carpet of Cannes or Hollywood and the tabloids are no longer the only places where self-staging takes place – in fact, social media and fashion blogs have become the new catwalk and our intimate advisors. Artists such as Daniele Buetti, Esther Eppstein, K8 Hardy, Michael Smith, Tobias Kaspar and Jakob Lena Knebl address how fashion today is integrated into our lives in a greater, holistic, all-embracing understanding of the local and global. | <sup>Pages</sup> **295–304** | Fashion is no longer simply a projection screen of longing or the repressive instrument of a few in power. Rather, it is among us as an offer to shape our identity in order to stage ourselves as sometimes critical of capitalism, as sometimes playful, sometimes destructive or conceptual and to reflect on how we relate to the world.



**35**  An indispensable standard volume on the momentariness of fashion is: Gilles Lipovetsky, *L'Empire de l'éphémère: La Mode et son destin dans les sociétés modernes,* Paris 1987. For more recent articles on the ambivalent relationship of art and fashion see: Caroline Busta et al. (eds), *Texte zur Kunst,* Schwerpunktheft Fashion, no. 102, June, Berlin 2016 ; Catherine Chevalier et al. (eds), *May,* 'fashion issue', no. 15, June, Paris 2016. Prioritising the importance of the body as malleable material' is provided by Susanna Hoffmann-Ostenhof/Rita Vitorelli, *Spike Art Quarterly,* 'The Body', no. 47, spring 2016, Vienna/Berlin 2016, p. 9.

**36**  *Post Human,* Jeffrey Deitch/ Chantal Michetti-Prod'Hom (eds), exh. cat. FAE Musée d'Art Contemporain, Lausanne; Castello di Rivoli, Turin; DESTE Foundation for Contemporary Art, Athens; Deichtorhallen, Hamburg, Amsterdam 1992, pp. 52–55.

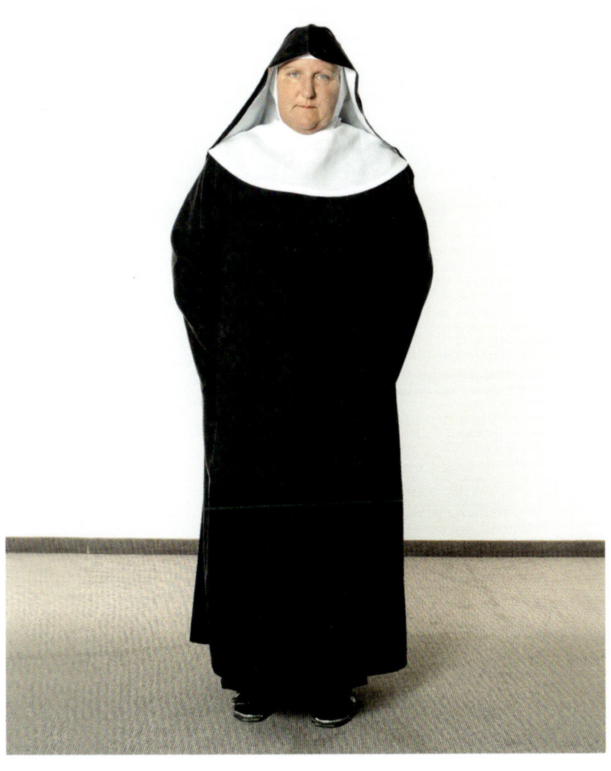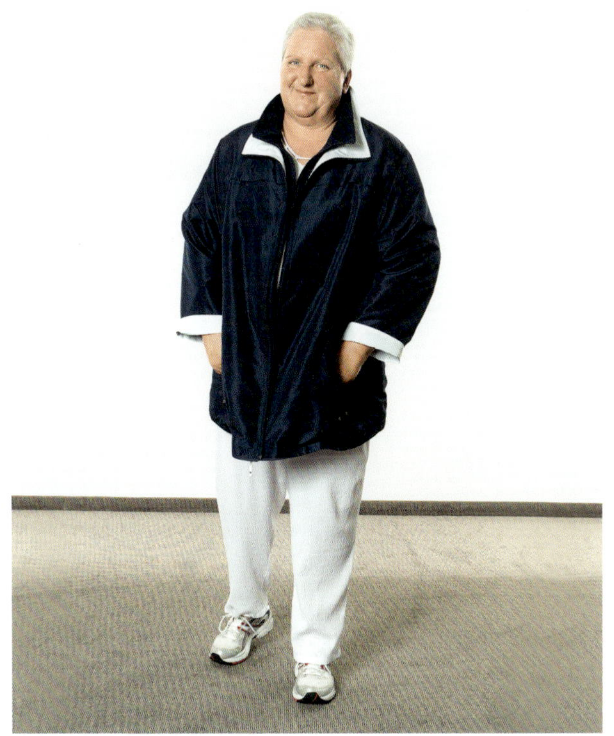

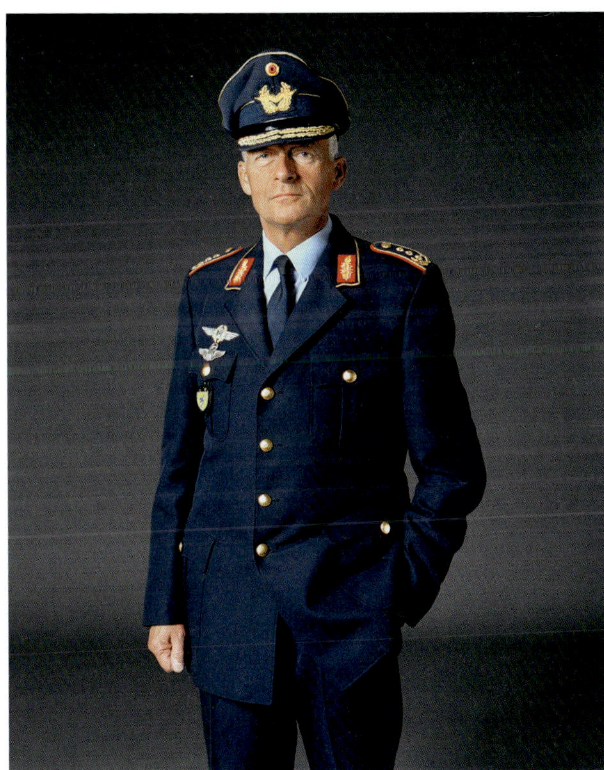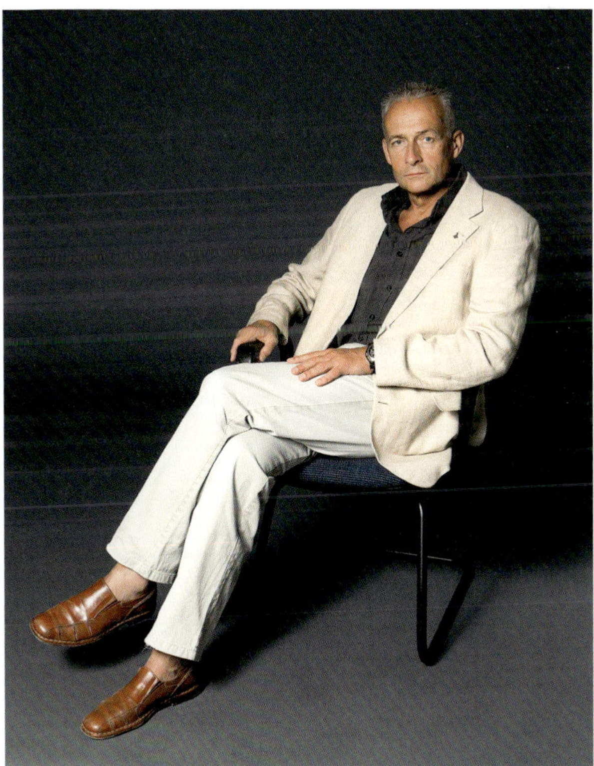



**186**  Herlinde Koelbl (b. 1939)
Philippa Rath, nun, Germany
Klaus-Peter Stieglitz, General Inspector
of the air force, Germany
From the series
*Kleider machen Leute,* 2012
Photographs
Courtesy of Herlinde Koelbl

# A Fold of is a

Peter McNeil

# Clothing Trace of Passion

**Fig. 1** Hikone screen,
Edo (1624–1644)
Six-panel folding screen
*(byōbu),* colour on gilded paper,
94.5 × 278.8 cm
Hikone Castle Museum,
Gift of Li Family

'Il n'y a point de Pays dans l'univers où la mode règne avec autant d'autorité qu'en France'.[1]

Histories of dress are often built around the lines of national borders. French and Italian histories tend to see 'fashion' developing in the period between 1300 and 1700. The British and German traditions often argue first for 'costume' and then 'fashion' or *mode* appearing in Western Europe from about 1700 on. Much of this argument rests upon theories and the pace of economic and urban development. Does fashion require a consumer base linked to industrialisation? As Europe and 'the rest' (Asia) developed within the uneven 'exceptionalism' (Kenneth Pomeranz's term) of European economies with their trade including slavery, overseas taxation and large militaries connected to their colonies – many scholars have argued that Europe 'had' fashion before Asia. Yet Asian textile cultures were the basis of many European fashions from the Roman and Byzantine period on, superior to what Europeans could achieve for centuries, and the subject of lust, adulation and emulation – even industrial espionage. Non-western societies including China and Japan had their own courts, merchant classes, stratifications, luxuries, trends and resorts of fashionable pleasures. | Fig. 1 | Textiles that make up this finery, unlike inert gems and precious metals, are often so fragile that their image survives mainly in art. After all, they come from animals that produce them for one season only, such as the silk from a cocoon, the wool from sheep, or the cotton and flax that bear seed on a seasonal basis. Their depiction by artists might involve a symbolic response, technical challenge or sensual pleasure in the act of representation.

Fashion is often linked to individuality, and the framing of the Italian Renaissance as the site of a new subjectivity by nineteenth-century thinkers is central. The idea of the 'rebirth' of Europe is nicely captured by Alain Erlande-Brandenburg on the late Medieval period: 'This nascent society was characterised by a belief in itself and in its future ... which was closely connected to trade, to wealth, to the birth, ... a new zest for life.'[2]

But people at that date were not 'individuals' like someone on Madison Avenue or Bond Street today. They had communal ties, their choice of

**Extreme:** reaching a high or the highest degree/very great/utmost/uttermost/maxima

**Fashion:** *fasun*/to make/shape/style /to shape appearance/ mode/etiquette/custom/usage/manner of dressing/adjusting oneself *façonner* – to fashion

1   [Gaudet], *Bibliotheque [sic] des Petits-Maitres [sic], ou Mémoires pour servir à l'histoire du bon ton & de l'extrêmement bonne compagnie,* Palais-Royal, Chez la petite Lolo, Marchande de Galanteries, à la Frivolité, 1762, p. 28.

2   Alain Erlande-Brandenburg, *The Cathedral: The Social and Architectural Dynamics of Construction,* trans. Martin Thom, Cambridge 1994 [1989], p. 88.

3   Fernand Braudel, *Civilisation and Capitalism, 15th–18th Century. Volume I: The Structures of Everyday Life: The Limits of the Possible,* translation Siân Reynolds, Berkley 1992 [1979]), p. 333.

4   Braudel, 1992, p. 323.

5   Braudel, 1992, p. 316.

Peter McNeil

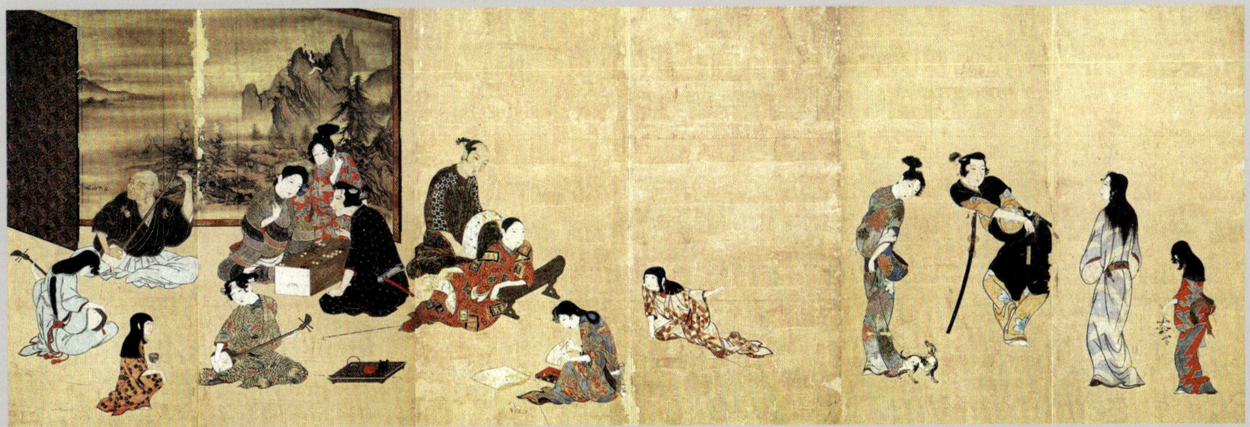

clothing was often determined by others, by imposed rules, and some-times their clothes were given to them – literally – 'livery'. Renaissance society did not mark a complete rift with the Middle Ages, and it continu-ed the important precepts of gift exchange, rank and order, of dynastic, family-related and historical memory-traces. Some things were changing, however, and starting to look more 'modern'. As social practices and ur-ban spaces developed, in wealthy societies such as Stuart England, there was a shift from the public to the private, for example the taking of shield-ed coaches and dining in private. The exponential rise of print culture from the sixteenth century on spread ideas about what was fashionable and how to look fashionable beyond borders and national settings. | <sup>Pages</sup> 110 |

There are many different ways we can think about fashion. All of them are brought out in different ways in this exhibition. There might be a fash-ion system, a fashion mind-set, a fashion mentality, fashion materiality and fashion production. All of these come together to create the strange beast 'fashion'. Much of this thinking has already been done for us by the great historians of Europe such as Fernand Braudel (1902–1985). In his clas-sic work *Civilisation and Capitalism, 15<sup>th</sup>–18<sup>th</sup> Centuries,* he makes an impor-tant space for sartorial fashions within 'those strange collections of com-modities, symbols, illusions, fantasms and intellectual schemas that we call civilisations'.[3] Braudel disputed that fashion is frivolous and unworthy of investigation, asking instead whether it is 'an indication of a deeper phe-nomena – of the energies, possibilities, demands and *joie de vivre* of a given society, economy and civilisation?'.[4] He also made the important point that fashion is not just about access to money but must consist 'of making a quick change at the right moment'.[5] Braudel's account looks Eurocentric nowadays. He acknowledged that European culture could not exist without the ideas, materiality and exchange with Asia. But he did contribute to the commonly held view that Europe developed fashion whereas other people had costume or dress, stating that fashion in societies such as China was 'immobile'. Im-mobile dress is an impossible position to argue from within any anthropologi-cal framework, and also flies in the face of many of the rewritings of fashion

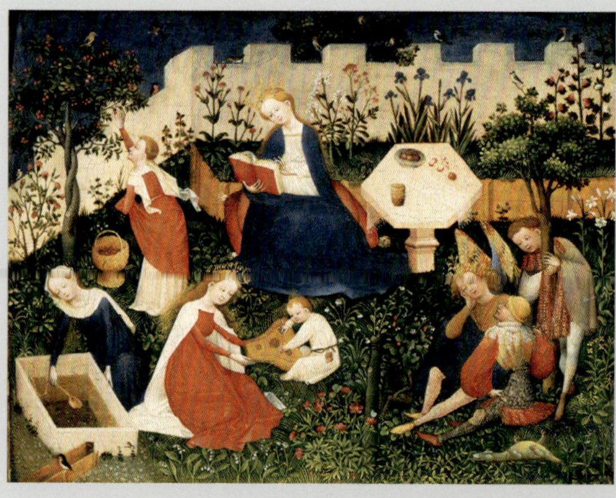



**Fig. 2** Upper Rhenish Master
*Garden of paradise*, c. 1410
Oil on wood, 26 × 33 cm
Frankfurt am Main,
Städelsches Kunstinstitut

history since the Ancient World. There is, however, one key issue that remains somewhat unresolved. Does the very fast – beyond the annual, to the seasonal, or even monthly – fashion change that we associate with European fashion for the upper male and female elites by the late eighteenth century – make European fashion distinctive? Here we have to accept that ideas about fashion do not necessarily match the lived experience of it – even very wealthy people in the past wore clothing from different dates, had their clothes refreshed and remade, and clung to personal preferences and eccentricities.

Braudel therefore saw fashion as an aspect of historical civilisation in which fashion was a part of aesthetic self-realisation (later modernist *Bildung*) as in the earlier writing of Johann Herder (1744–1803) and Jacob Burckhardt (1818–1897) in the nineteenth century. And central to this was the theorising of personal beauty. It is therefore not surprising that the first sociologists of fashion such as Georg Simmel (1858–1918) emerged in Berlin from an ethos saturated with concepts of art for art's sake (*l'art pour l'art*) – a literary and artistic movement involving the likes of Oscar Wilde (1854–1900), Walter Pater (1839–1894) and Stéphane Mallarmé (1842–1898) (all of whom wrote keenly on fashion and male/female beauty) – a transcendental horizon of beauty in all things, whether it be a poem, a piece of porcelain or a dress. Simmel's modern individual has both endless choice but also a veil of social conformity (unless belonging to the world of the outsider, of actors and the demi-monde).

Luxury, too, was often considered synonymous with fashion and held negative moral, often sensual, connotations. It continued to do so well into the twentieth century, in the writings of anti-Semite Werner Sombart (1863–1941). Sombart connected luxury with the rise of capitalism and argued this was largely connected to the domain of women. Sombart blamed the rise of luxury on the consumption habits, including tea, coffee and sugar, of eighteenth-century women, the proliferation of sex workers in nineteenth-century Paris and London and the mobility of cosmopolitan Jews. Luxury was bad, Sombart argued, as it was removed from ideal values (art) and had become base (animal or man). He was reacting in many ways to the mannered society in which he lived, fin-de-siècle Europe. The bizarre distortion of dress and body, the odd mixtures of historicism, and the exploitation of the workers labouring in the fashion industries led to a cultural backlash, generating oppositional dress, dress reform for women and men, | <sup>Pages</sup> **212**<sup>f.</sup> | and the fashion experiments of avant-garde artists. | <sup>Pages</sup> **128, 236, 233** |

It is tempting to see universals in all of this – the idea that all young men like to experiment with fashion and that all women resist the effects of age. But Steven Meisel's (b. 1954) late twentieth-century 'retro' Bel Air (Los Angeles) ladies (actually famous models aping the likes of Betsy Bloomingdale) in their air-conditioned and elegant drawing rooms are not the same as a lady sitting in the *hortus conclusus*. | <sup>Fig.</sup> **2** | We can examine how their fashions, the set of their face, bodies and hair might relate to ideas and ideals of feminine beauty and patriarchy across time and place. However, the mindset and the cultural horizons of these women are completely different. For example, the theorist of court societies, Norbert Elias (1897–1990), would argue in 1933 that court culture inhibited bodily function and was very much a product of observing and describing others, in 'memoirs, letters and aphorisms'.[6] Putting such works from different times and places together, as the exhibition *Fashion Drive* does, is a productive exercise. It makes history *strange,* reveals the arbitrary nature of our gendered and class-based worlds, and also underlines the fact that the bizarre appearance of clothed bodies from the past is not so strange compared to our own. How we interpret these fashions from the past is a fascinating and contested matter. We tend to imagine that people from the past were just like us. But rather than seeing women, for example, in the past as *empowered* by their clothes, we could think about the fashions differently, in a pre-emancipatory/liberation context. Fashion in the past often supplied women with a voice and an arena for symbolic gesture and affiliation – when often they had few other avenues open to them (private and professional embroidery was one, explaining one part of the significance of embroidered fashion and upholstery in the past).

Many of the fashions we see in *Fashion Drive* were the product of princely courts, towns and later cities. They raise the question as to who decides and determines fashion and whether it is a mainly urban phenomenon. Within Tudor and Stuart power dressing, the court and monarchs set fashions, which extended from dress to all things. The profligacy of Henry VIII (1491–1547) was infamous. Becoming very overweight in middle age because he could no longer play his favourite sports, Henry disguised his weight in a padded Germanic style. His waist expanded from 38 to 54 inches. His codpiece remained sturdy; it was separate, laced to the hose and doublet, and cod was, of course, slang for scrotum. Henry's 'cod' was boned and padded and must have made quite an impression as he swept into a room. An early extreme exemple can be found on armour. | <sup>Page</sup> **19** | The cod did not survive the next generation, when the masculinist prosthetic fell out of

6    Cited in Peter McNeil, *Fashion: Critical and Primary Sources, Volume 2: The Eighteenth Century,* London 2009, p. XVIII.

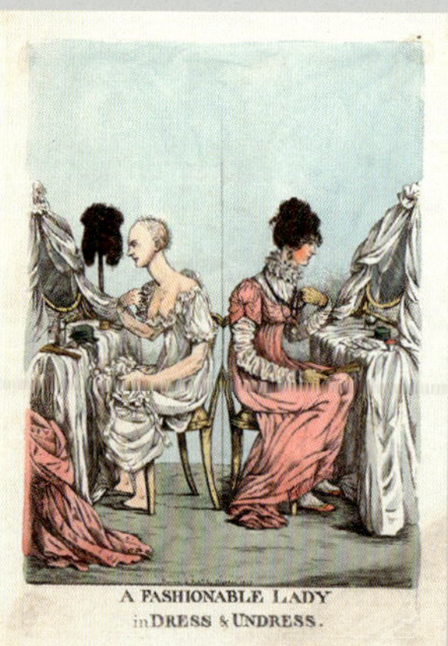

**Fig. 3** Robert Dighton (1786-1865)
*A fashionable lady in dress & undress,* 1807
Etching, hand-coloured, sheet: 33 × 23 cm
Lewis Walpole Library, Prints and Drawings,
Yale University

fashion across Europe. They are one of the only clothing moments for men when the scrotum was foregrounded – apart from the years following the French Revolution when breeches (worn by the *Incroyables* and in the *Directoire*) were scandalously sheer, and the peacock revolution of the 1960s. Today anyone can see through any man's grey track suit and Instagram sites are devoted to such lofty delights. Clothing often holds and manages these bodily analogies and amplifications. The notion of the 'erogenous zones' (an idea coming from John C. Flügel, 1884–1955, in the 1920s–30s) is well known today, but it is not a modern concept. In the Renaissance, a bodice could be called a pair of body parts, laced at the sides. Sleeves were separate and sometimes multiple sets were worn over each other. This type of 'extreme' fashion appears at various times and dates – in the period around the French Revolution, men's fashion included enormously high collars and elongated waistcoat collars flapped down over their equally large jacket revers, having no function apart from suggesting that fashion had exceeded the human form and also social needs. | <sup>Pages</sup> 112<sup>f.</sup> | Fashionable clothes were very expensive in the past compared to other costs of living and remained so until the 1950s. Some prominent royals had fewer clothes than many wealthy people today. Marie-Antoinette (1755–1793) ordered 36 dresses three times a year from the fashionable designer Rose Bertin (1747–1813) and many more informal gowns and also had her old dresses remade. But Empress Elizabeth of Russia had 15,000 dresses when she died in 1761, certainly extreme fashion holdings. Despite what is often said about the French, they maintained an earthy humour closely grounded to reality. The very precise Daniel Roche tells us that 12% of French proverbs concern clothes: they include 'she who neither sews nor patches needs a large income' and 'for every wash a tear'.[7] Colours, as in the Middle Ages, continued to be precise and also often bodily – queen's hair, king's eye, bull's blood, Paris mud and goose shit.[8]

Fashionable appearances were often associated with disappointment and deception. Jacques-Henri Meister (1744–1826), who visited England from Switzerland in the late eighteenth century, noted the fine black or dark

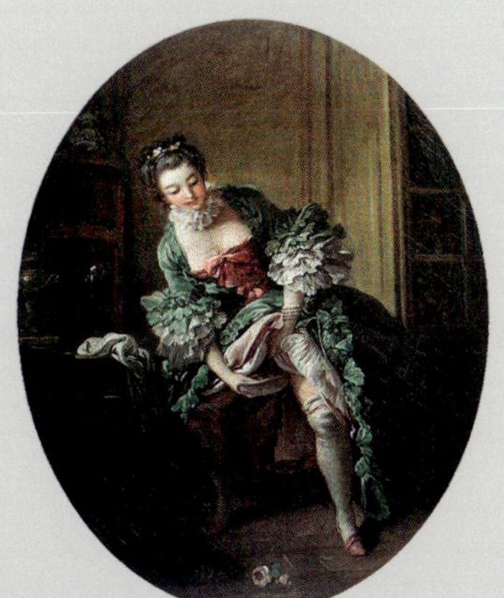

**Fig. 4** François Boucher (1703–1770)
*La Toilette intime* ou *La Jupe relevée,* 1760s
Oil on canvas, 52.5 × 42 cm
Current location unknown

chestnut hair of English ladies, only to learn that these colours were the fashion and many were wearing false hair.[9] | Fig. **3** | 'English beauty is more striking than attractive', he noted.[10] An Englishman, on the other hand, visiting France, note the artificial aids used by French women to improve their complexions, such as regularly inserting the glyster (enema) but noting that their faces could not be seen for the paint at any rate.[11] Fashion extended to gold, silver and Sèvres chamber pots for women *(bourdaloues),* depicted by the elegant pornographers and fine artists of the eighteenth century alike. | Fig. **4.** |

A text of the mid-eighteenth century was quite explicit on the difference between men's dress and *la mode de France* – for the travels of a gentleman it was recommended that he carry a dozen shirts, six pairs of shoes, silk stockings and a pair of buckskin breeches, but that this would still be inadequate: 'for at the first town you propose to reside at, you should fit out *à la mode de France,* and continue so as long as you stay in that country: don't think this advice unreasonable; as an *English* dress, is a sufficient object for *French* knavery'.[12] Here we find the deep oppositions between Protestant/Catholic, restrained/flamboyant, English/Continental and masculine/feminine that structure much thinking about fashion.

Fashion and urban space are very closely linked. The thinker Richard Sennett made this the basis of his *Flesh and Stone: The Body and the City in Western Civilisation* (1994). It was in Paris that the squares, streets and quais began to resemble a rational map, rather than the jumbled haphazardness of a medieval city. The multitude of streets and shops encouraged a new relationship of nineteenth-century city folk to their urbanity and their clothes. They needed clothes for showing off in good weather. The sociologist Zygmunt Bauman (1925–2017), too, contrasts the visual order that was so very important in the early modern city with the ambiguous, equivocal nature of the nineteenth-century city, full of transgression as well as regulation. In this modern centre might be found the *boulevardier,* the *flâneur,* the actress, the cross-dresser and the male or female prostitute. Nineteenth-century essayists thought fashion to be central to zeitgeist. Charles Baudelaire's (1821–1867) mid-nineteenth-century

<hr>

7    Daniel Roche, *The Culture of Clothing. Dress and fashion in the 'ancien régime',* trans. Jean Birrell, Cambridge 1994 [1st published as *La Culture des Apparences,* Paris 1989], pp. 376–77.

8    Roche, 1994, p. 143.

9    Jacques-Henri Meister, *Letters written during a residence in England, translated from the French of Henry Meister, containing many curious remarks upon English manners and customs, government, climate, literature, theatre, &c.&c.&c., together with a letter from the Margravine of Anspach to the Author (1799),* London 2010, p. 24.

10    Meister, 2010, p. 280.

11    [no author] *The Gentleman's Guide, in his Tours through France, Wrote by an Officer in the Royal-Navy…* Bristol (S. Farley) and Dublin (Smith and Son) 1766, p. 73.

12    *The Gentleman's Guide,* 1766, pp. 11–12.

A Fold of Clothing Is a Trace of Passion

opinion regarding the significance of fashion as extracting an essential *jus* concerning past and present is well known. Hippolyte Taine (1828–1893) used a similar approach in arguing why fashion mattered: 'I go up to Estampes [the print collection of the Bibliothèque Nationale] and I looked at the sixteenth-century masters … A fold of clothing is a trace of passion like an epithet. I endeavoured to rediscover and to experience those of the sixteenth century.'[13] Fashion continued to be an important topic for twentieth-century cultural and poetic thinkers. In 1967 the theorist Pierre Bourdieu with Yvonne Delsaut wrote a topical article 'Le couturier et sa griffe: contribution à une théorie de la magie' (the couturier and his brand *(marque)* – contribution to a theory of magic). Bourdieu and Delsaut were responding to the decline of the exclusive haute couture production of fashion and the rise of the Left Bank 'ready to wear' characterised by the meteoric rise of Yves Saint Laurent's Rive Gauche. | Fig. **5** |

The haute couture they call 'une opération de transubstantiation symbolique, irréductible à une transformation matérielle' (an operation of trans-substantiation, irreducible to a material form).[14] The essay goes on to remark that the contemporary 'crisis' of haute couture (many people believed it was about to disappear) is perhaps less a restructuring than the appearance of a focus on new signs of 'distinction', such as luxury sports, distant voyages and secondary or holiday residences. Bourdieu and Delsaut skilfully played with the words *la mode* (the fashion) versus *le mode* – the mode or manner of doing things – just as the word *costume* and *custom* have also been fruitfully connected for centuries by writers trying to define sartorial fashions. Throughout much of the twentieth century and our own times, critical fashion makers as diverse as Elsa Schiaparelli (1890–1973), Mai-Thu Perret (b. 1976) and K8 Hardy (b. 1977) have grounded the act of dressing and appearing with the artifice of fashion. | Pages **235, 239, 238, 276** |

On reflection, it seems that fashion requires either an elaborate court with many outlying suppliers or better still a metropolis, in order to flourish. It is thus hardly surprising that the three great metropolises

**13**    Hippolyte Taine, *Extraits* from Correspondence 23 November 1855, author's translation. 'Expositions sur la Gravure de Mode', Bibliothèque Nationale, Galerie Mansart, April 1961 [unpublished folio of photographs of the exhibit], BN. Est. Ad392, unpaginated.

**14**    Pierre Bourdieu and Yvette Delsaut, 'Le couturier et sa griffe: contribution à une théorie de la magie', *Actes de la recherche en sciences sociales*, 1.1, (1975), pp. 7–36, at p. 21.

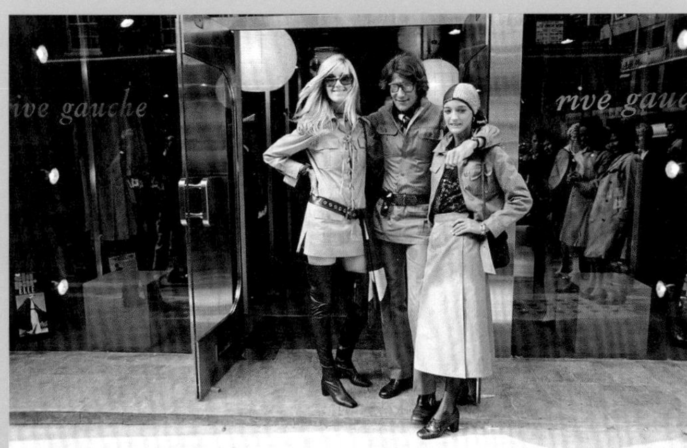



**Fig. 5** Yves Saint Laurent (1936–2008)
The designer pictured outside his first London
Rive Gauche store on New Bond Street, London,
on the opening day of the boutique, and with muses Louise
de La Falaise, aka Loulou (right) and Betty Catroux (left),
10 September 1969

with populations above 500,000 people that arose by the eighteenth century –
London, Paris and Edo (Tokyo) – were also great centres of fantastical fashion
expenditure, attenuation and excess. In many of these exquisite paintings,
sculptures, media works and prints, we see echoes of their extreme fashion
cultures, past and present.



A Fold of Clothing Is a Trace of Passion

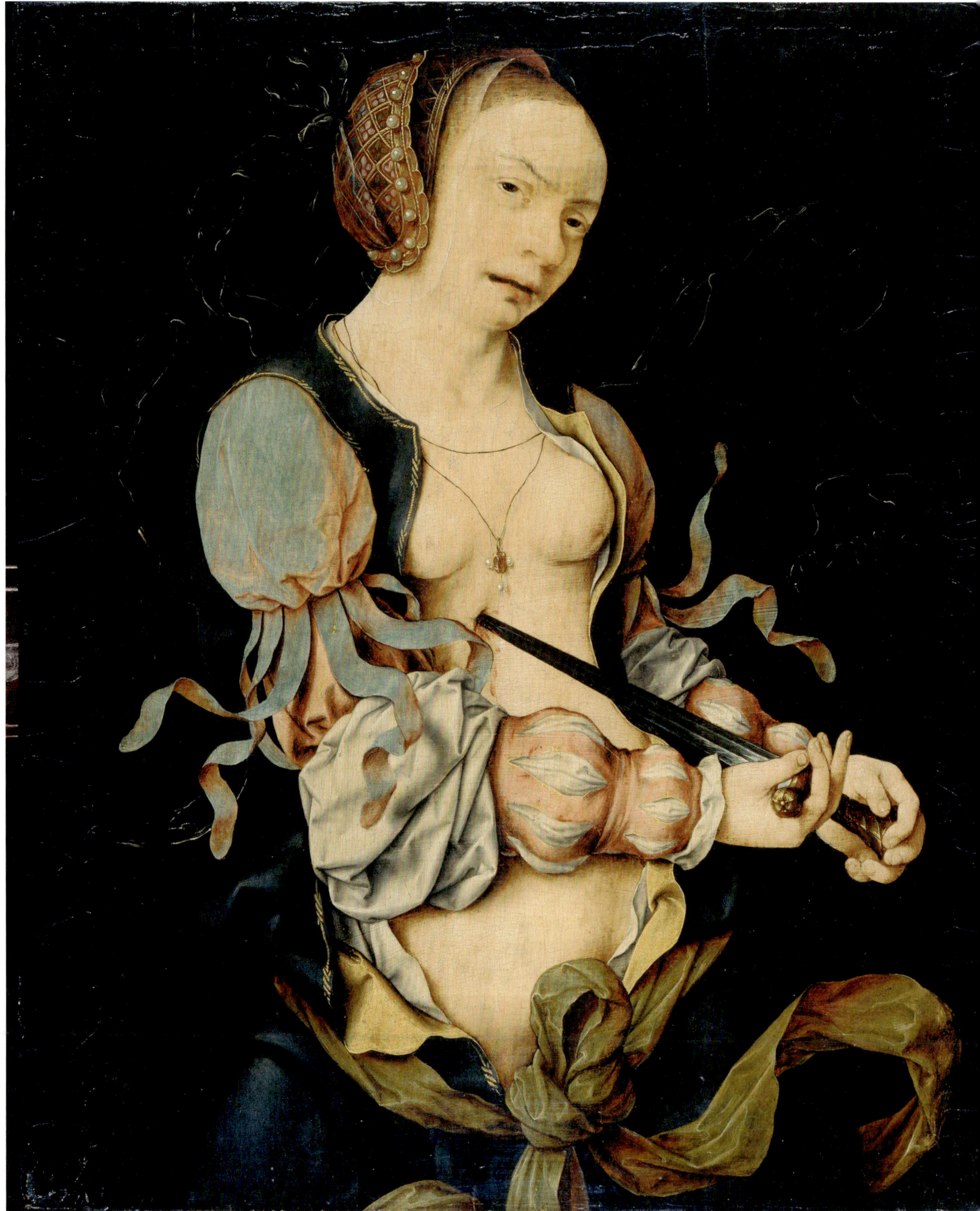

**76**  Joos van Cleve (1485–1541)
*Lucretia,* 1515/1518
Oil on oak, 47.7 × 35.3 cm
Kunsthaus Zürich, The Ruzicka Foundation, 1949

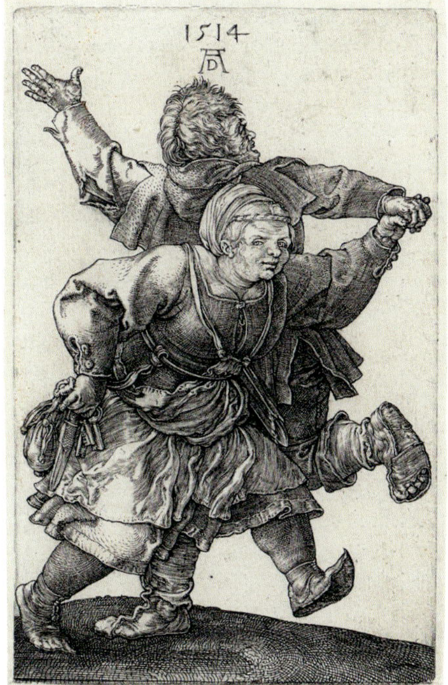

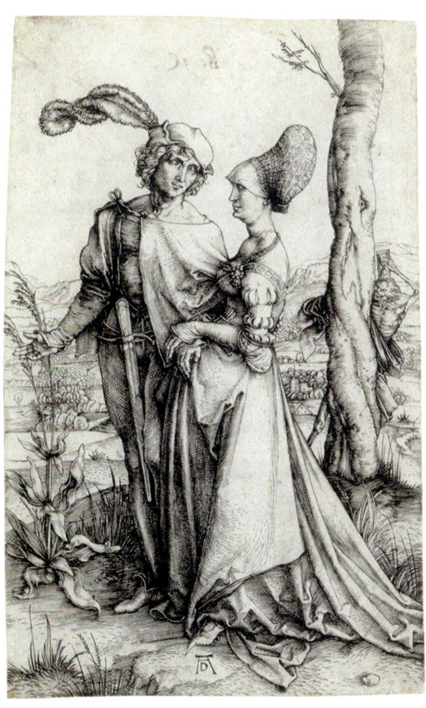

**125** Albrecht Dürer (1471–1528)
*Das tanzende Bauernpaar,* 1514
Peasant couple dancing
Copper engraving, sheet: 11.9 × 7.7 cm
Kunsthaus Zürich, Department
of Prints and Drawings, Sammlung
Landammann Dietrich Schindler, 2000

**122** Albrecht Dürer (1471–1528)
*Das Liebespaar und der Tod
(Der Spaziergang),* c. 1498
Young couple threatened by Death,
or The promenade
Copper engraving, image: 19.3 × 11.8 cm
Kunsthaus Zürich, Department
of Prints and Drawings, Sammlung
Landammann Dietrich Schindler, 2000



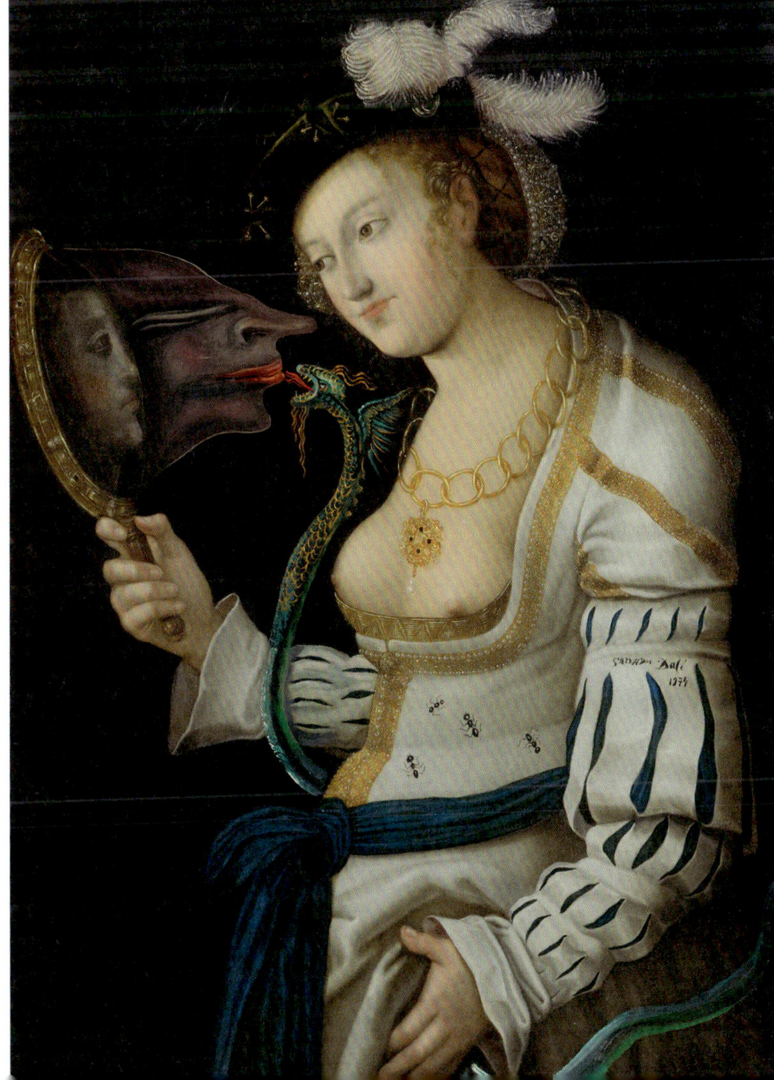

**86** Salvador Dalí (1904–1989)
*Transformación de una pintura
de Matthias Gerung,* 1974
Oil on wood, 82 × 60 cm
Private collection, Switzerland

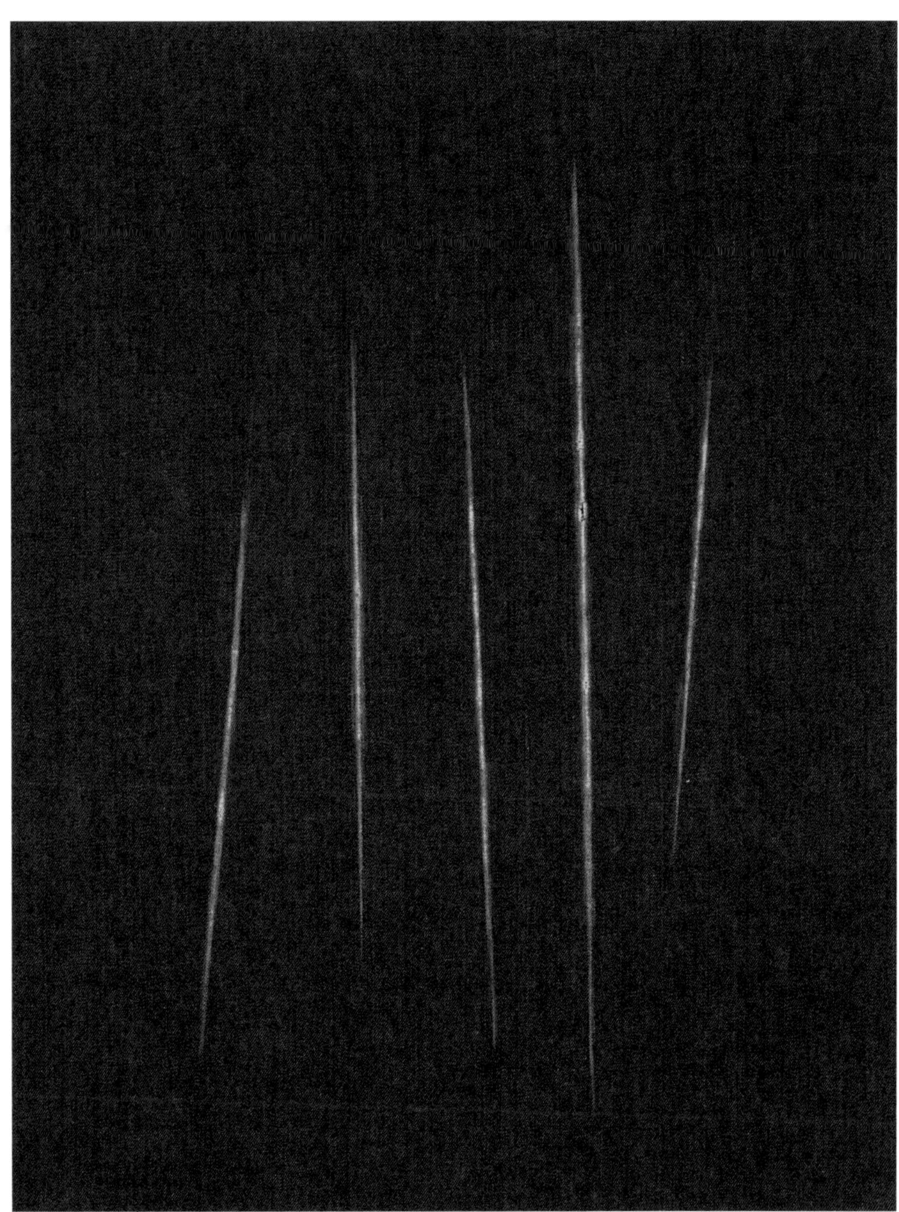

**138**  Sylvie Fleury (b. 1961)
*Concetto Speziale,* 2016
Denim on wooden stretcher, 80 × 60 cm
Private collection, Zurich

**239**  Francesco Salviati (1510–1563)
*Portrait of a young man,* after 1548
Oil on wood, 89 × 69 cm
Liechtenstein. The Princely Collections,
Vaduz-Vienna

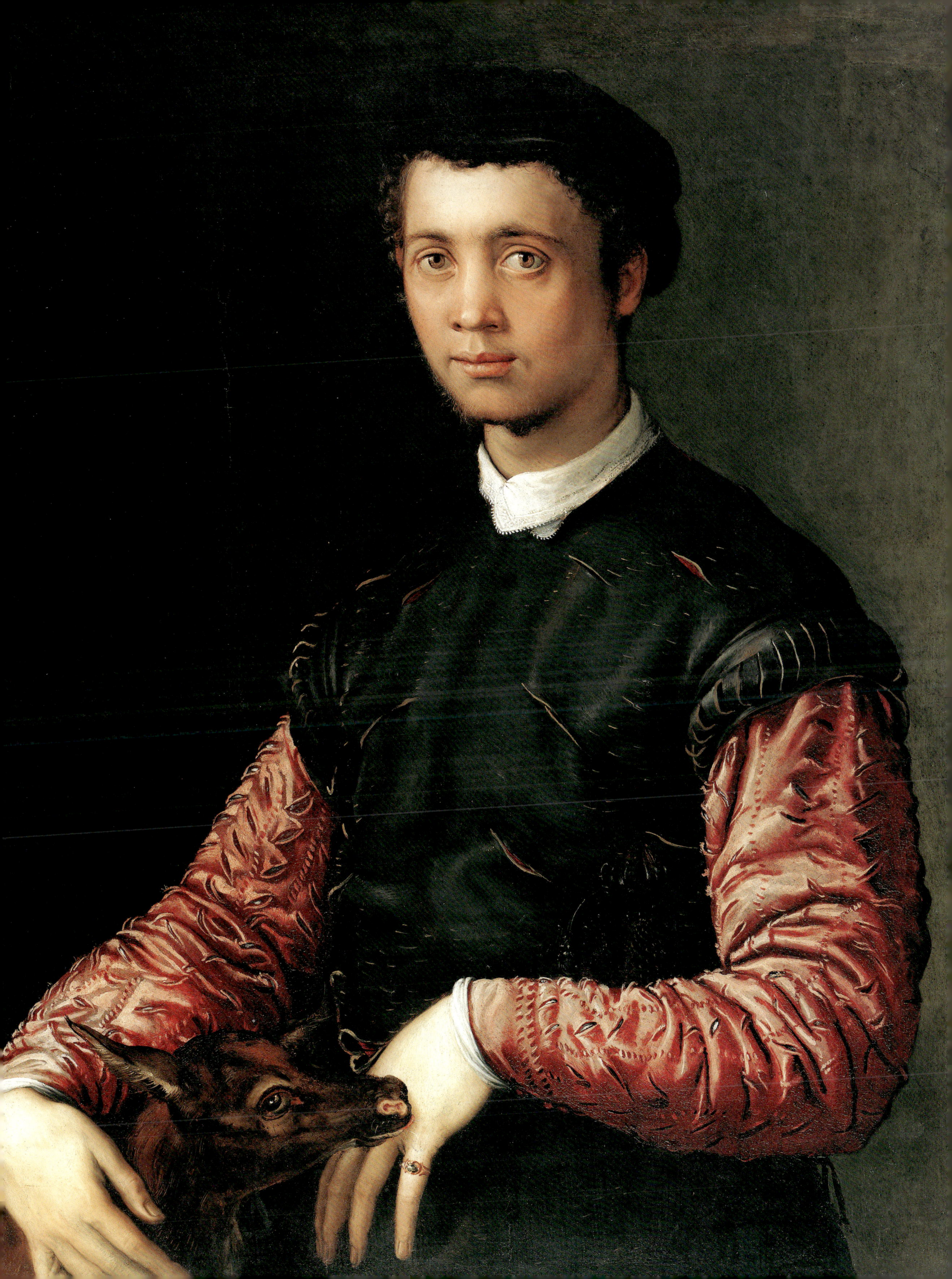

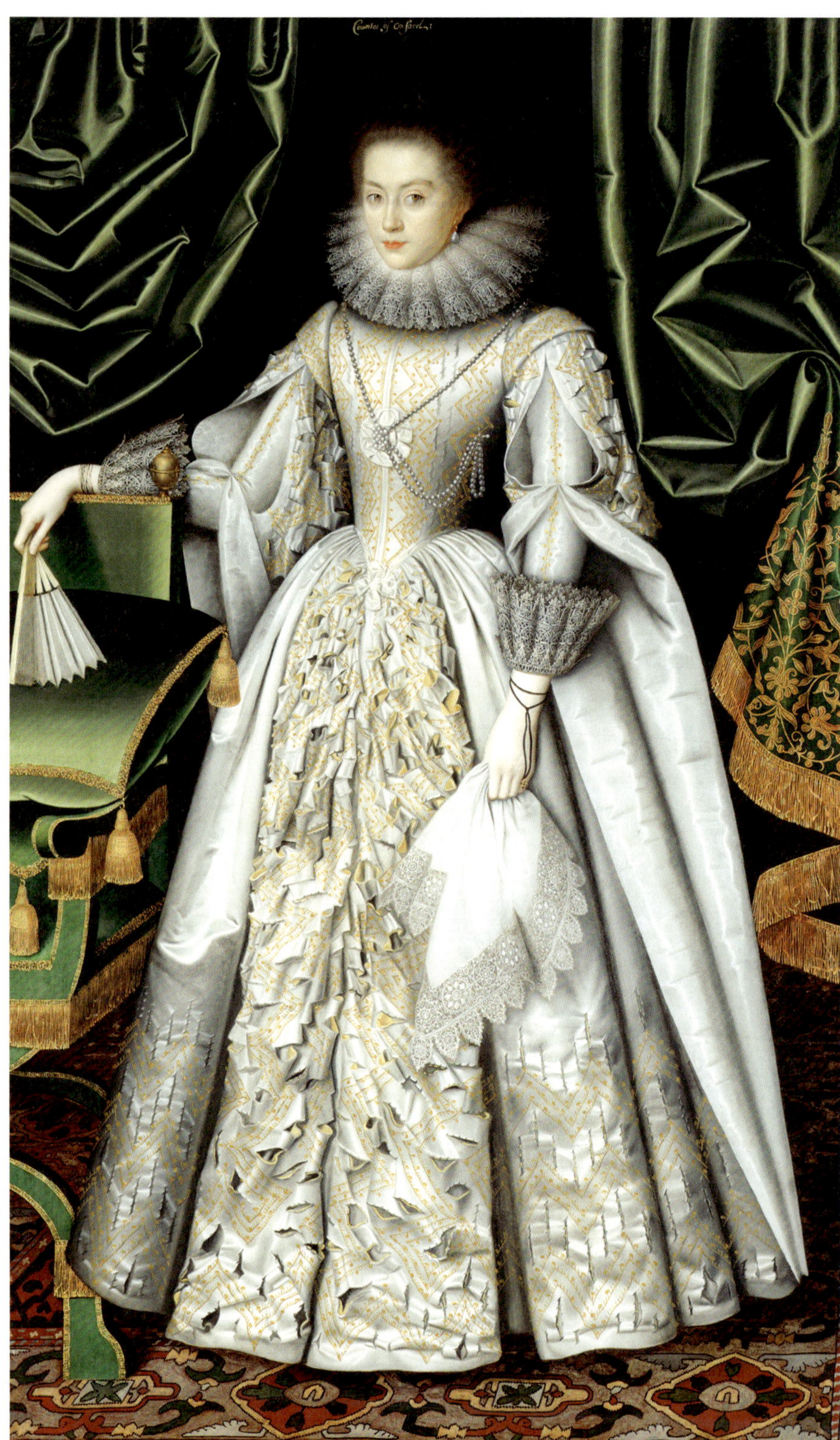





**192** William Larkin (1580–1619)
*Portrait of Diana Cecil, later*
*Countess of Oxford,* c. 1614–18
Oil on canvas, 205.9 × 119.5 cm
English Heritage, The Iveagh Bequest
(Kenwood, London)

# Silkworms for Daniela Hoferer

*The ability to reproduce the recorded in the light of the thread.*
*Not like that highly gifted child. Like the silkworm: physically!*
*Even the chameleon. It touches: you. And enchants: itself.*
*Because we now know each other across the countries,*
*she asks me, if the scars' new invisibility*
*will flow into the face. I say: as a fragment perhaps.*
*As leg of the spider, tail of the lizard, horn of the ox.*
*Everything that grows back is part of this world. So also her thread.*

*As an embroiderer, she stitches the minus to the plus in the system of coordinates,*
*connects worlds through threads, is pupil of the Moirai,*
*a diplomat of the horizon.*
*One like her embroidered a pillow with a love letter,*
*that was also a life story, both to frown upon.*
*Thus, the stitches are always the same. Only those that prick her vary.*
*She explains to me that the needles must be chosen exactly,*
*thread and stitch type dictated. I think, foil or sword?*
*To stabilise the flood of images is her Petersburg concept,*
*led by the thread through the labyrinth. It creates kaleidoscopes.*

*A hole is quickly punctured in the world. To fill it,*
*to fill it again and again, that's the lot.*
*The silkworm eats holes and absences into the world*
*and fills itself up with it.*
*When it eats white, it becomes wise,*
*when it eats black, depressed.*
*In it grows and from her threads itself the universe,*
*which according to Hawking is only absence and perforation.*

*I still want to say this:*

*Her gaze pierced me, to skilfully thread myself on it.*
*Me, the camel, through her eye.*



Nora Gomringer

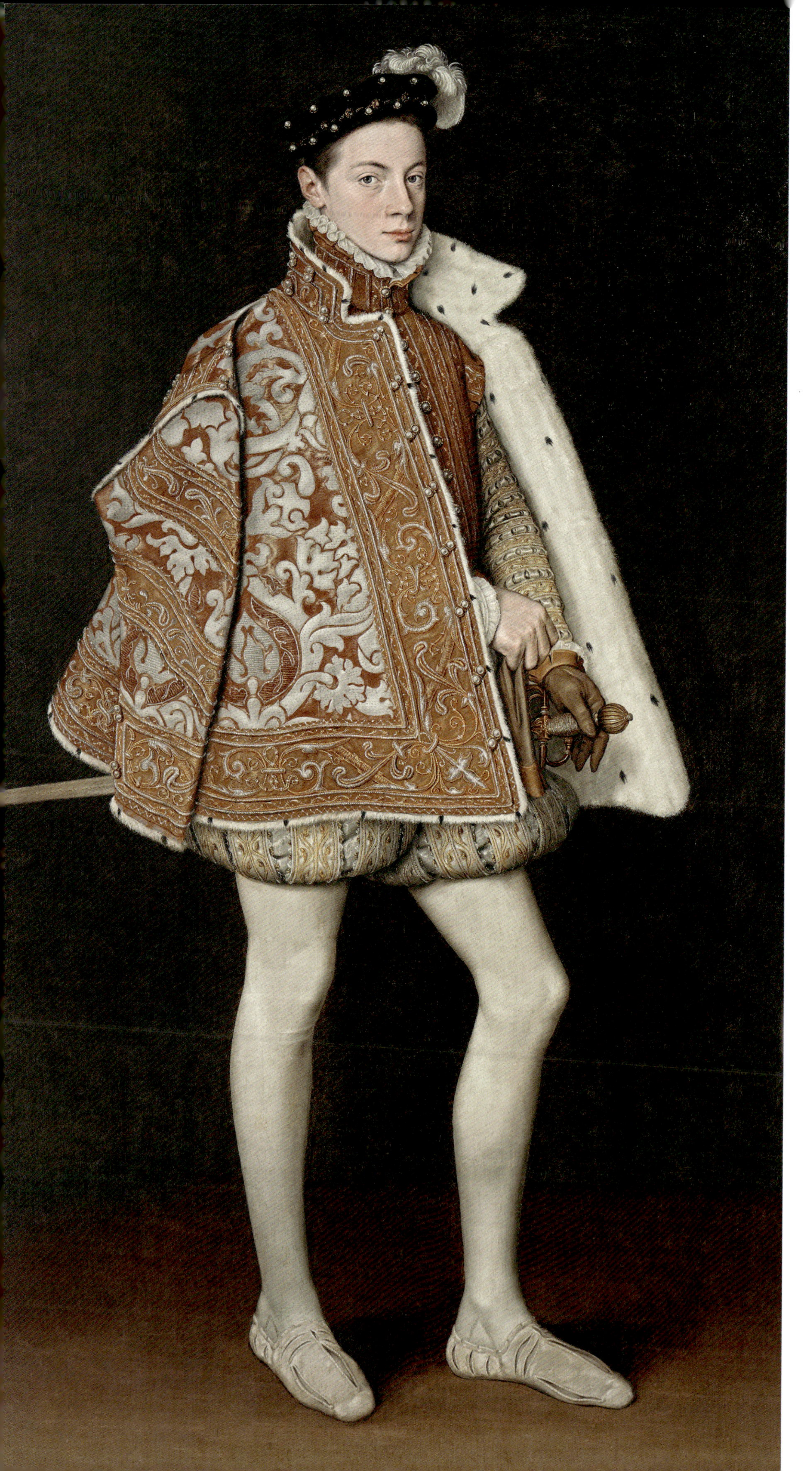

**218** Antonis Mor (1516/1521–1576/77)
*Alessandro Farnese in cape and cap,* c. 1560
Oil on canvas, 174 × 97 cm
Liechtenstein. The Princely Collections,
Vaduz-Vienna

**265** Unknown artist
*Portrait of Prince Hartmann
von Liechtenstein (1613–1686),* c. 1630
Oil on canvas, 201 × 98 cm
Liechtenstein. The Princely Collections,
Vaduz-Vienna

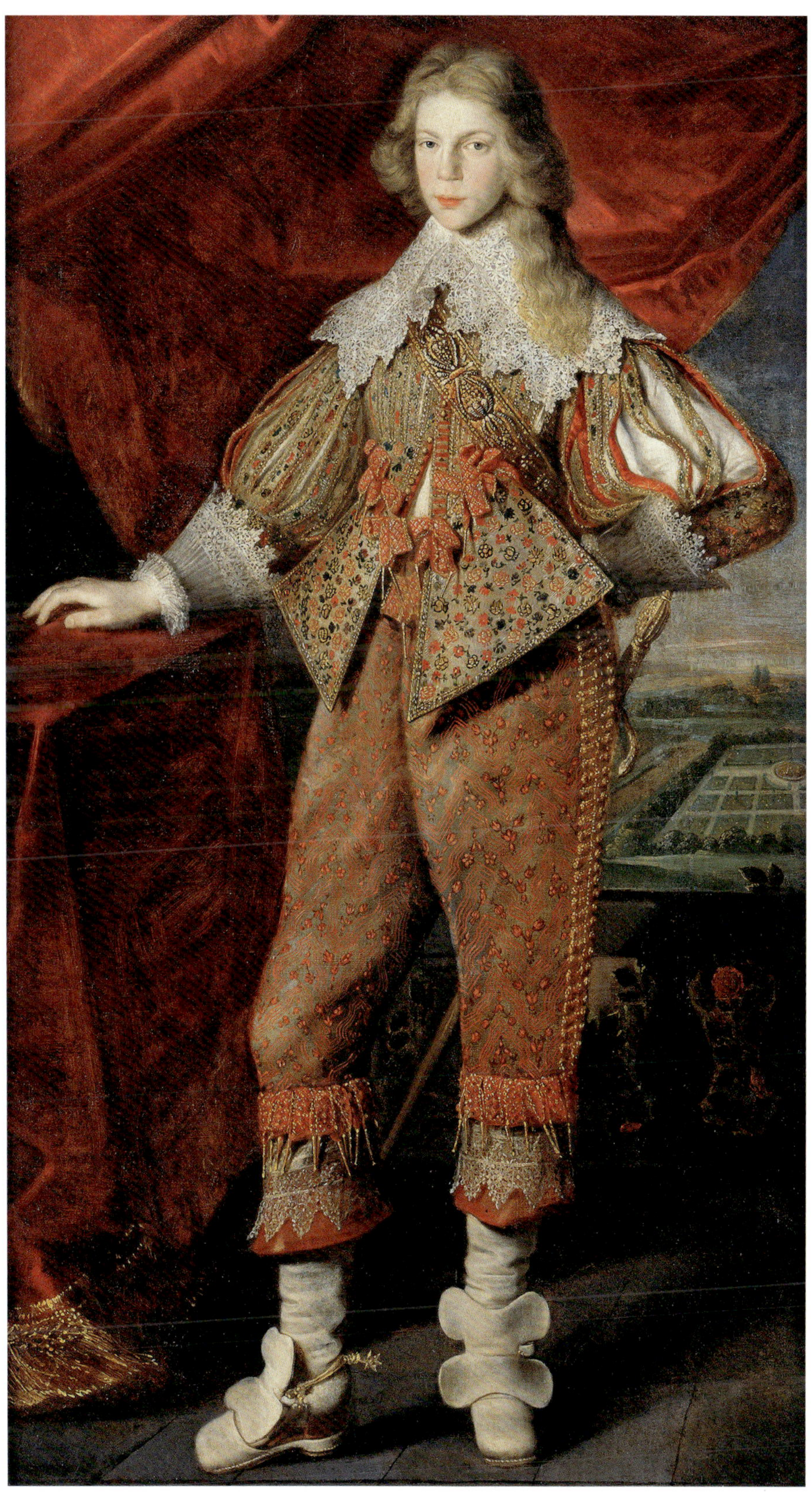

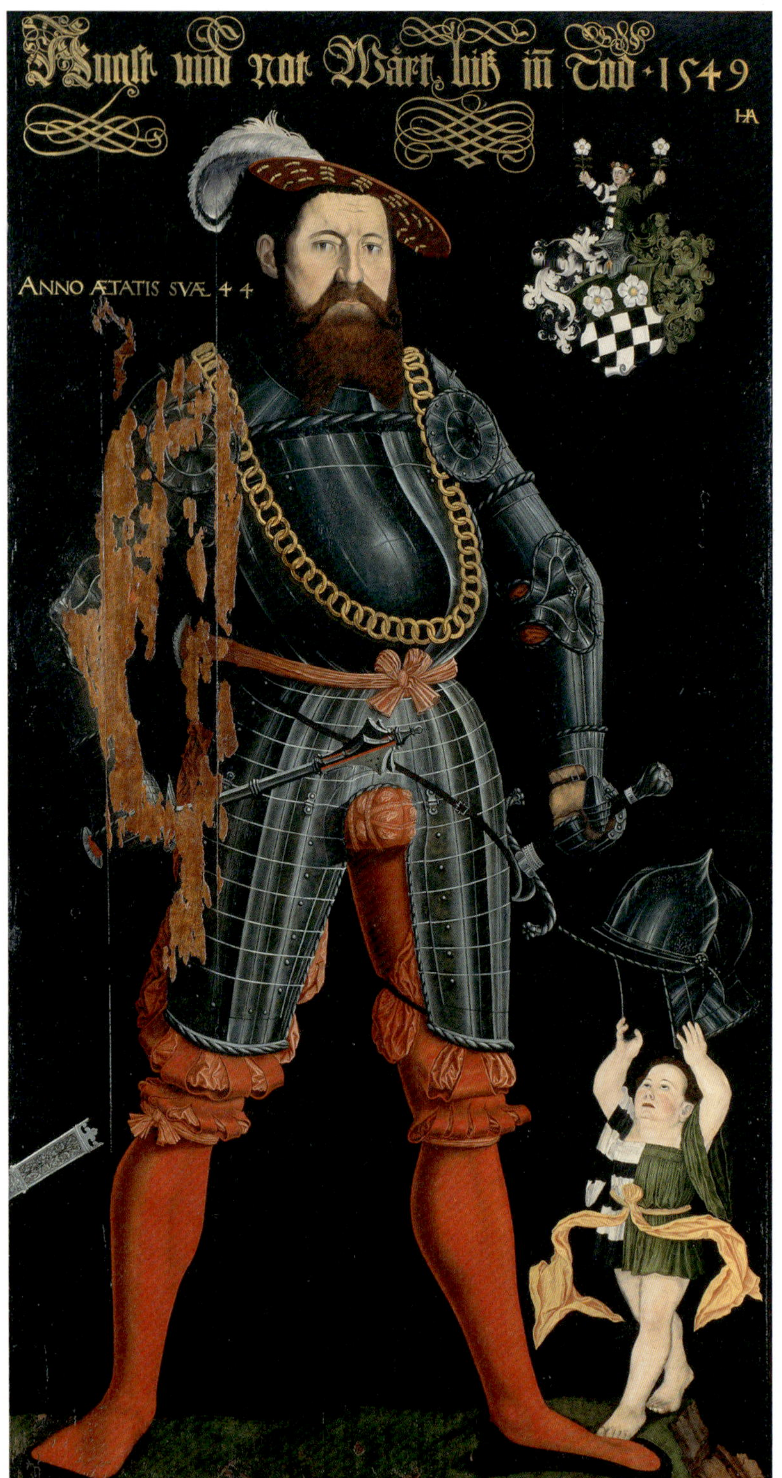


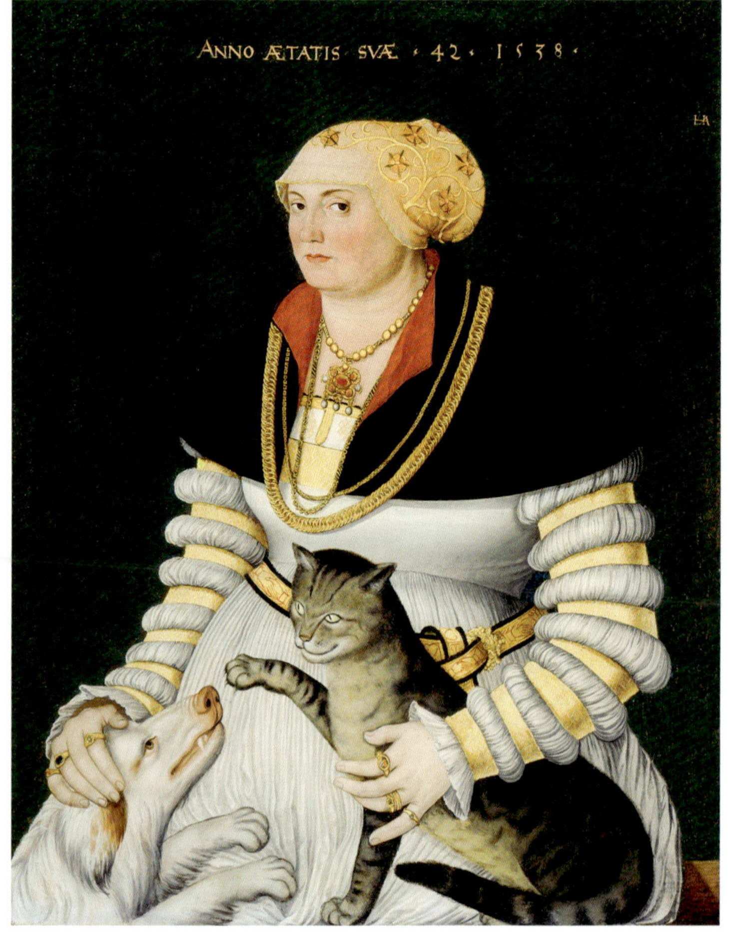


**45**  Hans Asper (1499–1571)
*Portrait of a gentleman: Wilhelm Frölich.*
*With the Frölich family's coat of arms and*
*upper coat of arms,* Solothurn 1549
Oil and tempera on wood, 213 × 111 cm
Schweizerisches Nationalmuseum, Zurich

**44**  Hans Asper (1499–1571)
*Portrait of Cleophea Krieg von Bellikon,* 1538
Tempera and oil on wood, 77 × 61 cm
Kunsthaus Zürich, Keller Collection, 1854

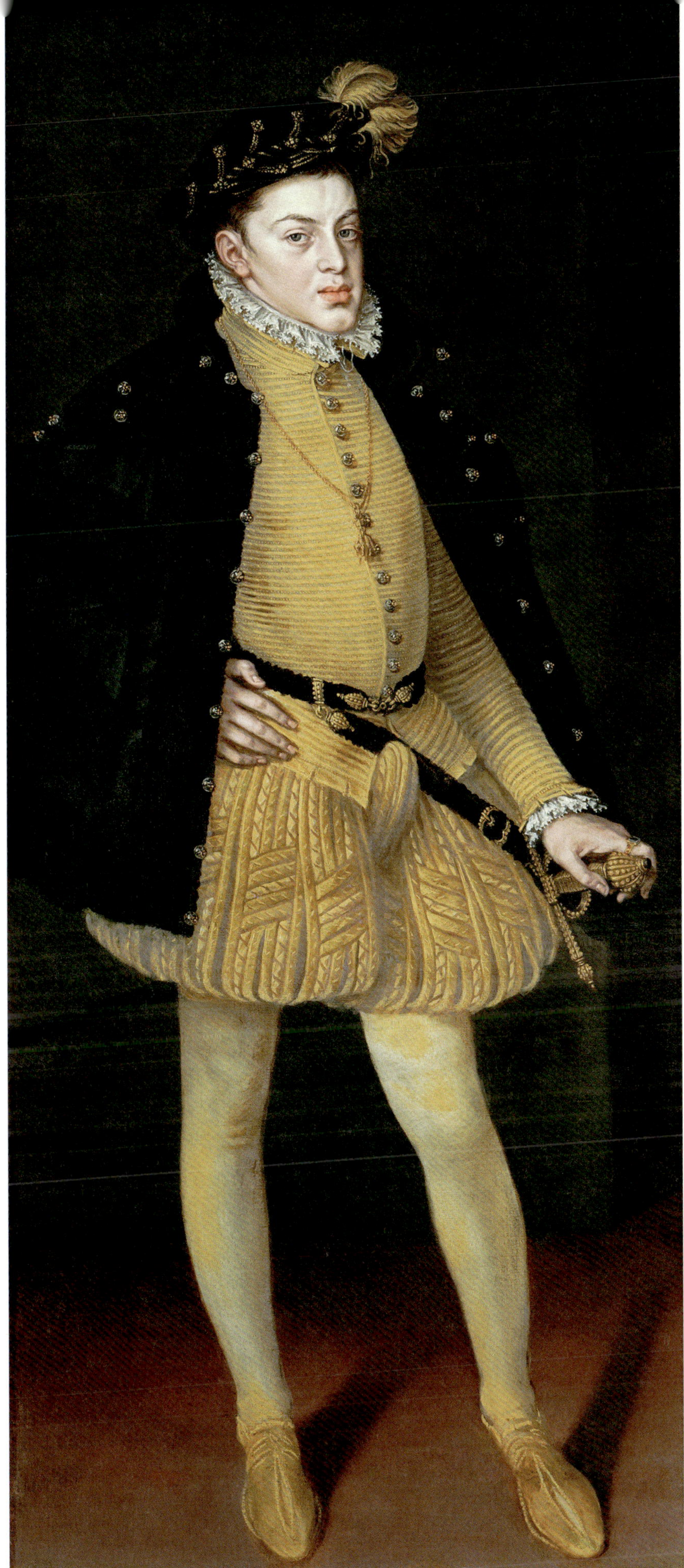

**77** Alonso Sánchez Coello (1531/32–1588)
*Infant Don Carlos (1545–1568),* 1564
Oil on canvas, 186 × 82.5 cm
KHM-Museumsverband, Picture Gallery

# Animals

## From Feathers to Fur and Their

Philipp Zitzlsperger

# in Fashion

## Silk to and Faux-Fur Sensual Appeals

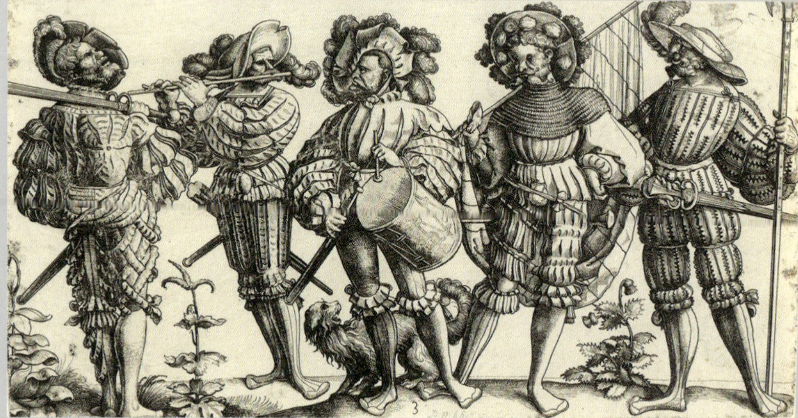

**Fig. 1** Daniel Hopfer (1470–1536)
*Fünf Landsknechte*
Five landsknechts
Iron etching, sheet: 20.5 × 37.6 cm
Staatliche Graphische Sammlung
München

Especially fine attire with decorations of animal origin has a long history, handed down to us primarily through works of art. History paintings, portraits, costume books and later also photographs are important sources for reconstructing the vestimentary culture of (pre-) modernism. Also, since the seventeenth century, the caustic mockery of caricatures provide important clues to social faux pas in clothing. Material evidence from real life began to accumulate in the eighteenth century and continued into the modern age. However, a complete picture of the fashion worlds can hardly be reconstructed because images can be misunderstood as direct reflections of a past reality. Even real artefacts sometimes provide only fleeting glimpses into the world of a particular fashion – a fashion that caused a sensation through their animal products alone, such as feathers, furs or silk.

Especially feathers were assigned a particular task as adornment. Like other accessories, they were ornaments, decorations or additional applications that were always part of a complex symbolic communication. As noted previously: What we see in images, does not necessarily correspond to real life. For this reason, clothing and its ornaments are, in pictorial representation, relevant to the interpretation of particular images, and only in a second instance does the question arise of their relationship to reality. Albrecht Dürer's (1471–1528) copper engraving *Der Fahnenschwinger* (The standard bearer, c. 1501) | Page **24** | epitomises the problem of interpretation. Viewed in isolation, the depiction of a flag-bearing landsknecht (mercenary soldier) might suggest that people obviously liked to wear feathers. This is also confirmed by written sources, which claim that the trade in ostrich feathers flourished in the early modern period.[1] And the soldier on Dürer's engraving wears extravagant, clearly visible, widely swaying ostrich feathers on a hat that cannot be seen because it is not worn on his head but resting on his back and held by a string around his neck. When one compares images, however, one quickly realises that the bushy feathers in such arm-length dimensions are rather rare. In Dürer, you will find an elaborate feather decoration in the form of two wings of an eagle in the copper engraving *Wappen mit dem Totenkopf* (Coat of

**1** Ingrid Loschek, *Reclams Mode- und Kostümlexikon*, Stuttgart 2011, p. 191.

**2** Cf. Lucas Cranach the Elder's *Portrait of A. of Rechenberg* (1535–40, Staatliche Kunsthalle Karlsruhe, inv. no. 122) with the ostentatious grasp of the sword's pommel. Portraits of ladies by the Cranachs are numerous. See, for example, Lucas Cranach the Elder's *Portrait of Three Ladies* (c. 1535, Kunsthistorisches Museum Vienna, inv. no. 877).

**3** *Albrecht Dürer: Die Druckgraphiken im Städel Museum*, Martin Sonnabend, exh. cat. Städel Museum, Frankfurt am Main, Cologne 2007, p. 194.



Philipp Zitzlsperger

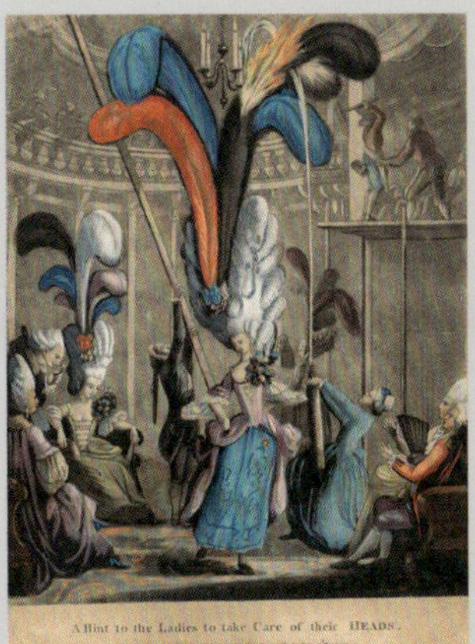

**Fig. 2** Philip Dawe (c. 1750–after 1790)
*A hint to the ladies to take care
of their heads,* London 1776
Mezzotint, hand-coloured,
sheet: 36.6 × 26.8 cm
Staatliche Museen zu Berlin,
Kunstbibliothek

**Fig. 3** Inez van Lamsweerde (b. 1963)
and Vinoodh Matadin (b. 1961)
*Fur – Kym,* 1994
Colour photograph, C-print, mounted on
aluminium plate, behind plexiglas,
183 × 183 cm
Kunsthaus Zürich, Zürcher Kunstgesellschaft

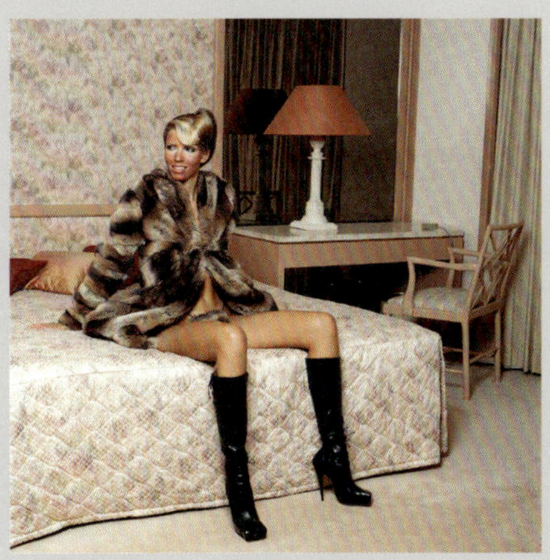

arms with a skull, 1503). They are the heraldic decor of a knight's helmet above the coat-of-arms cartouche with the skull. The hirsute man holding the coat of arms approaches a lady with a wide cleavage and, together with the oversized relief of a skull, the engraving gains a moralising element in which the feather decoration begins to appear as a supersized, extravagant, vain bric-a-brac. The suggestion, however, that feathers once again had a warlike connotation leads to a further search for evidence in visual images from Dürer's time: The exuberant feather decoration was reserved primarily for mercenaries and soldiers.[2] | Page 58 | Dürer's successors created numerous engravings of landsknechts; they were widely distributed, such as by the Augsburgian Daniel Hopfer (1470–1536), whose famous image *Fünf Landsknechte* (Five landsknechts) may have originated shortly after Dürer's *Der Fahnenschwinger* (The standard bearer). The illustration has five rustic soldiers in the then-typical style of slashed fabric and with exuberant headdresses. All have wide-brimmed hats with the familiar ostrich feathers. | Fig. 1 | In contrast, portraits of this period's social elites bear witness to a restraint in the use of feathers. Ostrich feathers appear on the men's hats – if at all – only as small accents, apparently avoiding exuberance. The cursory inspection of the paintings and graphics of the Dürer period indicate that – at least for men – it was not appropriate to don exuberant feather trimmings. In keeping with the decorum, the decorative ostrich feather was reserved for mercenaries as well as for women, but it rarely appears in the portraits of women. Only later, in the eighteenth century, do feathers count in standardised headdresses of the court ladies. | Fig. 2 | More often, however, they appear in boys' portraits, especially in the Baroque period, which could be interpreted as a reference to a future military career. | Page 79 | Here the circle closes with the landsknechte in terms of the feather decoration. Their costumes were not yet standardised into uniforms; they were dazzlingly colourful and covered with the slashed textile technique, which was elaborate and expensive to produce. Their feather ornaments crowned the (colourful) spectacle in the images, which must have been as lavish as it was frightening.

Exaggerated decoration was often beyond the decorum, that is, of premodern 'good taste'. That is precisely because, at the beginning of the sixteenth century, feather accessories in the men's world were apparently confined to the 'profession' of mercenaries or landsknechte; the obvious conclusion is that feathered decoration evoked something daring. The connotation of the lush ostrich feathers as a sign of lascivious waste and a celebrated affection for sinfulness finally seems to have found its confirmation in Dürer's *Der Reiter* or *Ritter, Tod und Teufel* (Knight, Death and the Devil, 1513). The image of the armoured rider completely without feather trimmings is popularly interpreted as *miles christianus,* the virtuous knight.[3]

Fur was also a popular vestimentary decoration of the early modern period, especially north of the Alps. In the premodern era, fur signified social rank, only privileged people were allowed to visibly wear it; in

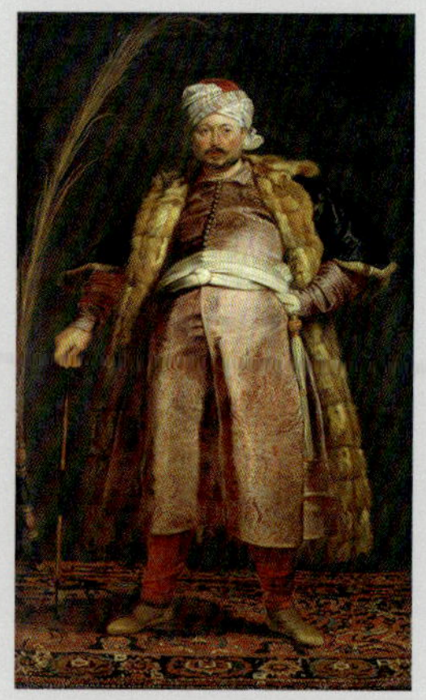



the modern age, fur became the insignia of luxury, decadence and also lasciviousness. For example, this is alluded to in Inez van Lamsweerde (b. 1963) and Vinoodh Matadin's (b. 1961) photograph *Fur – Kym* | Fig. 3 | depicting a model wearing a fur coat and slip designed by Vivienne Westwood (b. 1941). In 1994, this kind of use of fur in art was quite provocative from several perspectives. On the one hand, the 1990s are characterised by globally organised fur protests by different animal welfare organisations. On the other hand, the photograph associates fur with sex and prostitution. The hotel-room ambience and the fur wearer, who apart from a pair of patent-leather boots wears only a slip, are not only delicately provocative, but so too is the fact that Vivienne Westwood is, at least today, one of the most well-known eco-activists in the fashion industry. Despite all the criticism, fur still enjoys an undisturbed attractiveness, even in our time – a piquant detail revealed in closer inspection of Lamsweerde & Matadin's photograph is that it is faux-fur, for which no animal had to die, nevertheless, the acculturated desire can continue to be an irritation. Women are shown, especially in the (advertising) pictorial world, as passionate wearers of fur. In the past, in contrast, men initially had to rely on fur as a status symbol – as in the example of the feather decoration. In the early modern period, it was used mainly as adornment, as a more or less, large-scale ornamental trim. In paintings of the fifteenth and sixteenth centuries, men wore so-called cloaks (coats) trimmed with fur. It is important to note that in the early modern period, fur was generally a status symbol strictly regulated by the dress codes of the time and only awarded to certain high social classes. The dress code meticulously differentiated between lamb, fox, fitch, and marten (throat fur and back fur) – essentially furs that differed greatly in quality. In the fur hierarchy, for example, fox and fitch were among the inferior skins because their hair density is relatively low and their hair-colouring uneven. In contrast, the dense marten fur is particularly uniform and velvety in its colour, and was considered very valuable during the German Renaissance, which is why it was reserved for the social elite in the respective dress codes. In addition, the fur hierarchy had distinctions between the back and throat fur of martens,

4    Covered extensively in Philipp Zitzlsperger's *Dürers Pelz und das Recht im Bild: Kleiderkunde als Methode der Kunstgeschichte,* Berlin 2008.

5    The portrait of Hofmann was also engraved. There, the caption supplies the prosopographic life dates: 'Herr Melchior Maag ward gebohren 1570 [!] | ward Zwölfer auf loblicher Ehren-Zunft zun Schuhmacheren | 1591. Zunftm[eiste]r Nat. 1595. Amtmann zu Winterthur 1599[.] des Raths | Fr. Wahl 1607[.] Gesandter übers Gebirg 1608. BauHerr 1611[.] Landvogt | zu Kyburg 1612[.] Zunftm[eiste]r zum 2ten Mahl auf Joh. Bapt. 1619. | Statthalter 1620. starb 1643. aetatis 73.' {Mr. Melchior Maag was born in 1570 [!] | was local councillor on a commendable honour guild of shoemakers | 1591 guild master nat. 1595. district magistrate of zu Winterthur 1599 [.] of the council | fr. election 1607 [.] legate across the mountains 1608. builder 1611 [.] provincial governor | to Kyburg 1612. guild master for the second time on Joh. Bapt. 1619. | governor 1620. died 1643. aetatis 73.} Underneath is the motto from the Bible: 'Lebend Wir / so lebend Wir dem Herren: / Sterbend Wir / so sterbend Wir dem H[e]r[r]n! [If we live / we live for the Lord; If we die / we die for the Lord] (Romans 14:8)'. Cf. the online portrait collection database of the Herzog August Bibliothek Wolfenbüttel, edited by Peter Mortzfeld, http://portraits. hab.de/werk/28287/ [accessed: 29 August 2017].

6    Cf. Zitzlsperger 2008 (as in note 4), pp. 85–99.



Philipp Zitzlsperger

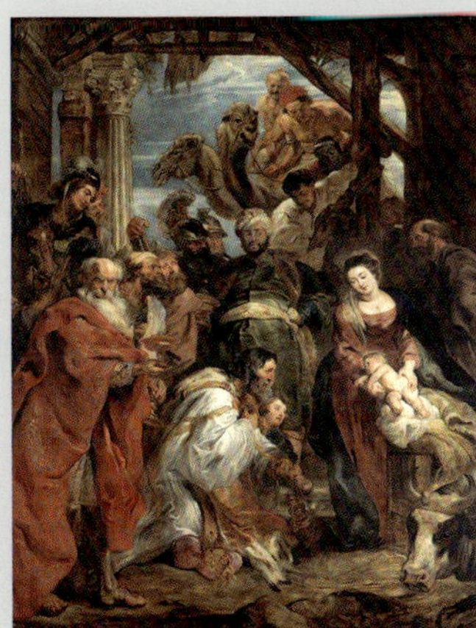



between the low-quality and light fur of the throat and abdominal region of the marten, and the high-quality, dense and dark-brown fur of its back.

A reference work for an imperial-wide dress code was the so-called *Reichspolizeiordnung* of 1530. This regulatory text, which served almost like a constitution for the entire Holy Roman Empire of the German Nation, summed up and standardised the previous common law. What was finally written in 1530 had already been applied, especially in imperial cities like Nuremberg. The *Reichspolizeiordnung* also contains a chapter focusing on the varieties of fur. Certain types of fur are ascribed to each social rank; however, farmers and day labourers are generally forbidden to wear fur. Their wives were only allowed to wear *schlechte belz* (bad furs) from lambs and goats. Only city dwellers were endowed with a fur privilege, but only if they enjoyed citizenship rights. *Gemeyne Burger und Handtwercker* (ordinary people and craftsmen) were not allowed to wear marten, but they were allowed fox, lamb and fitch. Merchants and craftsmen were, in addition to the common fitch, even allowed to wear the marten's throat fur, the more inferior part of the marten's pelt, provided they were members of the city council. The high-quality, dense fur of the marten's back was ascribed to distinguished citizens of the council identified by noble stock and aristocracy. The fur of the marten's back was therefore a high-status insignia that identified every wearer in urban everyday life as a rich citizen who did not have to be a member of the city government, but could be. While the fur of the marten's throat was only allowed to be worn by merchants who belonged to the city council, the fur of the marten's back pointed, above all, to the prosperity of its wearer, which enabled him to become a member of the city government.[4] The Portrait of Melchior Maag (1635) | Page 78 | by Samuel Hofmann (c. 1595–1649) is an example of the dress code shedding light on the not uncommon match between social status and clothing in a portrait. In this case, clothes worn in the portrait mostly correspond to the subject's reality. The portrait features the master of the shoemaker's guild, Maag, who in 1607 was councillor and from 1620 even governor of Winterthur; the flawless fur of the marten's back, which generously adorns the edges of the council cloak, was also worn in the Swiss region as the insignia of councillors.[5] That the fur of the council cloak was more than just an insignia, namely a symbol of administration of justice, cannot be further explained here.[6]

The *Portrait of Nicolas de Respaigne* (before 1620) by Peter Paul Rubens | Fig. 4 | is interesting in this context. The depicted bon vivant, a merchant born in Venice, was a jack-of-all-trades who travelled frequently to the Levant and to Jerusalem. He was a Knight of the Holy Sepulchre and had distinguished himself through his pious donations.[7] Rubens portrayed him as an exotic mix of merchant and pilgrim, with a turban on his head and a belly of prosperity that he proudly protrudes in the picture. This is framed by the fur-trimmed hem of his black-silk coat. It can be clearly seen that the fur is a 'patchwork' of many individual set pieces, in particular the already mentioned, lower-grade, throat-furs of animals that cannot be clearly determined; the judgement of a furrier would have to be obtained for this. Noteworthy, nevertheless, is that the wealthy merchant, who later appears prominently as an extra in the middle of Rubens's *Adoration of the Magi* (1624), |Fig. **5**| knows how to withdraw himself from all the splendour by remaining modest in his choice of fur.

The demand for appropriate clothing in art goes back to the early phase of modern art theory. Leon Battista Alberti (1404–1472) used the scholarly *ut pictura poesis* discourse to outline his criteria for pictorial depictions of history; he placed high priority on clothing that adequately represented the protagonists' dignity: 'So it did not behove, for instance, if Venus or Minerva were clad in coarse coats. Who, on the other hand, dressed Jupiter or Mars in the manner of women would also offend against the rule of the becoming person.'[8] Leonardo da Vinci (1442–1519) also discussed the aspect of decorum and *convenevolezza* without limiting himself to mythological themes, but to demand appropriateness and dignity also for the clothing of courtiers, kings and princes.[9] As early as 1500, the quest for historical authenticity in Raphael's circle was noticeable in Roman Renaissance painting, when ancient pictorial themes have real-life references, for example, to Trajan's Column.[10] In Mannerism, the eagerness to reconstruct costumes and locations subsided for a short time. But Lodovico Dolce's (1508–1568) *Dialogo della pittura intitolato l'Aretino* (1557) prominently addressed again the controversial issue of clothes in art. Dolce addressed the role of clothing most thoroughly when he demanded vestimentary appropriateness according to gender, class, age and nationality of the person depicted in the image. His pontifications concerning the historical dimensions of proper representation have subsequently been cited numerous times.[11]

Violations against decorum were therefore a problem of real life and of art theory. When fashion in the early modern period picked up pace and many complained that the vestimentary world was falling apart, *convenevolezza* became the order of the day.[12] This is when the caricature finally comes into play, which flourished in the seventeenth century for the first time and which, in the eighteenth century, gave rise to biting ridicule on a daily basis, as

**7**  Otto von Simson, *Peter Paul Rubens (1577–1640),* Mainz 1996, p. 191.

**8**  Leon Battista Alberti, 'De pictura, Lib. 2', in Oskar Bätschmann/Christoph Schäublin (eds), *Leon Battista Alberti: Das Standbild – Die Malkunst – Grundlagen der Malerei* (Latin and German), Darmstadt 2000, pp. 262–65.

**9**  On fundamentals of the *convenevolezza*, see Reiner Haussherr, *Convenevolezza: Historische Angemessenheit in der Darstellung von Kostüm und Schauplatz seit der Spätantike bis ins 16. Jahrhundert,* Mainz 1984 (= essays of the Akademie der Wissenschaften und der Literatur, Geistes- und sozialwissenschaftliche Klasse; 4).

**10**  Ingo Herklotz, *Cassiano Dal Pozzo und die Archäologie des 17. Jahrhunderts,* Munich 1999, p. 236.

**11**  Ingo Herklotz, 'Michele Lonigo als Kunstkritiker. Zu einer historischen Rezeption der Altarbilder von Sacchi und Passignano in St. Peter', in *Ars naturam adiuvans: Festschrift für Matthias Winner,* Victoria von Flemming/Sebastian Schütze (eds), Mainz 1996, pp. 413–29, here p. 427, note 40.

Philipp Zitzlsperger

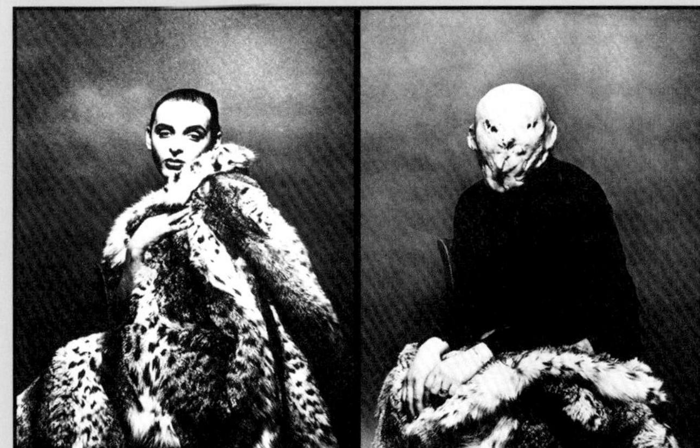



new fashions – predominantly from Paris – were worn on the streets of major European cities. Ladies' headdresses garnered special attention and gave reason for sarcastic comments because, again, it was the feathers that increasingly seemed to contradict the *convenevolezza.* | ^Page 111, 137 | In any case, the caricatures reveal that the ladies' tower-like hairstyles with colourful feather decorations could definitively be understood as a symptom of the decline of civilization. The print *A hint to the ladies to take care of their heads* (1776) satirises the fashion of feathers. The brightly coloured ostrich feathers have grown so high from the towering hairstyle that, up in the chandelier, they ignite and the staff stand around spraying water in an attempt to extinguish the fire.[13] | ^Fig. 2 |

Animals in fashion were popular vehicles of decorative exaggerations, as shown by the previous consideration of a caricature about feathers. Furs were also used for lavish self-staging and were initially, in the sixteenth and seventeenth centuries, worn as a strictly guarded class insignia until they became the decoration of dandies and bohemians with the increasing dissolution of social boundaries after the French Revolution.[14] Mary Wigman (1886–1973), | ^Page 229 | Urs Lüthi (b. 1947), | ^Fig. 6 | Francesca Woodman (1958–1981) or van Lamsweerde and Matadin | ^Fig. 3 | used furs in their photographs as symbols of well-being, and added a subtle criticism to the imagery when (in Woodman), for example, the fur hangs on the wall like a slaughtered animal or, when worn over the neck, finds its companion piece in the stuffed fox (?) on the floor.

**12**  See here, with many examples and sources: Gundula Wolter, *Teufelshörner und Lustäpfel: Modekritik in Wort und Bild 1150– 1620,* Marburg 2002.

**13**  For a fundamental discussion on clothing and moral ideas in premodernity, see: Aileen Ribeiro, *Dress and Morality,* London 1986. On headdress and feather decoration of the eighteenth and nineteenth centuries, see Ribeiro 1986, pp. 105–12.

**14**  See the essays herein by Barbara Vinken, pp. 96 ff., and Inessa Kouteinikova, pp. 160 ff.

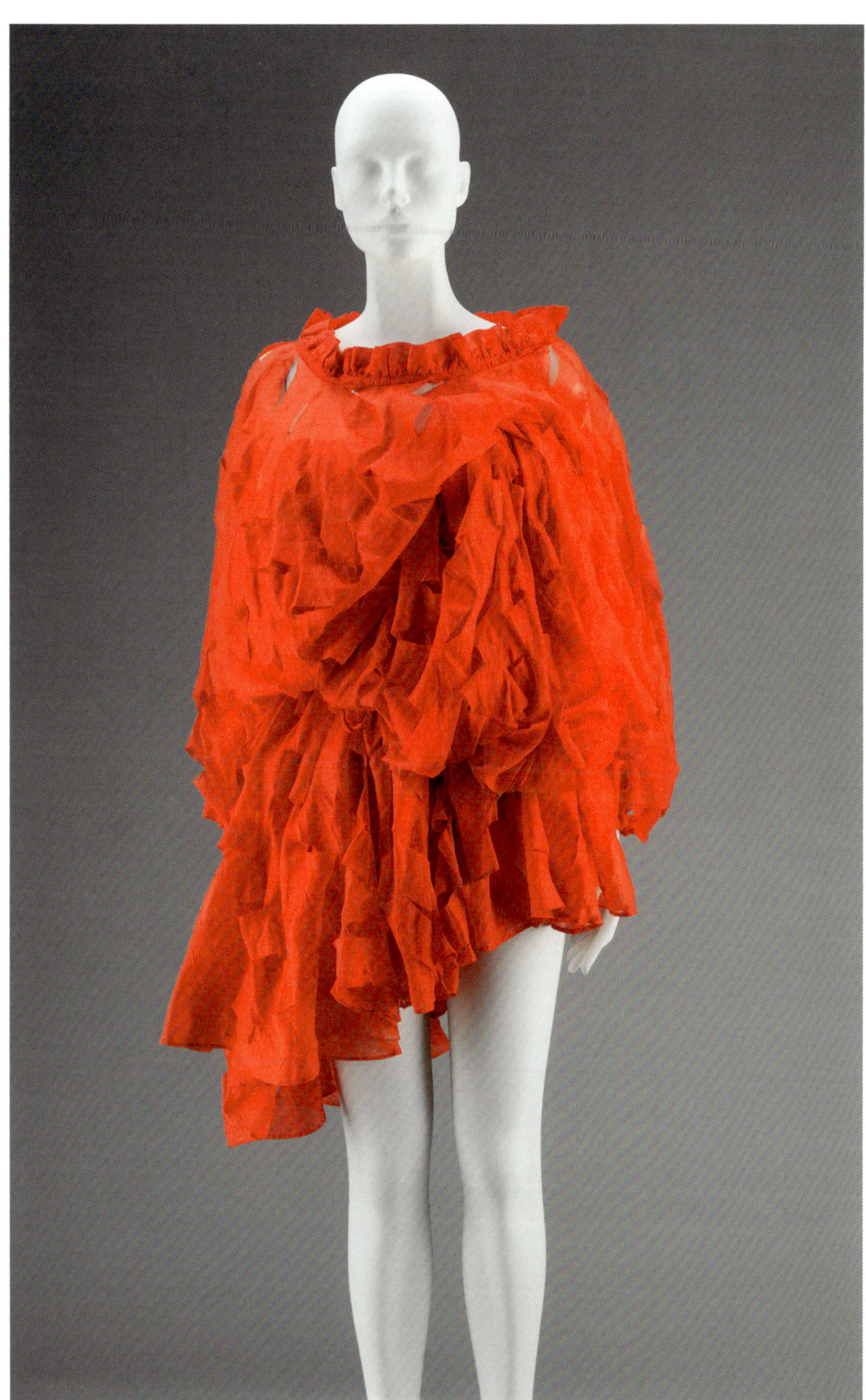

**42**  Vivienne Westwood (b. 1941)
Red dress from the 'Cut, Slash & Pull Collection',
spring/summer 1990, production 1991
Cotton voile with two sash belts
V&A, London, Textiles and Fashion Collection;
Given by Vivienne Westwood

**226**  Robert Peake (1551–1619)
*Catherine Carey, Countess of Nottingham,* c. 1597
Oil on canvas, 198.1 × 137.2 cm
Private collection

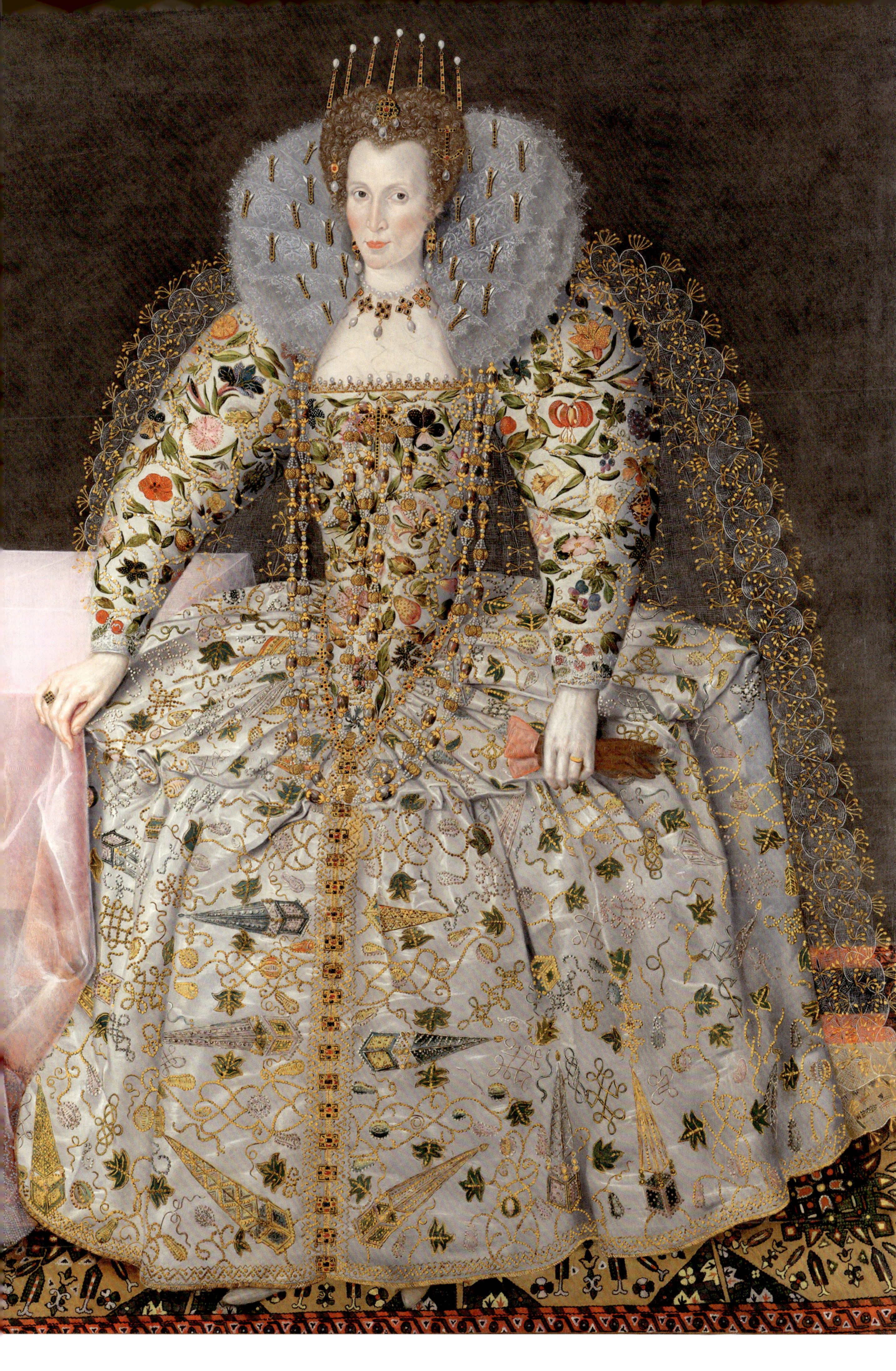

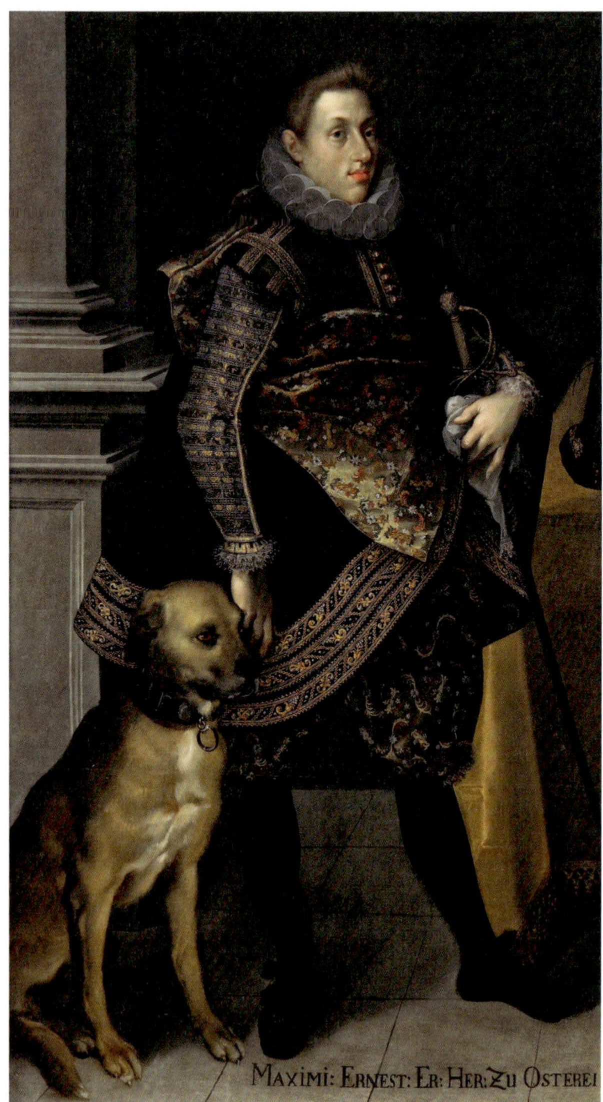



**171**  Joseph Heintz the Elder (1564–1609)
*Archduke Maximilian Ernst (1583–1616)*
*with hunting dog,* 1604
Oil on canvas, 191.5 × 105 cm
KHM-Museumsverband, Picture Gallery

**43**  Hans von Aachen (1552–1615)
*Archduchess Anna (1585–1618),*
*Daughter of Archduke Ferdinand II,*
*Territorial Prince of Tyrol,*
*Spouse of Emperor Matthias,* 1604
Oil on canvas, 58 × 48 cm
KHM-Museumsverband, Picture Gallery

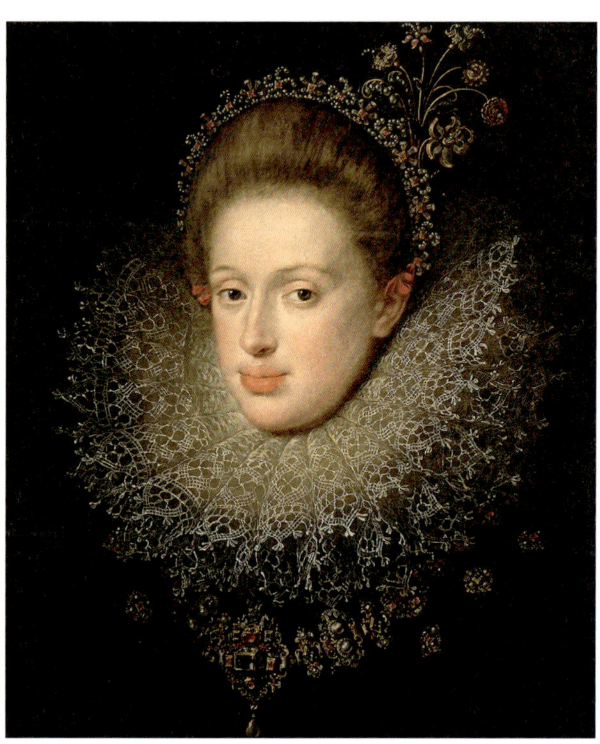

**300**  Jan Weenix (1642–1719)
*The white peacock,* 1693
Oil on canvas, 192.5 × 167.5 cm
Paintings Gallery,
Academy of Fine Arts Vienna

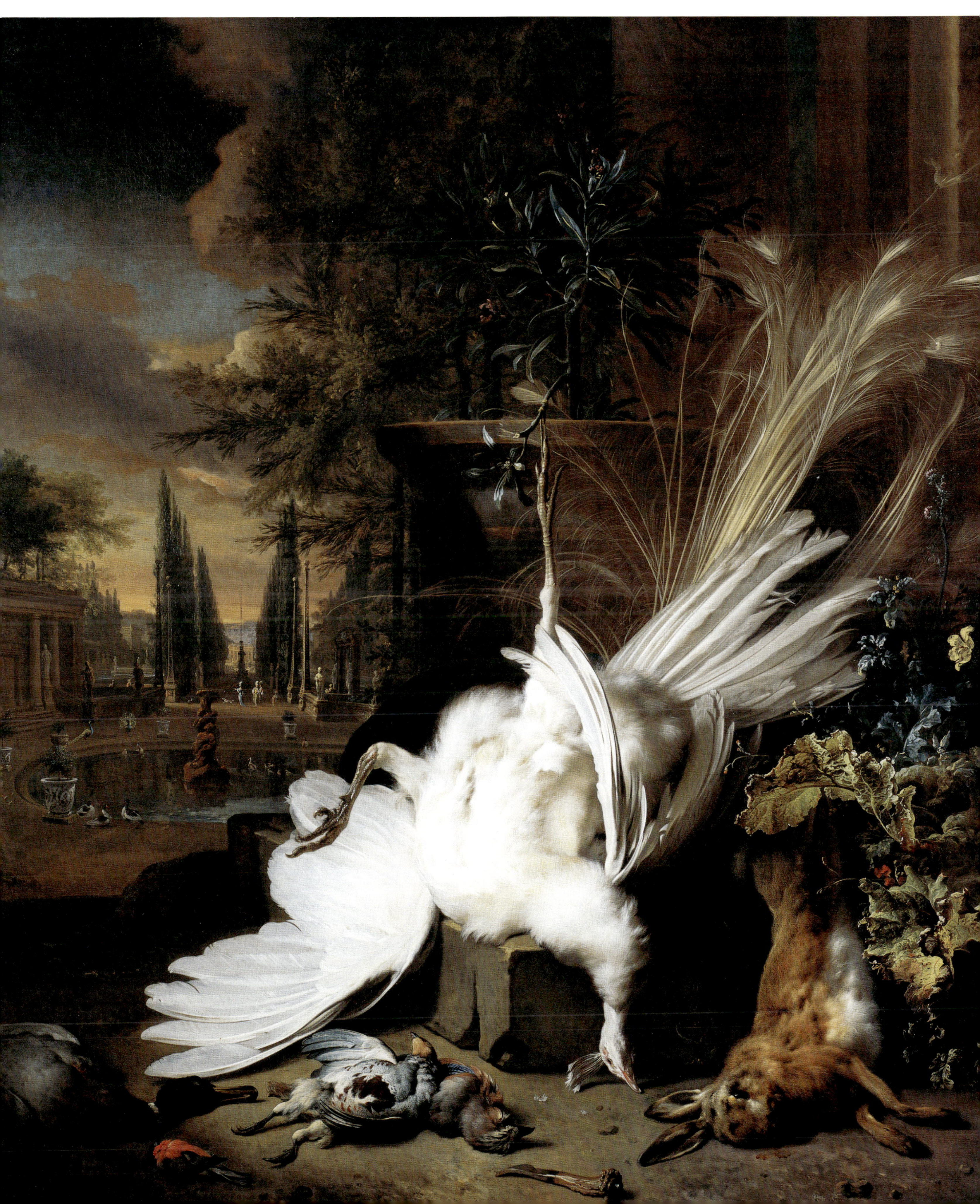

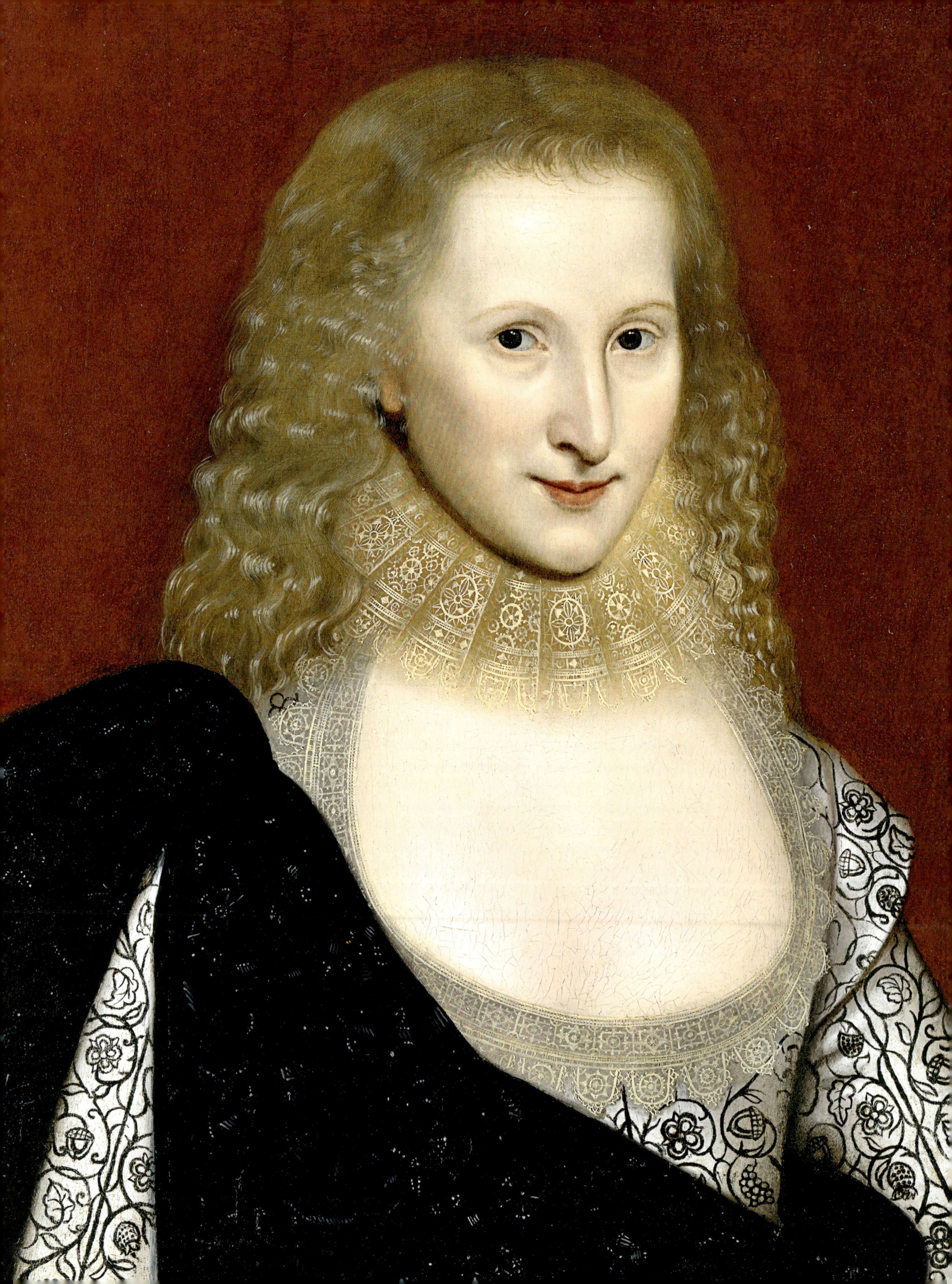

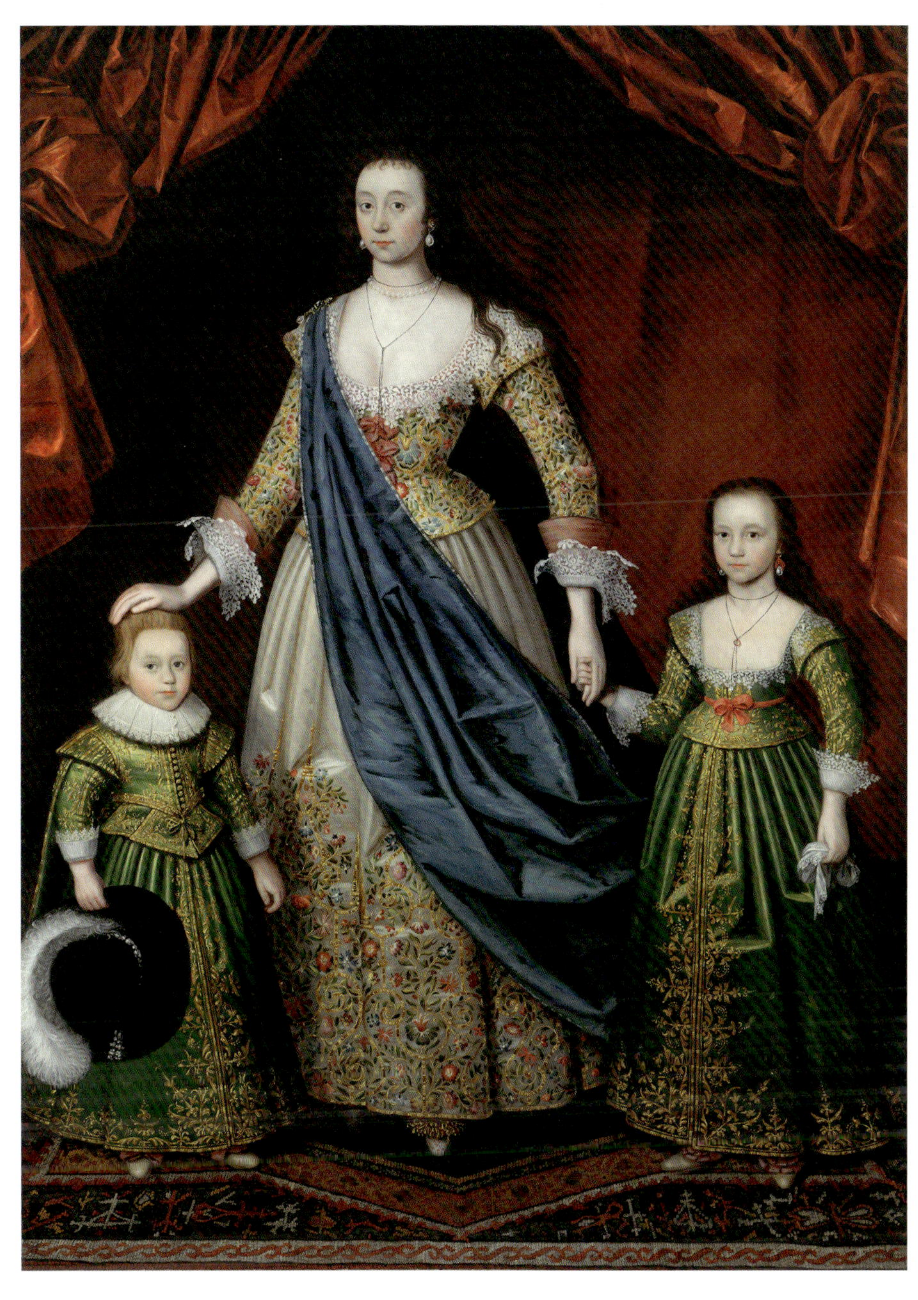

**130** English School
*Lady Elizabeth Pope, wife of*
*Sir William Pope (1596–1624),*
*with her eldest son Thomas,*
*later 2nd Earl of Downe*
*(1622–1660) and eldest daughter*
*Anne (b. 1617),* c. 1628–38
Oil on canvas, 202 × 147 cm
Orsay collection

**192** William Larkin (1580–1619)
*Unknown lady in a black and*
*white dress,* c. 1615–18
Oil on wood, 57 × 43.2 cm
Private collection

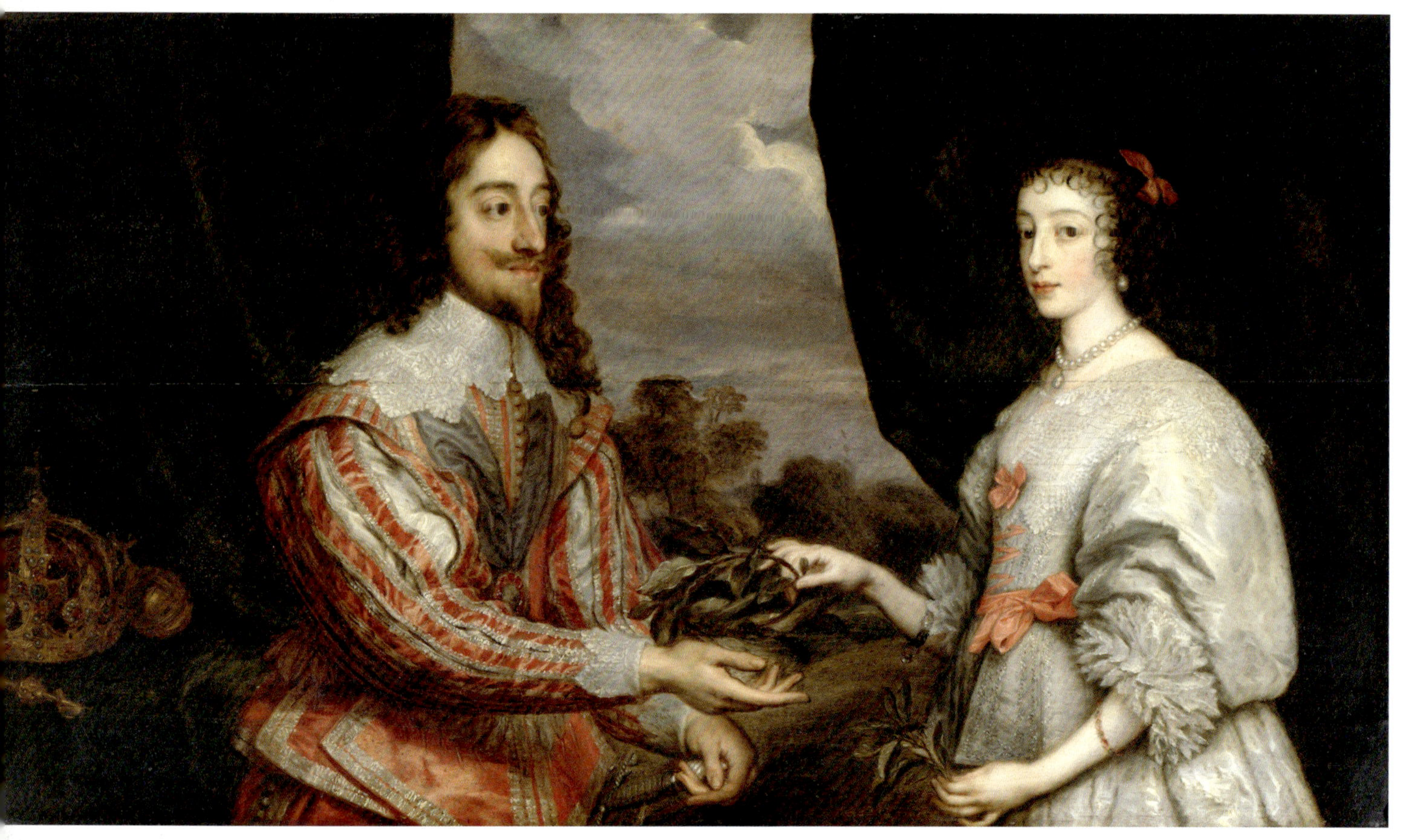



**80** Gonzales Coques (1614–1684)
*Charles I of England and
Queen Henrietta Maria,* undated
Oil on oak, c. 45.5 × 78.5 cm
V&A, London, Prints, Drawings & Paintings
Collection; Bequeathed by Rev. Chauncey
Hare Townshend

**136** Luca Ferrari (1605–1654), attributed
Tiberio Tinelli (1586–1638), attributed
*Portrait of a lady,* mid-seventeenth century
Oil on canvas, 205 × 115 cm
KHM-Museumsverband, Picture Gallery

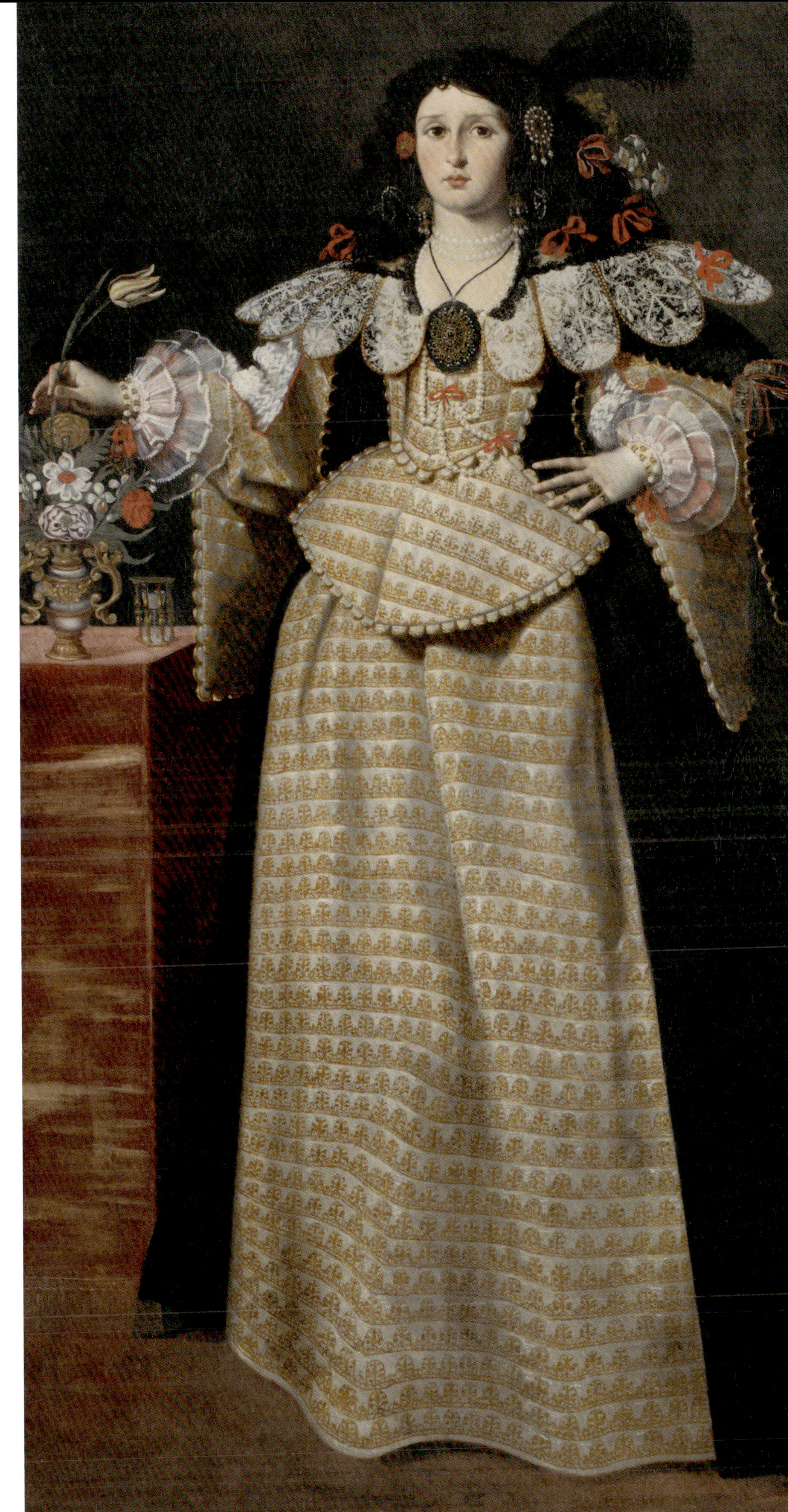

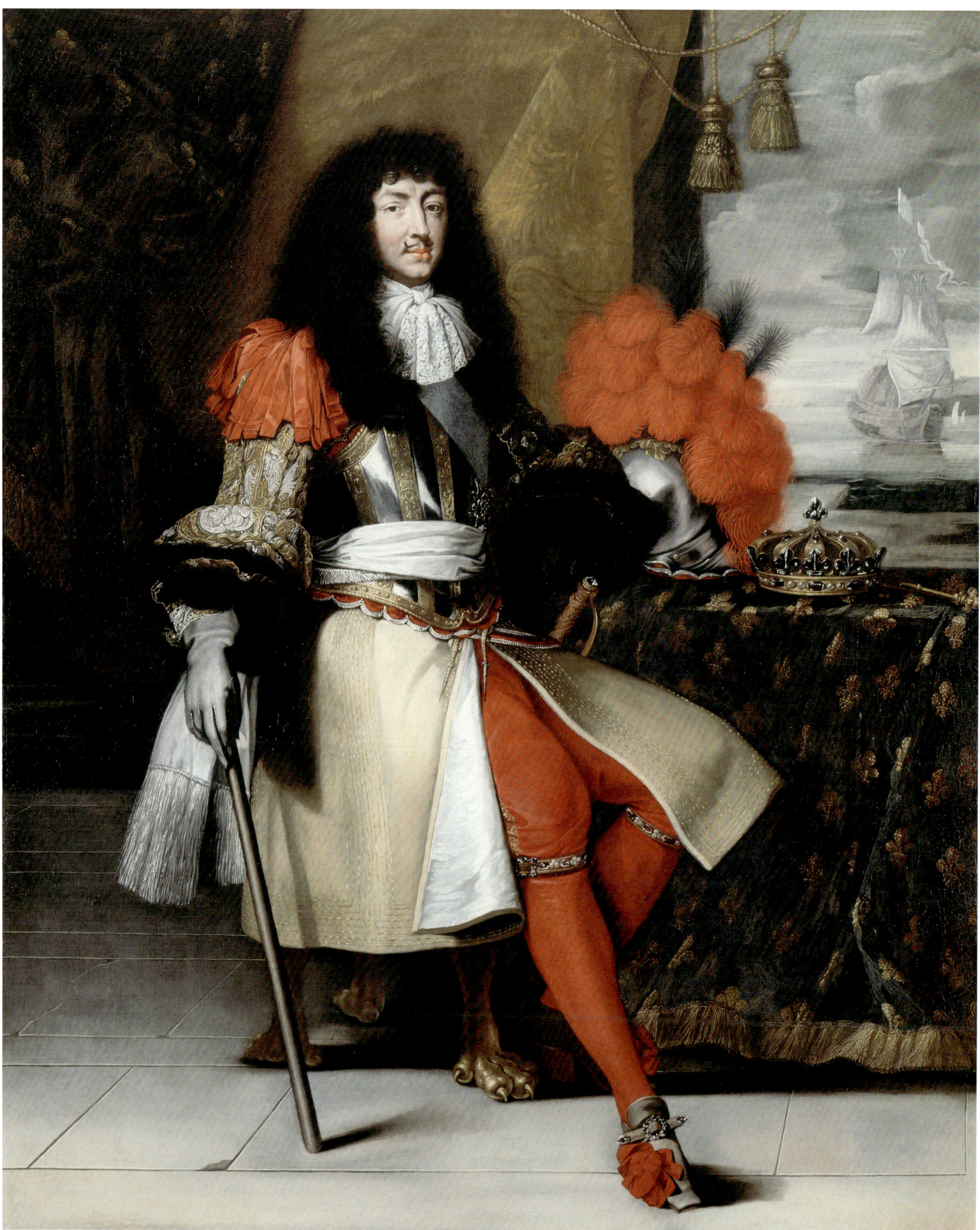

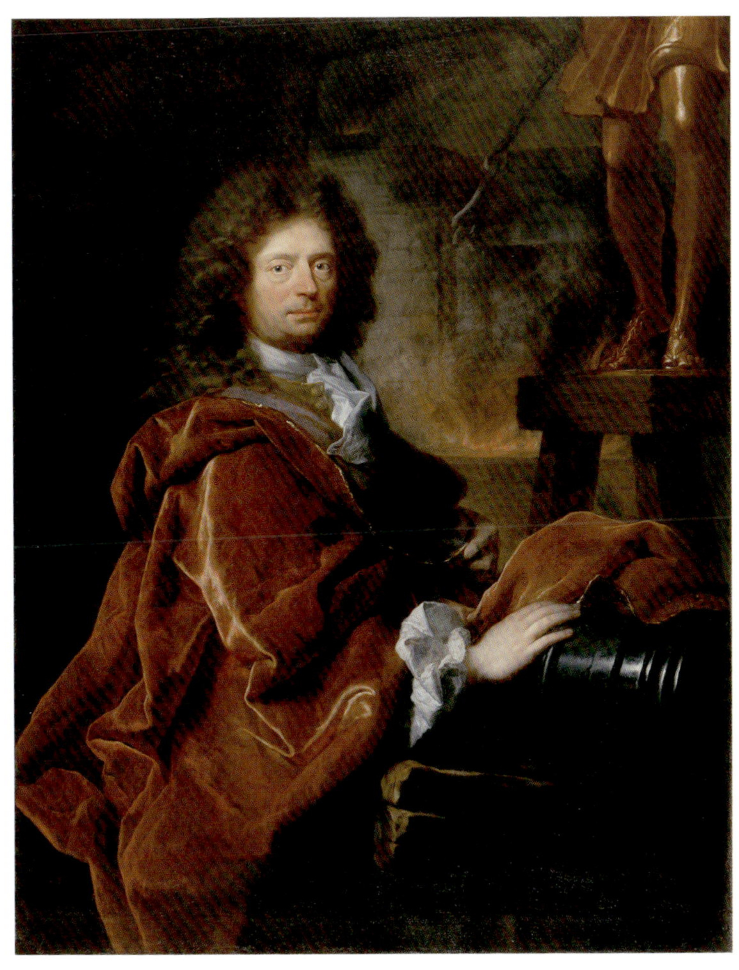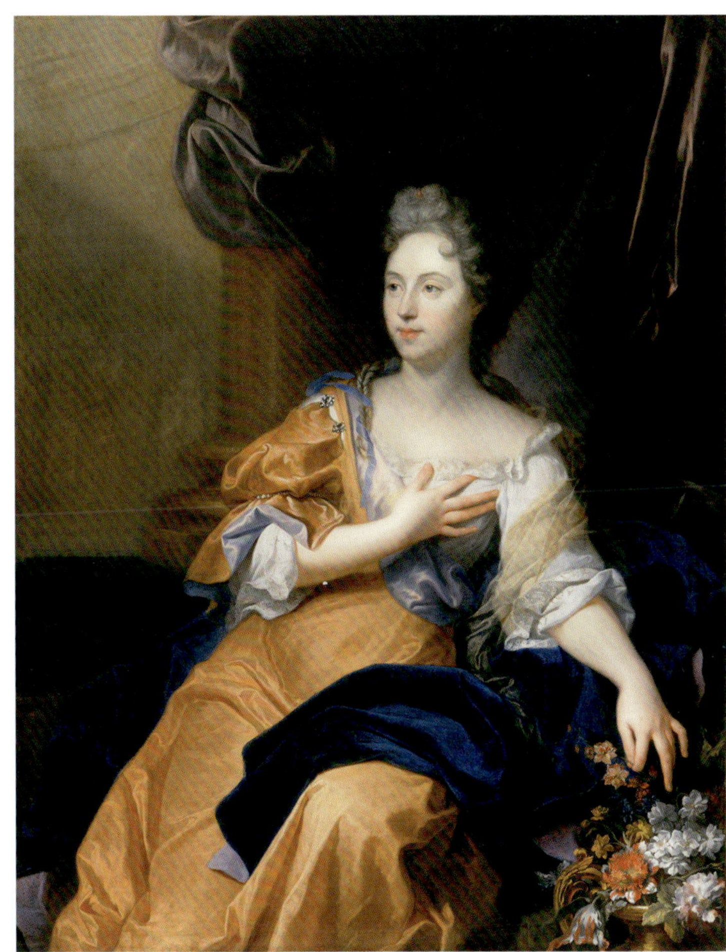



**194**  Claude Lefèbvre (1632–1675)
*Full-length portrait of Louis XIV (1638–1715), King of France
and Navarra. Equipped with crown and sceptre on a table
in front of a seascape with ship,* c.1670
Oil on canvas, 196.5 × 159 cm
Musée national des châteaux de Versailles et de Trianon

**235**  Hyacinthe Rigaud (1659–1743)
*Portrait of Balthasar Keller, brass-founder,* 1685
Oil on canvas, 140 × 107 cm
Kunsthaus Zürich, Keller Collection, 1854

**236**  Hyacinthe Rigaud (1659–1743)
*Portrait of Suzanne de Boubers de Bernâtre,
wife of Balthasar Keller,* 1686
Oil on canvas, 140 × 107 cm
Kunsthaus Zürich, Keller Collection, 1854

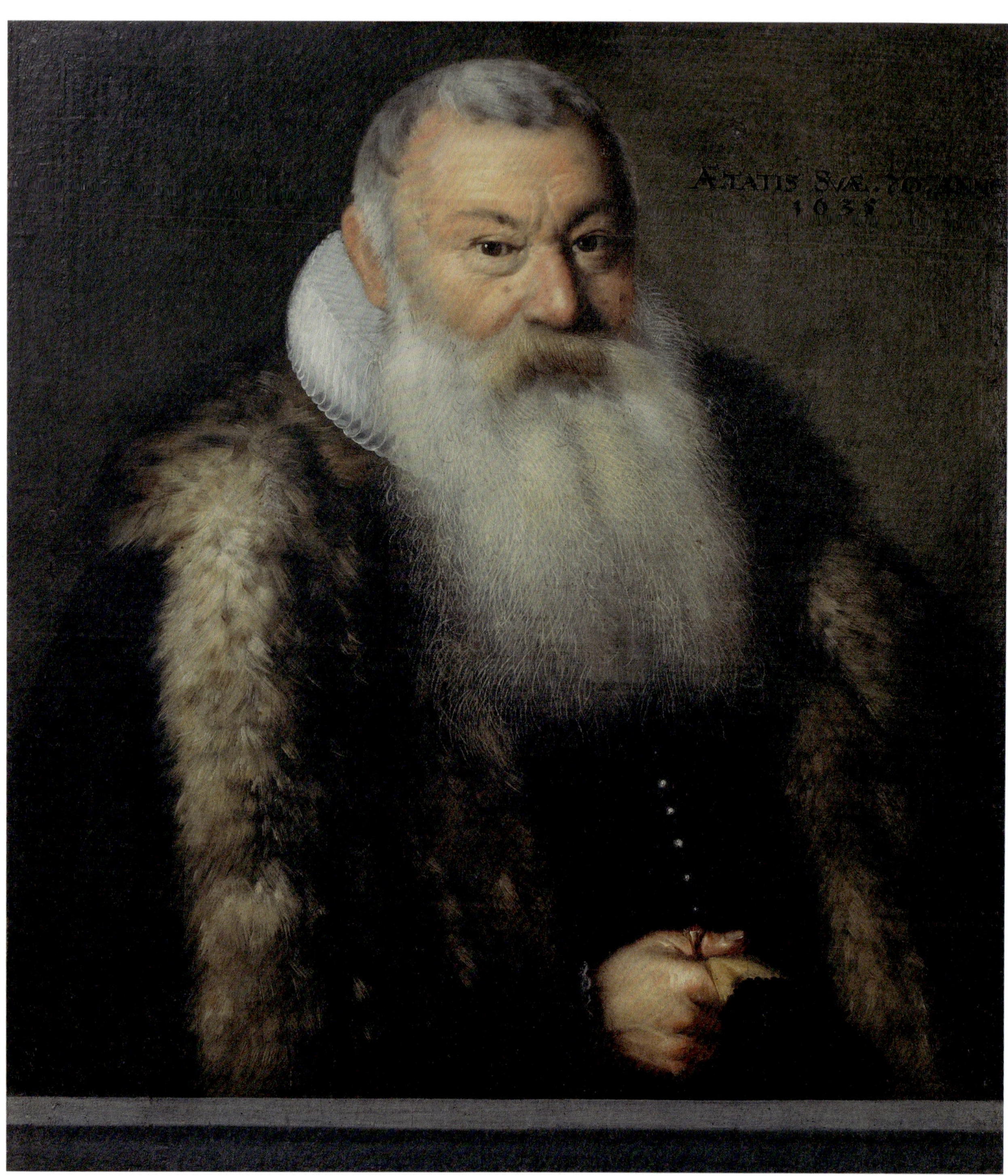



**177** Samuel Hofmann (1595–1649)
*Portrait of Melchior Maag,* 1635
Oil on canvas, 78 × 67 cm
Kunsthaus Zürich, Keller Collection, 1854

**210** Nicolaes Maes (1634–1693)
*Portrait of a young boy in*
*Adonis costume,* c. 1670
Oil on canvas, 55.5 × 42 cm
Paintings Gallery, Academy of Fine Arts Vienna

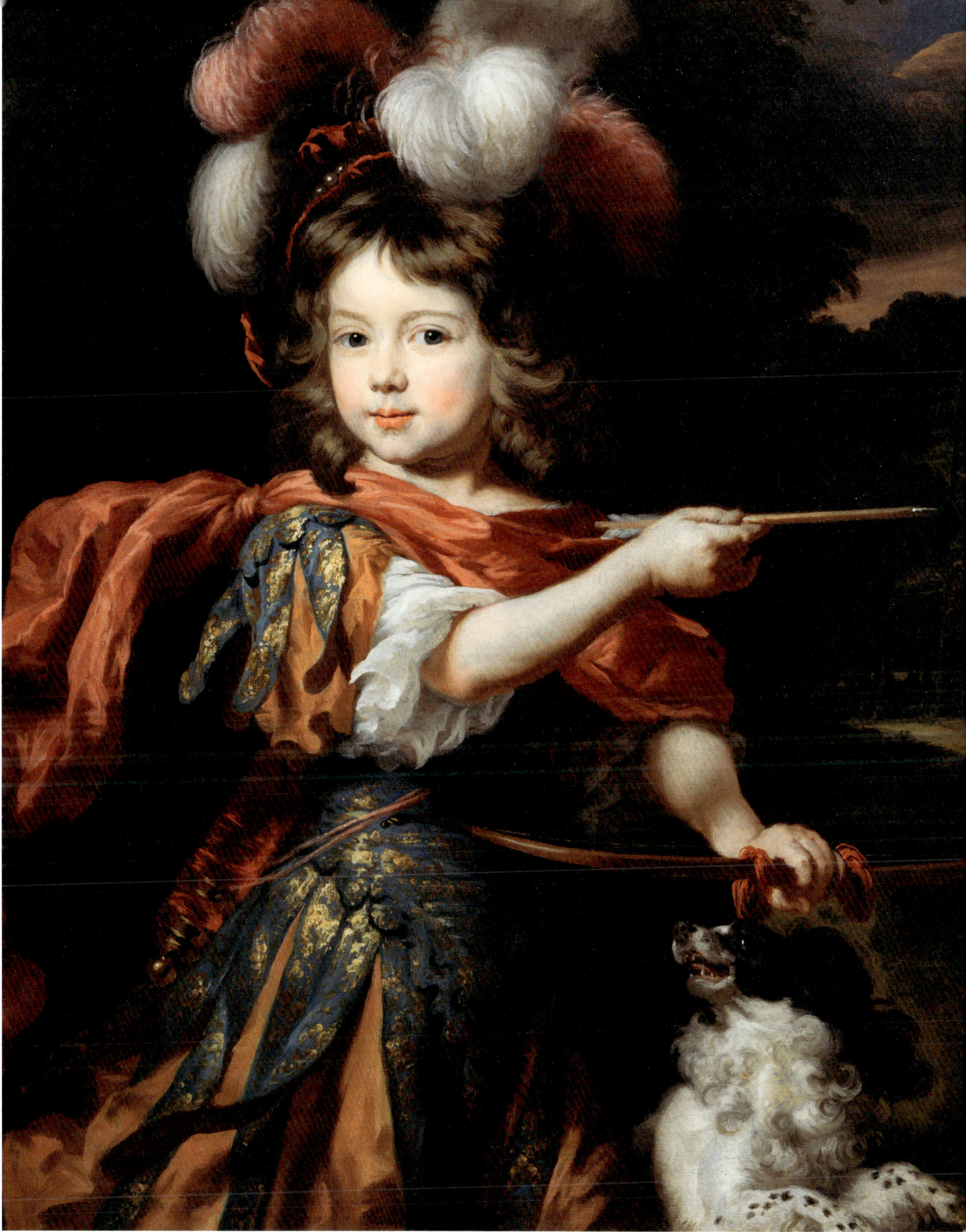

# Fashion of the Social Elite



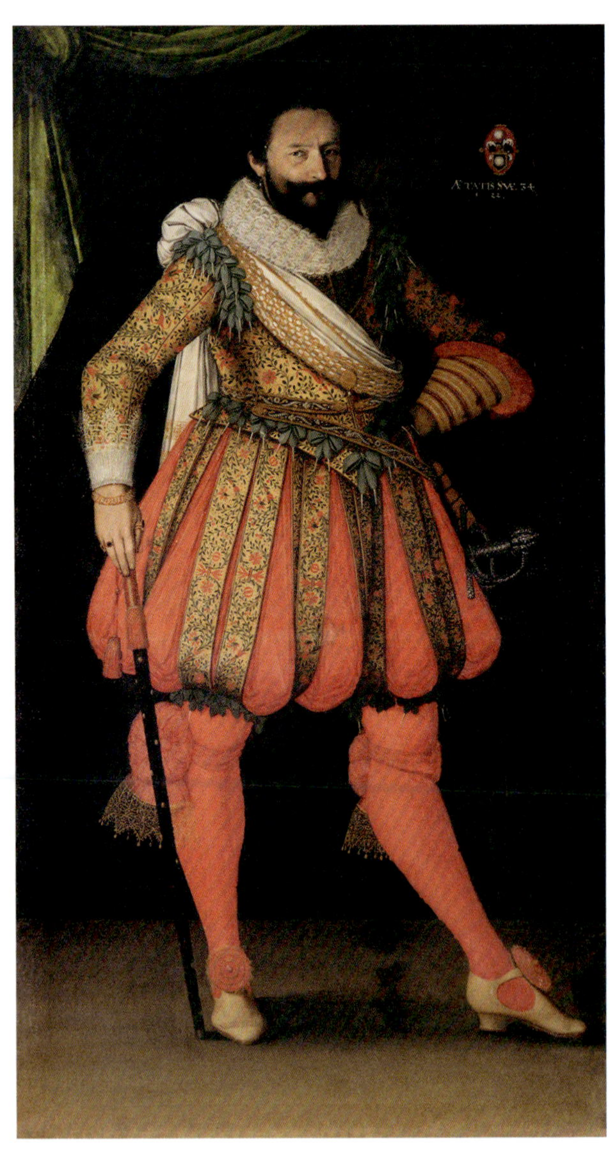

**Janine Jakob**

# Clothing, Accessories and Their Regulations by Sumptuary Laws in Swiss Cities of the Ancien Régime

Fashion as a cultural practice and symbolic language has always been subject to change. It takes on different, creative and 'extreme' manifestations that follow aesthetic and socio-cultural requirements. This article considers the fashion of the social elite[1] in Zurich, Basel and Lucerne during the time of the ancien régime of the seventeenth and eighteenth centuries. Clothing and accessories were important and popular instruments to express not only social status, economic power, wealth and prestige, but also religious affiliation in the hierarchical societies of Europe during this time. According to strict moral standards, however, luxury and 'haughtiness' – the fashion-driven luxuries – were understood as vices and sins. Therefore, the municipal authorities in Zurich, Basel and Lucerne forbade the immoral, lavish 'luxury of clothes' and the corresponding new *Alamodereien*[2] coming from French fashion.

The sumptuary laws regulated the extravagance in clothing and accessories to prevent indebtedness and to encourage thrift as well as a modest, pious and virtuous life. The authorities understood the splendour and 'excessive costliness of clothes' as both the 'main evil threatening the ruin of the country' and the 'downfall of many citizens'. Clothing and accessories should, however, help distinguish the estates and functions from each other, to identify persons of rank and, moreover, to prevent 'strife and jealousy' between the social classes.[3] Fashion was regulated according to a person's social status, gender and marital status, by weekdays and locations. Clothes, fabrics and accessories such as jewellery and headdresses were standardised according to their quality, authenticity, value and origin. As sanctions, fines were levied and prohibited objects confiscated.

## Doublet, Spanish breeches and lots of gold

Courtly clothing and sumptuous fashion in the context of noble lifestyles, although controversial, elicit a fascination. Full-length, life-sized portraits[4] depict a couple from Zurich, Nobleman Hans Caspar Schmid von Goldenberg and his wife Barbara Schmid born Wydenmann, in prestigious fashion with abundant gold. Hans Caspar Schmid | Page 80 | wears Spanish-style fashion. The Spanish breeches, fashionable since 1550,

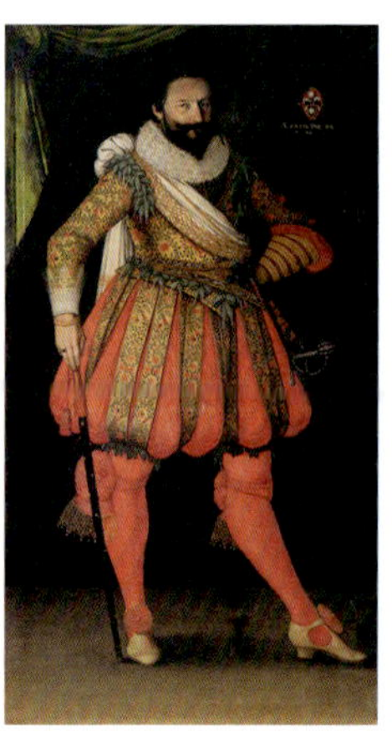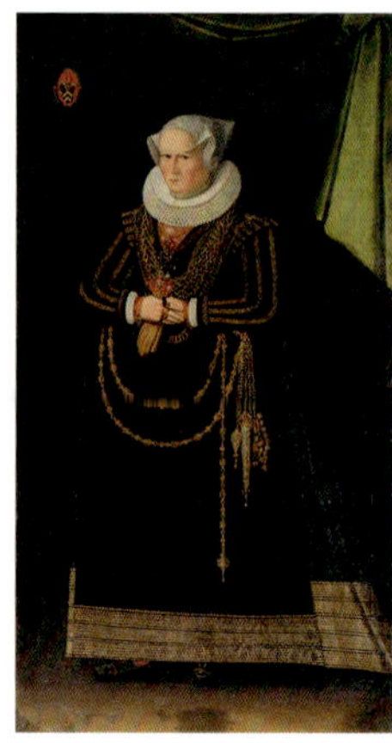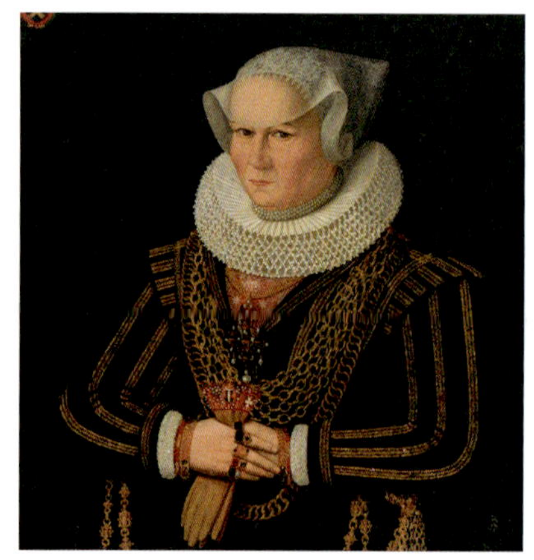

consist of vertically slashed upper breeches with wide vertical stripes of golden coloured fabric, probably atlas silk, that has an identical pattern to the upper garment's tendrils of green leaves and red fantasy flowers; the breeches have a puffy pants lining of bright red silk. The striking red is also evident in the stockings, the garters' ribbons adorned with golden lace, the rosettes of the light-brown, high-heeled leather shoes with decorative slits on the front, and the striped cuffs on the gloves. Schmid wears one glove on his left hand, which holds the other glove. Such elaborately decorated gloves belonged to the social elite, were considered a rule of etiquette and protected against the 'impure'.[5]

The doublet, with a peascod belly and a stiffened tip[6] extending below the waist, surrounds the body wrinkle-free and is closed at the front with red decorative buttons; the long closed sleeves have white lace-trimmed cuffs. Blue *Nesteln* – ribbons with metal ends – fasten the trousers and sleeves to the doublet; the ribbons' loops contribute to the sumptuous decoration. The doublet is complemented by an iron breastplate[7] decorated with ornaments, a white sash embroidered and trimmed with gold as a symbol of honour as well as with an overlying six-strand gold chain with a medallion and a pearl pendant.[8] As additional jewellery, Schmid wears a gold bracelet, four rings set with gems, and a golden earring adorned with pearls. The ruff, a status symbol and sign of purity, is made of precious white linen stiffened with rice flour starch and consists of about six layers of box (inverted) pleats.[9] A 'lovelock', a single strand of hair, falls down on the left – see also *Portrait of Prince Hartmann von Liechtenstein* (c. 1630). | <sup>Page</sup> **57** | As a man of high military rank, Schmid wears a beaded weapon belt with the partially visible vessel and basket of a rapier.[10] In his right hand, he also holds a staff made of black-painted wood with gold fittings as a symbol of authority.[11]

Barbara Schmid | **217**[b] | is depicted in a skirt, most likely in dark blue with a silver-grey pattern, as well as with a doublet and apron made of valuable black, fine-patterned fabric.[12] She also wears a red partlet with white embroidery. Golden trim adorns the doublet's long closed sleeves, small lapel, collar and padded shoulder rolls.[13] A wide gold border further decorates the hems of the unpleated apron and the skirt. Barbara also wears a ruff with six layers of dense knife (fan) pleats as well as hand ruffs and a white pinner cap. The bonnet comprises a tight lace cap that is worn underneath and attached to the upper bonnet. The latter curves over the forehead and stands outwards on both sides of the face in an S-shape.[14] Similar to her husband, she is portrayed wearing a pair of leather gloves with red, embroidered and beaded cuffs and red stockings and high heels opened on the side. Particularly valuable are the colourfully beaded shoes with pearls and a high sole and overhanging toecap.[15] Barbara Schmid wears numerous accessories, including jewellery that not only displays status symbols and represent the two families, but is also emotionally charged: She has two pairs of bracelets, of which the wider golden pair is decorated with the family crest Schmid and Wydenmann.[16] Of the nine

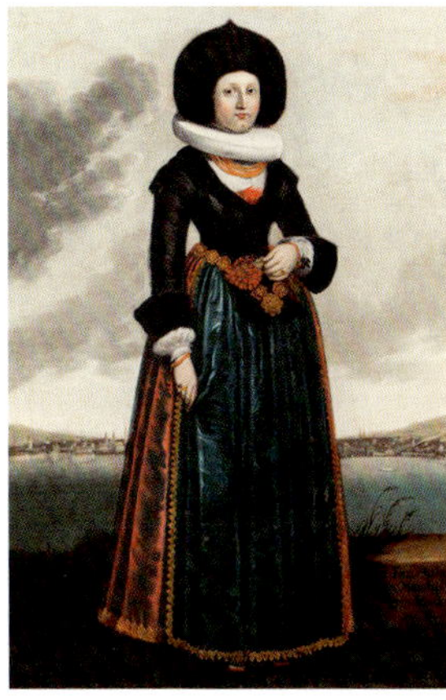



gold rings jewelled with pearls and gemstones, most probably some come from her husband and mother, the one on her right index finger is heart-shaped.[17] Her jewellery around the neck consist of a four-strand tight-fitting pearl necklace, a five-strand gold chain with coarse links in the style of her husband's chain, a golden chain reaching to the hip and a shorter more delicate gold necklace with a golden pendant. The latter is decorated with stones and pearls, and a representation of a women and an animal – a unicorn possibly with the Holy Mary. Objects of everyday use are attached to the metal chains on the châtelaine of the golden double belt: on the right, a colourfully embroidered bag, on the left, a quiver for cutlery lavishly decorated with a gold pattern, as well as another valuable container. Separately, a pear-shaped pomander[18] with a filigree mesh is attached to the long end of the belt for protection and as a remedy.

### Zurich Maiden with a large *Hinderfür* made of fur

In the full-length portrait, Susanna Meyer Murer |**214**| is depicted in the clothing of the 'Zurich Maiden'. The red skirt and the blue apron are made of silk, have evenly lined pleats and are adorned with a hem of golden lace. The black, tight-fitting doublet, closed at the front and most likely made out of velvet, with typical shoulder rolls and peplum and decorated with lace ribbon over the torso, spans the body wrinkle-free. The deep pointed neckline and the slightly funnel-shaped cuff of the long closed sleeves are trimmed with black fur. At the wrist, the white shirt sleeves are puffed and tightly closed with lace trim. |See **172**| She wears a fine white partlet made of lace combined with a red-golden fabric. This fabric is also used for the five layers of straps on the glove cuffs.

The voluminous headdress *Hinderfür*[19] consists of densely set black silk ribbon loops and is trimmed with valuable fur. The white ruff has a single layer of deep knife pleats and thus differs from those of the married couple Schmid. As jewellery, the Zurich woman wears a pearl necklace, three golden finger rings set with stones, a pair of gold bracelets with wide clasps, a five-strand gold chain and a metal belt with golden rosettes, which was possibly a bridal belt.[20] The upper garment, the *Hinderfür,* and the ruff were not exclusively worn by maidens in Zurich,

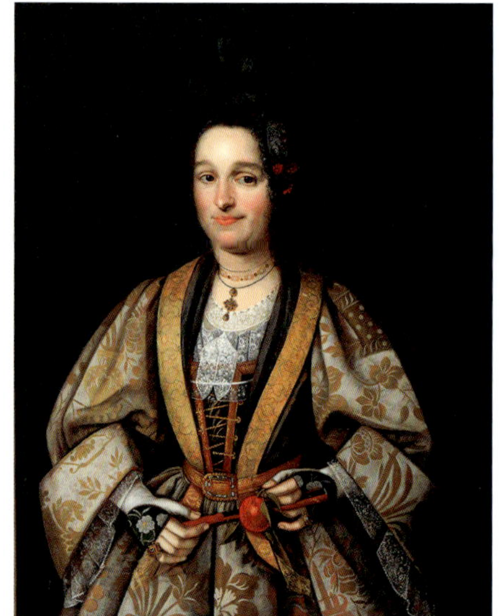

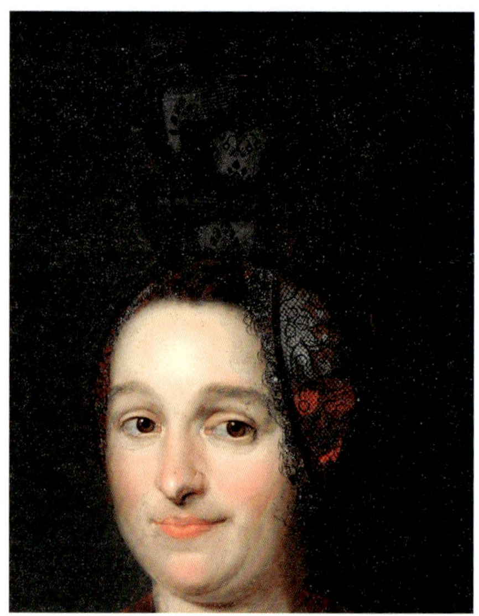

**266**  Unknown artist
*Portrait of Elisabeth Gossweiler
née Hirzel (1690–1762) from Zurich,
wife of merchant and Guild Master
Konrad Gossweiler from Zurich,* c. 1715
Damask dress patterned with
chinoiseries and corsage lacing
Oil on canvas, 96.5 × 74 cm
Schweizerisches Nationalmuseum, Zurich

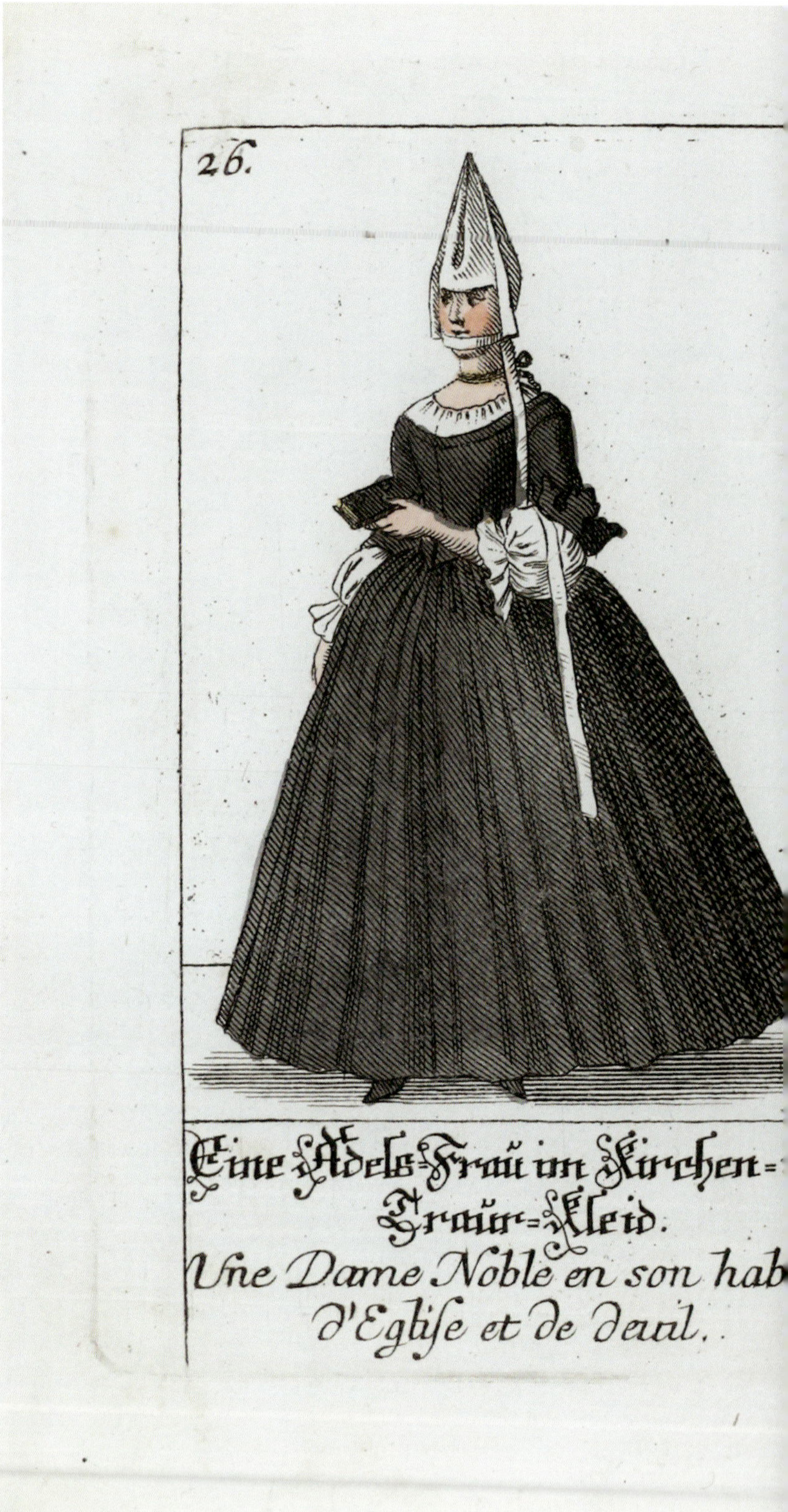


**172**  David Herrliberger (1697–1777)
*Zurich church habit – church and mourning dress,* 1749
26. Noblewoman in church and mourning dress
27. An elegant lady or maiden in church dress
28. A bourgeoise or maiden in church dress
Sheet IV, in *Zürcherische Kleider-Trachten*
Copper engraving, coloured, sheet: 10 × 15.4 cm
Private collection, Zurich



Janine Jakob

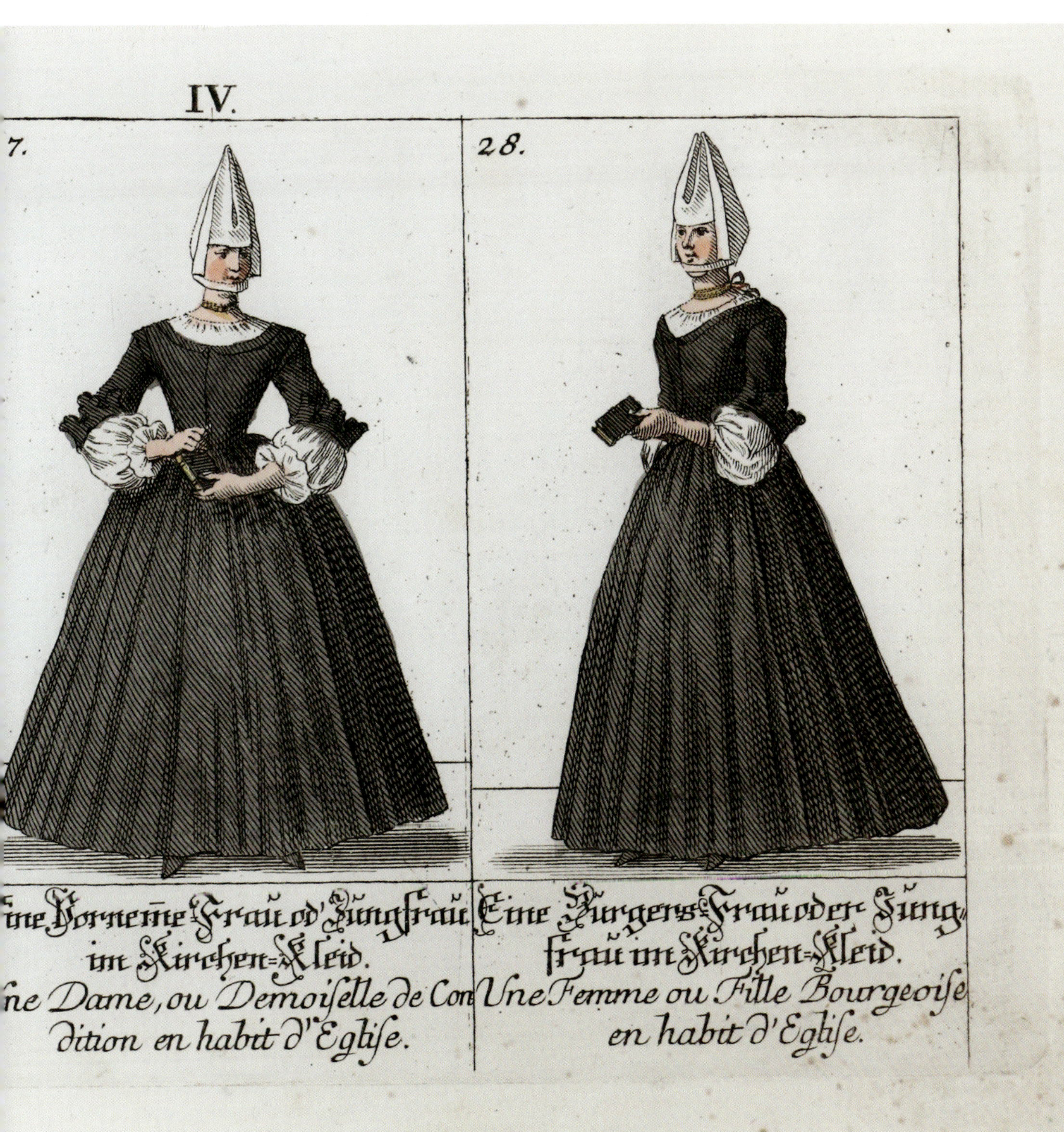



Eine Vorneme Fraŭ od Jŭngfraŭ
im Kirchen=Kleid.
Une Dame, ou Demoiselle de Condition en habit d'Eglise.

Eine Bŭrgers=Fraŭ oder Jŭngfraŭ im Kirchen=Kleid.
Une Femme ou Fille Bourgeoise
en habit d'Eglise.

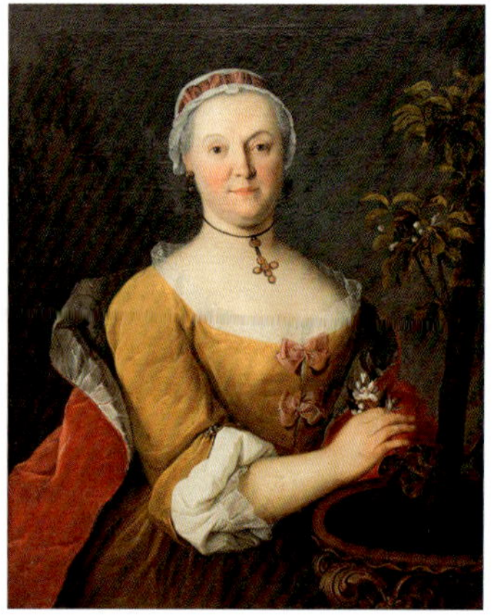

143 Johann Caspar Füssli (1706–1782)
*Portrait of Anna Ulrich*
*von Orelli (1705–1773) from Zurich,*
*wife of Johann Caspar Ulrich (1703–1778),*
*councilman and builder, daughter of*
*Hans Heinrich Orelli, merchant prince,*
*and Anna Margaretha Lavater,* c. 1730–45
Oil on canvas, 87 × 69.3 cm
Private collection, Zurich

Basel and Lucerne in the eighteenth century.[21] In Lucerne, these accessories had provided the reason for legal regulation, for example, in 1671.[22] Only a woman of high class was allowed to wear the *Hinderfür* from marten fur, but not of sable, and only persons of rank were allowed ruffs with up to four layers – less layers than the Schmid couple of Zurich had on their ruffs in 1622.

### Chinoiserie dress with an overhang and the *fontange* à la Zurichoise

In a half-length portrait, Elisabeth Gossweiler | 266 | is depicted in a silver-grey gown made of damask, patterned with large-format, gold-and-brown chinoiseries. The gown consists of a skirt with evenly spaced wide pleats and a tightly waisted upper garment with wide, three-quarter-length sleeves. In addition to vertical folds and an overhang above the wide cuff, the sleeves are equipped with wide *engageants* made of white lace. The colourfully embroidered bodice with golden lacing and lace ruffle trim is complemented by a fine, white partlet. A golden, quilted shoulder strap with heart-shaped leaf tendrils falls down on both sides of the belt buckle and is attached with a golden belt.

The white *mitaines* are folded backwards, revealing the inside of the mittens or half gloves with floral embroidery on a green background as well as two golden pairs of finger rings jewelled with gemstones. Of the three necklaces, one with a pendant, the middle one is made of fine filigree and enamel work, which the authorities permitted. The Zurich woman holds a valuable, closed fan and in her left hand a branch with leaves and a red fruit.[23] The headdress is also an extravagant, fashionable item. It represents an evolved form of the *fontange*[24] and can be called a *fontange à la Zurichoise.* | Detail 266 | Black lace and lace ruffles supported by wire and pleated grey-black patterned ribbons layered on top of each other protrude artistically upwards at the back of the head, at about a head's length over the close-fitting bonnet of grey-black silk with red patterning.

### The *Dächli-Tüechli* – the high, pointed church bonnet

The Zurich *Kirchenhabit,* the church dress | 172 | arising from seventeenth-century fashion, was prescribed in the sumptuary laws and was

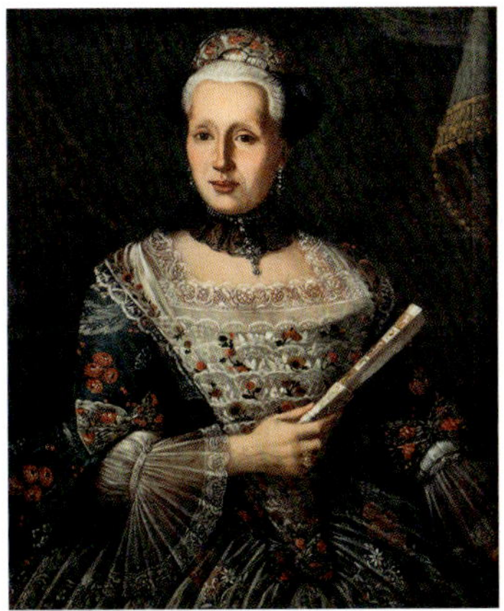



worn until the third quarter of the eighteenth century. As a symbol of Protestantism, it reinforced the group identity of the faithful. It corresponded to the authority's idea of morality and conveyed humility and modesty.

The three full-length illustrations[25] of the noble woman, the high-ranking woman and maiden as well as the simpler bourgeois woman and maiden are depicted in near-floor-length skirts and bodices or doublets with long sleeves, shoulder rolls and cuffs as well as white puffed sleeve borders, white partlet and black shoes. In addition, they wear the *Dächli-Tüechli,* a church bonnet tapering upwards, replete with a chin-band, and made of a starched white, fine canvas. The noble lady in mourning wears the white mourning ribbon, which hangs over her left shoulder and is attached to the bonnet (Fig. 26).[26] In seventeenth-century Basel, this ribbon was longer in size and also worn with black clothing.[27] Around 1730, the church dress included a golden, multi-rowed belt and necklaces as well as a ruff. At first, only women of the social elite could appear in church with the pointed, high *Dächli-Tüechli.*[28] By 1750, however, ordinary townswomen were also permitted to do so (Fig. 28). From 1744 on, it could not be made of silk or Crepe de Chine and had to be worn with a partlet that was closed around the neck. Offenses were punished with fines of 15 pounds or more.[29]

### Simple, but with a deep neckline

The comparatively simple fashion and small number of accessories in the portrait of Anna Ulrich from Zurich |143| shows a certain modesty in the context of the municipal authorities. The simple, yellow-brown dress of bodice and skirt consists of neither the forbidden multi-coloured taffeta nor the patterned brocade. However, the dress and the red cape may have been made of the unauthorised silk velvet and even have had a silver lining of quilted silk, which was also prohibited. If the person portrayed were to appear in this simple dress at 'all sorts of occasions', she would have faced fines of at least 50 pounds. The lace trim on the bodice and cuffs, whether of silk or linen, was punishable with a fine of 100 pounds. The bonnet with dark-pink ribbon and lace ruffle trim must have been produced in Zurich or in its 'region' and the lace must have been modest, up to an inch wide. The cross pendant |184| – albeit plain and symbolic of Protestantism – and the earrings, whether studded with real stones or imitations, would have been confiscated, and would have also resulted in a fine of 100 thalers.[30] In addition, 'outrageously frivolous disclosures' were prohibited, as in this low-cut bodice. The Zurich woman reveals refinement by holding a branch of white flowers of a precious, exotic lemon tree, thus embellishing her hand without any jewellery.

### *Bollekappe* and dress with elaborate stomacher

Maria Anna Barbara Xaveria Zur Gilgen |184| from Lucerne is shown in half-figure with a fan in her hand and wearing a blue dress probably made of silk. Over the skirt with panniers, she wears a delicate white apron decorated with flowers through which the red flowers of the skirt pattern are visible.[31]

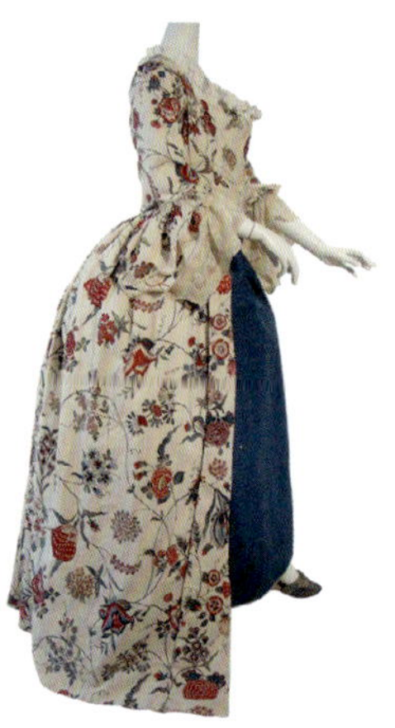
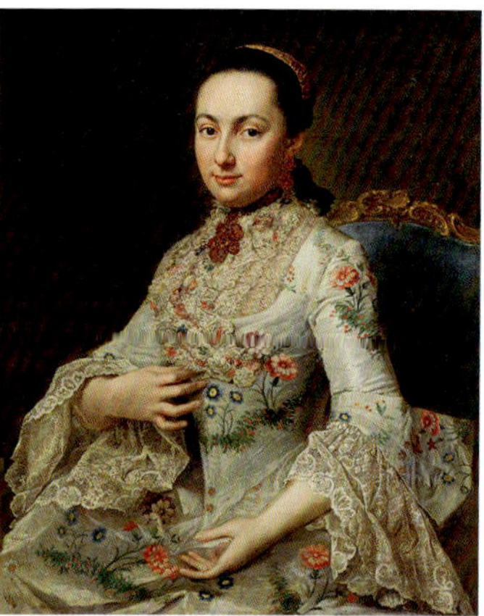





The elaborate stomacher is decorated with about ten rows of white lace ruffles and colourful flowers.[32] Above the black lace collar, the cross pendant on the necklace, decorated with stones and filigree work, has an elegant effect. The matching ear-pendants with crosses allude to Catholicism. Her golden, stone-set ring is similar to that of Elisabeth Gossweiler. | See **266** | Maria Anna wears the *Bollekappe*[33] as a headdress, which was popular with the ladies of Lucerne's upper class. The cap was patterned colourfully, with an arched wreath of ribbons and had the typical black *Bollen* (bulbs) which protruded laterally above the ears.

## Lots of lace and ruffles

According to Paragraph XIII 'Foreign Costumes' of the Basel Reformation Order of 1758, the 'modification of fashion' due to 'unnecessary costs' must be avoided. The 'introduction and wearing of a new costume' in public, 'in carriages' and outside one's 'own house' was punishable by a fine of a silver mark.

Valeria Hoffmann | **165** | is depicted in three-quarter view in a light-blue silk dress patterned with a colourful embroidery of flowers, grasses and leaves. As a lady of the social elite, according to Paragraph IV of the sumptuary law of 1758,[34] she was forbidden to wear a silk dress in church but could wear it outside the church without any restriction according to Paragraph XI.[35] The tight-fitting sleeves of the dress are decorated with conspicuously wide *engageants* made out of white lace.[36] Since these are not multi-layered but single-layered, they comply with the rule in Paragraph X, under the condition that they contain no gold or silver threads.

The décolleté is completely covered with white lace: Above the partlet, she wears an artfully arranged shoulder strap[37] in light-pink silk with floral-like lace ruffle trim and small colourful flowers as well as a lace jabot. Above it lies a necklace with a pendant, which, like her ear pendants, consists of numerous red stones set in gold. Paragraph XII generally prohibited, at a penalty of ten pounds, the wearing of all genuine gems and pearls, except on finger rings. However, women were allowed necklaces and earrings made out of gold, amber, mother-of-pearl, coral and garnets as well as 'black stones' or jet. If the jewellery consisted of garnets, no mandate was violated. However, if it were topaz, stones made of glass, real rubies or, as one might expect, cheaper red spinels similar to rubies, then the parure

Janine Jakob

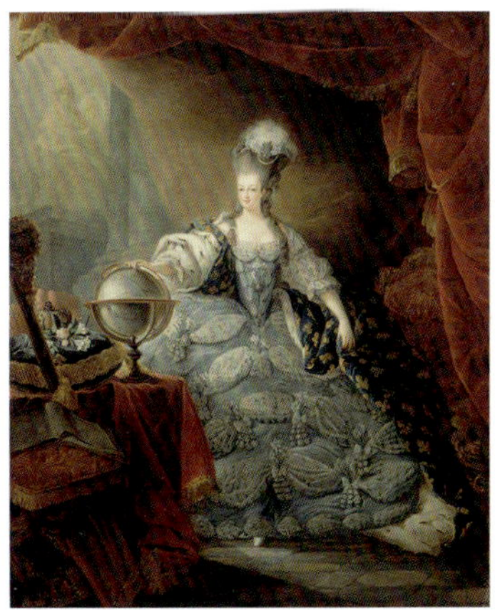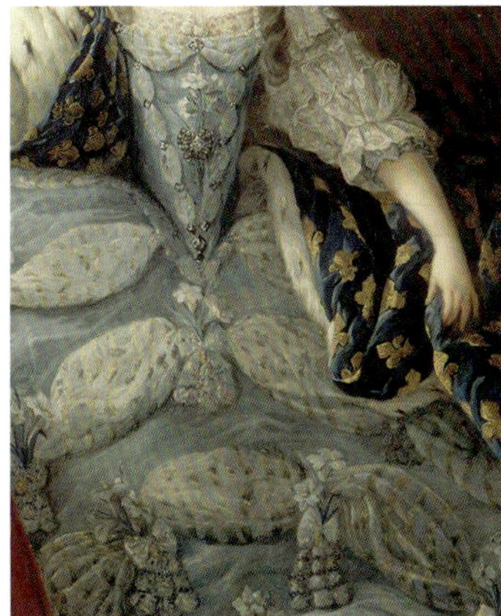



was prohibited under Paragraph XII. According to Paragraph X, 'coronets and embroidered items' were not to be worn if they were embroidered with gold or silver. But Paragraph IX, which regulated gold and silver on clothing, allowed citizens of Basel of all ages to wear 'silver or gold on their heads'; however, according to Paragraph XV, only citizens of a high status.[38] Therefore, Valeria Hoffmann was allowed to wear her dress, the *engageantes* and the *Baselhaube* – a cap of gold thread and wire with relief embroidery – outside the church.

### Queen Marie-Antoinette in the *grand habit de cour*

In this courtly full-length portrait, Queen Marie-Antoinette | [Fig. 1] | is depicted for the first time as the ruler of France in the *grand habit de cour* with the status symbols of globe, crown, numerous lilies, the bust of Louis XVI and her harp. The portrait shows, in comparison to the Swiss elite, other 'more extreme' expressions of fashion. The court dress is made of light-blue silk, with a wide pannier. The skirt is richly adorned with white, gold-striped, lushly draped tulle and flower tuffs and the sleeves are decorated with many lace flounces. The flower tuffs consist of three artificial lilies, three bows and three tassels each. The stomacher is adorned with lozenge-shaped stones and a brooch set with diamonds belonging to the diamond crown, and the brooch on the *bonnet à la draperie*.[39] This white-powdered, high hairstyle with a light-blue cap and a draped pearl row is complemented by valuable ostrich feathers.[40] The ermine-trimmed coat of dark-blue velvet is embellished with the golden lily, the symbol of the French monarchy. Coats with expensive fur were reserved for the highest circles. For example, in 1773, Lucerne forbade women of all social statuses from wearing coats made of fur, including ermine, sable and marten fur.[41] Despite the high artistic quality of the portrait, contemporaries criticised the depiction of the Queen's face but not her splendid fashion.[42]

### Pink *robe à la polonaise* and sparkly, decorated men's shoes

Anna Maria von der Mühl-Faesch | [Page **90**] | had a penchant for pink. In the full-length portrait of her sitting with a lute, she wears a light-pink *robe à la*

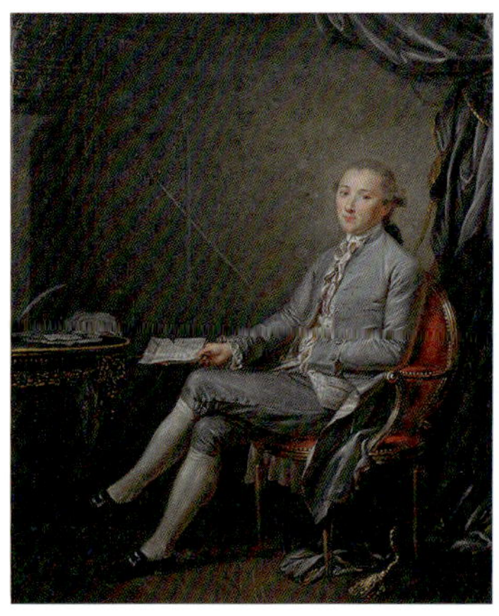 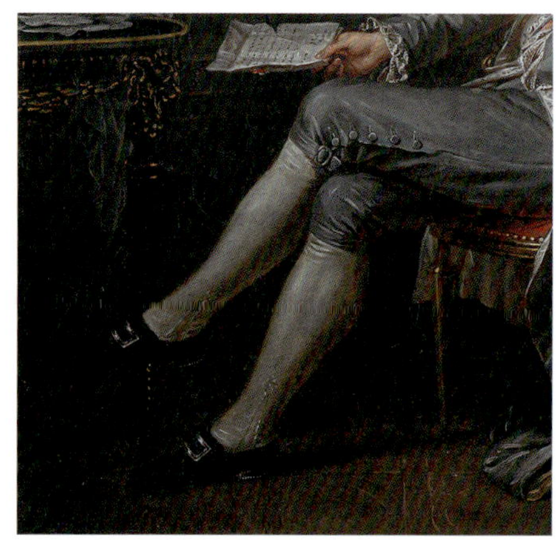

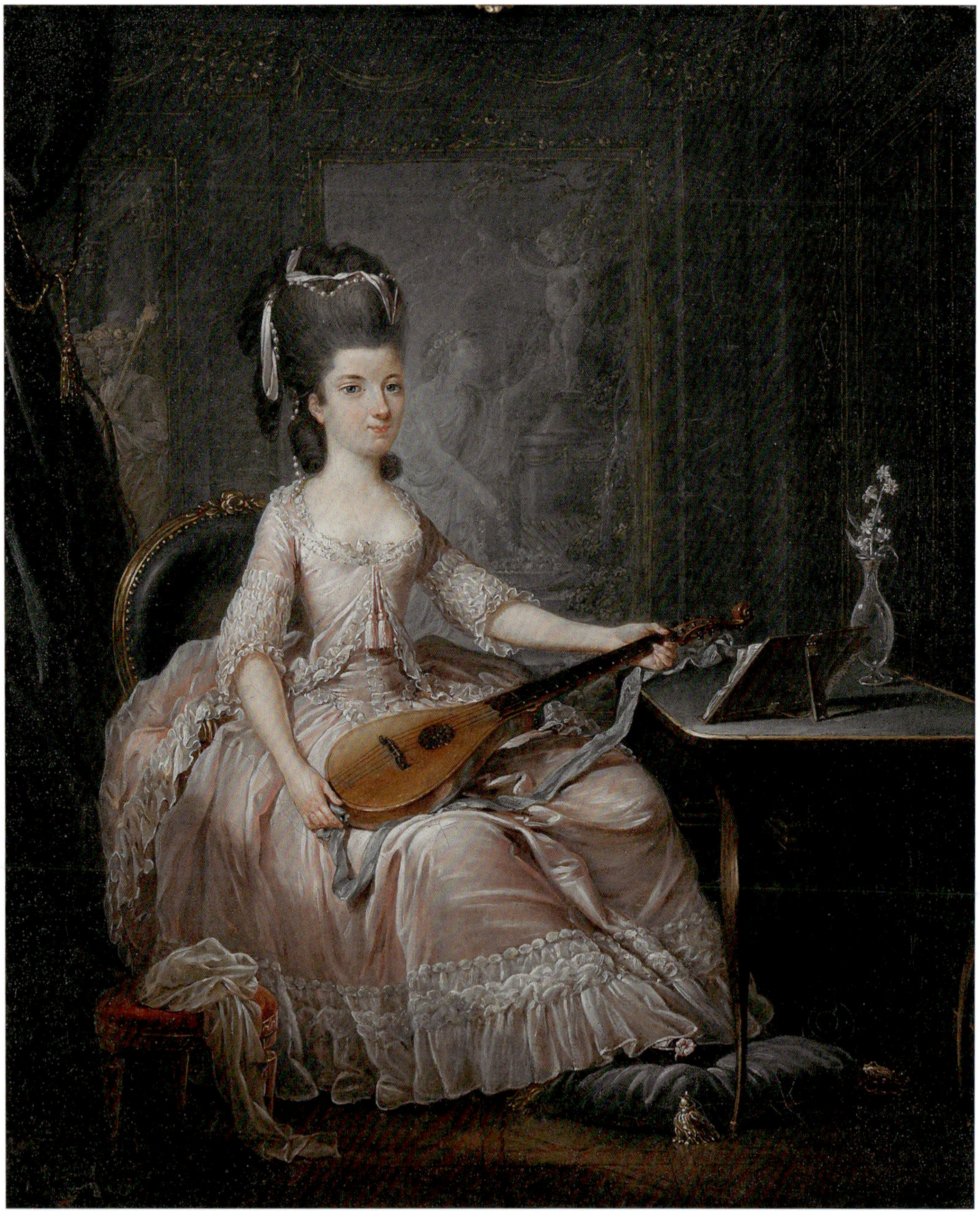

Janine Jakob

*polonaise*[43] with flounces, sleeves with sabot cuffs and a *manteau* draped at the back and closed with tassels at the front. The silk ribbon of the high coiffure with pearls and curls and the shoe rosettes are pink too. A sumptuary law not of Basel but of Lucerne explicitly permitted the wearing of French women's fashion: From 1773 onwards, colourful semi-silk dresses with a maximum value of twenty *Batzen* per cubit of fabric were allowed during the week, while on Sundays and public holidays only black clothes made of wool, pure silk or velvet were permitted in public.[44]

Johannes von der Mühl-Faesch in the full-figure portrait, | **197** | with a wig or long, tied-back hair, is dressed in French nobleman's clothing. The business man sitting on an elegant chair, holds a document in his hand. His important accessory, the rapier, hangs on the wall. He wears grey, knee-length breeches *(culotte)* with white silk stockings, a silvery-white, embroidered silk waistcoat, a shirt with jabot and neck stock, and a grey coat with a silver-white lining.[45] The latter features a stand-up collar and long sleeves with large cuffs and grey buttons. His black shoes with silver buckles have heels that add to his distinctively fashionable appearance. The silver nail-heads edging his heels give the shoes a special elegance.[46]

The portraits illustrate that despite sumptuary laws, there was a differentiated development of the social elite's fashion in Zurich, Basel and Lucerne during the ancien régime, and highly developed dress codes were in use. Fashion provided enough space for creative expression: Clothing and accessories charged with a symbolic meaning referred to personal values, identity constructs and worldviews, and thus represented high social status, power, political or military rank and family affiliation. To emphasise religious affiliation, Catholic women displayed more elaborate cross ornamentation than did Protestant women. Fashion imitated European fashion trends and also developed typical local forms, such as the Zurich church dress with the *Dächli-Tüechli,* the *Bollekappe* or the *fontange à la Zurichoise.*

1    Cf. Lucerne Sumptuary law of 5 April 1773, Historisches Museum Luzern, HMLU 12839. Wives and unmarried daughters of council officers and those who descended from 'persons and families by lineage and name' counted among the 'high class' or persons 'of condition'.

2    Cf. Ingrid Loschek, *Reclams Mode- und Kostümlexikon,* Stuttgart 2011, p. 379; Friedrich Jaeger (ed.), *Enzyklopädie der Neuzeit,* vol. 7, Stuttgart 2008, p. 644; Germ. Mode, lat. *modus,* meant right measure, way of life as well as tradition and customs in clothing. The French term *mode* indicated in the fifteenth century the changing way of dressing. From the mid-seventeenth century, fashion was ascribed to the new taste of clothing and from around 1770 to tradition, customs and etiquette. *À la mode* or *Alamode* characterised the exaggeration of French fashion while *Alamodereien* meant generally everything new coming from French fashion. Cf. Friedrich Staub/Ludwig Tobler (eds), *Schweizerisches Idiotikon: Wörterbuch der schweizerdeutschen Sprache,* vol. 1, Frauenfeld 1881, col. 1033. *Hoffärtig* (haughty) meant to be dressed impressively. Werner Sombart, *Luxus und Kapitalismus,* Paderborn 2011, p. 86: The French court of the eighteenth century symbolises the 'luxury of clothes'.

3    Sumptuary law of 13 October 1736. Staatsarchiv Basel, Bfl 1733–41. It refers to the Basel sumptuary laws of 1727 and 1733. Sumptuary law of Lucerne 1773 (as in note 1).

4    To the two portraits (cat. 217a/b) belongs a full-length portrait of Hans Rudolf Werdmüller (1614–1677), the first son of Barbara from her first marriage with Hans Rudolf Werdmüller, painted around 1625. They were created by the same artist and have been attributed to Dietrich Theodor Meyer the Elder. The fashion appearance corresponds with the fashion style in cat. 217a. See concerning the general ascription Leo Weisz, *Die Werdmüller,* vol. 1, Zurich 1949, p. XIV, as well as plates XI and XV; see also Hans von Meyenburg, *Die Schipf in Herrliberg: Chronik eines Landgutes am Zürichsee,* Zurich 1957, p. 148.

5    See Loschek 2011 (as in note 2), pp. 30, 38f., 271f., 407, and Ingrid Loschek, *Accessoires: Symbolik und Geschichte,* Munich 1993, pp. 79, 88. For the depicted shoe model, see June Swann, *Shoes,* London 1986, p. 13, no. 7.

6    Cf. Loschek 2011 (as in note 2), p. 215.

7    Cf. George Cameron Stone, *A Glossary of the Construction, Decoration and Use of Arms and Armor,* New York 1961, pp. 250f., ill. 308, types nos 2 and 9. The gorget is a kind of breastplate.

8    Cf. Loschek 2011 (as in note 2), p. 436. In the political or military field, the sash served as a symbol of honour. Martin Illi, *Die Constaffel in Zürich,* Zurich 2003, pp. 118f. From 1621 to 1638, Schmid belonged to the Zurich government, the council called *Kleine Rat* of Zurich as a *Constaffelherr* and served in the Zurich civil service and the French military service. During the Thirty Years' War, he was member of the Zurich Sweden Party *(Schwedenpartei).*

9    See Loschek 2011 (as in note 2), pp. 242f.; Johannes Pietsch/Sjoukje Colenbrander, *Netherlandish Fashion in the Seventeenth Century,* Riggisberg 2012 (Riggisberg Berichte; 19), pp. 30f., 93, 96; Wolfgang Glüber/Johannes Pietsch/Jutta Reinisch, *Chic! Mode im 17. Jahrhundert,* Regensburg 2016, p. 26. A reinforced or wired under-collar supports the stiffened, flattened ruff. It fell out of fashion after 1630, but was still worn into the eighteenth century.

10    Visible portions of the silver-plated hilt are the pommel, handle (grip), quillon, knuckle guard and inner guard. The distinction between stabbing weapons such as the rapier and sword are problematic and dependent on language. See Anthony North, *Schwerter,* Bern; Stuttgart 1982, pp. 7–14. Cf. also Angus Patterson, *Fashion and Armour in Renaissance Europe: Proud Looks and Brave Attire,* London 2009, pp. 58–64. Vladimir Dolinek/Jan Durdik. *Historische Waffen.* Hanau 1995, p. 100.

11    The staff is decorated with a fitting of golden nails arranged in a lozenge shape. The red-golden handle has a hanging tassel. Cf. Louis Carlen, 'Der Gerichtsstab in Bern', in *Berner Zeitschrift für Geschichte und Heimatkunde,* vol. 31, Bern 1969, pp. 112, 115.

12    Black clothing had a different symbolic charge. Black was a fashionable colour and expensive to produce; it stood, for example, for dignity, frugality and religion (see cat. 172). Cf. Aileen Ribeiro, *Clothing Art: The Visual Culture of Fashion, 1600–1914,* New Haven, Conn. 2017, p. 116.

13    The shoulder roll or epaulet is a short wing extending over the shoulder or also a roll in the form of a ring to broaden the shoulders; the roll was especially in fashion from 1575 until the first third of the seventeenth century. Loschek 2011 (as in note 2), pp. 39, 96f.

14    Cf. Loschek 2011 (as in note 2), pp. 195f. An invisible metal spring, the so-called *Ohreisen,* gives the desired lateral protrusion of the upper bonnet. Cf. Ribeiro 2017 (as in note 12), p. 120 and ill. 86, p. 116.

15    See Swann 1986 (as in note 5), p. 12, no. 5.

16    See Glüber/Pietsch/Reinisch 2012 (as in note 9), p. 28; Roswitha Rogge, *Zwischen Moral und Handelsgeist,* Frankfurt am Main 1998, p. 63. Bracelets were worn, mostly in pairs, by the richest women in the seventeenth century. Often, they were a gift of the groom to the spouse.

17    Cf. Will of Barbara Schmid from 5 February 1624, Zentralbibliothek Zürich, Ms T 75.64; Weisz 1949 (as in note 4), pp. 134–36. She owns 'six of the loveliest rings of her beloved mother', numerous belts, among them two 'especially beautiful' ones, a large, precious bracelet, necklaces, rings, gems, moreover an emerald, a ruby, a diamond and a 'large deep blue' sapphire of her husband as well as further gemstones.

18    Cf. Staub/Tobler 1881 (as in note 2), col. 383: The *Bysemöpfel* (Swiss German), German Bisamapfel, English also musk apple, is a small scent box belonging to the embellishments of the female costume. The additional object on the châtelaine is possibly a perfume flask.

19    Staub/Tobler 1881 (as in note 2), col. 1964.

20    Cf. Ulrich Barth/Christian Hörack, *Basler Goldschmiedekunst,* vol. 2, Basel 2014, p. 353, see fig. no. 598.

21    See Johann Andreas Pfeffel, 'Schweizer Trachte-Cabinet oder allerhand Kleidungen, wie man solche in dem löblichen Schweizer-Canton Zürich zu tragen pflegt' in *Hoff-Kupferstecher Cum Prvil. Sac. Caes. Maj,* Augsburg: Johannes Andreas Pfeffel, c. 1725–31, sheet no. 14 (Private collection).

22    *Reformation Und Verbott Dess Köstlichen Uberflusses in Kleidern Etc. Sambt Etwelchen Anderen Ordnungen: Durch Ein Hohe Oberkeit Dess Löbl. Standts Unnd Orhts Lucern … auffgericht Und Beschlossen Im Jahr 1671.* Printed in Lucerne by Gottfrid Hautt, 1671. Zentralbibliothek Zürich, cat. no. 31.82,21.

23    Presumably, it is a plum. However, the leaves correspond more to a citrus fruit. Kind advice by Peter Enz (Botanical Garden of the University of Zurich).

24    See Loschek 2011 (as in note 2), pp. 196f. The *fontange* was fashionable in France from 1685 until around 1713. The coiffure of the Duchess of Fontanges, a mistress of Louis XIV, had loosened during the hunt, whereupon the duchess, to the delight of the king, tied up her hair with a garter. The whole coiffure is later named after the uppermost hairbow, *fontange.*

25    The noble and elegant women depicted (cat. 172, nos 26 and 27) are to be understood as part of the social elite permitted to wear the mourning ribbon.



Janine Jakob

**26**  Hans Wanner et al. (eds), *Schweizerisches Idiotikon,* vol. 12, Frauenfeld 1961, col. 330. The *Dächli-Tüechli,* also called *Tächlitüchlein, Tächleintüchlein* in the sumptuary law *Tüchli;* moreover called *Sturz* or *Stuche.* Cf. Conrad Ulrich, 'Das 18. Jahrhundert', in *Geschichte des Kantons Zürich,* vol. 2: *Frühe Neuzeit – 16. bis 18. Jahrhundert,* Zurich 1996, pp. 364–511, here p. 436; Jenny Schneider, *Schweizer Damenkostüme des 18. und 19. Jahrhunderts,* Bern 1967, p. 4; Julie Heierli (ed.), *Johann Andreas Pfeffel Schweizerisches Trachten-Cabinet oder allerhand Kleidungen, wie man solche in dem löblichen Schweizer Canton Zürich zu tragen pflegt,* facsimile edition from 1750, Zurich 1925, p. 3.

**27**  See also Hans Heinrich Glaser, *Basler Trachtenbilder,* Basel 1624. Depiction of high-ranking and other persons. HMB – Historisches Museum Basel, image archive inv. no. 1983.641. Sheet: *'Ein frau tregt leid umb ir mann'.*

**28**  Pfeffel c. 1725–31 (as in note 21), sheets 8–9. Noble woman or maiden in her church dress. The ordinary townswoman had to wear a folded *Dächli-Tüechli.*

**29**  Staatsarchiv Zürich, StAZH, III AAb I.II: *Mandat und Ordnung,* sumptuary law of 4 March 1744.

**30**  Staatsarchiv Zürich, StAZH, III AAb I.II: *Mandat und Ordnung,* sumptuary law of 4 March 1744 and of 8 April 1750.

**31**  Cf. Ribeiro 2017 (as in note 12), example of Hogarth, p. 177.

**32**  Cf. Loschek 2011 (as in note 2), p. 456. The stomacher is a separate, stiffened triangular or U-shaped breast panel which fills out the front opening of the bodice. Characteristic for the courtly fashion of the eighteenth century, it consisted mostly of brocade with rich gold and silver embroidery and is often decorated with ribbons (French: *échelle*). See Akiko Fukai et al., *Fashion: Eine Modegeschichte vom 18. bis 20. Jh. Die Sammlung des Kyoto Costume Institute,* vol. 1, Cologne 2015, p. 42. On the cuff in cat. 184, see original in Claire Wilcox, *Fashion in Detail 1700–2000,* London 2013, model from England from the 1740s, 'A woman's bodice of silk taffeta', p. 60.

**33**  Cf. Julie Heierli, 'Der Kopfputz der bürgerlichen Frauen in der Schweiz zu Ende des 18. und Beginn des 19. Jahrhunderts', in *Anzeiger für schweizerische Altertumskunde,* vol. 24 (1922), no. 1, pp. 45–48. The headdress makes the wearer look as though she has a kind of bulb over her ears. Those two bulbs are called *Bollen* and gave the headdress its name. The two bulbs are connected by the black *Bödeli.* This is completed by a curved wreath of ribbons which lies on top. The latter consists of pleated and stiffened silver ribbons and is patterned with large red and small yellow flowers and delicate green foliage (see cat. 184)

**34**  Basel sumptuary law of 24 July 1758 *(Reformationsordnung).* UB Basel, A Lambda I 3, no. 77, and Staatsarchiv Basel City, Bfl 1756–65.

**35**  At sermons, the women as well as the men had to appear in black wool clothing, if they could afford it – otherwise in 'decent dress'. Outside of church, men were allowed to wear silk clothes, however, women were forbidden to wear silk skirts and could be punished by a fine of ten pounds.

**36**  Cf. Anne Kraatz, *Lace,* London 1989, pp. 7, 72–80; Gisela Framke, *Spitze: Luxus zwischen Tradition und Avantgarde,* Heidelberg 1995, pp. 6, 10–12. Especially in the seventeenth and eighteenth centuries, products from the lace industry developed into social status symbols.

**37**  For the shoulder strap, see the depiction of David Herrliberger, 'Zürcher Kirchenhabit – Kirchen- und Trauerkleidung', in *Zürcherische Kleider-Trachten,* sheet IV, Zurich 1749. Ill. 6. V, 31: Noble woman dressed for social visits.

**38**  Basel sumptuary law of 11 September 1769, Staatsarchiv Basel City, Bfl 1666–71, supplemented by the regulation 'zweyten Theil zu Uebermässiger Pracht und Kostbarkeit zu verhüten' (Part two, To stay away from excessive splendour and preciousness) states in Paragraph I, 'Gold und Silber auf Kleideren' (Gold and silver on clothing): gold and silver, real and false, on everything is prohibited and is newly punishable by a fine of 20 pounds, with the exception of children's caps as well as the common Basel caps of women and men's hats.

**39**  Cf. Fukai et al. 2015 (as in note 32), p. 110. See also Maurice Leloir, *Dictionnaire du costume et de ses accessoires des Armes et des Étoffes des origines à nos jours,* Paris 1992, p. 97, nos 18, 19.

**40**  Cf. Dossier MV 8061 on the portrait of Marie-Antoinette (here fig. 1), inv. no. MV 8061, Musée national des châteaux de Versailles et de Trianon, and Juliette Trey, in the respective collection catalogue online under collections.chateauversailles.fr. It is quite probably the diamond jewellery that Marie-Antoinette was given from Louis XVI in 1775, with the request to replace the extravagant feathers with diamonds. She is wearing both accessories in the portrait. Cf. Galeries Nationales d'Exposition Du Grand Palais (ed.), *Marie-Antoinette: [exposition],* Galeries Nationales Du Grand Palais, Paris, 15 Mars-30 Juin 2008. Paris 2008, p. 140.

**41**  Cf. Lucerne sumptuary law of 1773 (as in note 1).

**42**  Cf. Trey (as in note 40).

**43**  Cf. Loschek 2011 (as in note 2), p. 426; Fukai et al. 2015 (as in note 32), pp. 76f. The French dress in Polish style is draped in the back into two or three puffed sections and is worn with a bodice or gilet as well as skirt and a hoop skirt.

**44**  Cf. Lucerne sumptuary law of 1773 (as in note 1).

**45**  Cf. Loscheck 2011 (as in note 2), pp. 50, 161. The coat, called *Habit* after 1750, is a further development of the *Justaucorps.* The coat extends below the knees.

**46**  This decoration on the shoe heel is unique according to current research. The silver nail heads are merely decorative. Kind advice by June Swann.

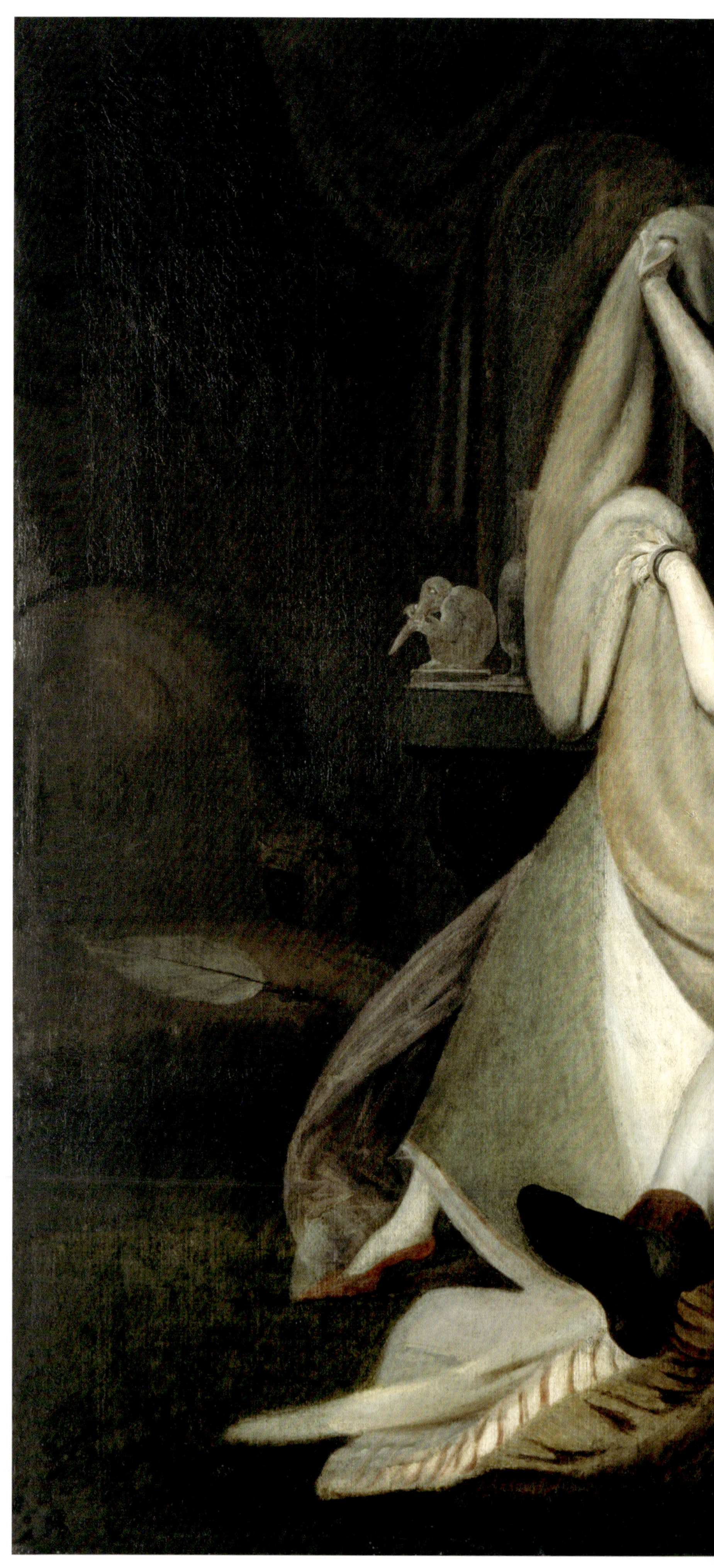

**144**  Henry Fuseli (1741–1825)
*Falstaff in the laundry basket,* 1792
Oil on canvas, 137.5 × 170.5 cm
Kunsthaus Zürich, 1941

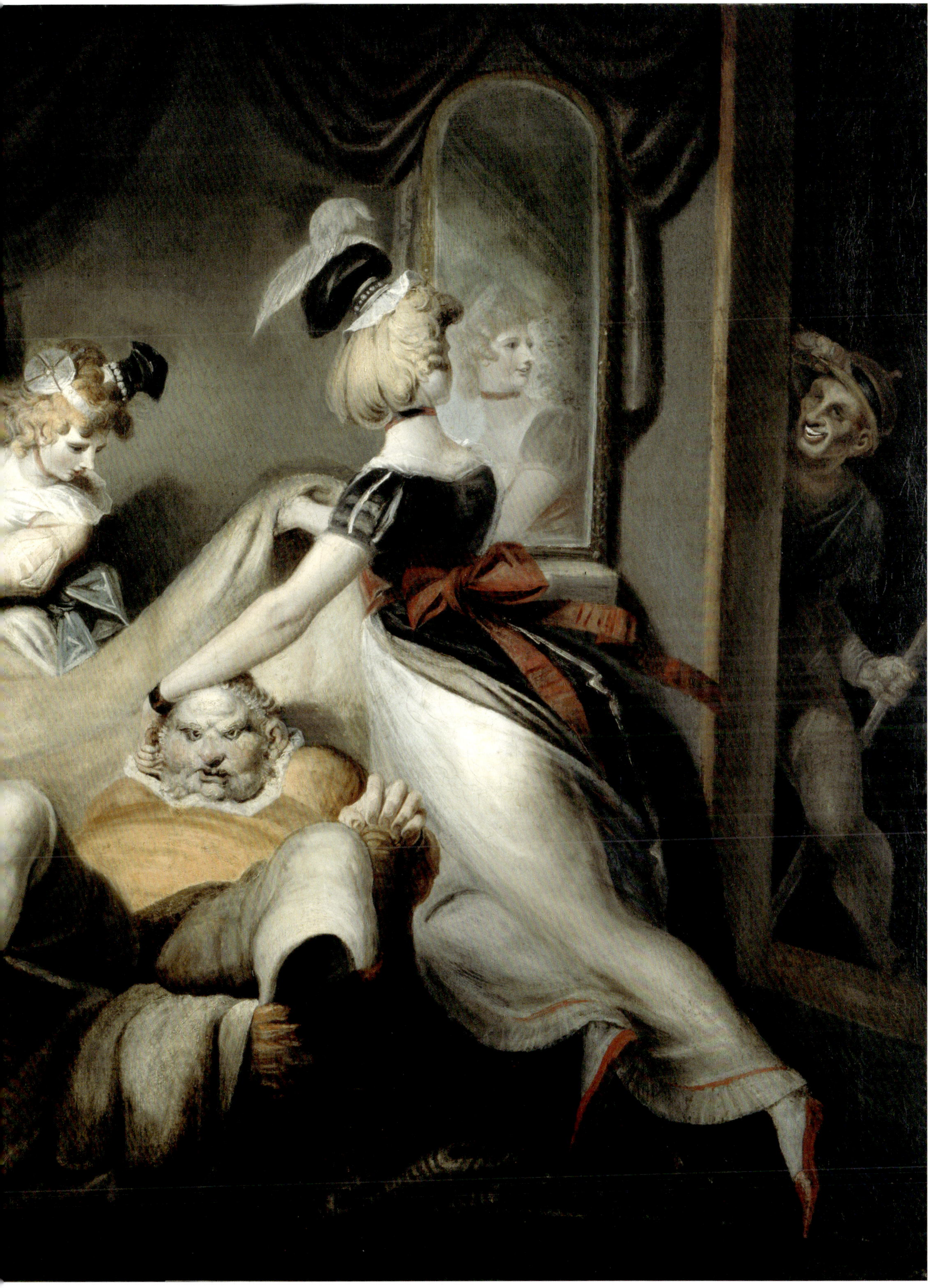

# Fashion Times Upheaval

**Barbara Vinken**

in

of Social

*The French
Revolution*

The French Revolution of 1789 led to a fundamental change not only in the political order but also in the dress code. The new social order that emerged with and after the Revolution and which manifested itself in clothing still prevails today. The importance of clothing for the Revolution can hardly be overestimated: this central political event, that radically changed the social, sexual and political order to bring about the modern republics, was named after a missing piece of clothing: those without breeches, the sans-culottes; the third estate and the people rose up against the culotte-wearing aristocracy. Of course, the sans-culottes were not really without trousers: They did not wear breeches, as the aristocrats did, but *pantalons,* drainpipe trousers not tied under the knee that we call trousers today. The original ridiculousness of this garment, the success of which was to become universal and today seems the most natural thing in the world, was immortalised in its name *pantalons*. The Pantalone, after whom the trousers were named in Romance languages, is a figure of the Commedia dell'Arte: an old, grotesquely vain fop who wants to imitate the aristocrats but wears the wrong trousers – ones that fall, precisely as the drainpipe trousers, smoothly onto the shoes. An absolute no-go at this time. That the parties opposing each other in the Revolution differed according to their clothes indicated a particular aspect of the upheaval that was to revolutionise the dress code. Fashion had divided the estates until the Revolution – 'what did custom stern divide' wrote Friedrich von Schiller (1759–1805) in his *Ode to Joy*.[1] Until then, clergy, nobility and the third estate distinguished themselves as a matter of course by their clothing. So that the order of the estates remained evident, luxury laws regulated what certain classes were allowed to wear until the reign of Louis XIV (1638–1715): the third estate, for example, could not have royal ermine trimmings or aristocratic ribbons of gold and silver on their hats.

After the Revolution, clothes did, nevertheless, provide a no less strict order. This time, it was not divine mandate but pretended to follow nothing but nature's own, proper voice. All humans had become brothers (again Schiller),[2] and thus turned out to be men. From now on, the clothes separated less the classes than the sexes. In fact, never were

1    Friedrich Schiller, 'An die Freude' [1785], in *Gedichte,* Heinz Ludwig Arnold (ed.), Frankfurt am Main 2008, p. 125. English version, see: https://www.schillerinstitute.org/transl/schiller_poem/ode_to_joy.pdf (accessed 11 December 2017).

2    Schiller [1785] 2008.

3    Cf. Edmond Goblot, *Klasse und Differenz: Soziologische Studie zur modernen französischen Bourgeoisie* [1925], trans. Franz Schultheis, cited after *Die Blumen der Mode: Klassische und neue Texte zur Philosophie der Mode,* Barbara Vinken (ed.), Stuttgart 2016, p. 237. Original French version: Edmond Goblot, *La barrière et le niveau,* Paris 1925.

4    Cf. John Carl Flügel, *Die Psychologie der Kleidung* [1930], trans. Matthias Müller, cited after Vinken 2016, p. 258. Original English version: John Carl Flügel, *The Psychology of Clothes,* Ann Arbor 1930.

5    Adolf Loos, 'Herrenmode' and 'Damenmode' [1898], cited after Vinken 2016, p. 137.

6    J.-A. Barbey d'Aurevilly, *Du dandysme et de G. Brummel,* Caen 1845, p. 27.

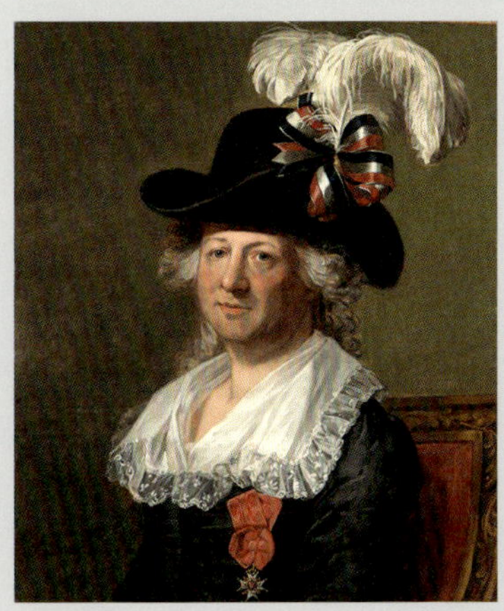



the sexes dressed as differently as in the nineteenth century. Regulations no longer determined which class was allowed to wear what, but rather, who was wearing the trousers. An infamous police regulation from the 16th Brumaire of the year IX forbade women from wearing trousers. To do so, they now needed a police permit. The sociologist Edmond Goblot (1858–1935) went so far as to speak of a 'dimorphisme sexuel', a 'dimorphism' of the citizens separated no longer by estates, but by the sexes.[3]

John Carl Flügel (1884–1955) famously coined the dictum the 'great male renunciation' as a parallel to the 'great French Revolution'.[4] From then on, men were to renounce everything that had made them the fairer sex for centuries: 'velvet and silk, flowers and ribbons, feathers and colours' as summarised by Adolf Loos (1871–1933).[5] No powder and perfume, no rouge, no red heels and shoes with bows, no lace, jewellery and embroidery, no lion's mane of curly wigs (such as Lord Bernard Stuart, 1622–1645, and his brother in the painting after Anthony van Dyck, 1599–1641). | Page **170** | Above all, men renounced the splendid display of a strong, swift, potent body, capable of fencing, riding, dancing and procreating. In Charles V's (1500–1558) time, the long, slender, stockinged leg jutted out from under the short balloon skirt, the Spanish breeches, or a tight, short upper hose. Henry VIII (1491–1547) himself and also Louis XIV (1638–1715) and Alessandro Farnese (1545–1592) displayed beautiful legs in precious silk hoses. | Pages **76, 58** | In the eighteenth century, the trousers became even tighter: As Barbey d'Aurevilly (1808–1889) states, the Comte d'Artois (1757–1836) had to be lifted by four servants into his skin-tight trousers.[6] Another courtier kept himself like those who wore the tight-fitting suits from Hedi Slimane for Dior at the beginning of the twenty-first century: The courtier had breeches in which he could sit, and others in which he could only stand.

With post-revolutionary fashion, the fashion of the modern age, men hid their charms. The modern man renounced to show leg, a lot of leg, leg to the crotch, possibly butt and manhood. The bourgeois was not provocative, not gorgeous and not beautiful; he was dressed 'correctly' for the office he held or wished to hold. The distinction lay in not distinguishing oneself through clothes. To the bourgeois, all ornament was suspect, all jewellery was sheer outwardness and nothing but a deceptive pretence that distracted from the true, inner values. Little by little, men's fashion in order to appear more plain speaking discarded everything that stood out, was imaginative and surprising. The vest, made of brightly patterned and colourful damask, brocade, plaid velvet or embroidered satin was the shrunken form of past glories. As early as around 1835, the vest was considered too conspicuous and hence whittled down to the tie. Male coquetry became ridiculous. To strive for elegance became inelegant. The bourgeois did not become weary of demonstrating day in, day out that he did not need to shine through clothes. Being properly dressed now meant not being dressed too well, and exactly that became the embodiment of the distinguished. The art of the artless had to be learned. It became a male science in itself. The eager effort to stage democratic equality

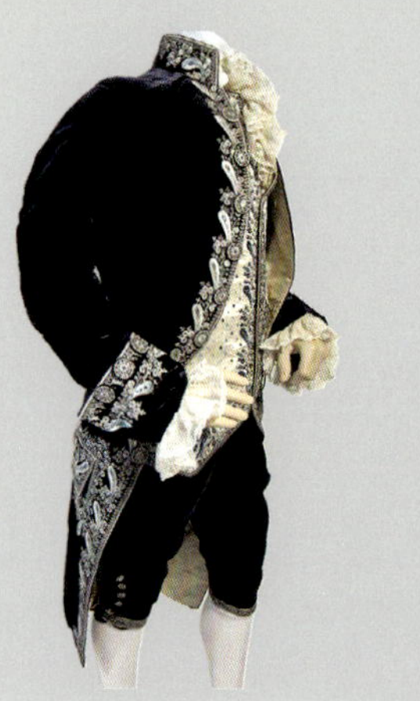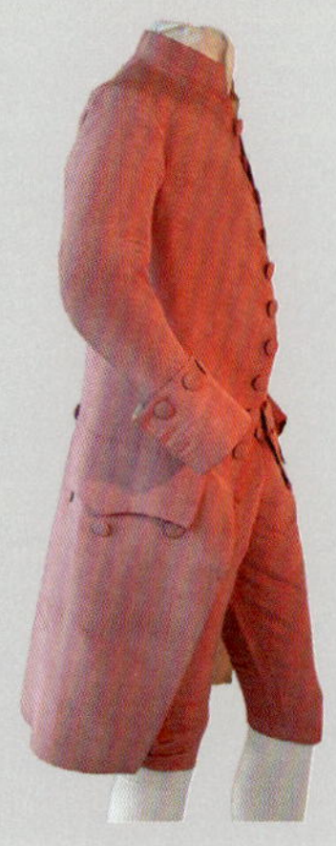



and the straddle-legged, heterosexual fraternity was thwarted by dandies whose only vocation was to wear clothes in style. | <sup>Pages</sup> **175, 176** | Women, on the other hand, became the indescribably feminine queens of hearts. From the world in which men, more or less brotherly, distributed power, authority and money among themselves, women were banished to the cosy home. Lost in the men's milieu were only disreputable females, women of the world. Fashion and femininity (or even the effeminate) became synonymous, fashion became the privilege and the stigma of the feminine. The bourgeoisie highlighted the nobility's disempowerment through their women, and, during major occasions, paraded them as trophies.

On the eve of the Revolution, the French court once more staged the traditional dress code that separated the estates in a spectacular way.[7] This was actually – and, most likely, without the parties being aware – a costumed farce. It was 4 May 1789 – the storming of the Bastille was not far off. Louis XVI (1754–1793) was forced, in view of the devastating economic situation, to convene the Estates-General to restructure the budget. This had not occurred since 1614, but facing bankruptcy, their approval was indispensable to raise taxes. A symbolic event, it was the afterimage of an epoch that had come to an end. The protocol, including the dress code, adhered to the meeting format 200 years prior. The estates' outfits were prescribed in meticulous detail.

King and queen appeared in full court following the old dress code. Marie-Antoinette's (1755–1793) dress was of silver silk brocade, Louis's coat made of gold-arrased, shiny fabric: Sun King – tradition bound – and Moon Queen. Louis XVI wore a diamond-studded sword, a coat with diamond buttons, diamond-clad shoes and the famous regent diamond; Marie-Antoinette plaited the flawless, 55-carat Sancy diamond into her hair. Sparkling and glittering, decorated all over with marvellous stones, the king and queen became the reflection of divine radiance. This couple mirrored heaven on earth. The clergy appeared in purple. The aristocracy wore feather hats and black velvet jackets richly embroidered in gold, lace ties, and black silk culottes with white silk stockings. The members of the third estate had to appear in simple black suits, cheap muslin scarves and crude black hats. The dull, dark suits of the third estate's representatives devoured the sunlight, forming the ideal dull-dark background for the glow of the colours, the sparkle of the rainbows. What had been perceived at that moment already as a humiliation of the third estate was later described as 'dress apartheid'.

In the performance staged on that day for the last time, the clothes suggested a philosophy of life. They were the opposite of any arbitrary, tyrannically ordered fashion. Personal caprice and self-fashioning could only express themselves to a very limited extent. In the dress code, the French monarchy illustrated its divine right. And as this monarchy was meant to be eternal, so the clothes were not meant to be subject to the whims of fashion. There was nothing arbitrary about them; they simply re-presented the cosmic order of being. For this reason, the main task of king, queen and court was to present their carefully clothed



Barbara Vinken

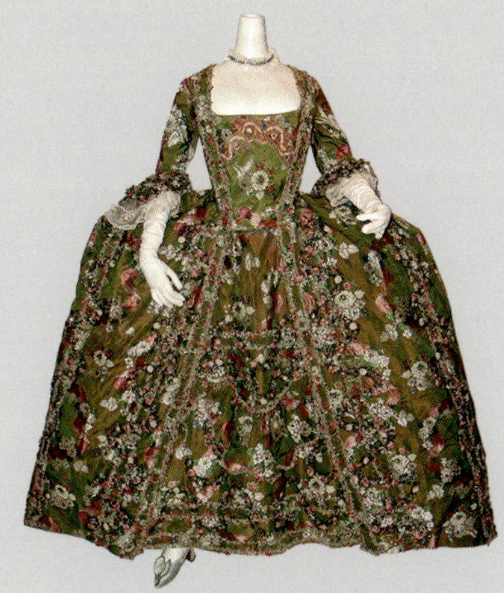

**3** Robe à la française
(à grand panier), c. 1765
Brocaded shot silk,
with adjustable petticoat,
stomacher recreated
Collection Kamer-Ruf

bodies to the eyes of the world. Clothes served to celebrate the beauty
of the God-created, hierarchical cosmic order. Queen and king in velvet
and silk with diamond bows and ribbons illustrated their participation
in the eternal stability of the cosmos, immune to the wheel of fortune,
immune to the deceptively trickling vanitas of all earthly transience.
This symbolic function of clothes, which in the late eighteenth century
was a fading wishful thought, came to light as an outdated fiction with
Louis XVI's summoning of the Estates-General. What clothes were meant
to symbolise turned out to be a vain claim. The meeting revealed that the
order of the Estates had become untenable: the emperor's new clothes.
With the constitution of the National Assembly on 17 June 1789 by the third
estate and defectors from the monarchy and clergy, the end of the absolut-
ist monarchy was sealed before the actual Revolution.
Marie-Antoinette, queen of France and daughter to the Habsburg Maria
Theresia, and Louis-Philippe (1747–1793) from the house of Bourbon-Orléans
illustrate the change of time that would soon be called 'old'. Orléans, known
as Philippe Égalité, seized the opportunity of the assembly of the estates to
abandon the splendour of the ruined Ancien Régime and defect sartorially
to the third estate – a class travesty. While his cousin the king, as descend-
ant of the Sun King, had no acute sense of the *zeitgeist* and sought constantly
to outshine everybody, Orléans, as a citizen and patriot, set aside velvet and
silk, embroidery, lace, feathers, gems and bright colours in favour of the dark,
muted hemp of the third estate. Instead of *culottes,* which showed off the legs
in skin-tight, shiny silk stockings, he wore the *pantalon,* which has since become the sign of the modern man. His own short-cut hair replaced the pow-
dered curly wig; no costly embroidery and lace adorned him. Philippe became a
forerunner of men's fashion by laying aside the luxuriant beauty of the aristocracy to appear as a bourgeois everyman.
Marie-Antoinette, who considered monarchy by divine right the most natural
thing in the world, had already damaged severely the dress policy of the
Ancien Régime. Since this regime was God-given for her, she was unaware that it
needed artful staging. For the assembly of the Estates General, she submitted to



**7**  See Caroline Weber, *Queen of
Fashion – What Marie Antoinette
Wore to the Revolution,* New York
2006.

**8**  Honoré de Balzac, 'Les Chou-
ans' [1829], in *La Comédie humaine,*
Paris 1977, p. 1124.

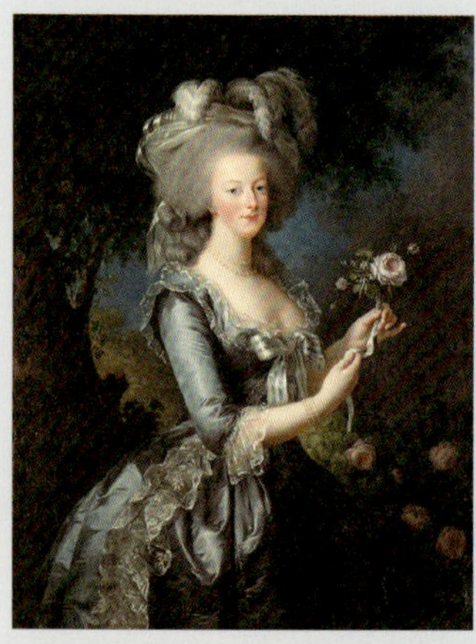



the protocol, but that meant that she, who had turned into a queen of fashion, must disguise herself as a French queen of the old kind. She wore the *robe à la française* of heavy silk brocade, stiffly corseted with flared *paniers*. |3, [Page] 122, [Fig.] 8 | It was her almost uncorseted, much lighter, simpler, virtuously natural, cotton muslin with but a small *panier* that was a trendsetter for the Neoclassical fashion revolution of flowing white fabrics. As *fashion à la grecque* of all things, this fashion would triumph in the Directoire and Empire styles. Marie-Antoinette had long since discarded the court's splendour and the corset, and abandoned the Baroque silk brocade and Rococo taffetas for cotton muslin.

The famous portrait *Marie-Antoinette en chemise* by Marie Louise Élisabeth Vigée-Lebrun (1755–1842) |292| shows her as early as 1783 swathed in pastoral white muslin with a straw hat: Marie-Antoinette was carefully staged as nothing but a natural woman. She revealed her femininity – and was, without the courtly garnish of armour, no longer a queen. This new, intimate, very unqueen likefashion was soon to be called *chemise à la reine*. The portrait provoked such a scandal that it had to be removed from the famous Salon exhibition in the Louvre in 1783 and replaced with a more acceptable (but practically identical – in pose and facial expression) image. | [Fig.] 1 | The spicy detail is that the artist Marie Louise Élisabeth Vigée-Lebrun was participating for the first time in the prestigious Salon, and was, at the same time, one of the few women who had been allowed to do so.

During and after the Revolution, the Neoclassical style triumphed. But it did not win under the name of *mode à la grecque* as an ideal veil of the beautiful soul, but disrespectfully as a 'fashion of nudity' – satirists claimed that one saw not the beautiful soul, but too much embarrassing flesh. Honoré de Balzac (1799–1850) depicts the new provocative shamelessness with a few strokes: 'A rather short dress made of Indian cotton, which looked like a damp cloth, underlined the delicacy of her shapes.'[8] As if naked, the beautiful Mademoiselle de Verneuil dances in this scandalous robe. Leo Tolstoy (1828–1910), in *War and Peace,* states without ado the shocking appeal of the 'Greek fashion': every woman is turned into a 'naked Elena'. The fact that what was to be seen under the very light, feathery cotton muslin or batiste was by no means the naked flesh but flesh-coloured jerseys did not change any of the criticism of public nakedness. | [Pages] 135, 137 |

The post-revolutionary opposition, which structures fashion, is the erotically marked (female) against the erotically unmarked (human/male). In the oldest misogynistic fashion, it opposes the (male) spirit to the (female) flesh, the superficial (female) dress to a deep (male) character. Fashion of the twentieth century – the fashion of the modern age – wittily shatters this bourgeois order of clothes and sexes, born with the Revolution.

---

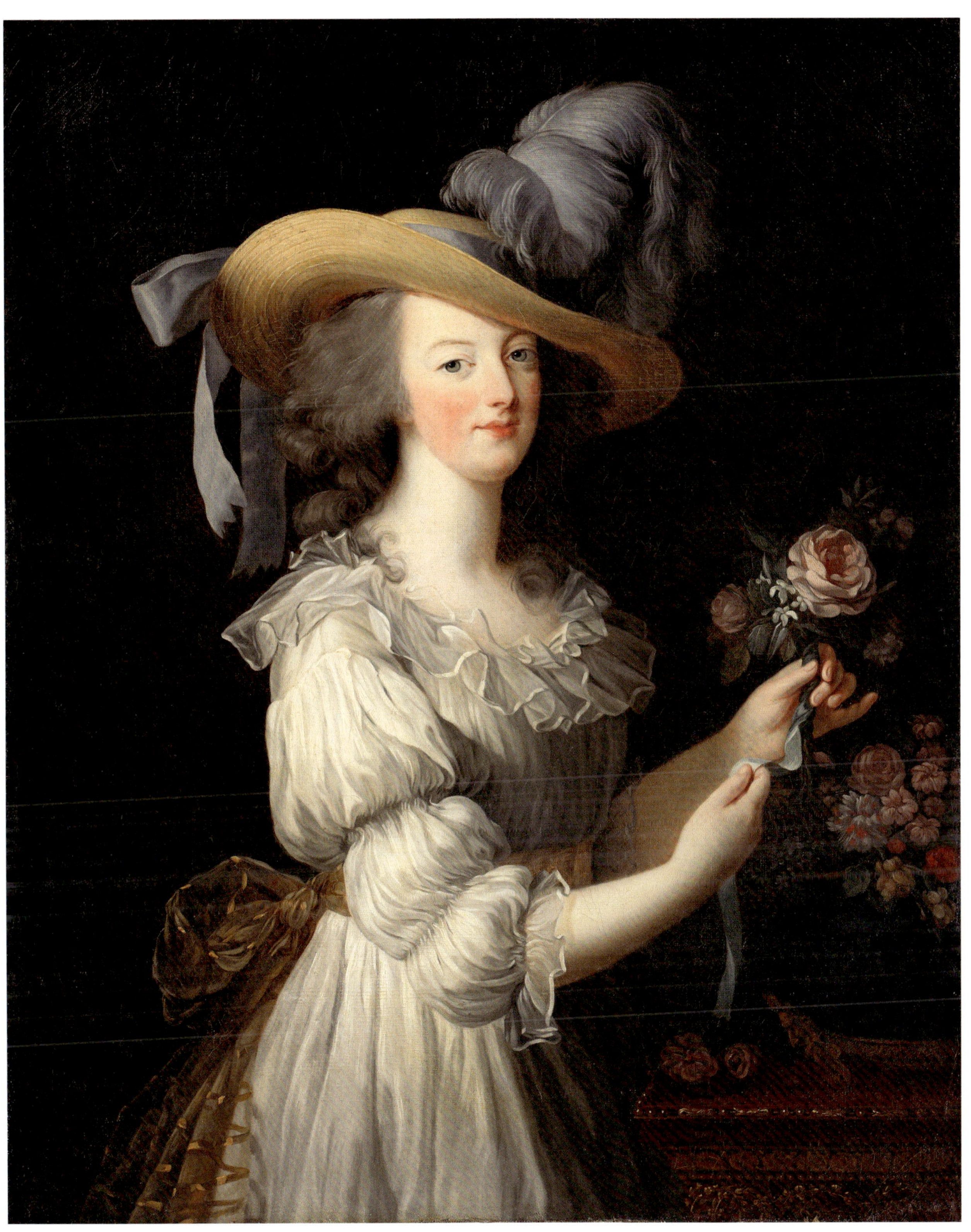



**292**　Marie Louise Élisabeth Vigée-Lebrun (1755–1842)
*Marie-Antoinette en chemise,* 1783
Oil on canvas, 89.8 × 72 cm
Hessische Hausstiftung, Kronberg im Taunus

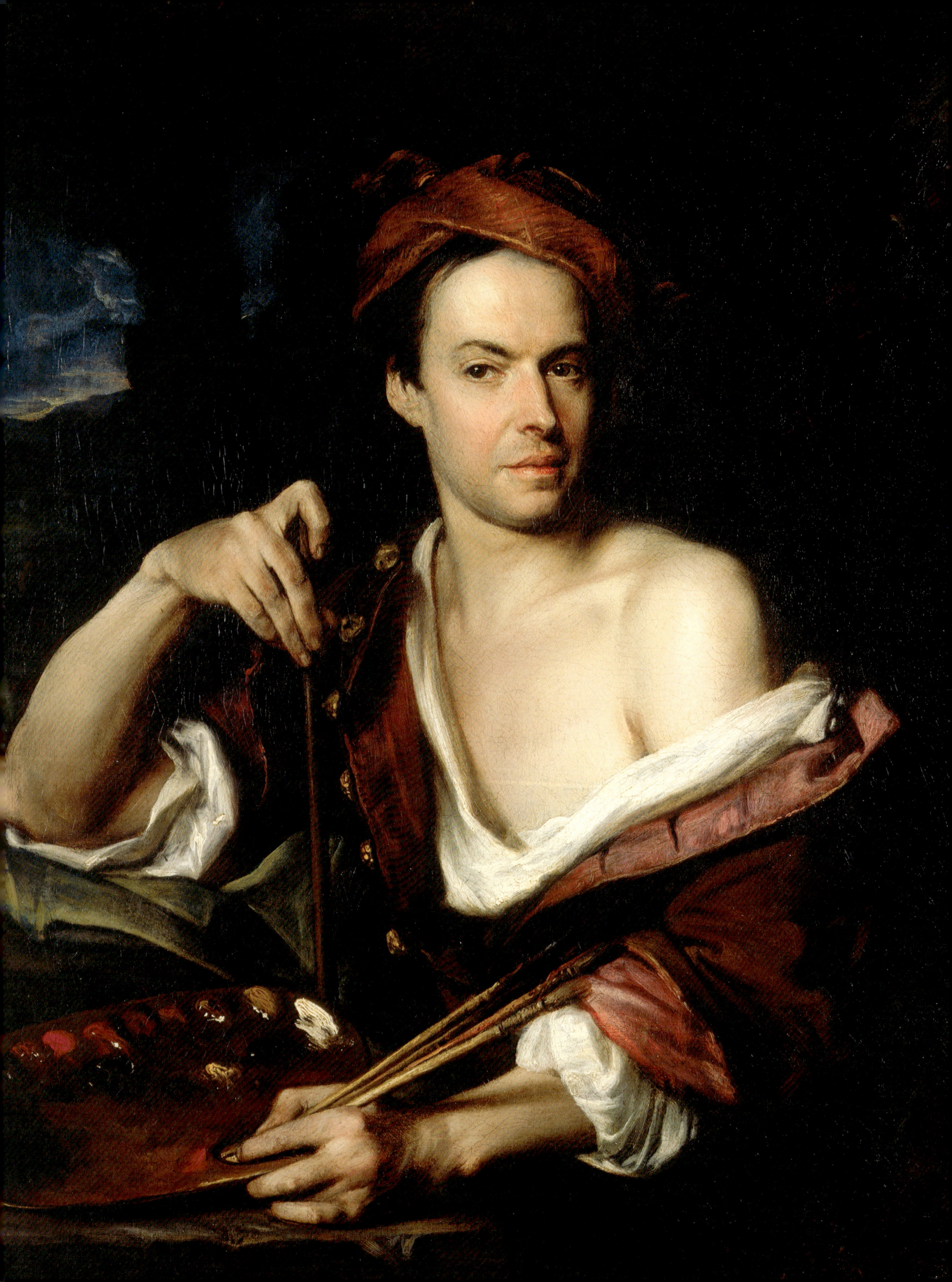

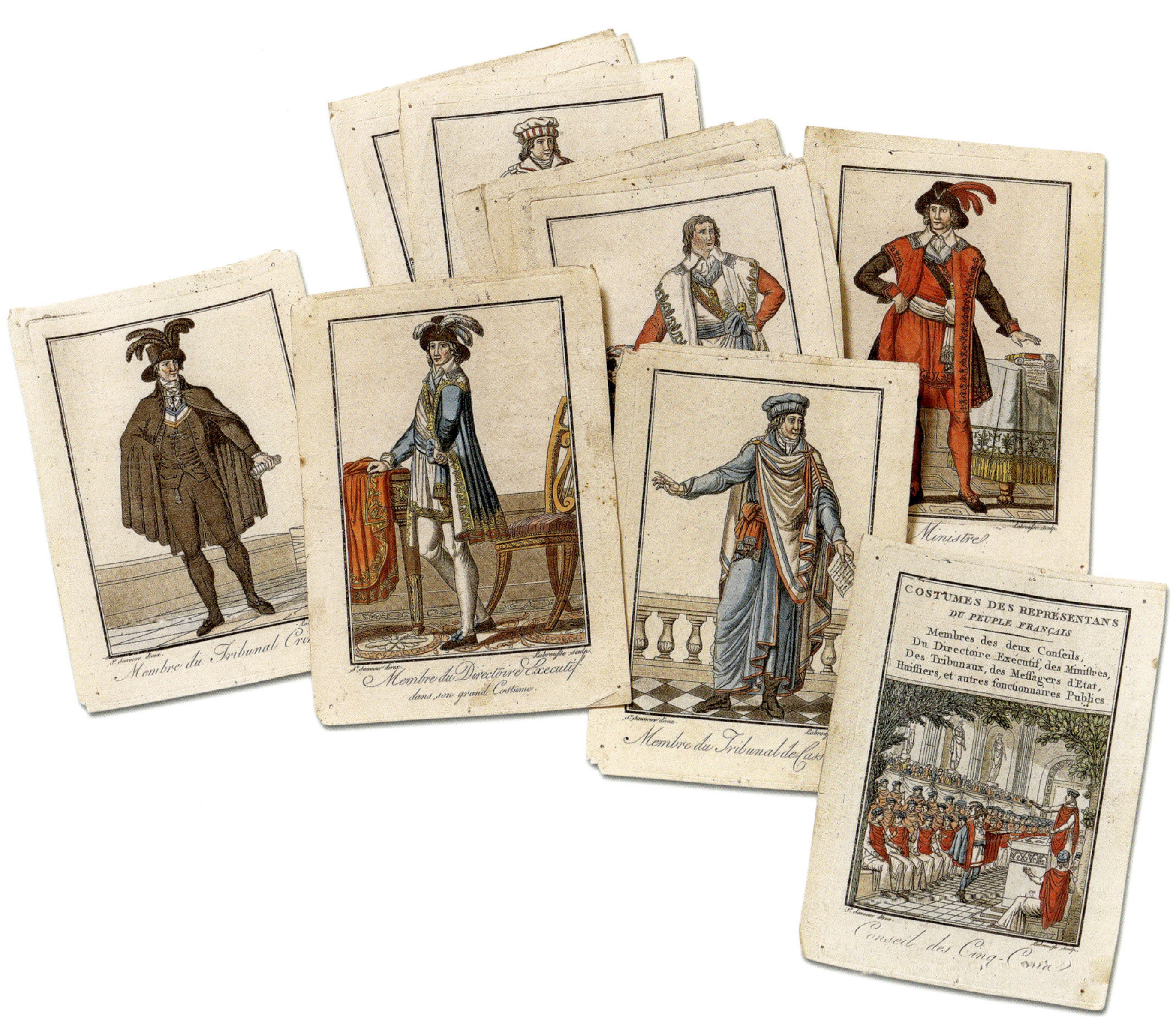



**189**  Johann Kupezky (1666–1740)
*Portrait of a young artist*
*(Christian Benjamin Müller?),* c.1705/1710
Oil on canvas, 94 × 74.5 cm
Kunsthaus Zürich, donated by August Abegg, 1925

**8**  Jacques Grasset de Saint-Saveur (1757–1810)
Series of 15 depictions of French municipal authorities
from the time of the Directoire, 1795
Copper engraving on paper, coloured, 16.8 × 11.7 cm each
HMB – Historisches Museum Basel

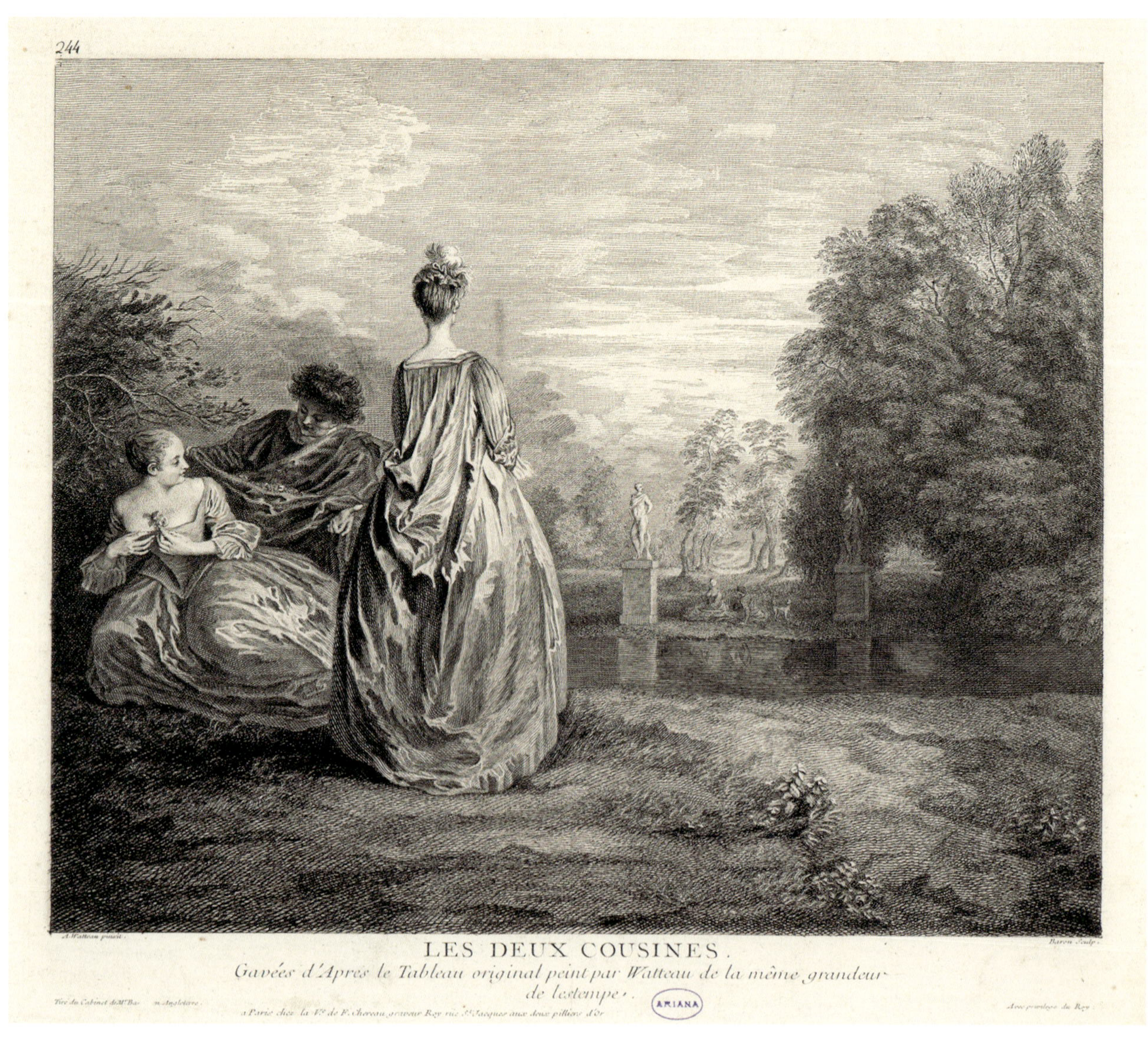
LES DEUX COUSINES.

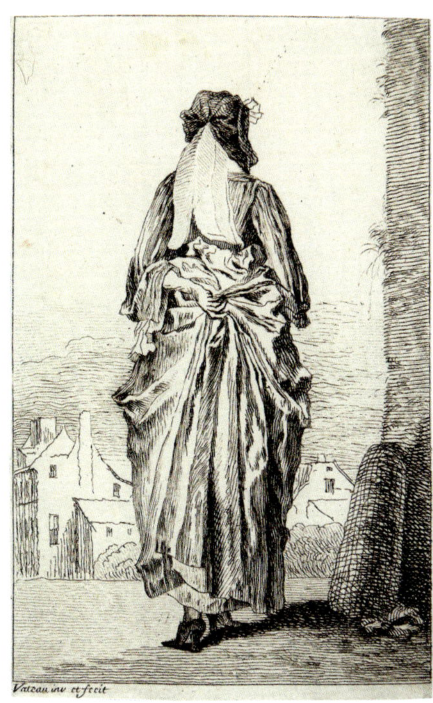


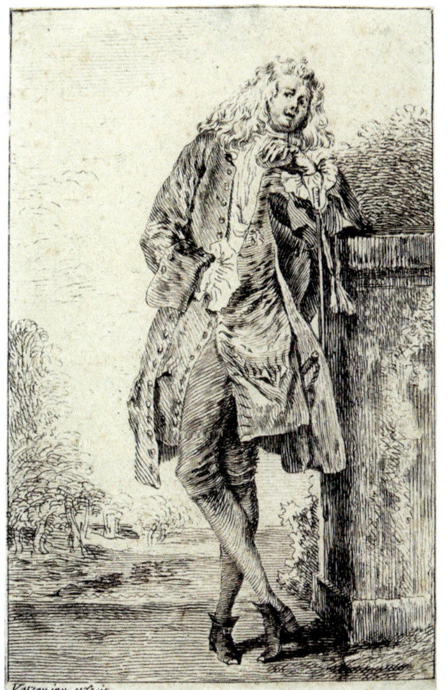


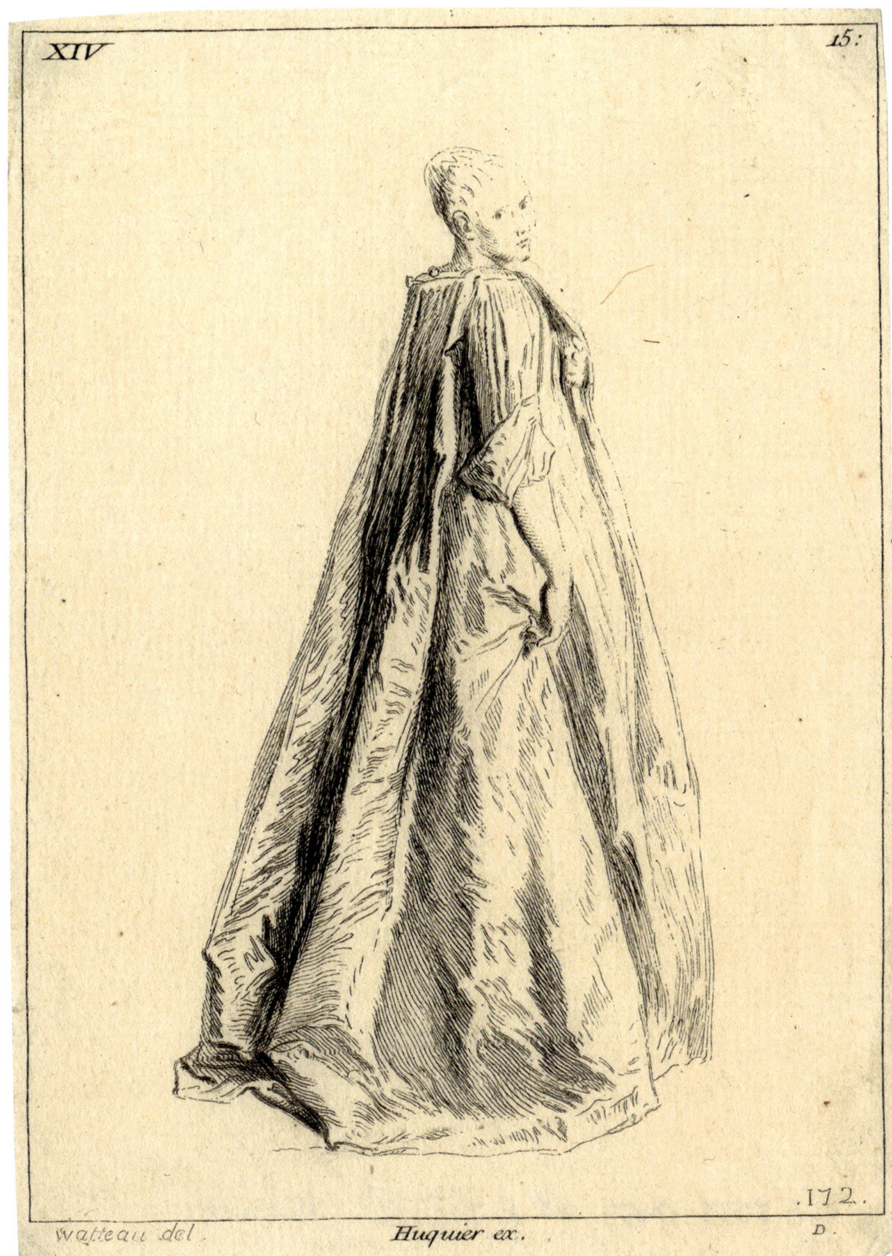


**297**  after Jean-Antoine Watteau (1684–1721)
*Figures de modes,* first quarter of the eighteenth century
Series, frontispiece and six of originally eight plates
Etching and etching needle, sheet: 11.5 × 7.5 cm each
Rennes, Musée des beaux-arts

**296**  after Jean-Antoine Watteau (1684–1721)
Louis Desplaces (1682–1739), etcher
Gabriel Huquier (1695–1772), publisher
*Jeune femme debout avec la tête tournée vers
le spectateur,* 1717–28
Etching and etching needle, sheet: 18.7 × 13.1 cm
Ville de Genève, Musées d'art et d'histoire

**67** Louis-Auguste Brun
called Brun de Versoix (1758–1815)
*Portrait équestre de la reine Marie-Antoinette
en costume de chasse montant un cheval
portant le harnachement des Gardes-Nobles
Hongrois à la Cour d'Autriche,* 1783
Oil on canvas, 59 × 64.5 cm
Musée national des châteaux
de Versailles et de Trianon

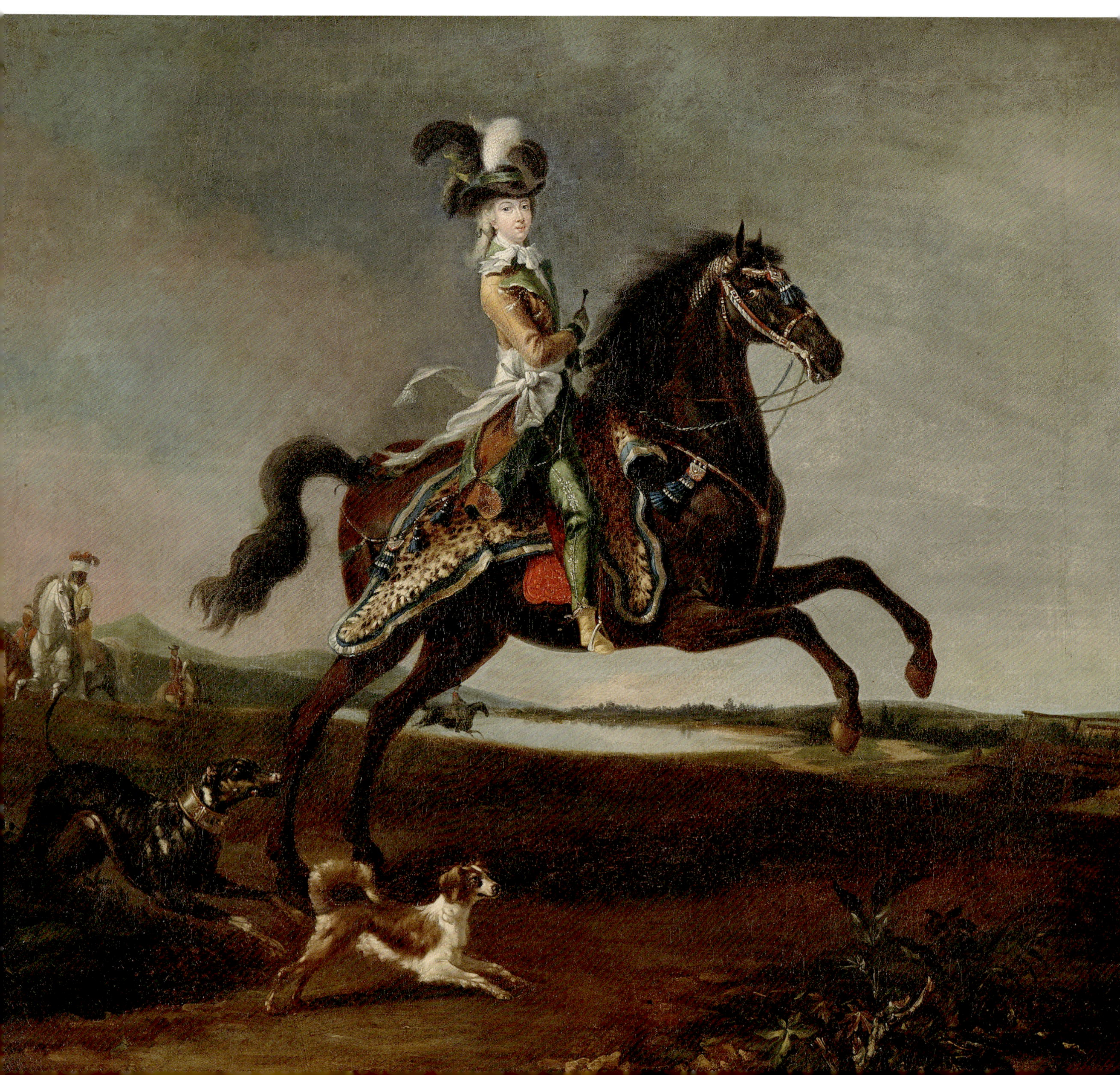

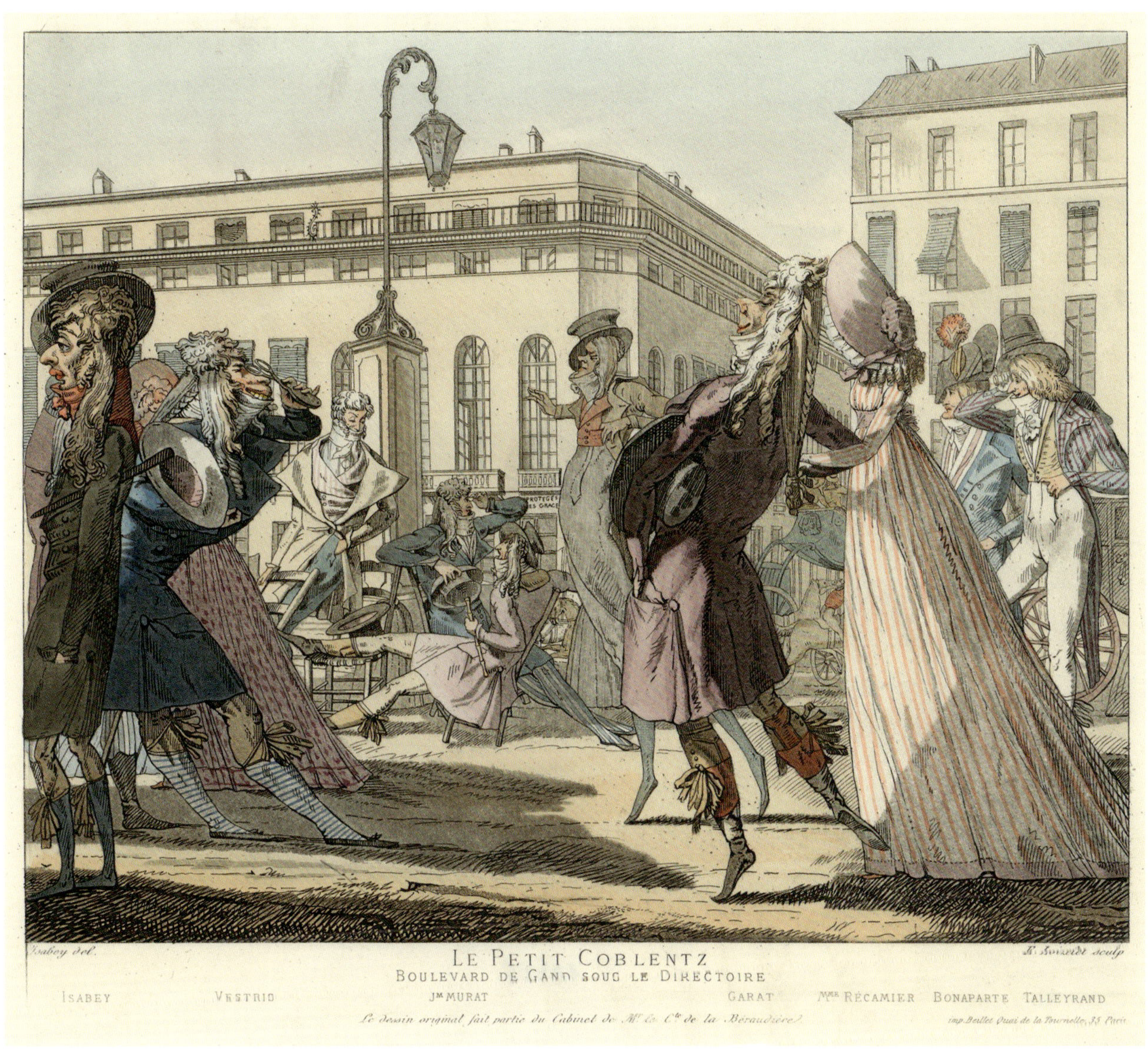


**181**  after Jean-Baptiste Isabey (1767–1855)
Eugène Loizelet (1842–1882), lithographer
*Le Petit Coblentz,* c. 1875
Lithograph, coloured, sheet: 38.5 × 50.3 cm
Staatliche Museen zu Berlin, Kunstbibliothek

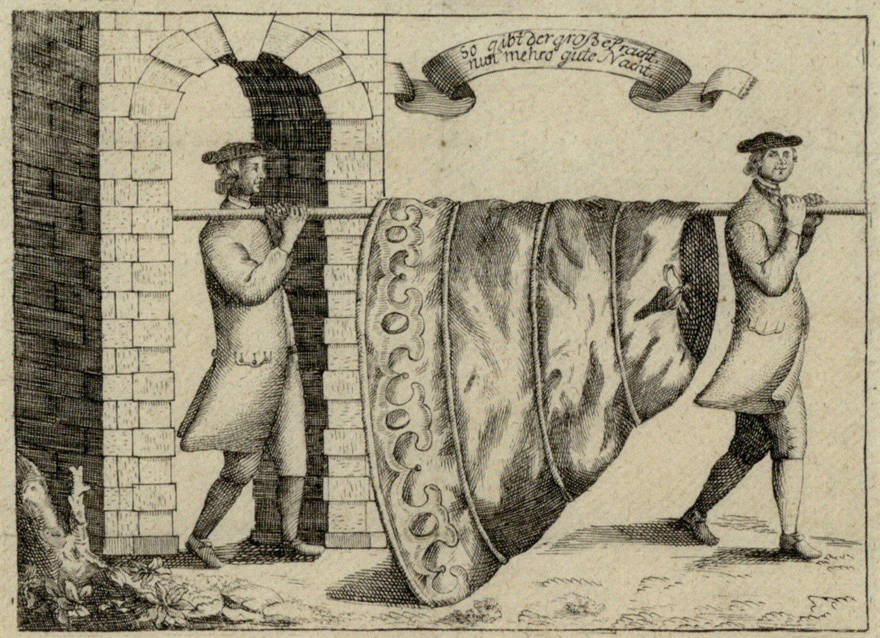



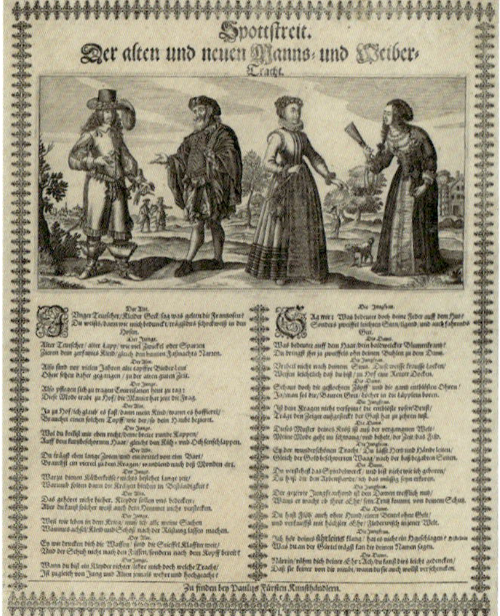



**267** Unknown artist
*Der weiten Reif-Röck Ehren-Ruhm*
*muss jetzt in das Exilium,* c. 1740
The honorary glory of the wide hoop-skirts
must now go in exile
Copper engraving, letterpress, sheet: 29.5 × 19.7 cm
Staatliche Museen zu Berlin, Kunstbibliothek

**142** Paul Fürst (1608–1666), engraver
*Spottstreit der alten und neuen*
*Manns- und Weibertracht,* c. 1650
Mocking quarrel about the old and new
costumes for men and women
Copper engraving, letterpress, sheet: 38.8 × 29.9 cm
Staatliche Museen zu Berlin, Kunstbibliothek

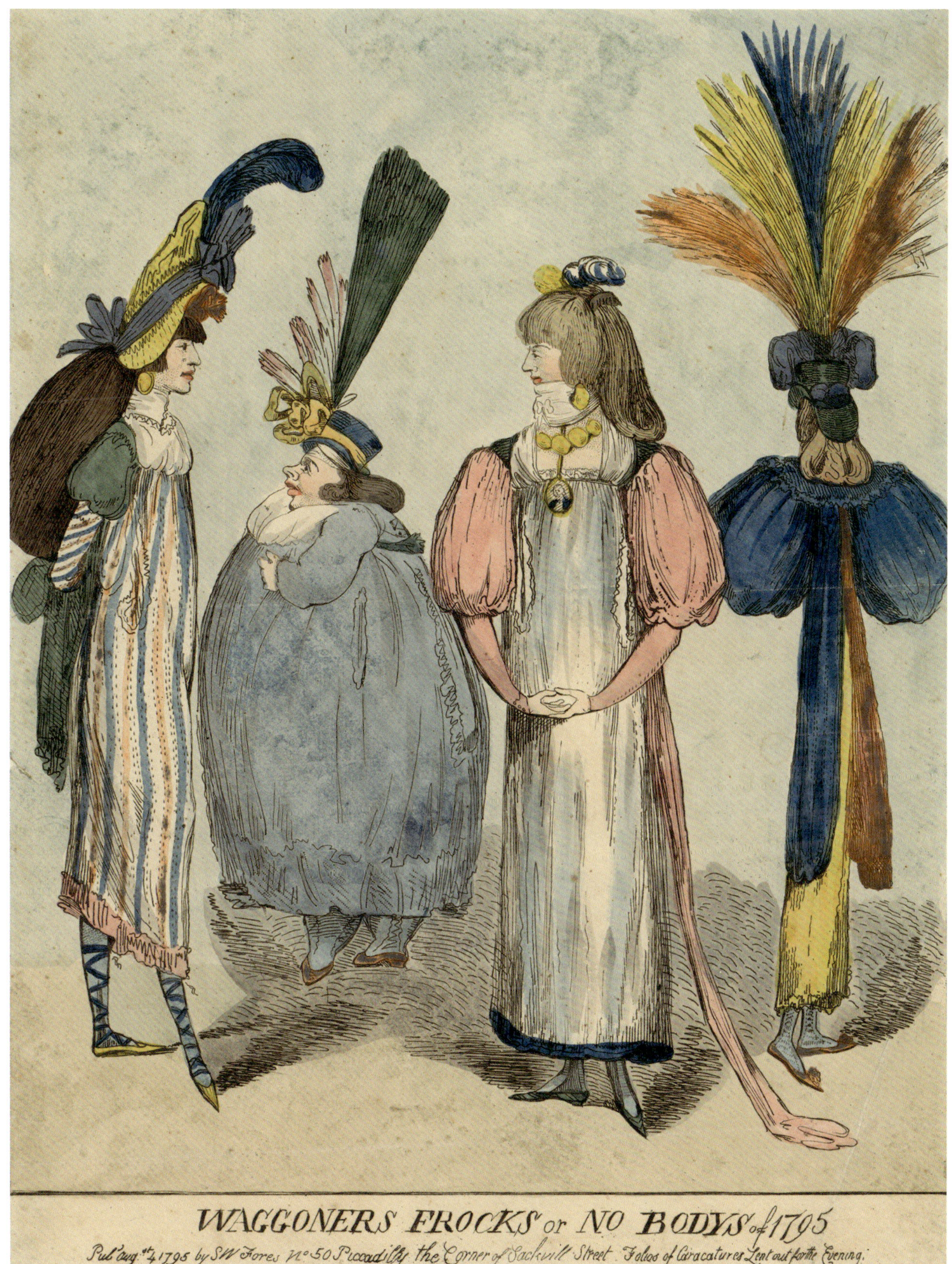


**140** Samuel William Fores (1761–1838), publisher
*Waggoners frocks or No bodys of 1795,* 4 August 1795
Etching, hand-coloured with watercolours, sheet: 38 × 28.4 cm
Staatliche Museen zu Berlin, Kunstbibliothek

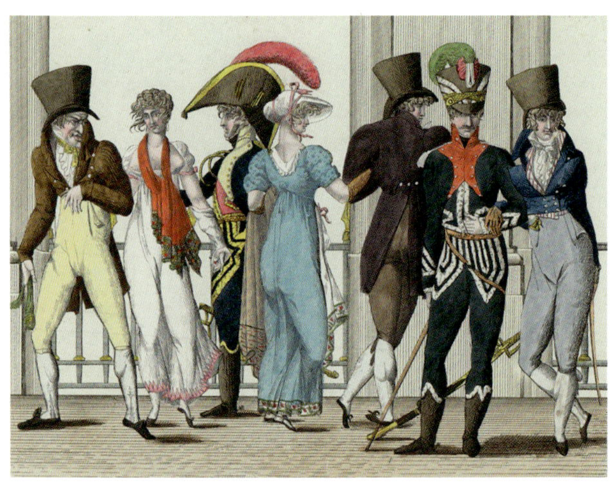

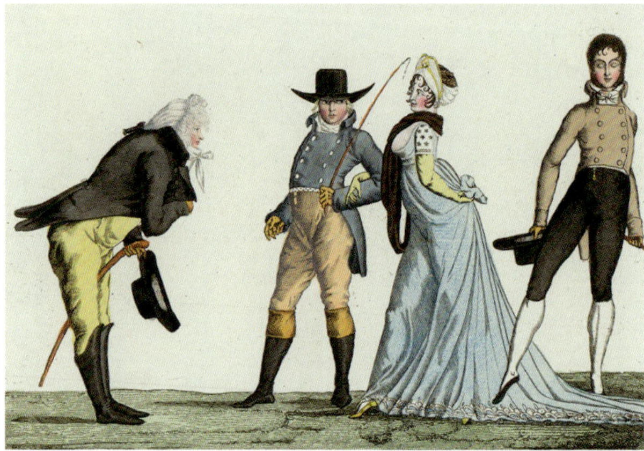

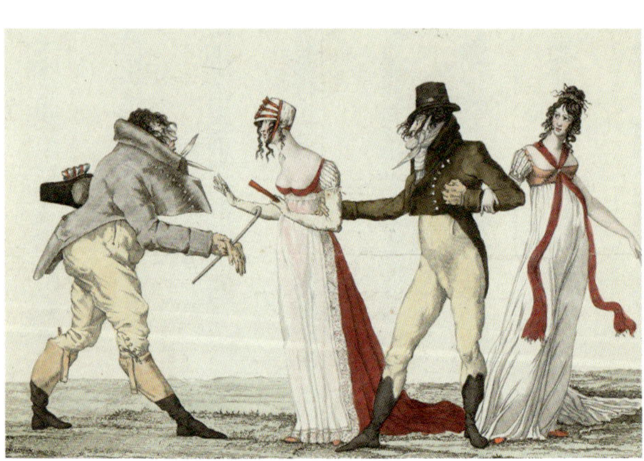

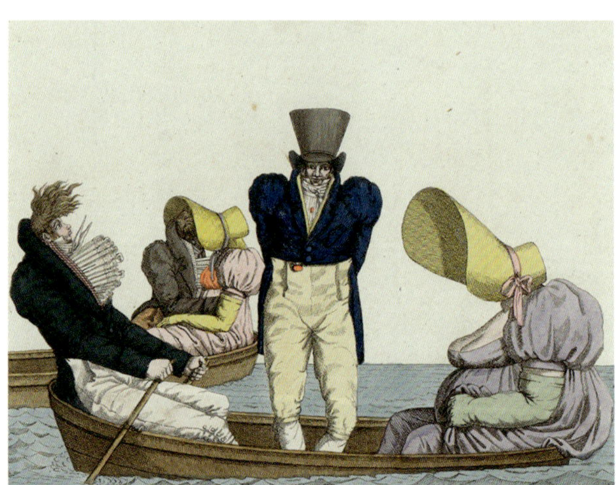



Rococo and Revolution

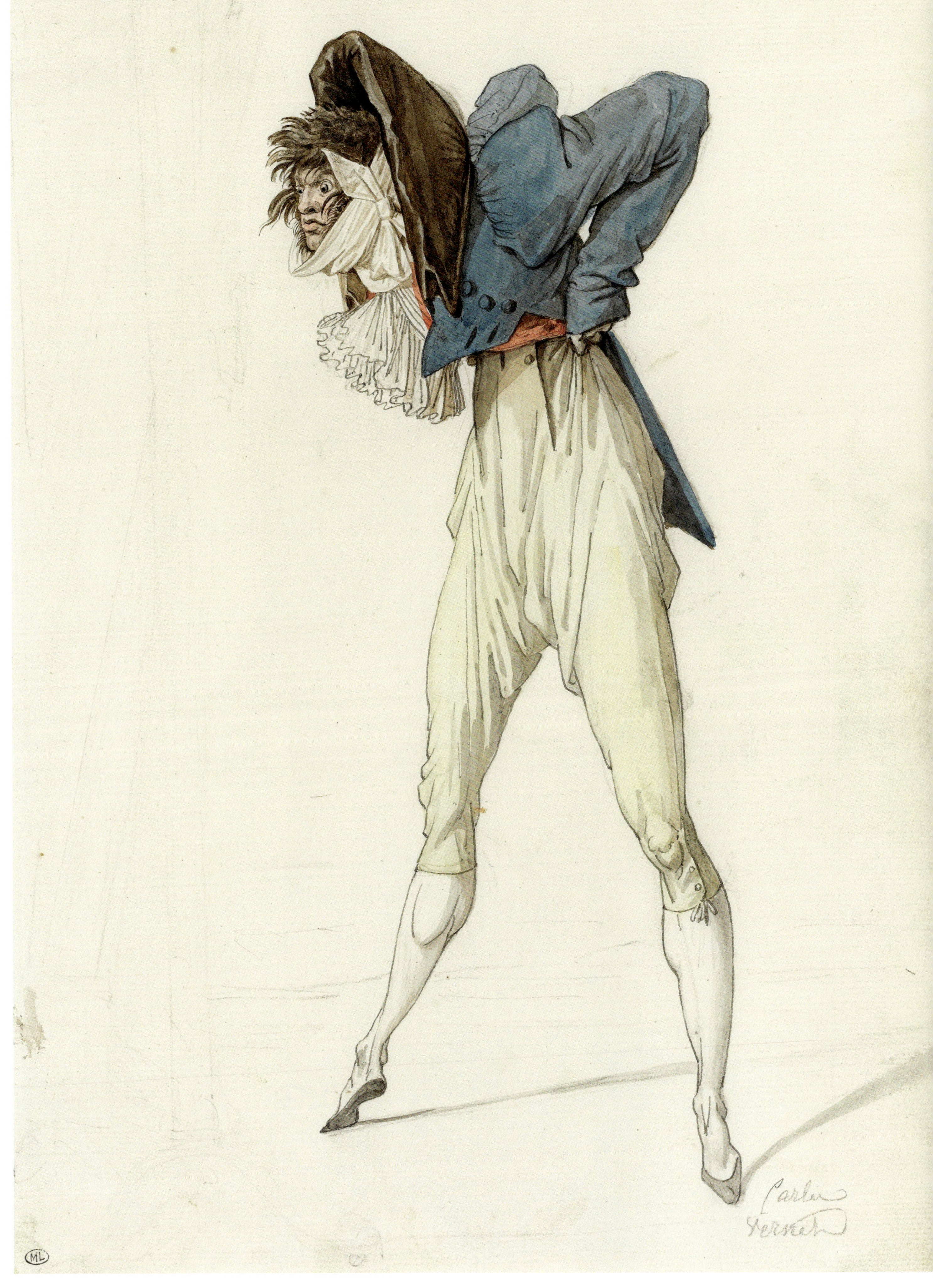

7 'Incroyables' suit, c. 1795
Striped silk coat (steel buttons), breeches,
embroidered waistcoat
and under-waistcoat
Collection Kamer-Ruf

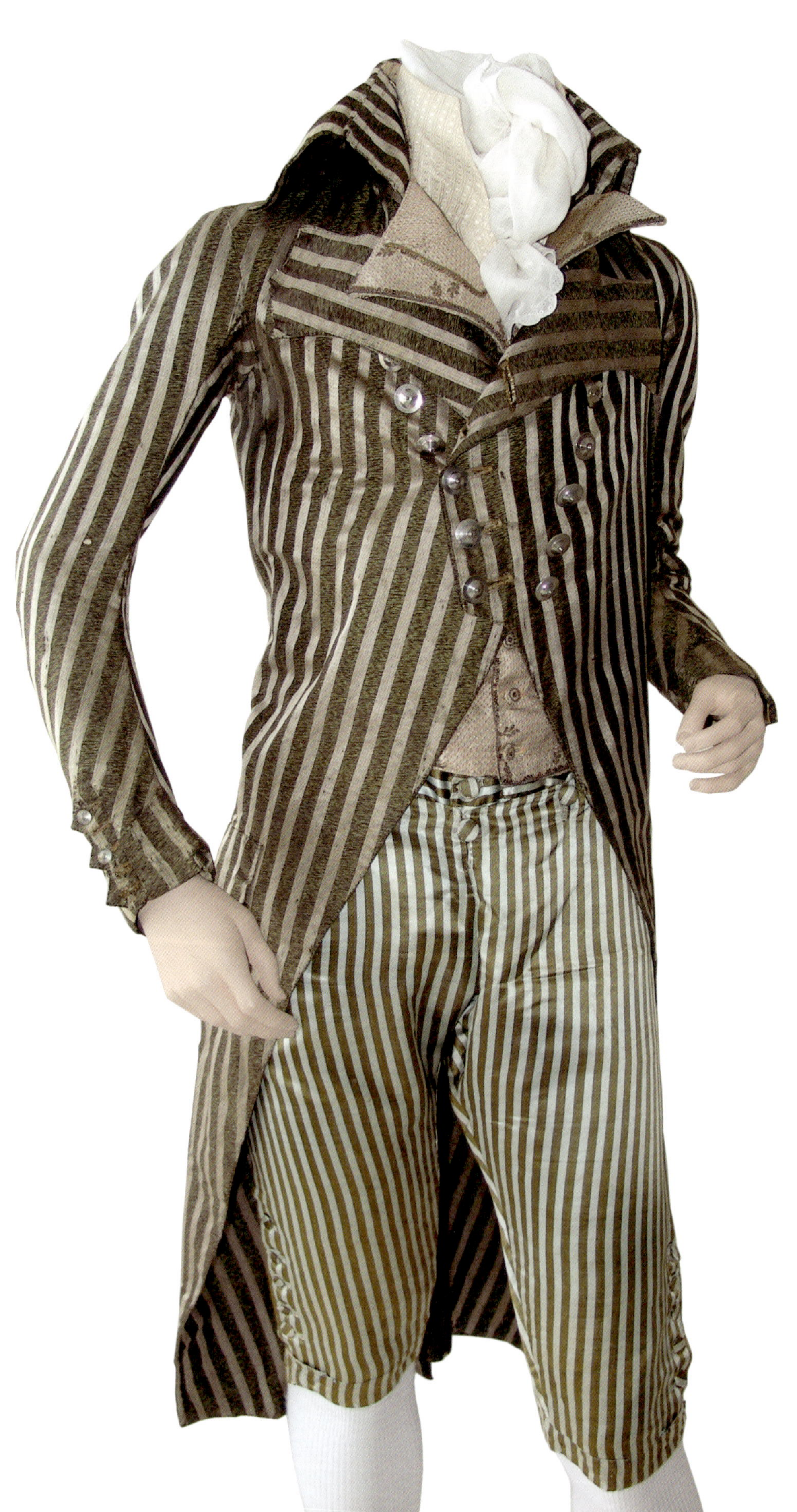

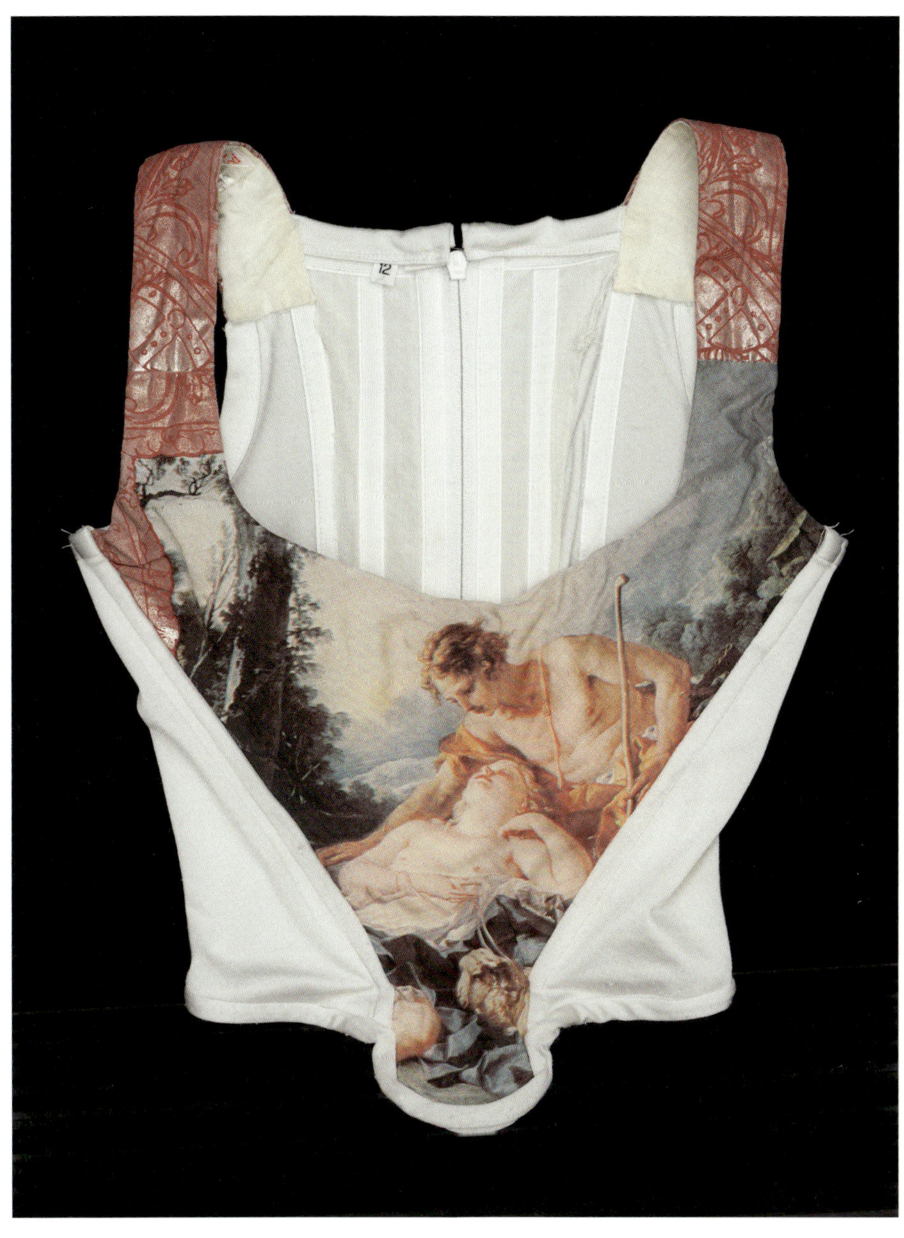

**41** Vivienne Westwood (b. 1941)
Corset from the 'Portrait Collection',
spring/summer 1990, production 1990
With a depiction of François Boucher's painting of
*Daphnis and Chloe* (1743, The Wallis Collection, London)
Shoulder straps feature classical motifs
Polyamide, polyester, Lycra, size 12
V&A, London, Textiles and Fashion Collection;
Purchased with the assistance of The Art Fund,
the Friends of the V&A, the Elsbeth Evans Trust,
and the Dorothy Hughes Bequest

# Anglo-Compari in

**Aileen Ribeiro**

# Some French sons Fashion

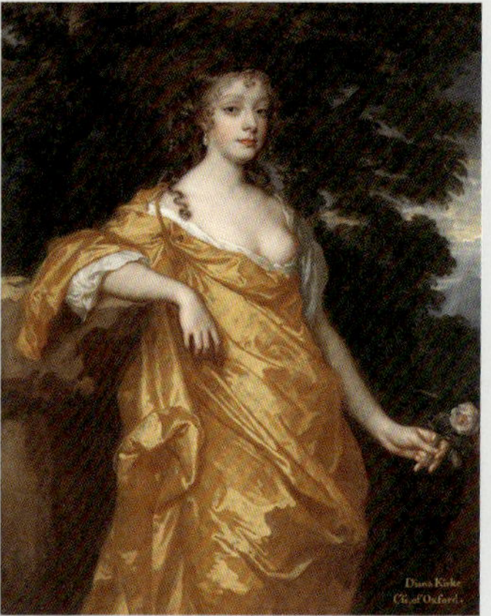



**Fig. 1** Sir Peter Lely (1618–1680)
*Diana Kirke, later Countess
of Oxford,* c. 1665
Oil on canvas, 132 × 104 cm
Yale Center for British Art,
Paul Mellon Collection

Where to begin on such a complex topic which involves not just the hazy and shifting concepts of 'nationality' but the often fraught relationship between England and France, two countries geographically close but often perceived as worlds apart in politics and culture? By stating perhaps that from the early modern period onwards, fashion gradually became dominated by France and to a lesser extent England, the latter with regard to menswear and informal clothing generally. Fashion follows power and by the eighteenth century these were the two dominant countries in Europe, a status confirmed by political events, warfare, trade and proto-colonial expansion. The history of dress in France and England has, to some extent, been seen as a conflict (or attraction) of opposites, the former linked to the relative uniformity and formality of high fashion, and the latter signified by democratic (sometimes eccentric) impulses manifested particularly in non-elite styles.

This essay sets out to consider the way artists in France and England 'saw' fashion in their work. Sight is significant here for we are concerned with what Daniel Roche refers to as the *'culture des apparences';*[1] a new emphasis on fashion among most classes in society is reflected in art of all kinds, including prints, fashion plates and caricatures. There are many questions to be asked about clothing in art, such as how far it is truthful and how far it incorporates various degrees of reality and even fiction (fantasy).[2] In the context of the exhibition *Fashion Drive,* questions need to be asked about the meaning of 'extremes' in clothing, and about the appearance of dress in art. With regard to 'extreme clothing', how far is this due to the intrinsic nature of the clothes themselves? For example, the highly structured garments which create a carapace which hides, or even moulds the natural shape of the wearer, such as the 'slashed', exaggerated and stiffened masculinity of northern Renaissance men's dress (echoed in armour, which is, after all, metal clothing); women's vast hooped skirts which appear and re-appear in the narrative of fashion over many years, an example of extremes becoming part of the mainstream; and obvious fashion victims such as the early nineteenth-century English dandies whose figures, created by artifice in the form of padded body aids, assume a parody of masculinity.

**1**  Daniel Roche, *La culture des apparences. Une histoire du vêtement XVIIe–XVIIIe siècle,* Paris 1989.

**2**  A question I discuss in Aileen Ribeiro, *Clothing Art. The Visual Culture of Fashion 1600–1914,* New Haven & London 2017.

**3**  Possibly copied from van Dyck's *Stuart Brothers* of c. 1638, The National Gallery, London.



Aileen Ribeiro

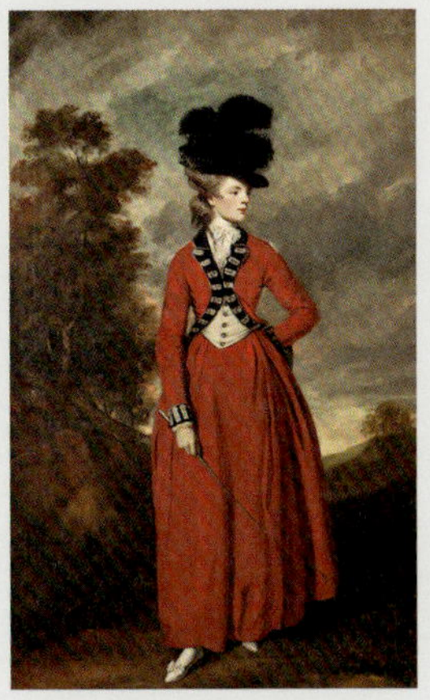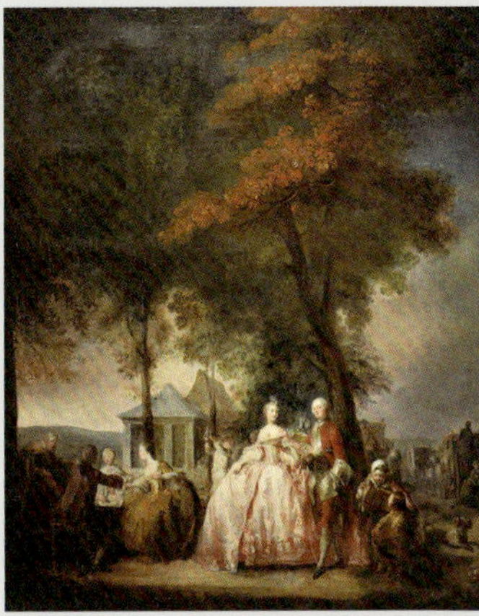



Dress becomes a laughing matter when it loses a sense of proportion and harmony, no longer relating to the natural body, and when artifice dominates appearance at the expense of restraint. On the other hand, extremes of dress may relate not to the clothes themselves, but to the way they reveal the body, notably the breasts; acceptable in the abstract, in art, such as in fanciful, imaginative and generalised images, but when actually seen in the flesh, such as in masque costume, or transparent neo-classical clothing, a woman's appearance was often subject to criticism and controversy.

Crucial to our consideration of clothing is the question: how is the representation of fashion in visual art the result of an artist's style and a response to the culture in which it is created? Does van Dyck, for example, exaggerate the careless throwaway elegance (which Castiglione in *The Book of the Courtier* (1528) refers to as *sprezzatura*) that we see in his images of cavaliers? The painting *Portraits of two young Englishmen*[3] | Page **170** | is a contrast between the romantic rather fanciful costume on the left and the slightly simplified version of real fashion on the right, altogether the kind of stylish, relaxed informality which was popular in England and carried to extremes in the work of Sir Peter Lely. His *Diana Kirke* | Fig. **1** | in only a white shift and loose satin drapery (mythological deities like Venus were allowed such sartorial license), is clearly an enticing sexual image, set in an Arcadian landscape, compared to which Hyacinthe Rigaud's *Portrait of Suzanne de Boubers de Bernâtre* | Page **77** | is the reverse, too stiff and completely lacking any sense of the poetic or pastoral, or indeed the love of the open air which characterises English painting (and clothing) throughout the eighteenth century. Since the seventeenth century, a popular and practical outdoors costume for Englishwomen was a jacket and skirt style (derived from masculine tailoring), worn both for riding and walking. Sir Joshua Reynolds' *Lady Worsley* | Fig. **2** | looks self-confident and elegant in her red woollen riding habit, adapted from the uniform of her husband's regiment, the Hampshire Militia. Frenchwomen were slower to adopt this style, and were rarely depicted wearing a riding habit until the reign of Louis XVI. It is something of a paradox that, while in England the riding habit was so utilitarian and forward-looking (and thus favoured by French feminists during the 1789 revolution), breeches were

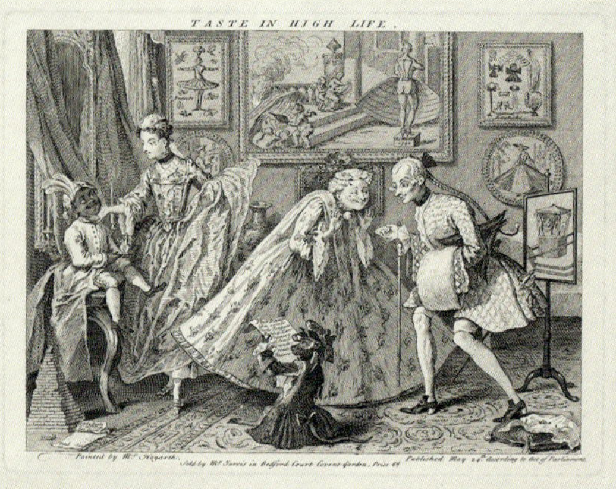


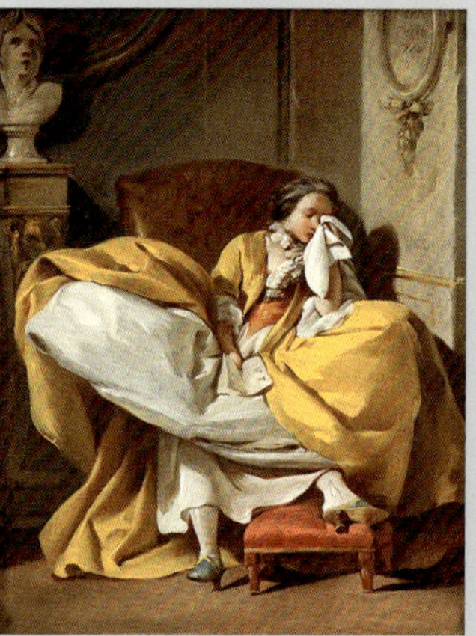


**Fig. 4**  after William Hogarth (1697–1764)
*Taste in high life,* 1746
Etching, sheet: 21.5 × 28 cm
British Museum, Department
of Prints & Drawings

**Fig. 5**  Jean-Baptiste-Marie Pierre (1714–1789)
*La Mauvaise nouvelle,* 1740
Oil on canvas, 23.5 × 18.5 cm
Paris, Les Arts Décoratifs,
musée Nissim de Camondo




not acceptable, whereas in France they were permitted for hunting, as in Louis-Auguste Brun's *Portrait équestre de la reine Marie-Antoinette* | Page **108** | in a *costume de chasse.* Along with a silk coat in military style, she wears tight pantaloons like those worn by Hungarian hussar regiments, here embroidered in silver. While Virginia Woolf remarks, with a nuanced concept of gender, that 'it is *"only"* [my accentuation] the clothes that keep the male or female likeness',[4] the early modern belief in strict sartorial difference between the sexes was widely held as a moral truth. There was a feeling that while women could 'adapt' menswear (as in riding habits), it was indecent for them to 'adopt' (wear) male garments, and especially inappropriate with regard to a Queen of France in a public portrait. Fashion in France, supported and promoted by the state, 'was' about display, and about luxury, especially in Paris, reaching an apogee, perhaps, in the reign of Louis XV. François Boucher's *Portrait of the Marquise de Pompadour* | Page **199** | is artifice, rococo-style, personified in the extravagance and luxury of her rustling green taffeta dress with its three-dimensional decoration of pink silk roses and ribbons; in Baudelairean terms, this is a woman as idol. Although elite English-women were often in awe of what they perceived as French superiority in style, Pompadour's extraordinary and absolutist 'statement' dress was not to their taste, preferring in general a muted version of French fashion on formal occasions, suited to a constitutional monarchy. Increasingly by this time in England, extremes in dress with sumptuous and costly fabrics were linked by many critics to the despotic political system they associated with France. The focus in Gabriel de Saint-Aubin's *Promenade à Longchamp* | Fig. **3** | is on the elegant courtiers, the man in a silk velvet suit, and the woman in a formal pink silk *robe à la française* (characterised by back pleats falling from the shoulders) over a large hoop. Such hoops (although originally an English invention), and the robe à la française, were sometimes criticised as unwelcome imports from France, especially when political tensions were high and both countries were at war. William Hogarth's *Taste in high life*[5] | Fig. **4** | is a satire directed against the slavish adoption of French fashions which, he claimed, unsexed men and made women look grotesque, although they were widely worn. In his *Analysis of Beauty* (1753) he remarks: 'Custom and fashion will … reconcile almost every absurdity whatever to the eye.'[6] Hoops


**4**   Virginia Woolf, *Orlando: A Biography,* London 1928.

**5**   Hogarth's original painting of 1742, Private collection, was etched anonymously, without the artist's permission, in 1746.

**6**   William Hogarth, *The Analysis of Beauty,* edited and introduction by Ronald Paulson, New Haven & London 1997, p. 37.

**7**   Thomas Murray, *William III,* c. 1691, National Portrait Gallery, London.

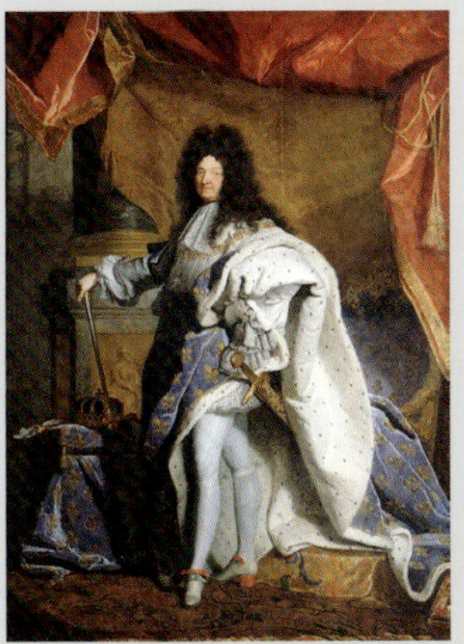
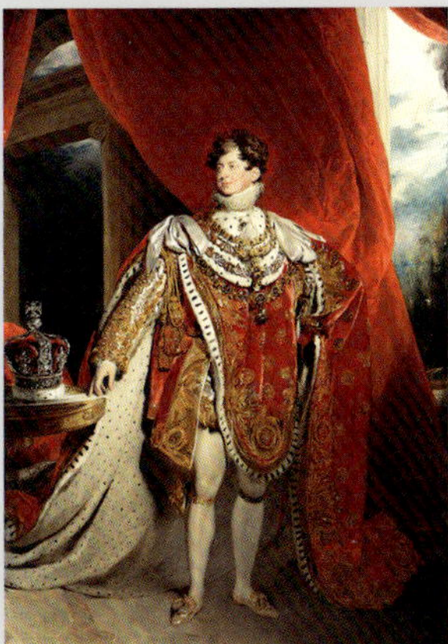



were particularly difficult to wear; in Jean-Baptiste-Marie Pierre's *La Mauvaise nouvelle,* | Fig. 5 | for example, emotion so overcomes the young woman that she is oblivious to her appearance, her hoops uncontrollable, her dignity vanished.

As fashion follows power, nowhere was this made more explicit than in the most splendid costume of all, that of ceremony, and at the apex of the hierarchy of appearances (which he had largely been instrumental in creating at the grandest court in Europe) was Louis XIV. Rigaud's astonishing portrait of Louis XIV | Fig. 6 | (so imbued with majesty that it was an offence to turn one's back to it) shows the monarch in the blue velvet coronation mantle lined with ermine, over the silver tissue costume of l'Ordre du Saint-Esprit. The political climate of England could not countenance such an image (indeed, as a riposte to French absolutism, William III had himself depicted in parliamentary robes[7]), and it was not until Sir Thomas Lawrence's portrait of *George IV* | Fig. 7 | in coronation costume that there is an English equivalent to Rigaud's *Louis XIV.* Determined to outdo Napoleon's coronation in 1804, and with the royal coffers augmented by French reparations in 1815, George IV's coronation was the grandest and most expensive in English history. The King, in love with fancy dress from his youth, looked back to the Elizabethan age for inspiration; in ruff, gold-encrusted and ermine-lined crimson velvet, and silver tissue doublet and matching trunk hose, Lawrence captures his monumental presence – 'un roi grand seigneur' (Charles-Maurice de Talleyrand-Périgord's words) – much inspired by Rigaud's portrait of the Sun King. Monarchy was about ostentatious display, and extremes of splendour were most in evidence at court. But whereas men wore luxurious versions of the current fashion, women had to appear in a specific dress, more elaborate in France than in England. The concept of court dress for women as a distinct and exclusive style, initially related to fashion but infinitely richer and more ornate, had been established by Louis XIV in the 1670s. With its heavily boned bodice, wide skirt, and a lengthy train, court dress kept to this style, augmented by large hoops which had, by the 1770s, disappeared from fashion elsewhere; it was uncomfortable to wear and difficult to move in, a costume of extremes. Marie



Some Anglo-French Comparisons in Fashion

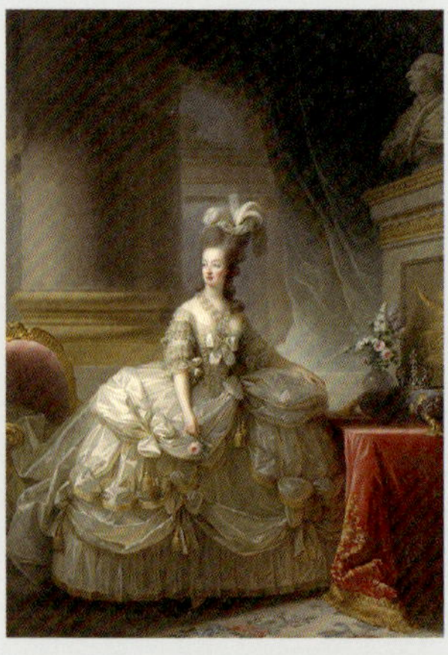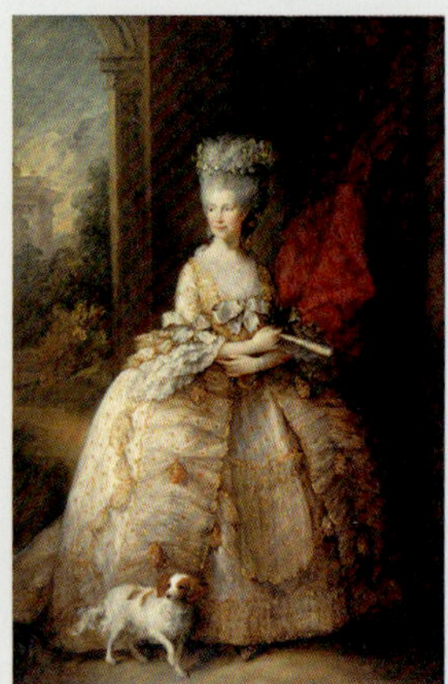



Louise Élisabeth Vigée-Lebrun's *Marie-Antoinette en grand habit de cour* and Thomas Gainsborough's *Queen Charlotte* present an example of how a similar kind of dress can seem in the hands of one artist pompous and ridiculous, and in the other graceful and dignified. | ^Fig. **8, 9** | Marie-Antoinette's unease in this archaic costume with its meaningless festoons of drapery, is palpable, as is the artist's dislike at having to paint it. It was symbolic of the meaningless and arcane rituals of the court, of a growing and dangerous resentment at the expense and isolation of the royal family from the everyday concerns of the people. Vigée-Lebrun preferred to depict the Queen in much simpler fashions, notably the innovative soft unstructured white muslin *chemise à la reine* in 1783, | ^Page **103** | although this portrait had to be removed from the Salon – the dress was, critics said, based on female underwear (i.e. the white muslin shift worn next to the skin), far too informal and undignified for a queen to wear. Compared to Vigée-Lebrun's image of Marie-Antoinette in the cumbersome *habit de cour,* Queen Charlotte looks at ease and quietly elegant, in a *robe à la française* (English royalty only rarely wore a version of the *grand habit*) of white spangled gauze over a more modest hoop. Critics might see such dress as absurd, but the traditionally conservative (and unfashionable) English court (described by one visitor as 'the residence of dullness') was able to ride out the storm engendered by the French Revolution.

The 1780s in France have sometimes been described – with the virtue of hindsight – as the 'waiting years'. They were also the years in which Anglomania flourished; philosophical writing and progressive thought promoted simpler styles of dress in more affordable fabrics, which were associated with the relative freedom of English laws and institutions. 'C'est aujourd'hui un ton parmi la jeunesse de copier l'anglais dans son habillement', claimed the journalist and playwright Louis-Sébastien Mercier in his famous *Tableau de Paris* (1781–88),[8] and an engraving of *A Frenchman and two Englishmen* | ^Fig. **10** | depicts the contrast between the former in his powdered wig, three-cornered hat under his arm and silk habit *à la française;* and the latter in the new wide-brimmed round hats placed firmly on their (own) hair, and caped woollen English greatcoats. Another illustration shows two young boys, one, says Mercier, dressed à la française, like a man of 30,[9] and the other in flowing hair and the English 'skeleton' suit i.e. an open-necked, short jacket buttoned onto trousers, a costume which, while greeted at first with some scorn, became adopted as a practical style, conducive to comfort and easy movement. Other admired, and copied, trends in dress from England included versions of the riding habit, plainly-styled morning gowns of linen or cotton, and the simple, short-sleeved, white muslin frocks worn by young girls, which anticipated the neo-classical dress linked to the revolutionary years of the 1790s and the first decade of the nineteenth century.

Dress has always reflected the moods and aspirations of a period, and nowhere was this more evident than in the French Revolution and its aftermath. Extreme political events in the early 1790s (the abolition of monarchy, the appearance of a republic and the violence of the Terror), and in the years following, leading to

Aileen Ribeiro

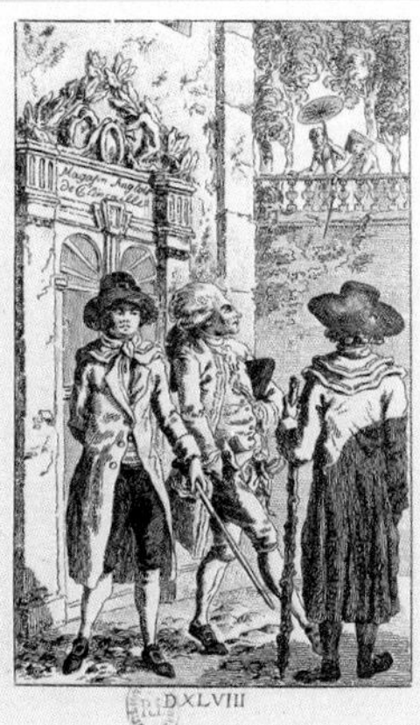

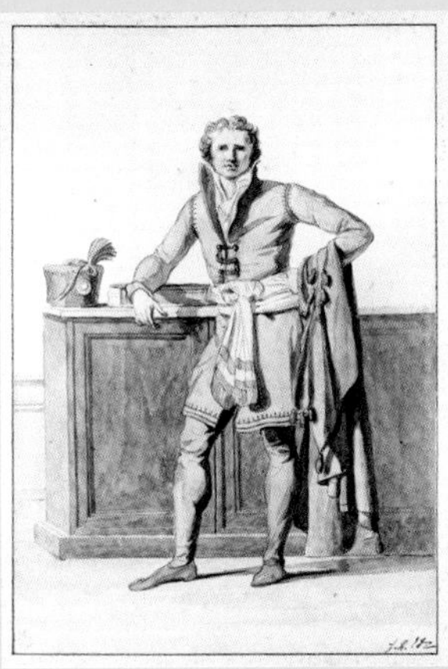

**Fig. 10** Balthasar Anton Dunker (1746–1807)
*A Frenchman and two Englishmen*
Engraving, in Louis-Sébastien Mercier,
*Tableau de Paris,* Lyon 1791
Bibliothèque nationale de France,
département Estampes et photographie

**Fig. 11** Jacques Louis David (1748–1825)
*Le Citoyen français, projet de costume,* 1789–99
Watercolour and pen drawing, 30.2 × 20.2 cm
Paris, musée Carnavalet

an empire, were bound to make an impact on clothing, the most visible signifier of status and identity. Some of the clothes were extreme in a political and ideological way, such as Jacques-Louis David's designs in May 1794, for the new republic's legislative and official costume, intended to be suitable for 'republican manners and the character of the Revolution'. How does one define and depict such an abstract idea? David's answer, apropos his projected *Le Citoyen français, projet de costume* (Civilian costume for a French citizen), | Fig. 11 | is a beautiful and imaginative design in which classical, Renaissance and theatrical elements are combined; it was too removed, however, from current male fashion to be accepted. Two or three years later, the clothing (this time, actually worn) of the *Incroyables* (literally unbelievable in their appearance) was an extreme reaction to politics, sending out confusing and conflicting signals; | Pages 144, 113 | these included exaggerated interpretations of English country clothing, *ancien régime* hair powder, knee-breeches and pumps, and the deliberately unkempt look which mocked the Jacobin supporters of the revolution. Like punks in the realm of Malcolm McLaren and Vivienne Westwood, their aim was to shock – a modern fashion manifesto. | Pages 260, 262 | This was also the effect created by their female counterparts, the *Merveilleuses* (literally marvels to behold) in their sleeveless, high-waisted, figure-revealing white neo-classical dresses, described by Mercier in *Le nouveau Paris* (1798) as dressing 'à la sauvage'. In England, there was no strong inspiration from antiquity, which the French so identified with their new republic. Associating immodest and bizarre styles of dress with extreme French politics (a rich source of inspiration in English caricatures), | Page 139 | English women preferred demure versions of the neo-classical fashion, or long-waisted clothes with vaguely historical (often Tudor) references which were greeted with amazement and some ridicule in Paris in 1814 and 1815, as we see in *Le Bon Genre*.[10] Ridicule, of course, was implicit in caricature,[11] an art form highly developed in England from the 1770s, combining the country's love of the extreme and grotesque, along with a fondness for moralising, in a tolerant political society; in France, caricature did not flourish in any serious and sustained way until the reign

8   Louis-Sébastien Mercier, *Tableau de Paris ou Explication de différentes figures gravées à l'eau-forte pour servir aux différentes Editions du Tableau de Paris,* Yverdon 1787, p. 46.

9   Mercier 1787, p. 35.

10   S.W. Fores, *English & French taste or A peep into Paris* (1818) is copied from 'Costumes Anglais & Français' by Horace Vernet (1814) in *Le Bon Genre*.

11   *Ridikül! Mode in der Karikatur: Mode von 1600 bis 1900,* Adelheid Rasche and Gundula Wolter (eds), exh. cat., Staatliche Museen zu Berlin, Gemäldegalerie, Cologne 2003.



Some Anglo-French Comparisons in Fashion

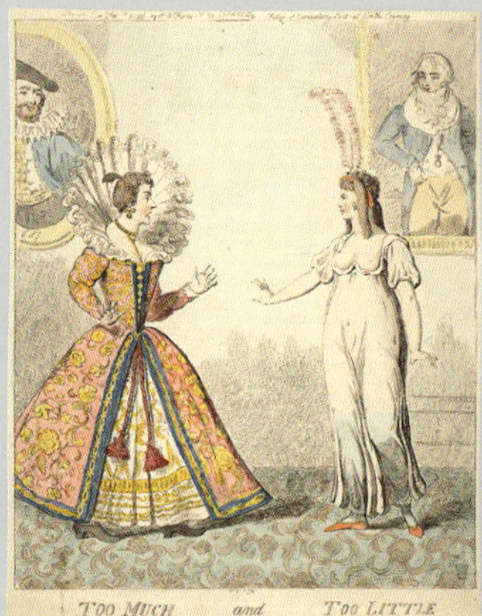

**Fig. 12**  Isaac Cruikshank (1764–1811)
*Too much and too little or*
*summer clothing for 1556 & 1796,* 1796
Etching, hand-coloured,
sheet (cropped): 37.8 × 29 cm
British Museum, Department
of Prints & Drawings



of the Citizen-King, Louis-Philippe (1830–1848), with Honoré Daumier, among others.  | ᴾᵃᵍᵉˢ **185, 189** | Like a fashion plate, a caricature is an exaggeration; unlike a fashion plate, it is not intended to be taken too seriously. In any caricature, such as Isaac Cruikshank's *Too much and too little,* | ᶠⁱᵍ· **12** | in which two women, one 'over-dressed' in mid-sixteenth century costume, the other 'under-dressed' in contemporary fashion, stare in horrified amazement at each other, we may see the clothes as absurd (although dress, after all, is inanimate except when on the body), but what we criticise are the people who wear them, and what their clothes seem to say about them. National differences in dress were knowingly exaggerated by caricaturists; the viewer immediately needed to get the point of the satire. In more subtle ways, artists (sometimes 'unknowingly') also responded to fashion by helping to create national stereotypes, for they are obviously part of the aesthetics of their own times and their own countries. All artists, including caricaturists, were instrumental in defining how we looked in the past.

124

Aileen Ribeiro

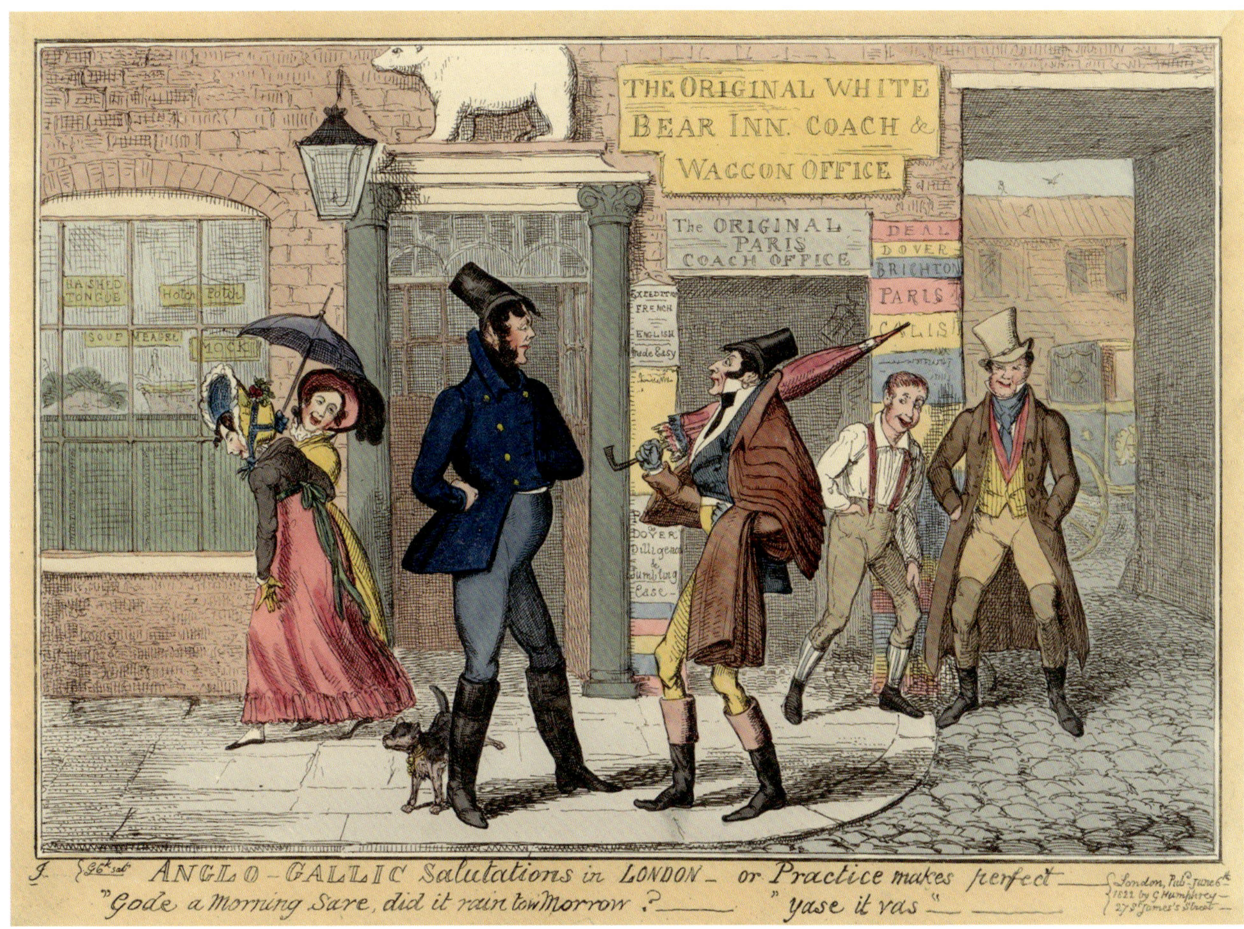


ANGLO-GALLIC Salutations in LONDON — or Practice makes perfect —
"Gode a Morning Sare, did it rain tow Morrow ?" ———— "yase it vas"

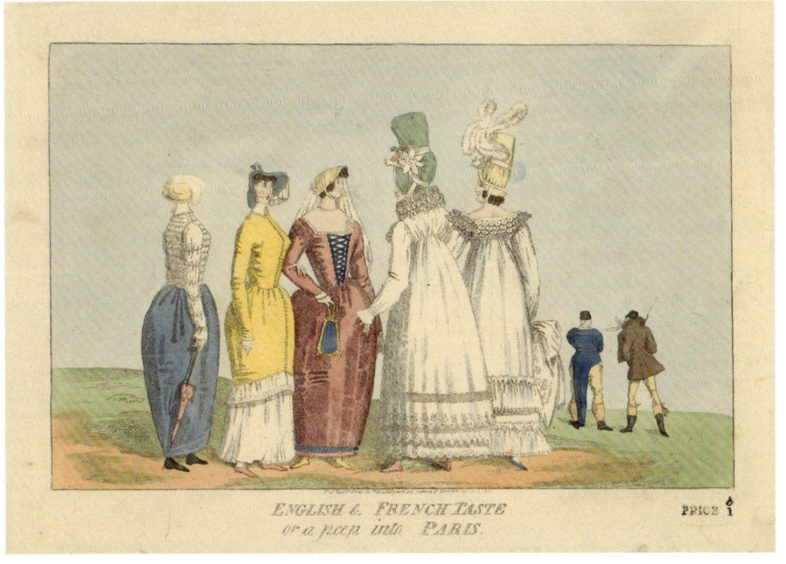


**83**  George Cruikshank (1792–1878)
*Anglo-Gallic salutations in London,*
6 June 1822
Etching, hand-coloured with watercolours,
sheet: 25.7 × 34.9 cm
Staatliche Museen zu Berlin,
Kunstbibliothek

**141**  Samuel William Fores (1761–1838), publisher
*English & French taste or A peep into Paris,*
14 April 1818
Etching, hand-coloured with watercolours,
sheet: 24 × 33 cm
Staatliche Museen zu Berlin,
Kunstbibliothek

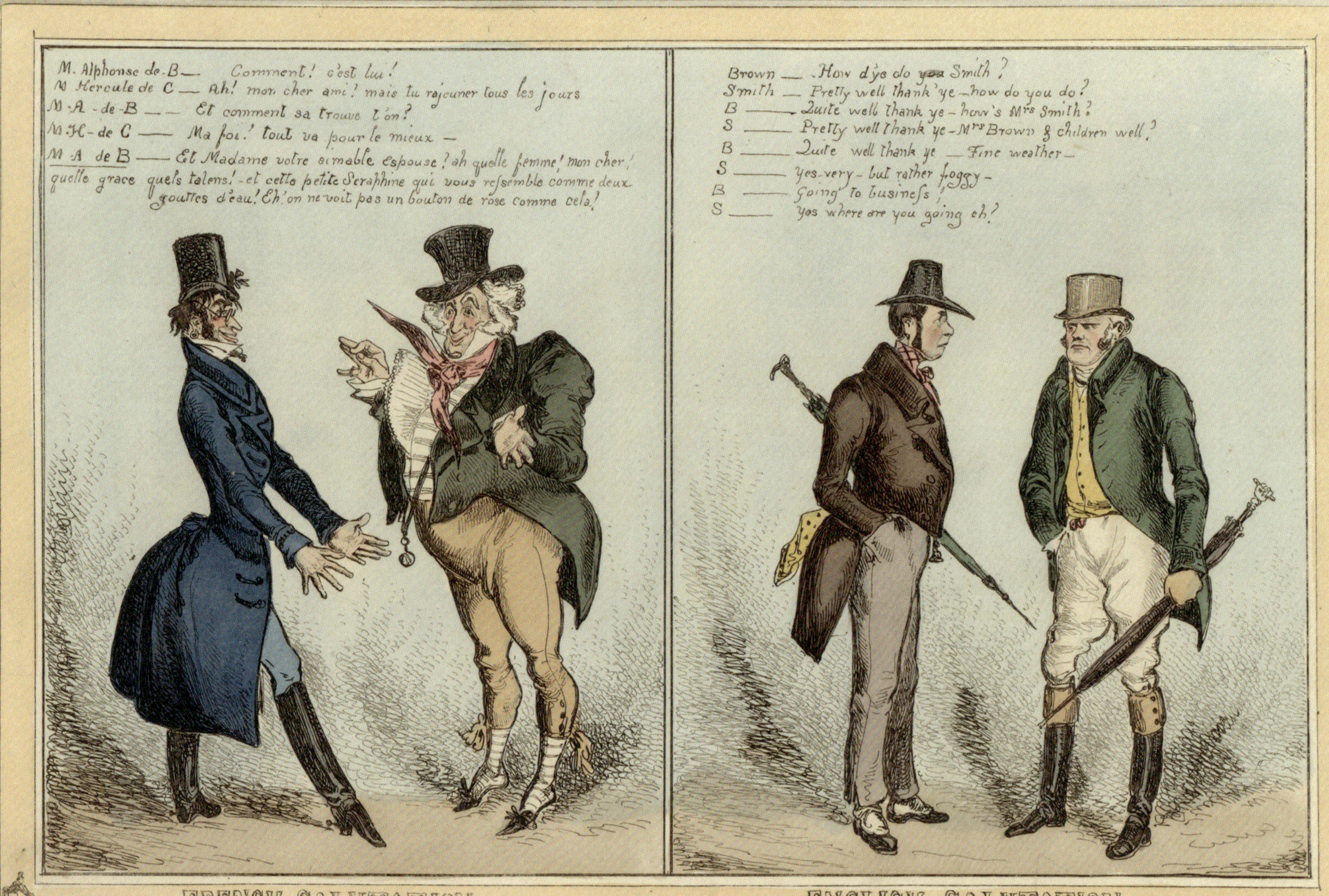



**170** William Heath (1795–1840)
*French salutation, English salutation,* May 1829
Etching, hand-coloured with watercolours,
sheet: 27.4 × 38.7 cm
Staatliche Museen zu Berlin,
Kunstbibliothek

**81** George Cruikshank (1792–1878)
*Monstrosities of 1816,* 12 March 1816
Etching, coloured, sheet: 25 × 35.4 cm
Staatliche Museen zu Berlin,
Kunstbibliothek

**82** George Cruikshank (1792–1878)
*Monstrosities of 1821,* 20 May 1821
Etching, hand-coloured with watercolours,
sheet: 25.3 × 35.2 cm
Staatliche Museen zu Berlin,
Kunstbibliothek

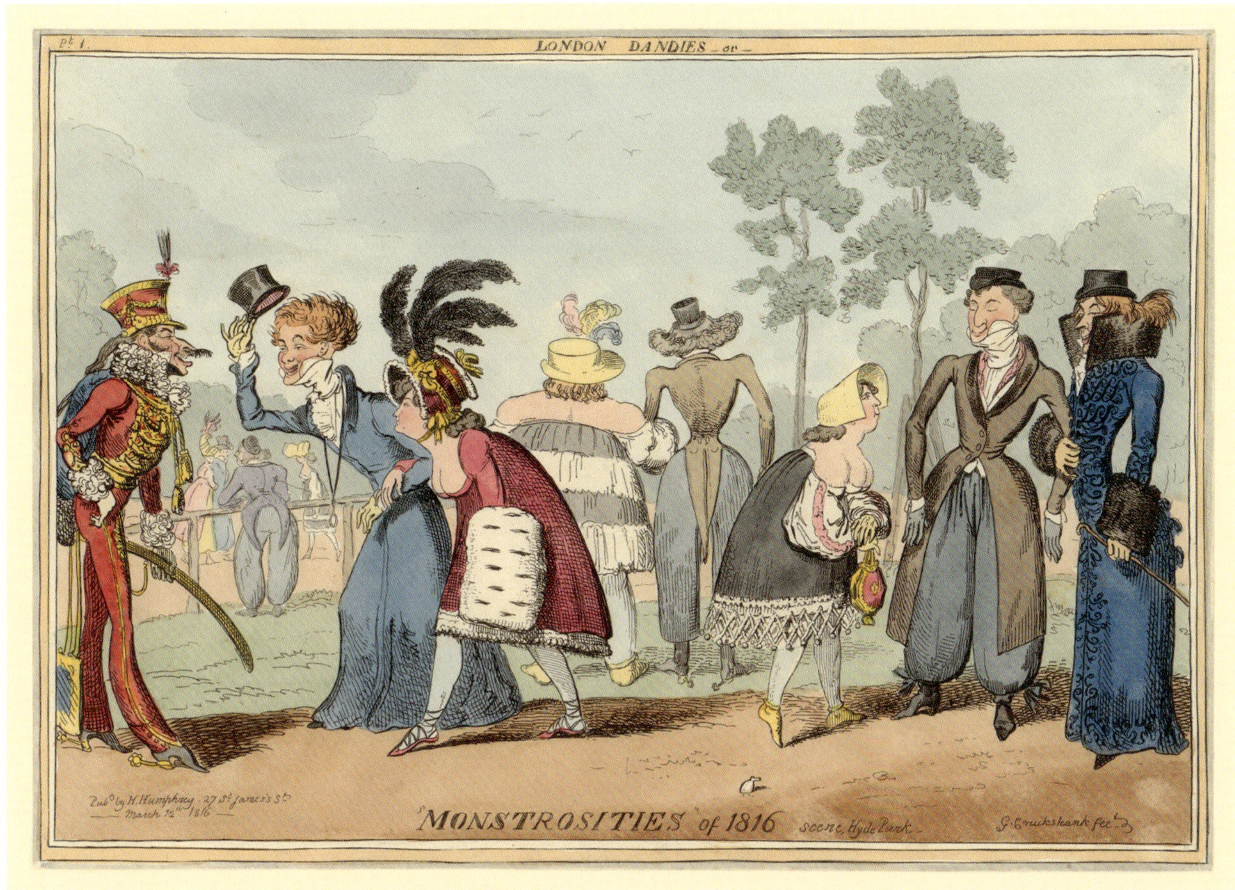

MONSTROSITIES of 1816     scene, Hyde Park.

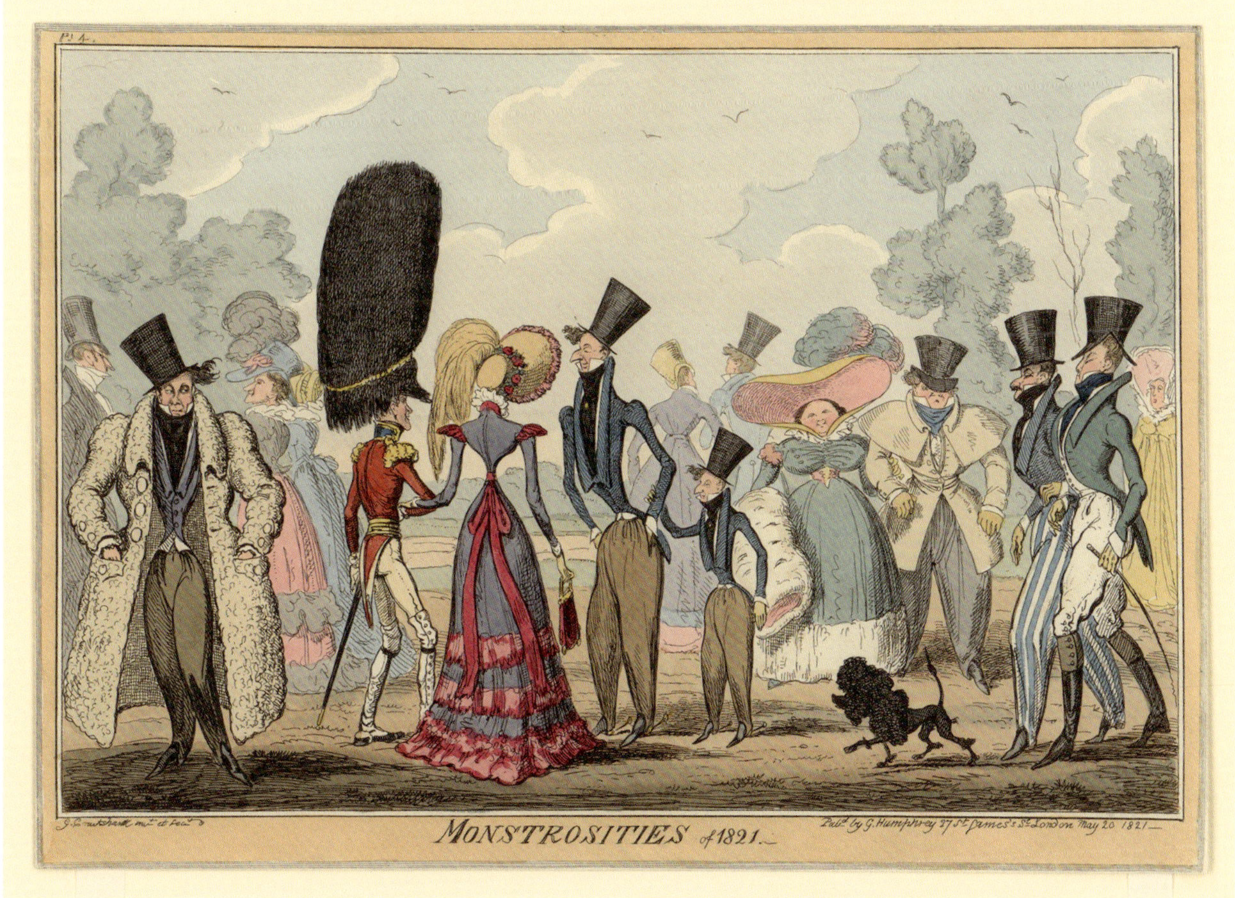

MONSTROSITIES of 1821.

# Uni

# National

## in the

## context after

Werner Telesko

*formity and
Fashions*

**European
the Fall of the
First French
Empire**

As a historic event of European dimensions,[1] the Congress of Vienna provided opportunities for a unique panorama of different (national) fashions within the framework of numerous diplomatic negotiations. Descriptions of the clothes worn for the various occasions and festive events often highlighted the extravagant; they depicted nationality less in the sense of its political origins and instead placed more emphasis on different regional and national tastes. The written reports compared the fashion consciousness and taste of different countries' representatives present at the Congress – customarily with, and not without reason, clear tendencies to perpetuate traditional stereotypes. Even before the official opening of the Congress, a report from Paris reveals that there could be no talk of a spirit of national community when fashion came into play: 'The political events did not remain without influence on the realm of fashion. Lilies are flaunted on women's hats, which, however, have not lost their height through this decoration. The small English ladies' hats therefore find little approval with the French ladies. Overall, to believe in a general reconciliation is the least one can do.'[2]

Numerous fashion magazines and newspapers, such as the *Journal des Luxus und der Moden* (1787–1812 under this title, and published under other titles until 1827)[3] and the *Friedensblätter: Eine Zeitschrift für Leben, Literatur und Kunst,* 1814/15), provided extensive reports on the Congress. Friedrich Justin Bertuch's (1747–1822) *Journal des Luxus und der Moden* did not, however, propagate an explicitly nationalist reading of fashion, but presented it as one of several options.[4] Not only were fashion styles presented through this form of publicity, but they also stimulated new trends. The widespread propagation of a 'new femininity'[5] in the wake of the French Revolution was unthinkable without the visualisation of different facets of female fashion.

The second factor that specifically allows an assessment of the 'nationality' of fashion at the Congress involves the various pictorial media that portrayed the holders of power, aristocrats, famous personalities et al and thus placed clothing at the centre of interest quite differently than what would have been possible in descriptions in the feuilleton. Most examples reveal that two outer garments

1     For a summary, see: Brian E. Vick, *The Congress of Vienna: Power and Politics after Napoleon,* Cambridge 2014.

2     *Friedensblätter: Eine Zeitschrift für Leben, Literatur und Kunst,* no. 19, Saturday, 13 August 1814, daily newspaper, p. 78 (information graciously provided by Alexandra Matzner, Vienna).

3     For basic information, see: Angela Borchert and Ralf Dressel (eds), *Das Journal des Luxus und der Moden: Kultur um 1800,* Heidelberg 2004.

4     Karin Wurst, 'Fashioning a Nation: Fashion and National Clothing in Bertuch's "Journal des Luxus und der Moden" (1786–1827)', *German Studies Review,* 28.2 (2005), pp. 367–86.

5     Viktoria Schmidt-Linsenhoff (ed.), *Sklavin oder Bürgerin? Französische Revolution und neue Weiblichkeit 1760–1830,* Frankfurt am Main 1989 (= Kleine Schriften des Historischen Museums Frankfurt; 44).

6    Cf. Philip Mansel, 'Monarchy, Uniform and the Rise of the Frac 1760–1830', *Past & Present: A Journal of Historical Studies*, 96 (1982), pp. 103–32.

7    Mansel 1982, p. 111.

8    Mansel 1982, pp. 123f.

9    Mansel 1982, pp. 125f.

10    Alexander Maxwell, *Patriots against Fashion: Clothing and Nationalism in Europe's Age of Revolution*, Hampshire, UK 2014, p. 58.

11    Maxwell 2014, p. 73.

12    Cf. Angelika Schmitt-Vorster, *Pro Deo et Populo. Die Porträts Josephs II (1765–1790). Untersuchungen zu Bestand, Ikonographie und Verbreitung des Kaiserbildnisses im Zeitalter der Aufklärung*, Ph.D. diss. Ludwig-Maximilians-Universität München, Munich 2006.

for men took a dominant position in Europe at the time of the Congress – the uniform and frock coat, which is also reflected in the corresponding representative paintings.

With the depiction of regents in civilian clothes, attention increasingly focused on the spectrum of the underlying roles for the bourgeois. This also resulted in expanding the possibility of depicting the ruler 'at work', that is to say, the increasingly important criterion of a record of civil performance, which was aimed directly at the third estate. The sphere of the 'indoor' now complemented in a new way the traditional perspective of the 'outdoor', that is to say the battlefield presence, which had always been closely linked to ruler iconography based on various personal unions (such as the monarch as commander).

To consider the distinct evolutionary lines of the epoch around 1800, Philip Mansel's groundbreaking study examined the use of the *habit habillé*, uniform and frock coat.[6] The declining importance of the French-style, aristocratically-based *habit habillé* went hand-in-hand with a growing popularity of uniforms, 'embodiments of monarchical authority';[7] the visual arts conspicuously represented this 'militarisation of the courts and monarchies'.[8] The use of the frock coat, in contrast, could by no means be taken as an indication of the bourgeoisie's ascent since it was also worn by reactionary regents such as Ferdinand VII of Spain (1784–1833) or Franz I of Austria (1768–1835).[9] While the King of Spain used inquisition and torture to repress every form of political renewal as well as the progressive Spanish Constitution of 1812, the Austrian Emperor especially targeted the 'Jacobins' and their revolutionary ideas.

Uniforms could, for the most part, more accurately and unambiguously display the social status of persons, thus enabling the presence of a 'visual hierarchy'[10] in which military uniforms occupied a special place and, in this way, most vividly represented the 'uniform mania'[11] of the late Enlightenment. In addition, 'national costumes' of male or female character – such as Justus Möser's (1720–1794) *'Landesuniformen'* (national uniforms, 1772) – played a special role. This underlines the new fact that wearing traditional costumes usually involved specific political messages. Even as early as the second half of the eighteenth century, one can observe a growing emancipation of the military portrait, which was expressed in the development that, on the one hand, a portrait in a uniform had increasing power to determine the ruler's image (in the Habsburg area, especially beginning with Emperor Joseph II, 1741–1790);[12] on the other hand, this resulted in the compositions directly integrating many factors explaining military actions (battle plans, background fighting, weapons, etc.).

As much as the uniform imagines uniformity in the sense of an aligned (military) consciousness, nevertheless, distinctive and differentiated meanings were attached to the colours and the different 'trimmings' (medals, rank insignia, epaulettes, etc.) of the uniform coat; this was described in detailed contemporary reports and visual testimonies, such as in the depiction of the military festival on 18 October 1814 in the Vienna Prater. | [Page 146] | This is also evident in,

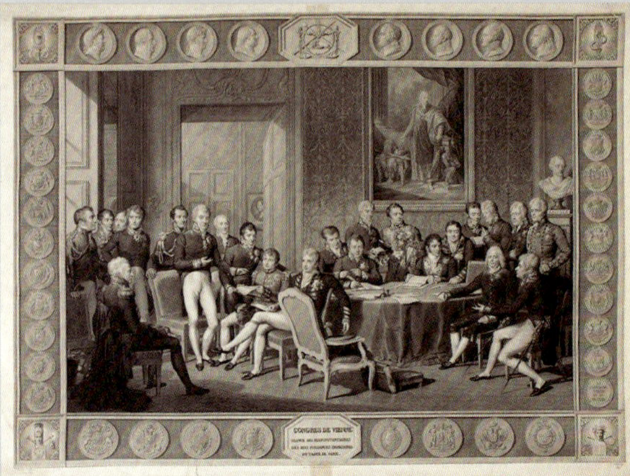

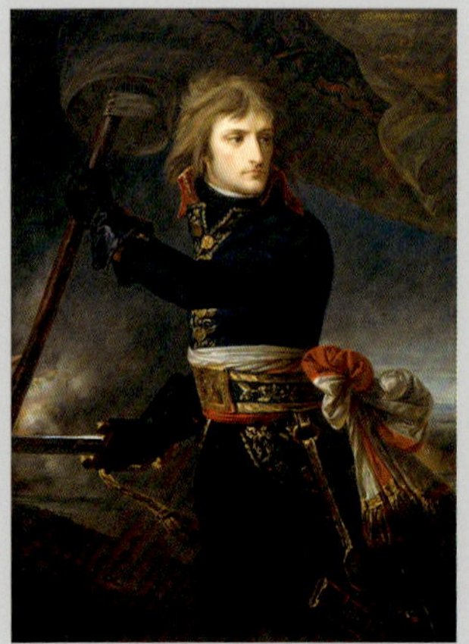

**Fig. 1** after Jean Baptiste Isabey (1767–1855)
Jean Godefroy (1771–1839), etcher
*View of a plenary session of
the Congress of Vienna in 1815,* 1819
Etching and copperplate engraving,
partly with roulette, sheet: 67.8 × 89.1 cm
Weimar, Klassik Stiftung Weimar

**Fig. 2** Antoine Jean Gros (1771–1835)
*Le Général Bonaparte sur
le pont d'Arcole,* c. 1796
Oil on canvas, 130 × 94 cm
Salenstein, Napoleonmuseum
Schloss Arenenberg

among other things, the famous stipple engraving of the Congress of Vienna (1815) | <sup>Fig.</sup> 1 | after Jean-Baptiste Isabey (1767–1855), that broke up the uniformity of fashion with different medals and decorative elements on the uniforms.[13] Furthermore, the uniform, naturally, emphasises the male body much more than coronation regalia, Spanish dress coat or ceremonial clothing. Thus, the militarism underlying the masculinity of the European monarchs was expressed in the uniform that both served as the benchmark and criterion of difference.

However, limited possibilities existed for the reception of famous works such as the advancing *général de division* Bonaparte on the Bridge of Arcole (1796) – as in the famous painting by Antoine-Jean Gros (1771–1835) | <sup>Fig.</sup> 2 | The emphasis shifts in several portraits in uniforms from the clearly emphatic dynamism in Gros's work with a sash tied with a large knot, whose colours, along with the uniform dress coat, indicate the French tricolour (!), to seemingly static mannequins in uniform, whose coloured distinction is underlined by corresponding sashes with the national colours.

For example, the Austrian Emperor Franz I, replete in a Field Marshal's gala dress, did not stand out among his entourage in crowd scenes at the Congress of Vienna, as depicted in the lithograph of Franz Wolf (1795–1859) after Johann Nepomuk Hoechle (1790–1835) | <sup>Page</sup> 147 | because of his luxuriant uniform splendour but because of his simplicity, military rigour and the concentration on colours of the Austrian barred shield. With their red-white-red, the colours let the heraldic tradition become a fixed part of the emperor's public presence by means of upper garments. It was not without reason that contemporary reports cynically remarked that the 'festive dress' of the overly frugal Austrian emperor was always the same.[14] In this sense, in the wake of the Napoleonic Wars of Liberation, the uniforms combined the commitment to the respective national origins with the willingness to take up arms for the interests of their own nation. From this perspective, the visual testimonies of military mass scenes at the Congress of Vienna served to propagate the colour canon of the nations present.



13 Werner Telesko, 'Jean-Baptiste Isabeys Kongressbild', in *Europa in Wien. Der Wiener Kongress 1814/15,* Agnes Husslein-Arco and Sabine Grabner (eds), exh. cat. Belvedere Wien, Vienna/Munich 2015, pp. 130f.

14 Hilde Spiel (ed.), *Der Wiener Kongreß in Augenzeugenberichten,* Munich 1978 (first edition 1965), p. 210.

15 Werner Telesko, *Napoleon Bonaparte. Der «moderne Held» und die bildende Kunst 1799–1815,* Vienna et al. 1998, pp. 85f.

16 Siegfried Müller, 'Die Nationalisierung der Kultur: Das Beispiel der ungarischen Nationaltracht', in Michael Reinhold (ed.), *Kleider machen Politik. Zur Repräsentation von Nationalstaat und Politik durch Kleidung in Europa vom 18. bis zum 20. Jahrhundert,* Oldenburg 2002 (= catalogues of the Landesmuseum Oldenburg; 19), pp. 23–31, here p. 26.

17 Christa Lichtenberger, *Der Einfluss des Wiener Kongresses auf die Entstehung der Wiener Mode,* diploma thesis Universität Wien, Vienna 2015, pp. 45f.

18 Lichtenberger 2015, p. 47.

Werner Telesko

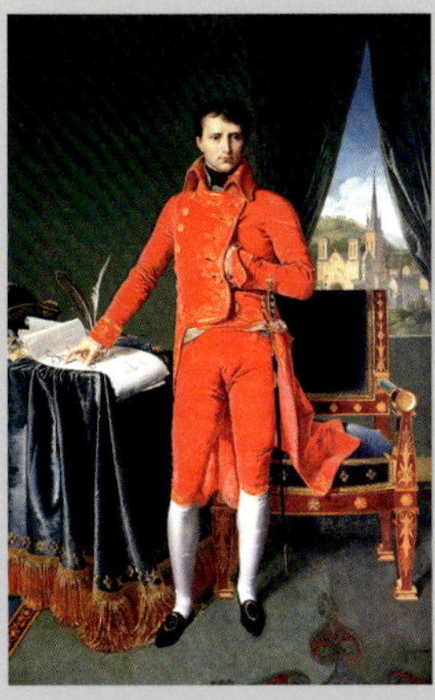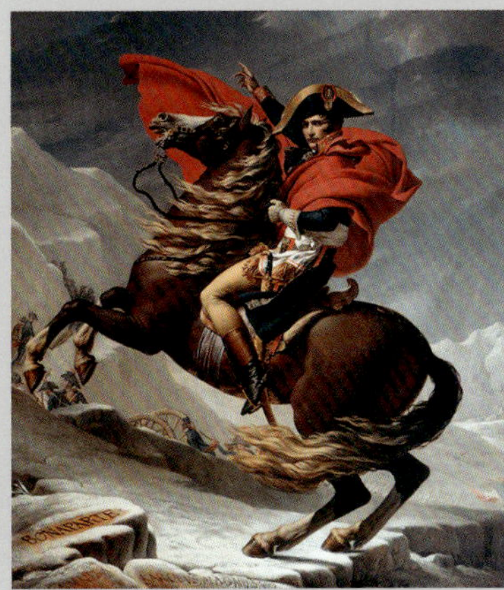



An exception in the early nineteenth century were explicitly political paintings such as the full-length portrait of Bonaparte as First Consul by Jean-Auguste-Dominique Ingres (1780–1867) in Liège (1803/04) that focusses on the scarlet consul uniform clearly signals imperial claims.[15] | Fig. 3 | The well-known equestrian portrait of 1800 by Jacques-Louis David (1748–1825) | Fig. 4 | simultaneously 'monumentalises' the Corsican's heroic habitus and projects the French colours of the tricolour onto the glorious tradition of a commander's portrait. For the first time, Napoleon's pictorial politics made representational clothing in its various forms a central subject of political strategies which, from 1804 onwards, the year of his coronation, primarily served as a link with the royal tradition of the Bourbons. The rapidly changing roles in Napoleon's career were finally illustrated and turned into the negative in caricatures, such as those by Thomas Rowlandson (1756–1827) and Karl von Steuben (1788–1856). | Page 142 | A 'Napoleonic stairs of life' (c. 1814) | Fig. 5 | illustrates how the rise and fall of the upstart inevitably came about with a radical change in outward appearance.

From the eighteenth century on, clothing (along with language), was the most apparent and effective sign of national renewal, as is especially evident in the Hungarian national costume. In multi-ethnic Vienna, for instance, wearing the Hungarian national dress, which can be understood as encompassing all estates, offered an almost ideal opportunity to protest against the Viennese court,[16] which, in any case, was very reserved towards nationalistic movements.

These conditions would have to be taken into account in the rich panopticon of costumes and the costumes of nationals that gathered at the Congress in Vienna. The Congress not only provided a stage for Europe, but also made its own 'Viennese fashion' an established term associated with master tailors such as Petko and Beer as well as the modiste Langer. Reports on Viennese fashion were surprisingly few and far between. The most significant was probably the *Journal des Luxus und der Moden,* which, in its November 1814 issue, describes Vienna as the meeting place of many cultures and fashions, but characteristically notes that an exact determination of modernity is difficult since the different fashions rank equally among each other and only Great Britain would have an exceptional position in this respect.[17] Although the April edition of the *Journal des dames et des modes,* dating from 1815, states that the ladies in Vienna dress very differently, the height of their hats, however, has come closer to English fashion. Furthermore, it was conspicuously emphasised that gentlemen favoured English fashion.[18] This could be well explained by the general political situation after the defeat of Napoleon, which placed Great Britain in a prominent position in the Concert of Nations after 1815. The dresses of the English Ambassador's wife Emily Anne Stewart, Lady Castlereagh (1772–1829) especially caused repeated admiration: at a ball in the House of Metternich in January 1815 she appeared in a self-designed (!) Austrian national dress while wearing the costume of a Vestal virgin together with her husband's Order of the Garter around her forehead,



Uniformity and National Fashions in the European context

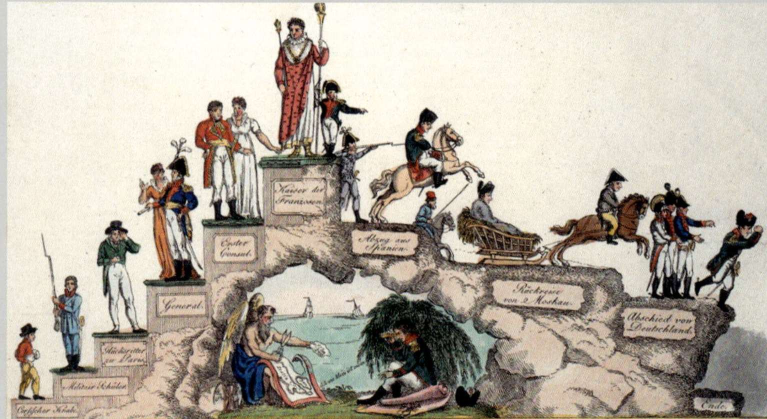



**Fig. 5** Unknown Artist
*Stufenleiter der Grösse und des Sturzes Napoleons,* c. 1814
Stepladder of the rise and fall of Napoleon
Etching, coloured, sheet: 22.8 x 36.8 cm
Berlin, Deutsches Historisches Museum

on which one could read the famous motto 'Honi soit qui mal y pense'.[19] The presence of many different nations at the Congress of Vienna also made it possible to intensify a practice that attested to friendship among nations in the nineteenth century – the wearing of traditional dress by representatives of other nations. Thus, the English women appeared on a *redoute parée* (literally: 'decorated redoute') at Metternich's palace in October 1814 in Russian (!) clothing.[20] The use of other monarchs' uniforms by the sovereigns of the three victorious powers of the Congress also sought to emphasise mutual understanding. The name *redoute,* which actually refers to a hall for balls, was subsequently transferred to the ball festivals that occurred especially at carnival time, and which enjoyed great popularity as public masked balls at the time of the Congress of Vienna. Often, several thousand people attended the events, which took place at irregular intervals several times a year. Men were usually required to wear a uniform. This made it clear that the Congress, as a world-historical event, guaranteed two things in the garments used for this occasion. On the one hand, the emphasis on nation-specific peculiarities was supplemented and transformed by lively cultural transfer, so that wearing clothing from other states also opened up the perspective to feel as part of a great family of peoples for the reorganisation of Europe after 1815. There was, on the other hand, still a long way to go for a deliberately provocative national instrumentalisation of fashion in the public sphere. When, after 1870, Prussia forbade the residents of Alsace-Lorraine to wear the colours of the tricolour, women found a creative response to their French identity by wearing blue, white and red dresses and carefully placing themselves side by side.[21]

19    Spiel 1978 (as in note 14), p. 169.

20    Spiel 1978, p. 145.

21    Coloured lithograph by A. Lemercier after Jan Baptist Huysmans, 1871 (Strasbourg, Cabinet des Estampes, EV 1870–74), cf. *Bismarck – Preußen, Deutschland und Europa,* exh. cat. Deutsches Historisches Museum Berlin, Berlin 1990, 390, no. 10/7.



Werner Telesko

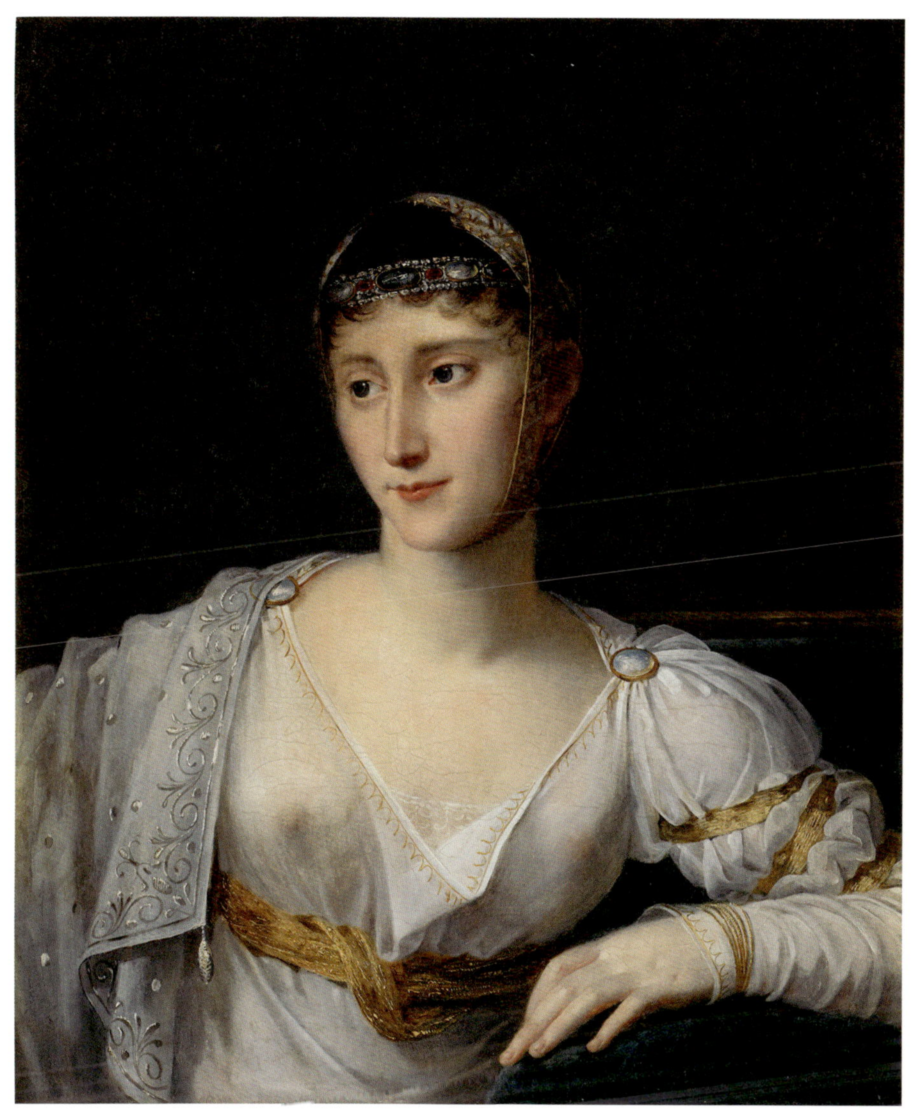

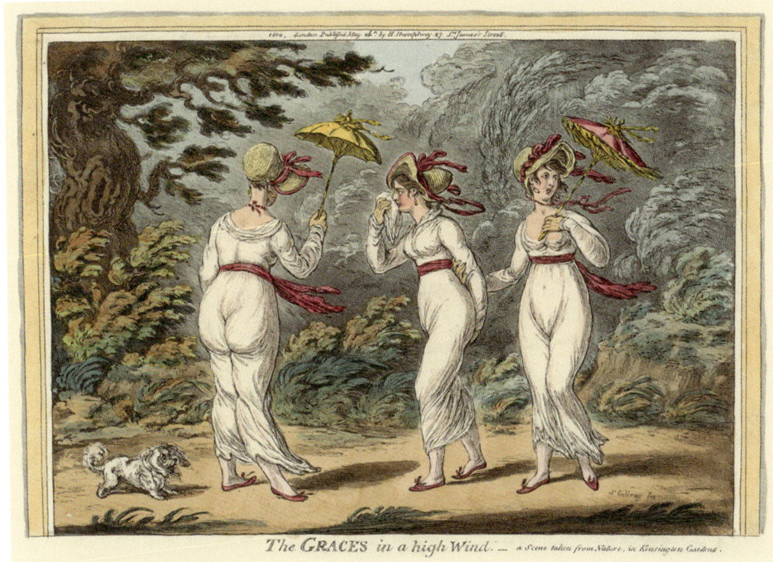


**195**  Robert Lefèvre (1755–1830)
*Half-length portrait of Pauline Bonaparte,*
*Princess Borghese, Duchess of Guastalla*
*(1780–1825),* 1806
Oil on canvas, 65 × 54 cm
Musée national des châteaux de Versailles et
de Trianon

**151**  James Gillray (1756–1815)
*The graces in a high wind,* 1797
Etching, coloured, sheet: 26 × 35.7 cm
Staatliche Museen zu Berlin,
Kunstbibliothek

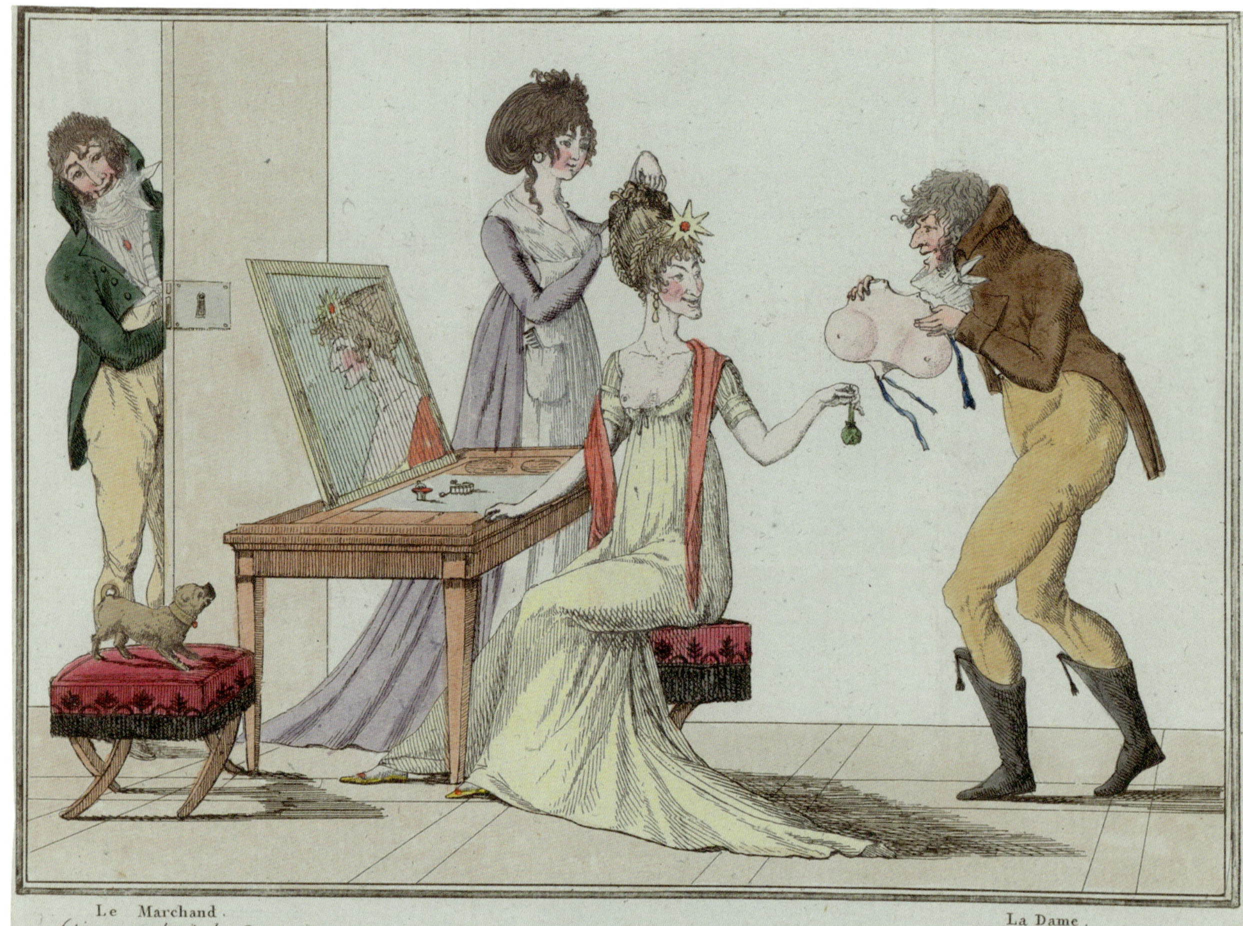


**107** after Defontaines?
*Les Suppléans,* 1801
The substitutes
Etching, coloured with watercolour,
sheet: 23.7 × 26.3 cm
Staatliche Museen zu Berlin,
Kunstbibliothek

**268** Unknown artist
*Quel est le plus ridicule?*, 1800/01
Who is the most ridiculous
Etching, hand-coloured with watercolours,
on light blue paper, sheet: 25.6 × 33.1 cm
Staatliche Museen zu Berlin,
Kunstbibliothek

**269** Unknown artist
*Le Coup de vent,* 1802
The gust of wind
Etching, hand-coloured with watercolours,
dotted, sheet: 24.6 × 31.8 cm
Staatliche Museen zu Berlin,
Kunstbibliothek

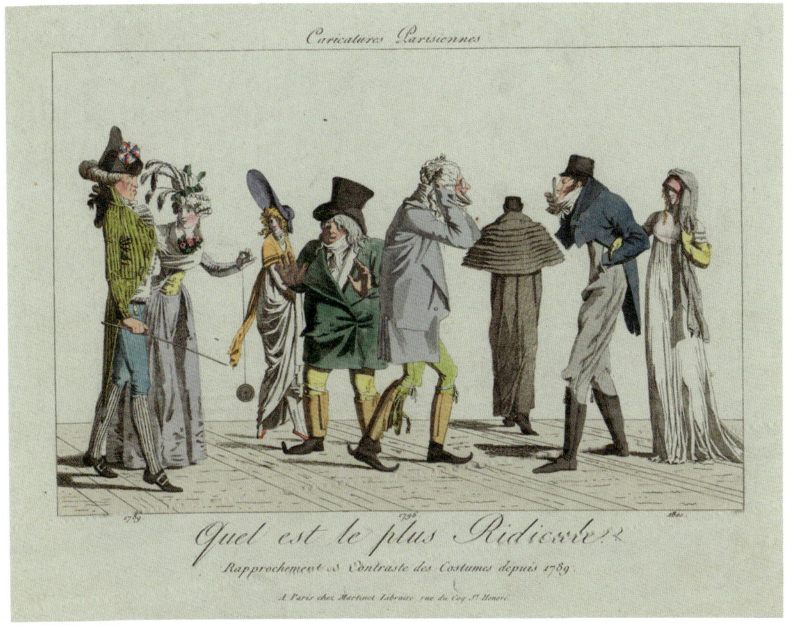


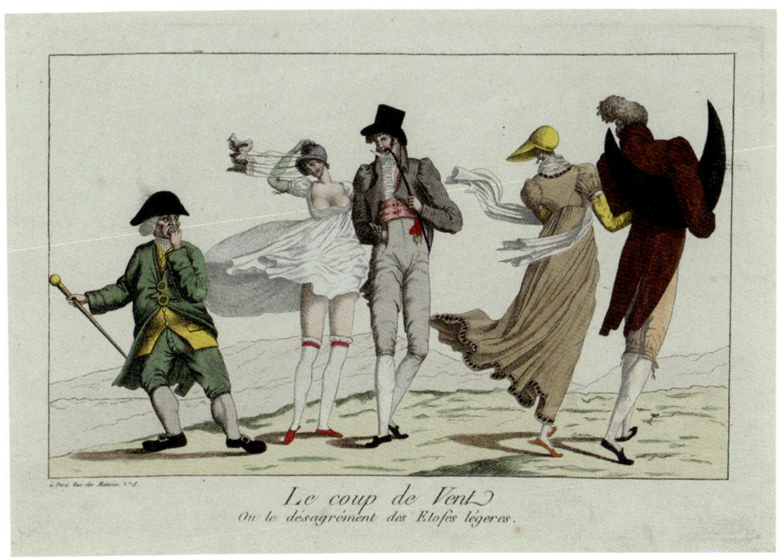

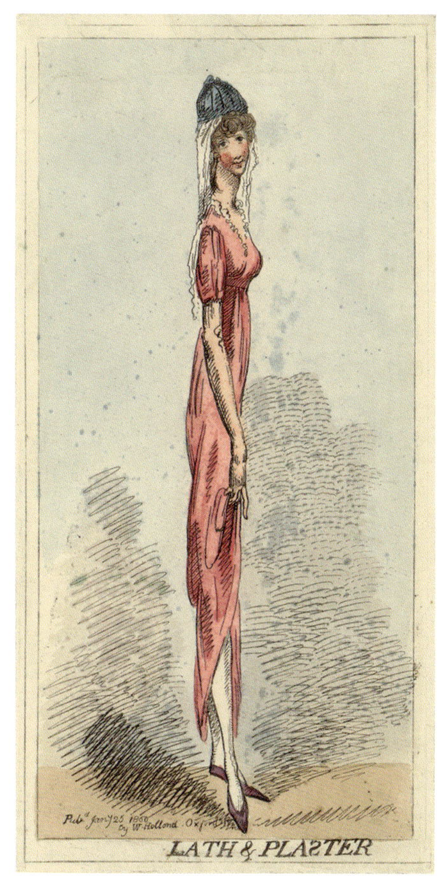


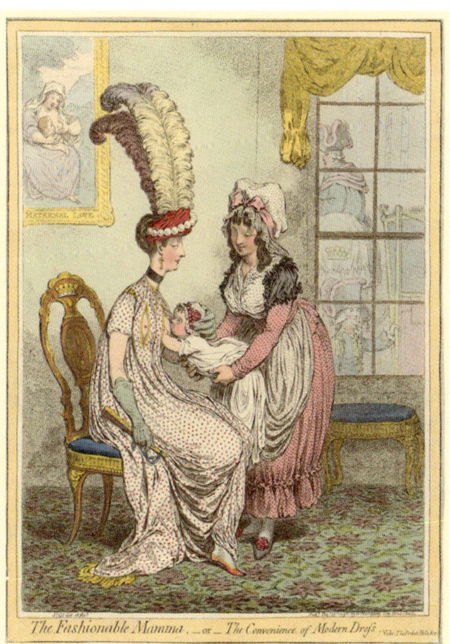



**179** William Holland (1757–1815)
*Lath & plaster,* 25 January 1800
Etching, hand-coloured with watercolours,
sheet: 30.2 × 14.8 cm
Staatliche Museen zu Berlin,
Kunstbibliothek

**150** James Gillray (1756–1815)
*The fashionable mamma, or The convenience
of modern dress,* 15 February 1797
Etching, hand-coloured with watercolours,
sheet: 34.2 × 24 cm
Staatliche Museen zu Berlin,
Kunstbibliothek

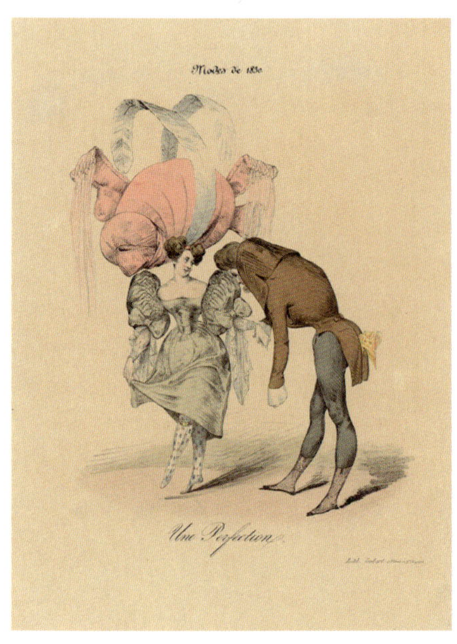

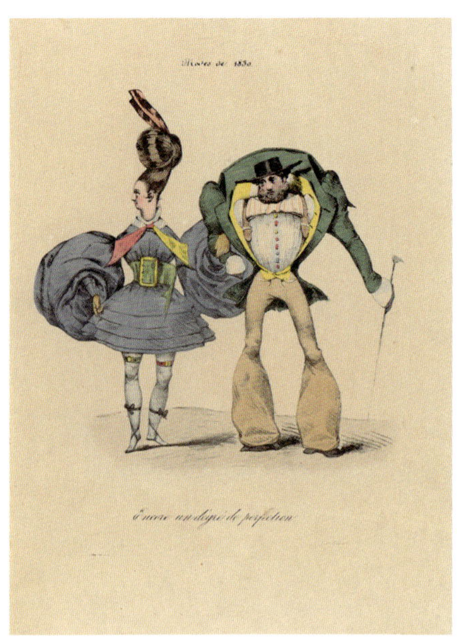

**155** Gobert, Lithographer
*Modes de 1830. Une Perfection,* 1829
Lithograph, sheet: 31.4 × 22.5 cm
Staatliche Museen zu Berlin,
Kunstbibliothek

**154** Gobert, Lithograf
*Modes de 1830. Encore un degré
de perfection,* 1829
Lithograph, sheet: 32.1 × 23.2 cm
Staatliche Museen zu Berlin,
Kunstbibliothek

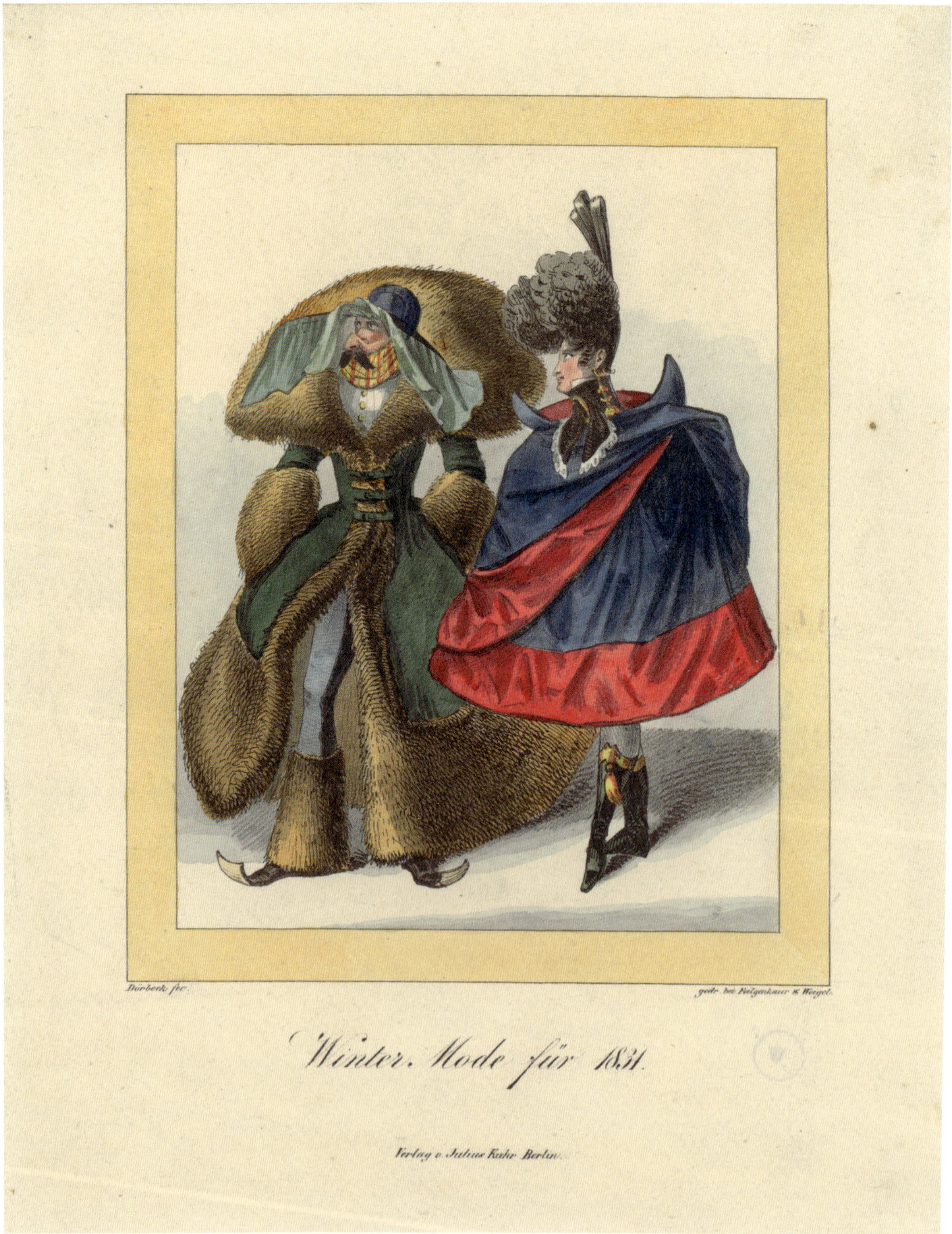

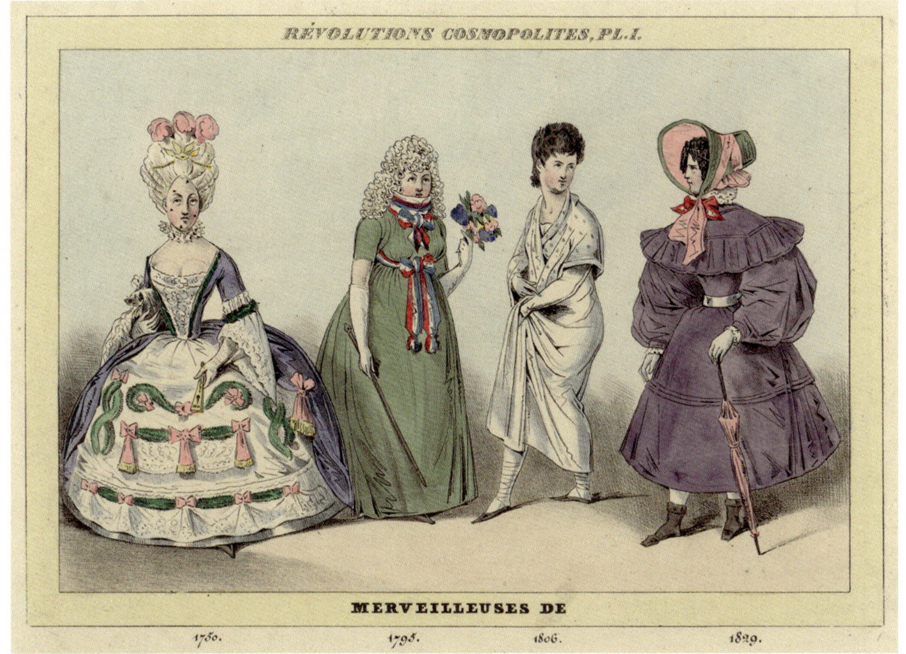



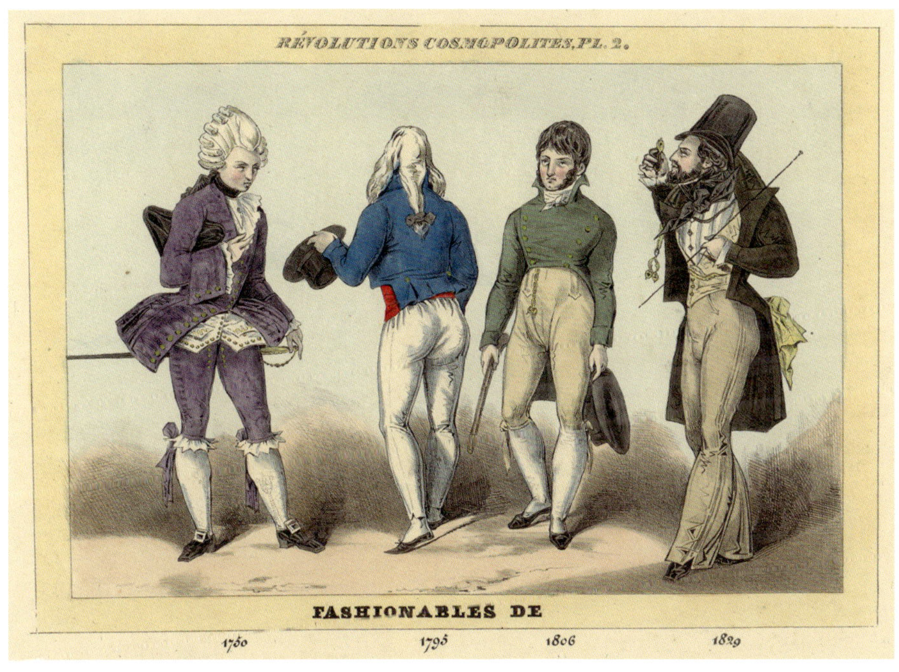





**231**  Victor Ratier (1807–1898)
*Merveilleuses*
Plate 1 from *Révolutions cosmopolites*,
after 1829
Lithograph, sheet: 26 × 32.4 cm
Staatliche Museen zu Berlin,
Kunstbibliothek

**232**  Victor Ratier (1807–1898)
*Fashionables*
Plate 2 from *Révolutions cosmopolites*,
c. 1830
Lithograph, sheet: 26 × 32.4 cm
Staatliche Museen zu Berlin,
Kunstbibliothek

**117**  Franz Burchard Dörbeck (1799–1835)
*Winter Mode für 1831*, 1831
Etching, hand-coloured with
watercolours, sheet: 28.5 × 21.8 cm
Staatliche Museen zu Berlin,
Kunstbibliothek

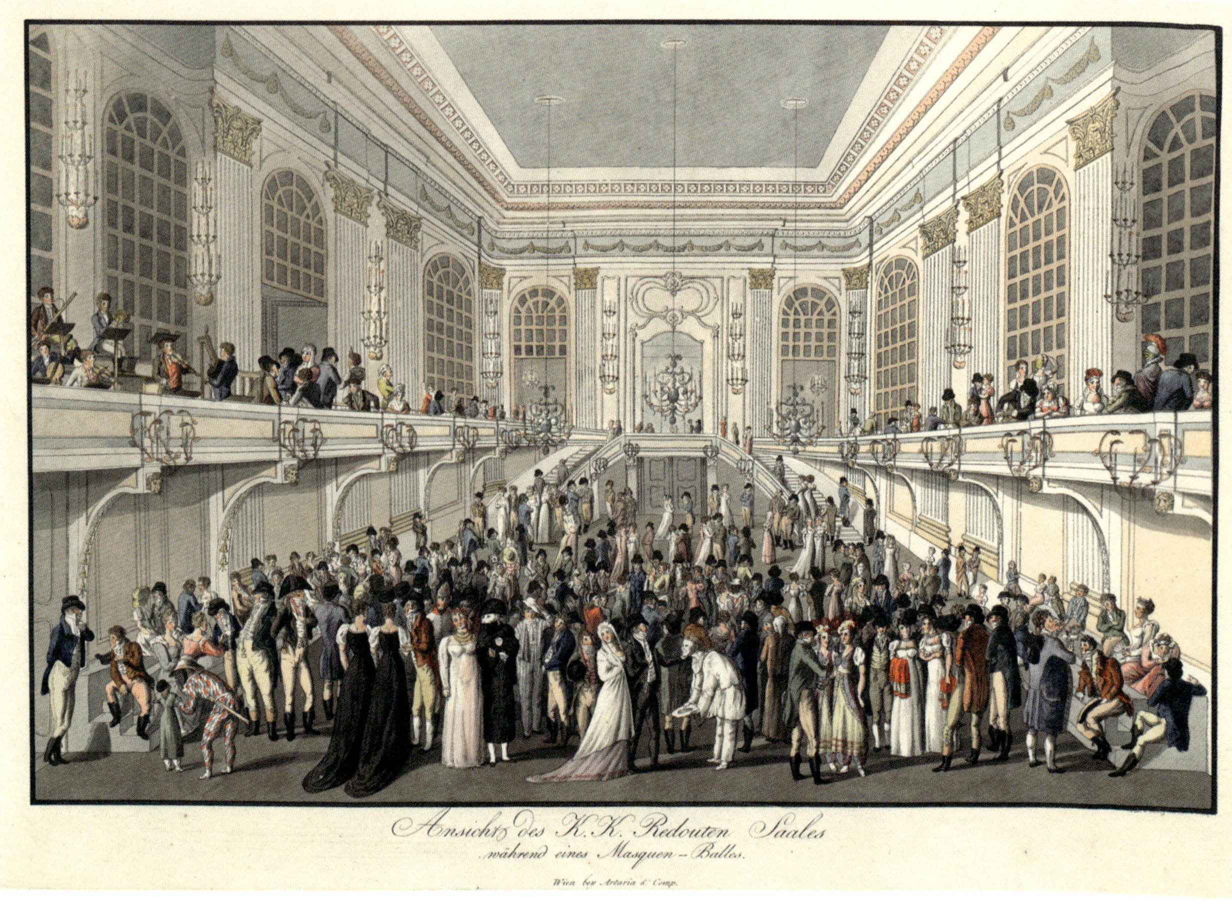

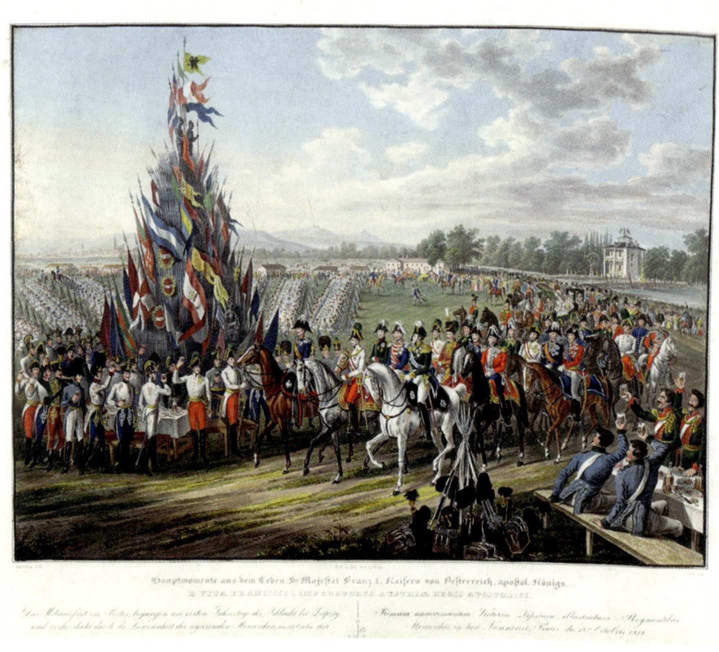

**242** Josef Schütz
*Ansicht des K.K. Redouten Saales
während eines Masquen-Balles,* c. 1815
Etching, coloured, sheet: 49.5 × 36.5 cm
Vienna, Österreichische National-
bibliothek, Map Department and Globe
Museum

**175** after Johann Nepomuk Hoechle
(1790–1835)
*Fest im Prater zum Jahrestag der
Völkerschlacht bei Leipzig 1814,* 1833
Lithograph, sheet: 45.9 × 58.9 cm
Vienna, Österreichische National-
bibliothek, Picture Archives and Graphics
Department

**188** Franz Krüger (1797–1857)
*Prinz August von Preussen,* c. 1828
Oil on canvas, 63 × 47 cm
Staatliche Museen zu Berlin,
Nationalgalerie

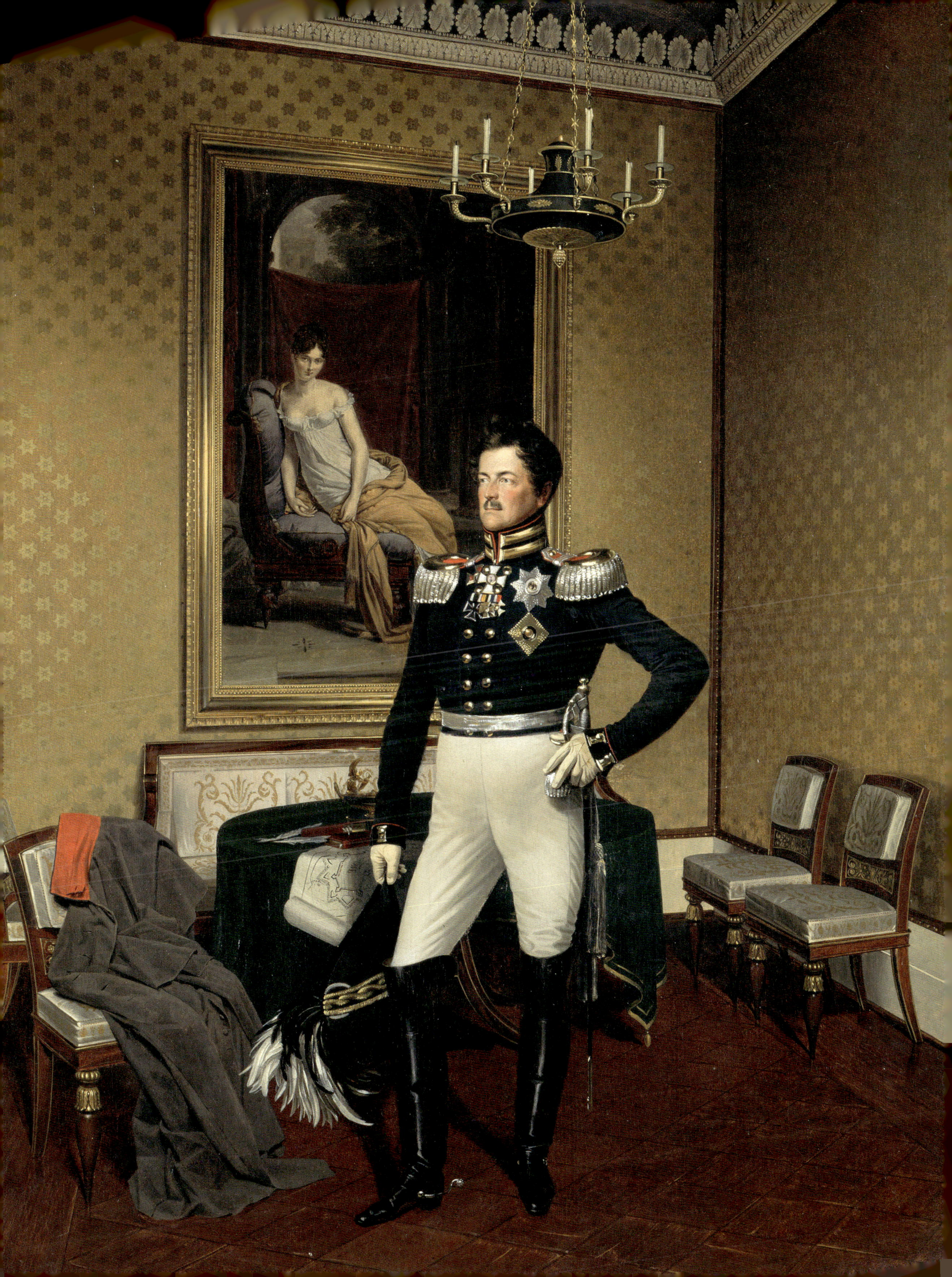

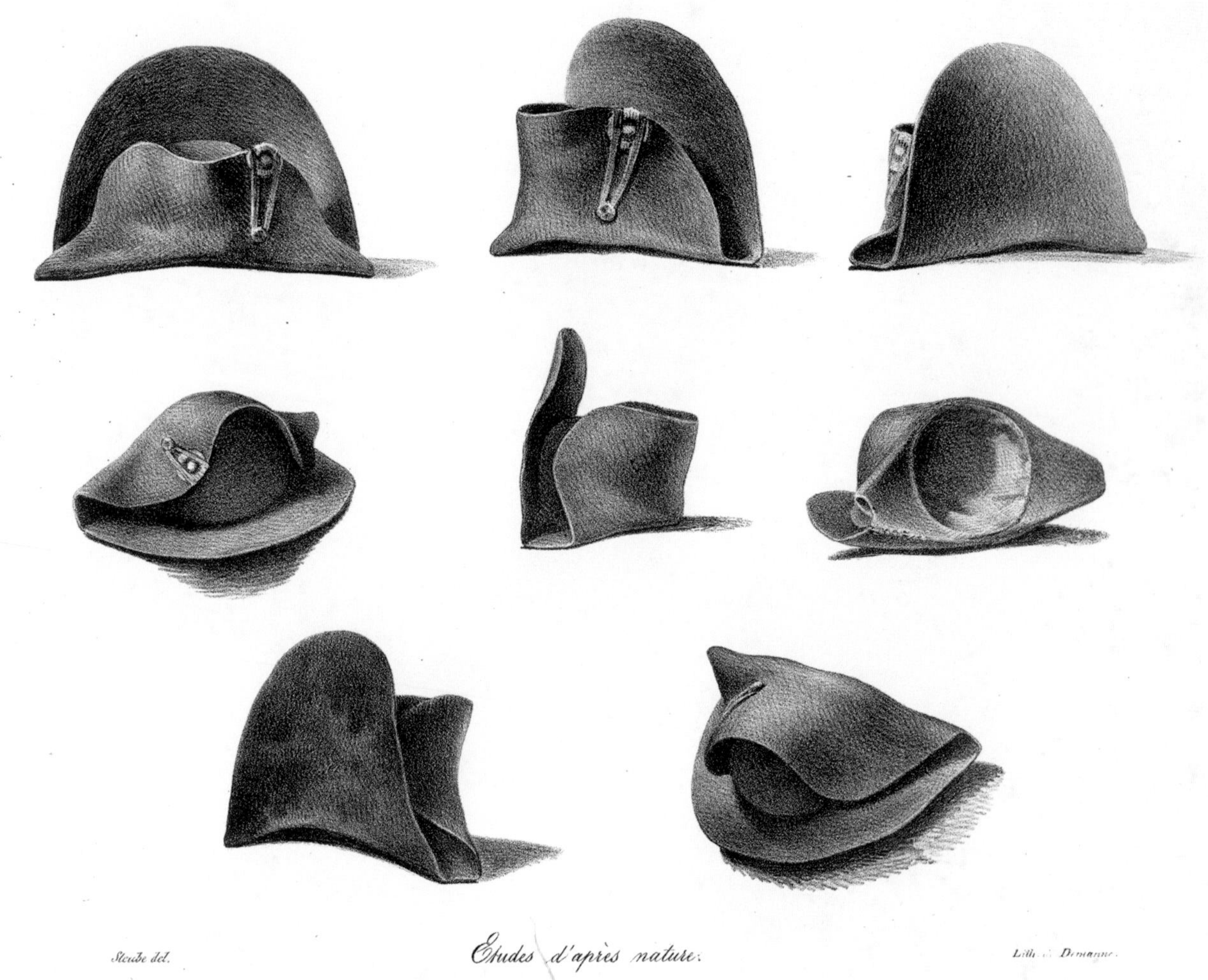





**246**  after Karl von Steuben (1788–1856)
*Der Hut Napoleons I in den verschiedenen*
*Lebensphasen des Kaisers,* after 1826
Napoleon I's hat in the various
life stages of the Emperor
Lithograph, sheet: 25.5 × 37.5 cm
Vienna, Österreichische Nationalbibliothek,
Picture Archives and Graphics Department

# Uniform

In uniform, the stooped walk upright.
The more metal on the collar, the
higher the ideals – so perhaps
does a veteran explain to the grandchildren
the costume.
Thus are old values and their echoes
on the stripes, in the foliage,
where it rustles and whispers of equality.
It remains a whisper when no one
recognises himself in the other.
When I turn against the light and thus
against others, I see through myself,
and there stands the will
to meet myself again and again.
In the uniform is the knowledge
about the extent of each mind and
the measurability of the bodies in the intentions
which have been clearly framed since Darwin.
It is the one form that binds all and
wants to keep them. No one may grow,
and if, then only in masses,
which are in stock in the warehouse.
The picture, in some rooms
it wears a black ribbon, the corner
encloses it smoothly and shiningly, but also firmly.
One hands the widow a country's flag,
when the husband lies in honour in the earth.
The buttons are then all
very dark bright stars on the one form.



Nora Gomringer

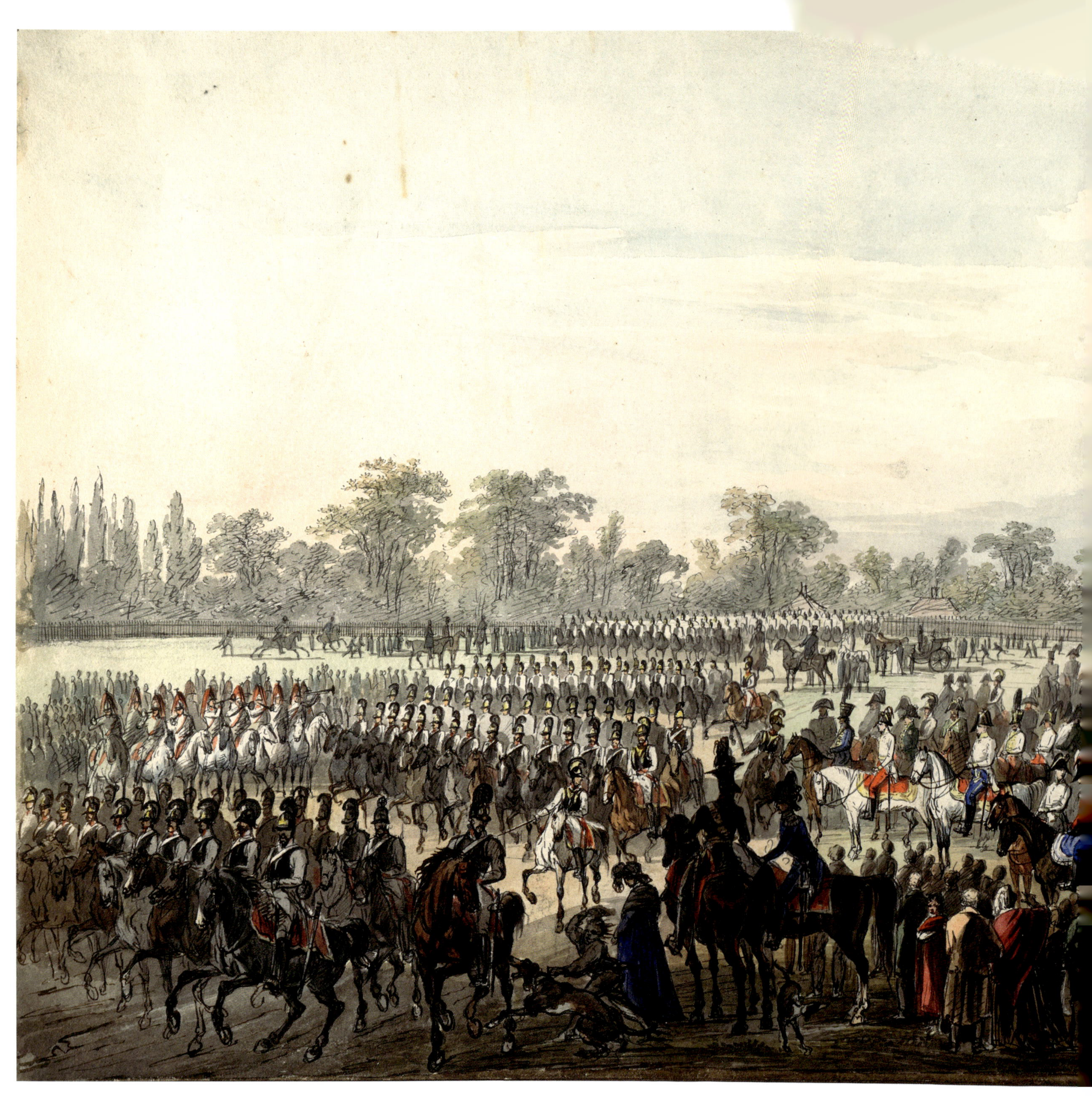

**174** Johann Nepomuk Hoechle (1790–1835)
*Parade während des Wiener Kongresses,* 1815
Parade during the Congress of Vienna
Pen and ink drawing, watercolours, 44.5 × 68.5 cm
Vienna, Österreichische Nationalbibliothek,
Picture Archives and Graphics Department

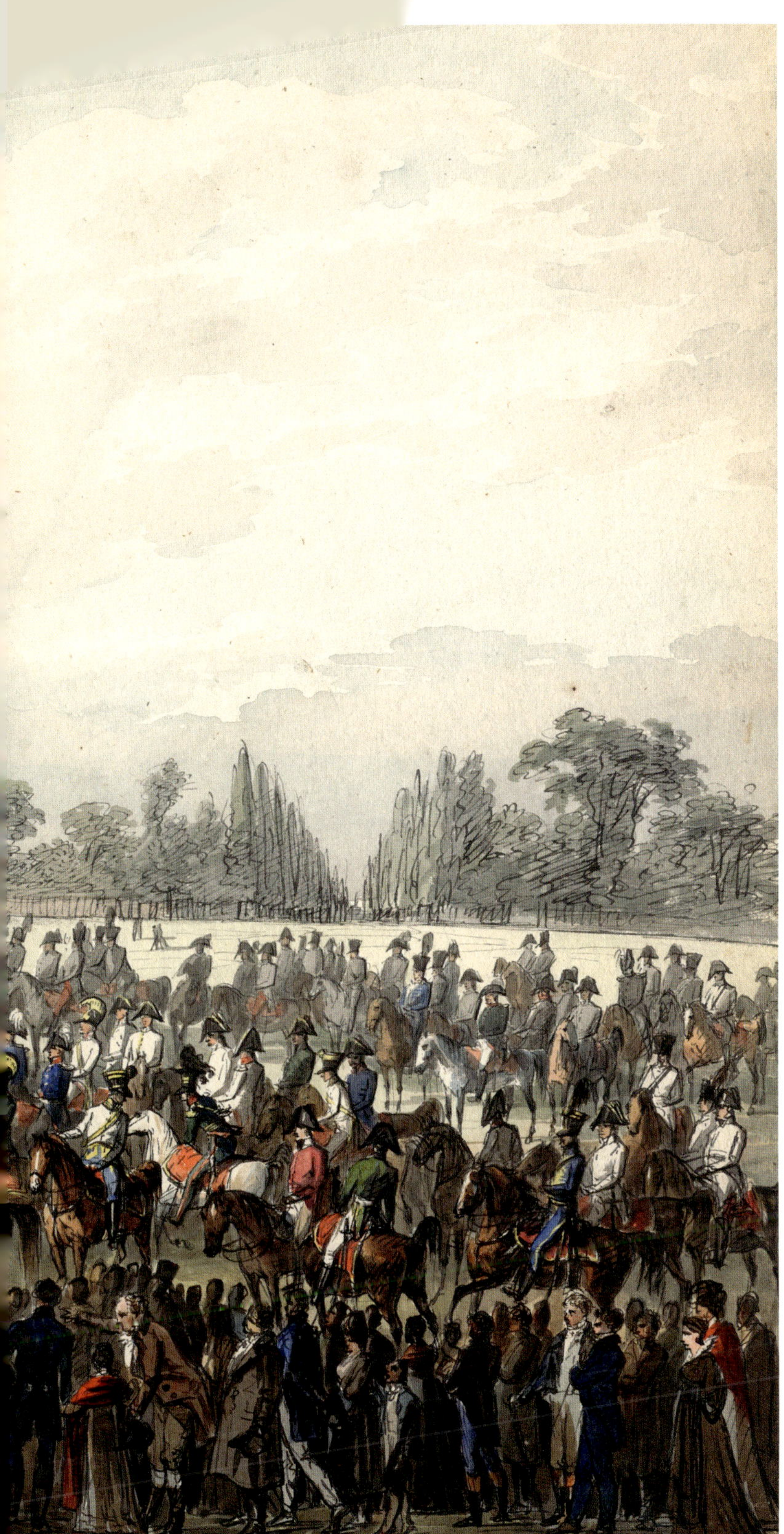

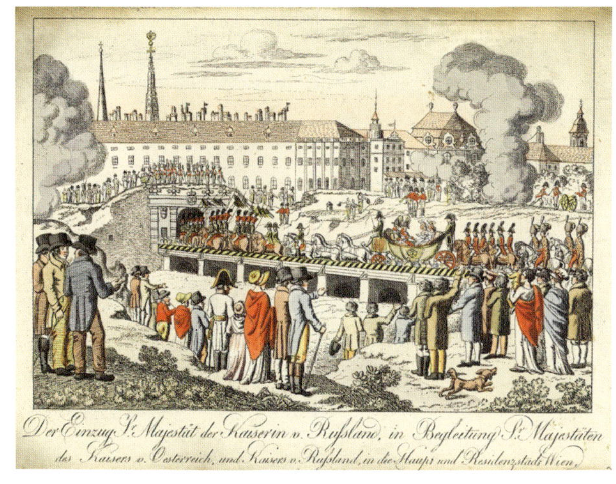


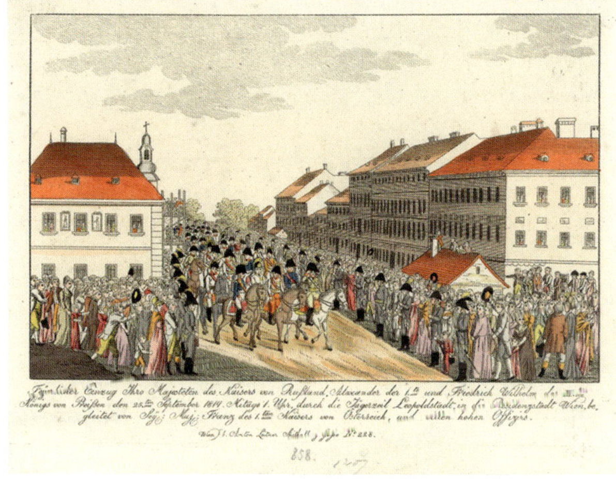





**275** Unknown artist
*The entry of Empress Maria Feodorovna
of Russia in Vienna 1814,* 1814
Etching, hand-coloured, sheet: 25.9 × 36.8 cm
Wien Museum

**276** Unknown artist
*Ceremonial entry of Monarchs Alexander I
and Frederick William III on 25 September 1814
in Vienna,* 1814
Copper engraving, coloured, sheet: 22.8 × 34.6 cm
Wien Museum

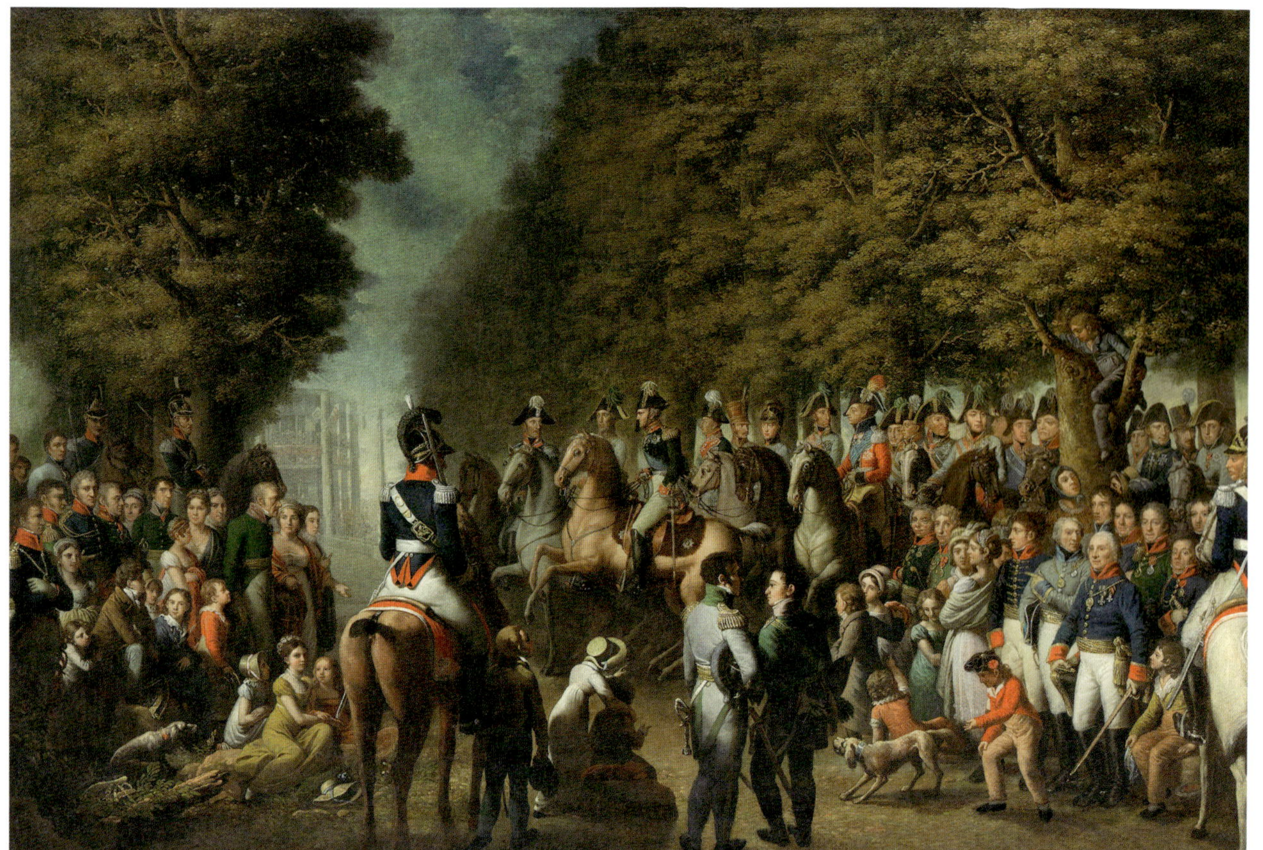

**274** Unknown artist
*The military festival in the Prater
on 18 October 1814,* 1814
Oil on canvas, 102 × 159 cm
Wien Museum

**176** Franz Wolf (1795–1859), lithographer
*Empfang der verbündeten Monarchen
in Wien 1814 anlässlich des Wiener
Kongresses,* 1833
Reception of the Allied Monarchs
in Vienna in 1814 on the occasion
of the Congress of Vienna
Lithograph, sheet: 45.8 × 58.6 cm
Vienna, Österreichische Nationalbiblio-
thek, Picture Archives and Graphics
Department

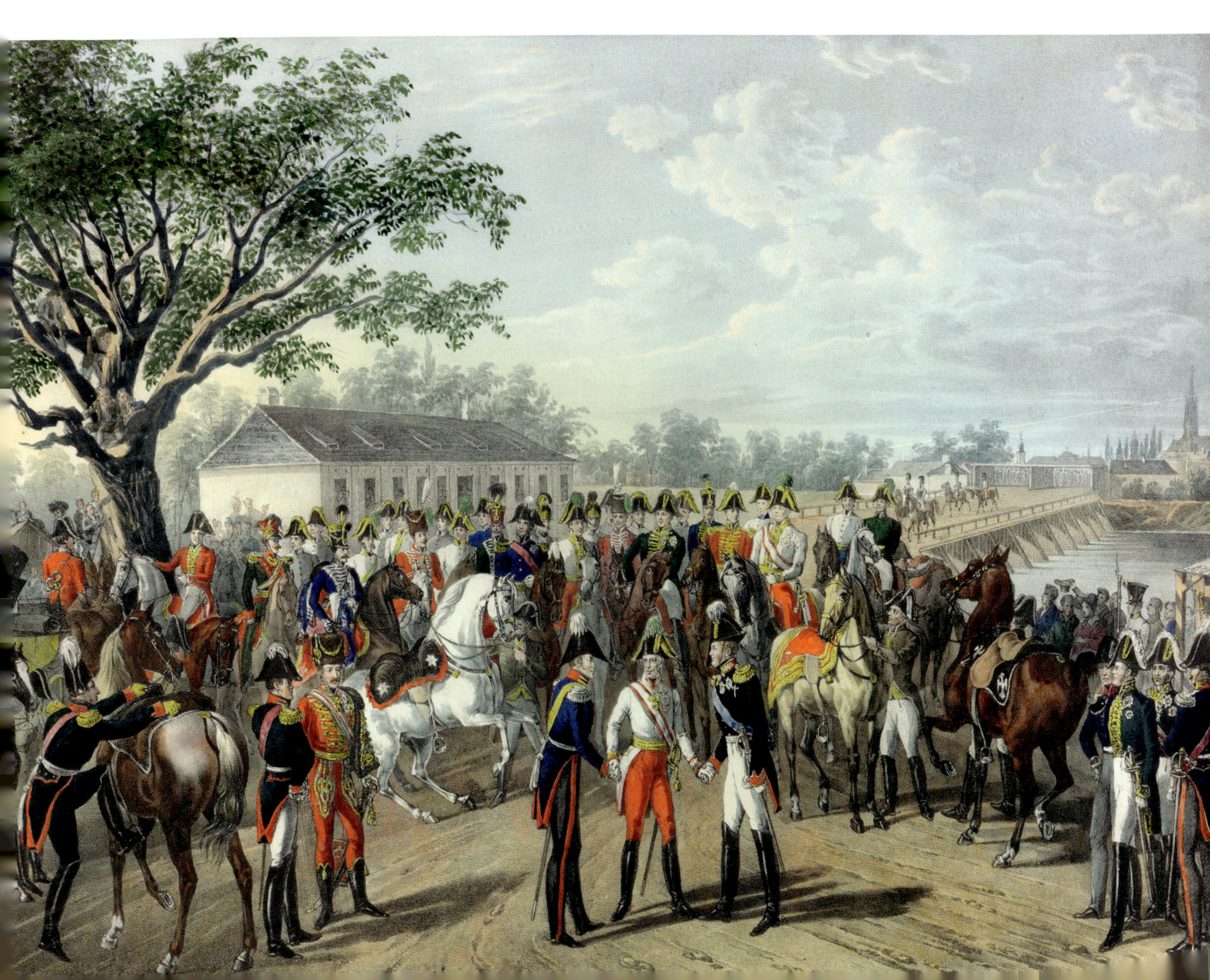

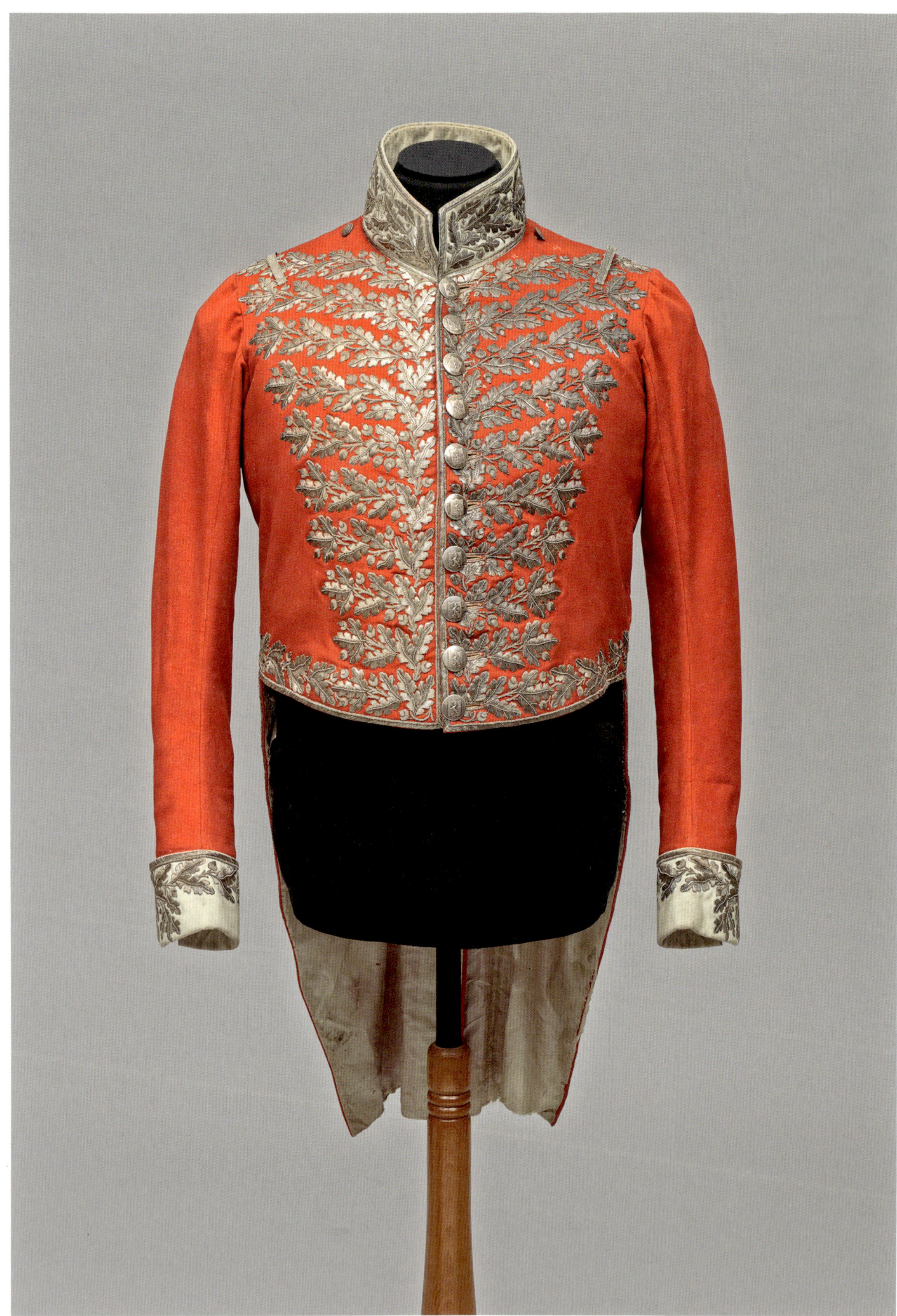



**9** Dress coat of the gala uniform
of a Bohemian Landstand, 1800–49
KHM-Museumsverband, Kaiserliche Wagenburg/
Department of Court Uniforms

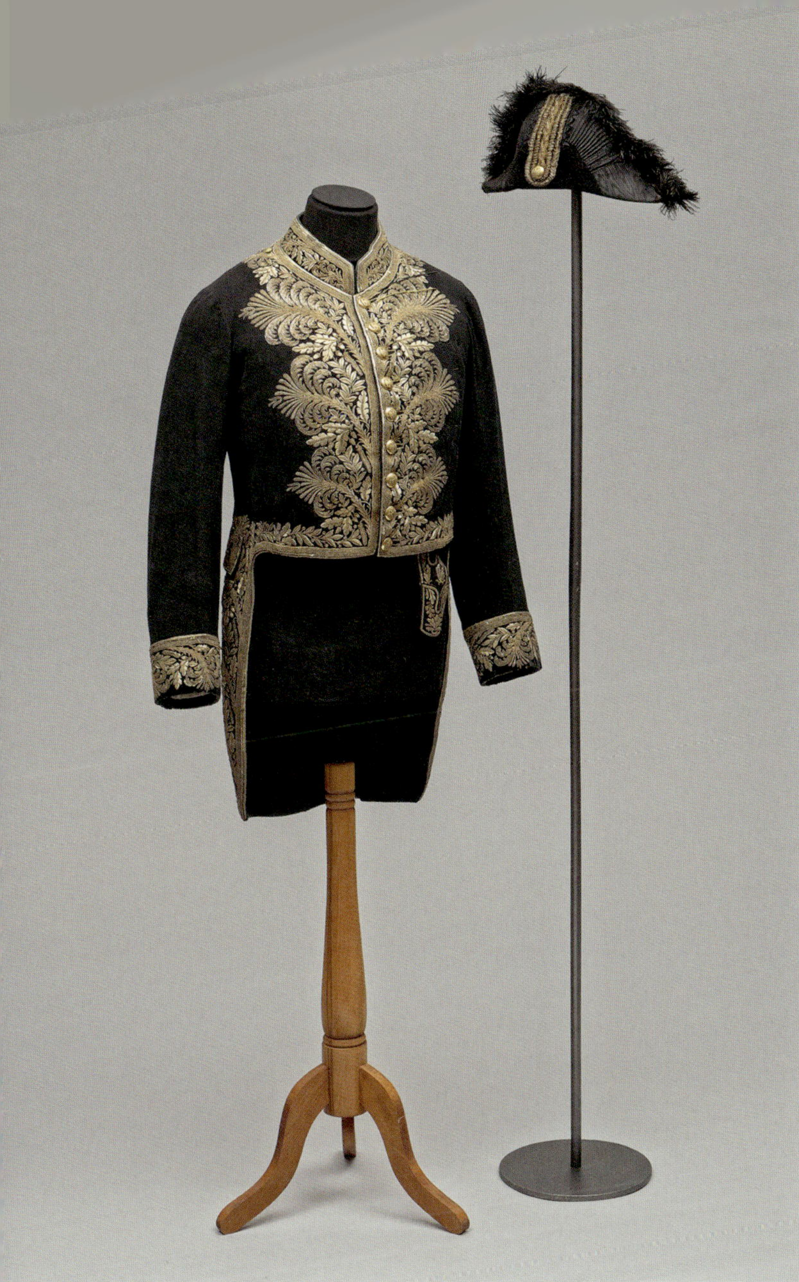





**10** Andreas Alkens, court gold embroiderer (design)
Anton Uzel & Sohn (production)
Dress coat of the gala uniform of an imperial
and royal privy councillor
KHM-Museumsverband, Kaiserliche Wagenburg/
Department of Court Uniforms

**11** Bicorn of a gala uniform of an imperial
and royal privy councillor
KHM-Museumsverband, Kaiserliche Wagenburg/
Department of Court Uniforms

**13** State dress coat, so-called Rococo dress coat,
and Habit à la française, c. 1815
KHM-Museumsverband, Kaiserliche Wagenburg/
Department of Court Uniforms

**14** Waistcoat for state dress coat, so-called
Rococo dress coat, and Habit à la française, c. 1815
KHM-Museumsverband, Kaiserliche Wagenburg/
Department of Court Uniforms

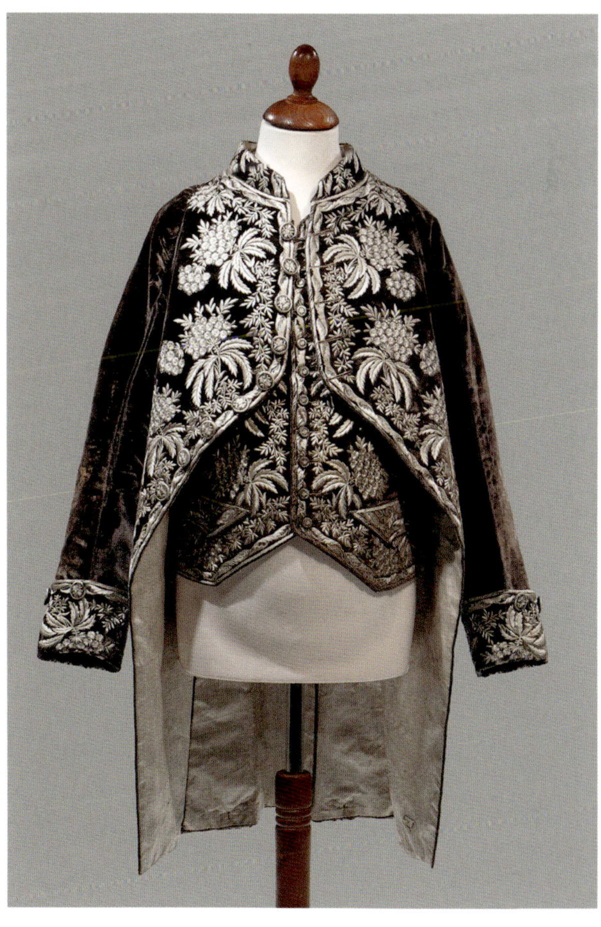

# The Magic

## Dress Codes and the Spread Uniforms

Monica Kurzel-Runtscheiner

# *of the Uniform.*

## *Fashion Dictates of Civilian through the Congress of Vienna*

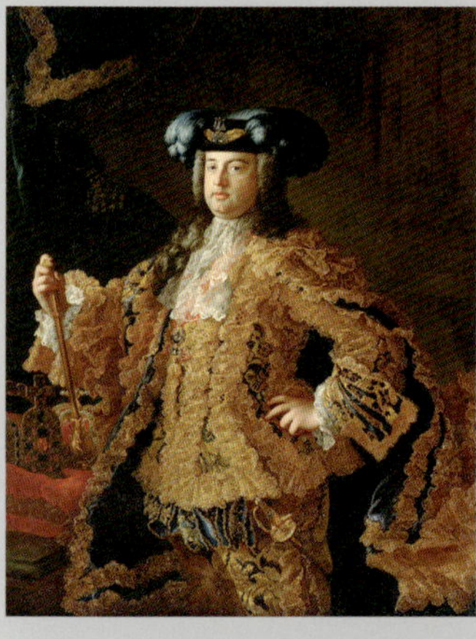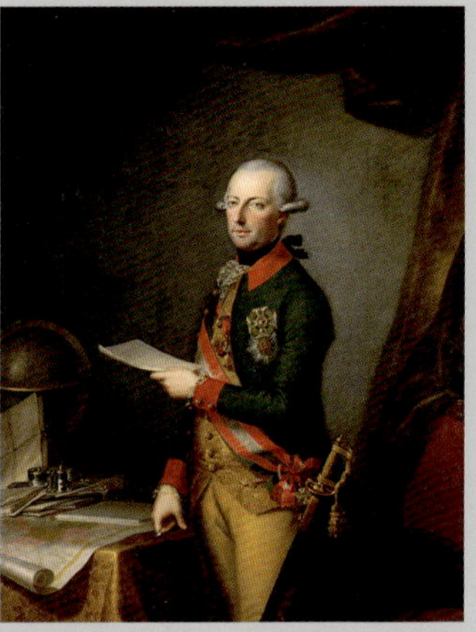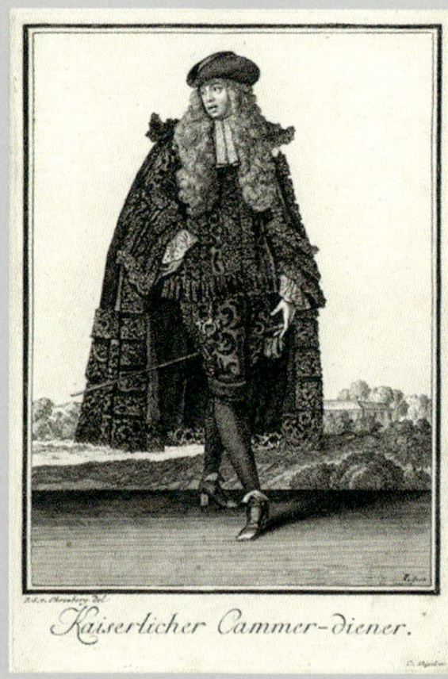



In the ancient régime, Europe's population was ascribed to hierarchically organised groups or 'estates': The nobility in its various gradations formed the apex of the social pyramid; the bourgeoisie found itself in the middle with state and university staff, merchants and craftsmen; and the base consisted of peasants, servants and day labourers. Women were assigned the status of their fathers or husbands. The external sign of the respective civil status was clothing, whose designs were regulated by special laws, so-called dress codes. Thus, visible symbols strictly demarcated the various statuses: For example, a wealthy merchant must forgo those luxury items reserved exclusively for the nobility – even though he had the means to acquire them. Through clothing, one could recognise a person's status and proper behaviour towards that person. Transgressions violated public order and were punished accordingly.[1]

The triumph of the Enlightenment encouraged challenges to this estates-based system throughout Europe, which would lead to a new social consciousness that depended less on factors such as birth or occupation and more on an individual's income and education. Consequently, clothing also expressed the new social order: By around 1750, dress codes disappeared and, for the first time, there was such a thing as an individual international fashion, where anyone who could afford it could wear it. The advent of fashion magazines spread, at unprecedented speed, the latest trends across the continent.[2]

In men's fashion, the courtier no longer served as a model: His magnificent, almost feminine-looking clothes | Fig. 1 | belied the new ideal of masculinity, which orientated itself towards antiquity's athletic man, believed to be reflected in a simple and functionally dressed soldier. Even rulers now appeared on official occasions primarily in military uniform, | Fig. 2 | and the suggested model for civilians became the simply dressed English country gentleman.[3] In 1766, Emperor Joseph II (1741–1790) abolished the 'Spanish mantle dress', the century-old garment of the court, | Fig. 3 | and so the male nobility lost its last visually distinguishing feature. Officers from noble families now always appeared at court in military uniform. The other courtly gentlemen had to appear in the most splendid, fashionable garments, which, however, could be worn by any citizen.[4] Suddenly,



Monica Kurzel-Runtscheiner

**Fig. 1** Martin van Meytens the Younger (1695–1770) *Duke/Emperor Francis I of Lorraine (1708–1765), in a Spanish mantle dress,* after 1745 Oil on canvas, 150 × 117 cm KHM-Museumsverband, Picture Gallery

**Fig. 2** Joseph Hickel (1736–1807) *Emperor Joseph II (1741–1790) in military uniform with red lapel, a globe and map,* c. 1785 Oil on canvas, 152 × 115 KHM-Museumsverband, Picture Gallery

**Fig. 3** after Peter Schubert von Ehrenberg (b. 1668) Caspar Luyken (1672–1708), engraver *Courtier in a Spanish mantle dress, Nuremberg,* 1703 Copperplate engraving, coloured, sheet: 32.2 × 20.2 cm KHM-Museumsverband, Kaiserliche Wagenburg Wien, Department of Court Uniforms

**Fig. 4** Wardrobe book of Prince Johann Wenzel II of Paar, 1795 Cover: c. 26 × 37.5 cm KHM-Museumsverband, Kaiserliche Wagenburg Wien

**Fig. 5** Design for the gala uniform of a member of the higher nobility of Lower Austria, 1811 Watercolour St. Pölten, niederösterreichisches Landesarchiv

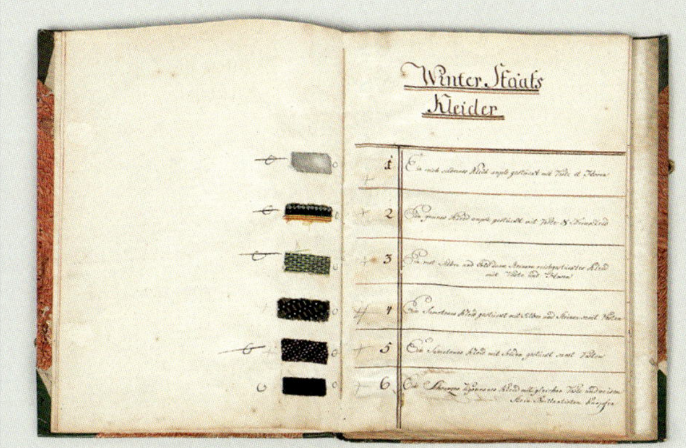 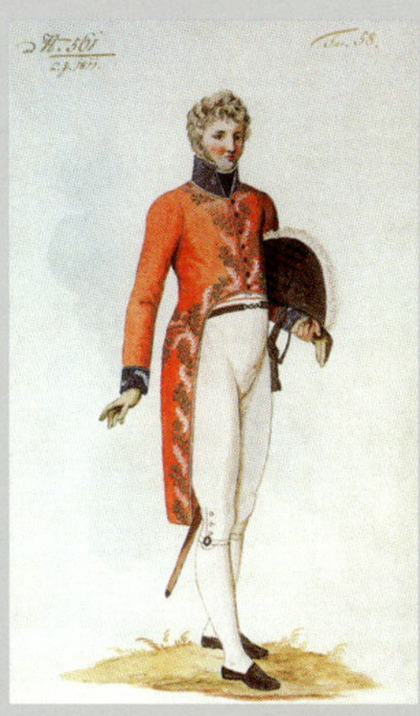

an aristocrat's clothes could be surpassed in modernity, beauty and exclusivity by those of a rich citizen. Those who wanted to express their prominence through clothing, therefore, had to spend enormous sums of money: The Austrian prince Johann Wenzel II von Paar (1744–1812), for instance, had a wardrobe in 1795 containing about 300 articles, which allowed for several hundred combinations and thus ensured that he would never suffer the embarrassment of appearing twice in the same outfit.[5] | Fig. 4 | Because only a few could participate in such a luxury, the fashion dictate became a real problem for those civilians who could not afford the extensive wardrobe required to participate in public and social life. The military, however, had the advantage that they were always adequately dressed in their magnificent uniforms at no great expense; they could show their rank and the associated prestige, and, moreover, they aroused the admiration of the ladies. All this led to many male civilians also wanting to benefit from the 'magic of the uniform'. From the 1770s on, the press had a lively debate on creating civilian uniforms that were actually introduced in various states in the last quarter of the eighteenth century.[6] In addition to various state officials, the nobility also received their own uniforms in many principalities. The Duchy of Westphalia justified this step in 1785 by noting that those who could not afford to follow in the ever-changing international fashion had increasingly become the target of ridicule.[7]

In Vienna, these developments were followed with interest[8] and, here too, voices were soon heard suggesting uniforms for civilian men.[9] That this did not happen was mainly due to political reasons: from 1789 onwards, the main impulses for the development of civilian uniforms came from the archenemy France, which, of course, did not qualify as a role model.[10] Only when the army of Napoleon (1769–1821) had already overrun large parts of the Habsburg Empire did Emperor Franz I (1768–1835) fulfil the long-cherished wishes of his nobility for uniforms, in order to gain their loyalty in the face of the crisis: | Page 147, Fig. 5 | The respective decrees expressly emphasised that these 'robes of honour' were a reward for the 'proven loyalty and strong allegiance to the Prince and the Fatherland' at the time of the 'presence of the enemy'.[11] The state officials' wishes for uniforms were, however, still ignored. Exceptions existed only for those, such as diplomats, who regularly dealt with dignitaries of other states and as a figurehead of the empire, therefore, needed appropriate clothing.[12] | Page 148, Fig. 8 | Only after Napoleon's defeat in 1814 and the decision to negotiate the now necessary reorganisation of Europe at a grand 'princely meeting' in Vienna did Emperor Franz abandon his opposition to uniforms for male civilians. With good reason: At this gathering of all political decisionmakers, later known as the 'Congress of Vienna', the emperor wanted to rebuild his battered reputation and assert his position as one of Europe's most important monarchs. He therefore gave the order to comprehensively restore Vienna, which had been severely damaged by decades of war, and to prepare numerous 'festivals appropriate to the dignity of the illustrious guests and the theme of celebration'.[13] To give these events the appropriate

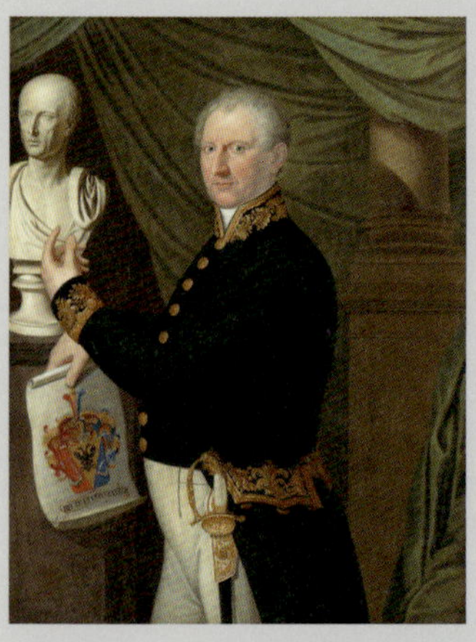 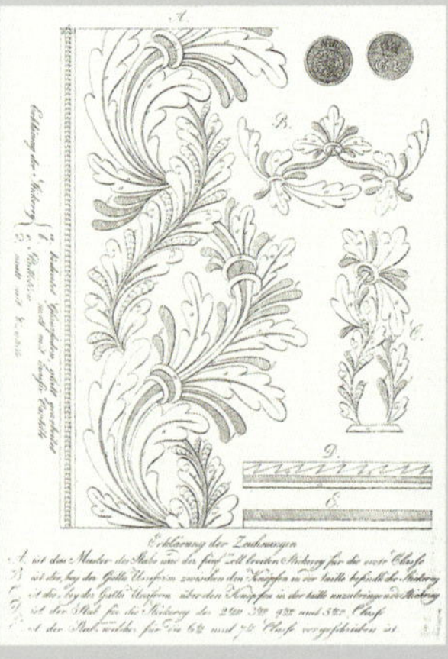 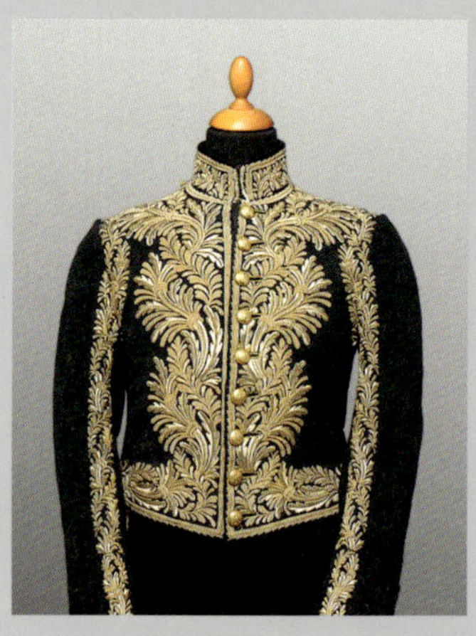

splendour, they needed many local visitors. The population was, however, so impoverished by wars and state bankruptcy that it was feared that even nobles and dignitaries would stay away from the festivals if they could not afford the necessary wardrobe. Thus, the emperor decreed that not only officials[14] and household servants,[15] but also the high-ranking dignitaries[16] should now immediately receive uniforms. For this group especially, which played a particularly important role in the countless festivals and ceremonies, it was a great financial relief not to have new, expensive gala garments made for every occasion, but instead to make appearances in the same luxuriant court uniforms. Thus, it was hoped that 'authorising court uniforms, in the presence of the foreign sovereigns, would result in more numerous appearances at court, and would therefore greatly enhance its splendour'.[17]

Like with diplomats some years earlier, now courtiers and civil servants received sumptuous dark-green cloth frock coats decorated with rich gold or silver embroidery. | Fig. 6 | The embroidery's pattern indicated to which professional or functional group the person belonged, while the luxuriance and breadth of the decoration indicated his rank within the respective hierarchy.[18] Hastily, thousands of new uniforms were made in Vienna and provided with the decorations designed by court embroiderer Andreas Alckens. | Page 149, Fig. 7 | When the congress started in September 1814, the court and officials were already beaming in their new uniforms and, as hoped, participated in the various festivities in large numbers.

Aristocratic civilians appeared either in their red estates uniforms introduced a few years previously | Page 148 | or in the brand-new, gold-embroidered chamberlain's dress coat. | Page 140 | Whoever was neither a member of the nobility nor chamberlain wore a so-called *habit à la française* with rich silk embroidery. | Page 149 | Together with the picturesque national garments of the Hungarians and the beautiful military uniforms of the victorious armies, they formed a splendid ensemble that aroused general admiration at balls, parades and other festivities. The satirical magazine *Eipeldauer* reported that at the large ball in the Vienna Hofburg the many hundreds of embroidered uniforms, which were richly decked out with gold and silver, shone as if all the stars had fallen from the firmament.[19] The ladies' robes, mostly white and markedly simple, appeared almost modest in contrast to this pomp. At the big festivals, female guests could make a mark, above all, with the lavish use of jewels and long 'court trains' made of colourful silk that were uncommon elsewhere.[20] Viennese tailors were able to produce, within a few hours, such trains to be attached over the dress for foreign ladies.[21]

The emperor's calculation to impress his powerful guests with generous hospitality, extraordinary festivals and a splendid royal household was more than successful: Even the spoiled Tsar Alexander I (1777-1825) emphasised repeatedly that he had never experienced anything like it.[22] Furthermore, along with its political significance, the Congress also became a catalyst for disseminating new trends and ideas.[23] On the one hand, the masses of foreigners of various

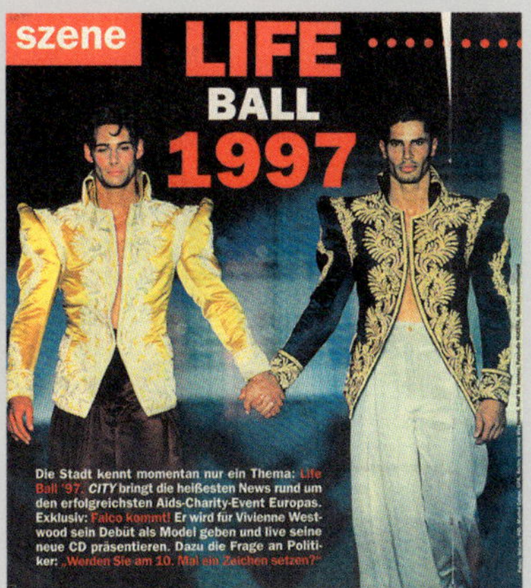



**Fig. 6** Unknown artist
*Portrait of Ignaz Grill Edler
of Warimfeld, Kanzleidirektor
of the Oberststallmeisteramt,
in the court official's uniform
introduced in 1814,* Austria c. 1830
Oil on canvas (?), 118 × 90.2 cm
KHM-Museumsverband,
Kaiserliche Wagenburg Wien

**Fig. 7** Embroidery pattern
for officials of the Kingdom
of Hanover, London 1816
KHM-Museumsverband,
Kaiserliche Wagenburg Wien/
Department of Court Uniforms

**Fig. 8** Dress coat of the gala
uniform of an imperial and royal
ambassador with the 'on all the
seams' embroidery introduced
in 1810, c. 1900
KHM-Museumsverband,
Kaiserliche Wagenburg Wien/
Department of Court Uniforms

**Fig. 9** Vivienne Westwood (b 1941)
*Life Ball 1097: Dress coats*
by Vivienne Westwood with
the pattern designed for
ambassador uniforms in 1810
In *CITY – Stadtzeitung für Wien,*
no. 12/1997 (21.3.–27.3.), p. 16

origins who spent months in Vienna brought their fashionable characteristics, and on the other hand, they eagerly accepted everything new. The English attracted special attention since they had long been isolated by the continental blockade and therefore had developed fashions and behaviours that seemed strange to the rest of Europeans. While the robes of the ladies looked ridiculous, the plain garments of the English gentlemen were admired and imitated. [24] | Pages 125, 126 | They, in turn, were drawn to the magnificent, gold-embroidered uniforms of the Viennese court, which meant that Count Ernst Friedrich Herbert zu Münster (1766–1839), who had travelled to the Congress as representative of the prince regent, had committed something akin to 'industrial espionage': In 1816, he introduced civilian uniforms in Hanover whose embroidery patterns were practically identical to those designed by the Viennese court embroiderer Alckens for Austrian diplomats and officials of the state chancellery. [25] | Figs. 7, 8 | In a slightly modified form, they are still in use today at the English royal court. [26] Although Austria's emperor had long resisted the introduction of civilian uniforms, the Congress of Vienna ultimately helped them break through across Europe. [27] With their splendour and diversity, they enriched the appearance of most major centres for about 100 years, until they disappeared almost everywhere at the end of the First World War. However, one of the uniforms had a long afterlife: At the Vienna Life Ball in 1997, Vivienne Westwood sent two models in frock coats on the catwalk, | Fig. 9 | whose splendid embroidery 'on all the seams' had been designed by Andreas Alckens in 1810 as a gala uniform for Austrian ambassadors. [28] | Fig. 8 | Thus, a uniform that was originally designed to curtail fashionable luxury was ultimately an inspiration for luxurious fashion.

1   For dress codes in the German-speaking countries, see Liselotte Constanze Eisenbart, *Kleiderordnungen der deutschen Städte zwischen 1350 und 1700: Ein Beitrag zur Kulturgeschichte des deutschen Bürgertums,* Göttingen/Berlin/Frankfurt am Main, 1962 (=Göttinger Bausteine zur Geschichtswissenschaft; 32). Various ambassadors' reports show that they were not always as ineffective as assumed here; see *Venetianische Depeschen vom Kaiserhofe (Dispacci di Germania),* Historical Commission of the Imperial Academy of Science, Alfred Francis Pribram (ed.), 2. dept., vol. 1, Vienna 1901, 229, 5 April 1659. Franz Christoph von Khevenhüller, *Annales Ferdinandei,* 14 vols, Leipzig 1721–26, vol. 1., 17, col. 61–62, 1578.

2   The *Journal des Luxus und der Moden,* which from 1786 appeared in slightly varying titles, was the leading journal in the German-speaking world.

3   Elisabeth Hackspiel-Mikosch, 'Stärke, Macht, Eleganz – Die Uniform als Symbol eines neuen Ideals von Männlichkeit', in *Nach Rang und Stand, Deutsche Ziviluniformen im 19. Jahrhundert,* exh. cat. Deutsches Textilmuseum, Krefeld 2002, pp. 15–27, here p. 16.

4   On the abolishment of the dress coat, see Monica Kurzel-Runtscheiner, 'Im Anfang war das "Mantelkleid". Zur Entwicklung der Ziviluniform in Österreich,' *Zeitschrift der Gesellschaft für historische Waffen- und Kostümkunde,* 47.1 (2005), pp. 25–42.

5   Wardrobe book of Prince Johann Wenzel II von Paar, 1795 (Kaiserliche Wagenburg Wien, inv. no. Z 287/007)

6   On the debate about uniforms, see Peter Albrecht, 'Die Nationaltrachtsdebatte im letzten Viertel des 18. Jahrhunderts', in *Jahrbuch für Volkskunde,* 10 (1987), pp. 43–66. Also Peter Albrecht, 'Die Schwedische Nationaltracht Gustav des III. in der deutschsprachigen Publizistik', *Jahrbuch für Volkskunde,* 15 (1992), pp. 177–206. On the introduction of civil uniforms in various imperial principalities, see Krefeld 2002 (as in note 3), pp. 66, 75, 145. In 1777, courtiers in Sardinia received civil uniforms upon their own request, see Marzia Cataldi Gallo, *Fasti della Burocrazia: Uniformi civili e di corte dei secoli XVIII–XIX,* Genoa 1984, pp. 19, 118f. In Russia, civil servants of the governments were given uniforms in 1782; see *Neues St. Petersburgisches Journal: vom Jahre 1784,* pp. 315–23.

7   Alheidis von Rohr, 'Zur Wahrung des Standes – Die Uniformen der deutschen Ritterschaften', in Krefeld 2002, (as in note 3), p. 146.

8   The *Wiener Diarium* repeatedly reported about the various debates on uniforms and took great note of the introduction of estates-based court uniforms in Sweden. See Albrecht 1992 (as in note 6), notes 2, 25, 28, 30. Justus Möser's *Patriotische Phantasien,* published in 1780, in which he also republished his treatise written in 1772 'Über die Vortheile einer allgemeinen Landesuniform' are still available in the private library of the imperial family (Fideikomiss-Bibliothek, now property of the Austrian National Library Vienna).

9   R- u- ff., *Gedanken über die Kleidertracht in Wien, und mir gutscheinende Kleiderordnung,* Weigandische Buchhandlung am Graben, Vienna 1781. *Bemerkungen über das Projekt einer neuen Kleidungs Ordnung in Wien, welche künftiges Jahr 1787 beobachtet werden soll,* Vienna 1786.

10   Madeleine Delpierre, 'Une Révolution en trois temps', in *Modes & Révolutions,* 1780–1804, exh. cat. Palais Galiera, Paris 1989, pp. 11–39. Jean-Marc Devocelle, 'D'un costume politique à une politique du costume', in Paris 1989, pp. 83–103.

11   Decree for the Carinthian Estates, 26 March 1808, Kärntner Landesarchiv, Gubernium Graz, fasc. 48. There were almost identical formulations also for the Lower Austrian Estates in 1806/07 and the Moravian Estates in 1807.

12   In 1810, in addition to diplomats, the relatives of the Geheime Hof- und Staatskanzlei were also given uniforms; see Kurzel-Runtscheiner 2005, (as in note 4), p. 33.

13   Österreichische Nationalbibliothek, Vienna, manuscript collection, cod. ser. no. 12158, Johann Baptist Skall, *Memorabilien vom Königs-Congresse zu Wien im Jahre 1814 und 1815,* T. 1 and 2, 1825, fol. 15v. On renovations, preparations of festivities and logistics of the congress, see Monica Kurzel-Runtscheiner in *Der Kongress fährt: Leihwagen, Lustfahrten und Luxus-Outfits am Wiener Kongress 1814/15,* exh. cat. Kaiserliche Wagenburg Wien, Vienna 2014.

14   *Vorschrift für die von Sr. k.k. Majestät sämmtlichen Staatsbeamten bewilligte Uniform,* from the kaiserlich-königlichen Hof- und Staatsdruckerey, Vienna 1814.

15   Haus-, Hof- und Staatsarchiv Wien, Vienna (in the following: HHStA), Obersthofmeisteramt, documents, column 18, carton 568, from 1849, regulation from 11 September 1814.

16   HHStA, OMeA, Staatskanzlei, Interiora fasc. 86, 'Uniformierung', regulation from 1 July 1814.

17   HHStA, OMeA, 1814, carton 200, no. 38, 245–48; 24 June 1814.

18   For a detailed description of the uniforming of wide sections of the Austrian civil public in 1814 and in the process the underlying, symbolic, formal language, see Kurzel-Runtscheiner 2005 (as in note 4), pp. 33–37.

19   *Der Wiener Kongress, 1. September 1814 bis 9. Juni 1815,* Walter Koschatzky, Bundesministerium für Unterricht, Verein der Museumsfreunde (ed.), exh. cat. Hofburg-Kaiserappartements, Vienna 1965, p. 248 (*Eipeldauer,* 1815, no. 2, pp. 14f.). Likewise, Anna Eynard on 19 October 1814, in Benoît Challand, Alexandre Dafflon et al. (eds), *Jean de Montenach, Anna Eynard-Lullin. Journaux du Congrès. Vienne 1814–1815, Archives de la Société d'histoire du canton de Fribourg,* Fribourg 2015, p. 204.

20   Commentaries and comparisons between men's and women's clothing are to be found in, among others: Henrich Graf zu Stolberg-Wernigerode, *Tagebuch über meinen Aufenthalt in Wien zur Zeit des Congresses: Vom 9. September 1814 bis zum April 1815,* revised by Doris Derdey, edited by Boje Schmuhl, Dössel 2004, pp. 34, 142. In addition, see Richard Bright, *Travels from Vienna through Lower Hungary: with Some Remarks on the State of Vienna During the Congress, in the Year 1814,* Edinburgh 1818, pp. 17f., and *Carl Bertuchs Tagebuch vom Wiener Kongreß,* Hermann von Egloffstein (ed.), Berlin 1916, pp. 79f., 108.

21   Challand and Dafflon 2015 (as in note 19), entry of Anna Eynard on 23 December 1814, p. 267.

22   At the Congress in Vienna, the extensive spying also reported on sovereign guests. In the protocols, one can repeatedly find statements of the Tsar which verify his enthusiasm for the emperor's hospitality and the splendour of the congress; see August Fournier, *Die Geheimpolizei auf dem Wiener Kongress,* Vienna 1913, pp. 44, 154. In addition, see also Kurzel-Runtscheiner 2014 (as in note 13), p. 34.

23   Thus, the *corporate identity,* developed for the imperial fleet of vehicles of the Congress of Vienna, was adopted by numerous European princely courts after 1815 (Kurzel-Runtscheiner 2014, pp. 14–18).

24   *Journal für Literatur, Kunst, Luxus und Mode,* November 1814, pp. 738f. ('Modebericht aus Wien').

**25**  Regulation for the 'sämmtliche
Civil-Staats-Diener Unsers Königsreichs
Hannover', enacted by Ernst Count of
Münster in the name of the prince regent,
Carlton House, 12 November 1816. The added
embroidery patterns matched those of
the uniform regulation of 1810 for Austrian
diplomats and members of the state chancel-
lery (HHStA, OMeA, Staatskanzlei, Interiora,
fasc. 86, 'Uniformierung', 169–90): Those
designs enclosed may be from Andreas
Alckens, who at least received an 'accord'
with a detailed breakdown of prices for the
manufacture of the embroideries (ibid.,
chancery regulation from 30 November 1810).
It can be assumed that the same patterns
were also used as models for those court
uniforms which the prince regent introduced
for his court and which are therefore pre-
cursors of the British uniforms still in use
today. See Valerie Cumming, *Royal Dress:
The Image and the Reality 1580 to the
Present Day*, London 1989, pp. 88f.;
in addition, see *The Annual Register for
the Year 1817*, London 1818, pp. 100f.

**26**  See description and illustration in
*Dress and Insignia worn at His Majesty's
Court, Issued with the Authority of the
Lord Chamberlain*, London 1921.

**27**  Among the countries which intro-
duced civil uniforms from 1815 onwards
were the Netherlands, Sweden and
Sardinia; cf. Philip Mansel, *Dressed to
Rule: Royal and Court Costume from
Louis XIV to Elizabeth II*, Essex 2005, p. 98.

**28**  The uniform was shown in the exhibition *Costumes à la Cour de Vienne* in Paris
a year previously. See *Costumes à la Cour
de Vienne, 1815–1918*, Odile Briot, Georg
J. Kugler, Monica Kurzel-Runtscheiner (eds),
exh. cat. Palais Galliera, Musée de la Mode
de la ville de Paris, Paris 1995, p. 80.

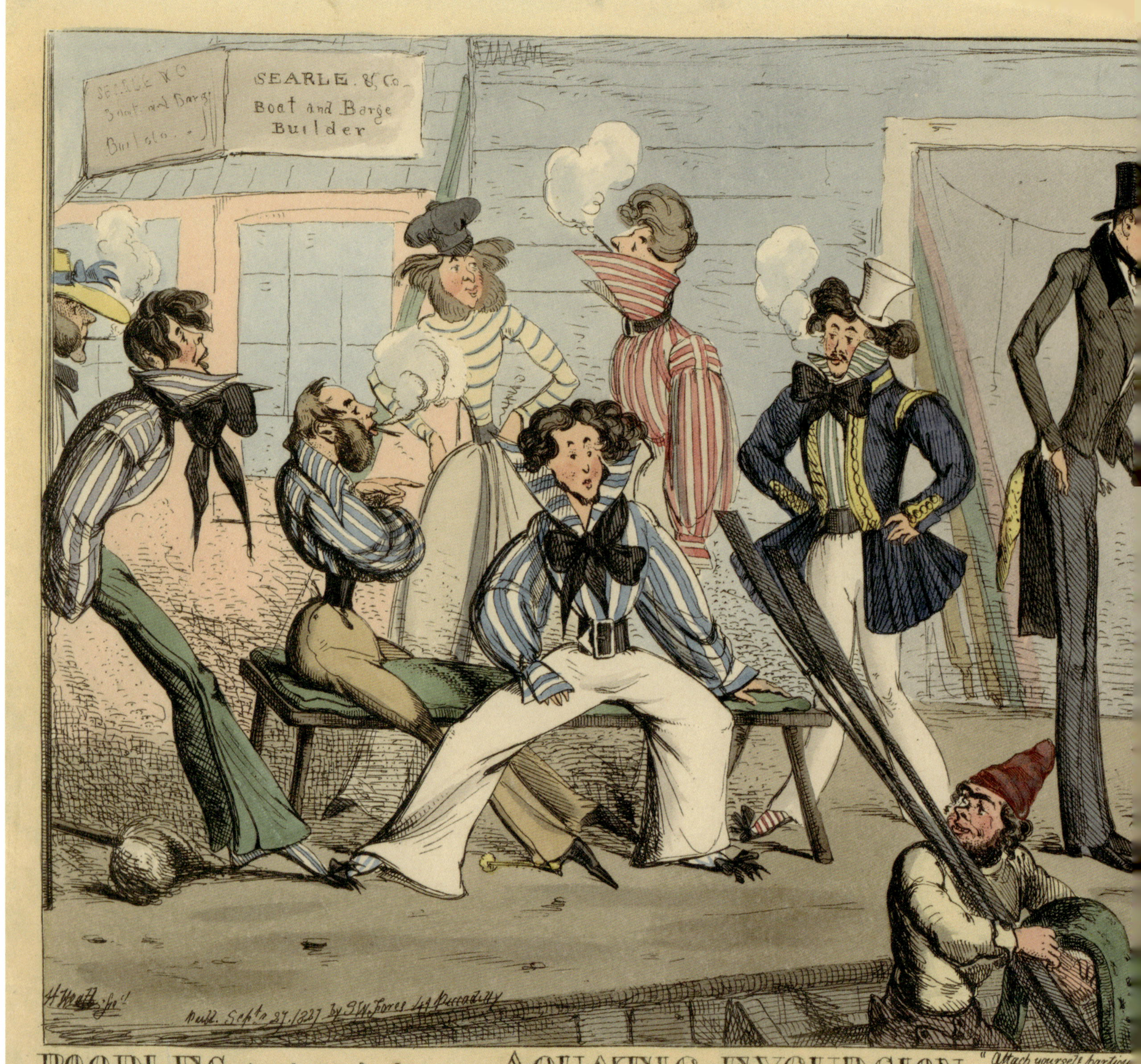


**169** William Heath (1795–1840)
*Poodles preparing for an aquatic excursion,*
27 September 1827
Etching, hand-coloured with watercolours,
sheet: 23.9 × 33.6 cm
Staatliche Museen zu Berlin,
Kunstbibliothek

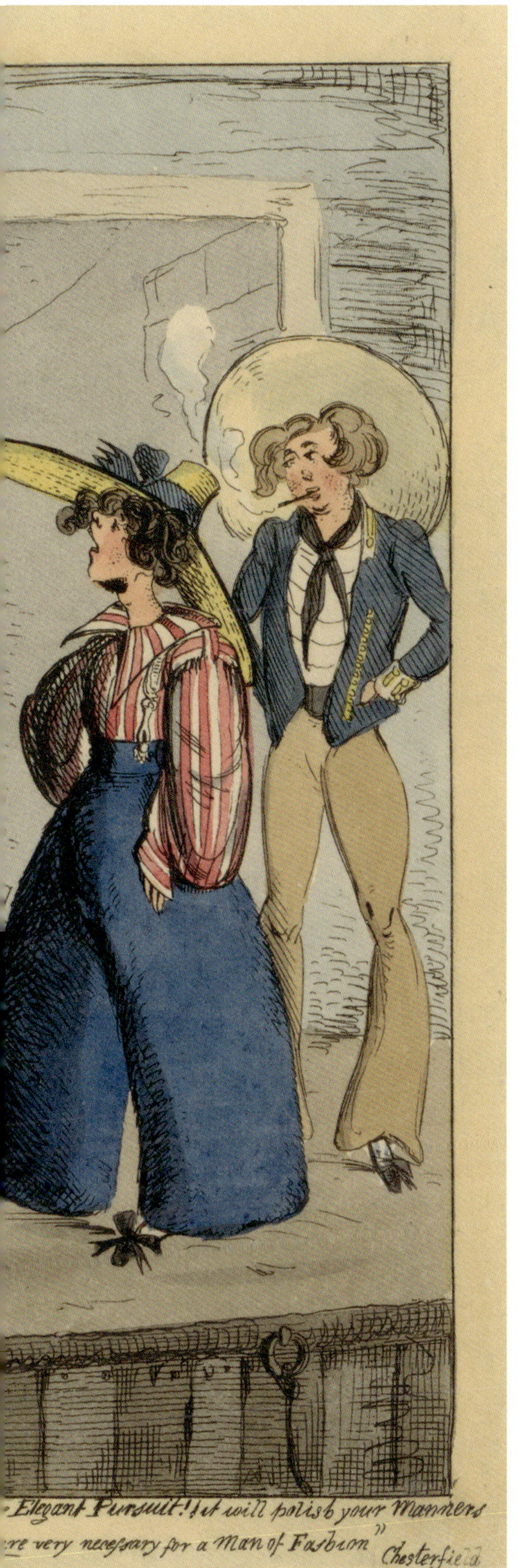


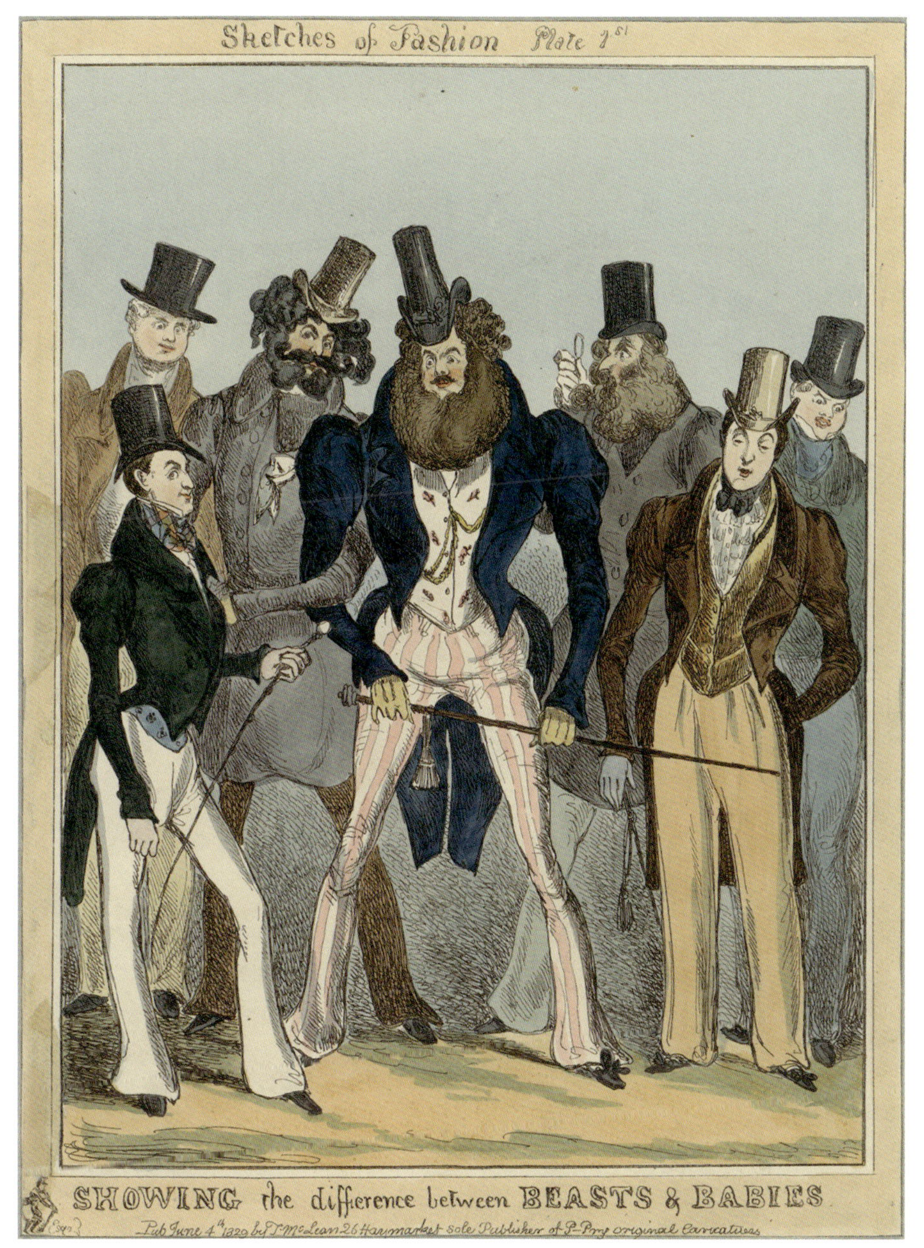




**277** Unknown artist
*Showing the difference between
beasts & babies,* 4 June 1829
Etching, hand-coloured with watercolours,
sheet: 33.8 × 24.2 cm
Staatliche Museen zu Berlin, Kunstbibliothek

# The Import-Being

*Inessa Kouteinikova*

# ance of
# a Dandy

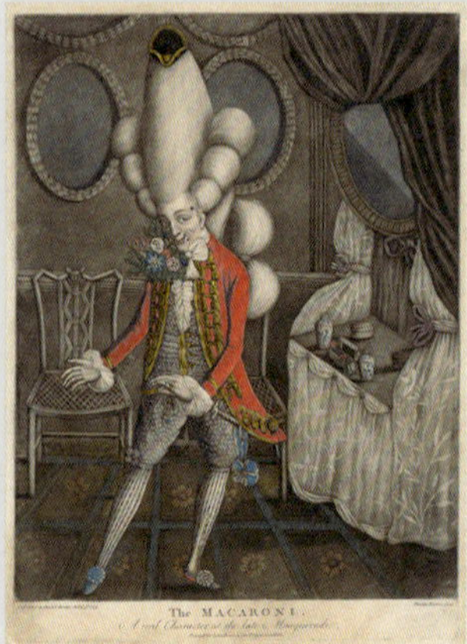

**106** Philip Dawe (1750–1790)
John Bowles, publisher
*The macaroni. A real character
at the late masquerade,* 3 July 1773
Mezzotint, coloured, sheet: 36.5 × 26.2 cm
Staatliche Museen zu Berlin,
Kunstbibliothek

Could it be that the times are now ripe for a renewed interest in the dandy, whose engagement with the history of fashion and dress code may prove to have been as ambiguous, contradictory and conflicted as our own?

We cannot begin to understand the dandy without looking back several generations to an outpouring of beautifully nuanced thinking and writing on the subject by two opposed schools of criticism, often aiming at destabilising each other's theories: the English and the French. Thomas Carlyle (1795–1881) may have been the first writer to conceive of the English aesthetical tradition in ways that unmade the dandy, suggesting that he might have no need for a pedestal. In the writings about dandyism by the French poet and journalist Charles Baudelaire (1821–1867), himself a dandy, we learn of ambitions and equivocations that lead directly and indirectly to Eugène Delacroix (1798–1863), to Edgar Allan Poe (1809–1849), to Vicomte de Valmont, the hero of Pierre Choderlos de Laclos' (1741–1803) *Les Liaisons dangereuses* (1782), and to Emma, protagonist of Gustave Flaubert's (1821–1880) *Madame Bovary* (1856). Baudelaire, whose work on dandyism often strikes readers as enamoured and ostentatious, considered writing a handbook on the topic covered by the nineteenth-century *dandys littéraires.* Though the guidebook never went to print, famous and often disparate figures such as Jules-Amédée Barbey d'Aurevilly (1808–1889), the Marquis de Custine (1790–1857) and the Vicomte de Chateaubriand (1768–1848) could have populated its pages.

So – what is a dandy? Thomas Carlyle thought he had the answer: 'A Dandy is a Clothes-wearing Man, a man whose trade, office and existence consists in the wearing of Clothes.'[1] The connection between usefulness and the dandy's idleness and fastidiousness is clarified by Carlyle's French opponent, Baudelaire: 'A dandy does nothing. To be a useful sort of man has always struck me as something utterly hideous.'[2] Baudelaire's words come far closer. Defining dandyism as an essential element of 'modern life', he characterises the dandy as a 'man, […] who has no profession other than elegance […].'[3] He instructs us further that 'Dandyism is an ill-defined social attitude as strange as duelling; it goes back a long way, since Caesar, Catilina, Alcibiades.'[4]

1    Thomas Carlyle, *Sartor Resartus. The Life and Opinions of Herr Teufelsdrökh,* New York 1846, p. 281; the novel was first published as a serial in 1833/34 in *Fraser's Magazine,* https://archive.org/details/sartorresartusli02carl [retrieved in August 2017].

2    Charles Baudelaire, http://www.nigelrodgers.co.uk/?page_id=23 [retrieved in November 2017].

3    Charles Baudelaire, 'The Dandy', in *The Painter of Modern Life,* transl. by P. E. Charvet, Paris 1863, http://www.writing.upenn.edu/library/Baudelaire_Painter-of-Modern-Life_1863.pdf [retrieved in November 2017], p. 9.



Inessa Kouteinikova

**4** Baudelaire 1863, p. 9.

**5** Oscar Wilde, *The Soul of Man under Socialism,* London 1900, p. 71, first published as an essay in *Fortnightly Review* February, London 1891.

**6** Elizabeth Amann, *Dandyism in the Age of Revolution. The Art of the Cut*, Chicago, London 2015, p. 165.

**7** Amann 2015, p. 165.

**8** Amann 2015, p. 165.

**9** Deidre Shauna Lynch, *Economy of Character. Novels, Market Culture and the Business of Inner Meaning,* Chicago, London 1998, p. 162.

**10** Ellen Moers, *The Dandy: Brummell to Beerbohm*, Lincoln and London 1978, p. 262.

Oscar Wilde (1854–1900), who was a believer in the great tradition of dandyism, also recognised the dangers incorporated in traditions – the programmatic solutions, the predictable emotions, the ready-made modes of thinking and dressing. In his remarkable essay 'The Soul of Man under Socialism' he wrote: 'The public clung with really pathetic tenacity to what I believe were the direct traditions of the Great Exhibition of international vulgarity, traditions that were so appalling that the houses in which people lived were only fit for blind people to live in. Beautiful things began to be made, beautiful colours came from the dyer's hand, beautiful patterns from the artist's brain, and the use of beautiful things and their value and importance were set forth. … And now it is almost impossible to enter any modern house without seeing some recognition of good taste, some recognition of the value of lovely surroundings, some sign of appreciation of beauty. In fact, people's houses are, as a rule, quite charming nowadays. People have been to a very great extent civilised.'[5]

### Decadence is in the air

Though little known, *downy calves* or false calves introduced by the *macaroni* in the 1770s in England were worn throughout the nineteenth century and into the early twentieth. Apparent physical strength was viewed as an equivalent of moral strength, and one could judge a man's virility from the circumference of his calves. Historian Elizabeth Amann points out how legend has it that 'the term *macaroni* derived from the upper-class youths returning from the Grand Tour who preferred Italian pasta to the hearty roast beef of British cuisine.'[6] She continues that 'these young men, who reputedly congregated at a Macaroni Club, imported not only the culinary, but also the sartorial taste of the Continent, adopting extravagant powdered hairstyles and intricately embroidered fabrics.'[7] Interestingly enough, Amann observes that the depiction of the *macaronis* in popular late eighteenth-century prints has been understood by some critics 'as an attempt to discredit aristocratic and Whig circles and particularly the opposition leader Charles James Fox (1749–1806) by associating them with an unpatriotic love of foreign luxury.'[8] | Page **162** |

The Regency dandy Beau Brummell (George Bryan Brummell, 1778–1840) located the dandy's essence in an overly conscious dress code, with those smaller touches of refinement, or 'insides of costly construction',[9] only apparent to the discerning eye of the gentleman in the know. Brummell is the kaleidoscopic product of many periods and consists of so many particles that he seems to require catalogue treatment. Barbey d'Aurevilly's 1845 biographical essay 'Du dandysme et de George Brummell' considers the subject of the dandy and Brummell's great unity in variety. He dresses his text 'as skilfully as Brummell tied his cravat'.[10] With dandyism, d'Aurevilly brings to the surface the changeable, unpredictable, roiled philosophy of the dandy. He turns the dandy into a landmark, embraced by the casual public. While no library could enable us to survey the entire story of dandyism, we can trace some influential observations in Lord Byron's (1788–1824) essays and novels, which gave

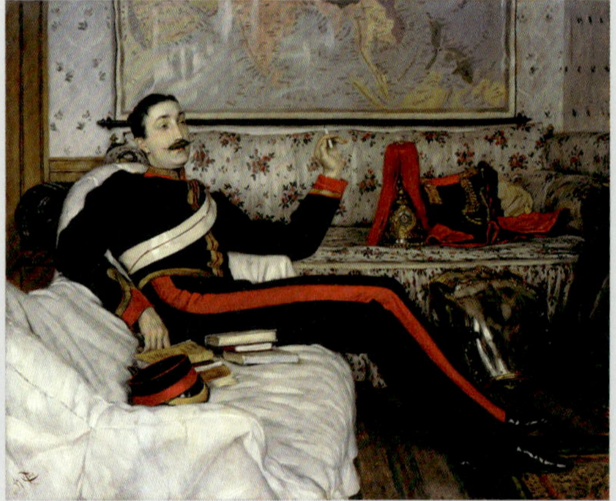



the dandy a central place in his critique of contemporary culture. Byron, whom Barbey d'Aurevilly describes as the 'solar plexus' of the nineteenth century, was still in his twenties when first celebrated as a dandy and a poet of decadence. His obscure aristocratic birth offered new opportunities to explore his power and influence as they resonate through history. In his poems, dandyism had reached a point of historical reckoning, taking into account precedent, genealogy and chronology – all the more reason to press for a reconsideration of the tradition beginning with Byron. His early epic poem *Childe Harold's Pilgrimage* (1812) circulated in high societies from foggy Albion to the Russian Empire, as a saga of a world-weary young man whose conflicted dependence on grandiosity and pleasure comes to an end. Byron celebrated the dandy as an embodiment of the Apollonian order, while embracing his demonic forces as the avatar of a new age. The new dandy, 'the Byronic hero', was born in myriad creative forms and artistic languages.

## How is the dandy depicted?

'There exist only three beings worthy of our respect: the priest, the warrior and poet,'[11] Baudelaire instructs us. |Fig. 1| Elements of all three can be glimpsed in the dandy, who created from them something utterly new: himself. Dandyism involves a complex range of visions, tastes and life styles. Being a dandy is an art form, lifestyle, philosophy or a psychological disorder – there are men who simply could not have existed in any other way. Baudelaire described it as an 'aristocratic superiority of [the] mind … the burning desire to create a personal form of originality'.[12]

To engage with questions about what defines dandies, in a way that goes beyond the traditional focus on the dandies of the Victorian and Edwardian era within the French-English circles, we might start by asking how artistic styles and epochs link in and through dandyism and what affective power it has on art. Is the dandy a vehicle for – dandyism even a form of – style? How can the dandy function in relation to style in artistic practice? The connection between the reigning norms of dress and how they are echoed in their

11   Charles Baudelaire quoted in Stephen Jay Gould, *The Structure of Evolutionary Theory,* Cambridge, Massachusetts and London 2002, p. 169.

12   Baudelaire 1863, p. 10.

13   See also Aileen Ribeiro's essay in the present publication, p. 116–24.

14   Aileen Ribeiro, *The Art of Dress: Fashion in England and France 1750 to 1820,* New Haven 1995 and 'Some Evidence of the Influence of the Dress of the Seventeenth Century on Costume in Eighteenth-Century Female Portraiture', *The Burlington Magazine,* 119.897 (1977), pp. 832, 834–40.

15   Giovanni Pietro Bellori, *The Lives of the Modern Painters, Sculptors and Architects (Le vite de' pittori, scultori et architetti moderni,* 1672), translation by Alice Sedgwick Wohl, introduction by Tommaso Montanari, Cambridge 2005, p. 218.

16   Bellori 2005, p. 220.



Inessa Kouteinikova

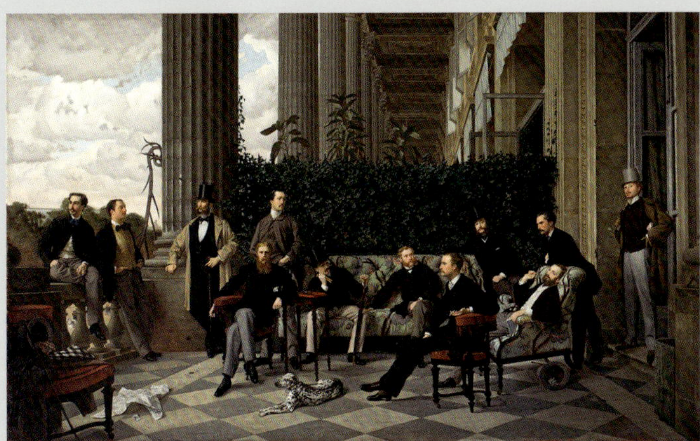



pragmatism in later stages was rediscovered in the early nineteenth century, as the fashion historian Aileen Ribeiro[13] reminds us. British attention to historical dress shifted away from the seventeenth century and its style, epitomised by the prominent Flemish portraitist Anthony van Dyck (1599–1641), towards Elizabethan costume.[14] Judging by van Dyck's portraits, the fashion aesthetic of the time based itself on a tight-fitting covering for the torso and an emphasis on the unbroken line of the legs. | ᴾᵃᵍᵉ **170** | By looking at van Dyck's sitters, one can imagine that a dandy is a personality who is at his happiest when he has achieved the status he craves – that of being the leading figure of his circle, the *primus inter pares, Le Cercle de la Rue Royale.* | ᶠⁱᵍ· **2** | A dandy himself, van Dyck dreamed of large capital cities embracing his talents while he searched for obsequious ways of remaking his noble sitters. Van Dyck's early biographer Giovanni Pietro Bellori (1613–1696) describes how the artist's succession of Peter Paul Rubens (1577–1640) in the graces of King Charles I of England (1600–1649) immediately 'increased his rewards and riches', 'to support the ostentation of his habits and the splendour of his way of life. He rivalled the magnificence of Parrhasius, keeping servants, carriages, horses, players, musicians, and jesters, and with these entertainments he played host to all the great personages, knights and ladies, who came daily to have their portraits painted at his house.'[15] Towards the end of his life, van Dyck had 'little wealth, as he spent everything on the sumptuousness of his way of life, more that of a prince than a painter'.[16] Could this strike us as the key to unlock not only the art of van Dyck but the fashion world more generally? Dandyism permeated every aspect of the early modern court, from the monarchs to their entourage, suitably magnificent to carry on the display of power. Their houses, spectacularly decorated with furnishings, artworks and luxury goods, were dominated by abundant quality and richness, and the monarchs dedicated themselves to their furnishing with alacrity. Splendour and magnificence were important but so was fashion: Italian silk, Persian carpets, Russian furs, French petticoats, Florentine taffeta, Genoese damask, French velvets, Flemish tapestries. In this regard, it is not just the story of a dandy, but a journey through the many pathways at court that offered the potential to express authority and allegiance, discernment and taste. These complex spatial dynamics within the



---

The Importance of Being a Dandy

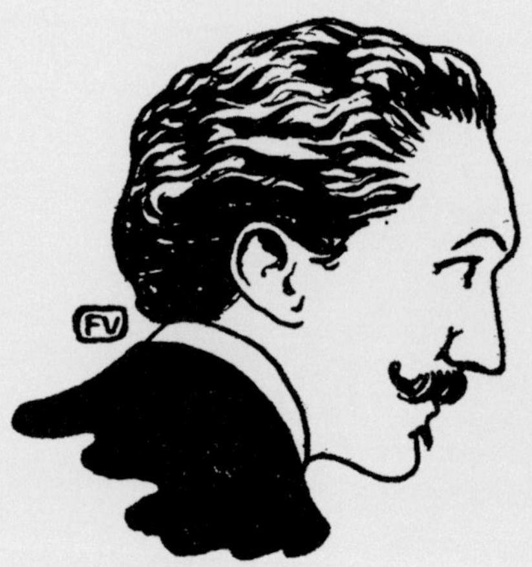



**287** Félix Vallotton (1865–1925)
*Le Comte Robert de Montesquiou
(1855–1921),* 1896
Reproduction of the woodcut,
in Rémy de Gourmont, *Le Livre des
masques. Portraits symbolistes,
Gloses et Documents sur les Ecrivains
d'hier et d'aujourd'hui,*
Paris 1896, p. 233
Kunsthaus Zürich, Library

larger geography of European fashion politics and the social lineage, as mediated by the presence of the dandies, and the display and mobility of artworks, tapestries, furniture and other luxury goods, mirrored the delicate negotiation of power in Europe.

In his book *L'Europe au Moyen Âge,* Georges Duby reveals *haute couture* to be an imaginary construction, often even a historical reconstruction of a dress code no longer apparent to us. He based his ideas on young noblemen with sumptuous garments and mannered gestures in the illuminated calendar of the *Très riches heures du duc de Berry,* painted by the Limbourg brothers between 1410 and 1416, depicting 'elegant men and women', 'frills', 'refinements', sophisticated and extravagant outfits, and even *haute couture.* It is precisely at the end of the Middle Ages, more than ever before, that one can measure the extent to which the clothing envelopes, disguises and masks the body.

### The nouveau-riche in focus

A visual marker of the new economic elite has been graphically described in the novels of Henry James (1843–1916) and Edith Wharton (1862–1937). When American tourists began to visit Italy in large numbers in the nineteenth century, their favourite destinations were Venice, Florence and Rome, 'an aesthetic luxury' tour according to James. A distinctive step in the history of taste and in the establishment of the new attitude towards the Tuscan painters occurred in 1853 when Sandro Botticelli's (1445–1510) *Primavera,* probably painted around 1480, was first displayed to the public in the Accademia Gallery in

Florence. Botticelli became instantly popular among the rich American expatriates, who were attracted by his beautiful settings, by the lilting, lyrical lines of his figures and loosely draped, floor-length robes in floral brocade, long sleeves that hid the hands and the magical twists of the drapery as if made by a sorcerer, that revealed the most voluptuous parts of the Renaissance bodies. The American painter John Singer Sargent (1856–1925), who studied at the Accademia di Belle Arti, also developed a fascination for Botticelli's beguiling theatrical display of fashion. Sargent found an ideal balance between the spirit of the Renaissance and the dazzling elegance and social hierarchy defining the new world. His invention of the nouveau-riche salon portraiture represents an astonishing attempt to catalogue its entire financial and philanthropic elite. His impulsive talent is matched by his admiration for the financial freedom of his sitters and the resulting selectness of their apparel. His love of fabrics becomes apparent in his portraiture. Their textures developed a life of their own and never failed to inspire him.

It is hard today to convey the significance and implications of the fashion described here: for the planning of the new look, but also for the daily lives of everyone else. As noted by Alison Syme, John Singer Sargent is a primary example of botanical artistry, a surprising accolade for a society portraitist; he used the 'the ideas of cross-fertilisation and hermaphroditic sexuality of flowers to "naturalise" sexual inversion'.[17] Sargent's characters are painted as themselves, but they are metamorphosed into gorgeous images overdressed as valuable statues in superior wrappings. | Page **175** | Sargent finds the truth in things and gives an intensive notion of the period by telling it entirely in fashionable manifestations. Sargent and the eccentric painter Giovanni Boldini (1842-1931) convey textures better than any other late nineteenth-century salon painters, the interaction between delicacy and crudity in a dandy's character, of bravado and refinement with the immediacy of artistic imitations. Sargent and Boldini had found a shortcut to fashion and dandyism through passions which do not usually make it into the record, a method which, in spite of the laboured painting, seems suspiciously easy. | Pages **176, 177** | Their portraits remind the viewers that fashion has not been and will not be waiting for everyone. By contrast, James McNeill Whistler's (1834–1903) female models posing for his paintings provide an odd parallel to the physician's relation to flesh, their famous 'white' dresses seem so transparent that the bodies resemble corpses. Whistler's women, even the most expressive and elegant, are always defined by his own being, a man who does not feel free but does not know why. The systematic, almost obsessive application of white was even more universal than a study of the fashion plates of the period might lead us to suppose: 'young girls were all dressed in white, fresh, light and floating, marvellously in harmony with our ideas of innocence, of virginity, and of chastity. They made one think of angels enveloped in their wings.'[18] | Page **192** |

### Félix Vallotton's elimination and illumination of excess

To be elegant in France in the early twentieth century, a woman's looks had to lend themselves to the ambient French Cubism, but the Swiss-born artist Félix Vallotton (1865–1925) had begun even earlier to analyse forms of clothing and to synthesise their basic elements into images that challenged the barriers of space and time. As a boy in Lausanne, he closely observed his family's dressmaking business. As in Émile Zola's (1840–1902) description of Nana at the Grand Prix de Paris, in Vallotton's dramatically lit portraits, we imagine 'the small bodice and blue silk tunic clinging to the body, raised behind the back by an enormous puffed bustle, outlining the thighs in a bold manner for these times

17    Alison Syme, *A Touch of Blossom: John Singer Sargent and the Queer Flora of Fin-de-Siècle Art,* University Park, PA 2010, p. 12.

18    Honoré de Balzac, *Ursule Mirouët,* introduction and translation by Donald Adamson, Harmondsworth, Middlesex 1976, p. 68; the novel was first published in 1841.

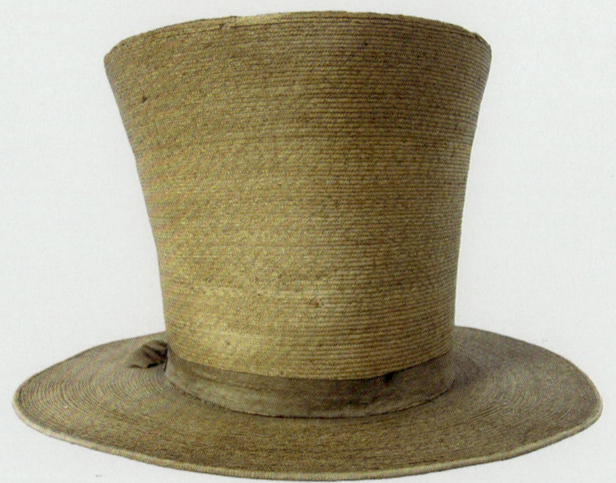



of bloated skirt'.[19] The expensive, impeccably cut, matt black suit of Vallotton's brother Paul draws the viewer's attention to the shining *haut-de-forme,* or top hat, in the sitter's hands. | Page 171 | For Vallotton, fashion is not a simple display of clothes but rather inhabits the models, revealing anatomical forms with a discreet eroticism and a clear colour palette. Modern painters such as Vallotton have a freshly vital attitude to dress in pictures, showing the psychological as well as social power that formal stylisation could bring to it. | Pages 196, 208 | The display in painting of stylised forms and patterns encouraged the idea that dresses and chairs, or automobiles and suits might themselves be designed according to analogous visual principles. As part of their combined interest in the way the look of all things natural and artificial might be similarly stylised, the design of actual clothing came to require serious aesthetic consideration. Fashion designers such as Charles Frederick Worth (1826–1895) | Pages 182, 186 | were becoming publicly famous for the first time in history: 'since artists now felt free to re-invent the world, they seized the right to infuse it with personal vision and idiosyncratic formal invention, to see and remake it again and again according to individual drive and need.'[20]

The enduring popularity of *haut-de-forme* became a recurring and beloved object of many artists.[21] | 15, Page 171 | On the canvases of Vallotton, Tissot, or Boldini, social life is thriving. The inclusion of top hats in their portraits is intentional – not for the sake of weather, but for the sake of status. Like many fashion accessories, hats convey many messages, both complex and meaningful. 'They were a source of psychological security and also an unavowed concession to vanity,' the wearers, with time, 'also becoming figures of fun and the objects of jokes'.[22] On most of the paintings by Boldini, Sargent, Édouard Manet (1832–1883), Amedeo Modigliani (1884–1920) or, René Magritte (1898–1967), *hauts-de-forme* stand out immediately, yet form an integral part of the costume and taste of the nineteenth and twentieth century. They are tireless advocates of the social and political atmosphere, forming part of a silent language and unconventional signs that also make top hats a prominent feature of influential nineteenth-century Russian, English and French novels.



Inessa Kouteinikova

## An example of the dandy today: The Sapeur

The Sape, Daniele Tamagni's book *Gentlemen of Bacongo* tells us, 'began when the Congo still was a French colony. Many Congolese people were fascinated with French elegance and decided to imitate the French look, a style which was further developed during the transition to independence.'[23] The picturesque modern tradition of the Sapeurs (Society for the Advancement of People of Elegance) has developed new symbolism, changed its allegiance from the Parisian diva to the dynamo. Though fiercely anti-intellectual and hostile to the contemporary ephemeral cultures, it is a popular movement, not an esoteric one. It presents itself as a peculiarly individual phenomenon in the vast non-individual space of Brazzaville. Their clothing is full of demonstrative statements, they profess admiration of impeccable tailoring, strong palette and memorable *accessoires*. Like their predecessors in London and Paris, they dream of making things over and questioning – in this case, colonial and post-colonial – social norms: there is an upside-down imaginative, consciously appropriative force of self-empowerment in deciding to make Congo just another dandyland by expending tremendous personal effort.




**19**   Émile Zola, *Nana,* translation cited in George Holden (ed.), London 1977, pp. 348, 668; the novel was first published in 1880.

**20**   Anne Hollander, *Fabric of Vision: Dress and Drapery in Painting,* London 2016, p. 177.

**21**   Timothy Campbell, *Historical Style: Fashion and the New Mode of History, 1740–1850,* Philadelphia 2016; Madeleine Ginsburg, *The Hat: Trends and Tradition,* London 1990.

**22**   Giuliano Folledore, *Men's Hats. The Twentieth Century – Histories of Fashion Series,* Modena 1989, p. 25.

**23**   Daniele Tamagni, *Gentlemen of Bacongo,* London 2009, foreword (unpaginated).

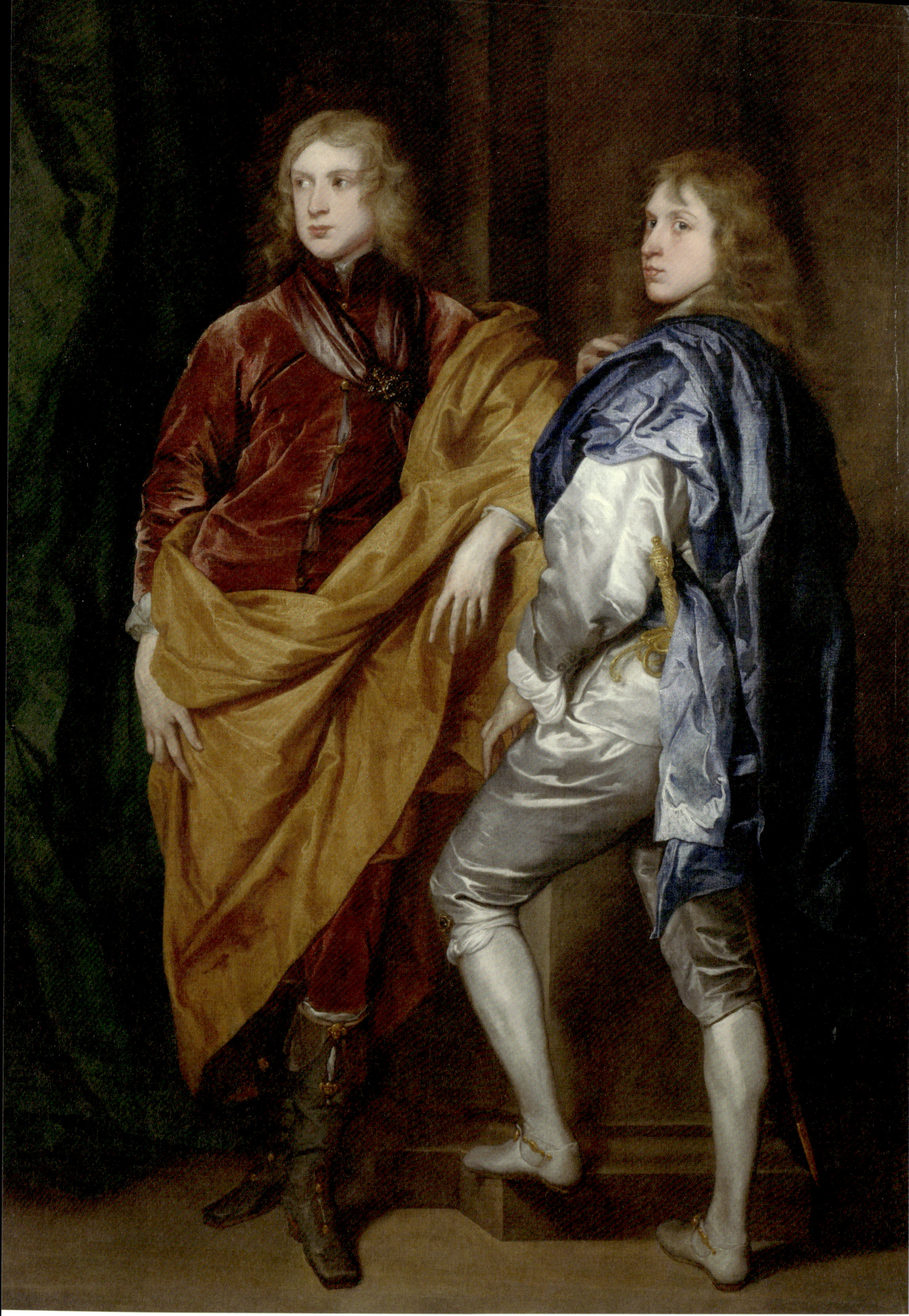

**128** after Anthony van Dyck (1599–1641)
*Portraits of two young Englishmen,*
c. 1635–40
Oil on canvas, 193.7 × 126 cm
The National Gallery, London

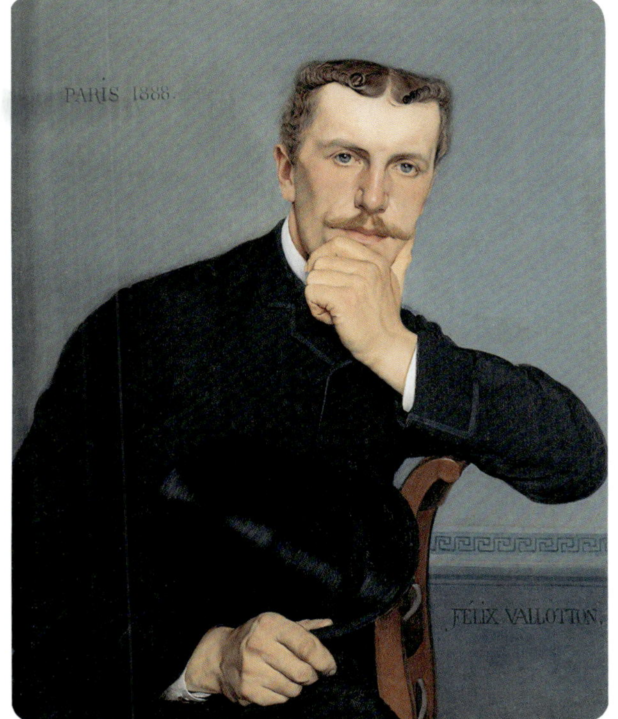


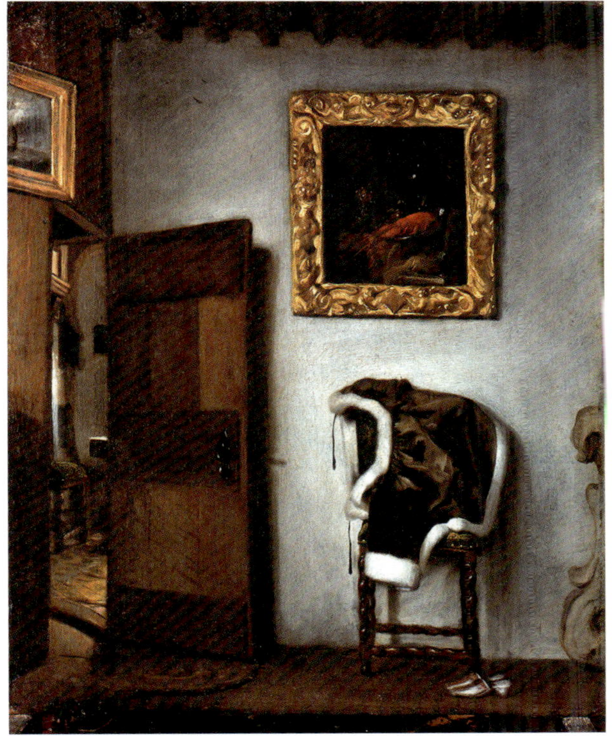

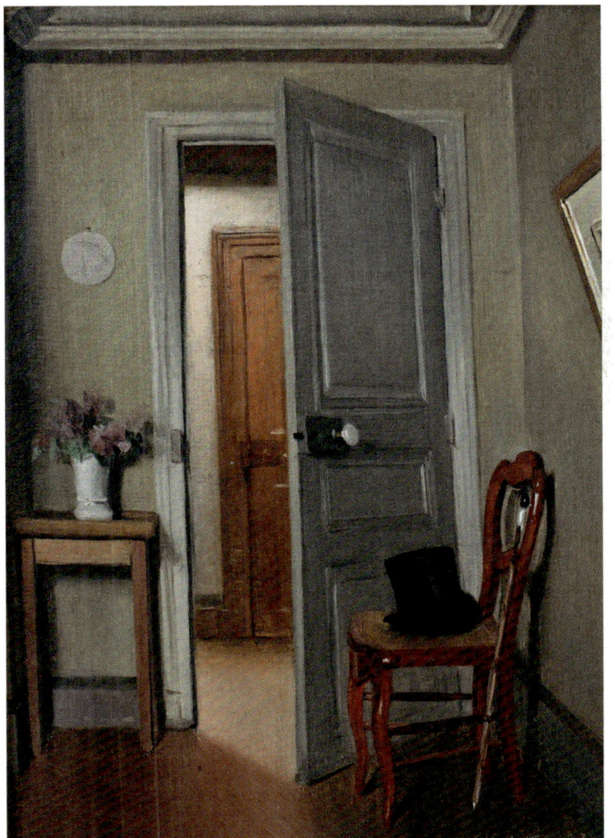

**61** Cornelis Bisschop (1630–1674),
attributed
*Interior with jacket on a chair,*
undated (c. 1660?)
Oil on canvas, 43.5 × 36.5 cm
Staatliche Museen zu Berlin,
Gemäldegalerie

**280** Félix Vallotton (1865–1925)
*Paul Vallotton avec son chapeau,* 1888
Oil on canvas, 76 × 61 cm
Private collection

**279** Félix Vallotton (1865–1925)
*Le Haut-de-forme, intérieur*
*or La Visite,* 1887
Oil on canvas, 31.7 × 24.8 cm
Collection Olivier Senn.
Donation Hélène Senn-Foulds, 2004.
Le Havre, Musée d'art moderne
André Malraux

**152** James Gillray (1756–1815)
*So skiffy-skipt-on,*
*with his wonted grace,* 1800
Etching, hand-coloured with
watercolours, sheet: 24.8 × 17.4 cm
Staatliche Museen zu Berlin,
Kunstbibliothek

**278** Unknown artist
*Longchamp,* 1840
Copper engraving, hand-coloured
with watercolours, sheet: 26.7 × 18.9 cm
Staatliche Museen zu Berlin,
Kunstbibliothek

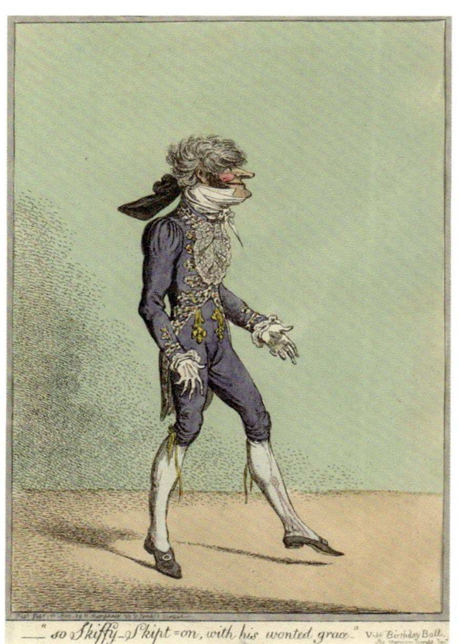

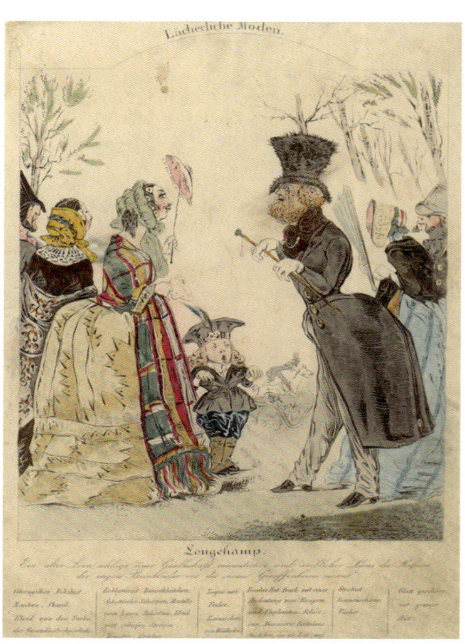

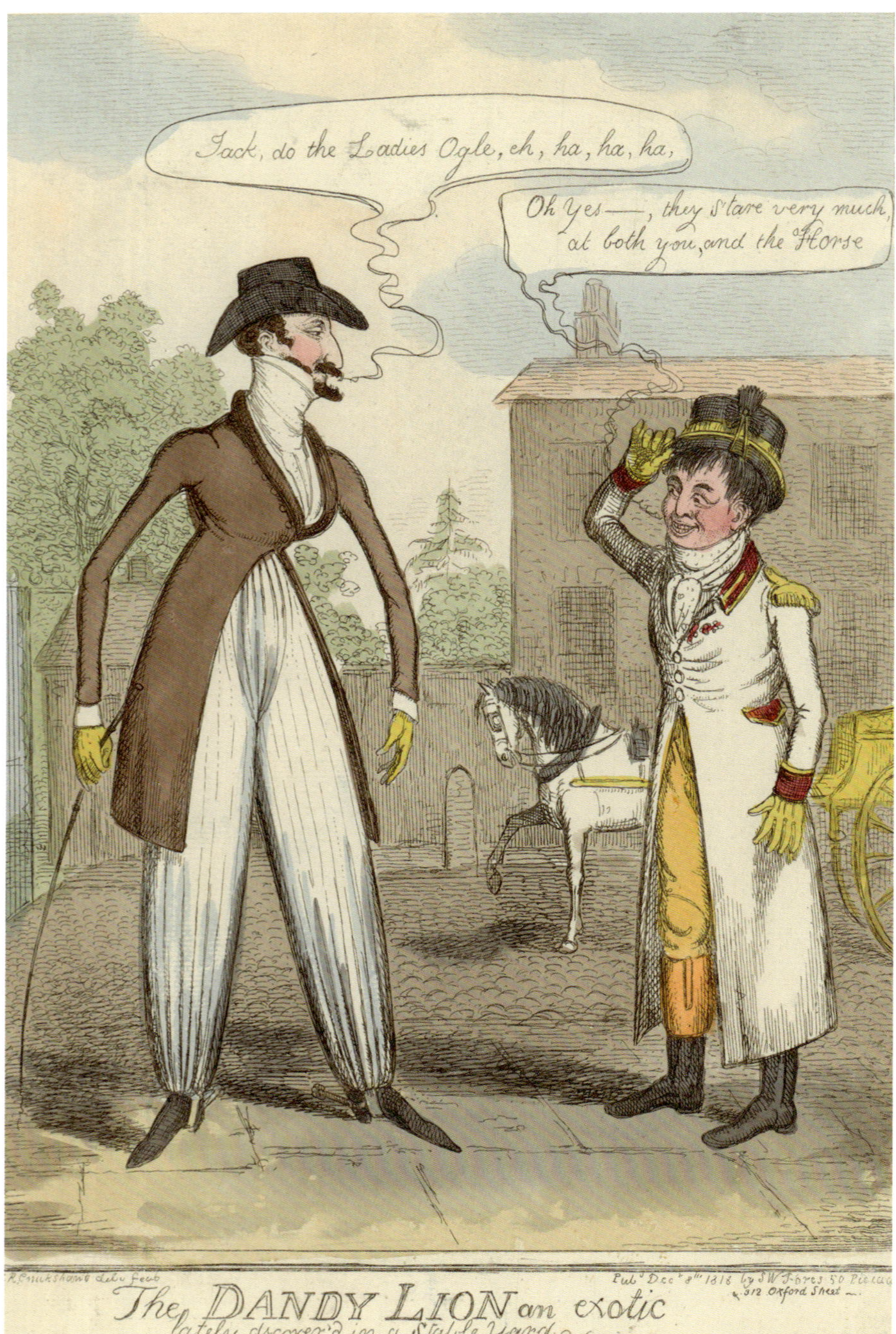


**85** Isaac Cruikshank (1764–1811)
*The dandy lion an exotic lately discover'd*
*in a stable yard,* 8 December 1818
Etching, hand-coloured with
watercolours, sheet: 32.9 × 21.6 cm
Staatliche Museen zu Berlin,
Kunstbibliothek

**84**  George Cruikshank (1792–1878)
*Neckclothitania*
Illustration in *Cravatiana Ou Traité Général Des Cravates: Considérées Dans Leur Origine, Leur Influence Politique, Physique Et Morale, Leur Formes, Leurs Couleurs Et Leurs Espèces, Ouvrage Traduit Librement De L'Anglais Sur La Huitième Édition; Orné De Vignettes, Fleurons, Et D'Un Gravure En Taille-Douce*, 1823
Book, 84 pages
Staatliche Museen zu Berlin, Kunstbibliothek

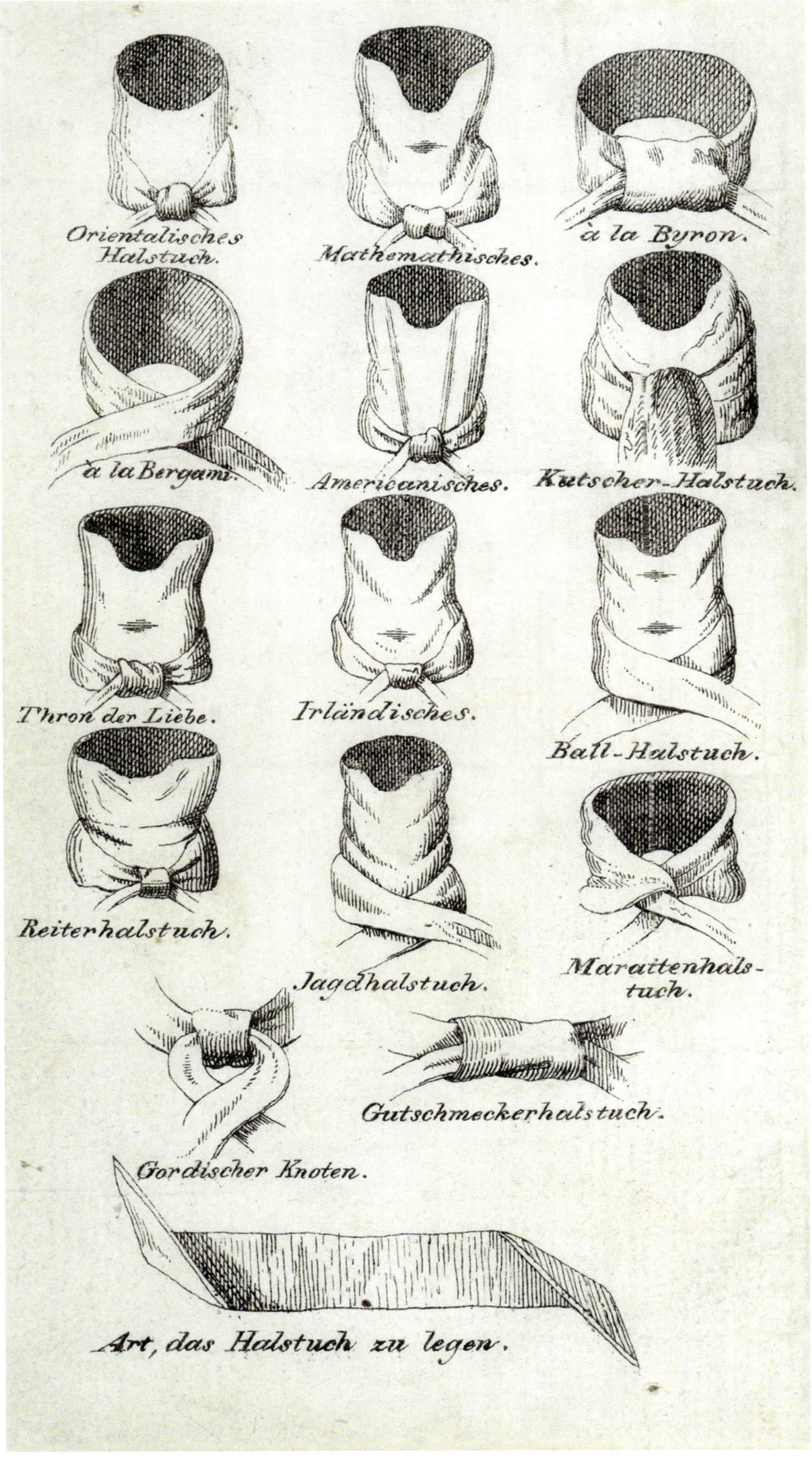

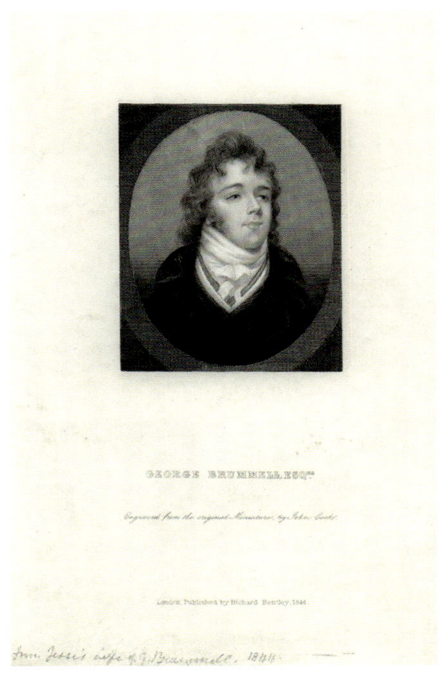


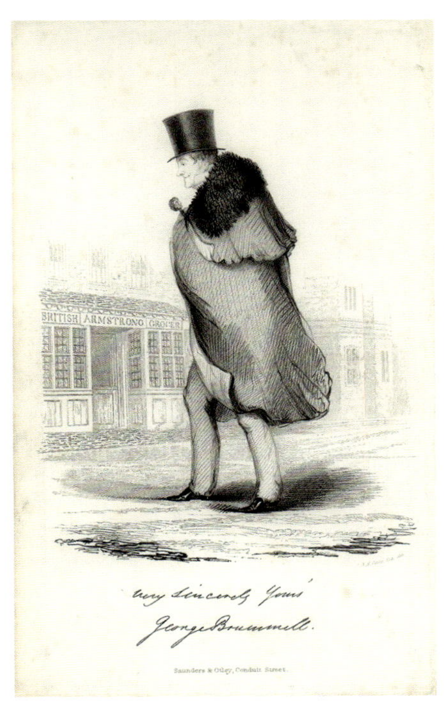




**78**  John Cook, engraver
After unknown miniaturist
*Beau Brummell,* published in 1844
Stipple and engraving, sheet: 18.2 × 11.8 cm
Lent by the National Portrait Gallery, London;
Given by Henry Witte Martin, 1861

**79**  R. H. Cooke, etcher
*Beau Brummell,* nineteenth century
Etching, sheet: 21.9 × 13.7 cm
Lent by the National Portrait Gallery, London;
Purchased with help from the Friends of the
National Libraries and the Pilgrim Trust, 1966

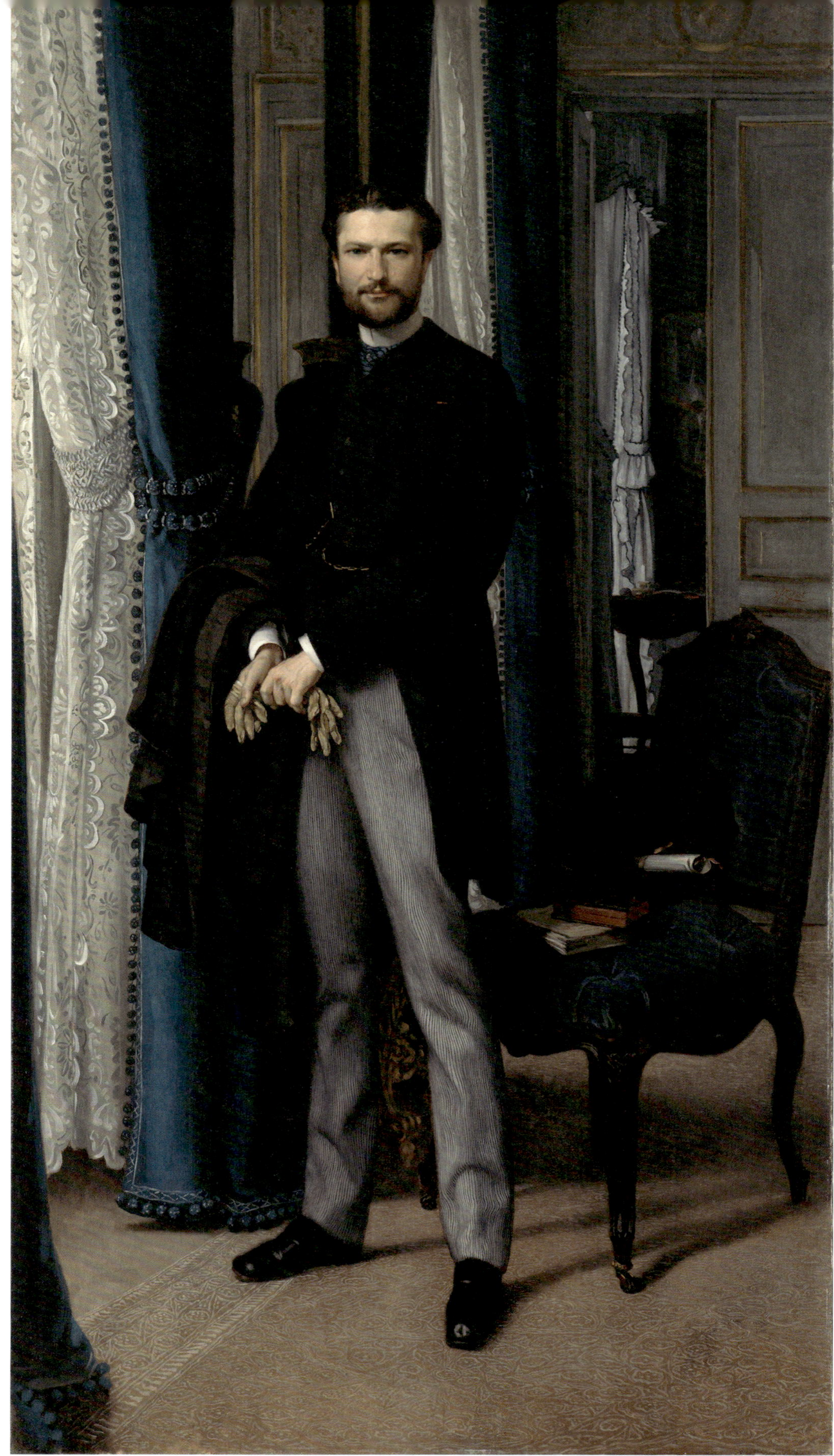

**260** James Tissot (1836–1902)
*Baron Aimé de la Seillière*, 1566
Oil on canvas, 128 × 71 cm
Staatliche Kunsthalle Karlsruhe

**240** John Singer Sargent (1856–1925)
*W. Graham Robertson*, 1894
Oil on canvas, 230.5 × 118.7 cm
Tate: Presented by W. Graham Robertson 1940

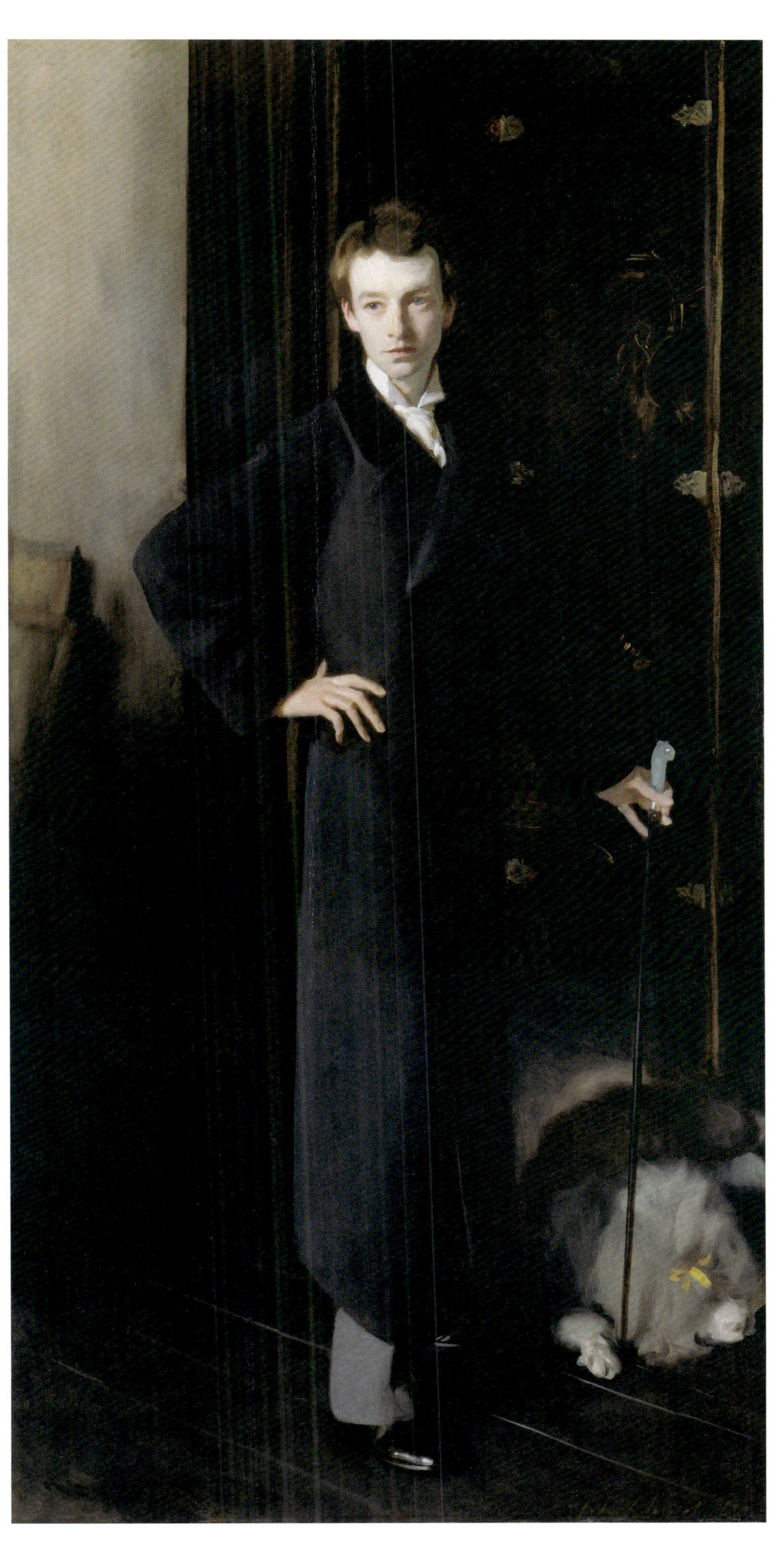

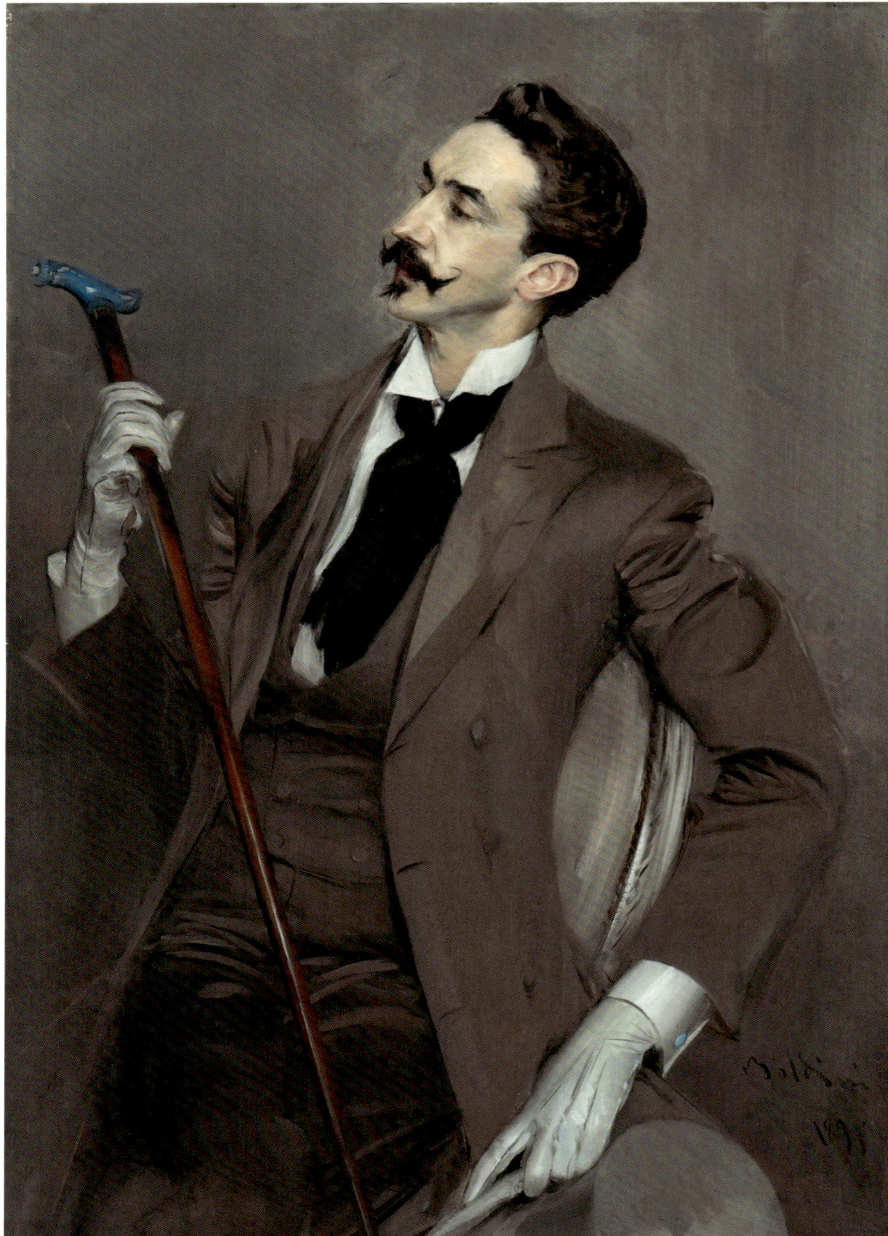

**64** Giovanni Boldini (1842–1931)
*Le Comte Robert de Montesquiou (1855–1921),* 1897
Oil on canvas, 115.5 × 82.5 cm
Paris, Musée d'Orsay, don d'Henri Pinard
au nom du comte Robert de Montesquiou, 1922

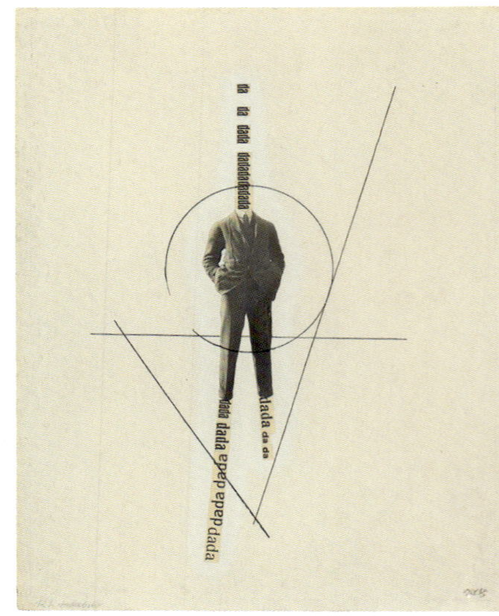

**166** George Grosz (1893–1959)
*Dadabild,* c. 1919
Photo and text collage, Chinese ink
and silver gelatin print on paper,
sheet: 37 × 30.3 cm
Kunsthaus Zürich, Department
of Prints and Drawings

**65** Giovanni Boldini (1842–1931)
*Portrait de Georges Goursat dit Sem,* 1902
Oil on canvas, 91 × 73 cm
Musée des Arts décoratifs, Paris

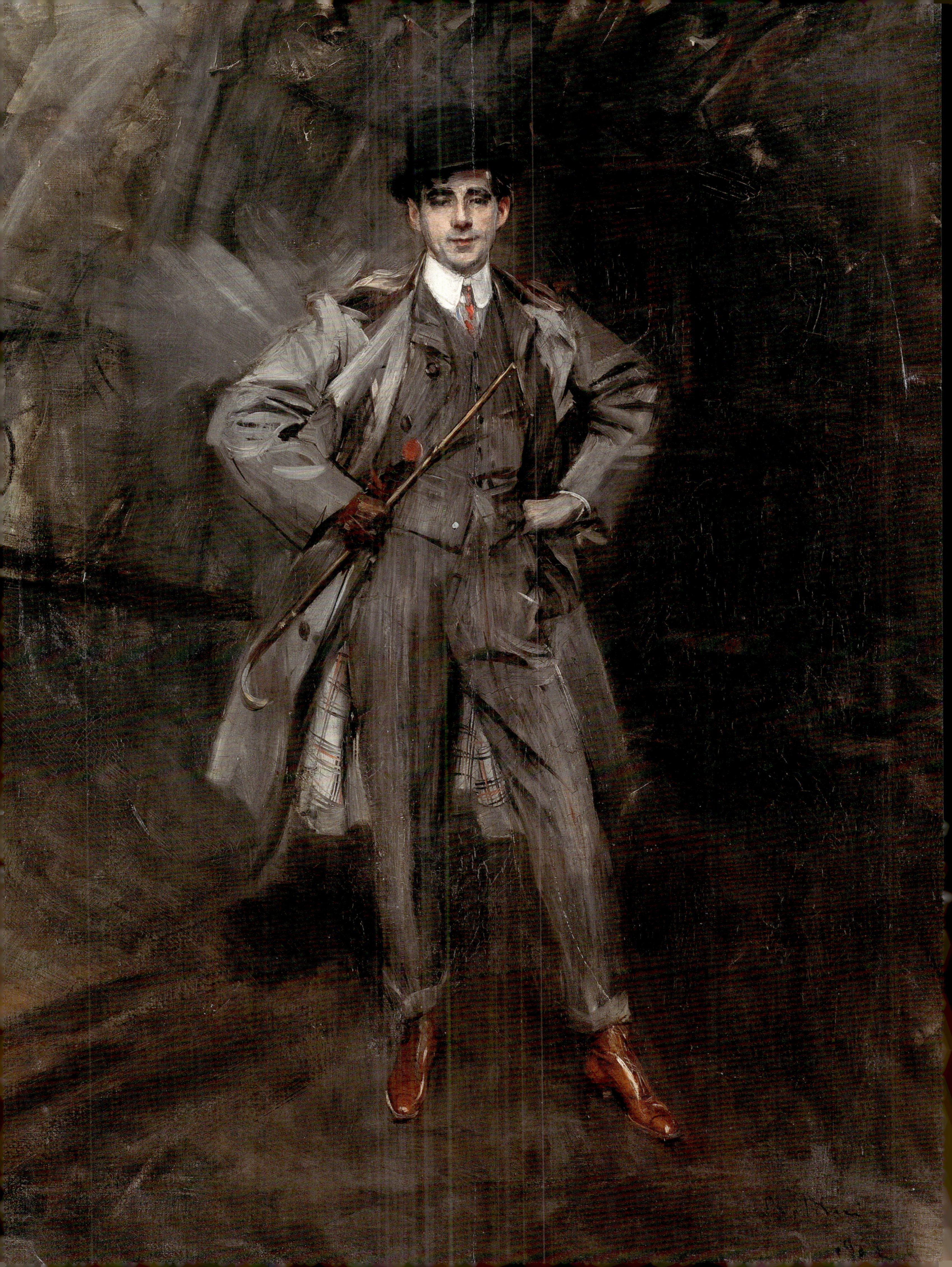

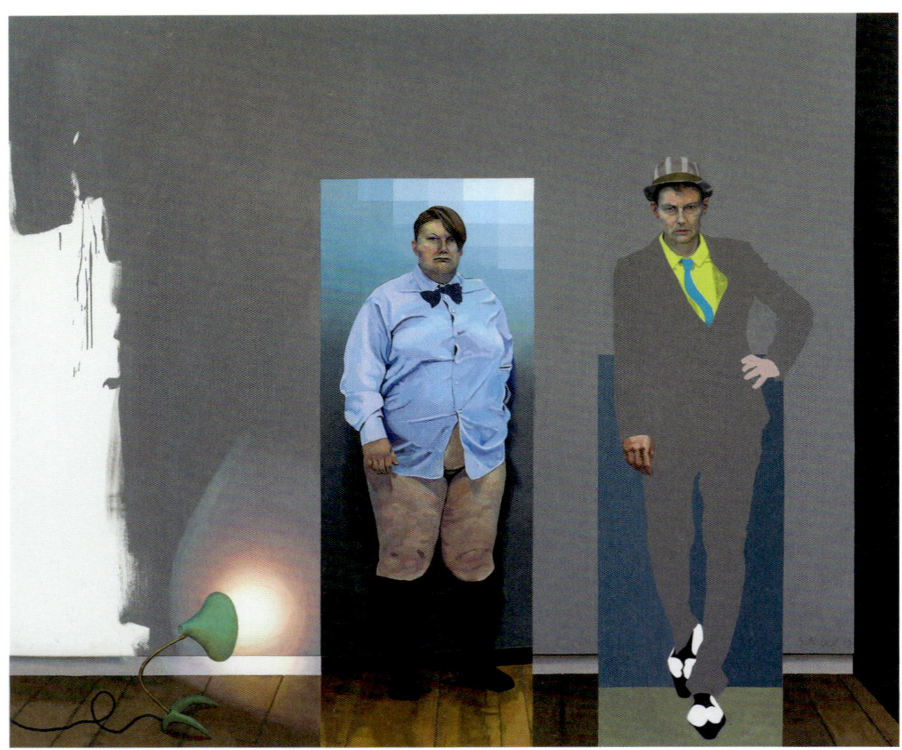

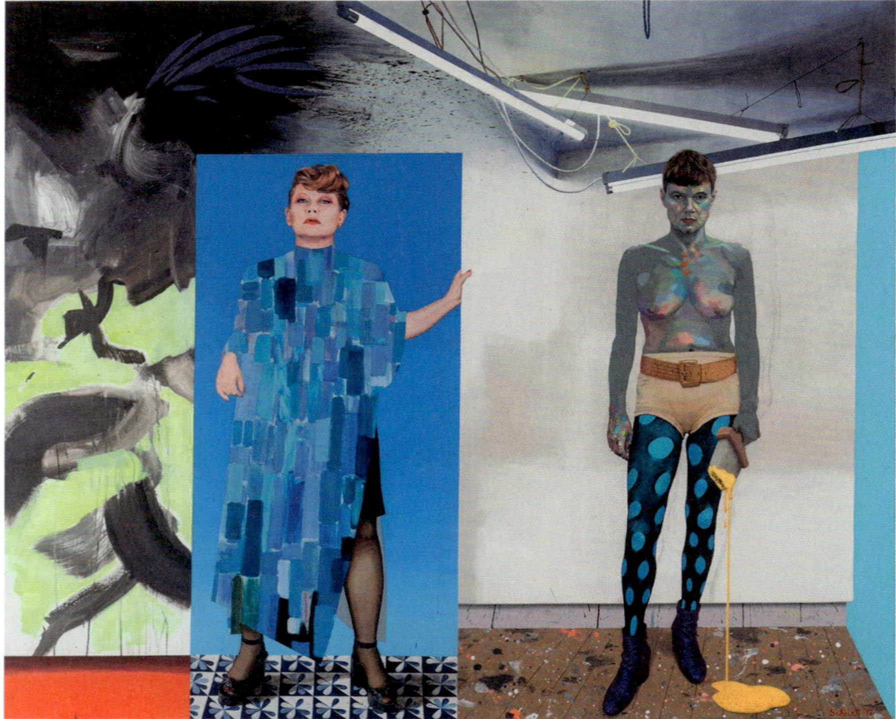

Ashley Hans Scheirl (b. 1956)
**top**  *Jakob und Hans mit Krähenfusslampe
vor monochromem Bild,* 2012
Jakob and Hans with crows-foot lamp
in front of monochrome picture
Acrylic on canvas, 280 × 230 cm
Courtesy of the artist, Private collection (not in the exhibition)
**bottom**  *Tina in Kupkakleid und ich mit Pinsel,* 2017
Tina in a Kupka-dress and me with a brush
Acrylic on canvas, 280 × 230 cm
Courtesy of the artist, mumok, Museum moderner Kunst
Stiftung Ludwig Wien (not in the exhibition)

**241**  Ashley Hans Scheirl (*1956)
New work for the exhibition, 2018
Acrylic on canvas
Courtesy of the artist
(no fig.)

# Farewell from the Emancipated Skirt

*The skirt went to work for me today.*
*Held position, A-line, neatly alphabetised.*
*Direct supervision, knees pushed through,*
*the fabric swirling around, the pros and cons.*

*In the catalogue it did look straighter.*
*Skirt shoved in walking, during the day*
*slowly up to the middle of the thighs.*
*Why these pictures, why so much likened noise about it?*

*Skirt silently separated from me and became undone.*
*Stayed a double A for me.*
*In the language of fabrics, A + A makes a type of circle.*
*I am now standing in trousers, in wide ones.*

*In the view from above, it results in an M or W.*
*In the beginning, it was still a fig leaf.*



Nora Gomringer

# *Under the Skirt. The as*

## *Katharina Tietze*

# Crinoline a Motif

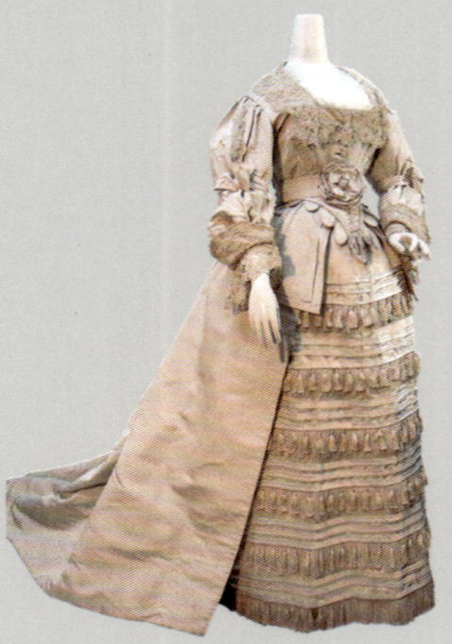

16 Charles Frederick Worth (1825–1895), design
Wedding or reception dress, France c. 1878
Labelled: Charles F. Worth
Cream silk faille with silk tassel trim
Collection Kamer-Ruf

'[...] the ladies' costume is characterised by quite unfavourable innovations. First, the unattractive hoop skirt regains prominence because of its bulges made of *crin* (horsehair), which holds it in shape, called crinoline, to which the three and fourfold flounces give a special plumpness: It now no longer acts as a bizarre yet graceful instrument of coquetry like the "chicken basket" of the Rococo or as a stiff but stylish grandiosity as was the "virtue guard" of the Counter Reformation, but in the new bourgeois and materialistic world, as an annoying and quirky adornment.'[1] In the mid-nineteenth century, women's fashion reached extreme proportions in its shape. The narrow-waisted dresses gained increasingly wider skirts, leading to a circumference unique in the history of fashion. How did this fashion come about and how is it reflected in art?

## Material developments

After the fashion of the Empire around 1800, when women wore high-girdled cotton dresses, | Page 141 | the hemlines became wider and wider. Supportive petticoats created a dome-shaped volume. From 1839 on, they received their support – that is to say, static quality – by horsehair, usually combined with cotton or wool.[2] Under the horsehair skirts were more petticoats, which made women's clothing very heavy and a reason to experiment with new materials and technologies. A peculiar invention used inflatable rubber air tubes. After 1856, steel-hooped cage crinolines were used effectively. | Fig. 1 | Thus, a significant material of the nineteenth century, previously used in architecture,[3] made its way into fashion. Skirts became simultaneously lighter and wider. However, in contrast to petticoats, crinolines could not be produced by individuals; Thompson & Co., a major manufacturer, had factories in places such as Saxony, London, New York and Paris. The crinoline gradually changed its shape, the volume shifted to the back, and the skirt narrowed in the front until the steel hoops went out of fashion in the late 1860s.

Not only did materials such as horsehair or steel play an important role in producing the volume, but also the sheer amount of fabric required for the upper skirt was remarkable. Ruffles and flounces added decorations to the

182

1   Egon Friedell, *Kulturgeschichte der Neuzeit (1927–1931)*, Zurich 2009, p. 1185.

2   *Zur Geschichte der Unterwäsche 1700–1960*, Almut Junker and Eva Stille, exh. cat. Historisches Museum Frankfurt, Frankfurt am Main 1988, pp. 118–23.

3   In 1851, steel found, for instance, visibly extensive use for the Crystal Palace of the first World's Fair in London.

4   Thorstein Veblen, 'Die Kleidung als Ausdruck des Geldes' (1899), in Sonja Eismann (ed.), *absolute Fashion*, Freiburg im Breisgau 2012, pp. 32–45.

5   Thanks to Martin Kamer for this information, along with many other suggestions.

6   See illustration of female workers in a crinoline factory, who wear crinolines themselves in Juncker and Stille 1988 (as in note 2), p. 123.

7   Eleri Lynn, *Underwear: Fashion in Detail*, London 2010, p. 20.

8   Gertrud Lehnert (ed.), *Die Räume der Mode*, Munich 2012, p. 13.

9   On the attributions, see also the very detailed article: Therese Dolan, 'Skirting the Issue: Manet's Portrait of Baudelaire's Mistress, Reclining,' *The Art Bulletin* 79.4 (1997), pp. 611–29.

Katharina Tietze

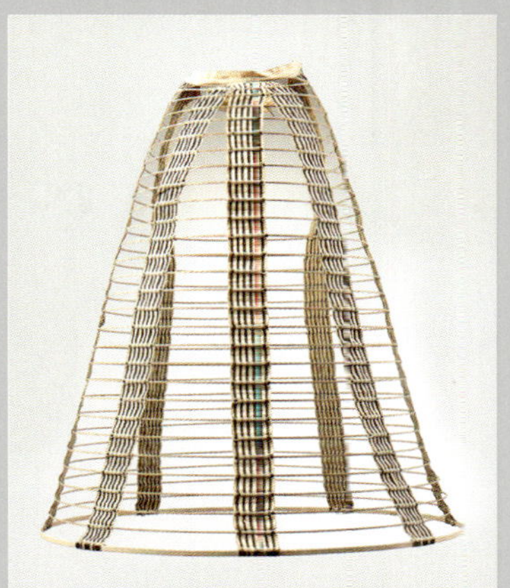



overall shape. Thus, women could display their financial purchasing power and their husbands' ability to spend money on expensive material and its fashioning, a phenomenon of dependency that the sociologist Thorstein Veblen (1857–1929) later described as conspicuous consumption.[4] The use of so much material also involved the aesthetic question of how to meaningfully design such a large surface. At the time, a particularly suitable material was Moiré that despite its complex production technique for its patterned repetition – produced by silk folded once and pressed – it was widespread and provided a magnificent display.[5]

## The bourgeois recourse to courtly forms

The crinoline as a variant of the hoop skirt was actually a courtly garment. It made its way into the bourgeoisie as an affordable steel-hooped crinoline; even working women[6] wore crinolines. As expected, the representative form collided with the demands of everyday life and was the subject of a deluge of caricatures. Eugénie de Montijo (1826–1920), born in Granada, the wife of Napoleon III (1808–1873) and Empress of the French, especially contributed to the spread of the crinoline. She was fascinated by her predecessor Marie-Antoinette (1755–1793) and with the crinoline alluded to early eighteenth-century Rococo motifs. As an anachronistic garment, the crinoline was worn in the nineteenth century by women from all walks of life before it went out of fashion. It also allowed a common woman to have a kind of majestic appearance in an era of the bourgeois.

## A woman's mobile space

Although women served, in a sense, as representative exhibits of their husbands, they occupied their own space with their voluminous skirts. They hid their abdomen and nevertheless garnered special attention to themselves due to the extreme size of the skirts. In terms of gender, the crinoline was thus ambivalent. It emphasised the charged space under the skirt. Not least, it became draughty underneath, which is why underpants increasingly came into use.[7]

The difference between body and dress plays an important role in the entire history of fashion, but with the crinoline it became especially distinct.[8] The steel-hooped cage crinoline required adept manoeuvring, for example, when sitting down or getting into a coach. However, because women had to pick them up to do so, it also made for a coquettish show of the legs. In its most extreme form, this gathering of the skirts was presented during the cancan, a show dance which originated in the 1830s in Paris, made famous by the operettas of Jacques Offenbach (1819–1880).

In 1862, Édouard Manet (1832–1883) painted a woman in a white dress with a crinoline, whose skirt fills a large part of the picture. | <sup>Page</sup> **191** | The work is known by the titles *La Dame à l'éventail* and *La Maîtresse de Baudelaire*. Pictured is Jeanne Duval (1820–1862), a Haitian-born actress and dancer, long-time mistress of Charles Baudelaire (1821–1867), a good friend of Manet.[9] As with the artist's other works, he surrounds this painting with many questions and allusions that can only be partially clarified with certainty. He portrays the approximately 40-year-old woman,

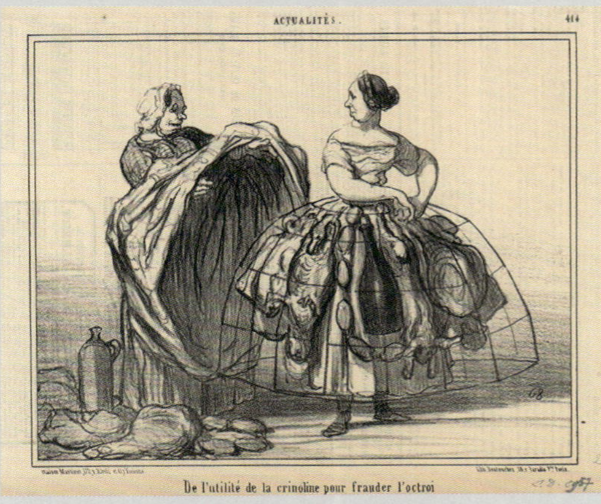

De l'utilité de la crinoline pour frauder l'octroi

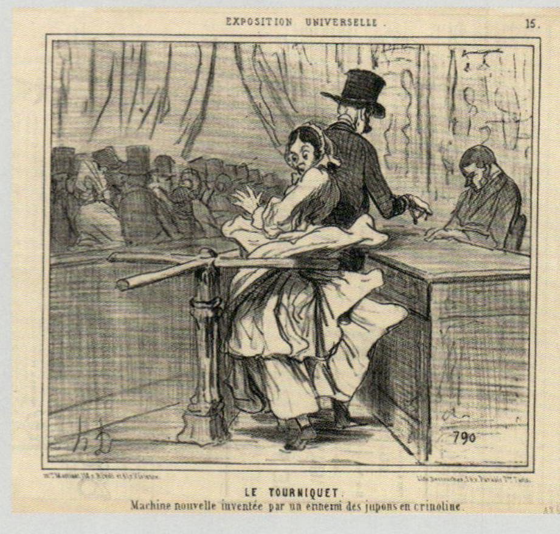

LE TOURNIQUET.
Machine nouvelle inventée par un ennemi des jupons en crinoline.

described by Baudelaire as his 'black Venus,' resting on a sofa in front of a lace curtain, the skirt of her dress roughly sketched with a few fleeting brushstrokes. The hand seems too big in proportion, and also the leg, which protrudes from under the skirt, does not seem to belong to her body. Duval holds a fan in her hand and looks directly at the viewer. Her white dress is accentuated with black details and is presumably striped inside. It is not a 'beautiful' image in the popular aesthetic sense, such as the contemporary portraits of Franz Xaver Winterhalter (1805–1873). In contrast to Manet, Winterhalter painted on behalf of the French and Austrian ruling houses and idealised the ladies of courtly society with his grandiloquent representations. Manet, however, cared not about the beautification of reality, but about sincerity.[10] He gives his friend's lover – she came from a humble background, her turbulent relationship with Baudelaire was fraught with money problems, and she was already sick – a grand appearance in the voluminous white dress that brings out her black hair and dark eyes. Manet portrays Duval in contemporary clothing. A brief time later, Baudelaire pleaded for this form of modern representation. In 1863, he wrote in an essay on the painter Constantin Guys (1802–1892) that 'the great majority of fine portraits that have come down to us from former generations are clothed in the costume of their own period. They are perfectly harmonious, because everything – from costume to coiffure down to gesture, glance and smile (for each age has a deportment, a glance and a smile of its own) – everything, I say, combines to form a completely viable whole. This transitory, fugitive element, whose metamorphoses are so rapid, must on no account be despised or dispensed with.'[11] Baudelaire, hence, considered clothing fashion with much seriousness and associated it with the concept of modernity: For Guys, 'it is his business to extract from fashion whatever element it may contain of poetry within history, to distil the eternal from the transitory.'[12] He appreciated the painter's colourful drawings, and how precisely they reflected situations, types and fashions of the many different classes. Baudelaire's text, which also pleads for makeup and remarks on the craving for distinction among dandies, counts as a foundational contribution to the textual canon of fashion history.

The American conceptual artist John Baldessari (b. 1931) comments on Manet's portrait of Duval in his series *Double Bill*. | Page 190 | He has made collages from the works of artists such as Marcel Duchamp (1887–1968) and Max Ernst (1891–1976) in combination with other paintings, and then partially transformed them by painting on the inkjet prints. In Manet's case, he changed the upper half of the picture and linked the crinoline skirt to a steamboat. This has increased the size of the skirt. Perhaps Baldessari wishes to draw attention to Jeanne Duval's overseas origin, and thus to an aspect of colonial history. In this respect, he might also have referred to Baudelaire's poems that, in the volume *Flowers of Evil*, also associate his beloved with harbours and ships: 'And your body, it bends and stretches like a noble ship [...].'[13] Duval, as a ship and as an exotic creature, has thus likewise become an object.

Katharina Tietze

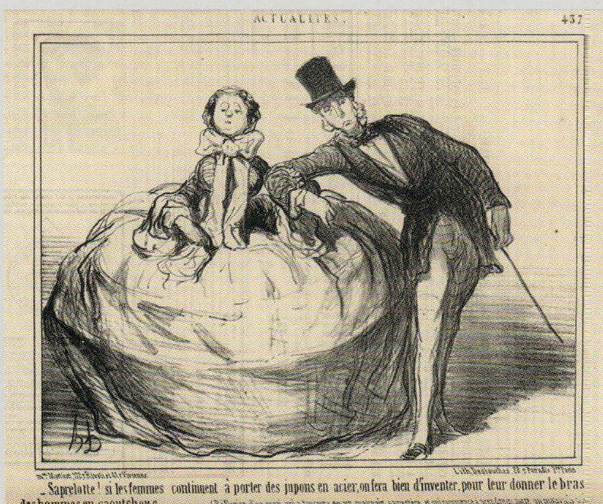

**103** Honoré Daumier (1808–1879)
*The usefulness of the crinoline when cheating the customs,* In *Le Charivari,* 19 June 1857
Lithograph, image: 20.8 × 26.7 cm

**100** Honoré Daumier (1808–1879)
*The turnstile. A new machine invented by the enemy of crinoline petticoats,* In *Le Charivari,* 26 June 1857
Lithograph, image: 19.7 × 22.8 cm

**105** Honoré Daumier (1808–1879)
*Damn it! If women continue to wear steel petticoats one will be forced to invent rubber men in order to give them an arm (Thoughts from a husband who always had a bad character, and now starts to have a bad back),* In *Le Charivari,* 9 September 1857
Lithograph, image: 20.3 × 26 cm

Al Kunsthaus Zürich, Department of Prints and Drawings

Highly regarded by both Manet and Baudelaire, Honoré Daumier (1808–1879) also dealt with crinoline fashion of the 1850s and 1860s. It offered a welcomed subject for his cartoons. Overall, fashion cartoons are a highly fertile source for fashion history. They describe contemporary reactions, provide information about a variety of details and illustrate the chronological course of certain fashions. In addition, they illustrate the social contexts of clothing, such as their use on different occasions, among social classes or in terms of gender relations.[14] Like fashion, caricatures exaggerate certain aspects; they react quickly and have entertainment value.[15] Daumier's trenchant drawings could be easily duplicated through the new medium of lithography and they benefitted from the development of modern journalism. The sheets shown in the *Fashion Drive* exhibition were published regularly in newspapers such as the *Charivari*. In the same medium, a whole series of caricatures by Charles Vernier (1813–1892) appeared under the title *Crinolonomanie*. Daumier dealt with the space that the crinoline forms and occupies. Thus, inflated into a balloon, it can let women fly off. The voluminous skirt provided plenty of wind surface and thus involuntarily enabled the (not discussed here) view of legs and underwear. Other sheets ask what might be underneath the skirt and imply that crinoline steel hoops were being used to transport smuggled goods. |**103**| The World's Fair in Paris in 1855 gave rise to more sheets. They show, by way of example, how modern developments collided with the hoop skirt. Thus, the crinoline is crushed by the turnstile, an almost symptomatic invention of the modern age as a system of separation. |**100**| Other cartoons deal with the fact that the crinoline does not allow you to walk through certain doors and practically prohibits getting in or taking a seat on public transport. In addition, they limit freedom of a man's movement since men must bend to offer an arm to a woman, as another sheet shows. |**105**| The London and Paris World Fairs marked the beginning of a new era. Design history began, in a stricter sense, with industrial mass production of the exhibited goods. Even crinolines were already being produced in factories in large numbers. There were always architectural analogies, since the exhibition building itself on the Avenue des Champs-Élysées was also


**10** Oskar Bätschmann, *Édouard Manet,* Munich 2015, p. 15.

**11** Charles Baudelaire, *The Painter of Modern Life and Other Essays,* translated and edited by Jonathan Mayne, London 1995, p. 13.

**12** Baudelaire 1995, p. 12.

**13** Charles Baudelaire, *Die Blumen des Bösen,* Munich 1997 (first 1857–68), p. 63.

**14** Adelheid Rasche and Gundula Wolter (eds), *Ridikül! Mode in der Karikatur,* Berlin 2003, pp. 34f.

**15** This even applies in the twentieth century, as Anna-Brigitte Schlittler shows in the example in the Swiss satirical magazine *Nebelspalter*. See Anna-Brigitte Schlittler, 'Bally-Schuhe sind tonangebende Modeschöpfungen. Schuhdesign im Zweiten Weltkrieg' in Rasche and Wolter 2003 and Katharina Tietze (ed.), *Über Schuhe. Zur Geschichte und Theorie der Fußbekleidung,* Bielefeld 2016, pp. 73–92.

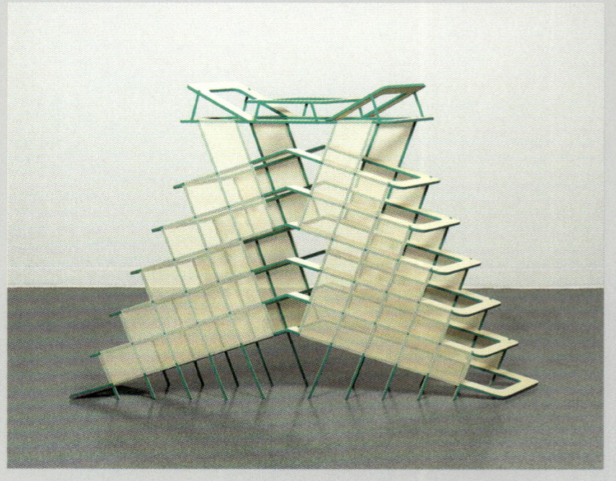
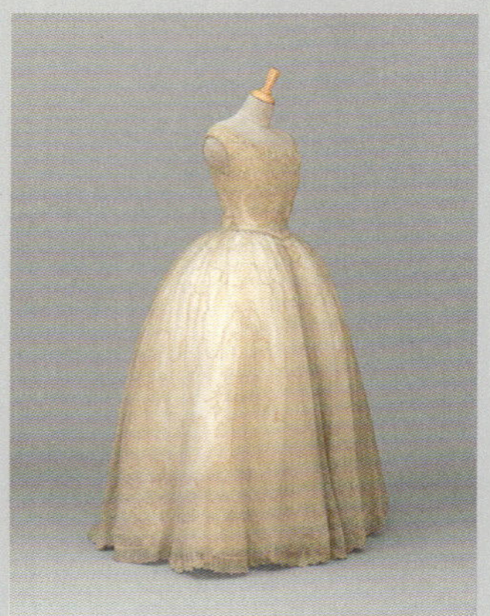



a construction made of iron. The static achievement that this material made possible, however, was hidden behind stone, just as the steel-hooped crinoline disappeared under masses of fabrics.

The American artist Diane Simpson (b. 1935) explores the connection between clothing and architecture in her work, for example, in building a sculpture inspired by a Baroque hoop skirt. | Fig. 2 | By eliminating soft and round shapes, the underskirt becomes a building. The horizontal layers as well as the actually movable vertical bands are cut from heavy medium-density fibreboard (MDF), whose edges are accentuated with mint green and covered vertically with fine cotton fabrics. Entitled *Underskirt* (1986), the artwork seems familiar in proportions and unfamiliar through material and formal abstractions. An apparent functionality makes it aesthetically appealing. The artist's theme is, at the same time, the complex construction of the petticoat and its very sight gives an idea of how difficult it was to move elegantly in it.

One of the most famous female wearers of crinolines was the previously mentioned Eugénie de Montijo, France's last Empress (from 1853 to 1870). She was a client of Charles Frederic Worth (1825–1895). A gown that presumably belonged to her and that came from Worth's workshop is now in the collection of the Textile Museum St. Gall.[16] | Fig. 3 | It is made of cream-coloured Aleçon lace and originates from the collection of textile merchant John Jakoby-Iklé.[17] The Empress, like the British Queen Victoria (1819–1901) and the Austrian Empress Elisabeth (1837–1898), was repeatedly portrayed by the popular society painter Franz Xaver Winterhalter. In the portraits, she often wears light-coloured dresses, just as Manet had depicted Jeanne Duval in a white dress. The light tones were flattering, but also stood for a certain intimacy. Street clothes of the time were, in contrast, often very colourful. Using precious lace for the fabric-devouring fashion was an especially exclusive enterprise. But in Manet's painting, the lace also appears as a curtain. Unfortunately, the matching crinoline to Eugénie de Montijo's dress is no longer preserved, so it is shown today with different substructures, and the circumference of the skirt can only be speculated.

16  The Textile Museum St. Gall cannot fully ascertain either Eugénie de Montijo's ownership or Worth's creation of that particular garment.

17  For more detailed information on this collection, see Hans Stettbacher (ed.), *Spitzen: [Sammlung Iklé und Jacoby] = Laces = Dentelles*, St. Gall, 1955.

18  Sigfried Giedion, *Die Herrschaft der Mechanisierung*, Frankfurt am Main 1982, pp. 405–16, as well as Regina Lösel, *Einkleidung von Bewegung: Eine textile Material- und Formgeschichte der Bewegung am Beispiel des Straßenkostüms zwischen 1850 und 1914*, Ph.D. diss. Carl von Ossietzky Universität Oldenburg, 2011, http://oops.uni-oldenburg.de/2040/1/loeein11.pdf (accessed 17 August 2017), pp. 65–68.



Katharina Tietze

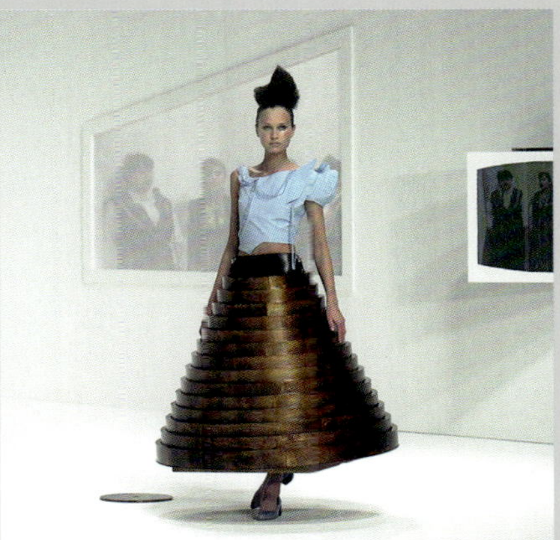
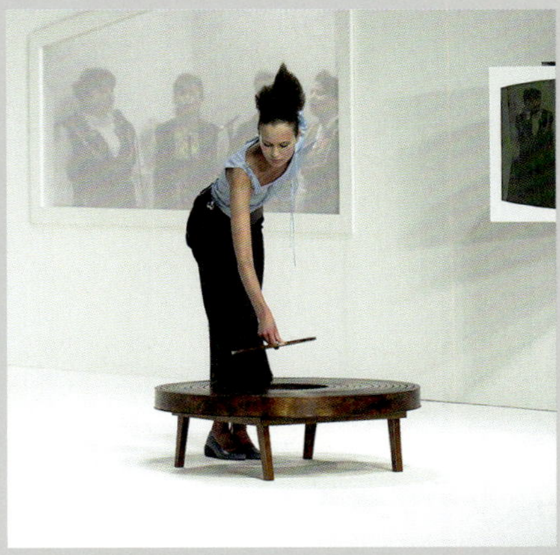

**Fig. 4** Hussein Chalayan
(b. 1970), design
Chris Moore (b. 1934),
photography/©Catwalking.com
*Afterwords,* 2000
Performance with detachable
low mahogany table-skirt during
the fashion show of the Collection
Fall 2000

The overly wide skirt reappeared in fashion of the 1950s as a petticoat and is currently experiencing a renaissance in bridal and ball gowns. Quite unromantically, in contrast, the fashion designer and artist Hussein Chalayan (b. 1970) has thematised a heavy skirt as a movable and changeable piece of furniture. | Fig. 4 | In the finale of his *Afterwords* collection (Fall 2000) show, the models take covers from armchairs and put them on, then a model climbs into the opening of a wooden coffee table, pulls it over her hips, which then opens up to become a skirt. The other models fold the chairs together like suitcases, whereupon everyone leaves the room with the furniture they are wearing. Here the crinoline is heavy and anything but comfortable, but it could symbolise that women virtually carry a house with them. Chalayan's designs are conceptually multi-layered as well as dressy. Given the then ubiquitous images of the war in former Yugoslavia, the collection has been read as a commentary on refugee flows. The designer was born in divided Cyprus and studied in London. He has repeatedly dealt with migration and nomadic life and stands at the interface between art and fashion. The show's video both documents a collection and serves as a repeatedly exhibited artwork. Chalayan uses the fashion show format to not only present clothes but also to make statements about their performative use, such as the previously-mentioned static table that turns into a mobile skirt.

With their decorations, the mid-nineteenth century clothes often appear like furniture. Similar materials were used, such as horsehair for upholstery or steel springs for seating comfort. Even comparable shapes were featured, such as those of a circular upholstered sofa with a centrepiece, the so-called borne.[18] The Viennese artist Jakob Lena Knebl (b. 1970) takes up this idea and turns herself into furniture in the so-called *Begehrensräumen* (spaces for desire) | Page **301** | The installation *Chesterfield* of 2014 includes a photograph showing Knebl as a light-green armchair. In the manner of Chesterfield upholstery, the body is painted plastically, the legs reduced to black furniture feet, and complementing this is the artist wearing thick velvet upholstery on her arms. In an inimitable way, she ironises body discourses and turns herself into an object that laughs back mockingly. The work of Knebl, who studied with the sculptor Heimo Zobernig (b. 1958) and the fashion designer Raf Simons (b. 1968), can also be read as a commentary on the history of fashion as a whole. While in the middle of the nineteenth century body extensions were external, today the body itself is shaped. | Page **136** |

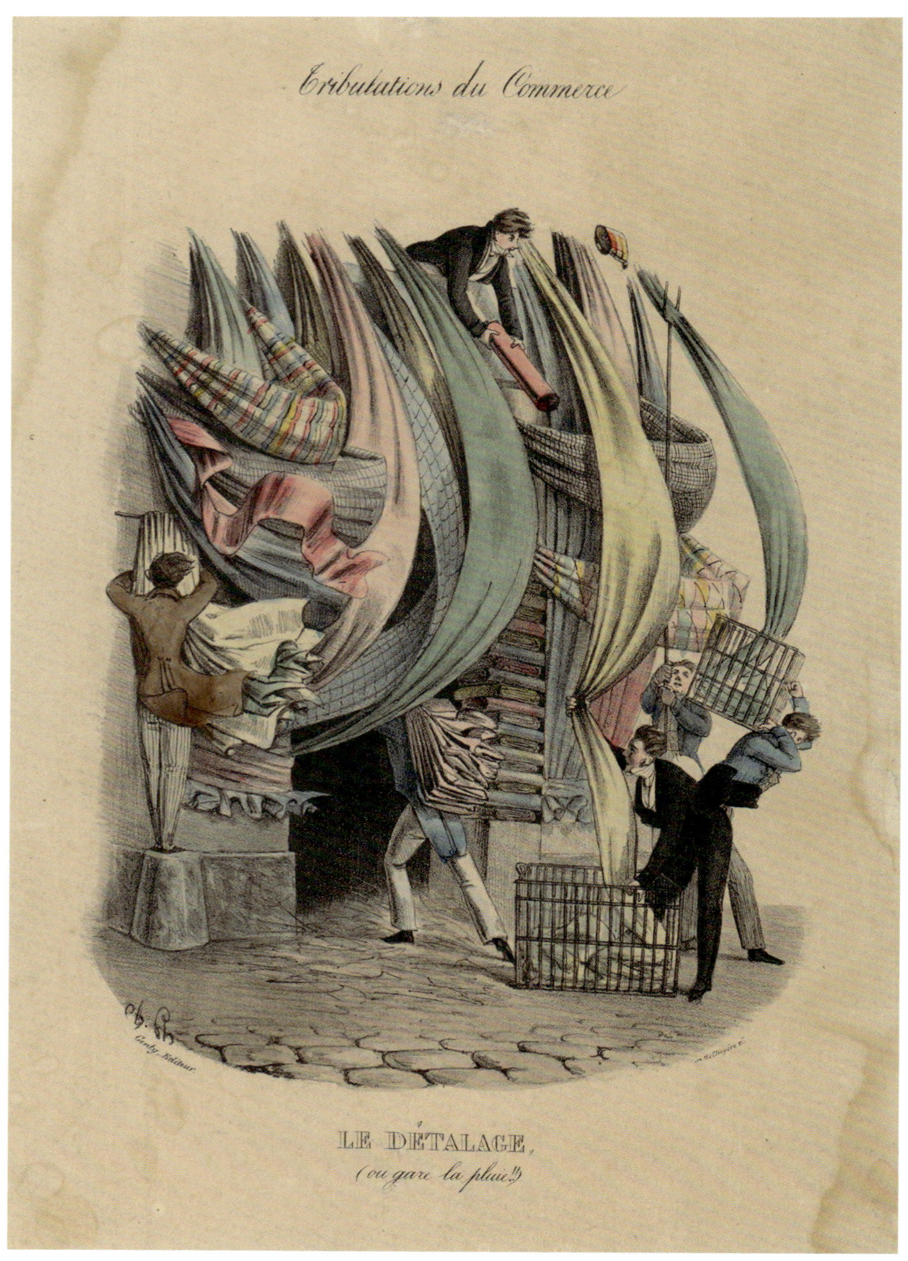



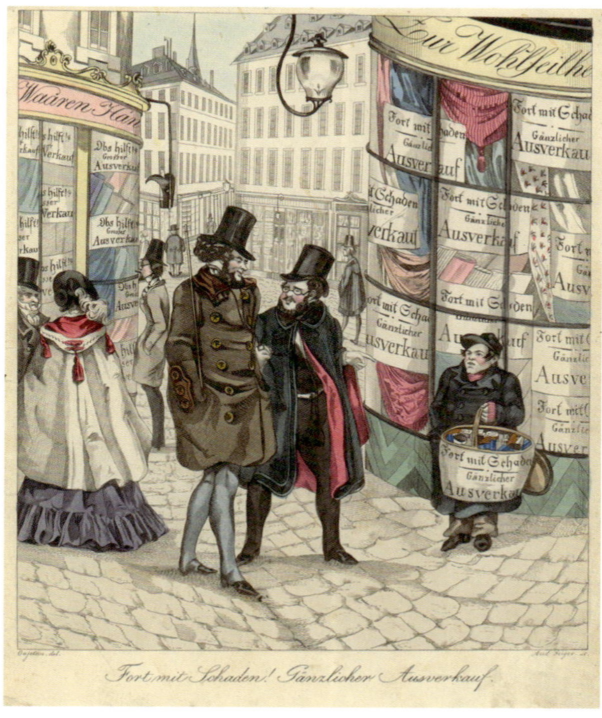



**228** Charles Philipon (1800–1862), lithographer
*Le Détalage*, c. 1827
Adversity of trade. Dismantling of the store display
Lithograph, coloured, sheet: 32.6 × 24.3 cm
Staatliche Museen zu Berlin, Kunstbibliothek

**74** after Joseph Cajetan (1821–1864)
Andreas Geiger (1765–1856), engraver
*Fort mit Schaden! Gänzlicher Ausverkauf!*, 1842
Away with damage! Total sale!
Copper engraving, coloured with
watercolours, sheet: 24.5 × 21.4 cm
Staatliche Museen zu Berlin, Kunstbibliothek

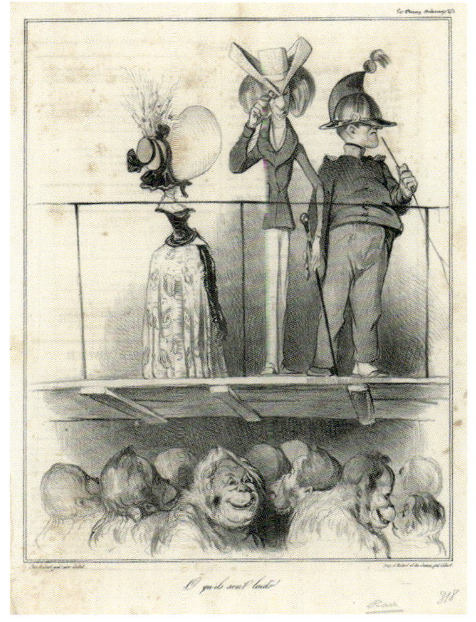

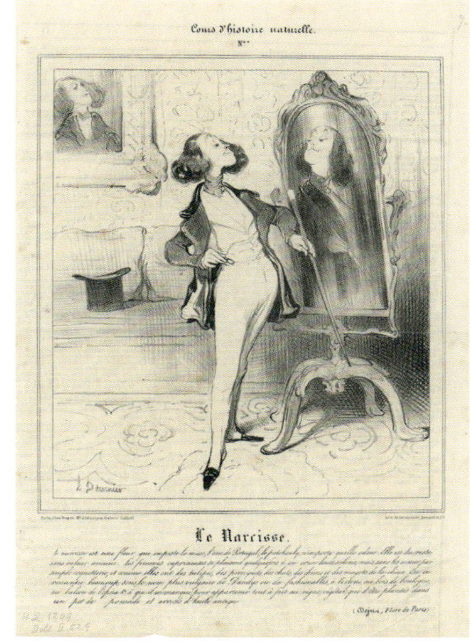

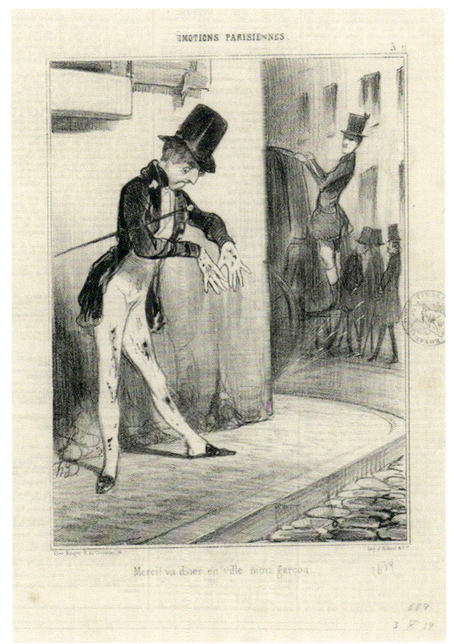

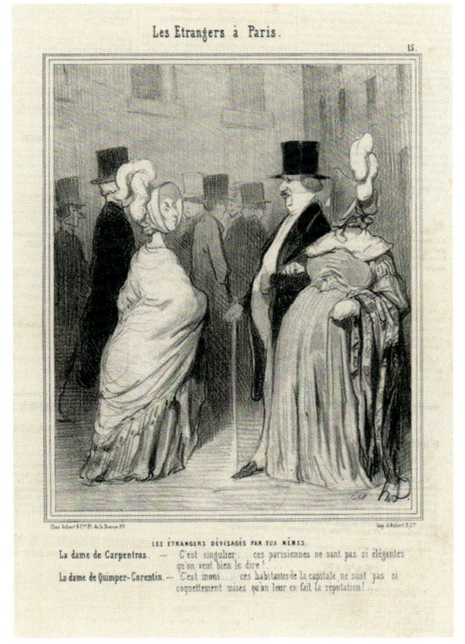

**90**  Honoré Daumier (1808–1879)
Oh how ugly they are!
In *Le Charivari,* 21 September 1836
Lithograph, sheet: 35.2 × 26 cm
Kunsthaus Zürich, Department
of Prints and Drawings

**91**  Honoré Daumier (1808–1879)
Narcissus. The narcissus is a flower that
stinks of musk, of Portuguese perfume,
of patchouli, of anything. Moreover, it is
absolutely worthless. Capricious women
sometimes enjoy using them as decoration
for their salons, but without really liking
them, just simple coquetry, like having tulips,
parrots, cats, dogs and Chinese porcelain
figures. They can be found often, under the
more vulgar name of dandys or fashionables,
in Tortoni, in the Bois de Boulogne, on the
opera balcony etc. where they are never
missing and where they are part of the floreal
décor, planted in a pot of pomade and watered
with antique oil. (De us, *Flore de Paris*)
Sheet 7 from the series *Cours d'histoire
naturelle 7,* in *Le Charivari,* 14 December 1837
Lithograph, sheet: 35.2 × 26 cm
Kunsthaus Zürich, Department
of Prints and Drawings

**92**  Honoré Daumier (1808–1879)
Thank you! Ready to dine out old boy!
In *Le Charivari,* 3 October 1839
Lithograph, sheet: 35.2 × 26 cm
Kunsthaus Zürich, Department
of Prints and Drawings

**95**  Honoré Daumier (1808–1879)
The lady from Carpentras: How peculiar,
but Parisian women are not at all as elegant
as one always says. ... The lady from Quimper-
Corentin: It's unheard of ... these women of
the capital are hardly as elegantly dressed
as their reputation has it!
In *Le Charivari,* 10 August 1844
Lithograph, sheet: 35.2 × 26 cm
Kunsthaus Zürich, Department
of Prints and Drawings

**47** John Baldessari (b. 1931)
*Double Bill: ... And Manet,* 2012
Varnished inkjet print on canvas with
acrylic and oil paint, 152.4 × 152.4 cm
Courtesy the artist and
Marian Goodman Gallery, New York

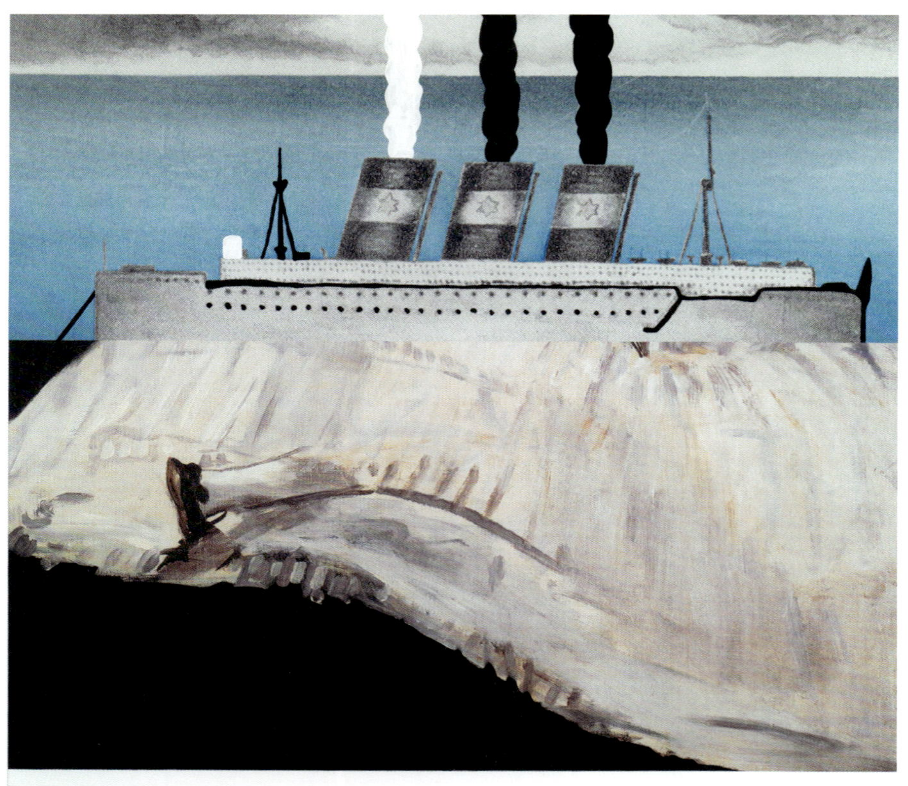

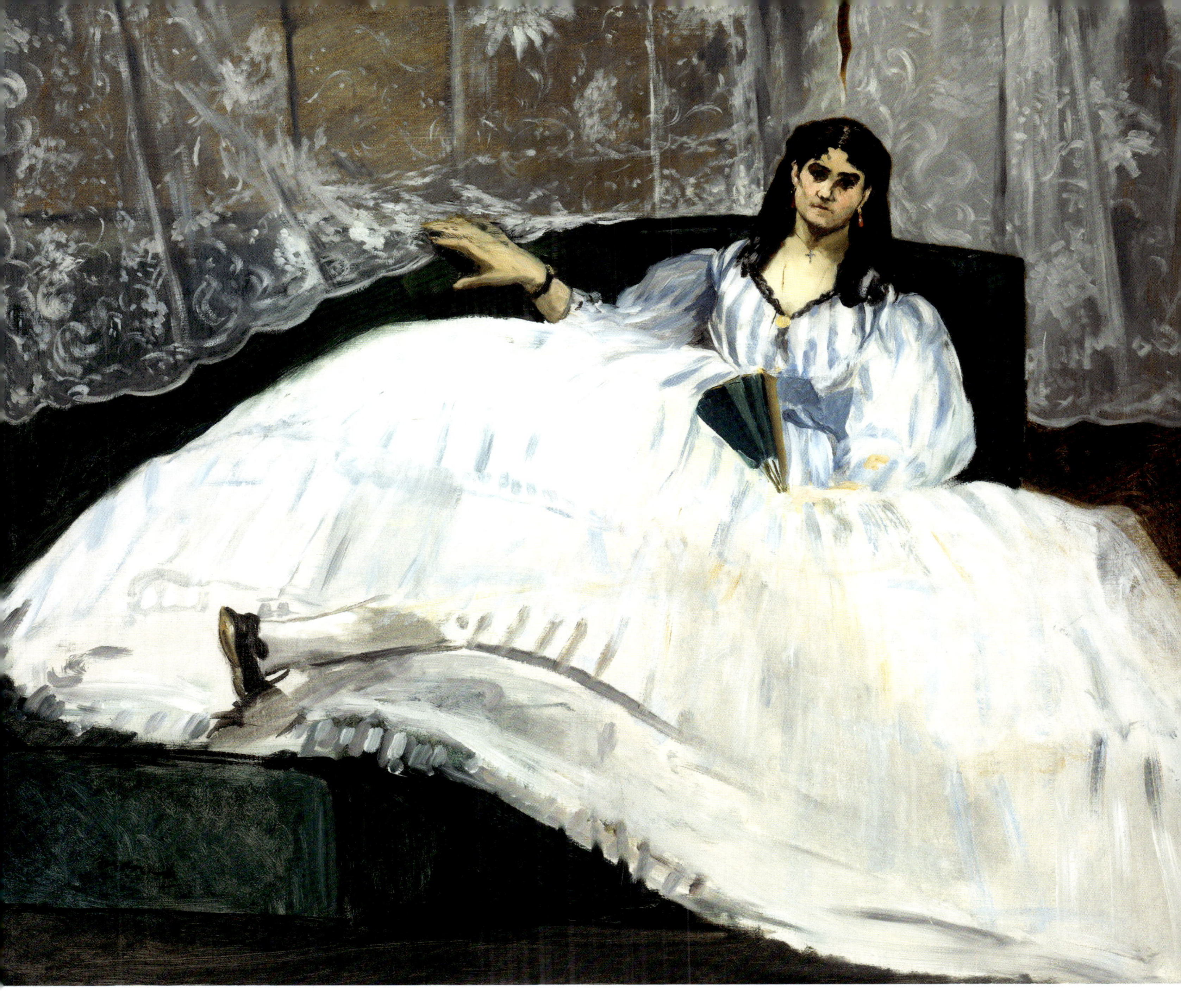

**211**  Édouard Manet (1832–1883)
*Jeanne Duval, la maîtresse de Baudelaire*
*(La Dame à l'éventail),* 1862
Oil on canvas, 89.5 × 113 cm
Museum of Fine Arts, Budapest

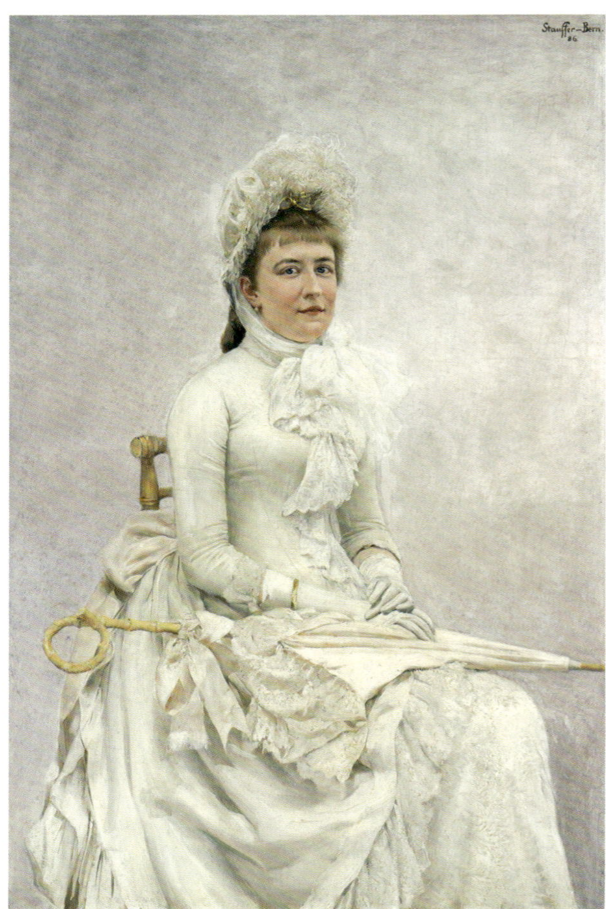

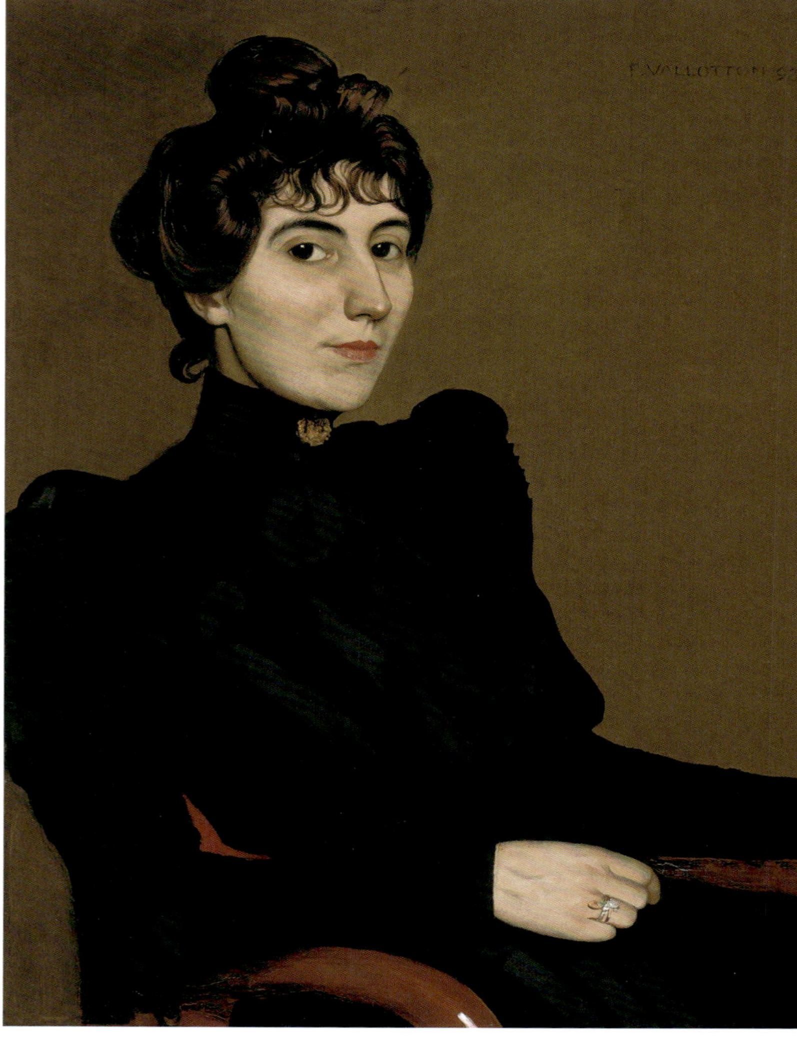

**245**  Karl Stauffer-Bern (1857–1891)
*Portrait of Lydia Welti-Escher,* 1886
Oil on canvas, 150.5 × 100 cm
Kunsthaus Zürich, loan from
the Gottfried Keller Foundation,
Federal Office of Culture, Bern, 1941

**288**  Félix Vallotton (1865–1925)
*Portrait of Marthe Mellot,* 1898
Oil on canvas, 73 × 60 cm
Kunsthaus Zürich, Vereinigung
Zürcher Kunstfreunde, 1938

**289**  Félix Vallotton (1865–1925)
*Le Chapeau violet,* 1907
Oil on canvas, 81 × 65.5 cm
Dauerleihgabe an die Hahnloser/Jaeggli-Stiftung,
ehemalige Sammlung Arthur und Hedy
Hahnloser-Bühler, Villa Flora, Winterthur

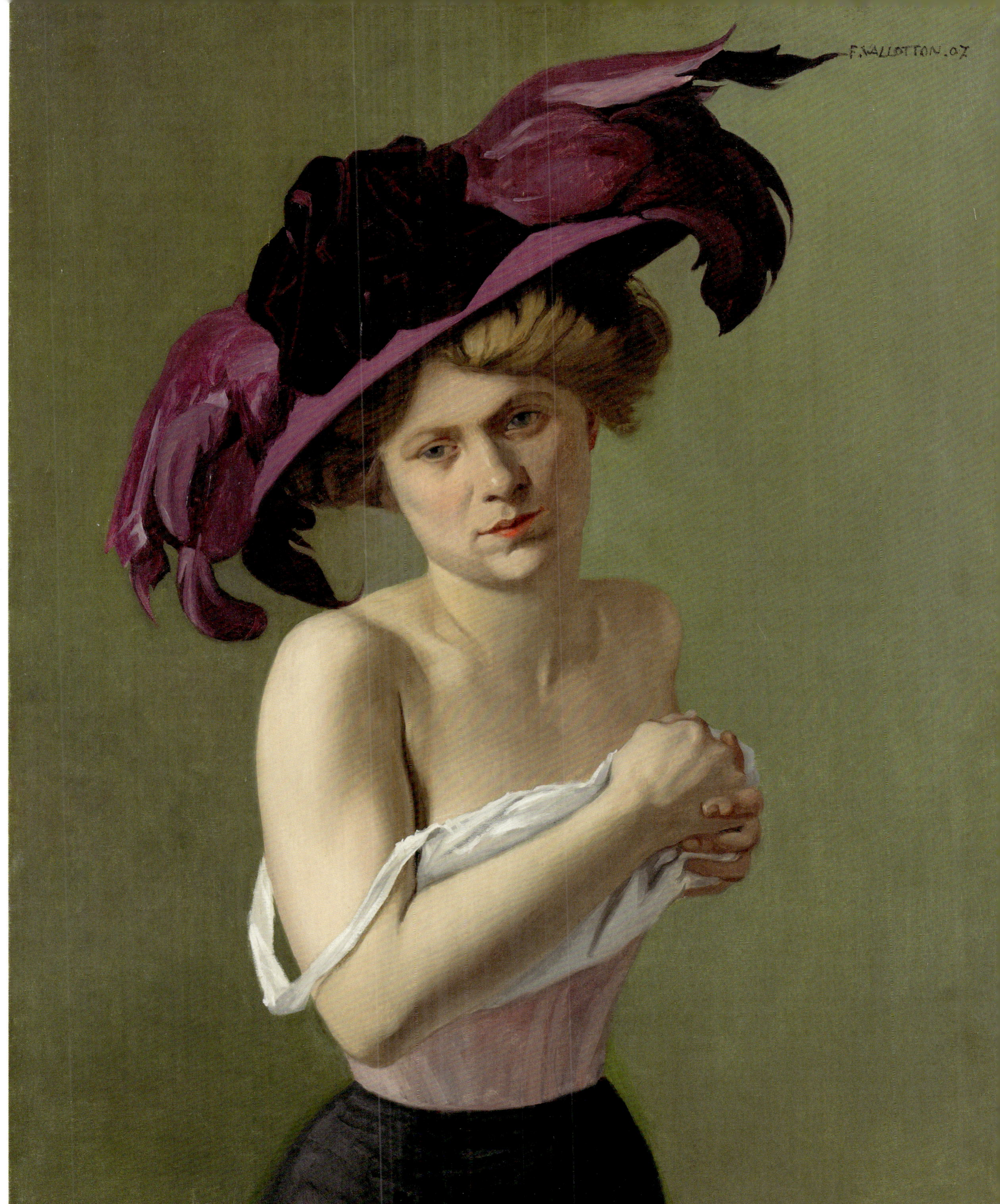

F. VALLOTTON. 07

# Fashion and in

**Cathérine Hug**

# Public Structural Change

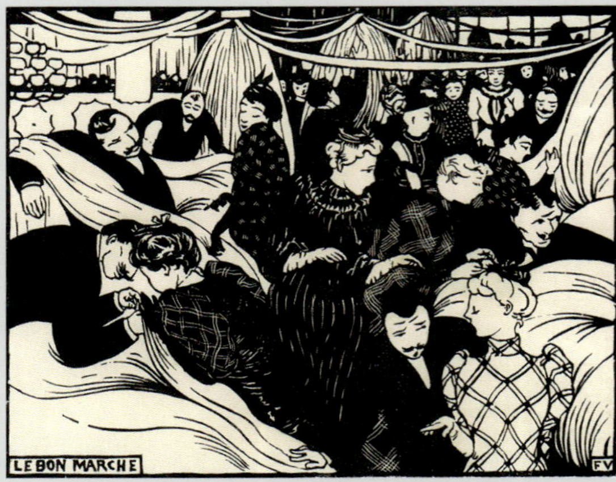


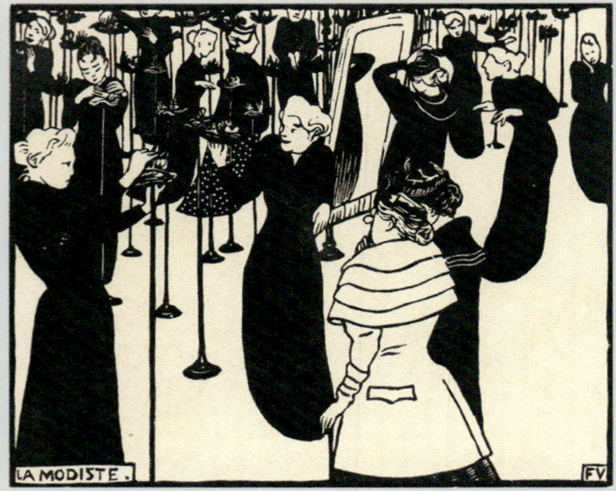




'However, when she was going through the silk scarves and glove departments, her will weakened once more. There, in the diffused light, stood a bright, gaily coloured display which made a delightful effect.'[1]

In 1883, Émile Zola (1840–1902) – at that time barely known beyond the borders of France – described in a surprising manner what we now call shopping fever or impulse buying. The author, famous for his socio-critical studies of society, became, from the late 1870s, increasingly interested in the ambivalent meaning of public or semi-public spaces such as the department store. He condensed his observations into his epochal novel *The Ladies' Paradise* (originally: *Au bonheur des dames)*. One should try to remember the following: exactly at that time, the department store, with its attractive displays of different brands, was created as we know it today; and with it came fashion-specific mechanisms such as the compulsion and even system-inherent necessity for innovation, on the one hand, and the emergence of standard sizes, and thus the longing for the ideal figure, on the other – along with a capitalist logic of growth that resulted in the concept of the clearance sale. Although all these aspects are now regarded as problematic and must be vigorously questioned, it should not be forgotten that the birth of department stores has also brought some positive effects, in that they have promoted – and in some cases even initiated – desirable changes for society, particularly with regard to equality between men and women. The following essay will consider the department stores' positive contributions, which tend to be forgotten, to expanding the public sphere.[2]

The concept of protected shopping arcades was already established as early as the 1770s; in particular, a law in 1791 – the *Loi Le Chapelier* – enabled the freedom to trade without restrictions.[3] The French Revolution set in motion a progressive democratisation of consumption; in the beginning of the 1870s, Auguste Hériot (1826–1879), with the *Grands Magasins du Louvre,* and Aristide Boucicaut (1810–1877), with his *Le Bon Marché,* heralded the start of a new era of the large department store.[4] On an artistic level, a fascinated and, at the same time, critical observer of this development was Félix Vallotton (1865–1925). His painting *Le Bon*

**281** Félix Vallotton (1865–1925)
*Le Bon Marché,* 1893
Woodcut on vellum, sheet: 23.6 × 33 cm
Kunsthaus Zürich, Department
of Prints and Drawings

**282** Félix Vallotton (1865–1925)
*La Modiste,* 1894
Woodcut, sheet: 23.6 × 30.7 cm
Kunsthaus Zürich, Department
of Prints and Drawings

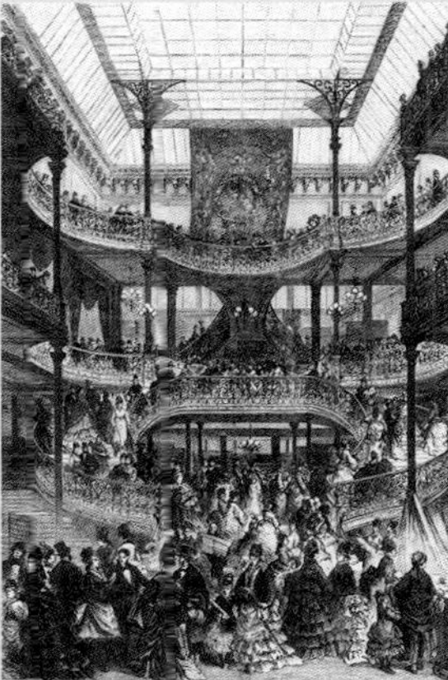

**Fig. 1** Frédéric Lix (1830-1897), after
Auguste Victor Deroy (1823–1906), etcher
*The new staircase* in *Le Bon Marché*
In *Le Monde Illustré,* c. 1875
Engraving
Private collection

*Marché* (1898, private collection) |<sup>Page</sup> 266| has the shape of a triptych and illustrates the artist's ambivalent, sacral disposition, towards what Zola described as *cathédrales du commerce moderne.*[5] Of astonishing timeliness in this painting is the sea of people: Then, as now, department stores are a collection of individuals who pursue their personal needs, indifferent to their neighbours' backgrounds. Even though then, as now, purchasing power still decides who leaves the place with more or fewer purchases, revolutionary developments emerged: A department store is historically seen as the first place after the church where women were allowed to leave the house unaccompanied and where, due to the lack of obligation to purchase, all social groups also mingled. The immersive character of the displayed merchandise and the fixed price tags, as seen in the outer wings of Vallotton's triptych, had not previously been shown in this way. The engaging character of the merchandise becomes even more obvious in Vallotton's woodcut *Le Bon Marché* (1893), |<sup>Page</sup> 196| executed five years before the painting, where the potential client seems virtually submerged in the touted merchandise, similar to the billowing waves of the sea. The association is not coincidental, the advent of railway travel at that time, strongly favoured a new leisure activity: beach tourism. The sensation of being in flux was also intensified by gas lighting, and at the turn of the century, electric lighting and glazed skylights. They were first used by architects such as Louis-Auguste Boileau (1812–1896), one of the inventors of iron architecture.[6] |<sup>Fig.</sup> 1| Conspicuous in Vallotton's print and the painting is the

interaction between men and women: In both cases, men serve the predominantly female clientele. The artist thus addresses the new issue of socially intolerable encounters between married women and unknown men. At the time of the artwork's creation, however, this perceived danger was already remedied by employing women as shop assistants. Women were previously employed mainly in home and factory work; however, with the *vendeuse,* the saleswoman, a type of work emerged that enabled women, for the first time, to advance in society regardless of marriage.[7] Zola addressed this new development in his novel *The Ladies' Paradise,* and those who read the book could follow the daily routine of a saleswoman. Remarkably, the author did long-term, on-site investigations of the real conditions in order to write as naturalistically as possible about a middle class that increasingly enjoyed consumption.[8]

The typical saleswoman could have looked like Vallotton's *Marthe Mellot* (1898). |<sup>Page</sup> 192| Although Mellot (1870–1947) was an actress in the ensemble of the famous Parisian avant-garde theatre Théâtre de l'Œuvre, the painter depicted her in a self-determined but inconspicuous manner. Black clothes were appropriate and, at the same time, fashionable with women who worked in public, such as actresses (while they were not on the stage) or simply saleswomen. Making a virtue out of necessity, Mellot decorated her black dress with shimmering silk ribbons on her chest, and she let their original spirals flow onto her fashionably pronounced shoulders. Black also befitted the female employees of *Le Bon Marché* because they had

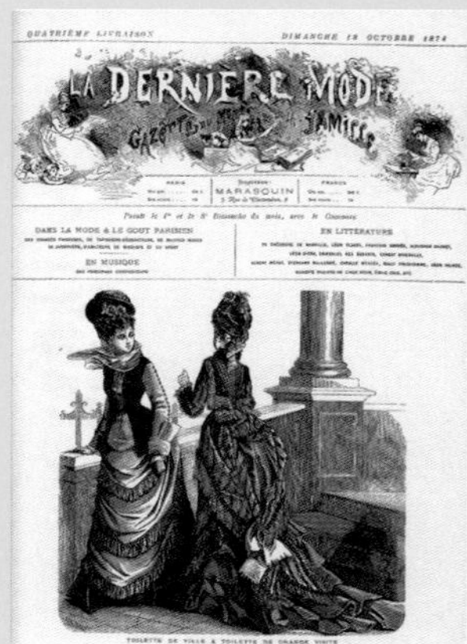 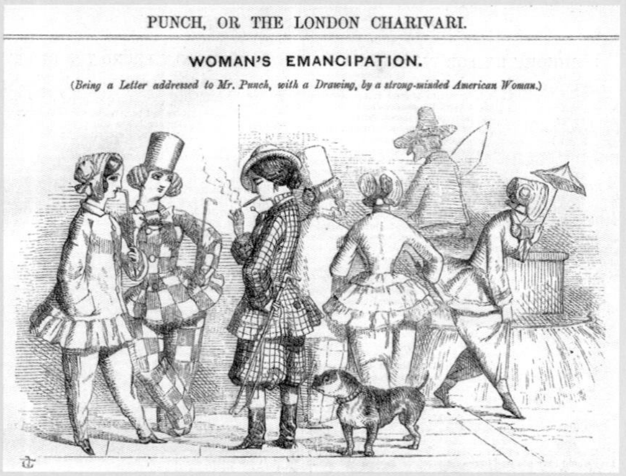



**Fig. 2** Stéphane Mallarmé (1842–1898), editor
Cover of his fashion magazine
*La Dernière Mode,* Paris 18 October 1874

**248** John Tenniel (1820–1914)
*Woman's emancipation (being a letter addressed to Mr. Punch, with a drawing, by a strong-minded American woman)*
In *Punch, or the London Charivari,* London, vol. 21, July–December 1851, p. 3
Kunsthaus Zürich, Library

to appear respectable and, at the same time, should not provoke any sense of competition with potential buyers.[9] In Karl Stauffer-Bern's (1857–1891) *Portrait of Lydia Welti-Escher* (1886), | Page **192** | the subject in her white dress seems to contrast with the black of Marthe Mellot, but is essentially another expression of the same tendency in fashion development that can be traced back to the *Mois du Blanc,* the Month of White.

This, in turn, harkens back to the entirely new sales strategy of *Le Bon Marché's* founder Aristide Boucicaut: Instead of a profit margin of 40 to 50 percent, there was only a 13 percent margin on goods.[10] As a result, *Le Bon Marché* was able to offer its products at the cheapest price and thus attracted the most female customers while it was at the same time bogged down with surplus goods. In January 1883, Boucicaut came up with the idea of a clearance sale in which he offered the remaining, regular-priced white clothes and top-quality goods – initially annually and then seasonally – at bargain prices. Thus, the portraits of Marthe Mellot and Lydia Welti-Escher stand for two contrasting and, at the same time, complementary dynamics. While the wealthy, non-working Welti-Escher indulges in the frivolous whims of fashion, Mellot's appearance suggests the ability to combine the reputable elegance of a public figure with the then disreputable occupation of an actress.[11] Thanks to the range of products on offer in the department store, the two women have a connection: they have been able to escape the conventional everyday work of sewing and thus can pursue other activities.

What began with individual persons, such as the Contessa di Castiglione (1837–1899) and her eccentric, but truly artful self-staging in elite circles which coincided with the beginnings of photography – in 1865, Pierre-Louis Pierson (1822–1913) took photographs of her | Page **278** | – became the general social credo of self-determination; the affordable[12] ranges of products increasingly penetrated the everyday life of the middle class. As one of many consequences of industrialisation, this development took place internationally: Department stores emerged not only in France, of course, but also in England, the United States, and soon afterwards in German-speaking countries. Prerequisites for this development included glass-iron architecture, which had first appeared on the occasion of the big world exhibitions, the invention of the industrially manufactured sewing machines by Isaac M. Singer (1811–1875) around 1851, and the growing mobility thanks to the railway that not only fuelled but also inspired the already existing rivalry between fashion nations France and Britain.[13] The fashion magazines, which enjoyed massively growing circulation, offered a means for those who could not afford such clothes to at least get a picture of what was *à la dernière mode* in the metropolises of Europe and especially in Paris (Stéphane Mallarmé, 1874).[14] | Fig. **2** | Regardless of whether the growing independence of the affluent middle-class woman correlated with an ever-greater reliance on insatiable consumption, Aristide and Marguerite Boucicault (1816–1887) laid a new groundwork for employee rights in their business *Le Bon Marché,* rights that we now take for granted.



Cathérine Hug

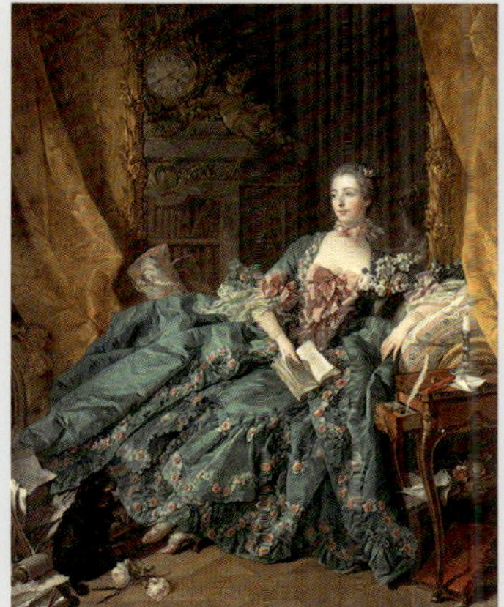





As early as 1877, *Le Bon Marché* employed around 1,800 people and, in 1887, operated 74 autonomously managed departments that included silk, women's clothing, ties, shirts and cosmetics, along with a mail-order business.[15] The Boucicaults, who were motivated not least by their experiences of social disturbances such as the July Revolution (1830) and the Commune (1871) as well as by their own modest origins, introduced social institutions such as company-owned housing, free evening training courses and a pension fund.[16]

Let us step back and turn our attention from the individual to the general, to what fashion can trigger when viewed by crowds of people. A huge change in public space, which became apparent during the 19th century, was the growing presence of elegantly and conspicuously dressed women in parks, on the streets, in cafés and tea houses, in railways, on racecourses, on beaches as well as at major events such as world exhibitions and, of course, in the grand magasins described above. Artists impressively revealed the transformations in how men and an increasing number of women staged themselves in the public space. |<sup>Pages</sup> **205–208** | These artists included around 1815, Johann Nepomuk Hoechle (1790–1835) in Vienna, Jean-Baptiste Isabey (1767–1855) in Paris and George Cruikshank (1792–1878) in London, Honoré Daumier (1808–1879) in the 1850s and then especially Félix Vallotton, Pierre Bonnard (1867–1947) and Édouard Vuillard (1868–1940). The latter three artists, all of them members of the artists' group Nabis, strikingly portray people merging with their environment – architecture and the crowd – yet standing out through the pattern of their garments' fabrics. Vallotton's *L'Arverse, Le Coup de vent* and also Pierre Bonnard's *Femmes au jardin* | <sup>Page</sup> **208** | clearly illustrate these two aspects: Certain fabric patterns occur repeatedly and thus demonstrate the industrial, inexpensive, mass production of printed cotton as well as its fashionable value. The fascination with the hypnotic power of fabric patterns continues in art to this day; for example, Sylvie Fleury (b. 1961) takes this up through her decontextualisation of a Valentino pattern in a painted tondo. | <sup>Page</sup> **218** | Difficulties such as weather conditions and road pavements made new demands on women's clothing. Although

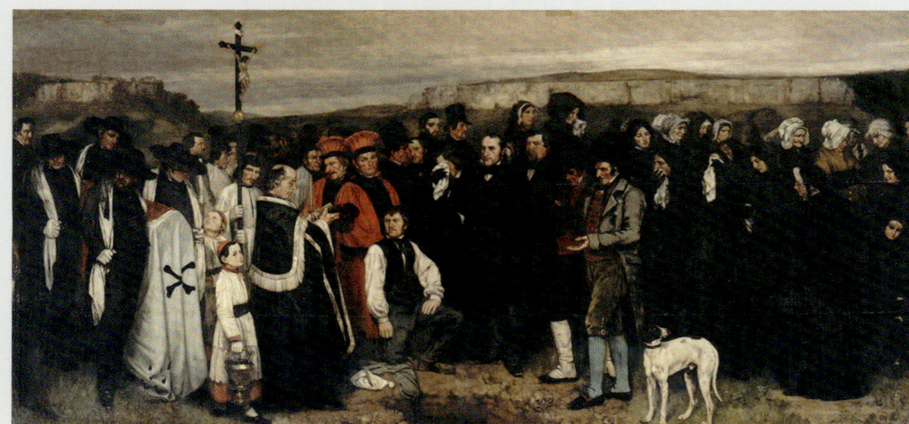



the restoration of the Second Empire resulted in a reactionary wind blowing again, the end of the cumbersome crinoline and constraining corset was inevitable, as short skirts | ^Page **234** | were already known as soon as the 1830s and women's trousers during the 1850s. | **248** | Overall, however, the increasing presence of women in public spaces also became apparent in the disconcerting development, which was already indicated in the prints of Daumier and Vallotton and which still seems to have general validity today: While a woman's wardrobe is becoming more diversified, a man's wardrobe is becoming more uniform and restrained. This corresponded (and still does today) with a male-dominated society which claims that to not be distracted from the externalities of one's counterpart when dealing with political and economic concerns, one should appear in a dark suit and with a top hat or in a military uniform.[17]

The ever-increasing mobility of women inevitably demanded more practical clothing. Thus, the clothing reform movements that began in 1881 with the Rational Dress Society in England and from 1887 in France gradually became institutionalised as an expression of a far-reaching profound social change, namely that of equality between men and women.[18] However, the most famous impulse of the reform dress movement came not from the country of the declaration of human rights, but from the German-speaking world and was initiated by Peter Behrens (1868–1940), Anna Muthesius (1870–1961), Henry (1863–1957) and Maria van de Velde (1867–1943), the Wiener Werkstätten, as well as Emilie Flöge (1874–1952) and Gustav

Klimt (1862–1918). This artists' movement is considered as one of the most important and most comprehensive contributions to fashion history. | ^Pages **210–214** | From today's perspective, Henry van de Velde's visionary and commendable claim, however, also leaves mixed feelings in light of his chauvinistic, patronising overtones: 'I think I can rightly say that the efforts we have made have also forced the big Parisian houses to follow the principle of "reasonable dress". [...] if reason sets a limit to the arbitrariness of Parisian fashion houses, we hope that they will learn more from us, but especially that the essential beauty of a fabric consists of the play and life of its drapery. On this basis, one must create cuts of clothes which produce these folds and give these fabrics this life that no "French" cut has offered for a long time.'[19]

Just as unflattering in terms of women's independent thinking and willingness to make decisions, the economist and sociologist Thorstein Veblen (1857–1929) was also influential in his time, seeing money as the main form of expression in fashion. In so doing, he ignored the fact that the new fashion industry was beginning to focus its attention mainly on the female middle class, which had risen through industrialisation, and had been neglected thus far: 'The assumption is that the more society, especially the affluent classes, develop, [...] the faster fashion changes and the more grotesque and unbearable forms it takes on.'[20] This polarising statement places much more emphasis on social differences than on the equally promising potential for equality, as also expressed in a problematic way in a work such as *An den Hallen in Paris*

Cathérine Hug

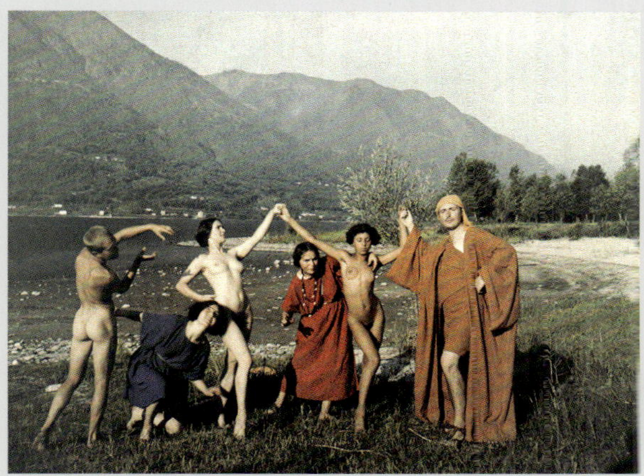
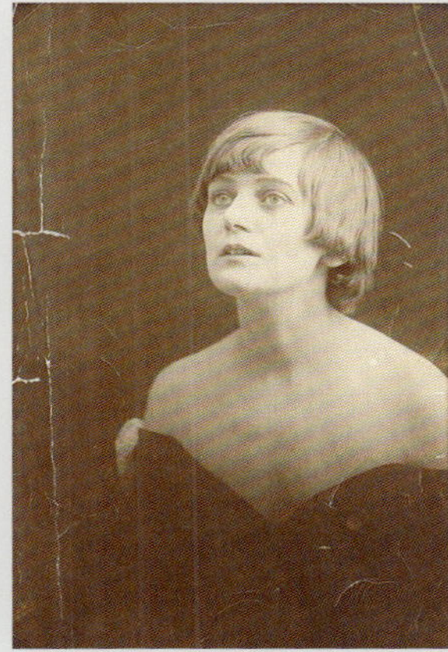

**213** Johann Adam Meisenbach
(1892–1959)
*Suzanne Perrottet and
Dancers at the Lago Maggiore
near Ascona,* 1914
3 photographs from
autochrome plates,
plates: 9 × 12 cm each
Kunsthaus Zürich, Library

**262** Unknown photographer
*Emmy Hennings,* Munich 1912
Black-and-white photograph,
14.5 × 10.5 cm
Kunsthaus Zürich,
Archive Zürcher Kunstgesell-
schaft and Kunsthaus Zürich

(At 'Les Halles' in Paris, 1903). | <sup>Page</sup> **205** | At a time when the choice of clothes became increasingly personal, motivated independently of rank and education, this painting shows, in the tradition of Gustave Courbet's (1819–1877) study of poor people in *A Burial at Ornans,* also called *A Painting of Human Figures, the History of a Burial at Ornans* (1849/50, Paris, Musée d'Orsay, | <sup>Fig.</sup> **4** | that dismantling old social barriers simultaneously created new ones, including those of money. And so, the new amenities of the exhilarating nightlife of the Belle Époque – in contrast to the new wholesale department stores – were reserved for the affluent. Although this charge against the elite is undoubtedly valid, an interesting observation emerges thanks to the images that highlight the nightlife: In the intoxicating and aphrodisiacal atmosphere combining dance, music and alcohol, norms of behaviour, as well as clothes, are stripped off in centrifugal movements, as in Giovanni Boldini's (1842–1931) *A l'opéra di Parigi* (At the Opra in Paris, 1886) | <sup>Page</sup> **206** | or Suzanne Perrottet's (1889–1983) naked dancers on Monte Verità and at Lake Maggiore (1914). | **213** | The worldwide, triumphant march of the myth of the Parisian woman as the epitome of the fashion-conscious and, simultaneously, self-determined woman was, however, unstoppable. Socio-politically important court ladies such as Madame de Pompadour (1721–1764), | <sup>Fig.</sup> **3** | the first fashion designers such as Rose Bertin (1747–1813) at the side of Marie-Antoinette,[21] the *merveilleuses* of the directorate | <sup>Page</sup> **139** | or Madame Récamier (1777–1849) | <sup>Page</sup> **141** | during the empire, laid the foundations for a long tradition that fell on fertile ground with the establishment of large department stores such as *Le Bon Marché.*[22] The series of postcards in mass circulation such as *La Journée de la parisienne* (The Day of the Parisian woman, c. 1900), | <sup>Page</sup> **207** | also provide information, little noticed by cultural history, on the true subversiveness of the Parisienne's lifestyle: As you can see here, the protagonist decides on her daily routine, and dresses appropriately for each part of the day (sometimes practical, sometimes jaunty, sometimes elegant and seductive), and even, at half past one, self-confidently enjoyed a relaxing cigarette, which at that time – as well as the bob hairstyle | **262** | and Marlene Dietrich's trouser suit thirty years twenty years later – was regarded throughout Europe as a distinguishing feature of the emancipated woman.[23]

201

1     Émile Zola, *The Ladies' Paradise: A Realistic Novel*, trans. Ernest Alfred Vizetelly, London 1886, p. 187.

2     Sonja Eismann offers critical observation of fashion as consumer goods, which would unequivocally crystallise in the second half of the 20th century, in this publication, pp. 264 ff.

3     Béatrice de Andia, 'Aux origines d'une révolution', in Béatrice de Andia and Caroline François (eds), *Les cathédrales du commerce parisien. Grands magasins et enseignes,* Paris 2006, pp. 14–16.

4     See Jan Whitaker, *Wunderwelt Warenhaus: Eine internationale Geschichte,* Hildesheim 2013 (first as *The World of Department Stores,* New York 2011); de Andia and François 2006 (as in note 3); Bernard Marrey, *Les grands magasins: des origines à 1939,* Paris 1979.

5     In the first edition of 1883, Zola talks of the *cathédrales du commerce moderne* on pp. 87, 282; see original under http://gallica.bnf.fr/ark:/12148/bpt6k1025132k/f11 (accessed 25 November 2017).

6     On the revolutionary character of iron and glass in the architecture of the modern department store, see Louis-Charles Boileau, 'Fondations des magasins du Bon Marché', in *Construction moderne: Revue mensuelle d'architecture,* vol. 2, Paris 1887, pp. 426–28; as well as the apt evaluation of Sigfried Giedion, *Raum, Zeit, Architektur: Die Entstehung einer neuen Tradition,* Zurich/Munich 1984 (first as *Space, Time, Architecture: The Growth of a New Tradition,* Cambridge 1941), pp. 170–73.

7     The changing working conditions of textile workers in the 19th century have been better researched for the United Kingdom, Germany and Switzerland than for France. See Phyllis G. Tortora, 'Tools that enable fashion change and innovations in dress', in Phyllis G. Tortora, *Dress, Fashion, and Technology: From Prehistory to the Present,* London 2015, pp. 125–40; Ruth Rhein-von Niederhäusern, *Leute machen Kleider: Arbeitsverhältnisse und gewerkschaftliche Organisation in der stadtzürcherischen Bekleidungsindustrie 1880–1918,* Zurich 1999; James A. Schmiechen, *Sweated Industries and Sweated Labor: The London Clothing Trades 1860–1914,* London 1984.

8     Zola's notes, encompassing around 380 manuscript pages, contain his hand-drawn room plans, statistics about the employees, analyses of their working conditions and habits and much more. See the digitalised archive material here: http://gallica.bnf.fr/ark:/12148/btv1b9079765s/f4.image.r=Au%20bonheur%20des%20dames%20Emile%20Zola (accessed 25 November 2017).

9     *Wünsche werden wahr – Die Entstehung des Kaufhauses.* Doku-drama/documentary, France 2011, 86 min., screenplay and directors: Sally Aitken and Christine Le Goff, production: arte France, Telfrance and Essential Viewing.

10     Monica Burckhardt, 'L'éclosion des Grands Magasins. Le Bon Marché', in de Andia and François 2006 (as in note 3), p. 46.

11     On the change in meaning of black in fashion, see, for example, Anne Hollander, *Seeing through Clothes,* Berkeley 1993 (first New York 1978), pp. 382–90.

12     Interestingly, the French expression *bon marché* is still synonymous for the cheap or low-priced, without the general knowledge (at least outside of France) of the connection to a particular department store.

13     Aileen Ribeiro elaborates on this rivalry, which, not least, also has its origin in the politics of the 18th century. See in this publication, pp. 116 ff.

14     The relevance of fashion magazines in forming the Western understanding of fashion, but also as a tool for the fashion industry, has been considered in many places and is not the focus of this publication. Stéphane Mallarmé's magazine *À la dernière Mode,* published eight times in 1874, is of particular artistic value. Mallarmé was de facto the only author in this publication, but wrote under various, predominantly female, pseudonyms, such as 'Miss Satin'. Instead of 'mode', he frequently spoke of 'fashion'. See also *Velours et guipure: Mallarmé et 'La dernière Mode',* Antoine Terrasse and Pauline de Lannoy (eds), exh. cat. Musée Mallarmé, Vulaines-sur-Seine 2003. The relationship between fashion and art in Mallarmé was explored extensively by Jean Pierre Lecercle, *Mallarmé et la mode: Le poëte en grève,* Paris 2014, pp. 187–203. Recent research shows that the poet Emily Dickinson played an important part in the debate on the fashion industry and their mechanisms. See the chapter 'Dress the Maker' in Daneen Wardrop, *Emily Dickinson and the Labor of Clothing,* Durham 2009, pp. 41–78.

15     Burckhardt 2006 (as in note 10), pp. 46, 48.

16     The role of Marguerite Boucicaut in the introduction of social welfare benefits was particularly important. See here Jean-Louis Debré and Valérie Bochenek, 'Marguerite Boucicaut et Marie-Louise Jaÿ. Les premiers magasins parisiens: du Bon Marché à la Samaritaine. Des patrons rouges', in *Ces femmes qui ont réveillé la France,* Jean-Louis Debré and Valérie Bochenek (eds), Paris 2013, pp. 374–76.

17     Inessa Kouteinikova's essay in this publication (pp. 160 ff) outlines how this development also relates to the history of the dandy. Thus far, the most expansive description of the suit's social history has been provided by Anja Meyerrose, *Herren im Anzug: Eine transatlantische Geschichte von Klassengesellschaften im langen 19. Jahrhundert,* Cologne/Weimer/Vienna 2016. With particular focus on artistic depictions, see Andrew Stephenson, 'But the Coat is the Picture': Issues of Masculine Fashioning, Politics, and Sexual Identity in Portraiture in England 1890–1900', in *Fashion in European Art: Dress and Identity, Politics and the Body, 1775–1925,* Justine De Young (ed.), London/New York 2017, pp. 178–206. With particular focus on the socio-political implications – especially also for women – of an increasingly more reserved men's fashion from the 1860s onwards, see Gesa C. Teichert, *Mode. Macht. Männer: Kulturwissenschaftliche Überlegungen zur bürgerlichen Herrenmode des 19. Jahrhunderts,* Münster 2013.

18     Diana Crane, 'Clothing Behaviour as Non-Verbal Resistance: Marginal Women and Alternative Dress in the Nineteenth Century', in *The Fashion History Reader: Global Perspectives,* Giorgio Riello and Peter McNeil (eds), London/New York 2010, pp. 334–53, here especially p. 343.




Cathérine Hug

**19** Henry van de Velde, 'Das neue Kunst-Prinzip in der modernen Frauen-Kleidung', in *Deutsche Kunst und Dekoration,* vol. 10, May 1902, reprint in *Gegen den Strich: Kleider von Künstlern 1900–1940,* Radu Stern (ed.), exh. cat. Museum Bellerive, Zurich; Musée des arts décoratifs, Lausanne, Bern 1993, pp. 106–07.

**20** Thorstein Veblen, 'Die Kleidung als Ausdruck des Geldes' (1899), reprint in *Absolute Fashion: Anthologie historischer modehistorischer Essays,* Sonja Eismann (ed.), Freiburg im Breisgau 2012, pp. 32–45, here p. 38.

**21** An important recent publication and first comprehensive study on Rose Bertin comes from Michelle Sapori, *Rose Bertin, couturière de Marie-Antoinette,* Versailles 2010.

**22** On the myth of the Parisian woman see, among others, Alexandra Bosc, 'Le mythe de la Parisienne', in *Paris 1900: La ville spectacle,* Christophe Leribault, Isabelle Collet and Dominique Lobstein (eds), exh. cat. Petit Palais, Paris, Paris 2014, pp. 218–63. In addition: Gloria Groom, 'Spaces of Modernity', in *Impressionism, Fashion & Modernity,* Guy Cogeval and Gloria Groom (eds), exh. cat. Musée d'Orsay Paris; The Art Institute of Chicago; The Metropolitan Museum of Art; New York, New Haven, Conn./London 2013, pp. 165–85.

**23** *Glanz und Elend in der Weimarer Republik,* Ingrid Pfeiffer (ed.), exh. cat. Kunsthalle Schirn Frankfurt, Frankfurt am Main/Munich 2017, pp. 152–72.

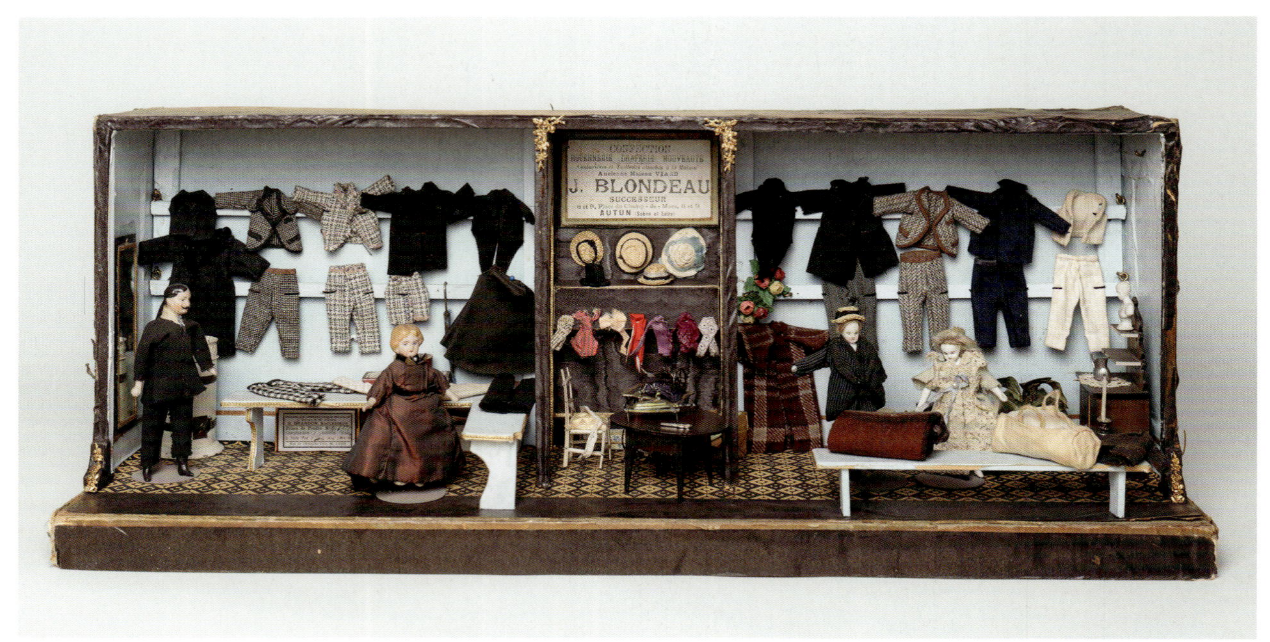

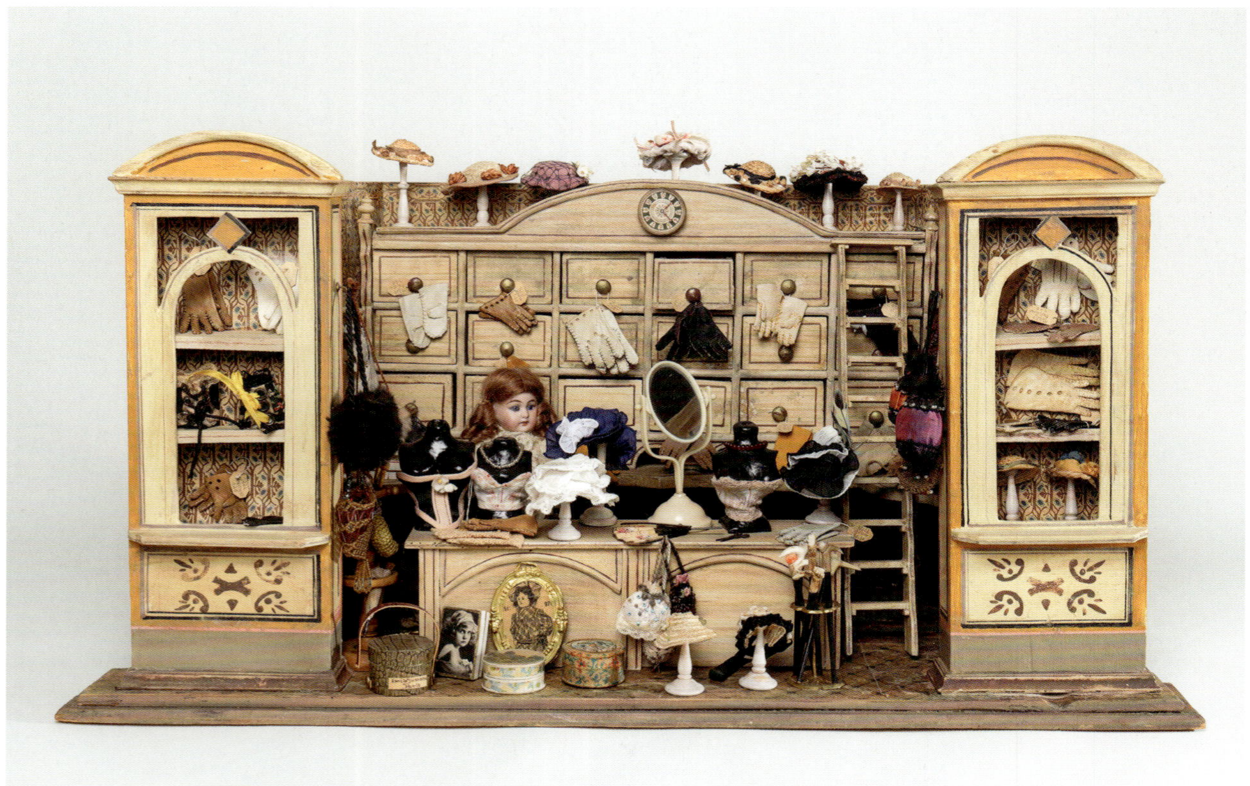

**17** Doll's house: gentlemen's outfitters, France c. 1880
Three-part with round arch joints, papered floor, patterned
in black and brown, light blue painted walls with sewn-on men's
clothing, two blue wooden counters and two dressed porcelain
dolls, completely furnished, 27.5 × 71 × 19.5 cm
Spielzeug Welten Museum Basel

**18** Doll's house: fashion accessories, Germany c. 1900
37 × 72 × 30 cm
Spielzeug Welten Museum Basel

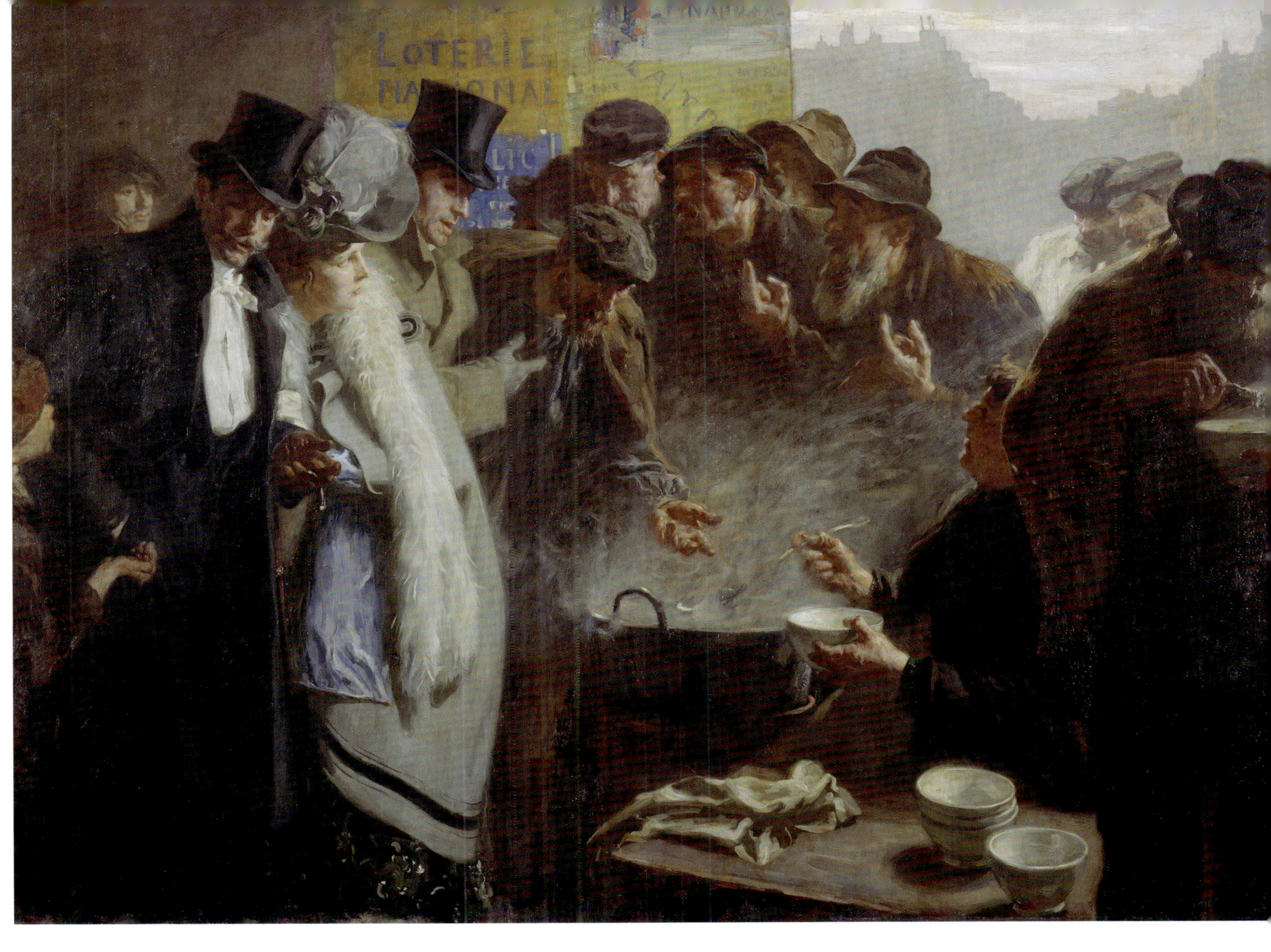

**182**  Arthur Kampf (1864–1950)
*An den Hallen in Paris,* 1903
Oil on canvas, 173 × 235 cm
Kunsthaus Zürich,
Bequest of Hildegard Reinelt, 1995

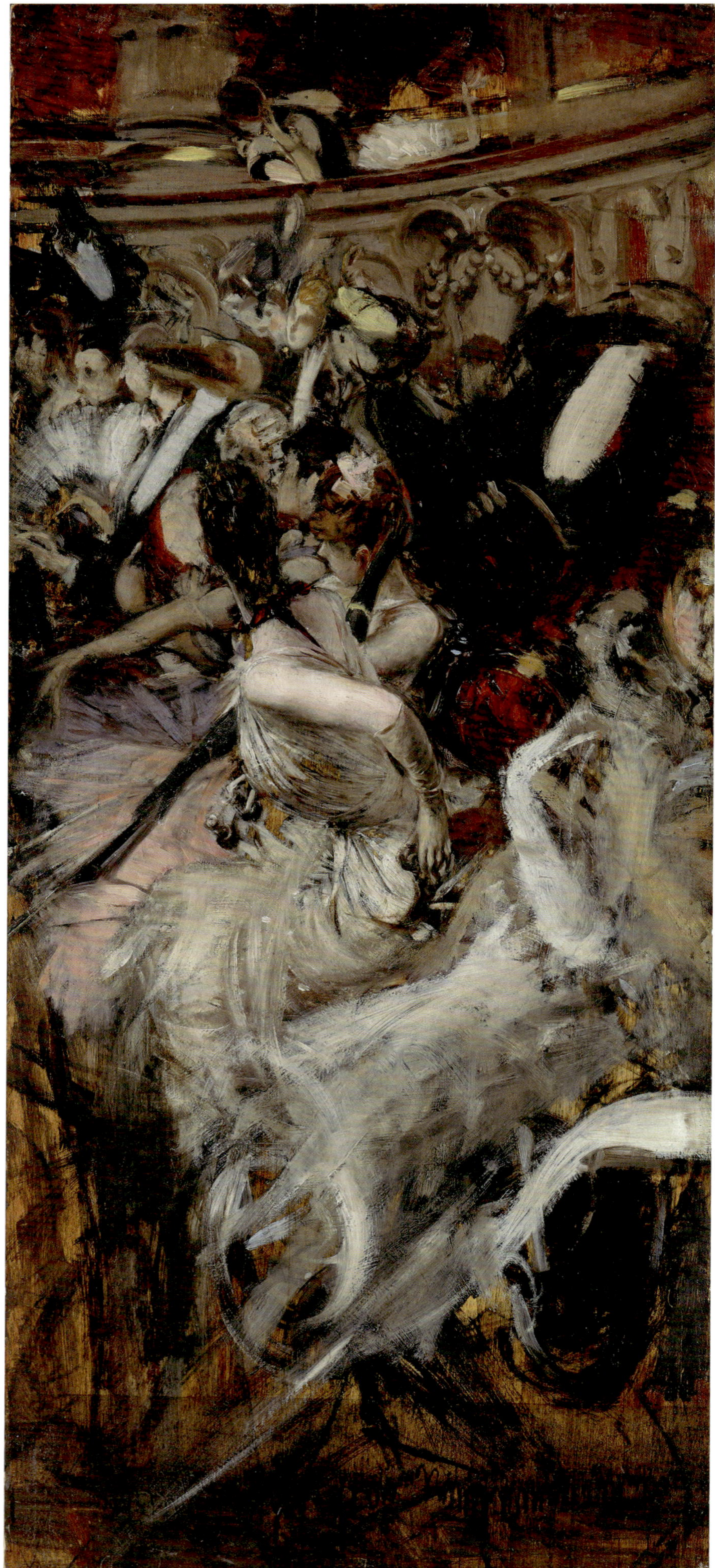



**63** Giovanni Boldini (1842–1931)
*A l'opera di Parigi,* 1886
Oil on canvas, 87.5 × 39 cm
Private collection
Courtesy Jean-Luc Baroni Ltd.,
London

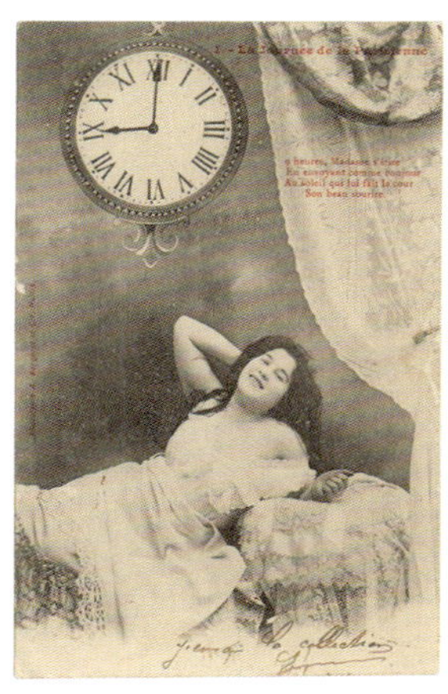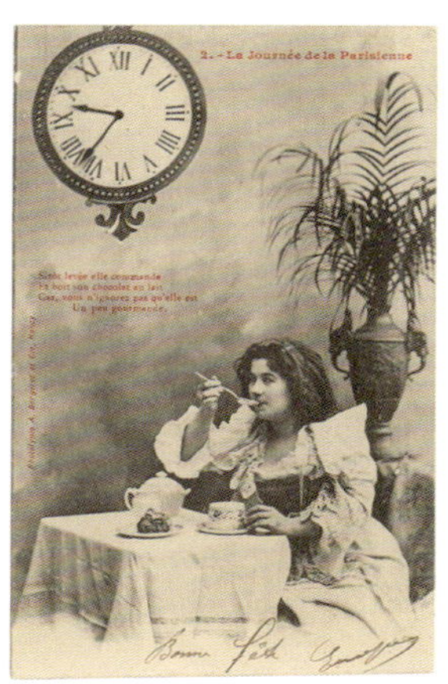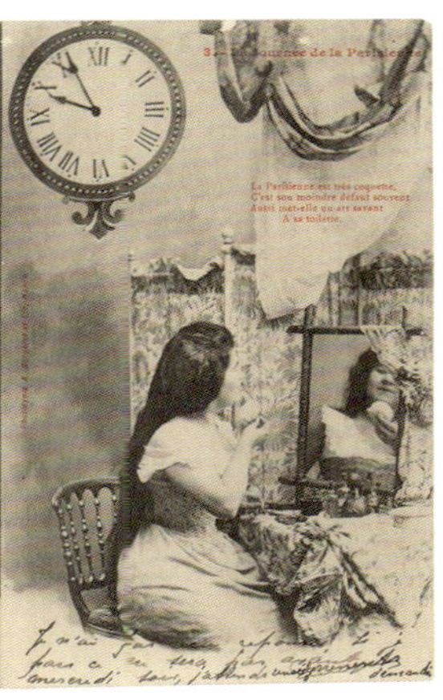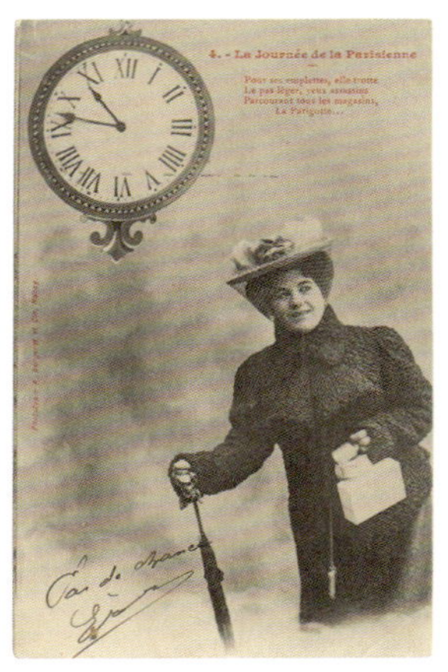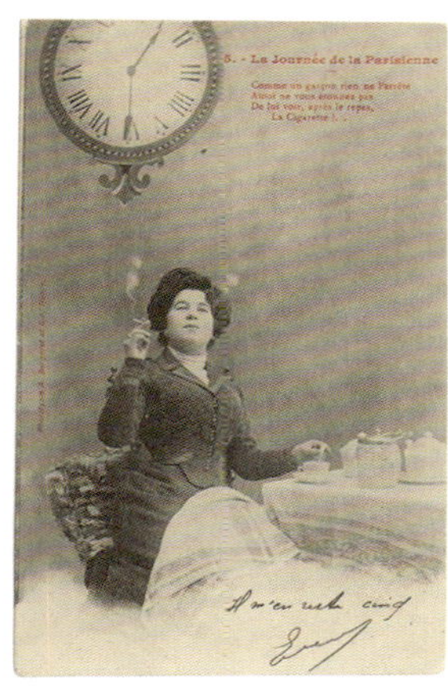
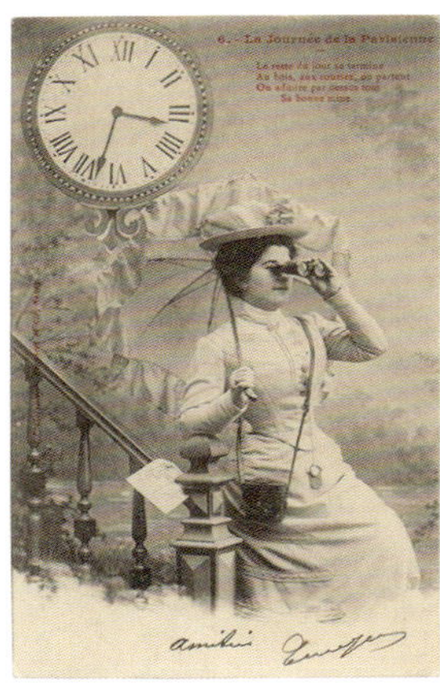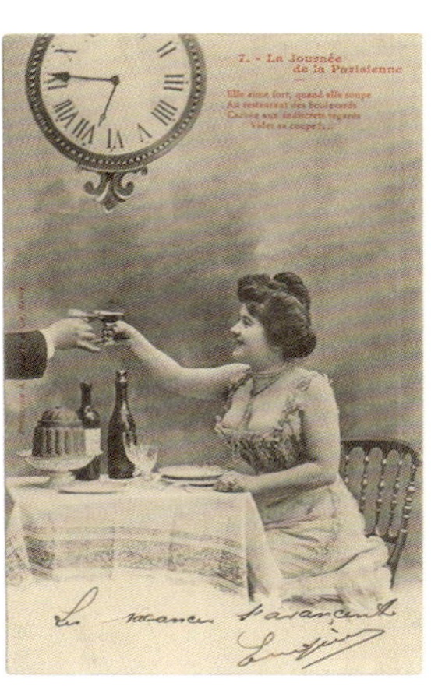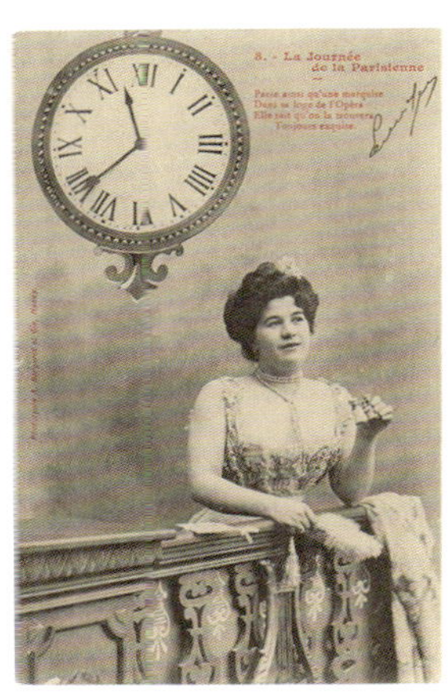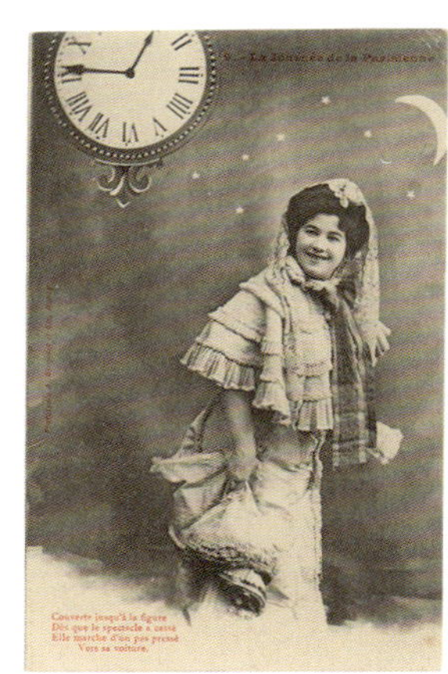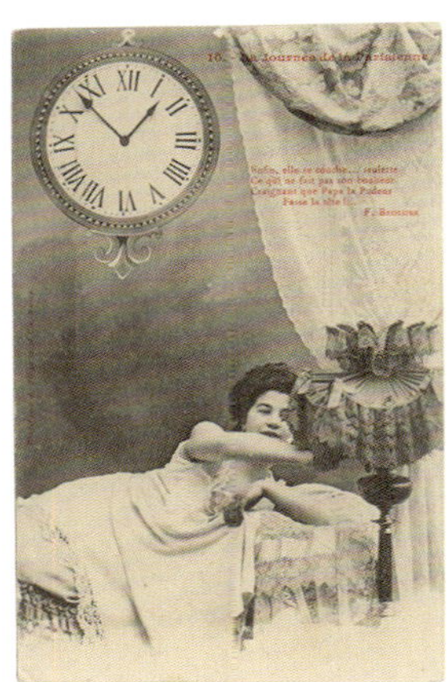



**19**  A. Bergeret et Cie, Nancy, Verlag
*La Journée de la parisienne,* c. 1900
10 black-and-white postcards,
phototype, sheet: 14 × 9 cm each
Private collection

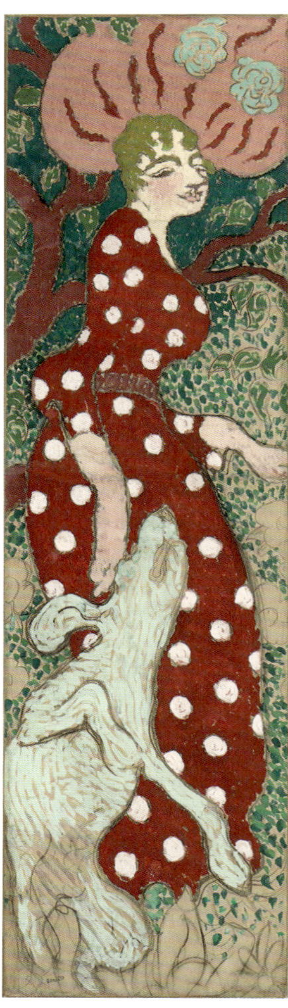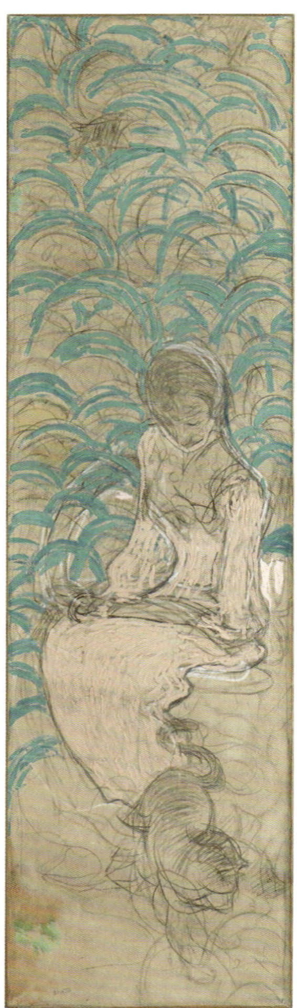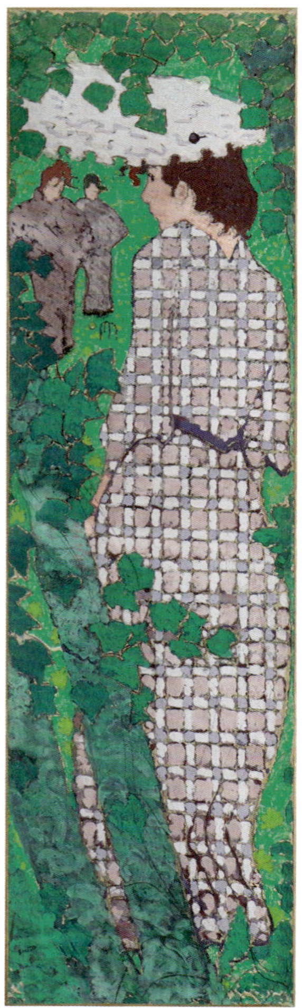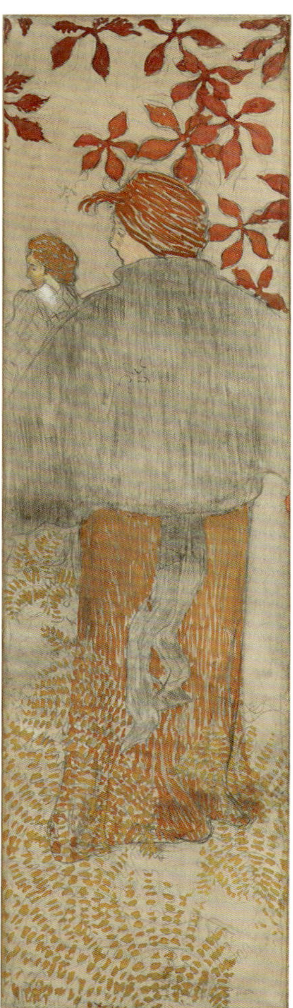

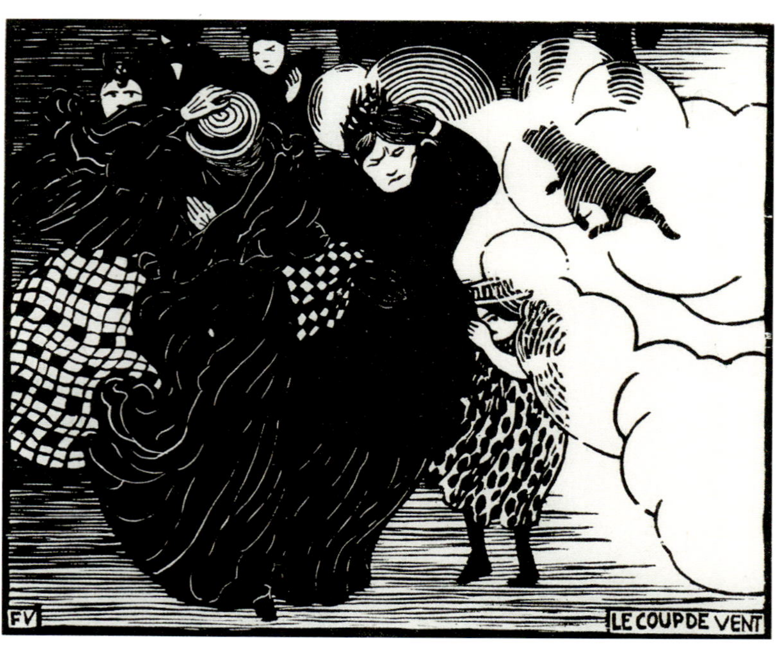


**66**  Pierre Bonnard (1867–1947)
*Panneaux décoratifs – Femmes au jardin,* 1890/91
Distemper on charcoal, pencil and
white chalk on paper, mounted on canvas,
154 × 47 cm each
Kunsthaus Zürich,
Vereinigung Zürcher Kunstfreunde,
donated in memory of Ernst Gamper, 1984

**285**  Félix Vallotton (1865–1925)
*Le coup de vent,* 1894
Woodcut on Japan paper, sheet: 25.3 × 31 cm
Kunsthaus Zürich,
Department of Prints and Drawings

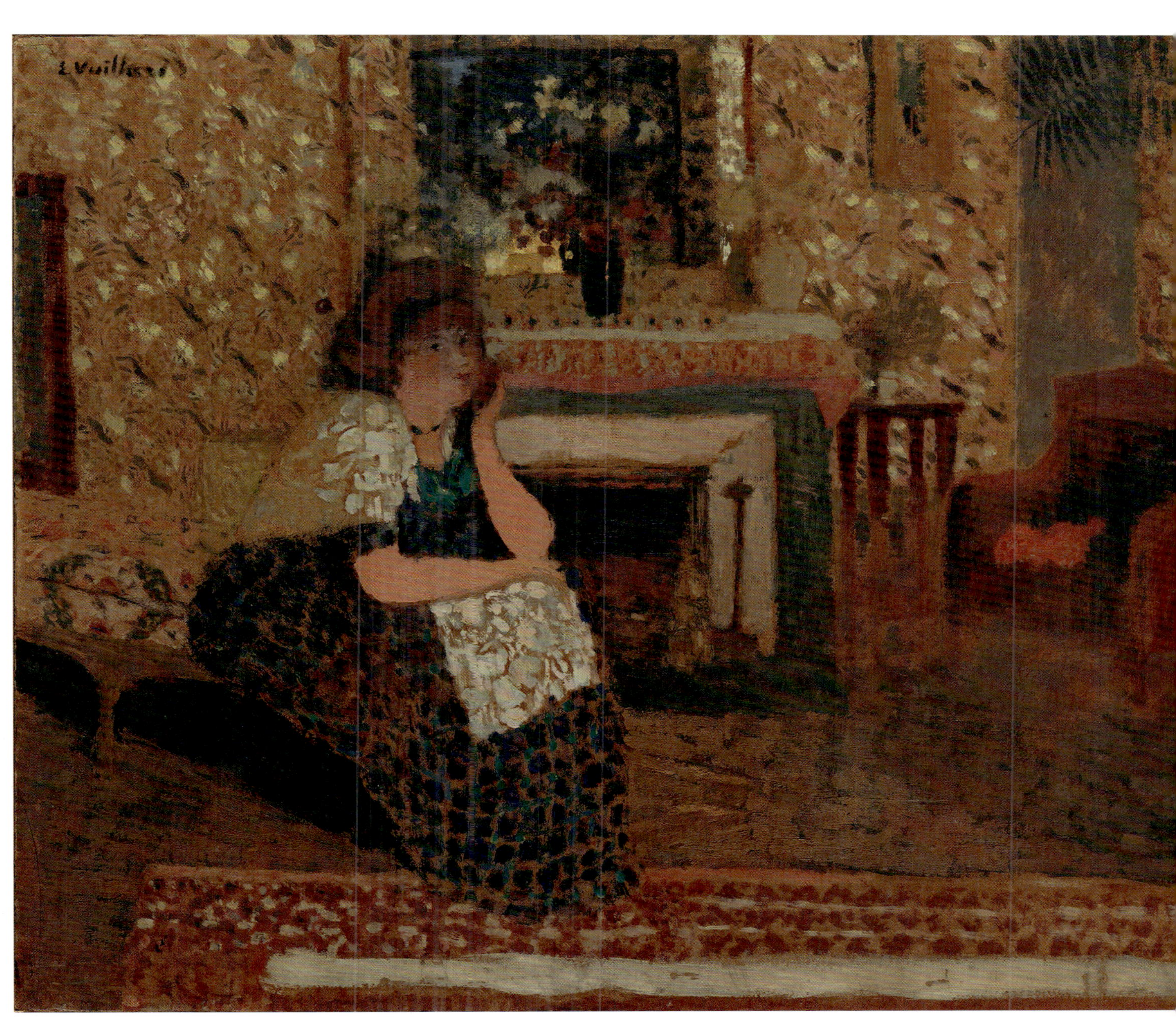

**293** Édouard Vuillard (1868–1940)
*Les bras nus,* undated
Oil on cardboard, 48.5 × 58 cm
Kunsthaus Zürich, Private collection

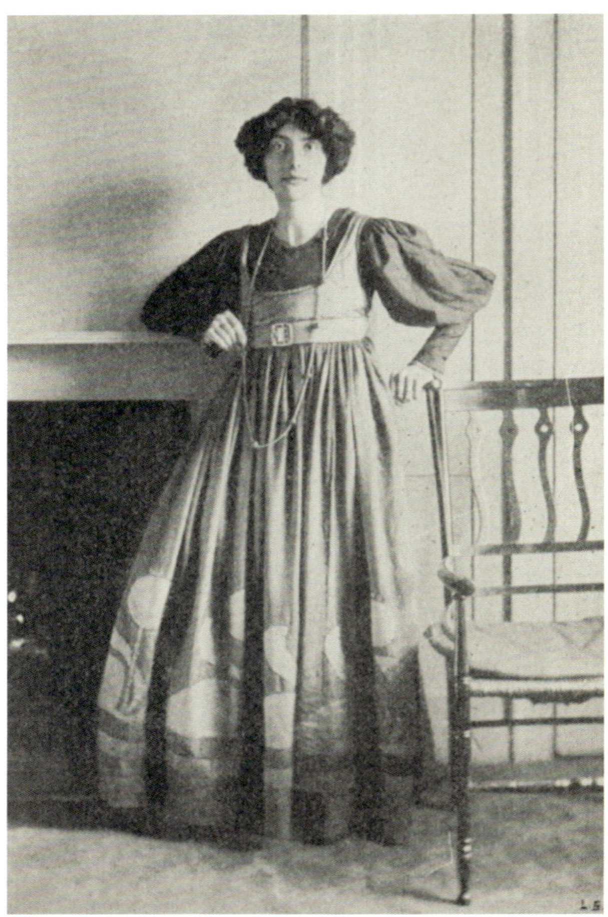
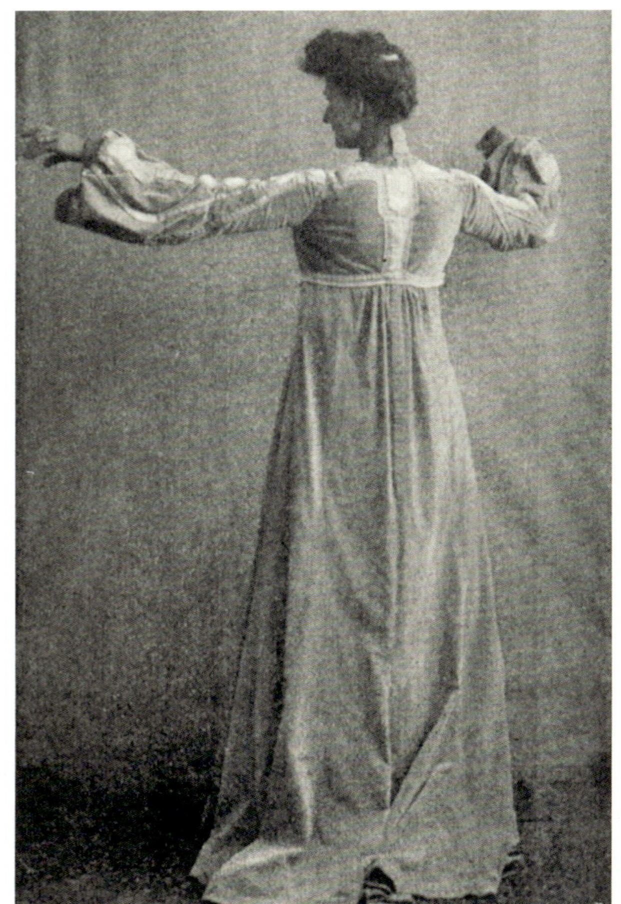
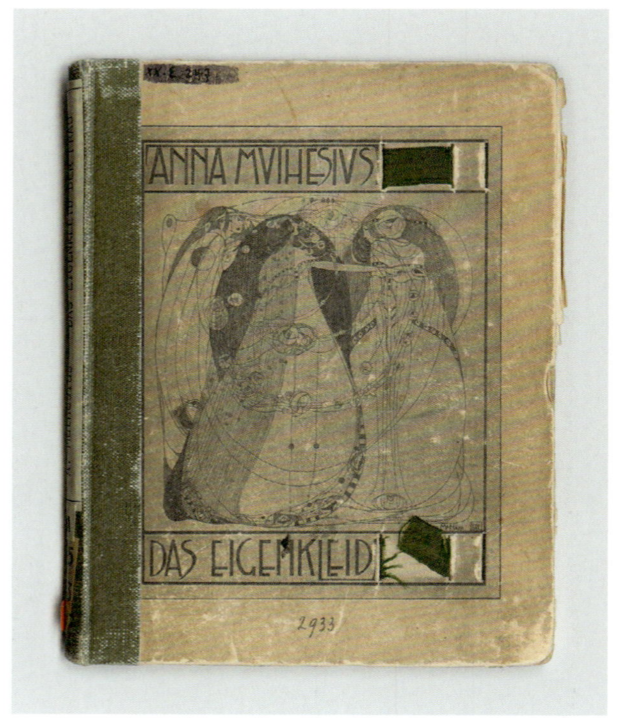





**21** Anna Muthesius (1870–1961)
Photographs of selected clothing designed
by Anna Muthesius
In *Das Eigenkleid der Frau,* Krefeld 1903,
Zurich University of the Arts, ZHdK/
Media and Information Centre MIZ

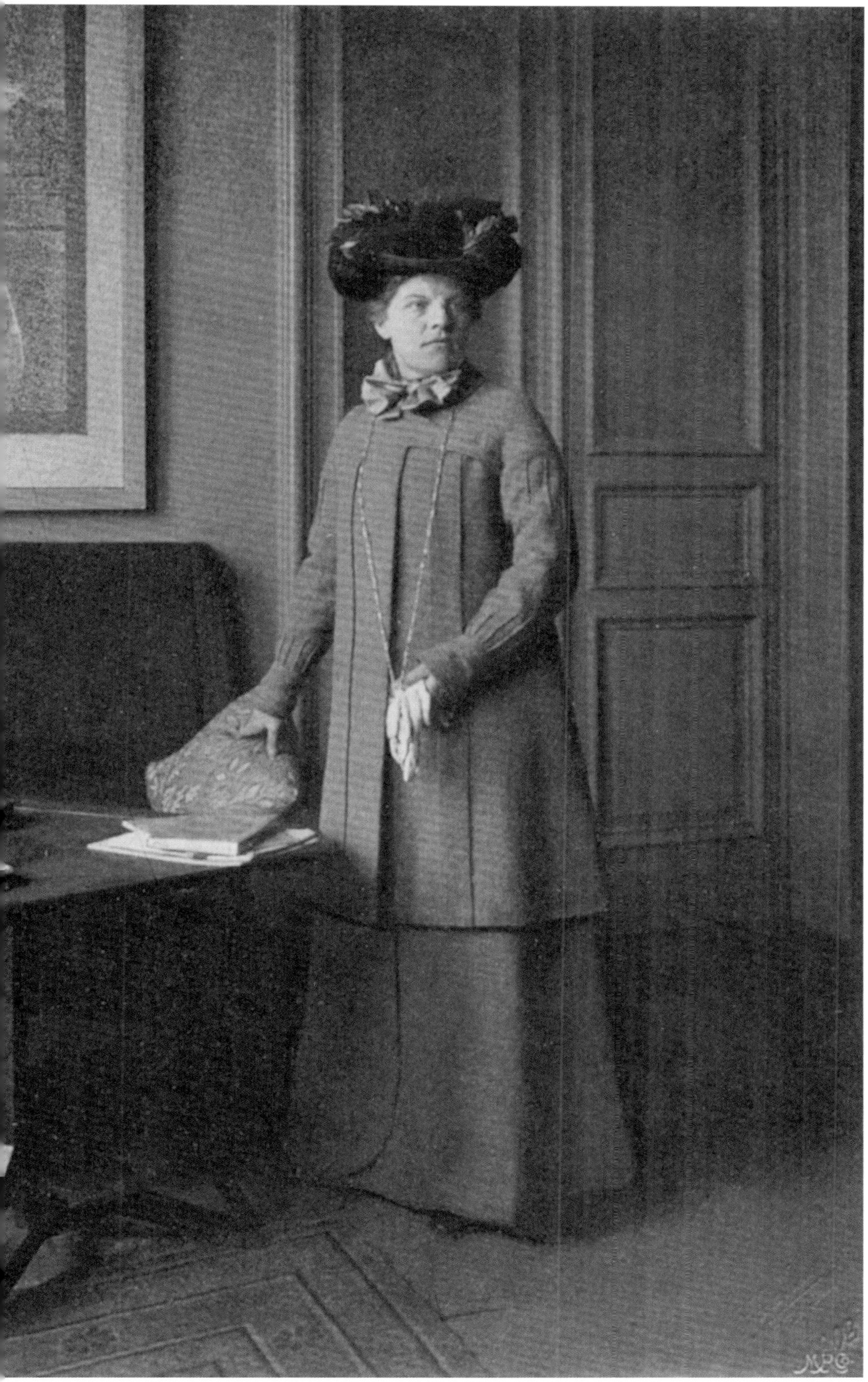

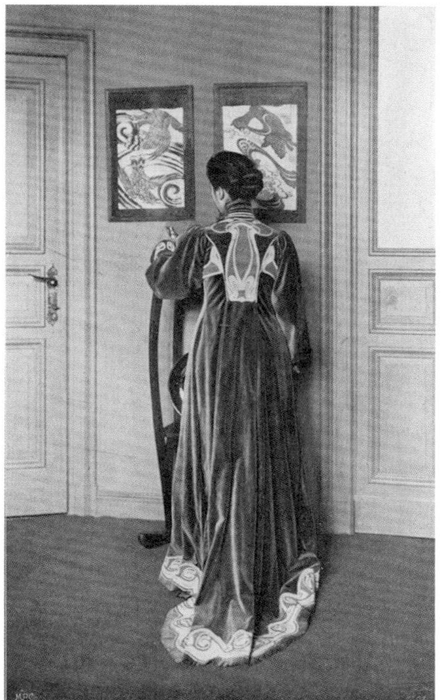

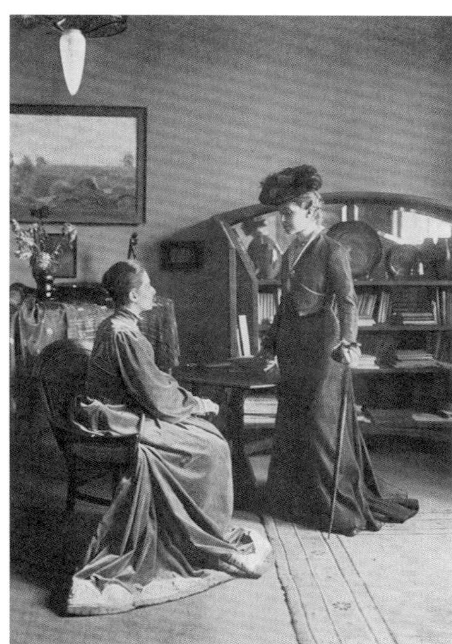

**20** Henry van de Velde (1863–1957) and
Peter Behrens (1868–1940)
Photographs of selected clothing designed
by Peter Behrens and Henry van de Velde
In Henry van de Velde, 'Das neue Kunst-Prinzip
in der modernen Frauen-Kleidung',
in *Deutsche Kunst und Dekoration,*
vol. 10, 1902, no. 5, pp. 363–86
Kunsthaus Zürich, Library

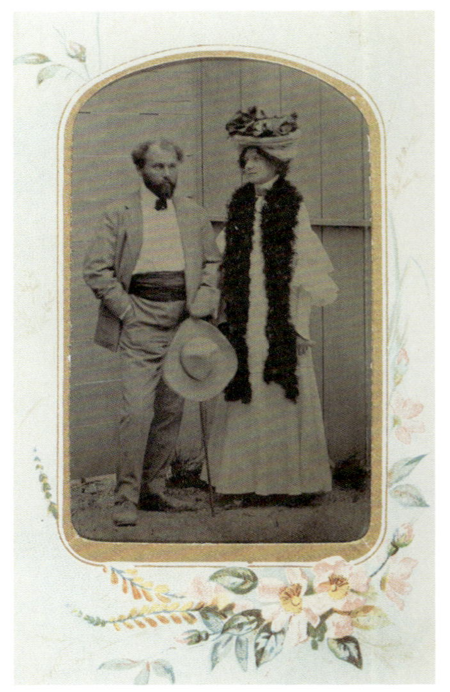

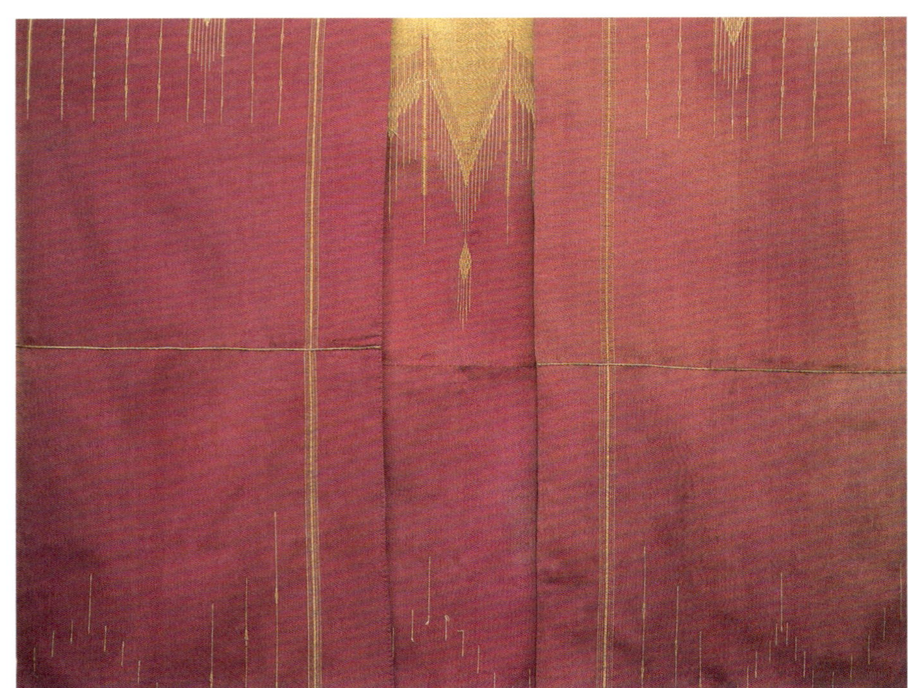

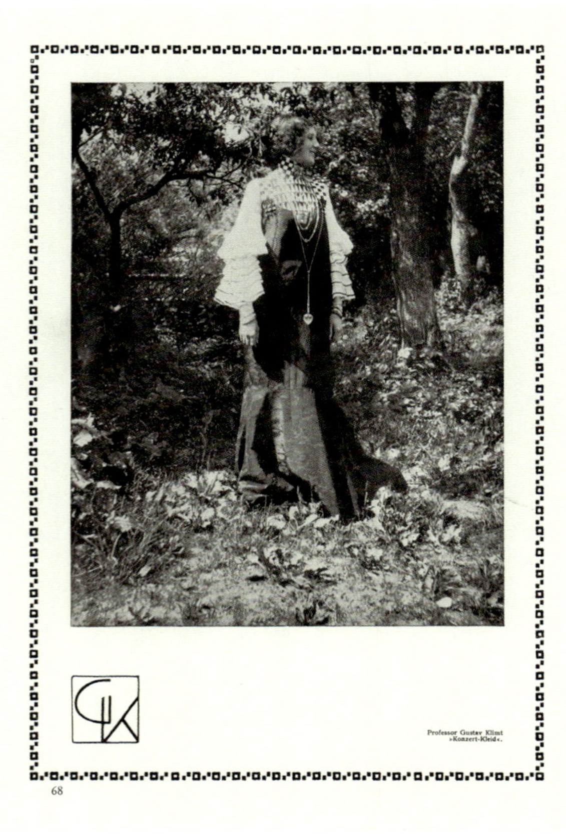


**22** Emilie Flöge (1874–1952), design
Gustav Klimt (1862–1918), photography
Klimt's photograph of a reform dress of his
companion Flöge, Litzlberg am Attersee 1906
In *Deutsche Kunst und Dekoration,*
vol. XIX, 1906/07, illustrations from pp. 69/70
Kunsthaus Zürich, Library

**23** Unknown photographer
Photograph of Gustav Klimt and Emilie Flöge
In a passe-partout typical for the current
prevailing taste of 1900
Ferrotype, 9 × 6 cm
Private collection, Vienna

**24** Unknown artist
Tunic for Gustav Klimt
Use of probably a North African fabric
From the textile collection of Emilie Flöge,
fashion designer and companion of Gustav Klimt
Private collection, Vienna



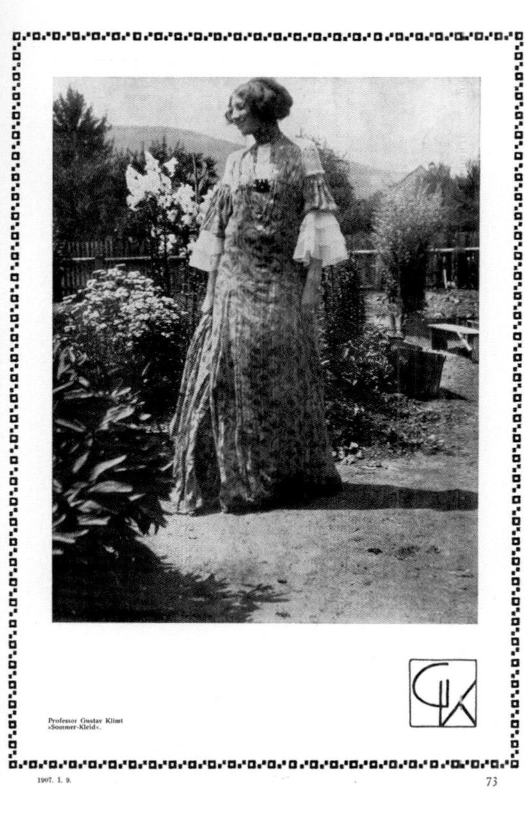



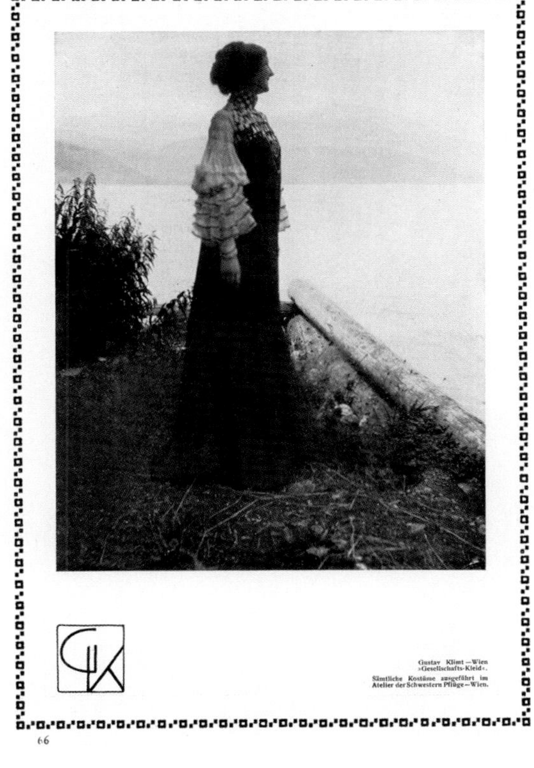

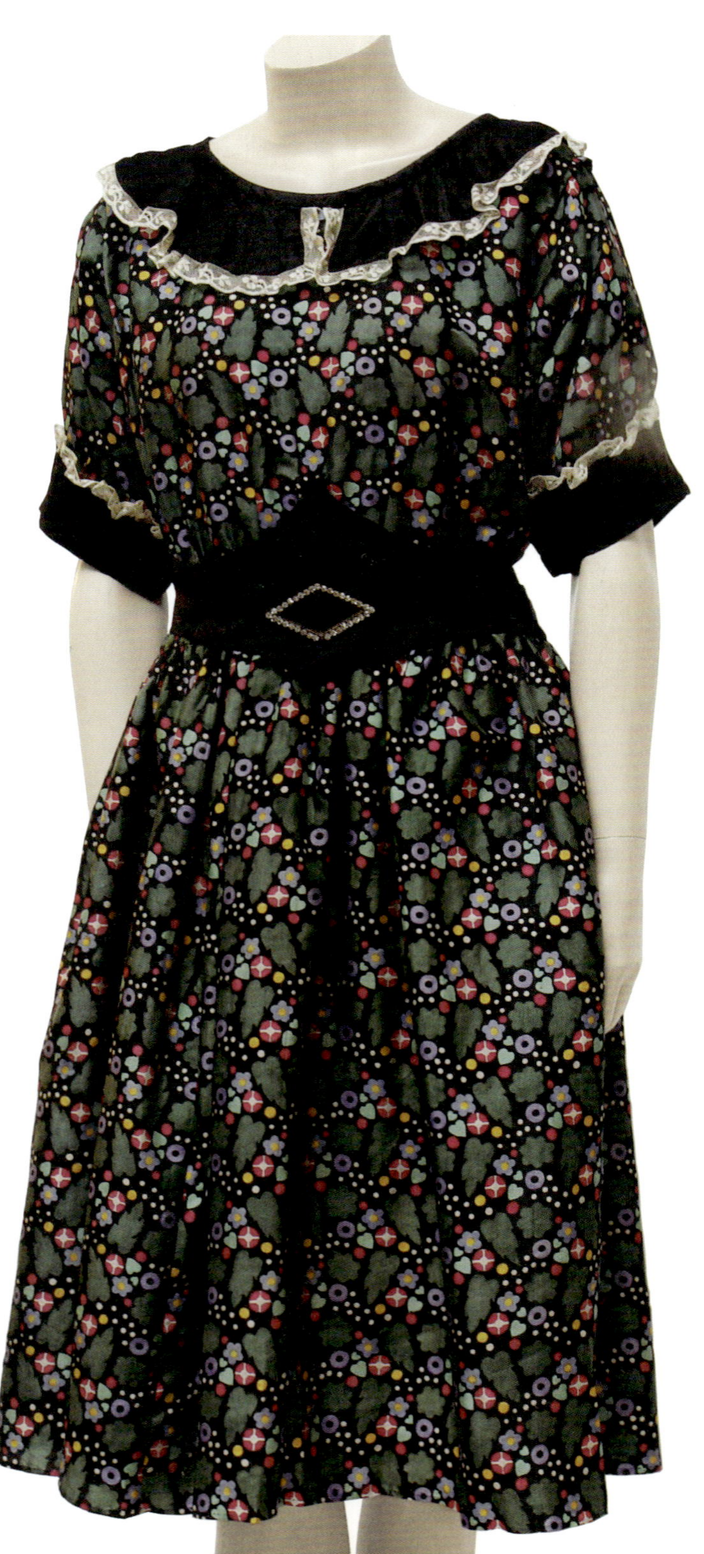



Fashion and Public

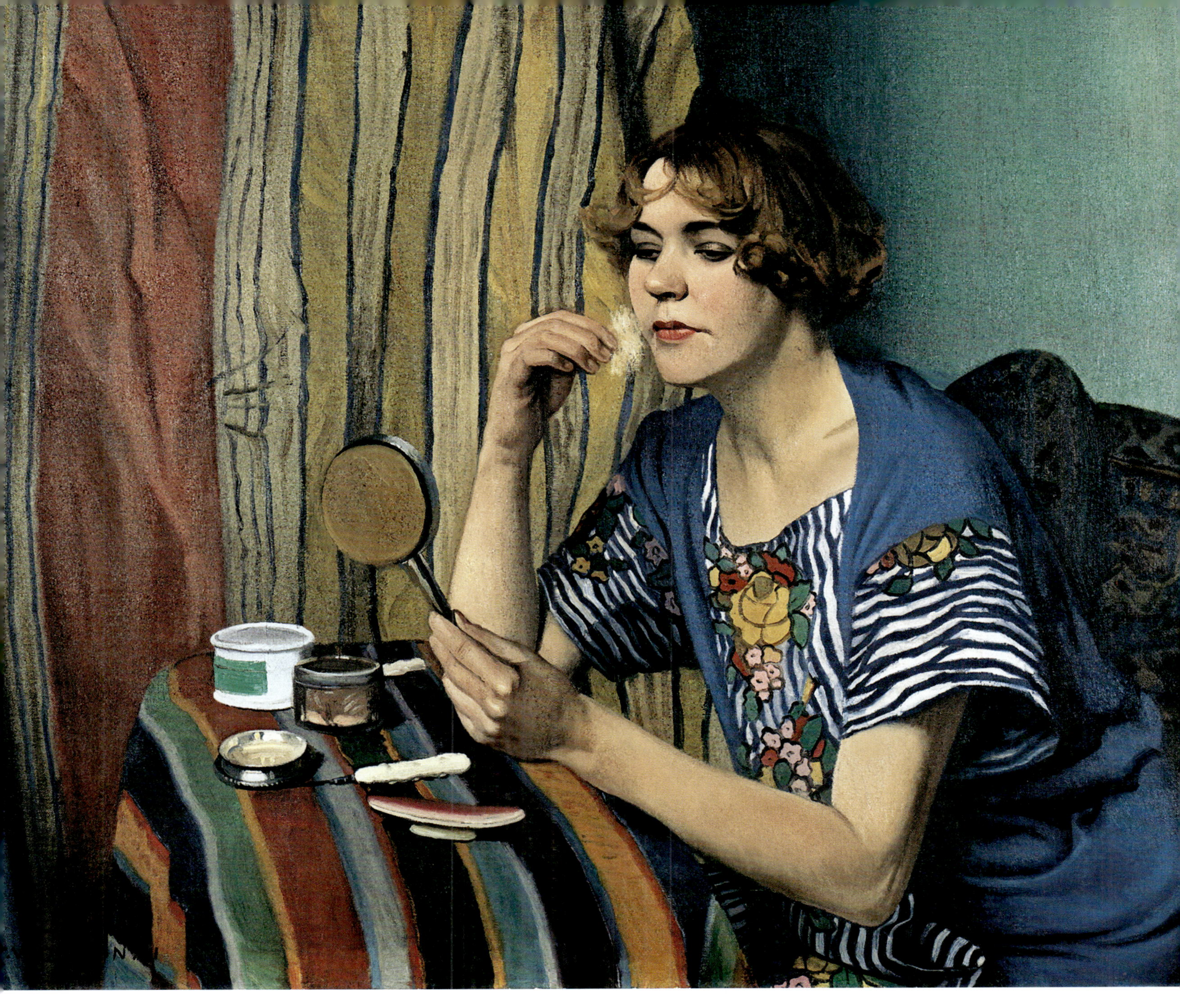

**290** Félix Vallotton (1865–1925)
*La Poudreuse,* 1921
Oil on canvas, 82 × 100 cm
Private collection

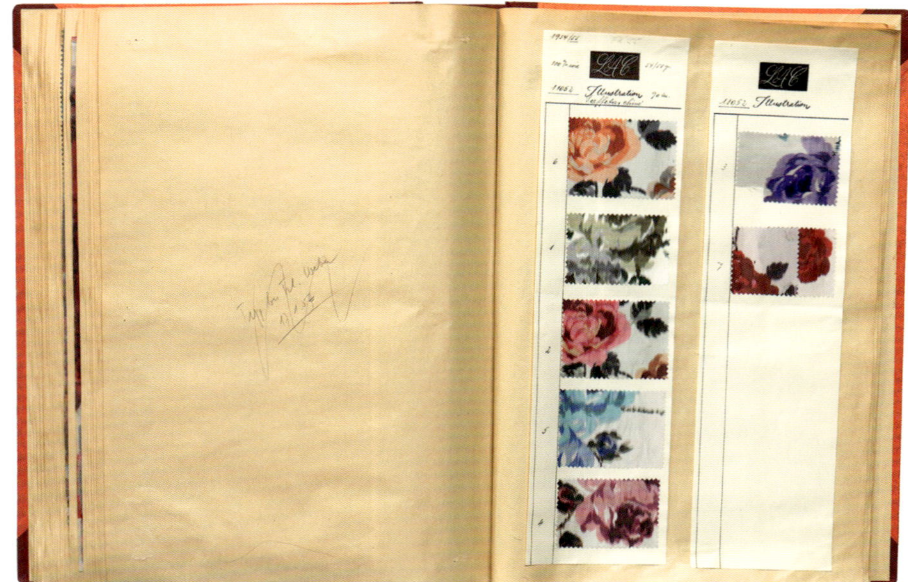

**30** Abraham AG (1941–2002)
Pattern book with fabrics by the Abraham company from winter 1953/54, 1955
On each page, a type of fabric in diverse colour combinations is presented, including the indication of quality, name, design number etc.
76 pages with fabric patterns from embroidered organza, organza with warp print and taffeta with warp print; hardcover, binding: linen, book cover: cardboard, 50 × 37.2 × 7.6 cm
Schweizerisches Nationalmuseum, Zurich

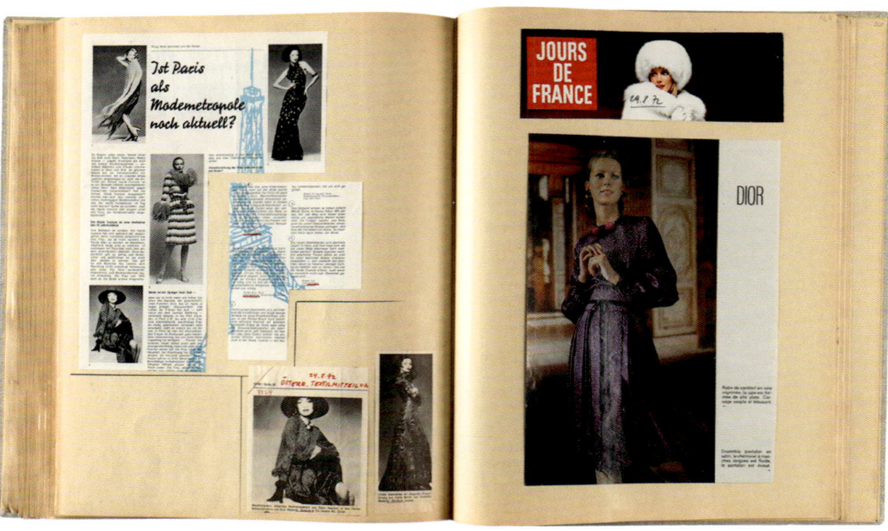

**31** Abraham AG (1941–2002)
Scrapbook, 1971/72
Collected press cuttings about topics related to the Abraham company from summer 1971 to summer 1972
179 pages; paper, hardcover, pasted, cover: linen, 51 × 43.5 × 7 cm
Schweizerisches Nationalmuseum, Zurich

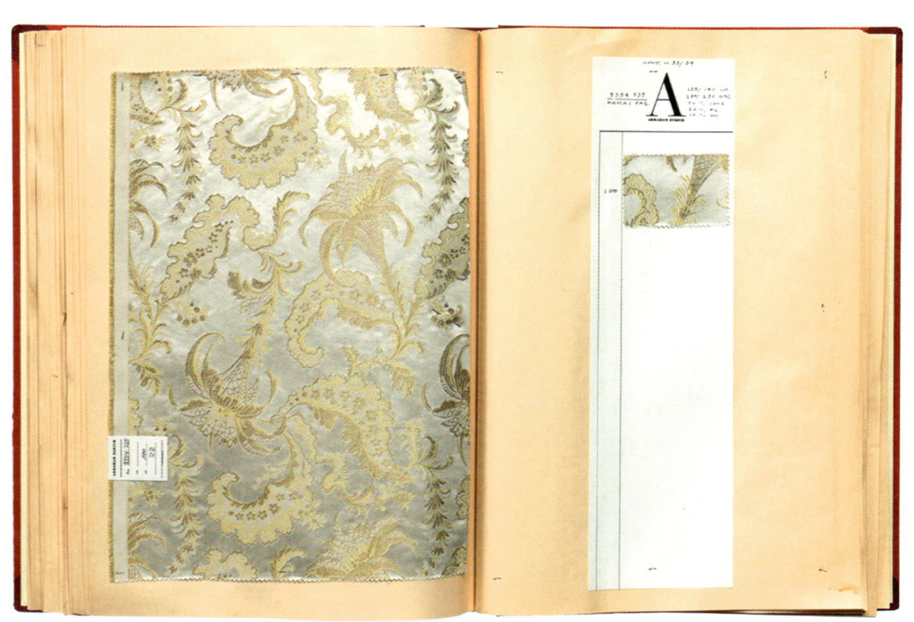

**33** Abraham AG (1941–2002)
Collection reference book with fabrics by the Abraham company from winter 1993/94, 1995
One double page per fabric.
Left: folded repeat pattern of the collection fabric; right: small design coupons in several colours, mounted on paper; inscription: article number, name of collection, indication of quality, fabric width, weight
Paper, hardcover, binding: linen, cover: cardboard, 50 × 37 × 7 cm
Schweizerisches Nationalmuseum, Zurich

Abraham AG (1941–2002)
Fabric sample: no. 267 Alvina,
Animal (textile motives), winter 1972/73
Crêpe de Chine, woven, printed with scale pattern in teal,
turquoise, light blue, beige and brown, 390 × 102 cm
Schweizerisches Nationalmuseum, Zurich

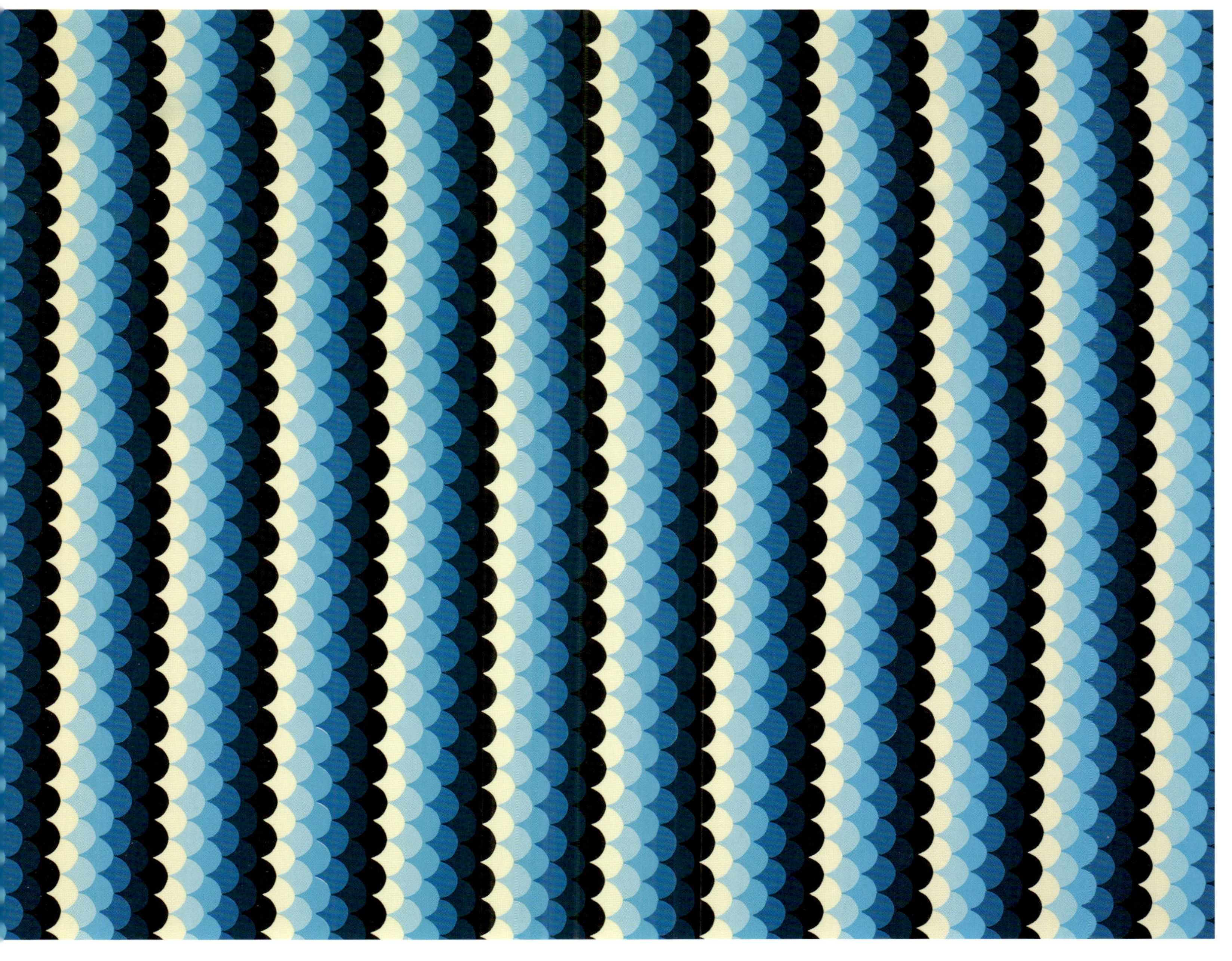

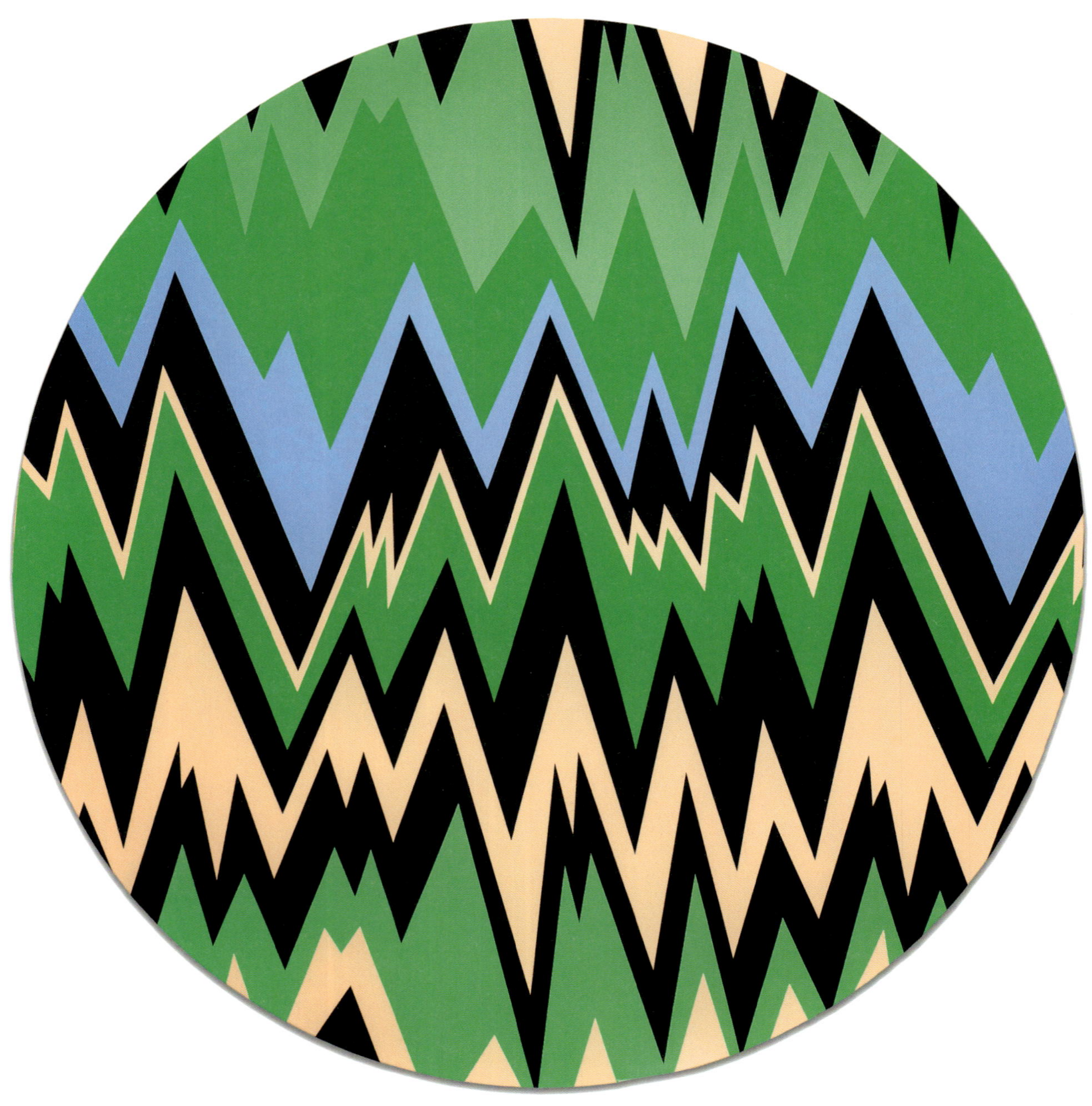

**139** Sylvie Fleury (b. 1961)
Untitled, 2016
Acrylic on canvas, frame: 125 × 125 × 10 cm
Private Collection, Courtesy the artist and
Karma International, Zurich and Los Angeles,
and Mehdi Chouakri Berlin

**25**  Madeleine Vionnet (1876–1975)
Black tango dress with open back, France 1917
Liquid silk
Martin Kamer

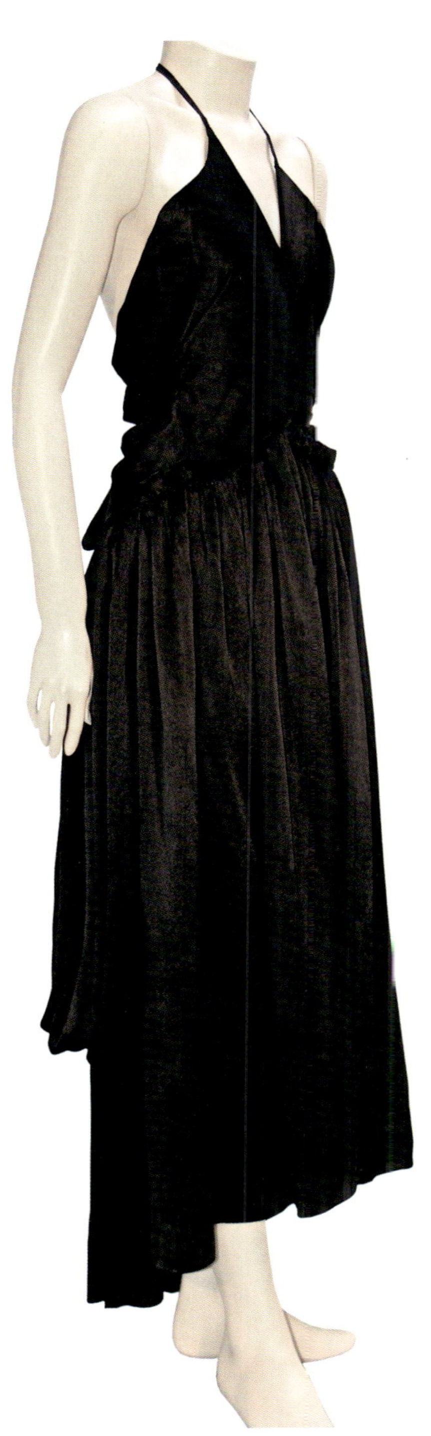
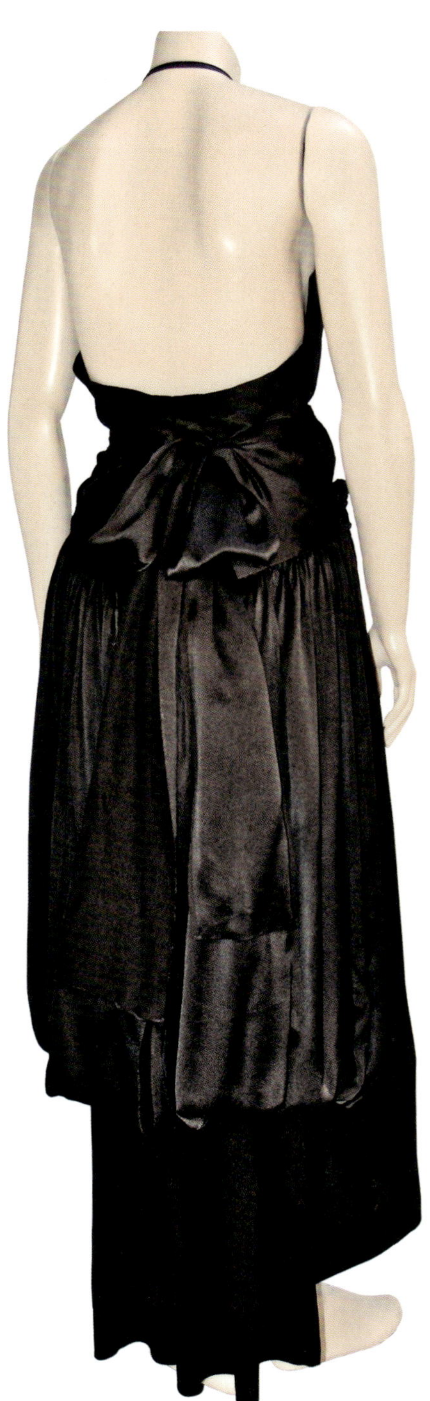

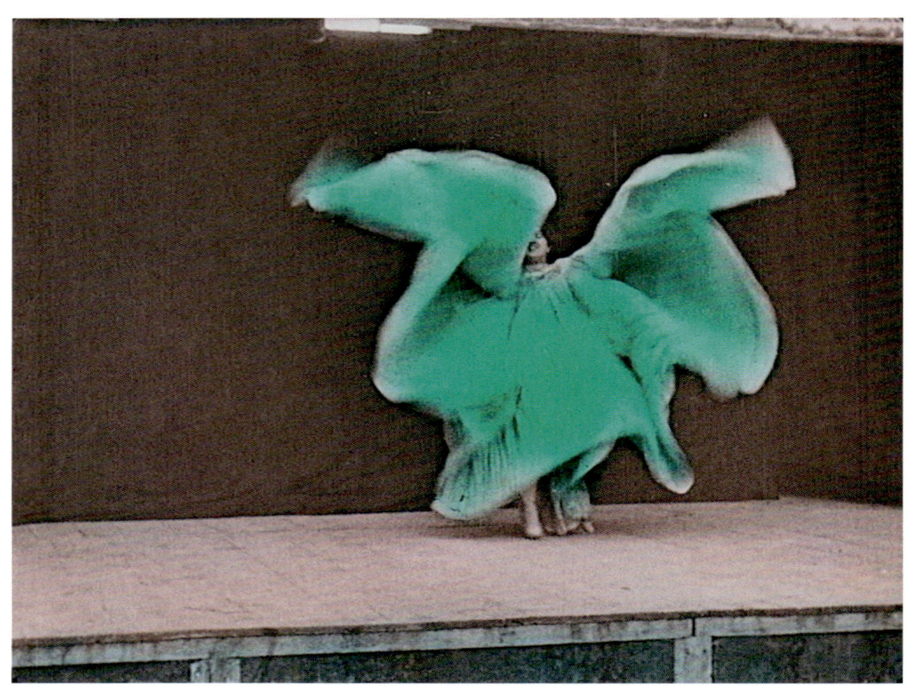

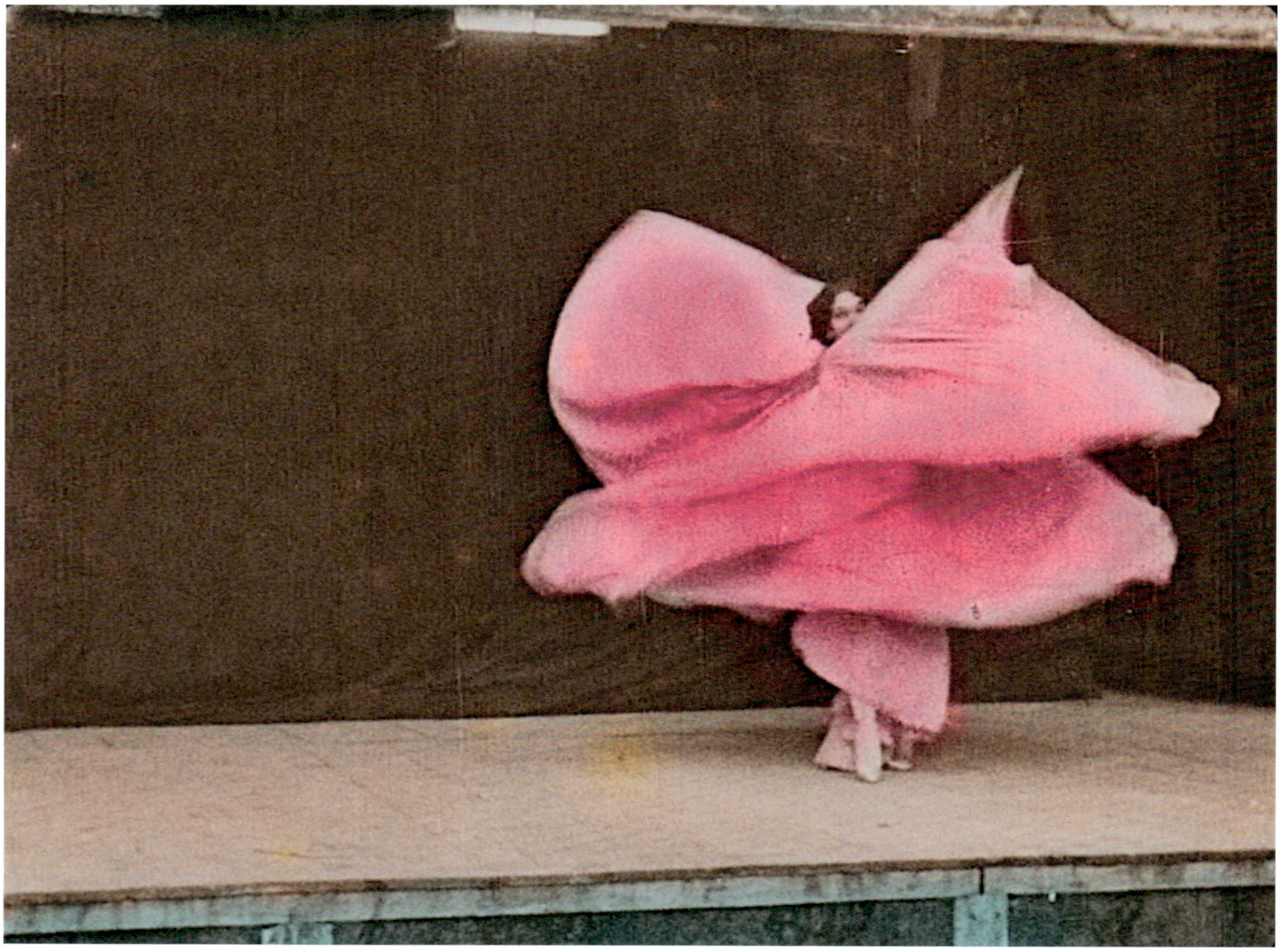

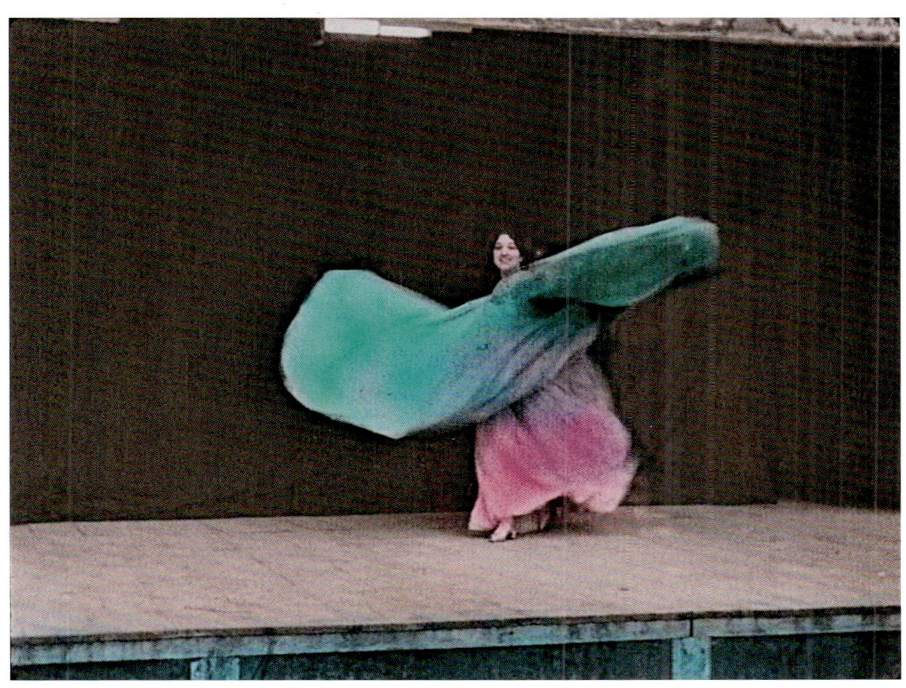

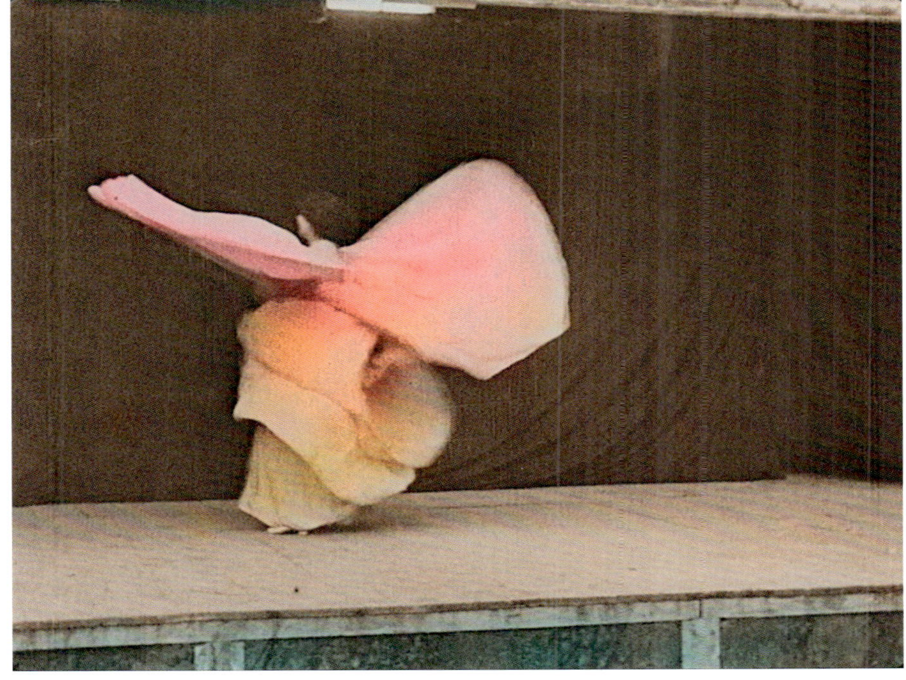

**209**  Lumière Brothers
(Auguste Lumière, 1862–1954, and
Louis Lumière, 1864–1948)
*Danse serpentine,* 1897
Choreography: Loïe Fuller,
Dance: Loïe Fuller and Papinta
Digitalised film, no sound
Duration: 59”

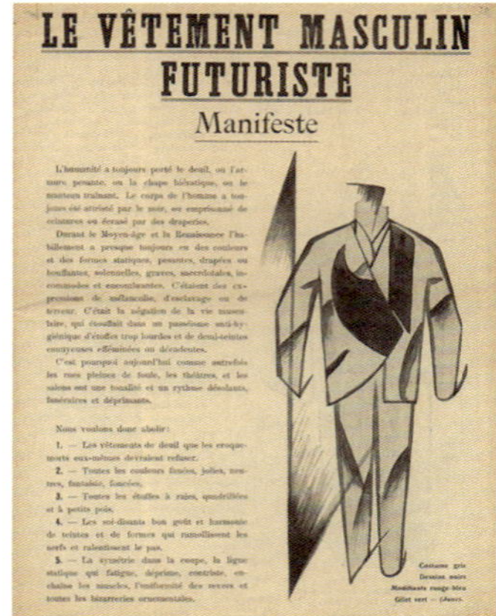



**54** Giacomo Balla (1871–1958)
*Le Vêtement masculin futuriste.*
*Manifeste,* Milan 1914
23.3 × 29.4 cm
Kunsthaus Zürich, Library,
Gift of Benedetta Marinetti, Rome 1951

# *Futurist Men's Apparel Manifesto*

Humanity has always dressed in mourning, or in
heavy armour, or in priestly robes, or in flowing capes.
Man's body has always been saddened by black,
imprisoned in belts or stifled by enshrouding cloth.
During the Middle Ages and the Renaissance,
clothing was almost always static in colour and
form, falling in folds or puffed out, solemn, grave,
priestlike, uncomfortable and cumbersome.
It was an expression of melancholy, enslavement,
or terror. It was a negation of the life of the muscles,
which suffocated in an unhygienic passéism
of excessively heavy fabric and boring, effeminate
or decadent half-tones.
That is why today, as in the past, the crowded
streets, theatres and salons  are so dismayingly
funereal in tone.

**We therefore want to abolish:**

**1.** – Mourning clothes that even undertakers
should reject.

**2.** – All faded, pretty, neutral, fanciful and
dark colours.

**3.** – All striped, checked and polka-dotted
fabrics.

**4.** – The so-called good taste and harmony of
shades and forms that soften one's nerves and
slow down one's pace.

**5.** – Symmetry in the cut, the static line which
tiringly and depressingly shackles the muscles,
the uniformity of the lapels, and all other
bizarre ornamentation.

**6.** – Useless buttons.

**7.** – Detachable collars and starched cuffs.
We want to liberate humanity from slow Romantic
nostalgia and the weight of life. We want to
colour and rejuvenate the crowds on our streets
through Futurism. We want finally to give
men beautiful, celebratory clothes.

**Futurist clothing shall therefore be:**

**1.** – **Dynamic,** by means of the dynamic patterns
and colours of the fabrics (triangles, cones,
ellipses, spirals, circles).

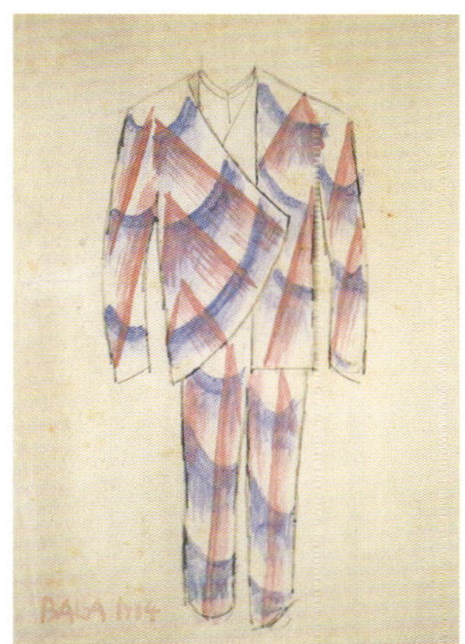

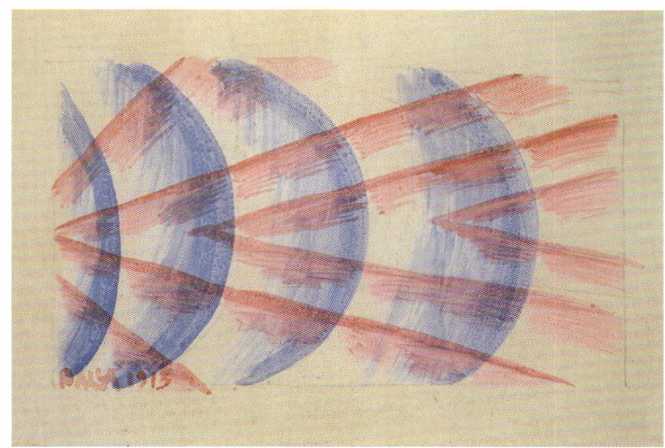

**2. – Asymmetrical.** E.g., the ends of the sleeves and the front of the jacket will be rounded on the right side and squared on the left. Same for waistcoats, trousers and short coats.

**3. – Agilising,** that is, tending to enhance the body's flexibility and favour its movement.

**4. – Simple and comfortable,** that is, easy to put on and to take off. With a few indispensable buttons.

**5. – Hygienic,** that is, cut in such a way that all pores can breathe easily. To this end, avoid any snug parts and tight belts.

**6. – Joyous.** Exuberant fabrics with iridescent colours, fabrics with muscular colours, insanely purple, very very very very red, 300,000 times green, 20,000 times blue, yellow, oooorange, verrrrm·illlllion.

**7. – Illuminating.** Phosphorescent fabrics that can shed light all around when it rains, and offset the melancholy gloom of the dusk.

**8. – Wilful.** Violent, aggressive colours, imperious and impetuous. Skilful use of skeletal tones: white, grey, black.

**9. – Flowing and airy,** that is, linked to the atmosphere through a gradation of tones and the sweep of its dynamic lines.

**10. – Short-lasting,** so that we may endlessly renew our body's pleasure and liveliness, and support the textile industry.

**11. – Variable,** by means of 'modifiers'. Such is the name I give to overlays of fabric (of varying size, thickness and colour) to be applied whenever and wherever one wants on any point of the garment, through the use of pneumatic buttons. This way, at any moment, anyone can not only modify, but also invent a new garment in keeping with one's changing state of mind. The 'modifier' can be imperious, loving, caressing, persuasive, diplomatic, monochrome, polychrome, shocking, discordant, decisive, scented and so on.

From all this will spring forth an astonishing variety of garments that will unceasingly shed a light of playfulness upon our cities, even if their inhabitants are utterly devoid of imagination and colour sense.

The dynamic joy of this clothing, as we drive down the bustling streets between Futurist buildings, will everywhere multiply the prismatic sparkle as from a jeweller's gigantic display window. Within us and around us, we shall have an acrobatics of volumes and colours without end, which will arouse, in the growing Futurist sensibility, countless new abstractions of dynamic rhythms.

MILAN, 20 May 1914

Giacomo Balla
Painter

Futurist Movement Management Offices
Corso Venezia, 61 MILAN

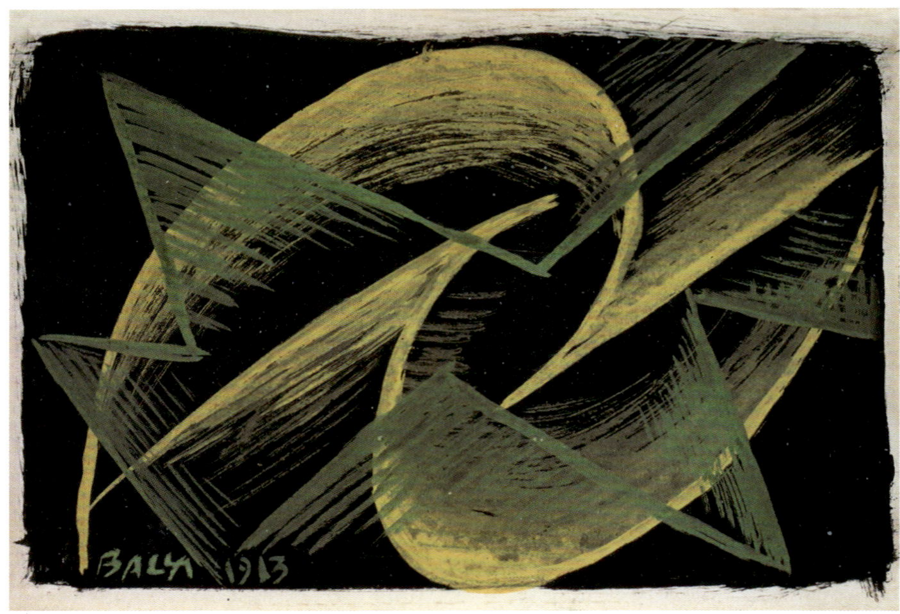

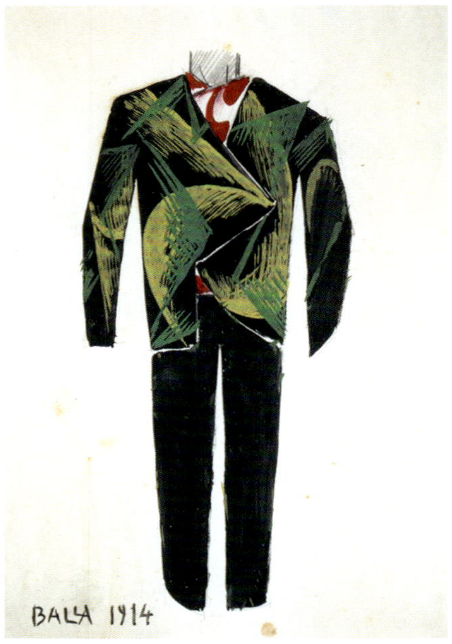

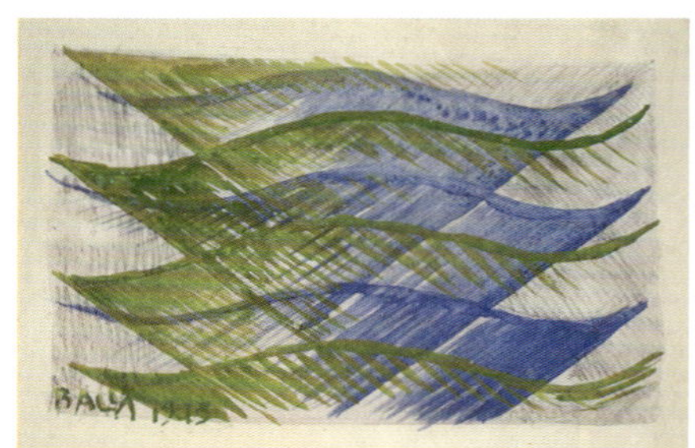

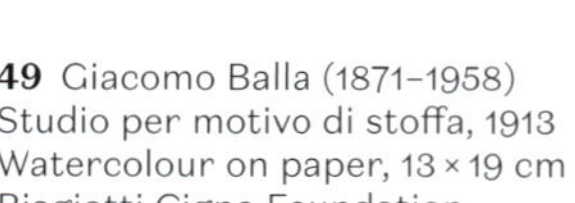

224

**49** Giacomo Balla (1871–1958)
*Studio per motivo di stoffa*, 1913
Watercolour on paper, 13 × 19 cm
Biagiotti Cigna Foundation

**52** Giacomo Balla (1871–1958)
*Bozzetto per vestito da uomo*, 1914
Watercolour on paper, 29 × 21 cm
Biagiotti Cigna Foundation

**50** Giacomo Balla (1871–1958)
*Studio per motivo di stoffa*, 1913
Watercolour on paper, 13 × 19 cm
Biagiotti Cigna Foundation

**51** Giacomo Balla (1871–1958)
*Bozzetto per vestito da uomo*, 1914
Watercolour on paper, 29 × 21 cm
Biagiotti Cigna Foundation

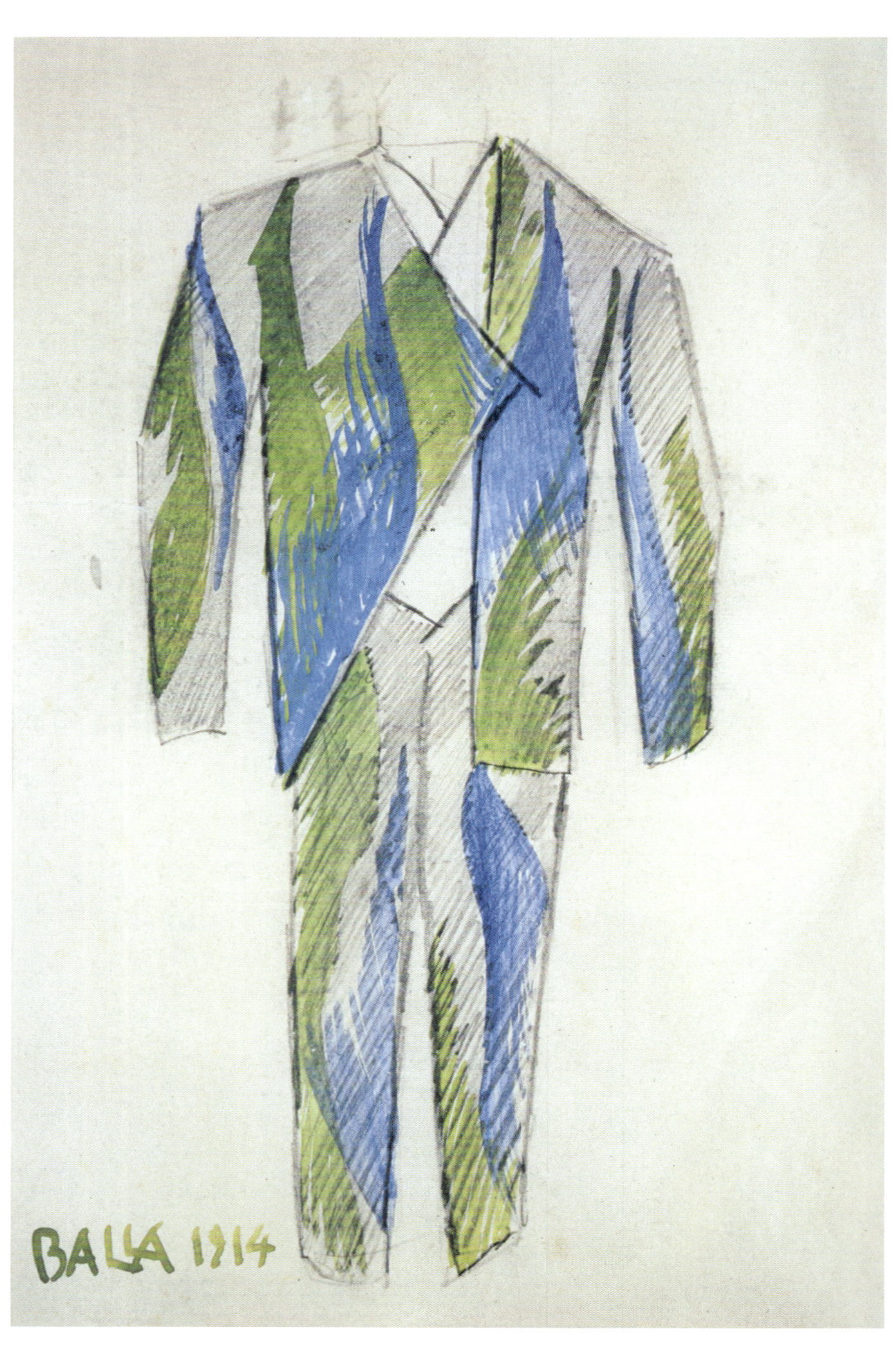

**57** Giacomo Balla (1871–1958)
*Vestito di luce*, 1930
Fabric, clasp from enameled wood, 121 × 141 cm
Biagiotti Cigna Foundation

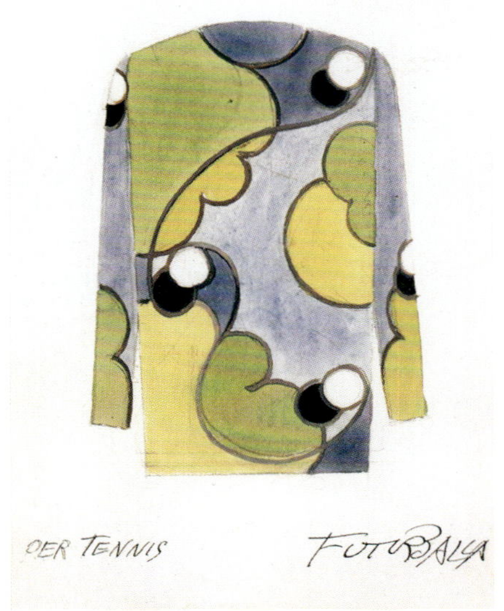


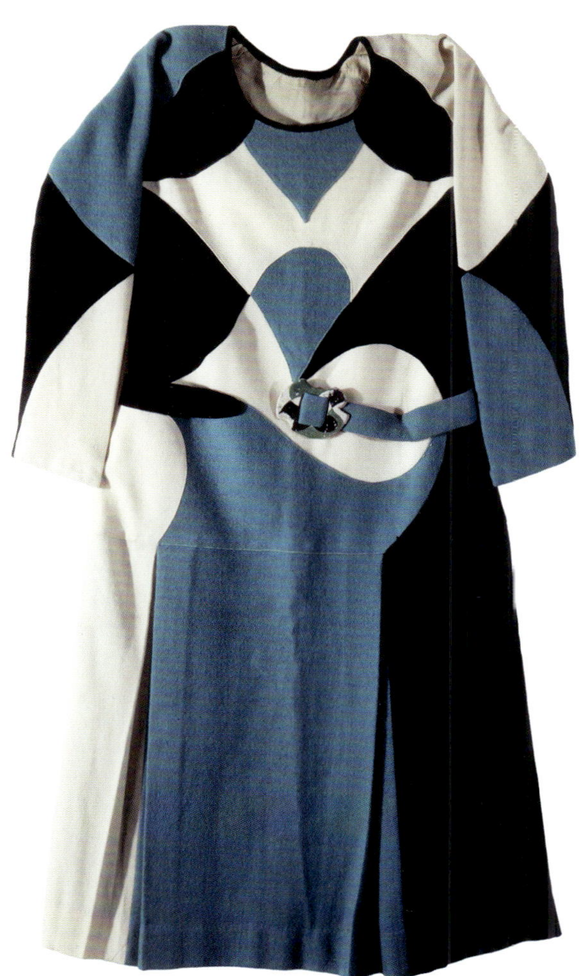

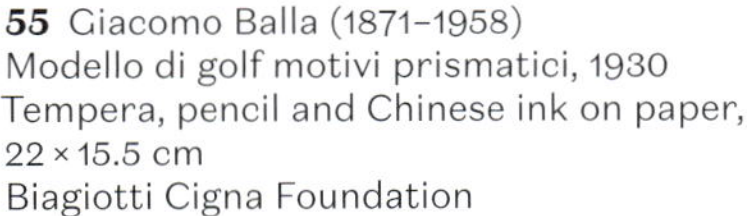


**55** Giacomo Balla (1871–1958)
*Modello di golf motivi prismatici*, 1930
Tempera, pencil and Chinese ink on paper,
22 × 15.5 cm
Biagiotti Cigna Foundation

**56** Giacomo Balla (1871–1958)
*Modello di golf per tennis*, 1930
Tempera, pencil and Chinese ink on paper,
22 × 15.5 cm
Biagiotti Cigna Foundation

**58** Giacomo Balla (1871–1958)
*Modello di golf futurfascista*, 1930
Tempera, pencil and Chinese ink on paper,
22 × 15.5 cm
Biagiotti Cigna Foundation

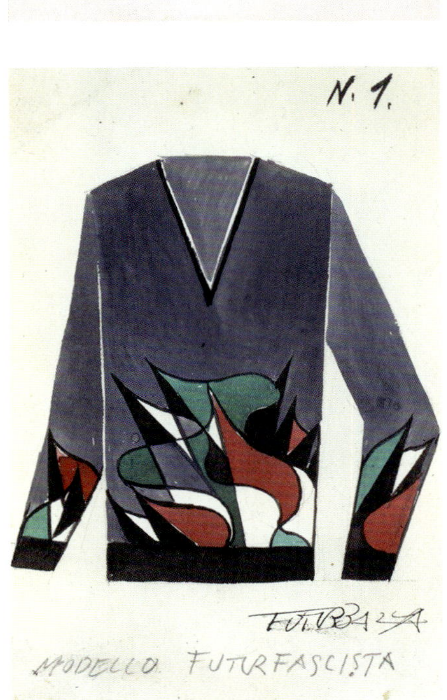

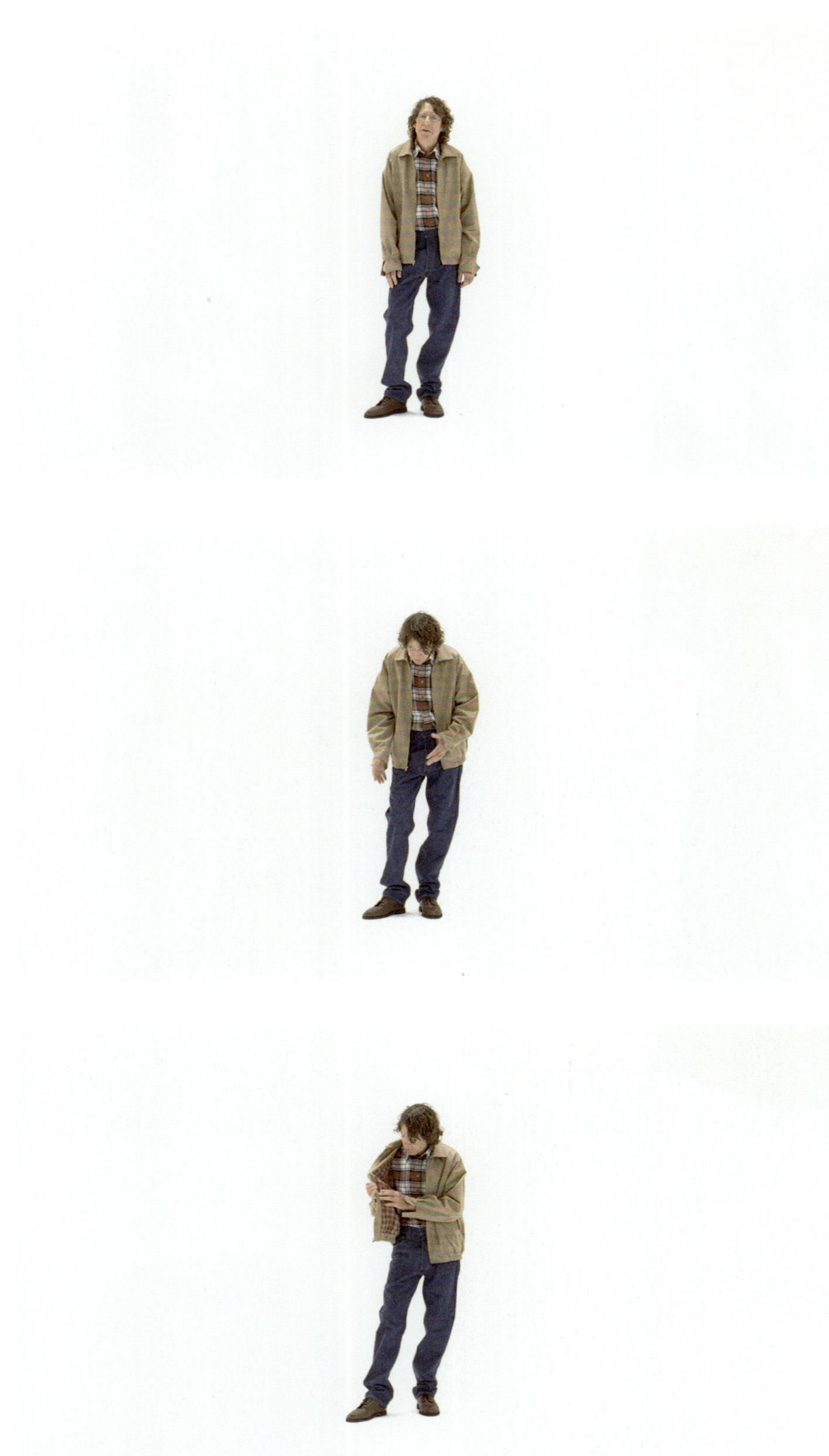

**233**  Charles Ray (b. 1953)
*Self-portrait with Homemade Clothes,* 2015
35-mm film, duration: 3'23"
Courtesy Matthew Marks Gallery

**263** Unknown photographer
*Verse ohne Worte in kubistischem
Kostüm,* 1916
Hugo Ball in the Cabaret Voltaire,
reciting his sound poems
Photograph, 71.5 × 40 cm
Kunsthaus Zürich, Archive Zürcher
Kunstgesellschaft and Kunsthaus Zürich

**62** Erwin Blumenfeld (1897–1969)
*Bloomfield, President-Dada-Chaplinist,* 1921
Collage with portrait photograph by
Blumenfeld, halftone printing and Chinese ink
on photograph of a female nude
Sheet: 13.4 × 8.8 cm
Kunsthaus Zürich, Department
of Prints and Drawings

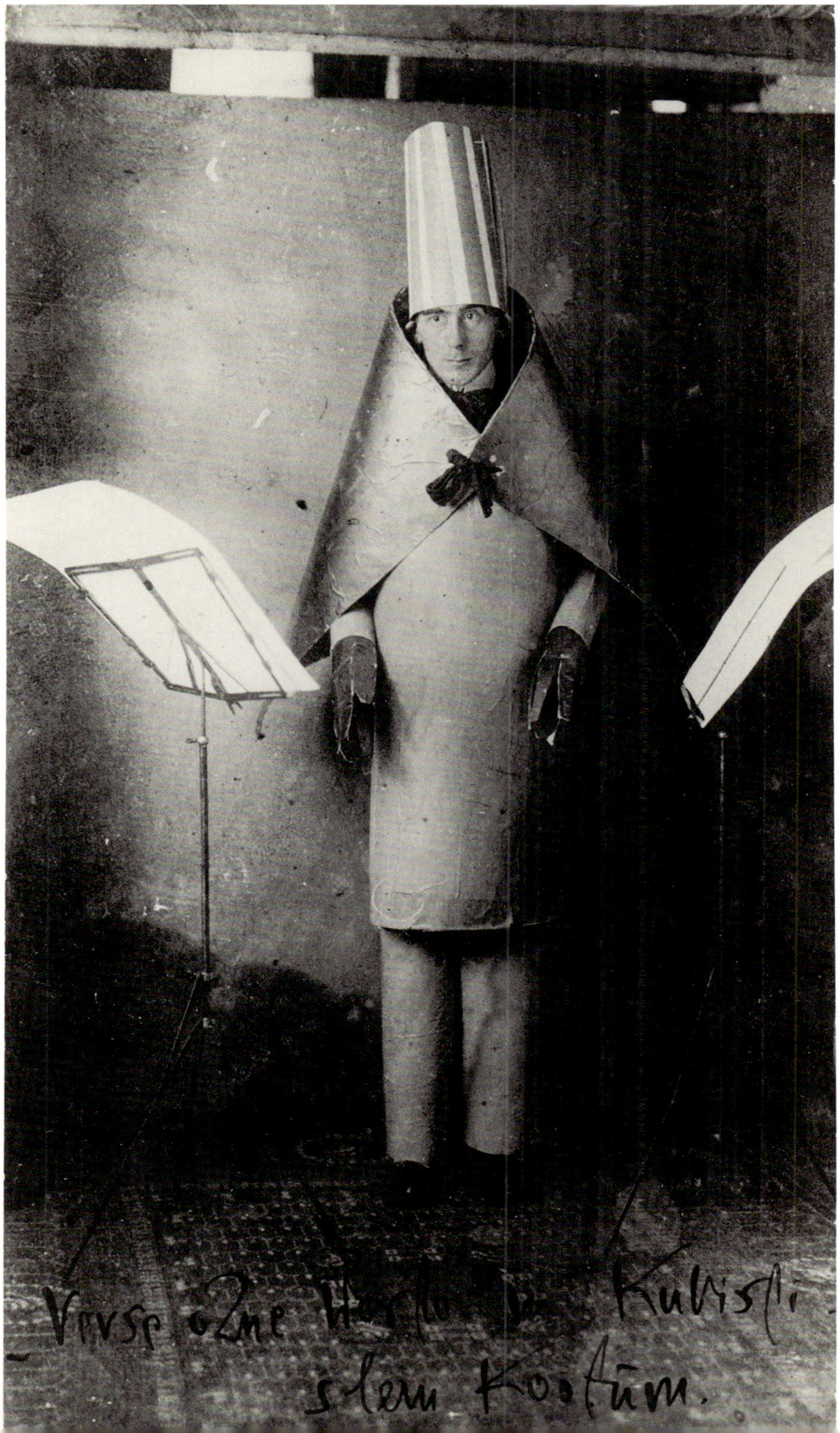

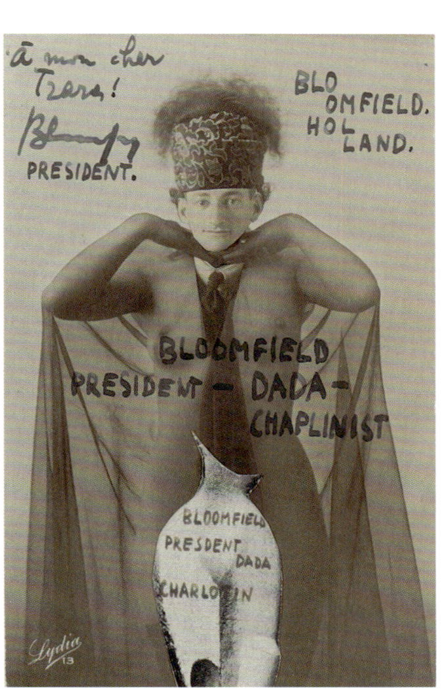

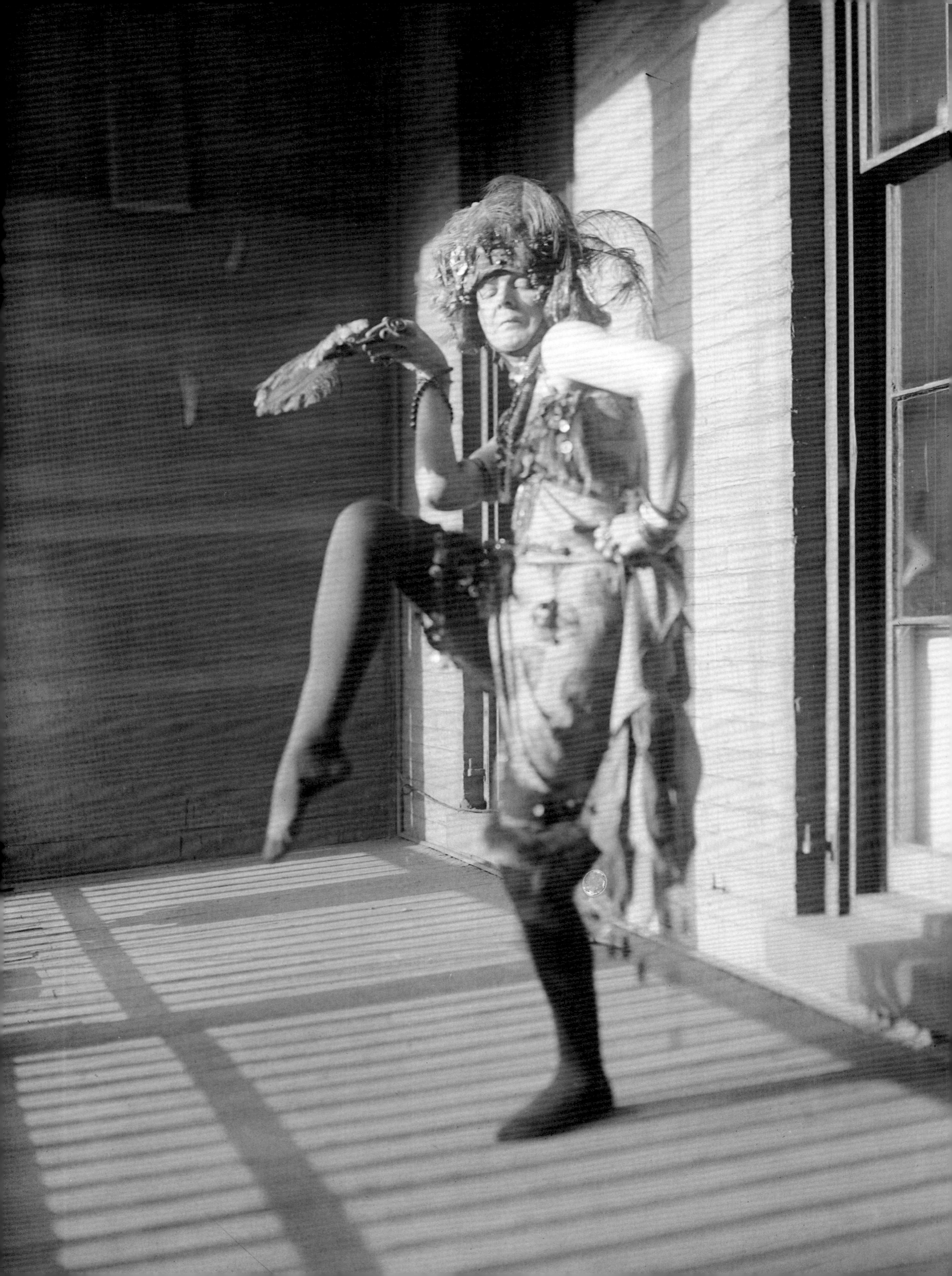

261 Unknown photographer
*Baroness von Freytag-Loringhoven,*
between 1910–20
Photograph of digital plot from
original glass negative image
Library of Congress, Washington, D.C.,
George Grantham Bain Collection

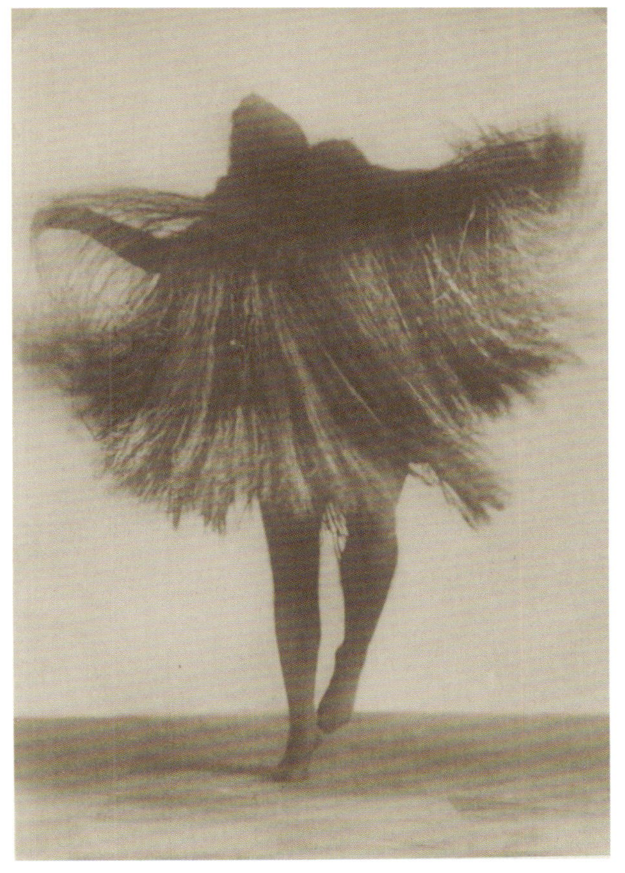



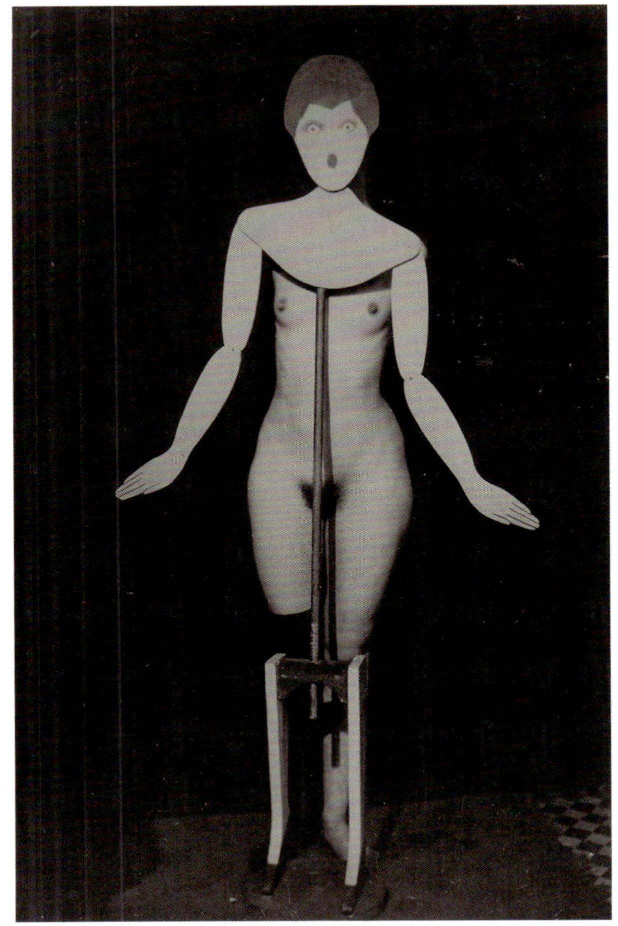

132  Hugo Erfurth, photography
*Mary Wigman. 'Götzendienst',* [1918/19]
Photo postcard, 13.5 × 8.6 cm
Kunsthaus Zürich, Archive Zürcher
Kunstgesellschaft and Kunsthaus Zürich

234  Man Ray (1890–1976)
*Portemanteau,* 1920
Silver gelatin photograph of a collage
of objects (original photograph)
Sheet: 25 × 16.5 cm
Kunsthaus Zürich, Collection
of Photography

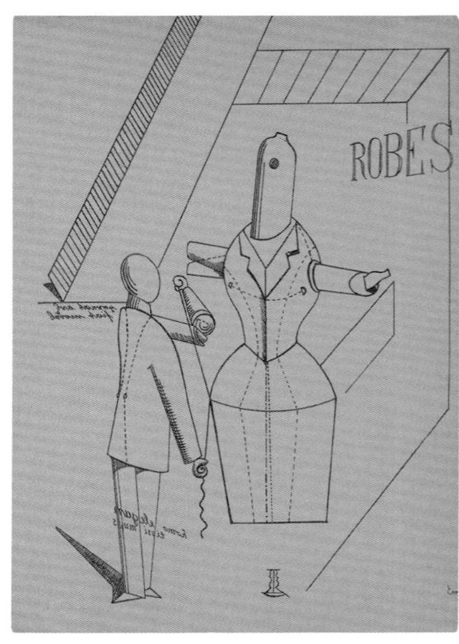

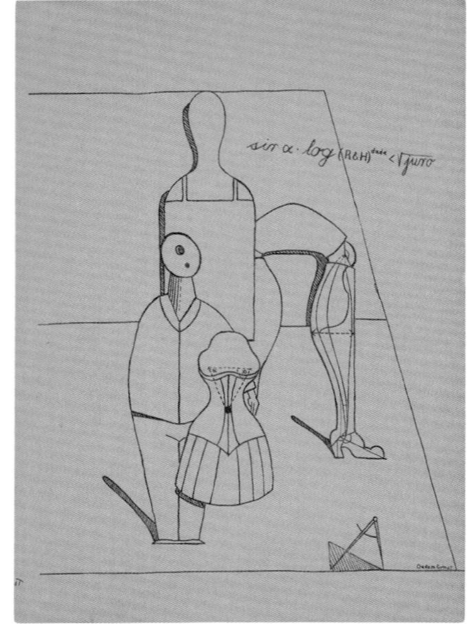

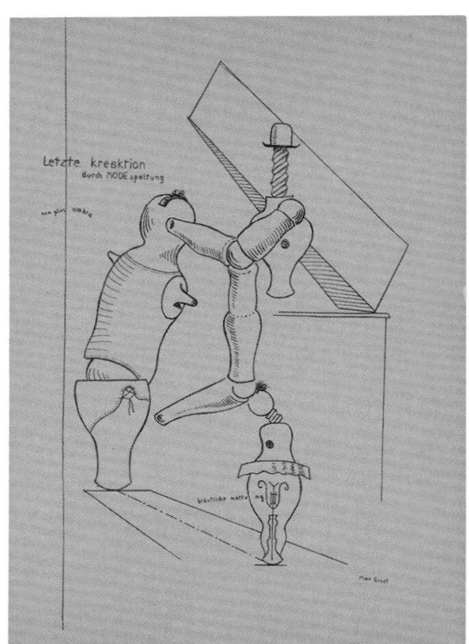

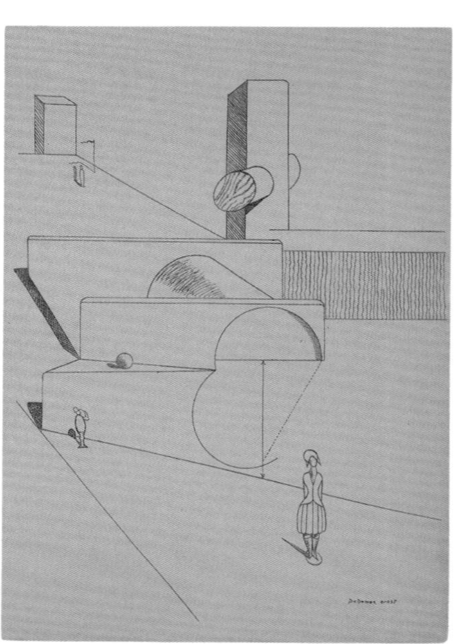

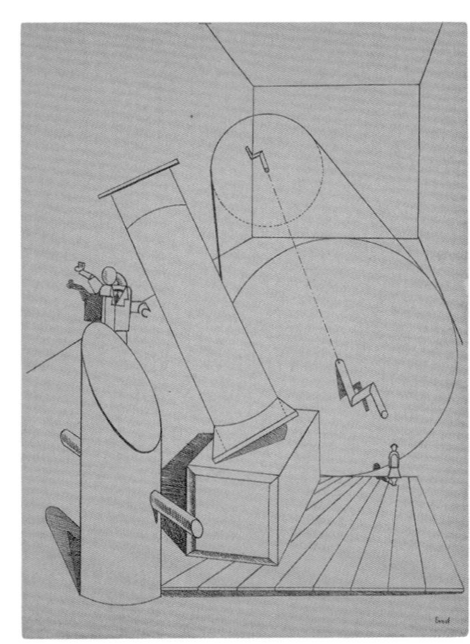

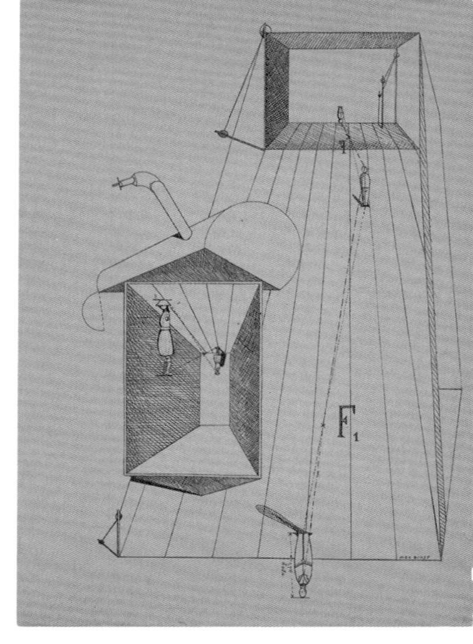

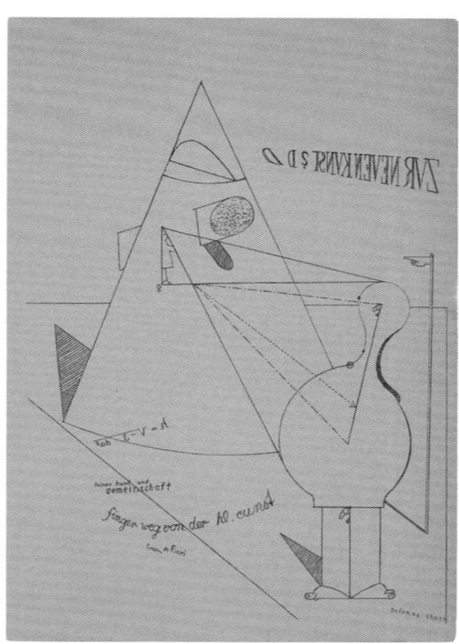

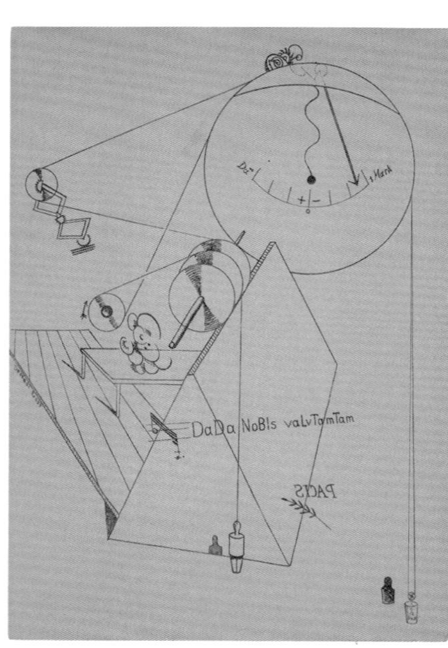

**133**  Max Ernst (1891–1976)
*Fiat modes – pereat ars,* 1919
8 lithographs on sturdy yellow typing paper,
cover with block print on white vellum paper,
folder with mounted title label on bluish glossy
paper, printed, a collaged fragment of
wallpaper on the lower edge of the sheet
Folder: 45.5 × 33 cm
Kunsthaus Zürich, Department
of Prints and Drawings

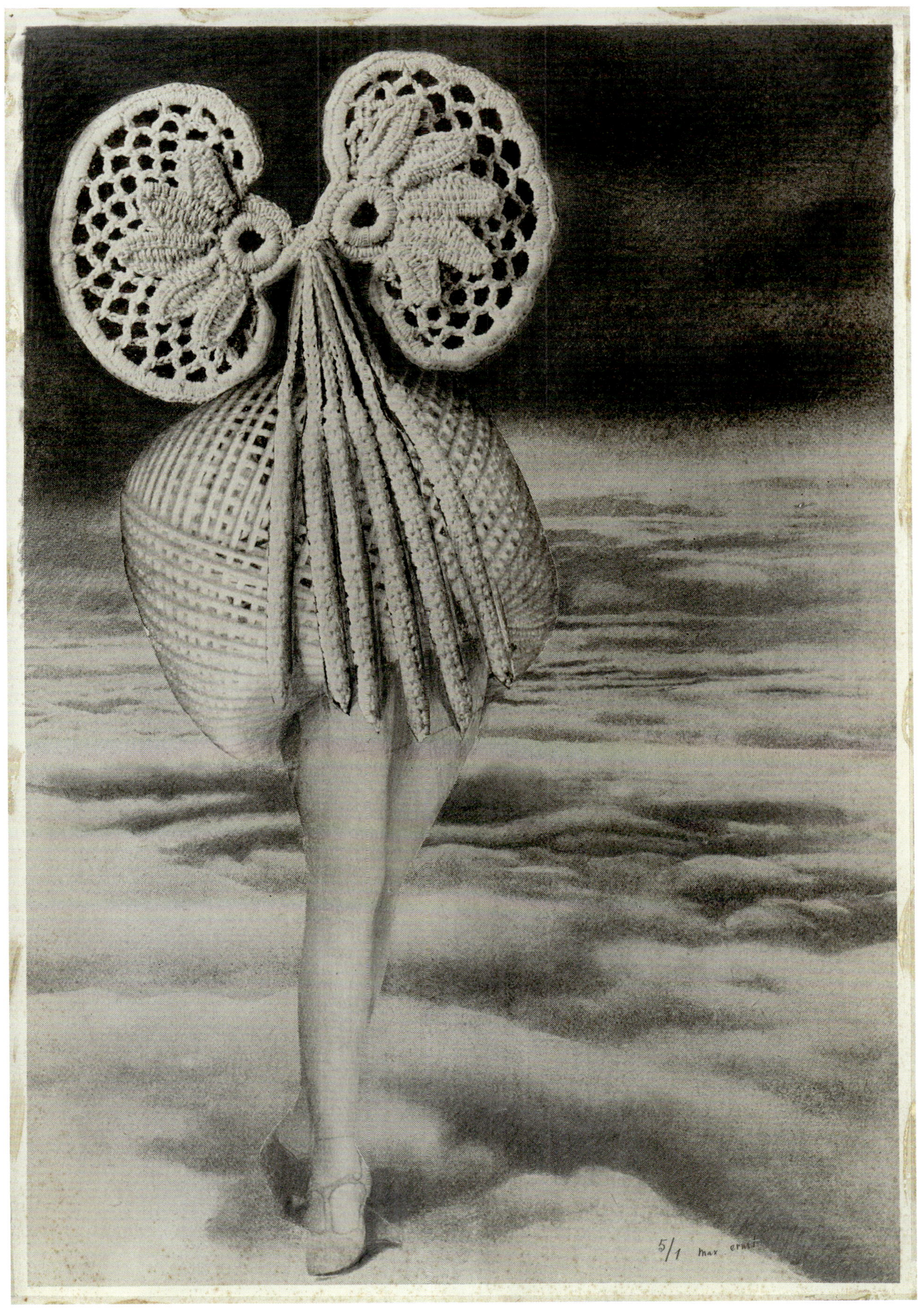



**134** Max Ernst (1891–1976)
*Au dessus des nuages marche la minuit. Au dessus de la minuit plane l'oiseau
invisible du jour. Un peu plus haut que l'oiseau l'éther pousse et les murs et
les toits flottent*, 1920
Photographic enlargement after the photomontage of the same name, sheet: 73 × 55 cm
Kunsthaus Zürich, Department of Prints and Drawings

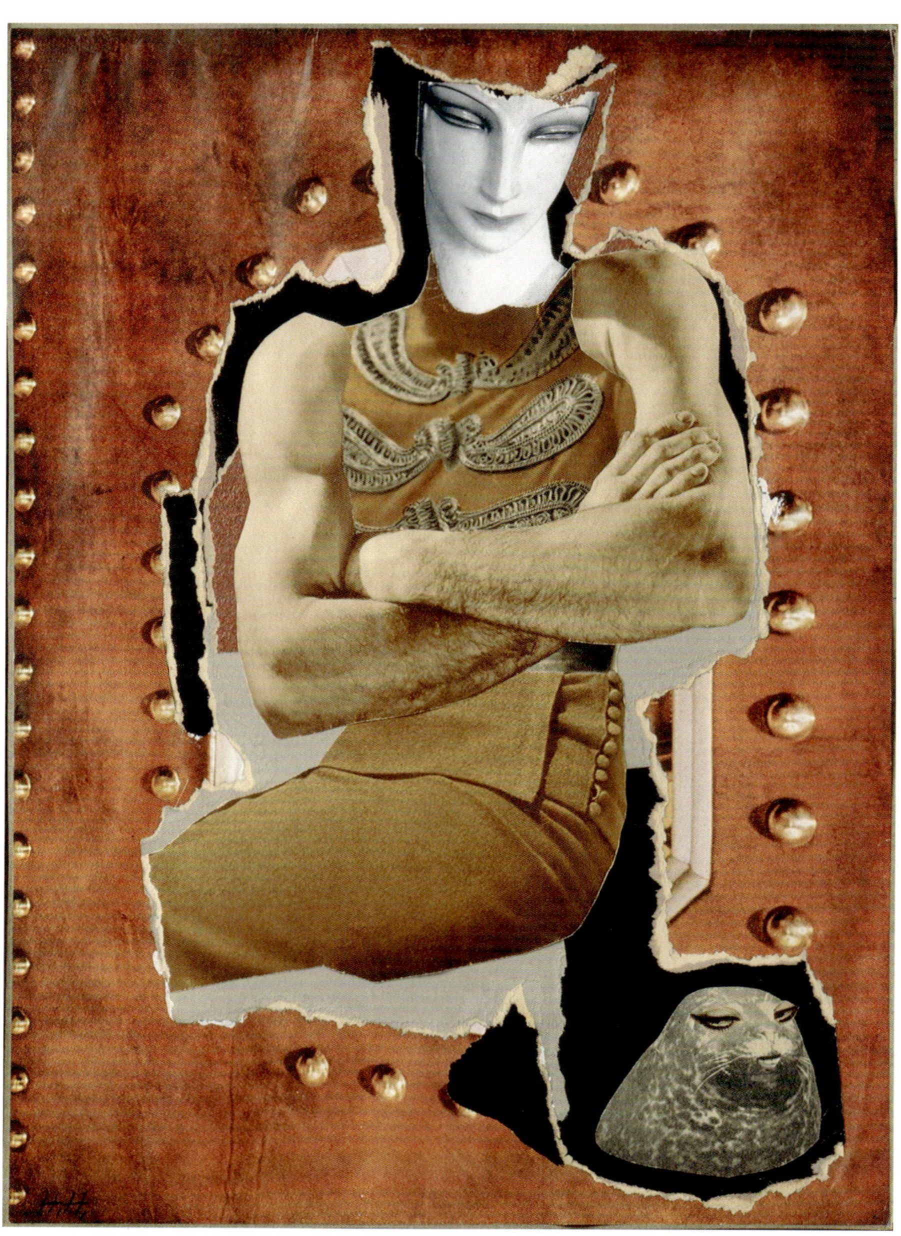

**173**  Hannah Höch (1889–1978)
*Domteuse,* c. 1930/1964
Animal tamer
Collage and photo montage; paper on cardboard,
numerous illustrations in colour and bronze
adhesive tape, mounted on cardboard, with an
artist's frame with suede cover, 35.5 × 26 cm
Kunsthaus Zürich, Department of Prints and Drawings

**156–164**  Natalja Gontscharowa (1881–1962)
9 designs, 1920s
Mixed media on paper,
frames: 56 × 39.5 cm each
Martin Kamer

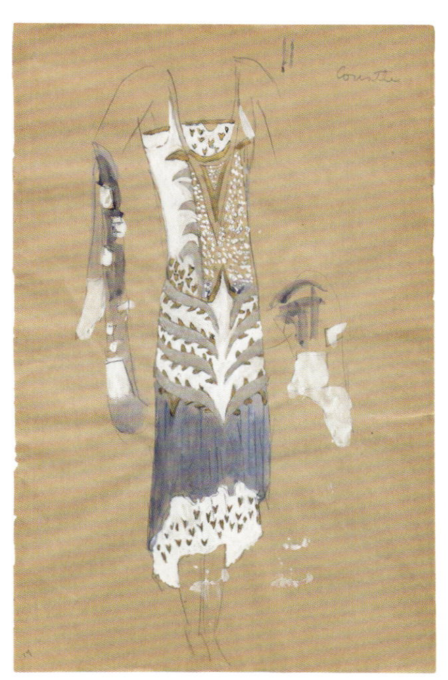
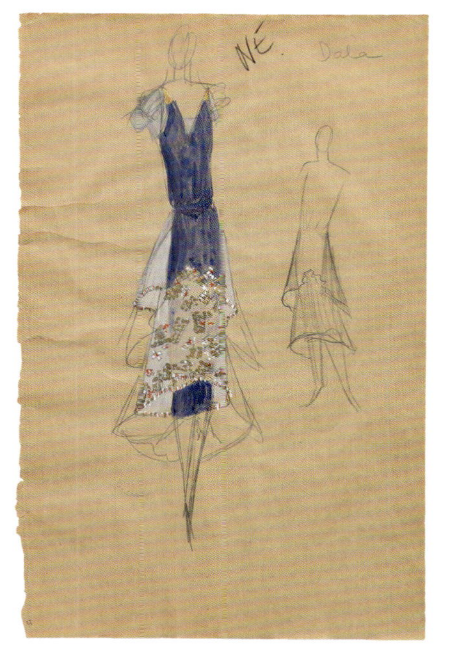
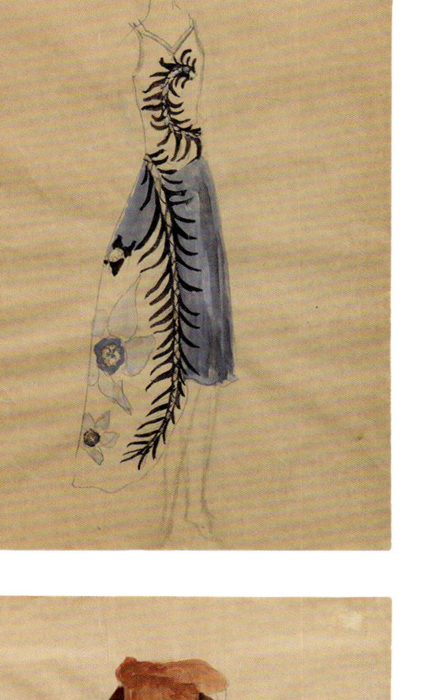
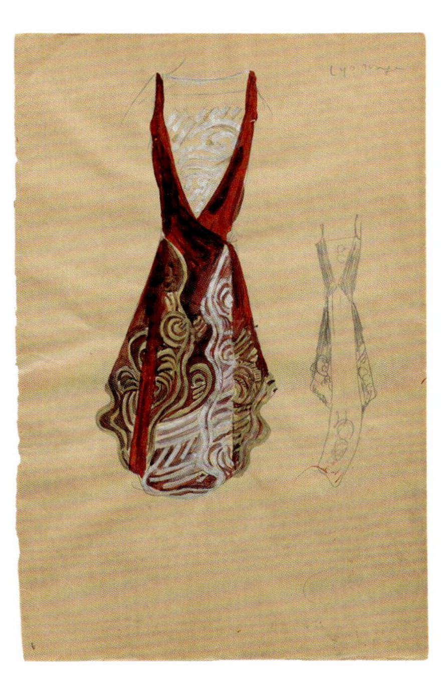
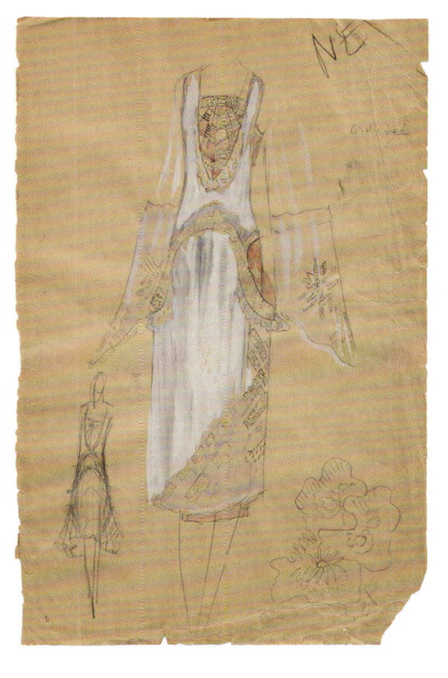
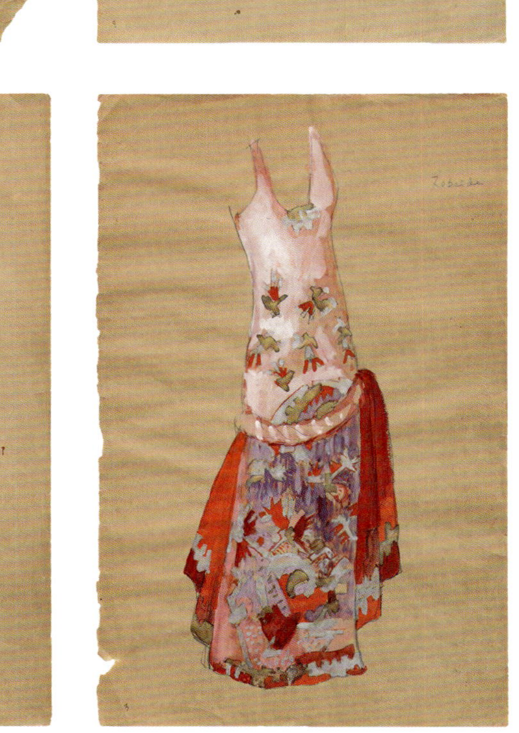
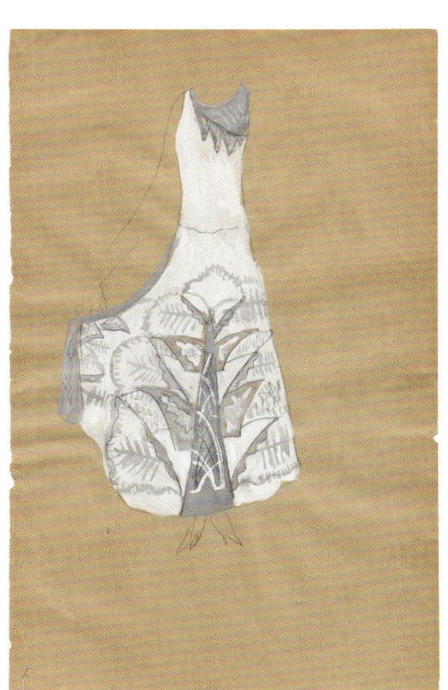
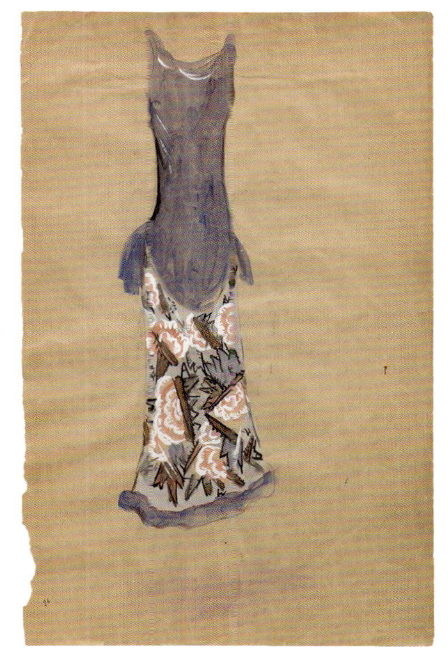

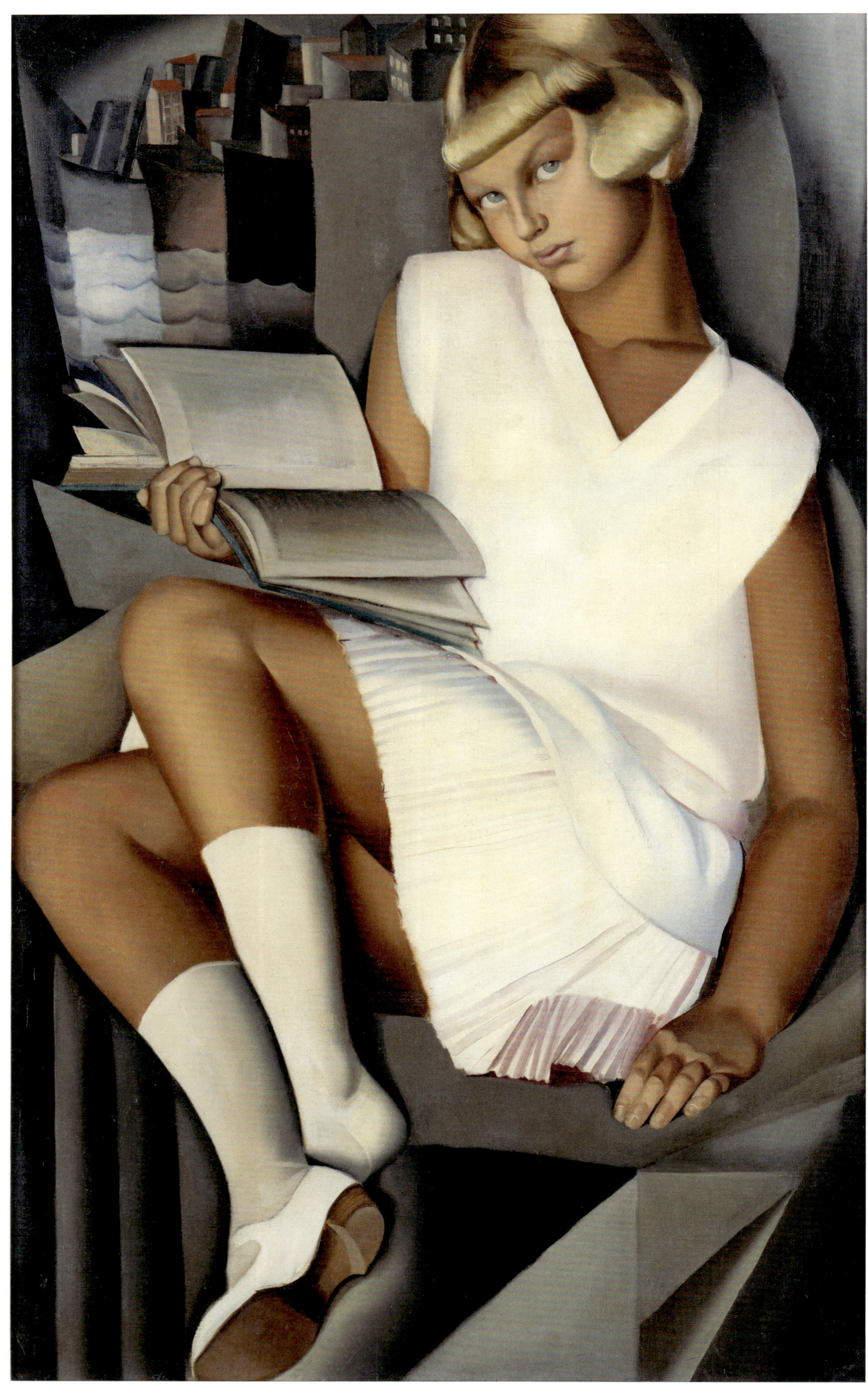



Artists Design Clothes

**198** Tamara de Lempicka (1898–1980)
*Kizette en rose,* 1927
Oil on canvas, 116 × 73 cm
Musée d'Art de Nantes

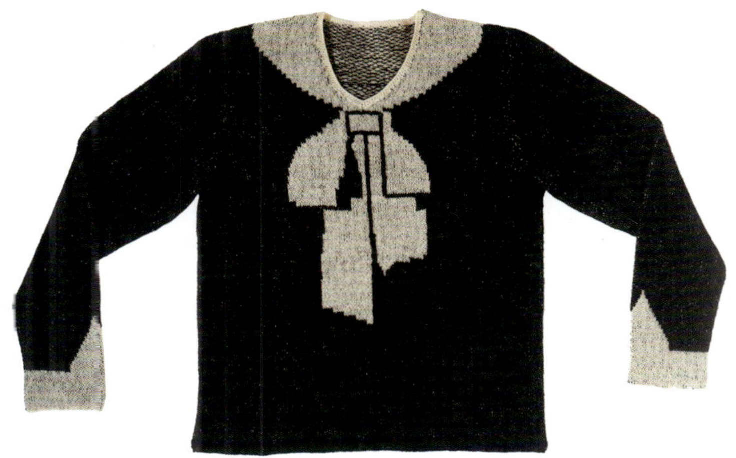

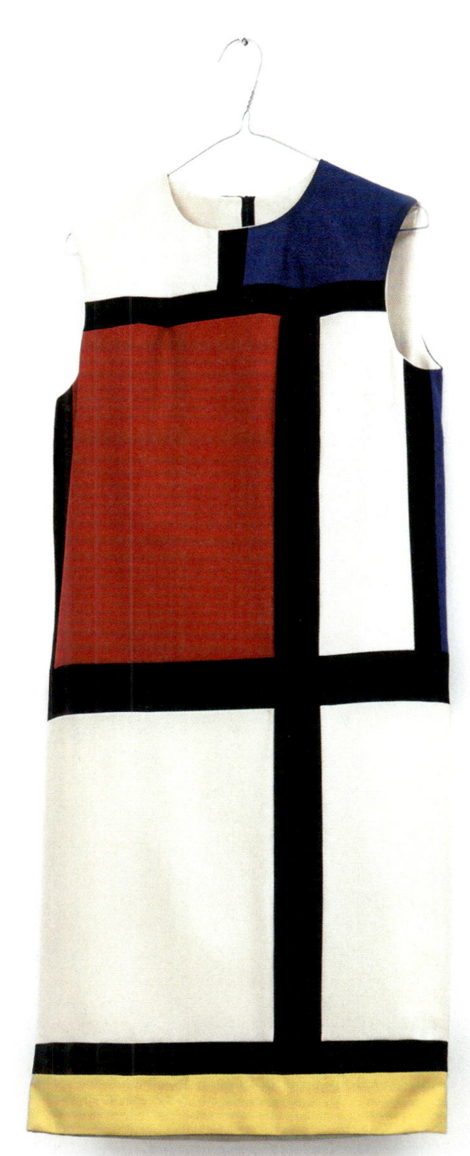

**27** Elsa Schiaparelli (1890–1973)
Cravat (jumper), 1927
Wool, hand-knitted
V&A, London, Textiles and
Fashion Collection

**137** Sylvie Fleury (b. 1961)
*Mondrian Dress Rack,* 1993/2016
3 Mondrian dresses,
1 clothes rack, 3 hangers
Courtesy the artist and
Karma International,
Zurich and Los Angeles

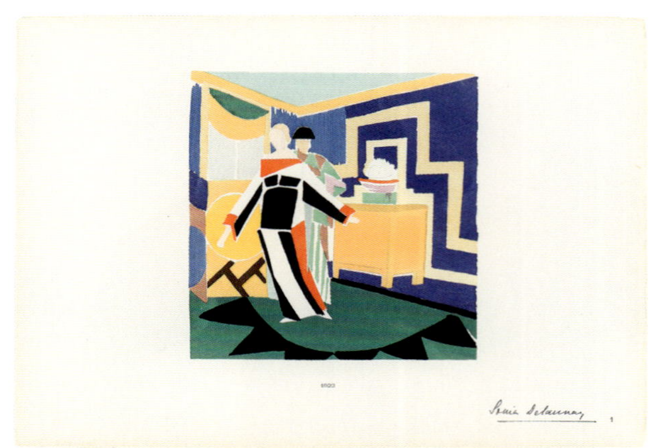

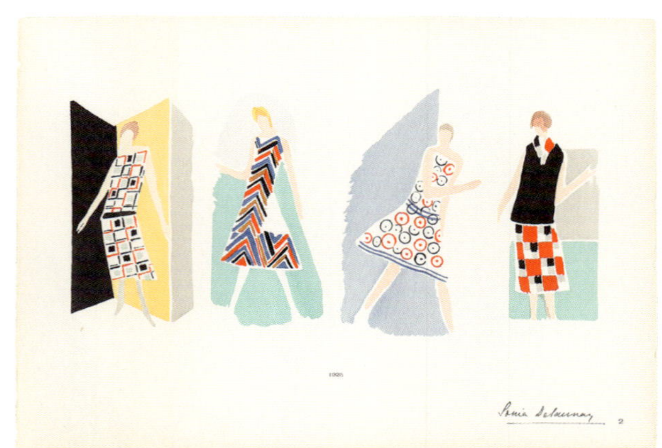

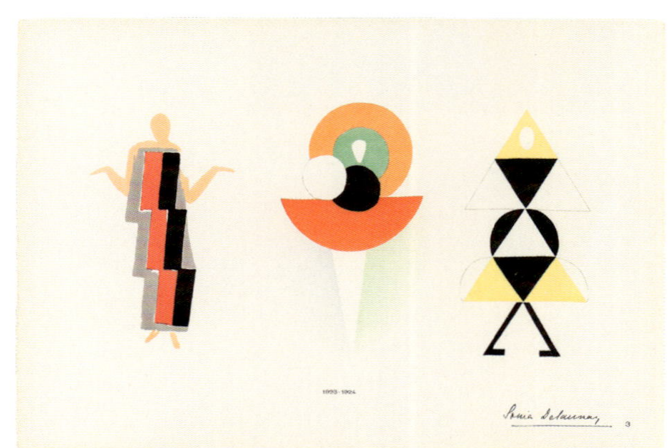

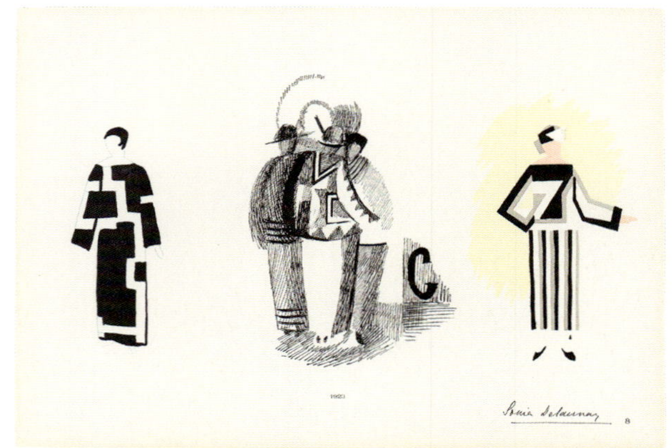

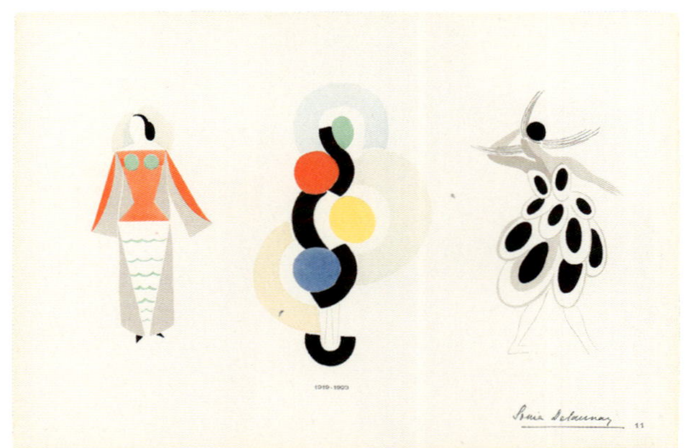

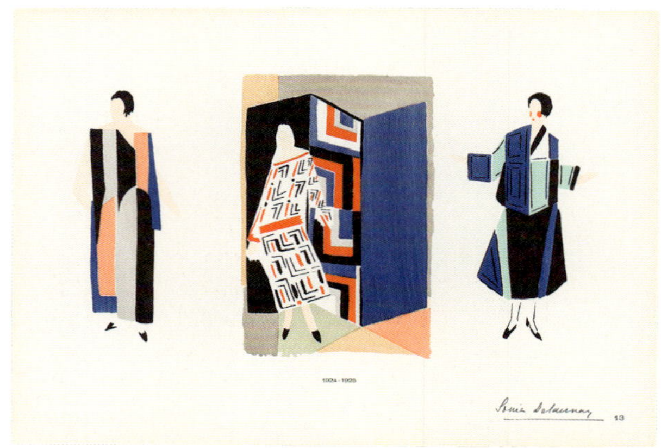

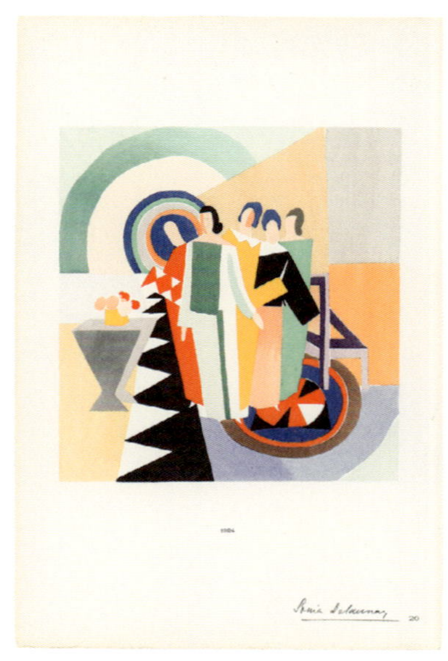

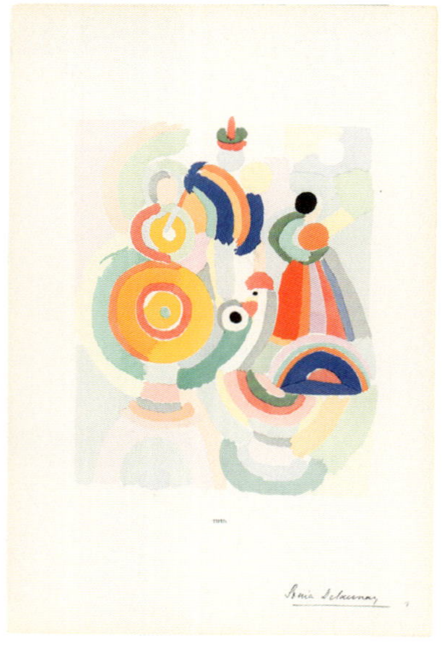

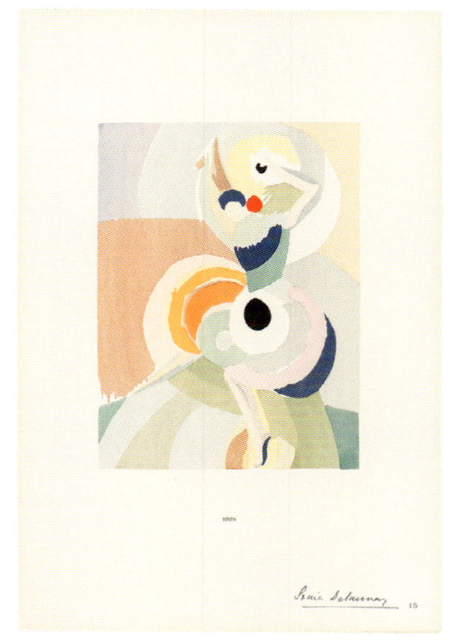

**108–116** Sonia Delaunay (1885–1979)
Clothing designs, 1915–25
Pochoir print and serigraph on
thin board, sheets: c. 56.2 × 38 cm each
Zurich, University of the Arts, ZHdK,
Museum für Gestaltung Zürich,
Graphics Collection

**75** Paul Camenisch (1893–1970)
*Café Commerce Suisse,* 1928
Oil on canvas, 115 × 140 cm
Collection Pictet

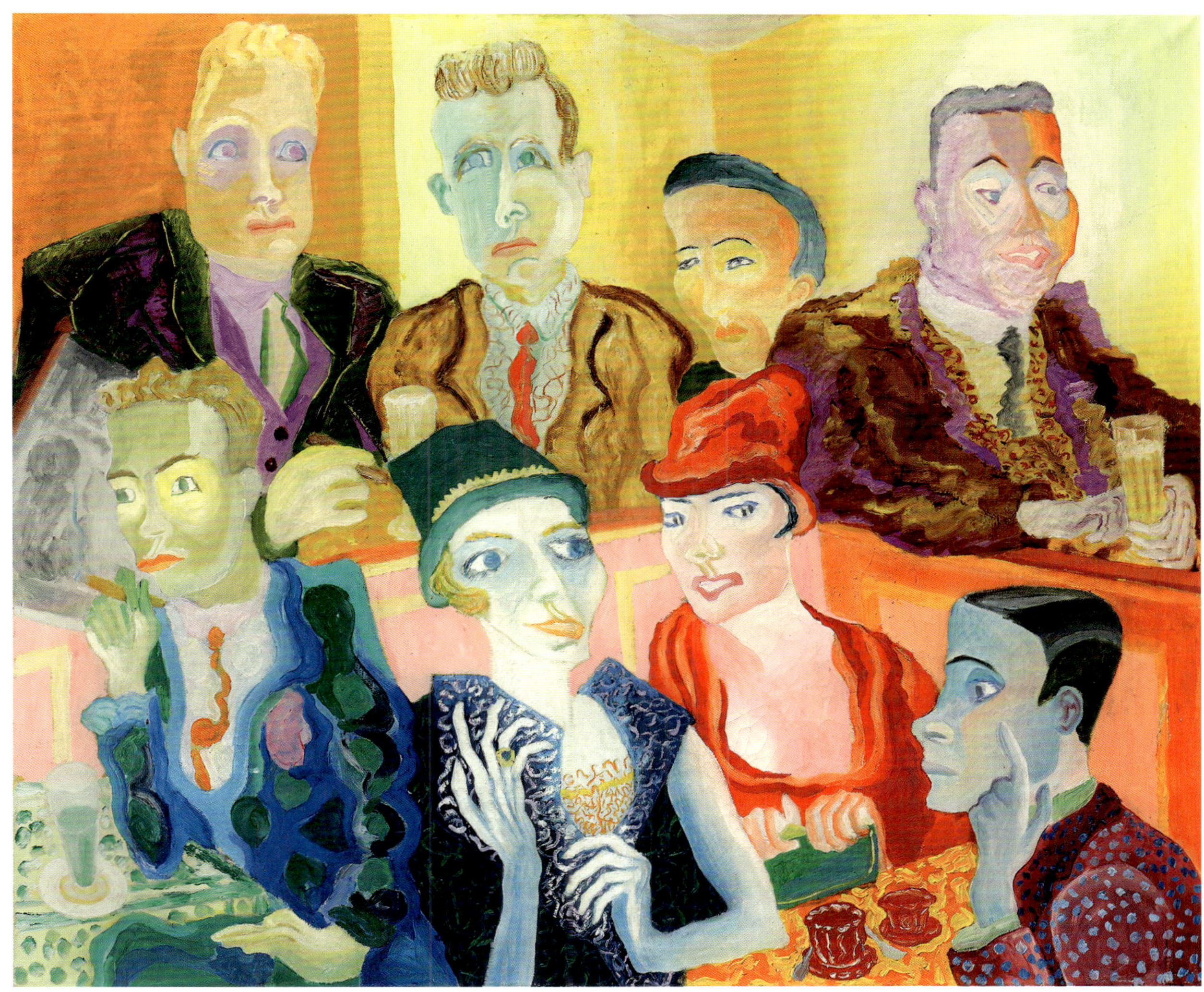

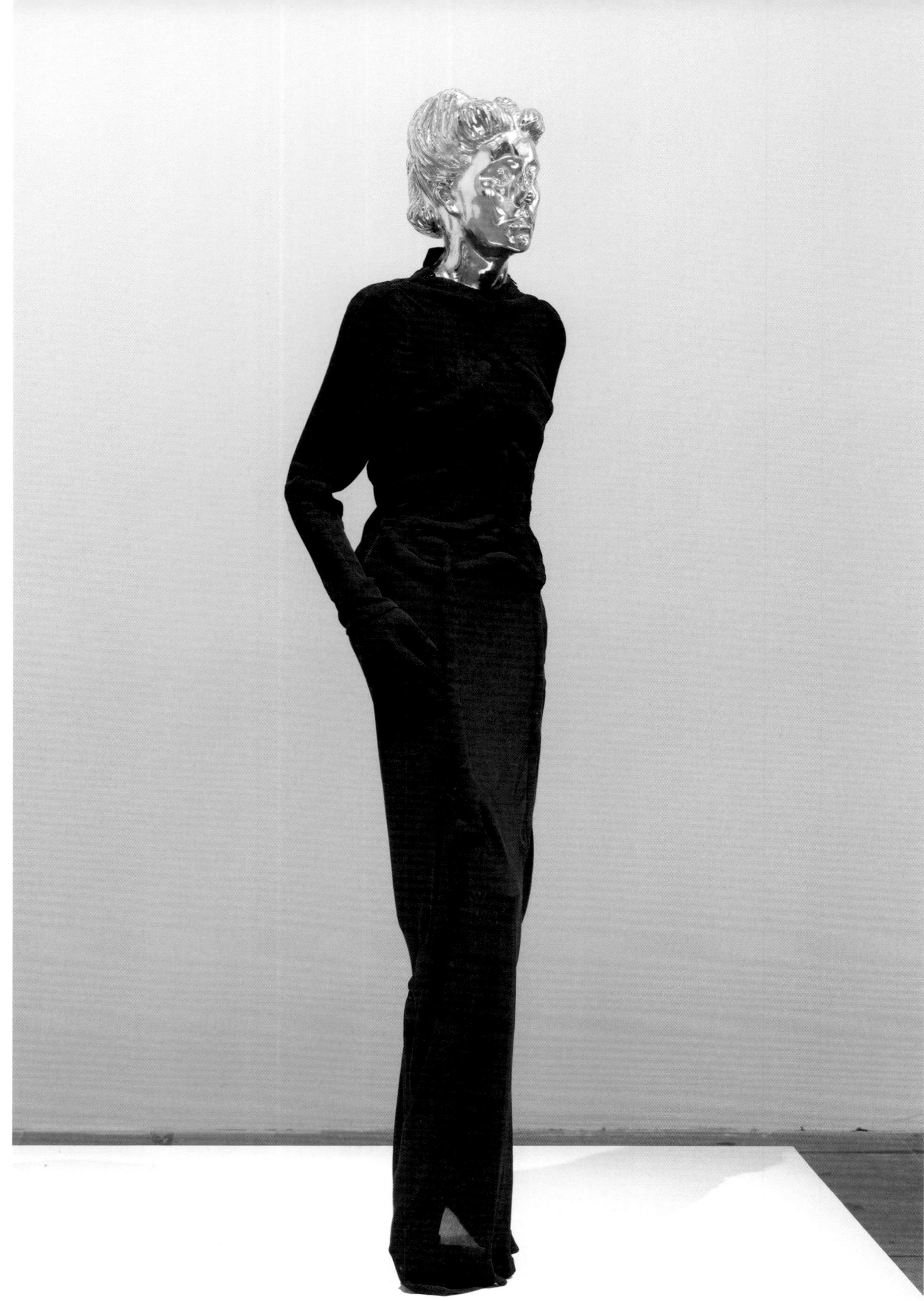



**227** Mai-Thu Perret (b. 1976)
*Flow My Tears I,* 2011
Mannequin with glass head, copy of Elsa Schiaparelli's
'Skeleton' dress, in cooperation with Salvador Dalí, 1938
made by Naoyuki Yoneto, 175 × 70 × 70 cm
Courtesy of the artist and Galerie Francesca Pia, Zurich

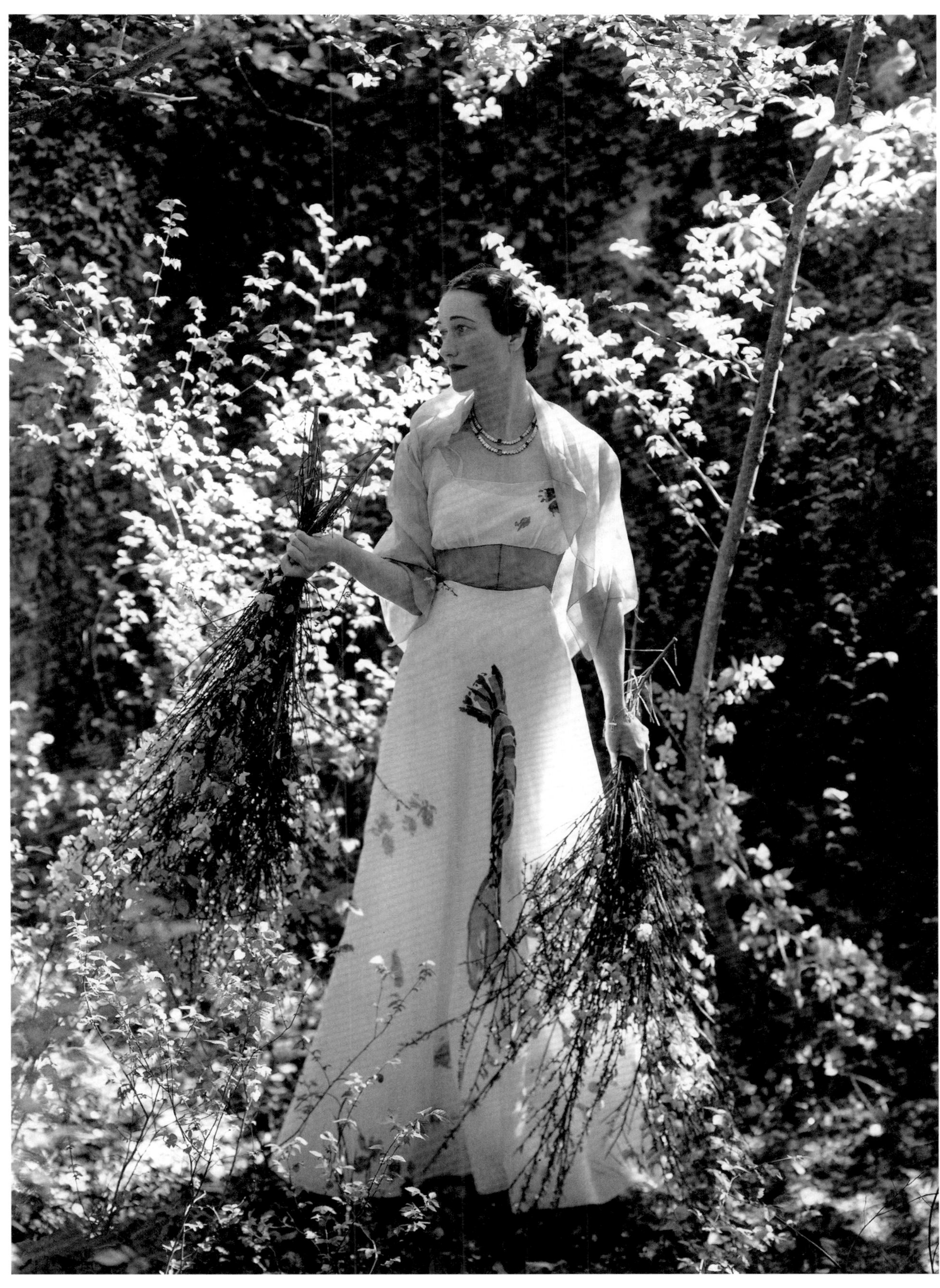

**59**  Joseph Beuys (1921–1986)
Felt suit, 1970
Wool felt, sewn, 170 × 60 cm
Collection Ph. Konzett, Vienna

**60**  Joseph Beuys (1921–1986)
*The Orwell leg: Trousers for
the 21st century,* 1984
Collection Ph. Konzett, Vienna

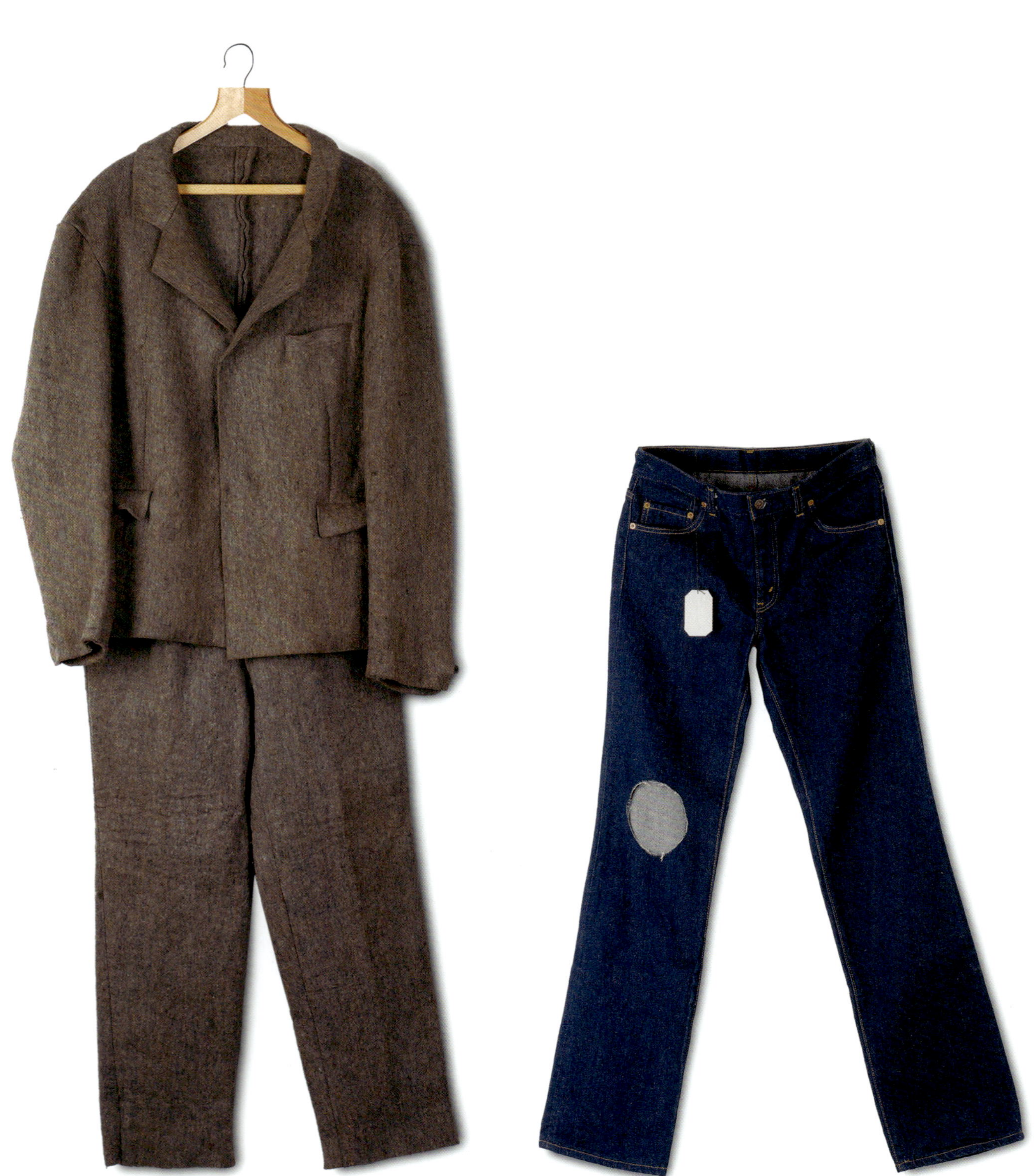

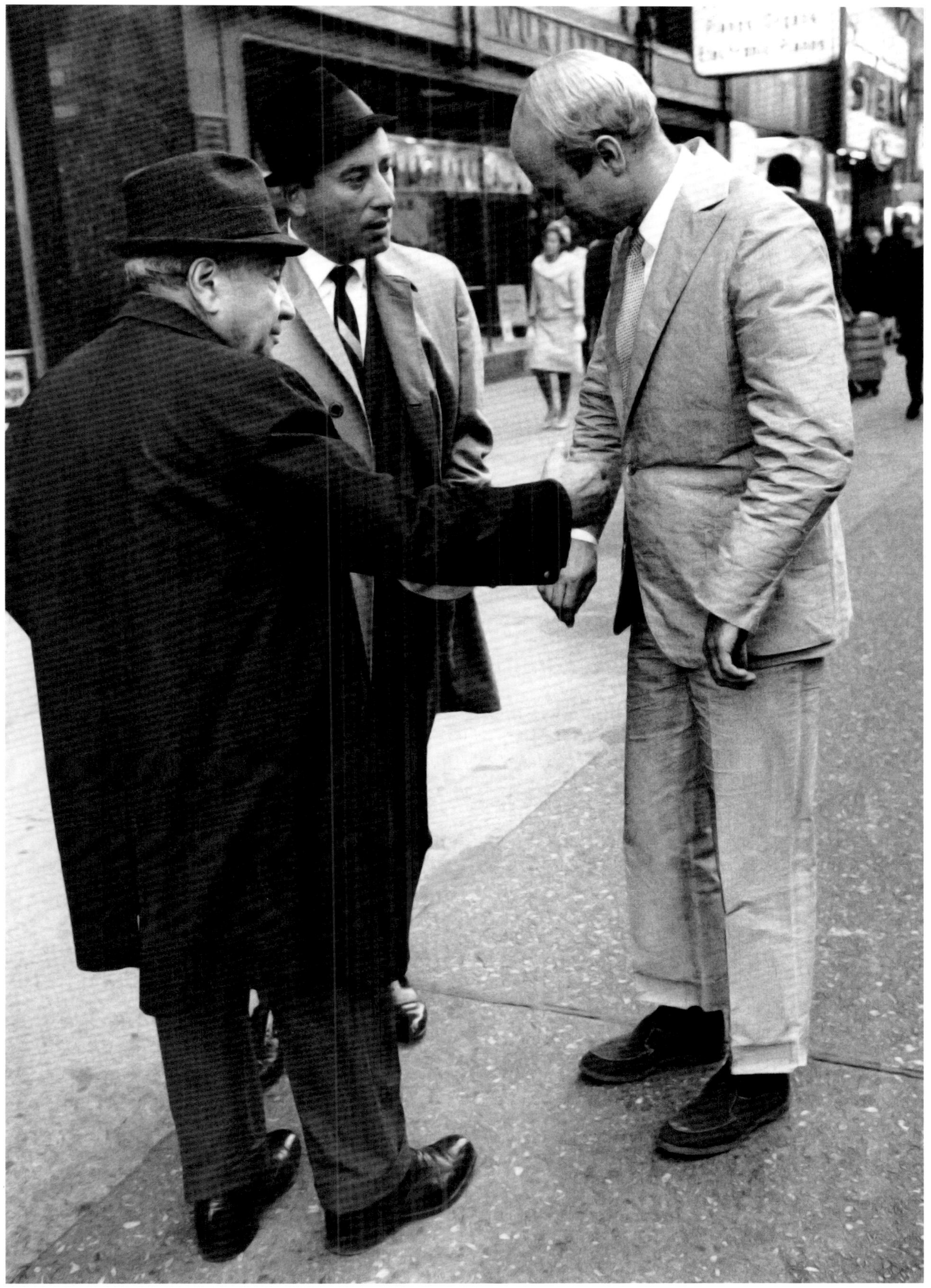

**237**  James Rosenquist (1933–2017), design
Steve Schapiro (b. 1934), photography
*Paper suit,* 1998
James Rosenquist in his *Paper suit,*
New York City 1966

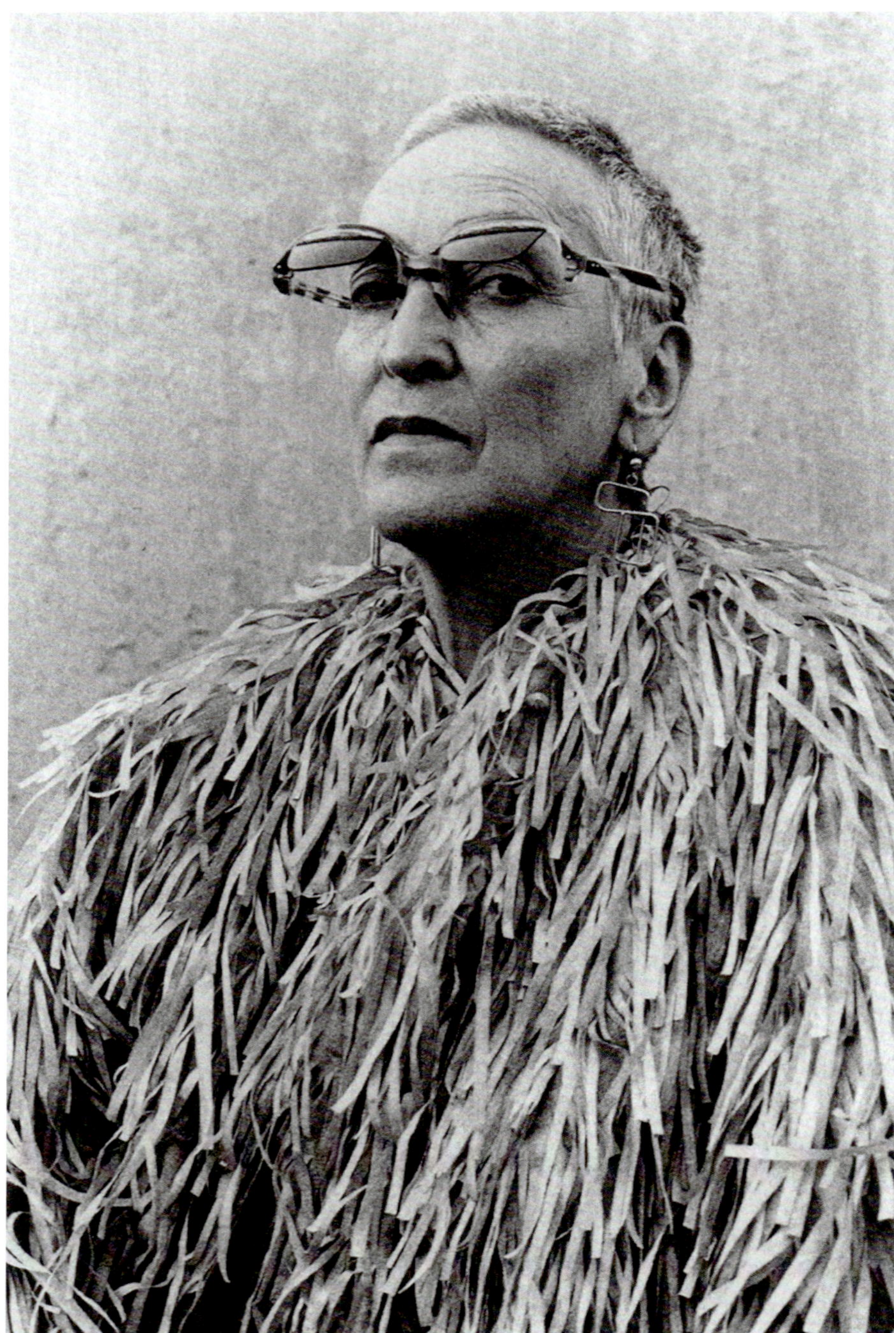

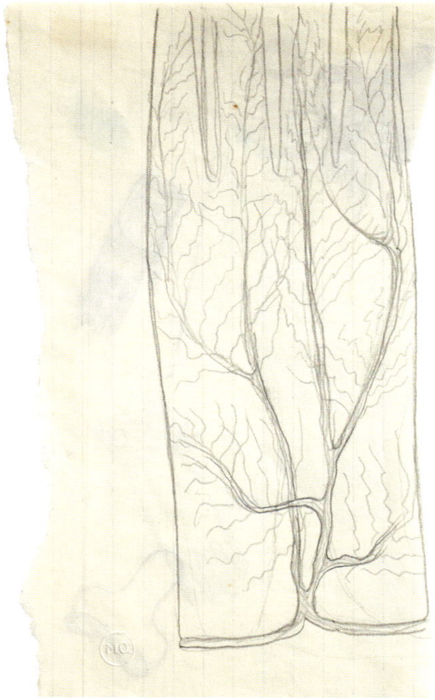

**222** Meret Oppenheim (1913–1985)
*Design for gloves with veins,* 1942–45
Pencil on paper, sheet: c. 19 × 11 cm
Private collection Basel
The artsist had the idea for these gloves
realised for the luxury edition of *Parkett,*
no. 4/1985 (cat. 225)

**225** Meret Oppenheim (1913–1985)
*Glove,* 1985
Edition for *Parkett,* no. 4/1985
Gloves made from goat suede, trimmed with
piping by hand and equipped with serigraph
Kunsthaus Zürich, Department
of Prints and Drawings

**224** Meret Oppenheim (1913–1985), design
Claude Lê-Anh (b. 1936), photography
*Meret Oppenheim with a model of her paper
clothes collections and one of her sun protection (half)glasses, designed by herself,* 1967

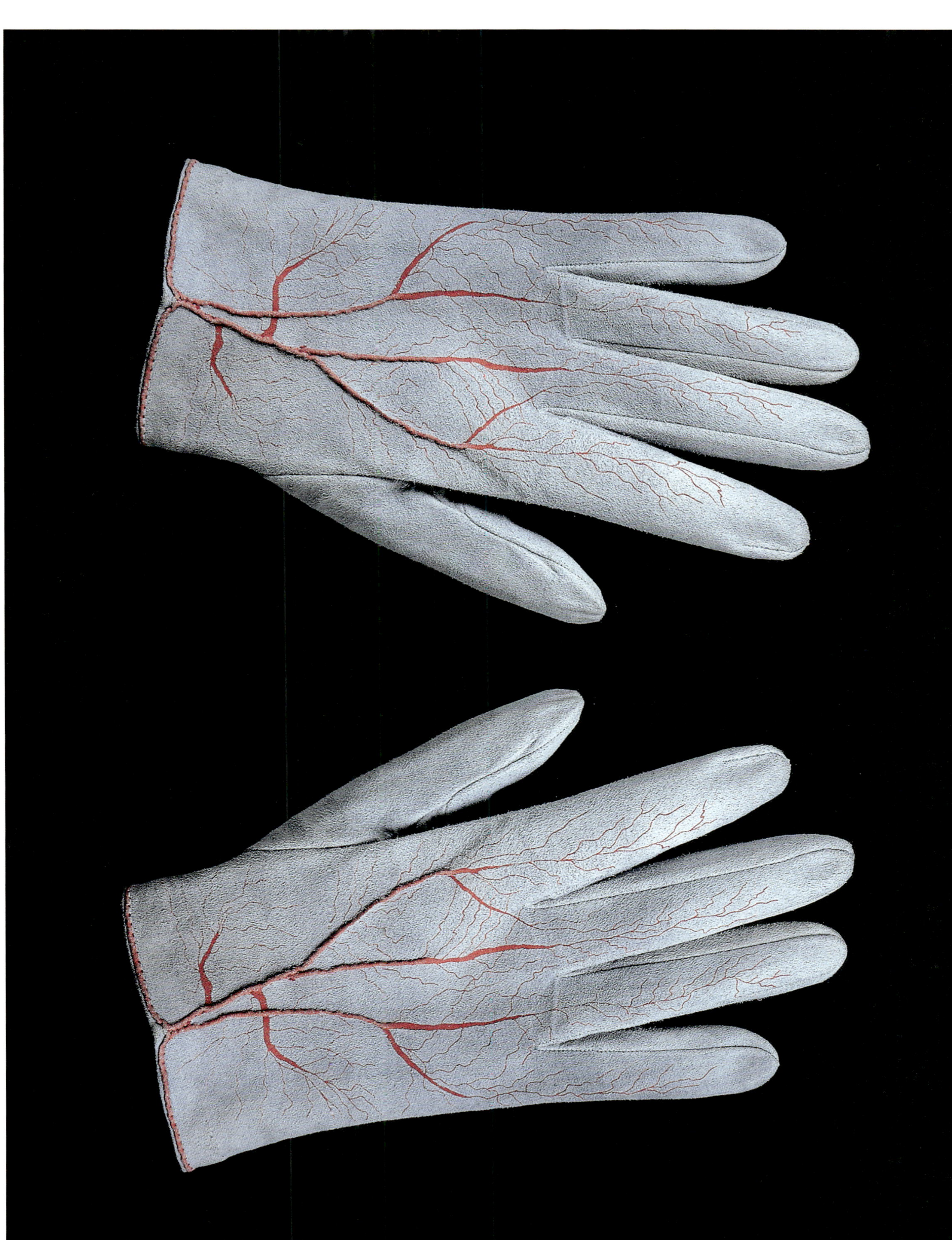

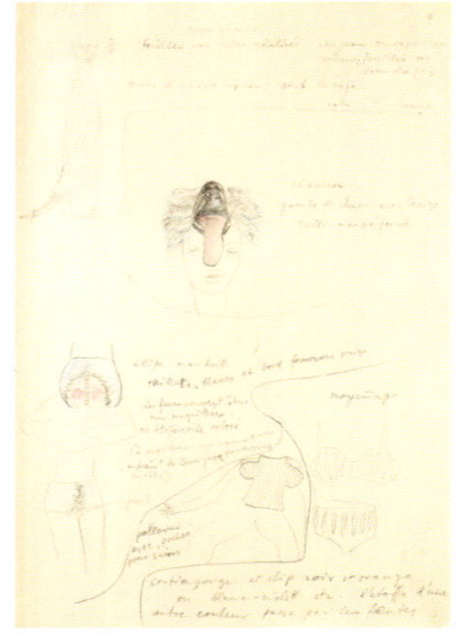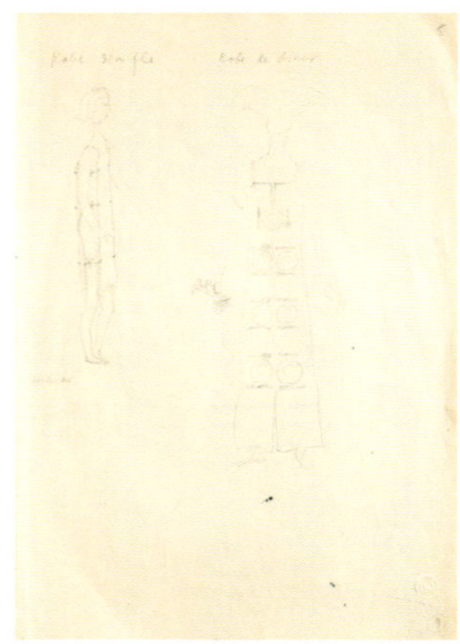

# *Paper Dresses*

Have the advantage over 'proper' dresses of
being cheap. After wearing them for a short while,
you throw them away. With 'proper' clothes you
make sure that you can wear them often, which
means that a dress that is too extravagant,
extremely noticeable, can really be worn only once.
That's why you should make the most extreme
models out of paper. Apart from that and on the side
you should also, however, make a standard-dress,
a sheath dress, which is made only in mono-colours,
black, white and all the colours that are in fashion
(or 3–4). Like paper handkerchiefs 10. – The cut of
this sheath dress changes, at most, once a year,
but many imaginative accessories are created for
this sheath: sleeves on chains (plastic) attached
to each other (and lifted over the head).
Smocks tied at the side with little bows (these
flat parts printed with totally 'dumb' patterns).
Or material like grass, bright green. These smocks
would be nicer over a trouser-dress, continuous
from top to bottom (made of paper?). Short or long
Cossack over-jackets, kimonos with or without
sleeves; e.g. orange-and-black shapes – flowers only
connected to each other with stems or lines etc.
(Also symmetrical or asymmetrical ornament
over the whole to 2/3 transparent top.) It would be
nicer if 'nothing' were in between, but that doesn't
work because you would get caught on everything.
Therefore: joined with a fine grid or, better,
a completely transparent material.

Over the standard-dress: garlands or snakes

Dresses that can be buttoned together
lemon yellow
buttons black
black
buttons dark grey
dark grey

The same dress, black at the bottom, then dark grey,
light grey-white (only neck and shoulder part) and
bright vermillion sleeves buttoned on.
The individual parts of these buttoned dresses
could also be narrower, so that the nice mini-dress
'for the office' becomes a mini-mini.
Alternatives for over the standard-dress:
fantasy collars, capes, lace sleeves

back
embossed patterns, colour or tone-in-tone
strongly 'lacquered' – carousel horse

On the back of the standard-dress material a grid
of centimetres so that it is always possible to say
at which points buttons, hooks or 'adhesive tape'
should be attached for fastening the accessories.

d'après Strasberg

**220** Meret Oppenheim (1913–1985)
Designs for cape, cap and
varieté lingerie, c. 1942
Pencil and crayon on paper
Sheet: 29.7 × 21 cm
Private collection, Basel

**221** Meret Oppenheim (1913–1985)
*Robe simple, robe de dîner,* 1942–45
Sketches, pencil on paper
Sheet: c. 29.7 × 21 cm
Private collection, Basel

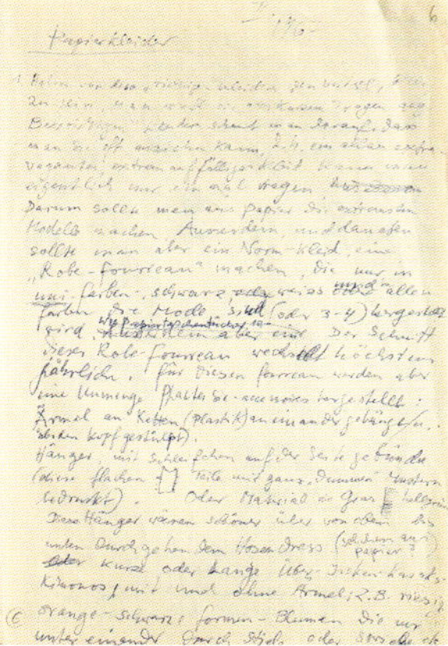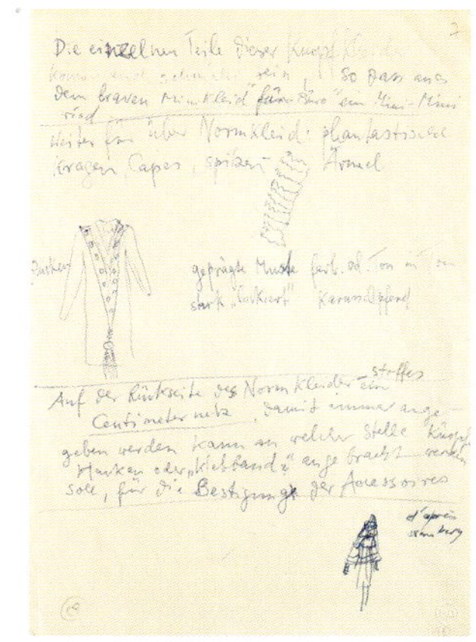

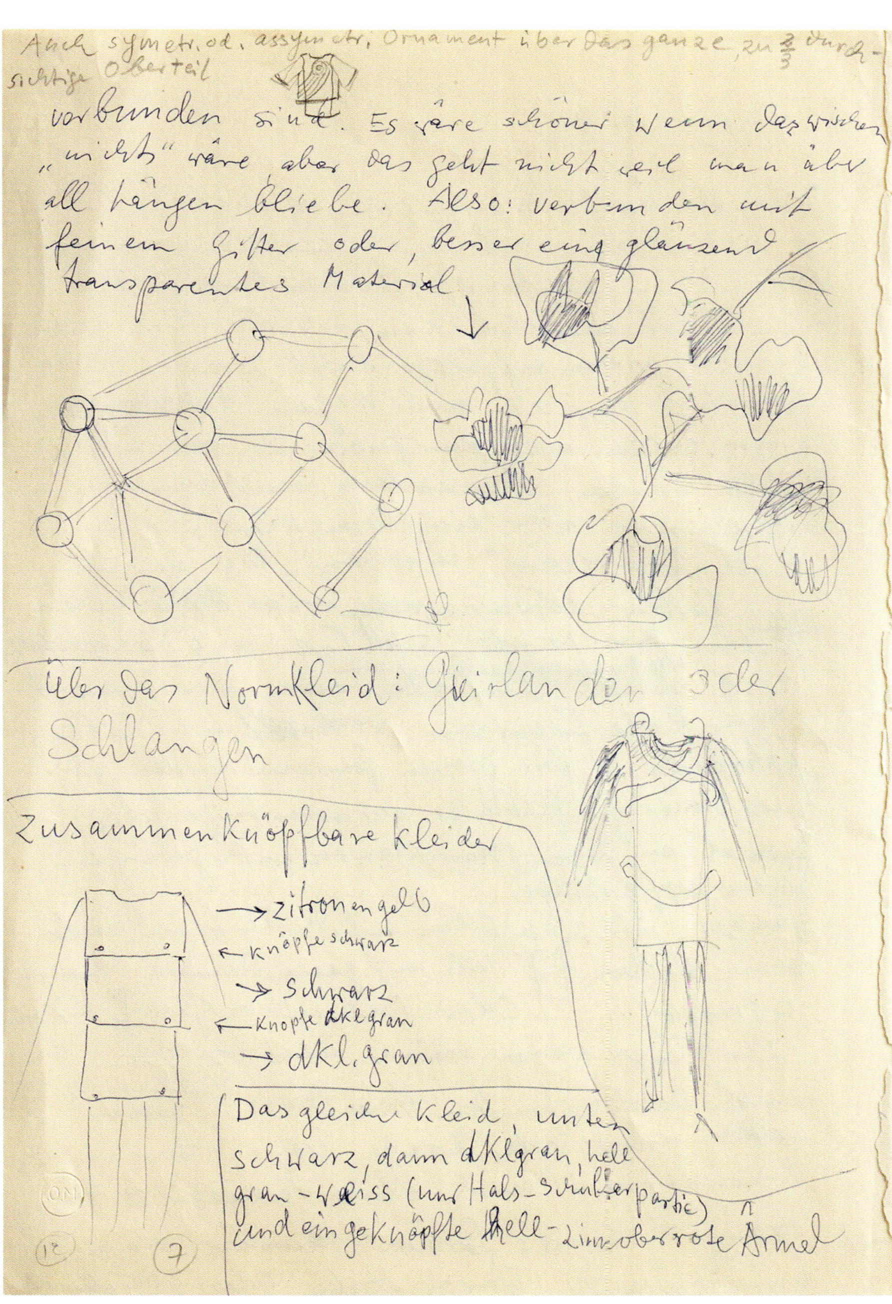

**223** Meret Oppenheim (1913–1985)
*Notes and sketches for paper clothes,* 1967
3 pages from an exercise book,
pencil and Chinese ink on paper
Sheet: 29.7 × 21 cm
Private collection, Basel

# Military

Franz
Schuh

# Look
# 68

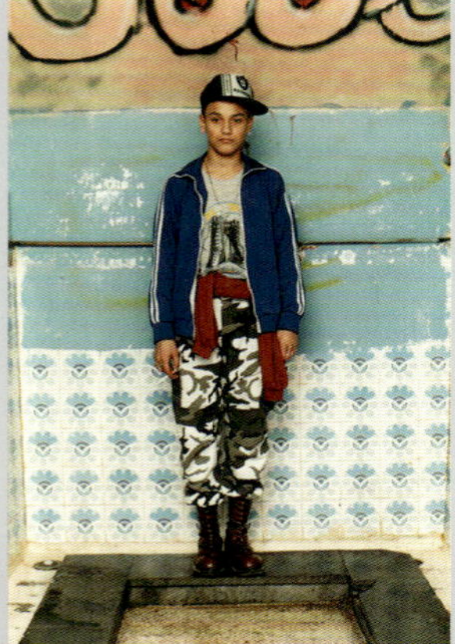

**251** Wolfgang Tillmans (b. 1968)
*Christos,* 1992
Colour photograph, 60.8 × 50.7 cm
Kunsthaus Zürich,
Collection of Photography

**253** Wolfgang Tillmans (b. 1968)
*Travis with tree,* 1994
Colour photograph, 50.8 × 50.7 cm
Kunsthaus Zürich,
Collection of Photography



'The singer Herbert Lippert, first tenor of the Vienna State Opera, is also a painter, not an occasional painter, but an accomplished artist in both of his fields. On 28 October 2017, the midday news of an Austrian television station featured the painter and singer, who had displayed his own artworks in an exhibition in Franz Schubert's opera *Winterreise.* One saw the paintings and Lippert singing: "Fremd bin ich eingezogen, / Fremd zieh' ich wieder aus…" (I came here a stranger, / As a stranger I depart…).'

One saw the artworks and heard the beautiful singing. Wonderful, but for the one-and-a-half-hour show, something else captured my attention: During this performance, the singer and painter Herbert Lippert wore a jacket copied from the military: The jacket had the brownish inconspicuousness of the military colour, a camouflage, but above all, those pockets, which was one reason why I wore military jackets in the 1960s and 1970s. Deep and wide pockets into which the magazine of an assault rifle would easily fit.

In the 1980s, when everyone was allowed to wear anything, when the promiscuity in fashion had become bold, Götz George played Horst Schimanski, a detective of the German crime series *Tatort* who celebrated such a happy state with military jackets. 'His trademark', says the German Wikipedia page on Schimanski, 'was his beige-grey M-65 field jacket, now colloquially known as the "Schimanski jacket".' But in my time of military looks, you could not turn it into a personal brand, at least not one that would get you anywhere. It was a time when the choice of clothes could result in social sanctions. First and foremost, the old declared war against hairstyles: long hair stung their eyes – and the old denounced the so-called 'moptop' as unkempt, and indeed, care was not my primary concern at the time.

In my case, the criticism went very far: As I gradually tried to gain a public foothold, an editor of the former *Arbeiter-Zeitung* wanted to hinder my career by, among other things, pointing out that I looked ugly: dressed as though I was terribly neglected. My first international appearance as an Austrian writer was in Berlin at the Café Einstein. A criticism about the presentation was published. I had read a text about buying clothes in Venice. A strange thing, if I may digress: Back then, Venice was a kind

Franz Schuh

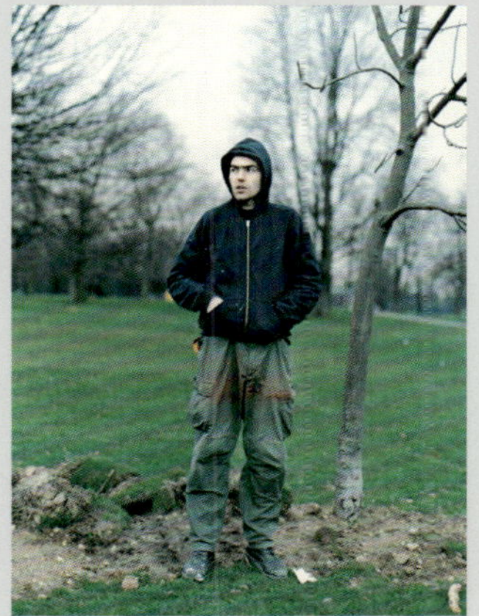



of erotic parking lot of Vienna. Couples who preferred not to be seen in Vienna strolled happily in Venice. However, Venice was also then a fashionable shopping centre, an El Dorado for women's fashion, while in Vienna's boutiques, an isolated-inelegant taste still prevailed. My text described a clothes purchase in Venice, and criticism quickly followed: First, my entire story about fashion was reminiscent of Max Frisch (who could do that better!) and second, I was, without doubt, a 'sloppy' person generally, which could be immediately ascertained from my clothes.

I had put on a US military jacket for the reading, and underneath I also wore a black V-neck T-shirt like the singer Herbert Lippert in 2017 under his military-inspired jacket. Yes, yes, that the times are changing is the most beautiful banality, which also exists in Latin: *Tempora mutantur.* For me, as a nostalgic individual, it remains astounding: Today, every allotment gardener, who is not suppressed and square, wears blue jeans and drags his rake through his little paradise; the car key stuck in his back pocket. And, at the time, it was exactly these people who persecuted with biblical hatred their blue-jean-wearing sons and daughters. However, perhaps, my nostalgic astonishment will, once again, focus more attention to another solely self-evident phenomenon: 'history' plays a role in today's everyday events related to costumes. This noticeably applies to the life story of individuals: The *caesura* in the history of self-dressing is the transition from being dressed by the parents and leaving the parents, which is also symbolised and realised by finally choosing your own garment. The dress codes

for people in my youth were paternalistic, and I assert that their deeper meaning was to be able to treat adults like children so that they, in every respect, do not have any ideas of their own. The biblical maxim from Deuteronomy, the fifth book of Moses, was de facto relevant in the 1960s: 'The woman shall not wear that which pertains unto a man, neither shall a man put on a woman's garment for all who do so are an abomination unto the Lord your God.' The struggles of girls to wear trousers to their secondary school are legendary. The other commandments from the Bible: 'You must not wear clothes whose fabric is mixed with wool and flax,' or 'You should attach four tassels on the corners of your upper garment,' have unfortunately worn off historically, and tassels are even incorporated today in the realm of individual arbitrariness. One could also interpret the caesura ironically, namely not as progress in the consciousness of freedom, but as a modernisation of coercion: from the fiat of the father (or any other superego) to the coercion of fashion, to voluntarily uniform oneself, and paradoxically – like everyone else – to give oneself a personal style. But I prefer to speak of personal oppression and of whatever temporary emancipation I experienced: I had a cap trauma in my childhood. That's because my father put caps on me that violated my aesthetics as well as my sense of freedom. All the other horrible things I had to wear to honour my parents, such as second-hand anoraks for the skiing course, put less strain on me than the damned shapeless caps. Their only legal justification was that they were cheap, and my dad would stand first in the line wherever there were cheap things for me. That was because we were poor – in the 1950s, even very poor. The cheap deal is the pauper's utopian profit. My father was at least as obsessed with this profit as the capitalist of his profits in the Communist caricatures. I was laden with ugly things, and today I still remember the triumph when I bought, by myself, my first things. Alas, I cannot say, unfortunately, that it was self-earned money that I had invested, for example, in a tweed jacket. No, I 'saved it from my mouth' – in the literal sense: It was saved from my food allowance in England. Sometimes I see the photograph, still lying around, that shows me with my tweed blazer during biology lessons: I stand next to the school skeleton, which allows his thin fingers to rest in solidarity on my left shoulder.

I have to admit that fashion responds to an appetite that is not strange to me and that not uncommonly leads to social distinction (to the demonstration of a social status). The first suit, a black, double-breasted one with a double vent at the back, was bought with self-earned money in Sweden, where I had worked hard for a summer with a construction company. I bought that suit, as well as my British tweed jacket, at a clearance sale. On the return flight from Stockholm to Vienna, I got into a conversation with a noble gentleman, who made fun of 'the primitives' already flying everywhere these days. The gentleman excepted me, who was, in truth, a showcase primitive, from his collection of curios: By my suit, he said, one can clearly see that I am by no means a member of the flying hordes. As for the appetite, it was a dark blue shirt in a window display in Edinburgh that awakened my instinct for possession. There again, I had some money that I had 'saved from the mouth'. What the hell – today the shirt is worn-out and hunger forgotten. What has remained is the reminiscence of the overwhelming influence that encouraged, so to speak, seduced, me to buy an unaffordable shirt. The appetite for stylish: The shirt in the Edinburgh display had a detail, a subtle difference that I knew only from the films: It was a shirt with a button-down collar.

Clothes, it seems to me, have two functions at the lowest level of their being. One is the 'moral', that is the concealment of nakedness, from which the erotic also results, since one does not show one's nakedness to everybody, but only a chosen few. And this status of being chosen creates the erotic feelings that are the same as the desire you, often enough, must feel for yourself. Then there is also the 'pragmatic' function: One wraps one's body in clothes in order to not surrender oneself, without defence, towards the outside world, especially its temperatures. The poverty of my parents during my childhood resulted in two things: My objections against forced happiness, especially through caps, remained unrecognised. These objections were, after all, purely 'aesthetic' and had nothing to do with the need to protect the child's head from a cold. The second, a consequence of poverty, was the huge fuss that had to be made with every purchase of a piece of clothing. To put an ugly cap on me, to buy me a pair of lederhosen or a sweater, all cheap, became an inner domestic and state act. The family celebrated their plight with every payment that, thank God, could be made for the child. Thus, one learned of the happiness in having a jacket in a storm and the rain. But one, however, learned nothing about the happiness in owning a 'beautiful' piece of clothing. It's like eating. Food intake is known to be pure necessity. When there is enough and more than enough food, there is a cultural space that includes culinary judgement and, in the end, food to simply quash hunger is considered primitive. Haute cuisine creates its own decadence, a refinement that wants to be disconnected from its original vital need. Clothes, too, when they no longer have to carry out their protective function as their only function, enter into an area in which necessity hardly matters, but choice is almost everything. In my youth, for a time, a third possibility existed in fashion: the systematic neglect of the external, the indifference to any choice in fashion issues, a defiance against the pretensions that annoyingly keep the decadent fashion business going. I have found among moving media images a figure that symbolises a variant of this indifference. It is one of the main characters in the television series *Gilmore Girls*. The series is about the life of single mother Lorelai Gilmore and her daughter Rory. They live in an intact America, in the (fictional) small town of Stars Hollow, where Luke Danes runs the restaurant in town: Luke's Diner. The series is instructive regarding the performers' outfits: Even though the *Gilmore Girls* have found fashion imitators in real life, their clothes, in my opinion, have no noteworthy fashion accent; they are rather casual.

Fashionable accents can be found especially in two figures: Rory's grandmother Emily; she belongs to the upper class and relentlessly stages this in all situations of life. Her clothes are unobtrusively conspicuous, solid, dignified, expensive, but not in the least pretentious. The only radical stylish accent in the series rests with Luke: The man wears his baseball cap front to back, but not in the rascal's way, but first, because his hair is thin and he thus always has something to hide, and second, for professional reasons: He must see exactly what is to be done in his restaurant and also what is going on there. In this instance, the peak of the baseball cap can only interfere.

Luke is a tall and strong man, his upper body, which he prefers to wrap in flannel shirts, is no small matter. And he wears military jackets, tight and short, his collar open. The T-shirts, the flannel shirts and the military jacket form a strong personal style that, paradoxically, is not really wanted by its wearer. Luke's resistance to style is an extra narrative in the series. In fact, in the 20th episode of the first season, Luke buys a gift for his girl-friend Rachel, I believe it is a disgusting potholder, and Lorelei finds the gift terrible. Lorelei offers to buy something better for Rachel, and with that opportunity she also buys some snazzy clothes for Luke. He does her a favour and plays the model for her, looks fabulous in the suit, but hates all this from the bottom of his heart: This is not his style!

Without a doubt, military jackets can be worn because of a need for such clothing: Such jackets do not limit physical flexibility; they are 'comfortable' and, as previously mentioned, in my case, I particularly appreciated the jacket's big and numerous pockets. However, I am convinced that even in the aforementioned television series, Luke's figure alludes to the military, to a soldier. The jacket is not neutral.

Before that, however, an illustrative error of judgement: I have always had a fashion appetite for leather coats, and a leather coat was, of all places, at a flea market in the Catholic parish of Maria Hietzing, a noble Viennese suburb. Cheap, yes, almost a gift. I came home wearing the gift, and my father was flabbergasted. He was an enemy of Hitler, even during the Third Reich. The coat, on the other hand, was the trademark of the 'Gestapo', and for that reason I was also an unbearable sight for my father. However, by discarding the coat, not really on the garbage heap of history, but at least in the dustbin of our council housing, I stood by him in solidarity.

So, I wore US military jackets, inherently un-ironed and greasy. The messier, the better, wasn't life a fight, a dirty one? A lean and tall Greek also visited the University of Vienna's Philosophy Department, and in Greece it was easier to get hold of the specialties of American military fashion. My Greek colleague had an overlong army coat. I bought a coat like it in Turkey and swaggered around in it. Why though, why?

After all, I'm peace-loving, a pacifist within the limits of reason; the charm of uniforms is strange to me. Wearing military clothing in civil society has an unresolvable dilemma: Is it militarising civilian life, or vice versa, does the military jacket demilitarise itself in civilian use?

I am not trying to answer, but remember that military jackets were cheap, and because of a second-hand trade with them, you could even dress in the American style of the Korean War: an obscene style, but 'practical' nevertheless. Last but not least, the style was also fashionable; among certain young people, the military look was a harmless mark of shared identity. Of course, even then some analysts had suspected the peace campaigners of not wanting peace – they were peace-activists only out of fear of their own aggressive impulses. With militant pacifism, they calmed their own belligerence. I think it is possible that this fashion was a reflex of the social unconscious: The Vietnam War, which cost the lives of so many people of my generation, had, unnoticed, infiltrated our mimetic behaviour.

This is how it was. Is it like this? Anyway, today any such background has vanished from superficial military fashion. In October 2017, the actor Sven Martinek, a tall and strong man, appeared on the German TV show *Inas Nacht*. He also wore something between a military jacket and a shirt, underneath a black T-shirt. He had his sleeves rolled up and, nonchalantly bending over the bar of the show, he looked like an American general issuing orders.

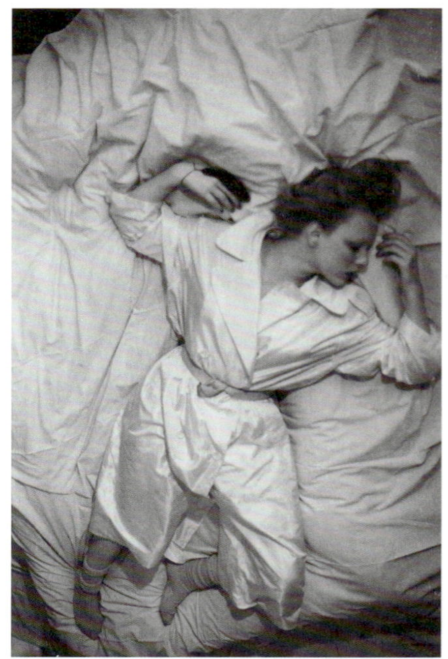 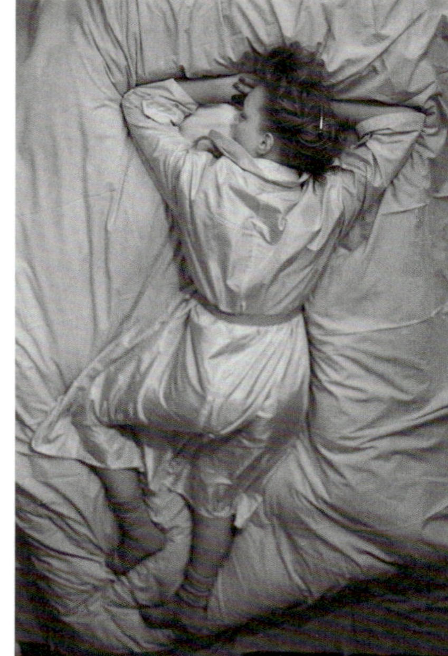 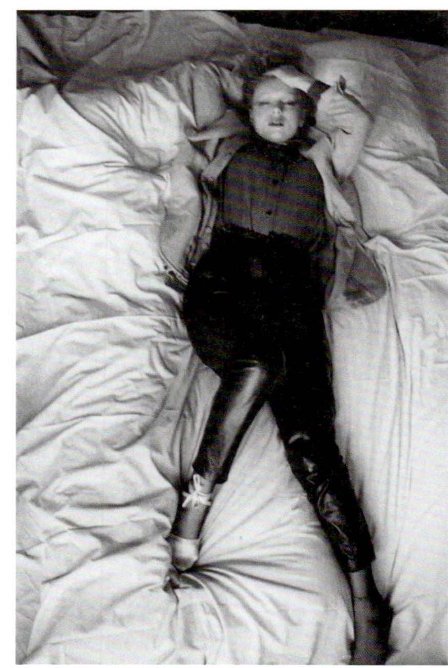



**238**  Tula Roy (b. 1934) and Christoph Wirsing (b. 1950)
*Lady Shiva, oder: 'Die bezahlen meine Zeit',* 1974
With Irene Staub aka Lady Shiva
Script, production, editing: Tula Roy
Cinematography, sound, editing: Christoph Wirsing
Concept and interview: Sissi Zöbeli
Super-8 blow-up on 16 mm, digitalised,
Colour, sound, 4:3 aspect ratio, duration: 40'
Courtesy Tula Roy and Christoph Wirsing

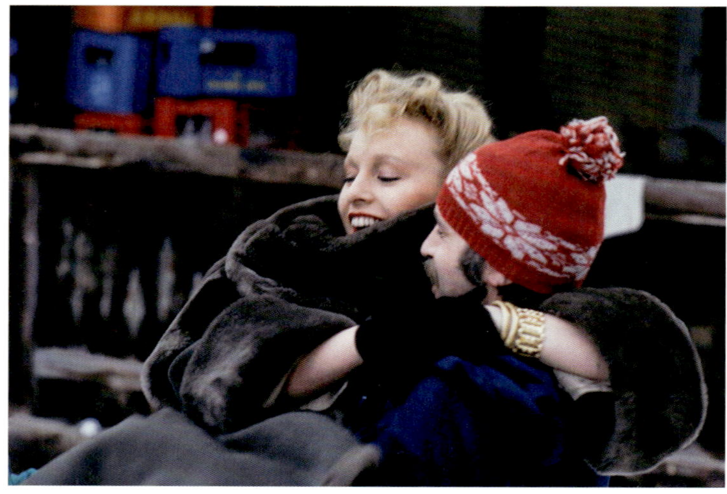

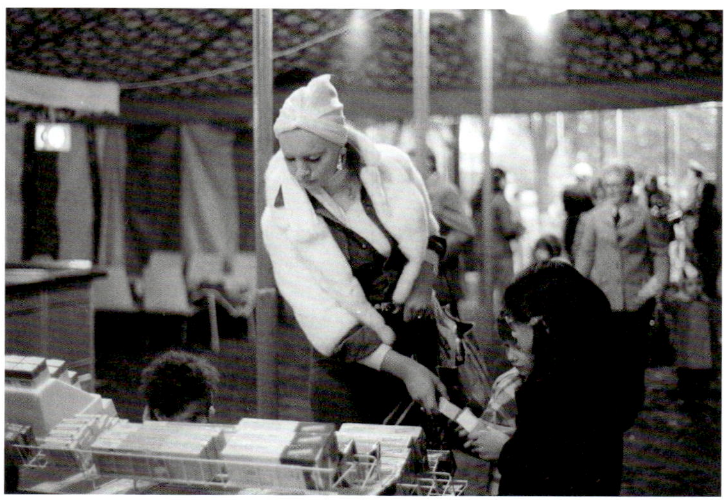

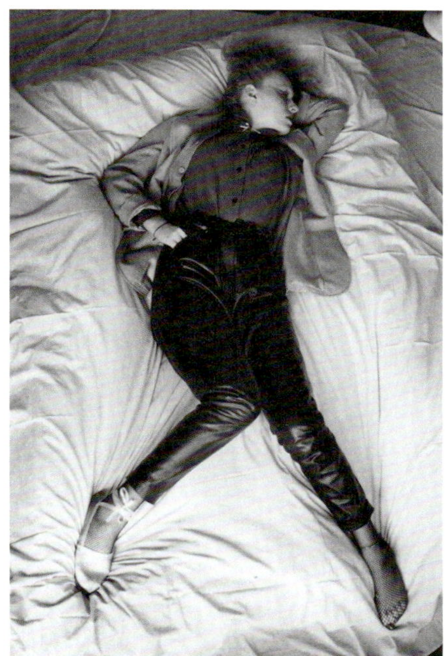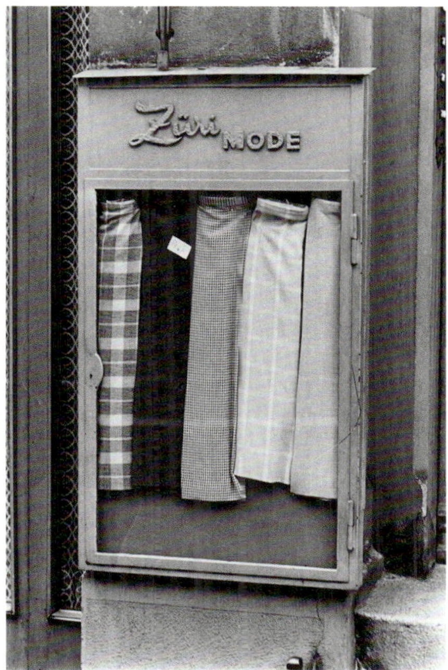

**303** Andreas Züst (1947–2000)
*Lady Shiva*
From the series *Menschen,
Tiere, Abendteuer, Lady Shiva*, 1973–83
9 black-and-white photographs on
Baryta paper, 23.7 × 15.8 cm each
Estate of Andreas Züst with Mara Züst, Zurich
Courtesy Galerie & Edition Marlene Frei,
Zurich



**303** Andreas Züst (1947–2000)
*Lady Shiva*
From the series *Menschen,
Tiere, Abendteuer, Lady Shiva*, 1973–83
9 black-and-white photographs on
Baryta paper, 23.7 × 15.8 cm each
Estate of Andreas Züst with Mara Züst, Zurich
Courtesy Galerie & Edition Marlene Frei,
Zurich

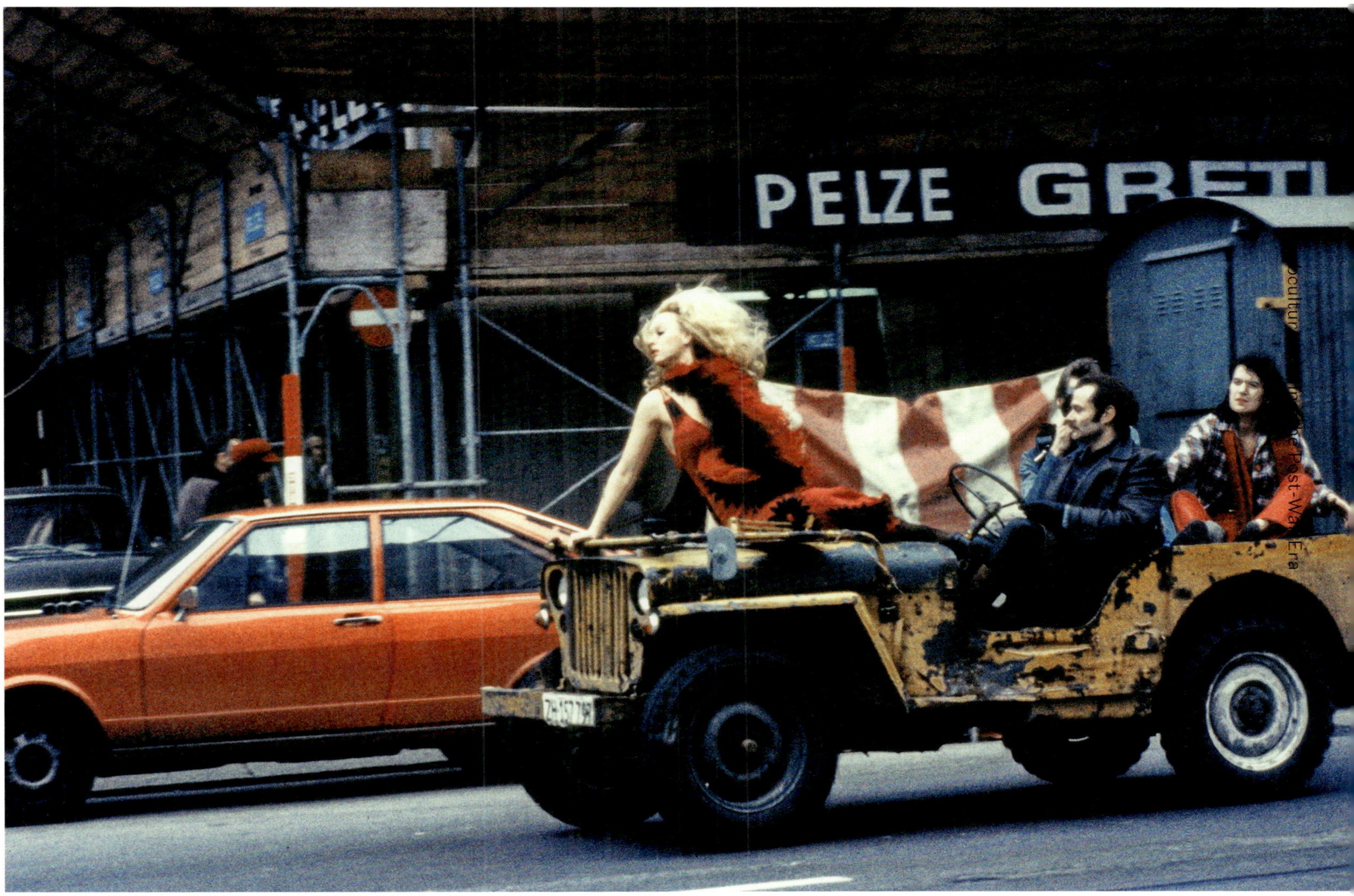

**149** Franz Gertsch (b. 1930)
*Franz and Luciano,* 1973
Acrylic on cotton, 198 × 298 cm
Kunsthaus Zürich, 1977

**187** Eva Kotátková (b. 1982) and
Jiří Kovanda (b. 1953)
*Hanging Sleeves, Hiding Hands,* 2013
Daily performance and two second-hand
trench coats, dimensions variable
Courtesy the artists

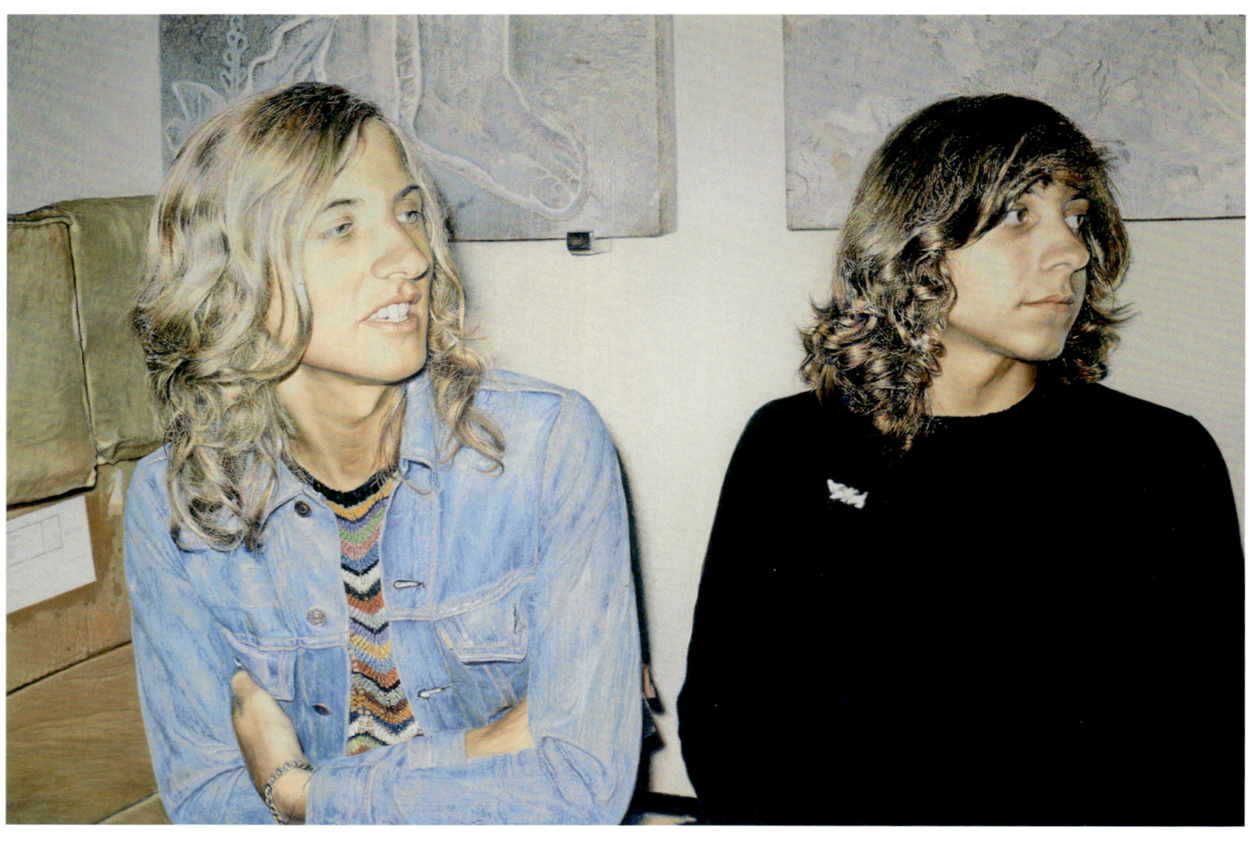

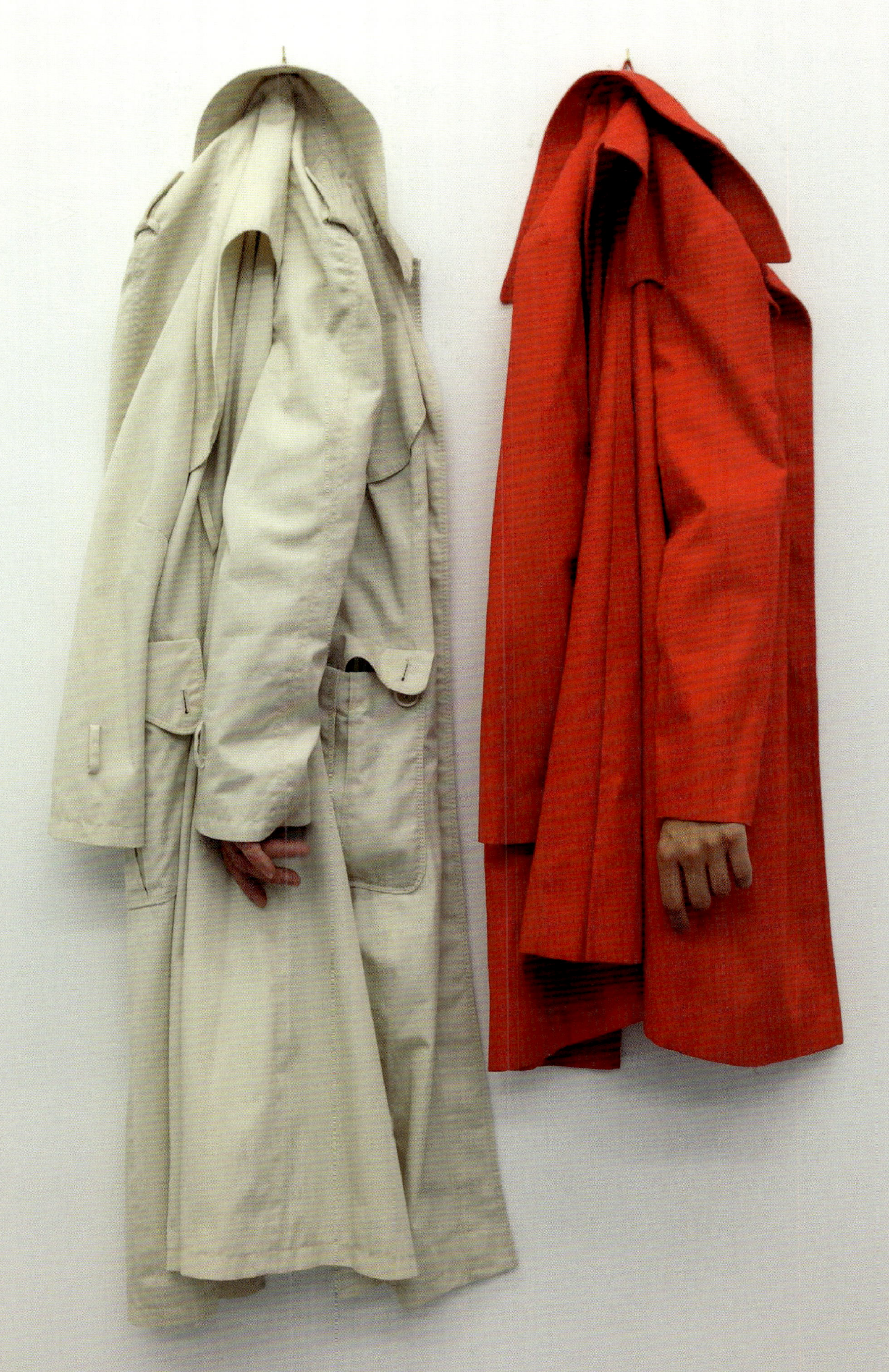

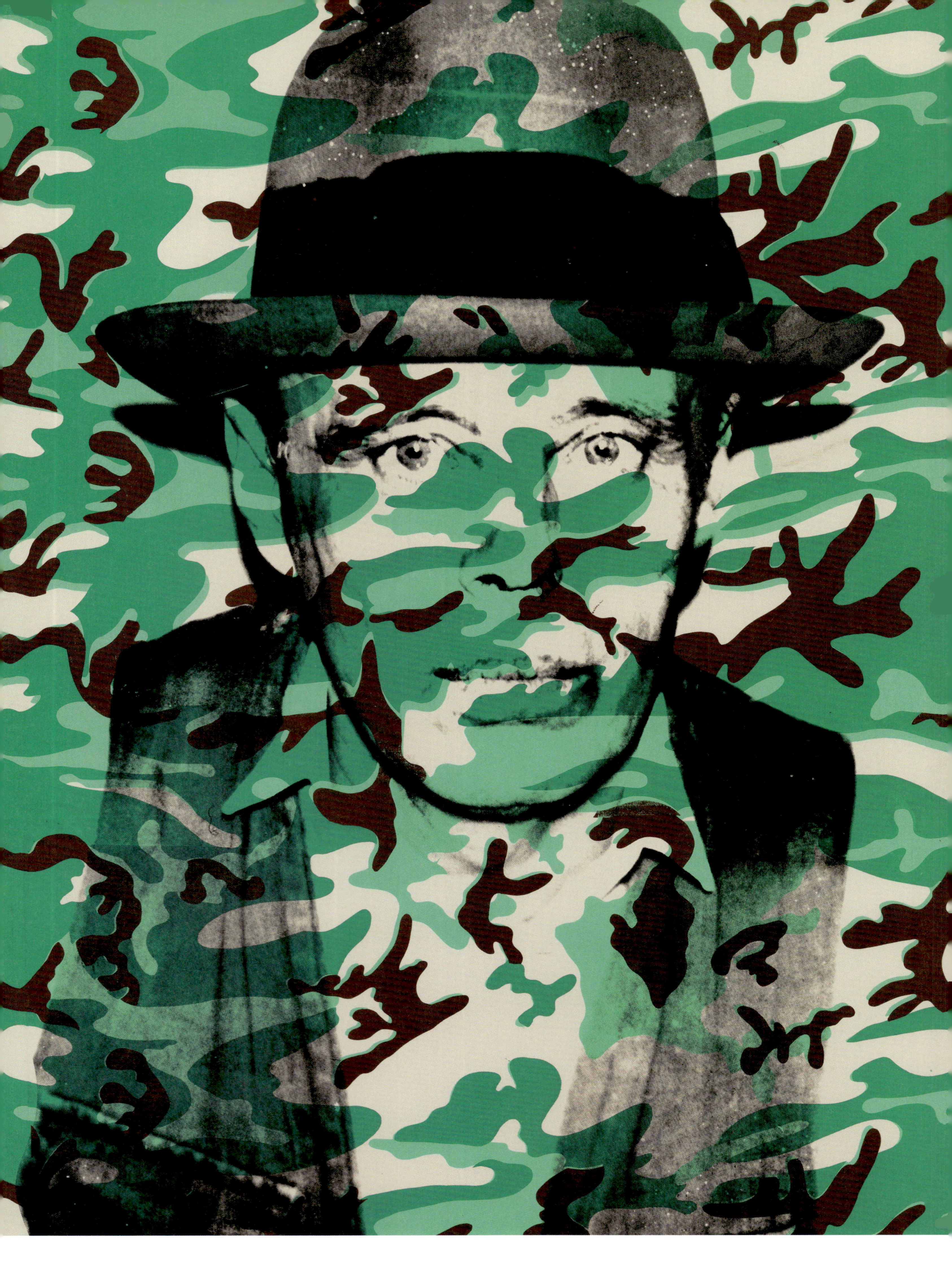

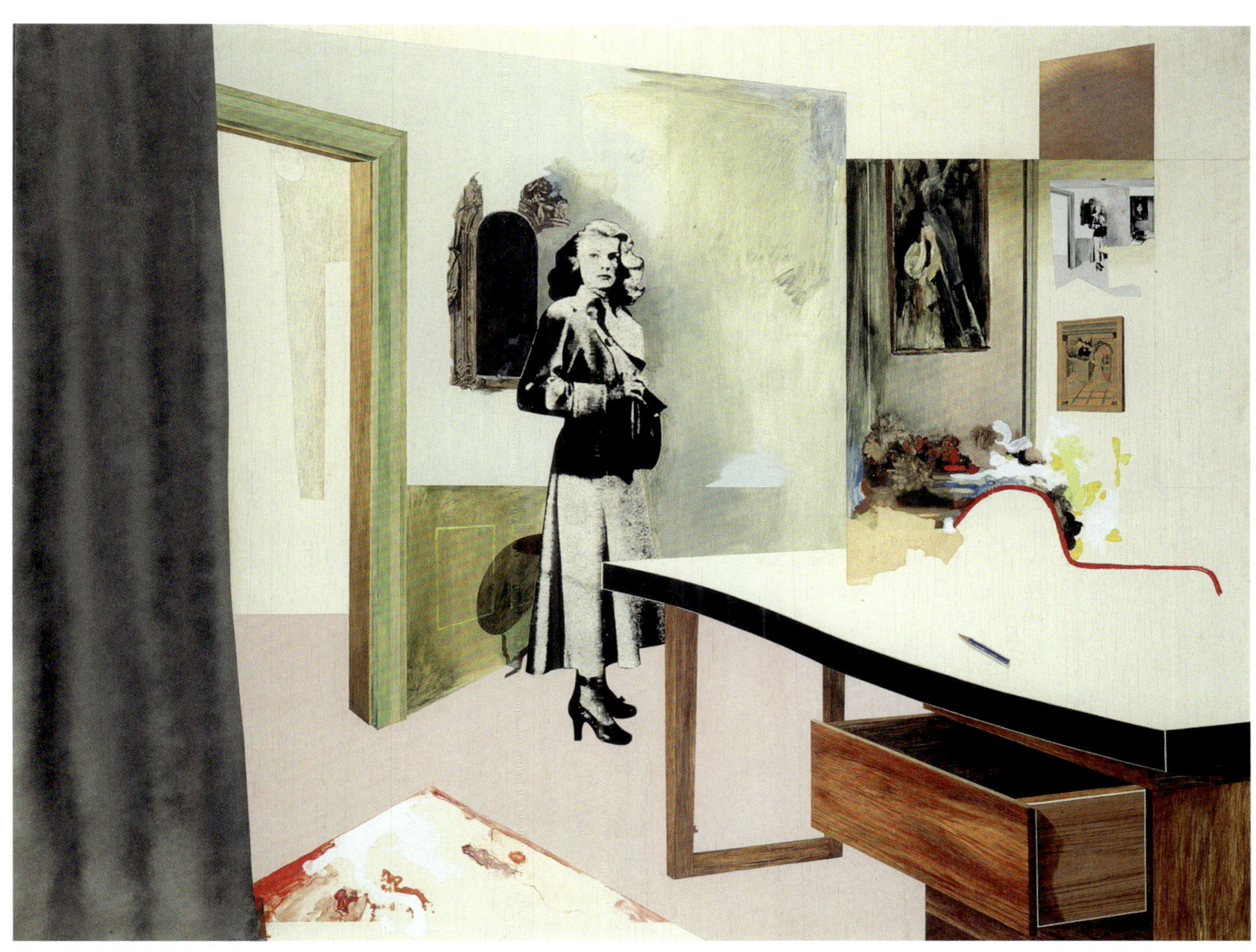



**294** Andy Warhol (1928–1987)
*Camouflage. Joseph Beuys,* 1986
Synthetic resin and silk screen colour
on canvas, 254 × 204.3 cm
Udo and Anette Brandhorst Collection

**167** Richard Hamilton (1922–2011)
*Interior I,* 1964
Oil and collage on wood with
inlaid mirror, 122 × 163 cm
Kunsthaus Zürich, bequest of
Erna and Curt Burgauer, 2002

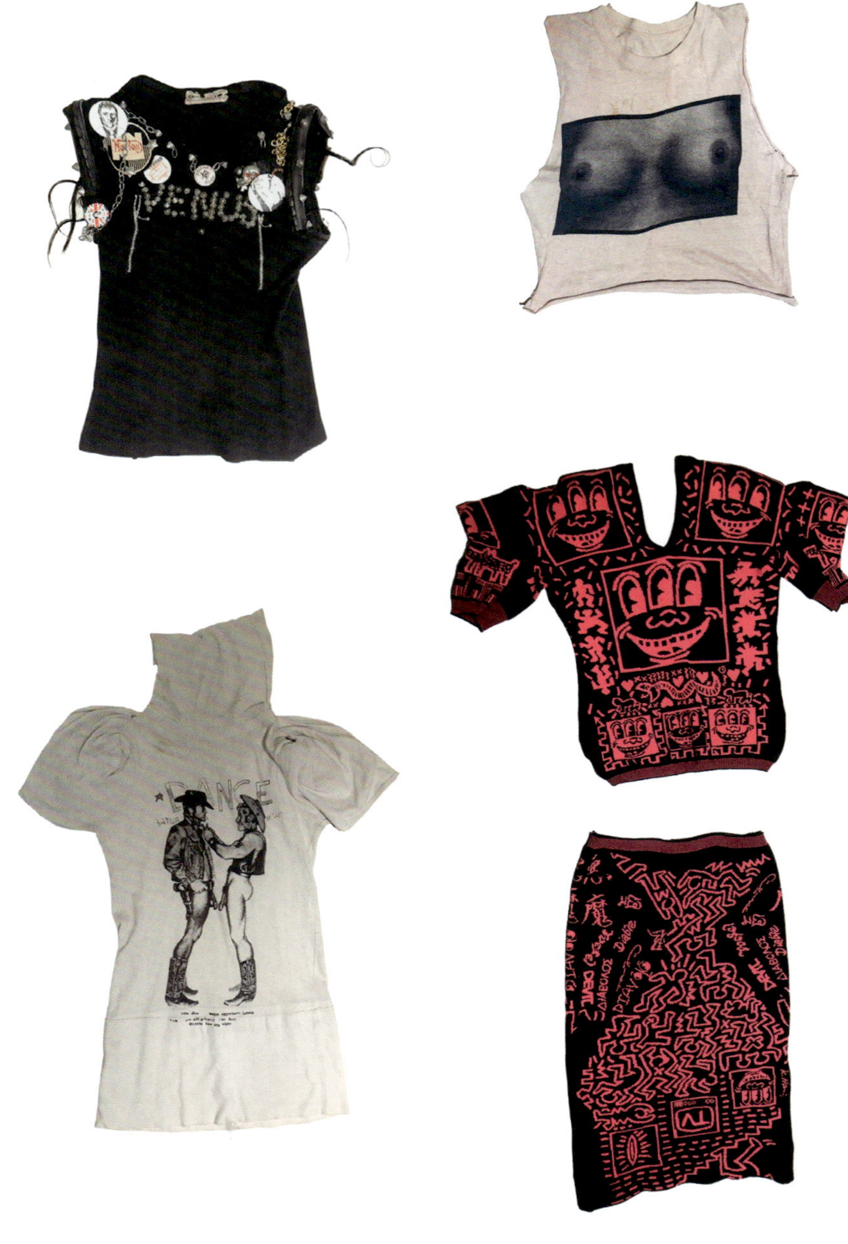



**34**  Malcolm McLaren (1946–2010) and
Vivienne Westwood (b. 1941)
'Venus' T-Shirt, 1975
Labelled: Let It Rock
Black cotton jersey, the armholes edged with
studded rubber tyre bands with black horse-
hair fringes, two diagonal zips placed over
the breasts, adorned with chains and assorted
badges, 'Venus' written in metal studs
Collection of Kim Jones

**35**  Malcolm McLaren (1946–2010) and
Vivienne Westwood (b. 1941)
Sleeveless, cropped T-shirt, c. 1976
Labelled: Sex
Collection of Kim Jones

**36**  Malcolm McLaren (1946–2010) and
Vivienne Westwood (b. 1941)
Short-sleeved T-shirt incorporating a Jim
French illustration from 1969, c. 1976
Labelled: Seditionaries
Collection of Kim Jones

**38**  Malcolm McLaren (1946–2010) and
Vivienne Westwood (b. 1941)
'Witches' sweater and skirt
with Keith Haring print, 1983
Labelled: World's End
Collection of Kim Jones

# Karl, Vivienne, Marc

*Like three heirs of a Lear who asks about*
*temperatures of the hearts*
*and minds, they prepare*
*their gifts very distinctly.*
*I love you like the fabric,*
*I love you like the scent,*
*I love you like the leather!*
*The old man gives his money to the forever young*
*and where the cats are walking*
*the tomcats' meow becomes loud from all sides.*

*The seasons are saisons*
*and therefore always pincushions full of vanities.*
*Fashion dolls are being draped, gathered;*
*the real ones are being tweaked and tightened.*
*Stella, Michael, Victoria, Paris can't comprehend,*
*that Vera still*
*sews most of the wedding dresses.*
*These are the guarantees*
*of life after the collection.*
*If you have questions, it has applied for several decades:*
*Open Vogue, Elle and Marie Claire*
*and only in case of the greatest doubts*
*if out of the bags, the flacons,*
*the coats, vases, clothes*
*everything is silent, address Anna specifically.*

*Brave, the half-lioness, before the eyes.*
*With a steak, we know who's grilling it.*
*And so soothed, the sphinx will*
*maybe pose a riddle*
*of next spring with its colours,*
*shapes, feathers, furs.*
*You just have to know how to read the signs*
*then robes receive Oscar statuettes*
*and department store chains, oligarchs' wives*
*buy what hangs designed.*

*Manolo reddens soles again*
*and Carrie's young sisters blog,*
*post, chat, comment on this crimson.*

*What you wear, you are so rarely today*
*like never before, because he who constantly skins,*
*is a wounded animal. Writes here the one,*
*who does not have to stride through a wardrobe*
*to enter new countries.*
*Even before she stands in one,*
*that shows her as threadbare.*



---

Nora Gomringer

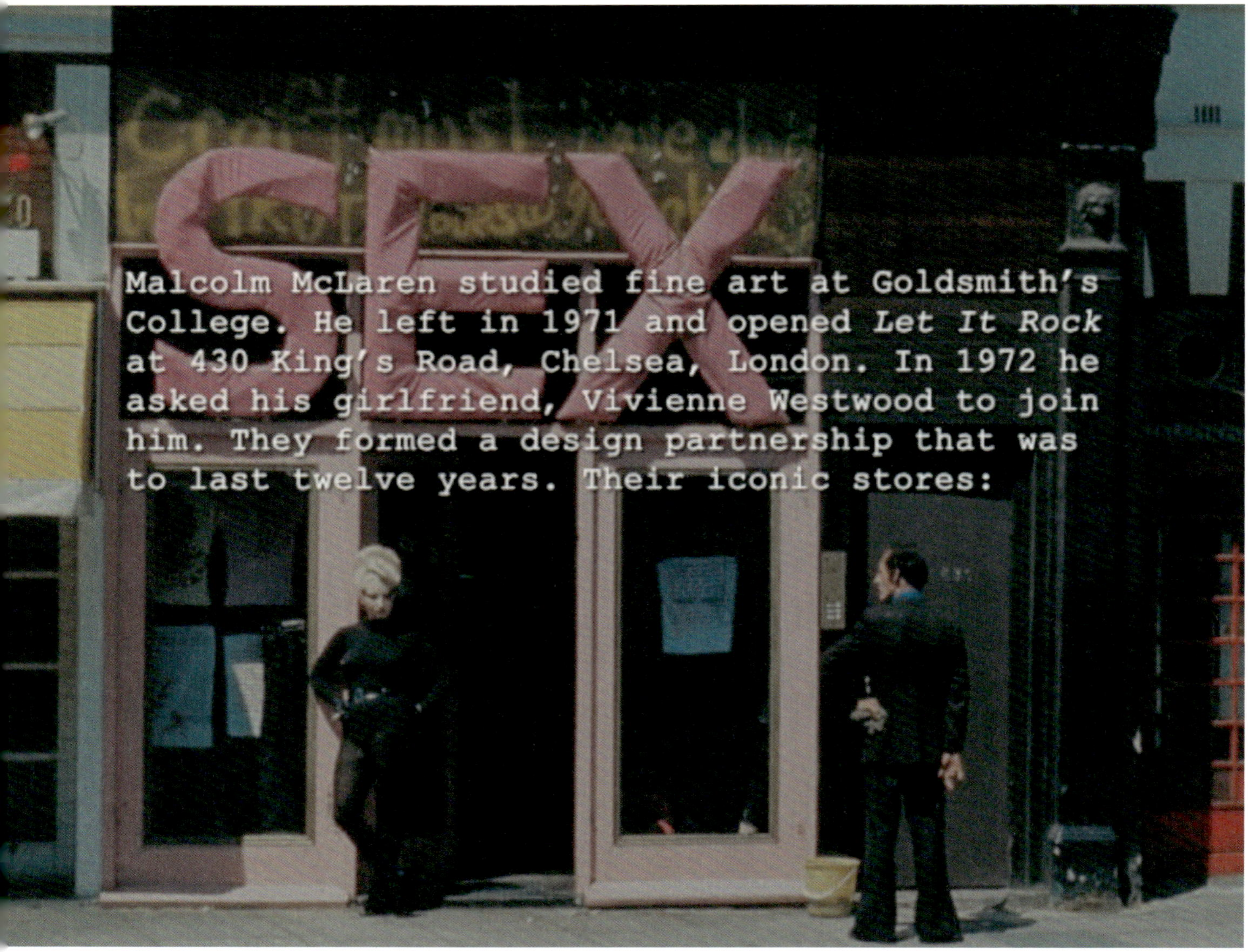

Malcolm McLaren studied fine art at Goldsmith's College. He left in 1971 and opened *Let It Rock* at 430 King's Road, Chelsea, London. In 1972 he asked his girlfriend, Vivienne Westwood to join him. They formed a design partnership that was to last twelve years. Their iconic stores:

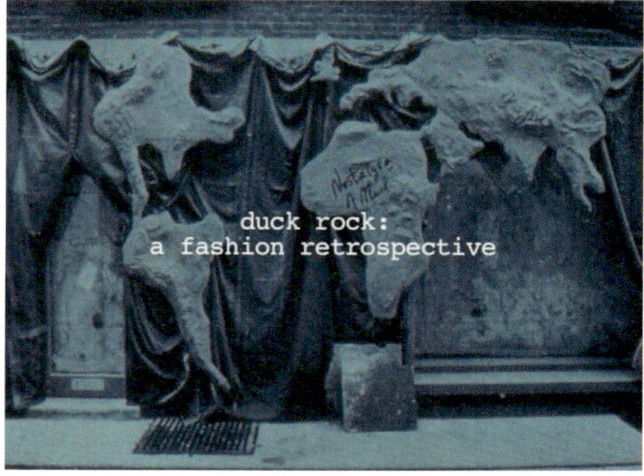


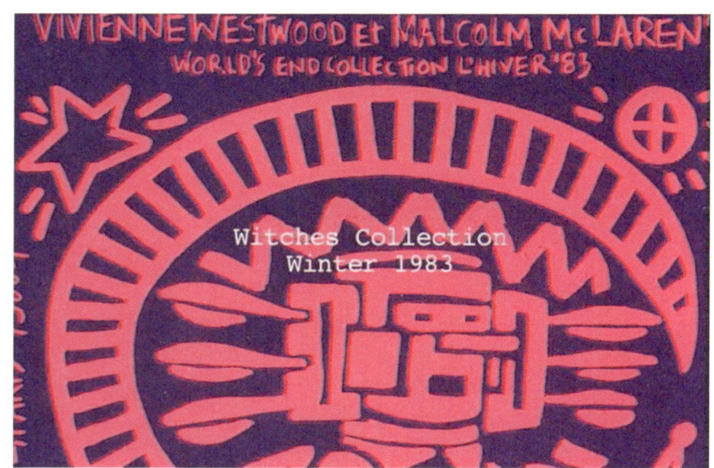


**40**  Malcolm McLaren (1946–2010)
*Duck Rock,* 2008
A fashion retrospective featuring excerpts
from the catwalk shows of McLaren/Westwood
World's End fashion collections:
'Savages' (1981) and 'Witches' (1983)
Arranged by Malcolm McLaren
Video, colour, duration: 4'49"
Courtesy Young Kim, Estate of Malcolm McLaren

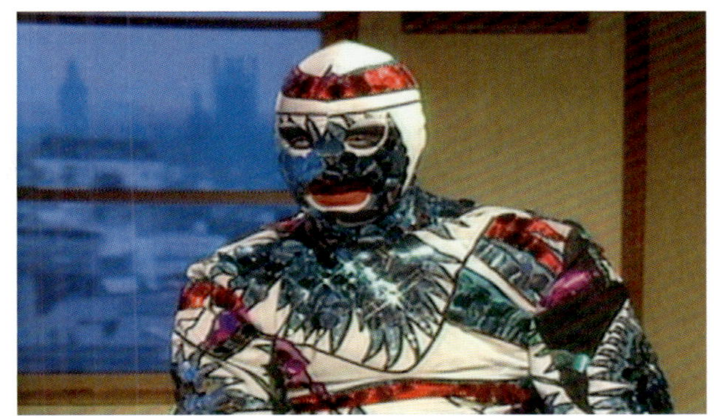

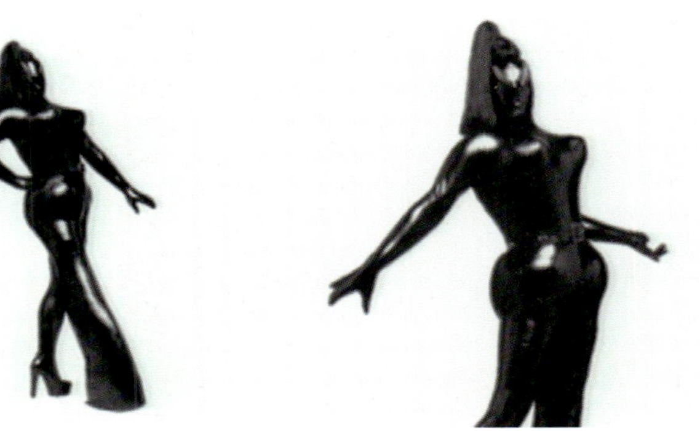

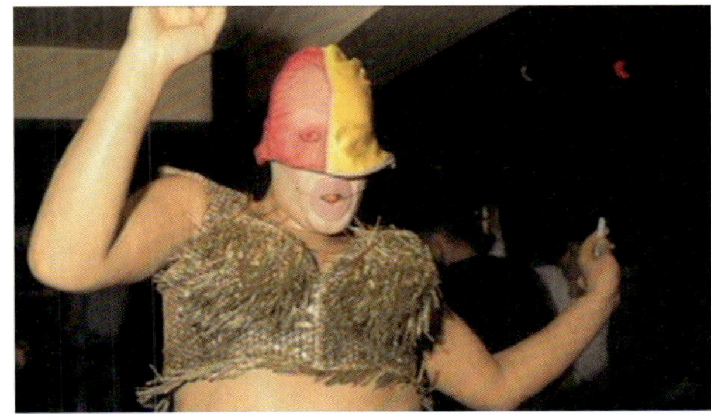

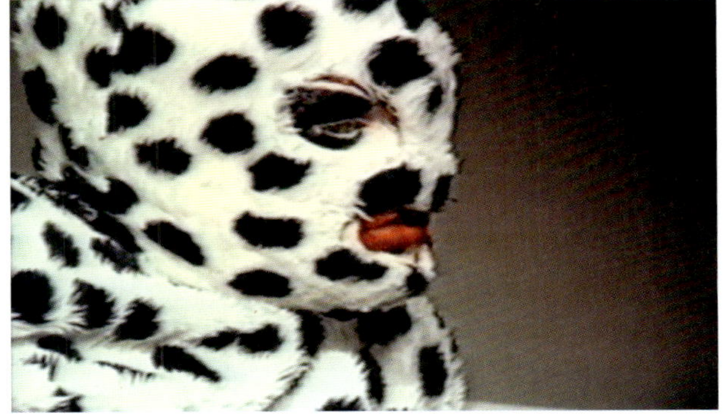



**46** Charles Atlas (b. 1949)
*The Legend of Leigh Bowery,* 1980s/2002
Film (video and super8) on DVD,
Colour, sound, duration: 82'
EAI, New York

# I Shop Therefore

## The Female Fetish between and

**Sonja Eismann**

# I Am (Female)

## Commodity
## Sacrality
## Pornography

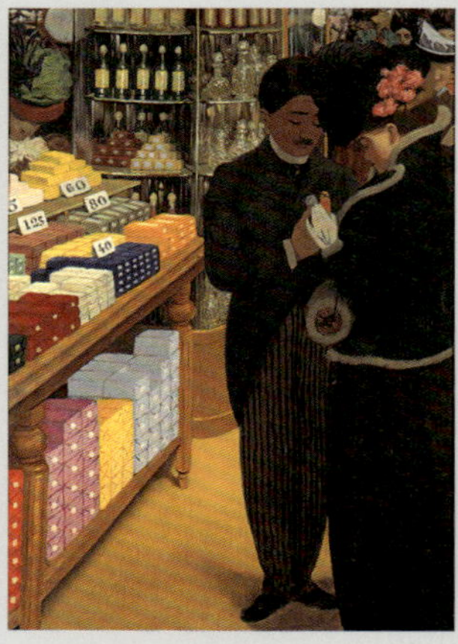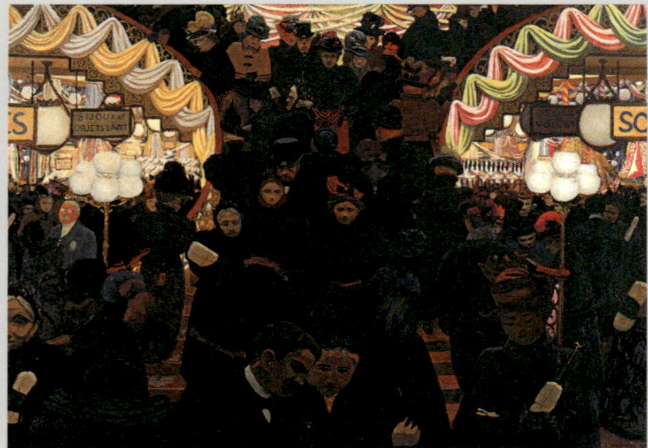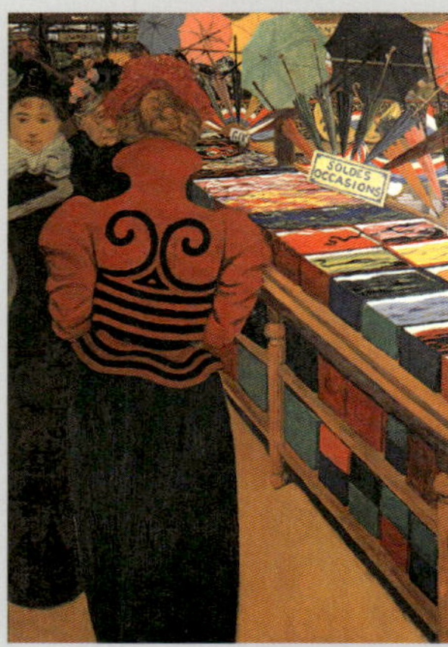

'There appeared to be an immense clearance sale going on; the establishment seemed to be bursting with goods, blocking up the pavement with the surplus,' writes Émile Zola (1840–1902) in the first chapter of his 1883 novel *Au bonheur des dames* (The Ladies' Paradise) about the eponymous department store.[1] In this eleventh part of the *Rougon-Macquart* cycle of novels, Denise, a young saleswoman from the countryside, comes to Paris and is hired in the 'Cathedral of Modern Commerce', modelled after the still existing department store *Le Bon Marché,* the world's first modern temple of goods.

'The well-rounded neck and graceful figures of the dummies exaggerated the slimness of the waist, the absent head being replaced by a large price-ticket pinned on the neck; whilst the mirrors, cleverly arranged on each side of the window, reflected and multiplied the forms without end, peopling the street with these beautiful women for sale, each bearing a price in big figures in the place of a head.'[2] The young woman who has just arrived in the capital to help out in her uncle's shabby fabric business looks at the store's display as though hypnotised. Soon, the girl will be part of the merciless struggle between the *petites boutiques* and the *grand magasins,* which Zola, after meticulous sociological and economic field research, stages as an examplary triumph of modern commodity capitalism.

In his triptych *Le Bon Marché* (1898, Private collection), | Fig. 1 | Félix Vallotton (1865–1925), a Swiss immigrant in Paris, captures this fetish of the commercial object that Zola, using sacred-sensual metaphors, repeatedly denounces as consumerist idolatry. In the artwork, the almost exclusively black-clad customers, an amorphous mass driven by stress and pleasure, provide the dull beat to the siren song of brightly lit, colourful goods to their left and right. The merchandise, a uniform variety of colourful, quasi-identical small boxes, emits an almost pornographic radiance – apart from the constant buzzing of the desire for possession, the only 'conversations' that can be heard in this shop are about the sale and price tags, which manifest as well as quantify the omnipresent possibility of possession. The accusation of fashion's immorality – always connoted as feminine – is as old as fashion itself, but only industrialisation and the resulting


1   Émile Zola, *The Ladies' Paradise: A Realistic Novel,* trans. Ernest Alfred Vizetelly, London 1886, p. 2.

2   Zola 1886, p. 3.

3   Zola 1886, p. 3.

4   Friedrich Theodor Vischer, 'Mode und Zynismus', in *Die Listen der Mode,* Silvia Bovenschen (ed.), Frankfurt am Main 1986, pp. 33–79, here p. 37. For Vischer's English version, *Fashion and Cynicism* (1879), see, for instance, *The Rise of Fashion,* Daniel Purdy (ed.), Minneapolis 2004.

5   Eduard Fuchs, 'Ich bin der Herr dein Gott!' in Vischer 1986, pp. 156–78, here p. 173.

6   Vischer 1986, p. 156.

7   Vischer 1986, p. 175.

8   Vischer 1986, p. 176.


Sonja Eismann

mass production emerging in the nineteenth century led to increased condemnation of shopping. Due to the rationalisation of the means of production, as well as society, after the upheavals of the French Revolution, the objects appealing to ardent consumers were no longer affordable only to the affluent. Now consumption was possible across all social classes – Zola's *Au bonheur des dames* has everything, from 'cheap goods, bargains' piled up outside to the 'velvet mantle' for 'eighteen hundred [francs]'[3] – which causes the stigma of availability to be transferred from the goods to the female buyer. It is not for nothing that the German literature professor and author Friedrich Theodor Vischer (1807–1887) spoke of women's fashion of the time as 'fashion of whores' in his 1879 diatribe *Mode und Zynismus* (Fashion and Cynicism).[4] Eduard Fuchs (1870–1940) clearly diagnosed in his essay 'Ich bin der Herr dein Gott!' (I am the Lord your God!) in 1906 that 'the modern capitalist enterprise based on mass sales must systematically push that not only small circles follow changes in fashion, but preferably everyone.'[5] In the introduction, Fuchs directly describes 'women's clothing' as an 'erotic problem'.[6] He assumes that 'the passive role in sexual life [forces] the woman to make fashion her most important advertising medium in the fight for the man'[7] and wanting to inevitably win the 'wedding veil as a prize'.[8]

The 70 photographs of the series *Alle Kleider einer Frau* (All the clothes of a woman, 1970) | Page **296** | by Hans-Peter Feldmann (b. 1941), with their sober black-and-white cataloguing of a female's complete wardrobe, serve as a persiflage of the dictum of the erotic features of women's clothing by rendering the lifeless garments without sexual tension. Feldmann's work thus enters the conflicted area in popular fashion discourses that began with the debates on fashion's democratisation at the end of the nineteenth century and are still widespread today. Hence, fashion can, on the one hand, develop emancipatory potential through its nonverbal visual communication that mark distinctions shaping identities, especially in socially marginalised groups such as women, but also LGBTIQ or People of Colour; think of the 1920s Flapper fashion of showing legs, the militaristic style of the Black Panthers in the 1960s or the 2016 movie *Express Looks (of Outfitumentary)* by K8 Hardy (b. 1977) | Page **276** | on queer-feminist dress codes. On the other hand, fashion can also be perceived as an instrument of repression, subjecting its wearers to socially standardised views; shopping is practised as a drug-like stultification as well as prolonging disgraceful manufacturing practices. The many garments shown initially seem, through sheer numbers, to confirm the preconception of women as fashion victims, but the sobriety bordering on sadness with which these inconspicuous items are set – or not set – in scene, contradicts and ironises the image of the vain self-actress, who wants to express her ego as favourably as possible with clothes. When viewing from today's perspective, one must add the piquant detail to Feldmann's previously mentioned work *Alle Kleider einer Frau* that while people in the 1970s owned an approximate average of 70 garments each, today they have nearly 100 (not including underwear).[9] Today, one third of consumers have around 300 items of clothing in their closets; a considerable part will be thrown away unworn (of the 27 kilogrammes of new clothing bought on average per capita per annum in industrialised countries, usually 14.8 kilogrammes are discarded unused).[10]

For a long time, Elena Esposito's (b. 1960) findings on fashion, 'the individual thus does what others do to be different',[11] seemed to apply to all society; then subcultures emerged that turned this upside down – and affirmed it simultaneously. After World War II, with the global triumph of pop culture and, in particular, during the heyday of the countercultures of the 1960s to the 1980s, sub- or underground cultures developed that did not want to be perceived by society as 'fashionable'. Rather, they opposed fashion but at the same time wanted to be recognised by their peers on an equal footing. Thus, they released themselves from the constant change of typical fashion cycles, but simultaneously became impulses for them. Subcultural styles are usually masculine because they are perceived as rebellious and directed against the establishment; thus, as an 'anti-fashion', they are diametrically opposed to a 'fashion in itself' constantly associated with rule-conforming, passive femininity. In his treatise *Subculture: The Meaning of Style* (1979), written under the impact of the development of punk, the British theoretician Dick Hebdige (b. 1951) describes subcultures initially as 'noise', 'dissonance', 'disorder' and as a 'temporary blockade in the system of representation'.[12] However, he assumes an inevitable

restoration of the broken order that includes, among others, 'the conversion of subcultural signs (dress, music, etc.) into mass-produced objects (i.e. the commodity form)'.[13] He goes on to say: 'Indeed, the creation and diffusion of new styles is inextricably bound up with the process of production, publicity and packaging which must inevitably lead to the defusion of the subculture's subversive power – both mod and punk innovations fed back directly into high fashion and mainstream fashion. Each new subculture establishes new trends, generates new looks and sounds which feed back into the appropriate industries [...]. Youth cultural styles may begin by issuing symbolic challenges, but they must inevitably end by establishing new sets of conventions; by creating new commodities, new industries or rejuvenating old ones...'[14]

Vivienne Westwood (b. 1941) and her former partner Malcolm McLaren (1941–2010), who also managed the Sex Pistols, show, in an extremely exciting manner, the contradictory nature of these processes. With the avant la lettre punk creations sold since the early 1970s in their London boutique, with changing names such as 'Let It Rock', 'Sex', 'Too Fast To Live Too Young To Die' or 'Seditionaries', they were architects of the movement with their 'shocking' clothing that was influenced by bondage and biker styles. This simultaneously paved their way to the world of high fashion. Today, Westwood, appointed Queen of the Order of the British Empire in 1992, is considered one of the pioneering fashion designers in England. | [Page] **260** |
In the last few years, she no longer concentrates her (fashion-)political statements and actions on the

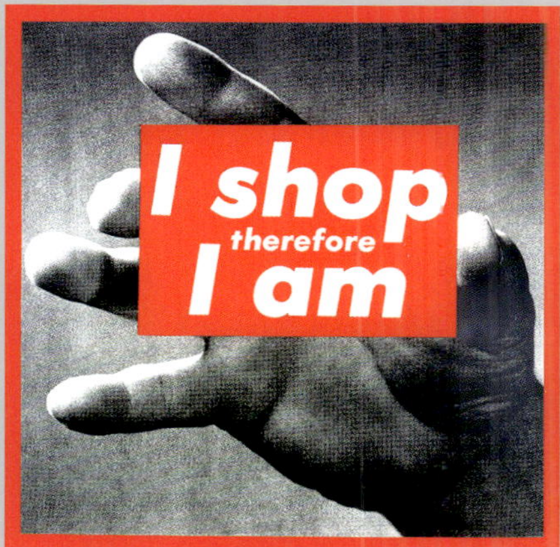



**Fig. 2** Barbara Kruger (b. 1945)
*Untitled (I shop therefore I am),* 1987
Photographic silkscreen on vinyl,
284.5 × 287 cm
Courtesy Sprüth Magers



subversion of the 'deadly' status quo[15] through a no-future-punk ethos, but on a growing awareness of ecology and sustainability. Under the motto 'Reduce, Reuse, Recycle, Rethink',[16] she wants to, as a public figure, create an awareness of the finiteness of our natural resources in times of climate change and, according to her own statements, is committed to the maxim of 'quality over quantity'. In an interview with *The Guardian*, she said, 'In my view, it is worse for someone to come out of a shop with an armful of new T-shirts made in a sweatshop, than it is for a rich lady to buy one beautiful dress.'[17]

In contrast to the 'trickle-down theory' of the German sociologist Georg Simmel (1858–1918),[18] the author and curator Ted Polhemus (b. 1947) characterised the 'bubble-up theory' based on 'cool' or subcultural street fashions in his exhibition catalogue *Streetstyle* (1994), which accompanied the exhibition of the same name in London's Victoria and Albert Museum. Polhemus assumes that fashion influences do not 'trickle down' from the upper to the lower classes, but 'bubble up' from below, from a variety of different street styles or subcultural groups. While many of these groupings through their self-conception were and are critical of capitalism – and therewith also critical of consumerism – and so actually – rejecting the classic overheating cycles of fashion, there were and are *tribes* like the *casuals* or the UK garage movement that, like a short-circuit, pre-empted these utilisation cycles. The *casuals,* for example, with an ostentatious fixation on traditional UK sportswear brands such as Fred Perry and Lyle & Scott, and the UK garage movement, with their Italian 'bling bling' brands such as Versace, Moschino or Gucci – displayed, from the beginning, an affirmative relationship with the fashion industry. Also, the protagonists featured in the early photographs of German photographer Wolfgang Tillmans (b. 1968) such as *Lutz & Alex, climbing tree* (1992), | <sup>Page</sup> 277 | often derived from the club, rave and gay scenes, due to their hedonistic attitude, harbour no reservations about fashion design or brand culture. Concurrent with these (pop-) cultural developments are attempts in the field of cultural studies to analyse the act of consumption not as conforming to the system but potentially dissenting. The cultural scholar John Fiske (b. 1939), referring to Michel de Certeau (1925–1986)


**9**    For further information see, for instance, http://www.fastfashion-dieausstellung.de/ (last accessed 31 October 2017).

**10**    Cf. Sonja Eismann and Nina Lorkowski, *Warum Nachhaltigkeit mehr ist als nur 'bio',* Weinheim 2016, p. 81.

**11**    Elena Esposito, *Die Verbindlichkeit des Vorübergehenden. Paradoxien der Mode,* Frankfurt am Main 2004, p. 13.

**12**    Dick Hebdige, *Subculture: The Meaning of Style,* London/New York 1979, p. 90.

**13**    Hebdige 1979, p. 94.

**14**    Hebdige 1979, pp. 95–96.

**15**    Cf. https://www.theguardian.com/lifeandstyle/2014/feb/08/vivienne-westwood-arctic-campaign (last accessed 31 October 2017).

**16**    Cf. https://elizabethgalloway.co.za/reduce-reuse-recycle-textile-waste/ (last accessed 31 October 2017).

**17**    Cf. *The Guardian* (as in note 15) 2014.

**18**    *Streetstyle: From Catwalk to Sidewalk,* Ted Polhemus, exh. cat. Victoria and Albert Museum, London 1994.

in *Understanding Popular Culture* (1989), speaks of 'tactical consumption' and postulates that every act of commodity consumption is an act of cultural production since consumption always includes the production of meaning. He even compares the marginalised youths hanging out in shopping malls with Vietcong guerrilla tactics: The art of moving between production and consumption is 'using their products for our purposes'.[19]

The affirmative handling of commodity cultures, which feeds on the cultural history of the generational conflict between the 1968 critics of the system, and a post-no-future generation[20] that excessively embraces technologised commodity culture, was followed by the cold shower of the man-made ravages of the Anthropocene. The fast-response strategies of contemporary 'fast fashion' infest the globe with ever-faster changes of up to 24 fashion collections per year (rather than the previous two), with big discount clothing chains and with bloggers showing on YouTube channels their huge masses of purchased clothing; at the same time, increasingly louder criticism develops over inhumane production conditions in sweatshops, the natural waste of resources, and the growing mounds of textile garbage.

This context shapes Michelangelo Pistoletto's (b. 1933) installation *Metamorfosi* (1976–2016) | Page 302 | in which fabrics, one part white, one part colourful, pile up on the left and to the right of a mirror, and evoke the immense consumption of textiles in so-called developed countries. Every year, the unimaginable quantity of 80 billion pieces of clothing are produced worldwide (many of which are worn by buyers only once or never – before they are thrown away).[21]

Some solutions to this devastation have fine-sounding names like 'clean fashion', 'green fashion', 'fair fashion', 'slow fashion', 'ethical fashion' or 'zero waste fashion'. With different emphases – for example, on fair working conditions, the use of ecological materials, or a low waste of resources – they attempt to solve the problem of rising global mass consumption. However, experts such as Christiane Schnura (b. 1958), coordinator of the German campaign for clean clothing, points out that 'within a certain framework' it may be possible to 'build a kind of island as an [idealistic] enterprise', this framework would, however,

---

19 John Fiske, *Understanding Popular Culture*, London/New York 1991, Chapter 2.

20 Cf. also the B-side of the EP *Herz aus Stein* (music label ZickZack) of the German band Band Freiwillige Selbstkontrolle, the piece *Moderne Welt* from 1980, in which it says 'Wir sagen ja zur modernen Welt' (We say yes to the modern world).

21 Cf. Eismann and Lorkowski 2016 (as in note 10), p. 81.

22 Sonja Eismann, 'Freiwillige Selbstverpflichtung ist nicht genug!,' interview with Christiane Schnura, in Eismann 2016, pp. 87–91, here p. 90.

23 Elke Gaugele in an unpublished interview with the author, Berlin 2014.

24 Jacques Rancière, 'Die ethische Wende in Ästhetik und Politik', in *Das Unbehagen an der Ästhetik,* Vienna 2007, pp. 125–54. English version: Jacques Rancière, 'The Ethical Turn of Aesthetics and Politics' in *Dissensus: On Politics and Aesthetics,* New York 2010.

be 'tiny' since it would require a 'change in society as a whole' rather than just new marketing strategies.[22]

Elke Gaugele (b. 1964), Professor of Fashions and Styles at the Academy of Fine Arts Vienna, sees even neo-bourgeois and colonialist strategies of distinction in the quest for 'cleaner' fashion, in which the 'developed' world is condescendingly patting the head of the 'less developed' world: 'Since the mid-aughts, the United Nations' policy has been moving away from blue helmets and focusing increasingly on the production of ethical textiles, fashions and luxury goods as pacification strategies and forms of developmental aid.'[23] This is precisely the opportunity for so-called developing countries, who are unable to compete with high-tech, low-wage countries. Eco-slogans such as 'jute instead of plastic' are now returning in conscientious fashion in a Western class-specific habitus, in which the ethical, sometimes with religious undertones and always with the connotation of (class-specific) charity, has become even a part of a new definition of luxury. Ethics, Jacques Rancière (b. 1940) wrote in 2007, was merely another form of honour that would equip itself with a new form of domination.[24]

In the meantime, the previously described department store imagined by Zola has expanded across the entire globe and is still bursting with cheap or outrageously expensive products, while underpaid seamstresses toil in sweatshops in its many basements. The happiness of the ladies – which was already a double-edged sword in Zola since it meant the demise of the small retail sector – seems today to have finally turned into a feminine disaster. While the victims of modern clothing production are mostly women and girls with miserable working conditions, the surrounding discourses present the problem of clothing consumption in a feminine way, as if female consumers, through their infinite desire, bear the lone responsibility to buy clothes and to present their selves; however, corporate, production and marketing managers escape any responsibility. Indeed, our material handling of consumption needs to change, but we also need to change our fixation on fashion as a simultaneously sacral as well as quasi-pornographic object of desire, which is so eerily similar to a mechanism intrinsically oriented towards femininity.

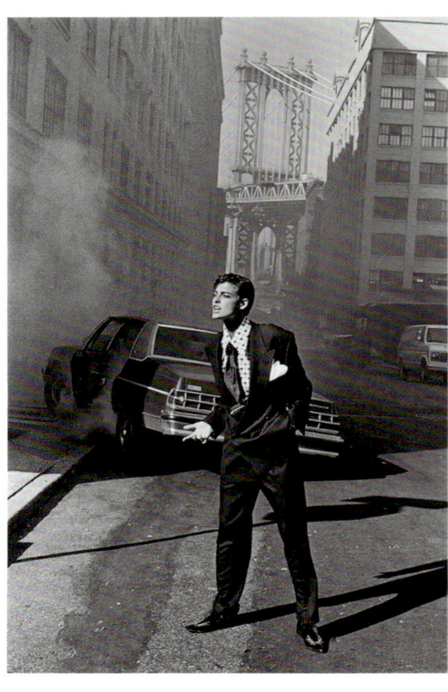

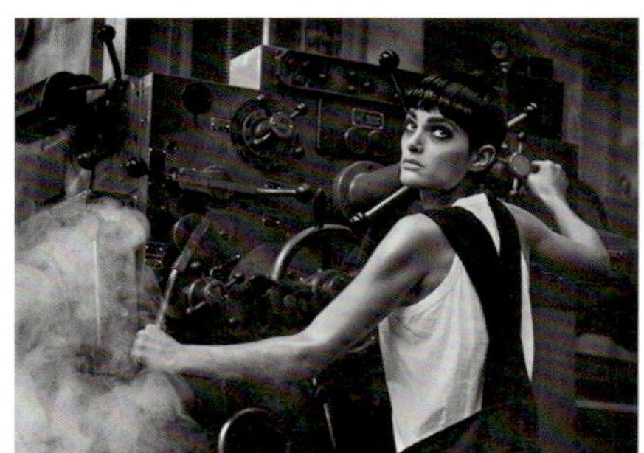

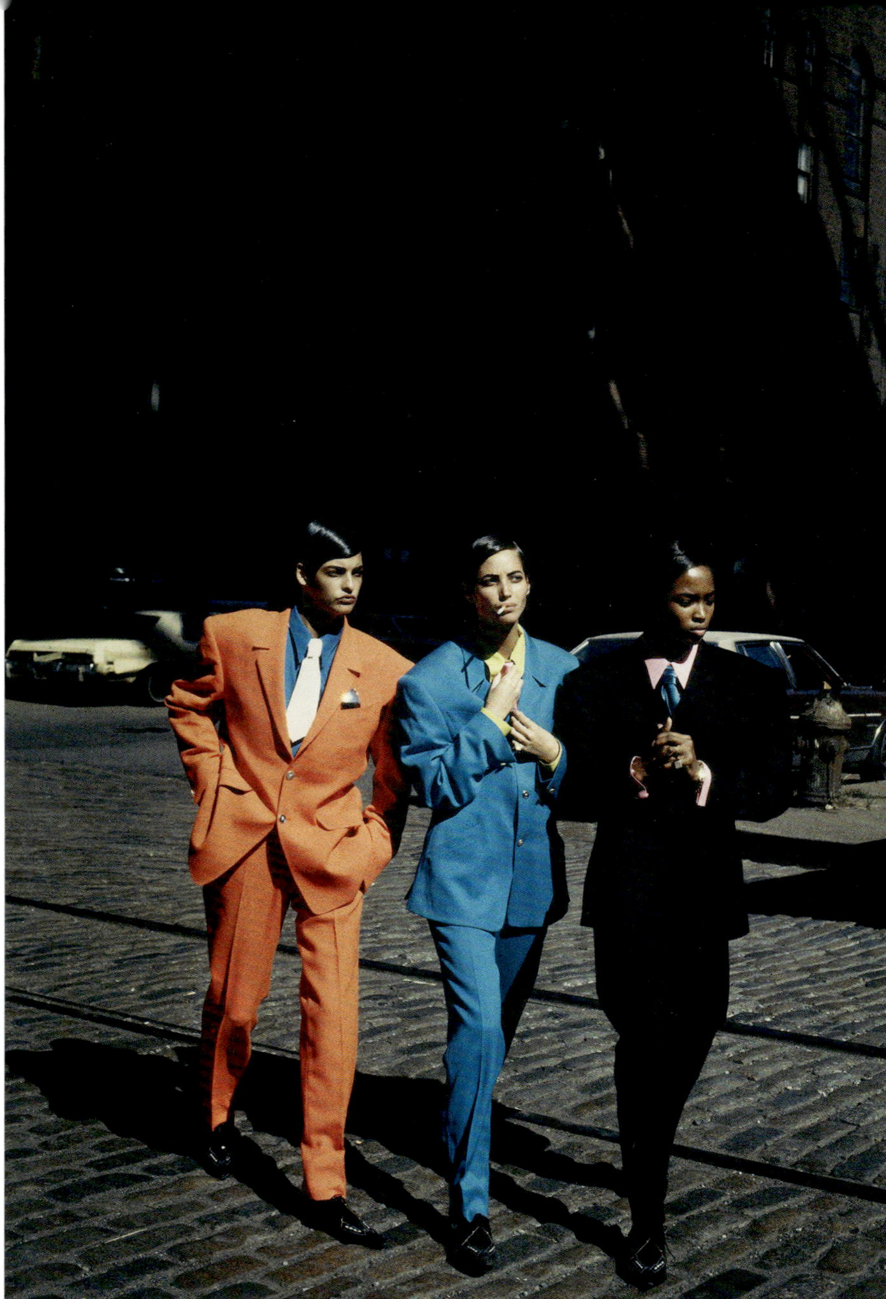

**202**  Peter Lindbergh (b. 1944)
*Linda Evangelista, Brooklyn,* 1990
Exhibition print; Hahnemühle
Photo Rag® Baryta 315 gr, 60 × 50 cm
Courtesy Peter Lindbergh, Paris

**200**  Peter Lindbergh (b. 1944)
*Lynne Koester, Paris,* 1984
Exhibition print; Hahnemühle
Photo Rag® Baryta 315 gr, 60 × 50 cm
Courtesy Peter Lindbergh, Paris

**203**  Peter Lindbergh (b. 1944)
*Linda Evangelista, Christy Turlington &*
*Naomi Campbell, Brooklyn,* 1990
Exhibition print; Hahnemühle
Photo Rag® Baryta 315 gr, 60 × 50 cm
Courtesy Peter Lindbergh, Paris

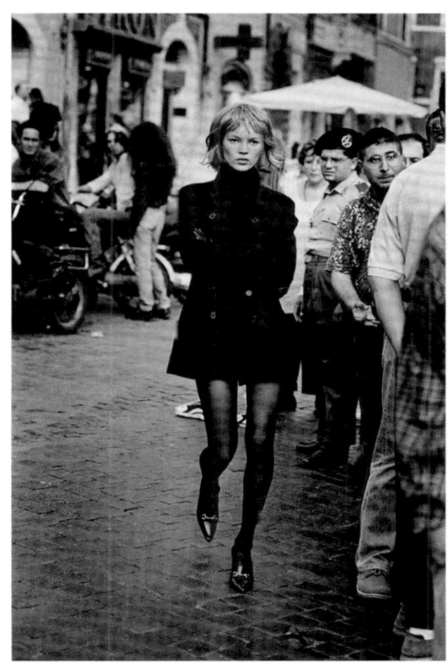

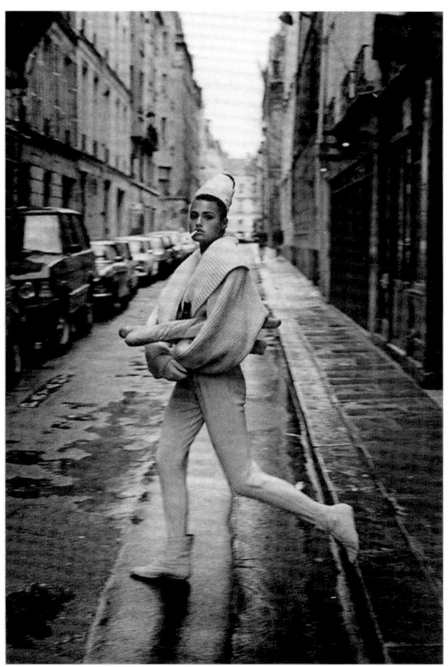

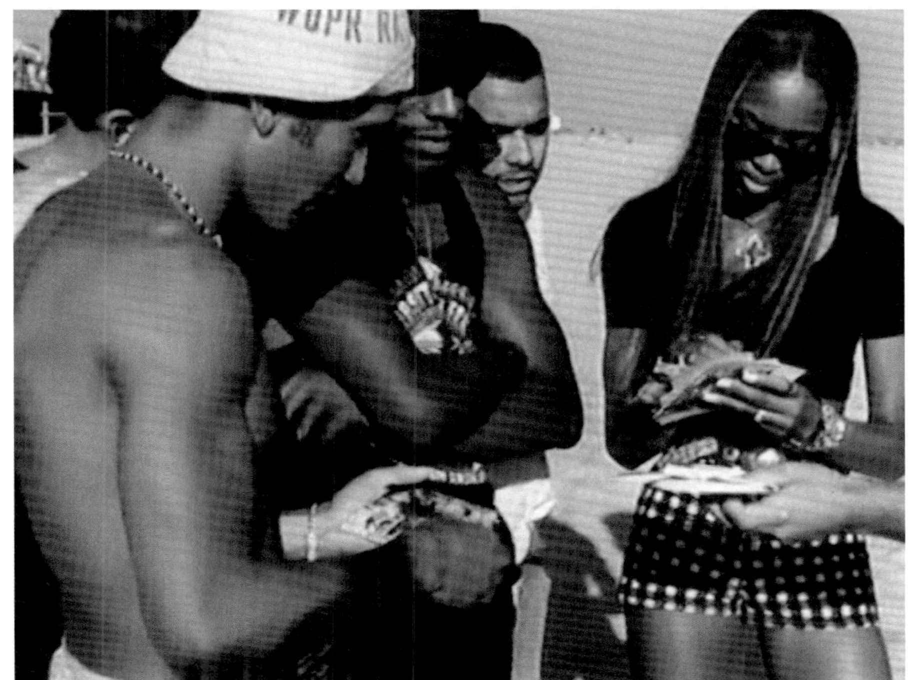



**205**  Peter Lindbergh (b.1944)
*Kate Moss, Rome,* 1994
Exhibition print; Hahnemühle
Photo Rag® Baryta 315 gr, 60 × 50 cm
Courtesy Peter Lindbergh, Paris

**201**  Peter Lindbergh (b.1944)
*Yasmin Le Bon, Paris,* 1985
Exhibition print; Hahnemühle
Photo Rag® Baryta 315 gr, 60 × 50 cm
Courtesy Peter Lindbergh, Paris

**204**  Peter Lindbergh (b.1944)
*Models: The Film,* 1991
16-mm and 35-mm film, digitalised,
black-and-white sound, curation: 48'57"
Courtesy Peter Lindbergh

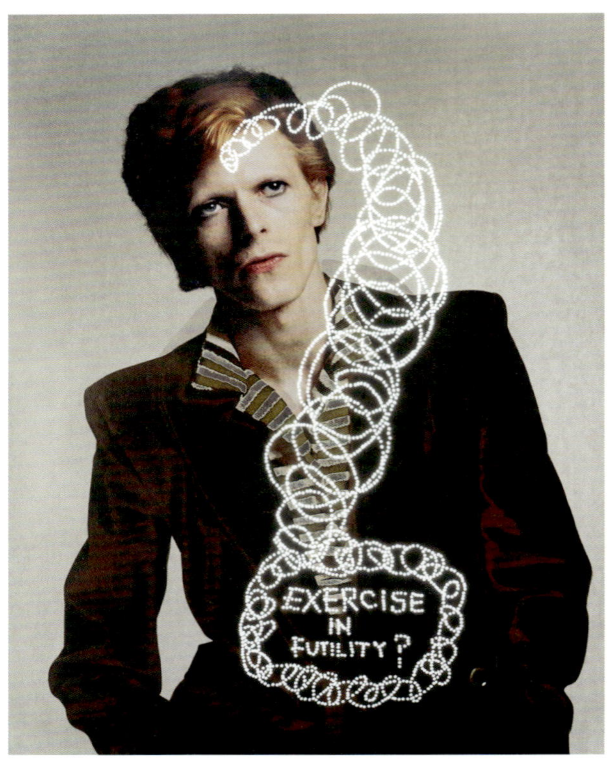

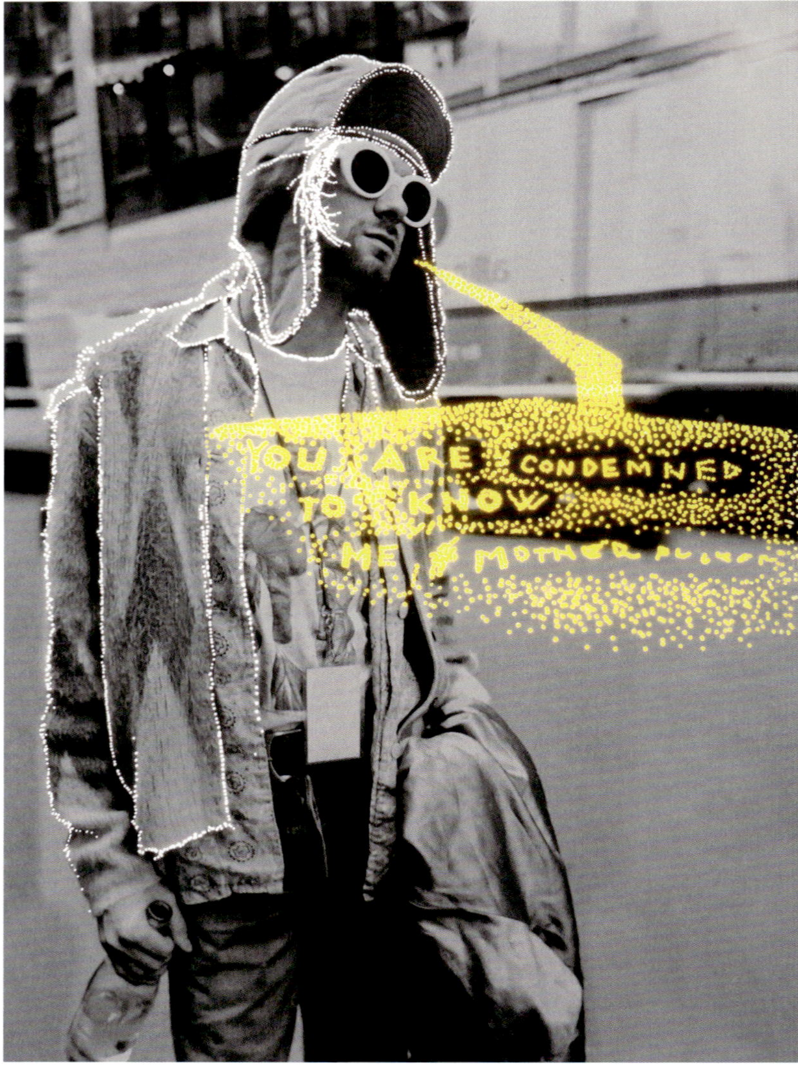



**70**  Daniele Buetti (b. 1955)
*Exercise in futility?*, 2016
Perforated photograph in light box
Photograph: 50 × 40 cm
Light box: 51.5 × 41.5 × 7 cm
Courtesy Feldbusch Wiesner
Rudolph Galerie

**71**  Daniele Buetti (b. 1955)
*You are condemned to know me,
motherfucker*, 2016
Perforated photograph in light box
Photograph: 50 × 40 cm
Light box: 51.5 × 41.5 × 7 cm
Courtesy Feldbusch Wiesner
Rudolph Galerie

**145** General Idea
*FILE magazine, IFEL,* Special Paris Issue,
vol. 2, no. 3, September 1973
Stampa Galerie, Basel

**146** General Idea
*FILE magazine,* Glamour Issue,
vol. 3, no. 1, autumn 1975
Stampa Galerie, Basel

**147** General Idea
*FILE magazine,* Special People Issue,
vol. 3, no. 3, summer 1977
Stampa Galerie, Basel

**148** General Idea
*FILE magazine,* Punk 'Til You Puke! Issue,
vol. 3, no. 4, autumn 1977
Stampa Galerie, Basel

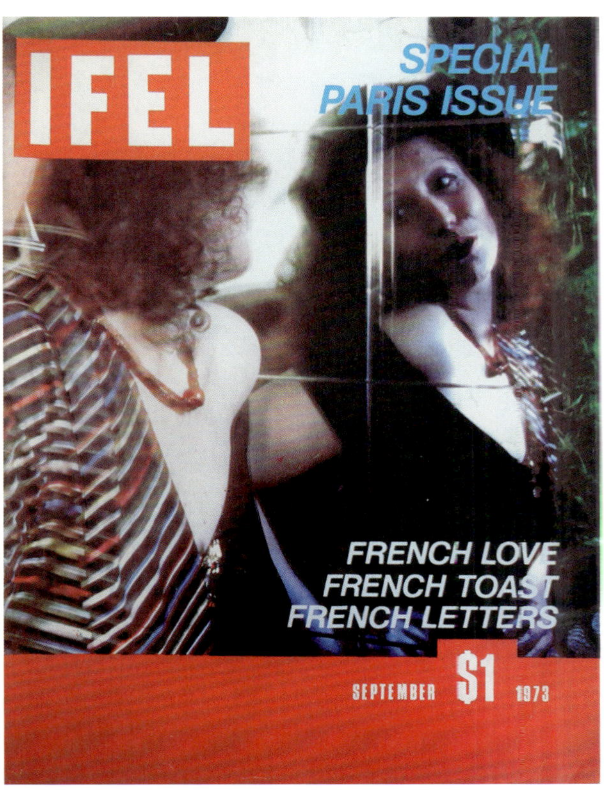


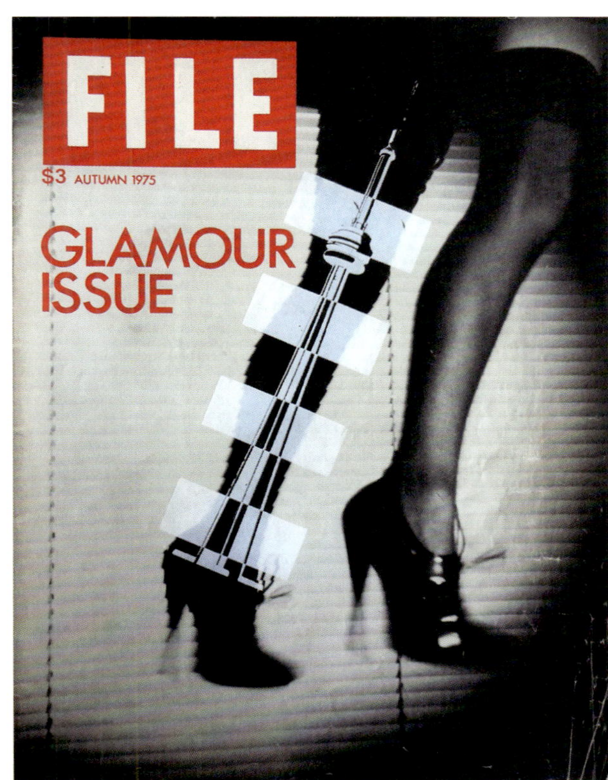


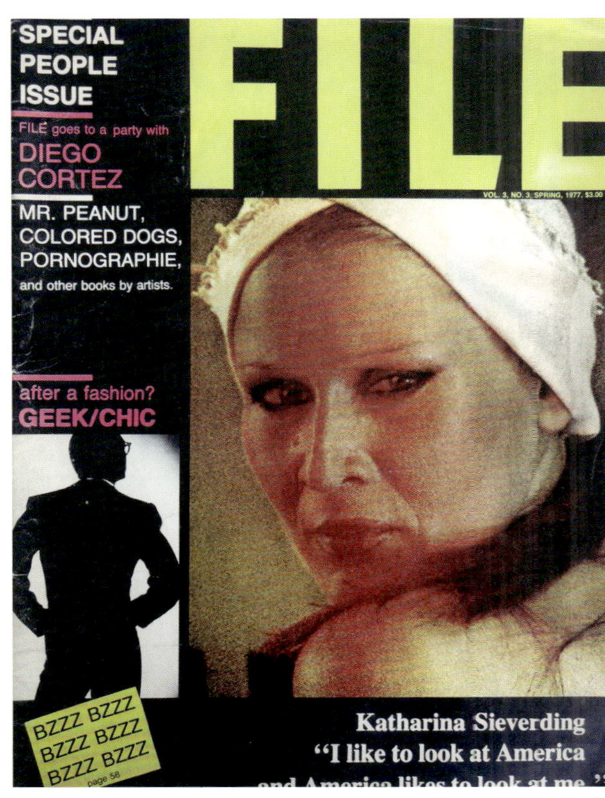


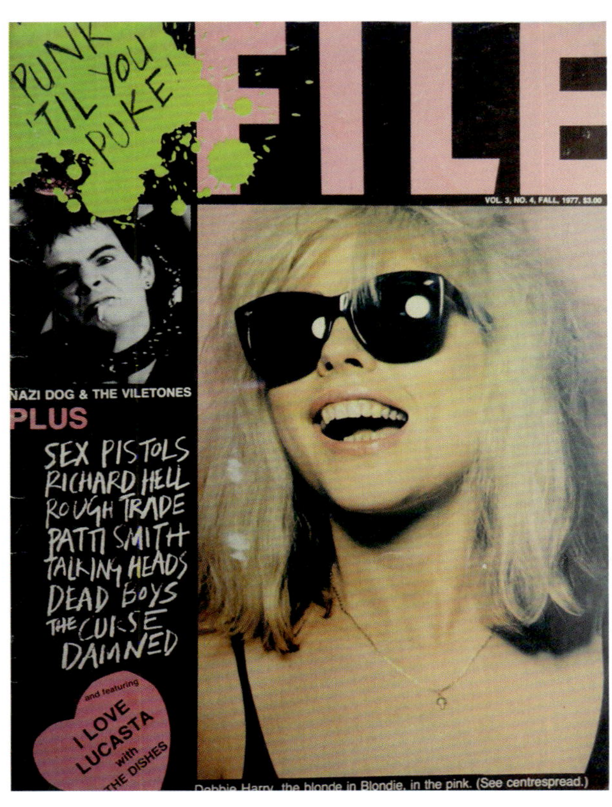

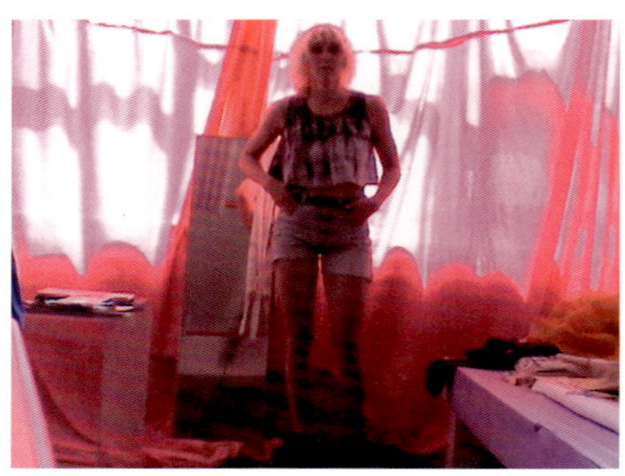
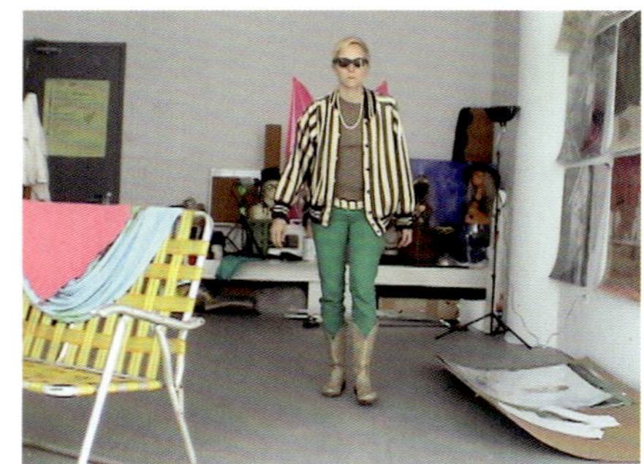

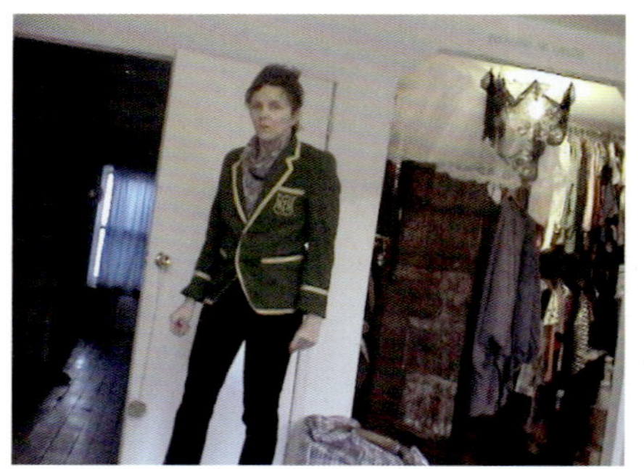
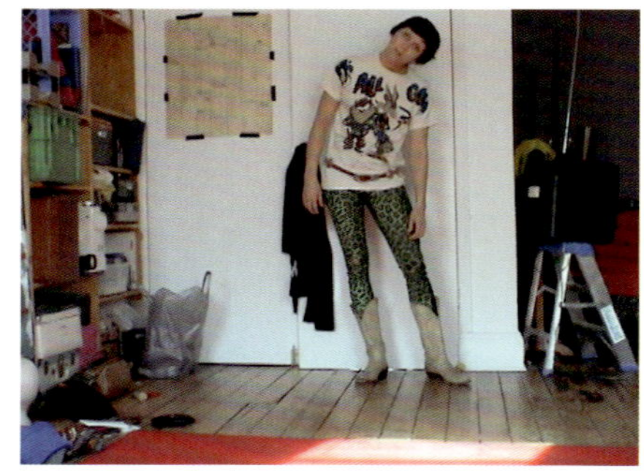

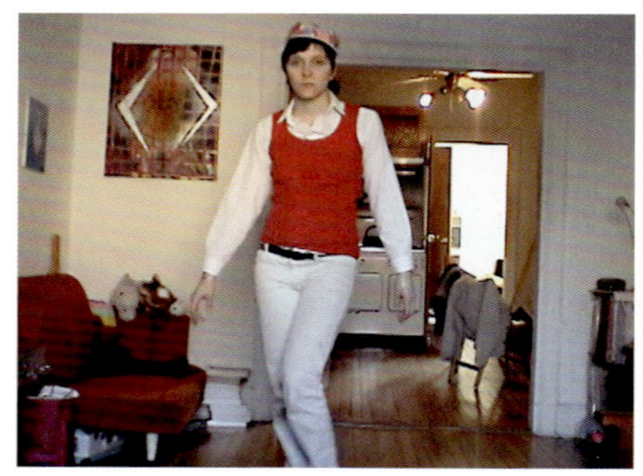
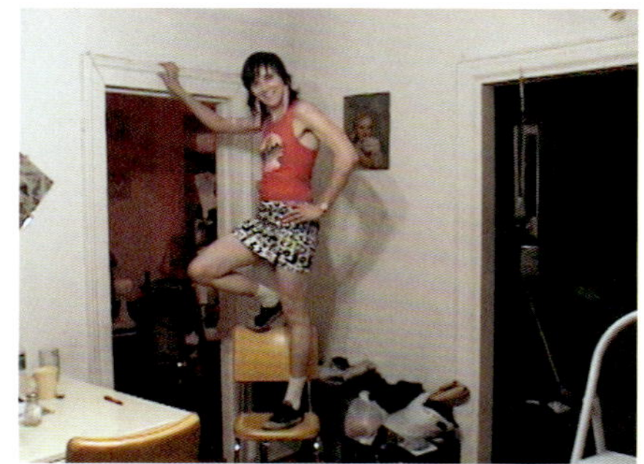

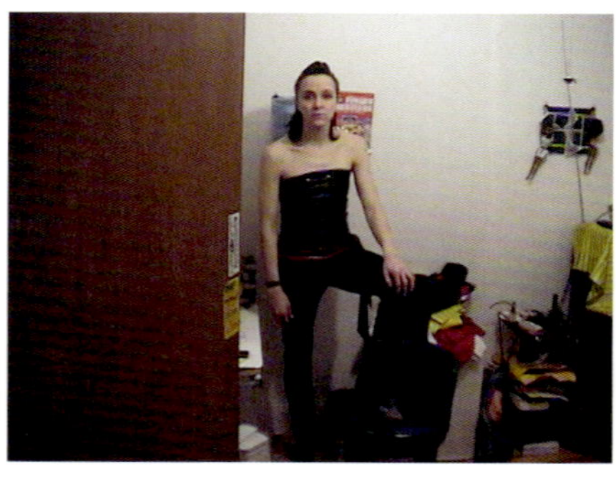
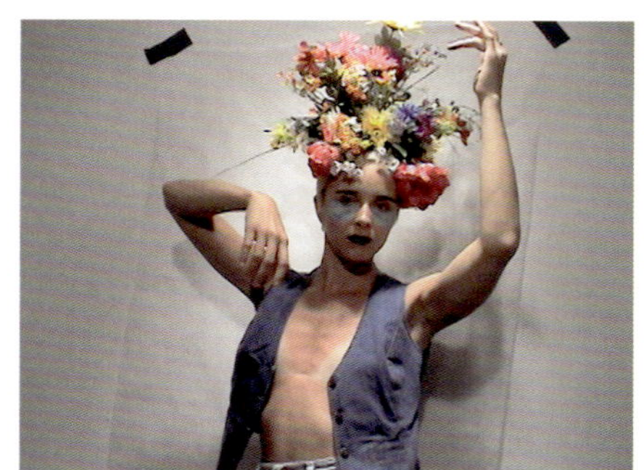

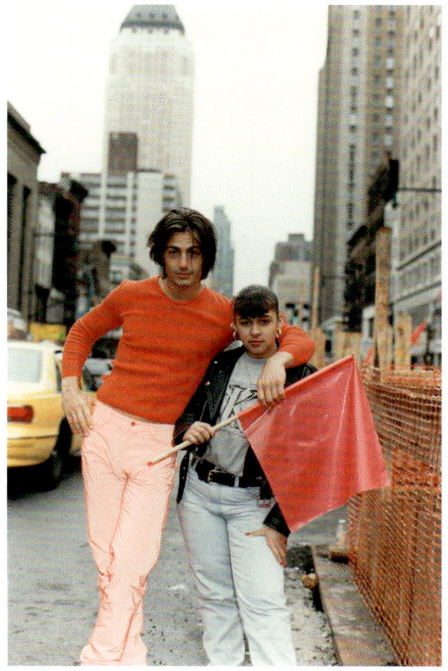

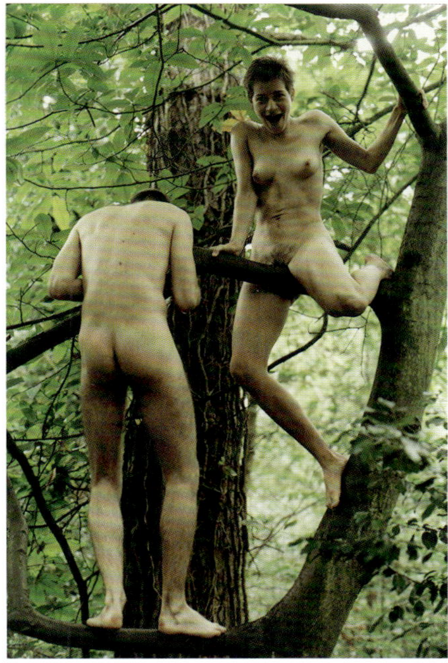

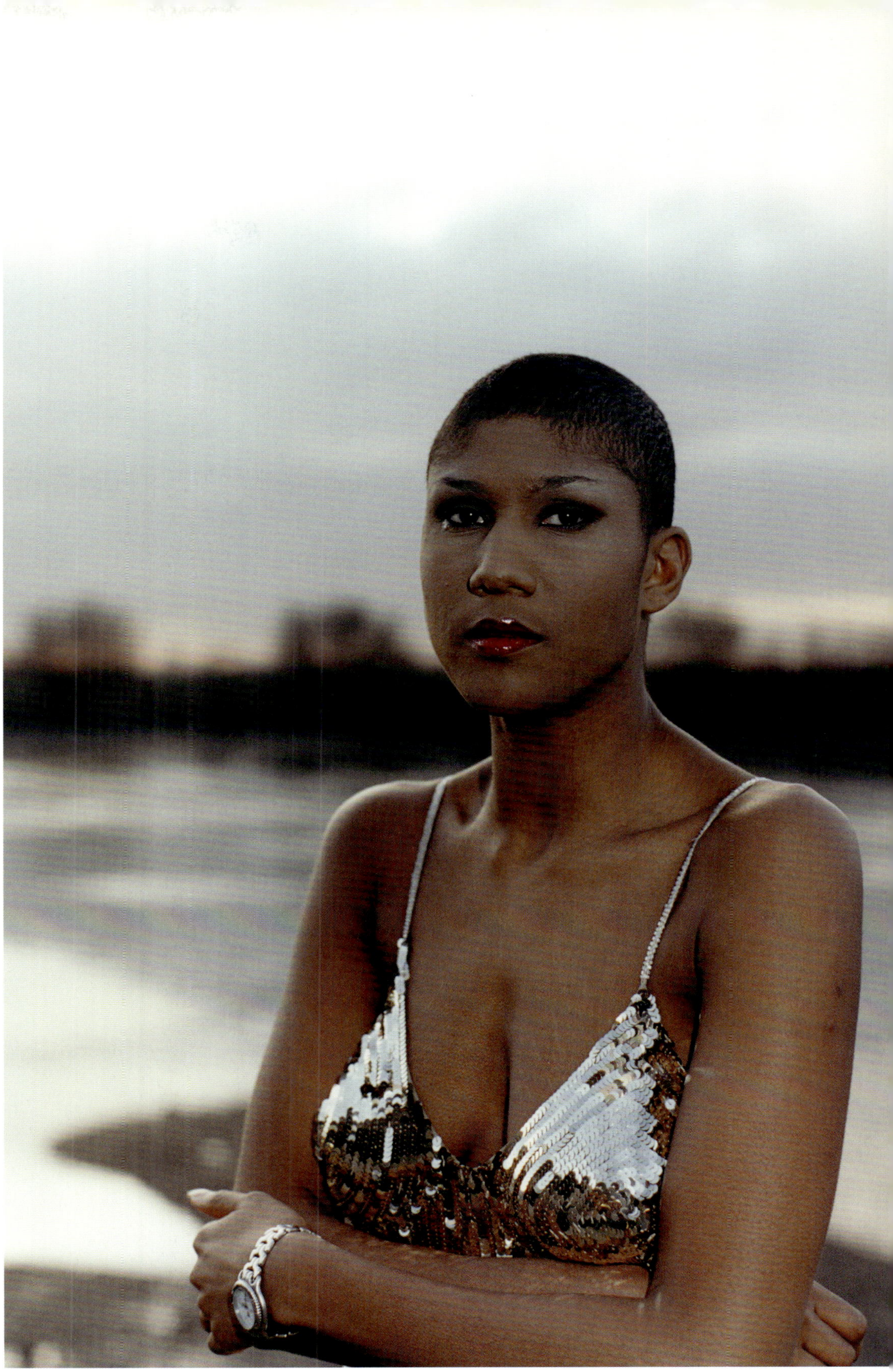

258  Wolfgang Tillmans (b. 1968)
*Michael Bergin & fan,* 1995
Colour photograph, 60.8 × 50.7 cm
Kunsthaus Zürich,
Collection of Photography

252  Wolfgang Tillmans (b. 1968)
*Lutz & Alex, climbing tree,* 1992
Colour photograph, 40.6 × 30.5 cm
Kunsthaus Zürich,
Collection of Photography

256  Wolfgang Tillmans (b. 1968)
*Smokin' Jo,* 1995
Colour photograph, 60.8 × 50.7 cm
Kunsthaus Zürich,
Collection of Photography

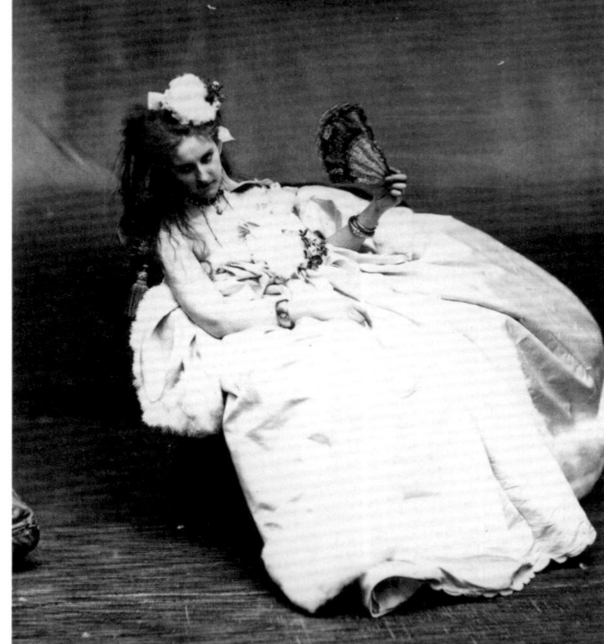
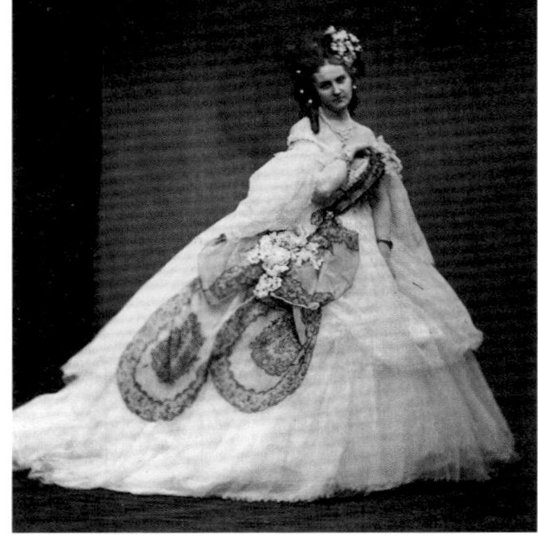
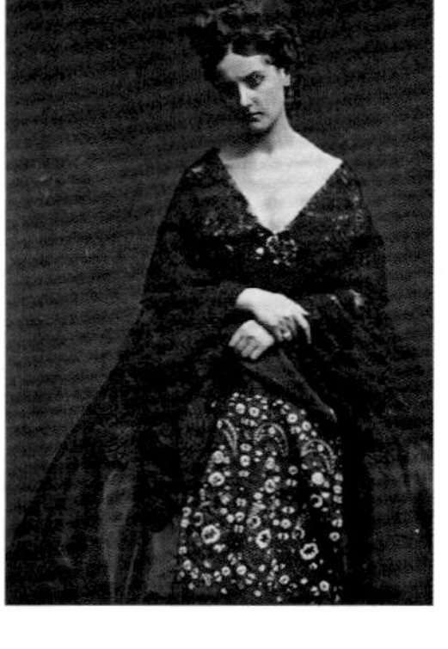
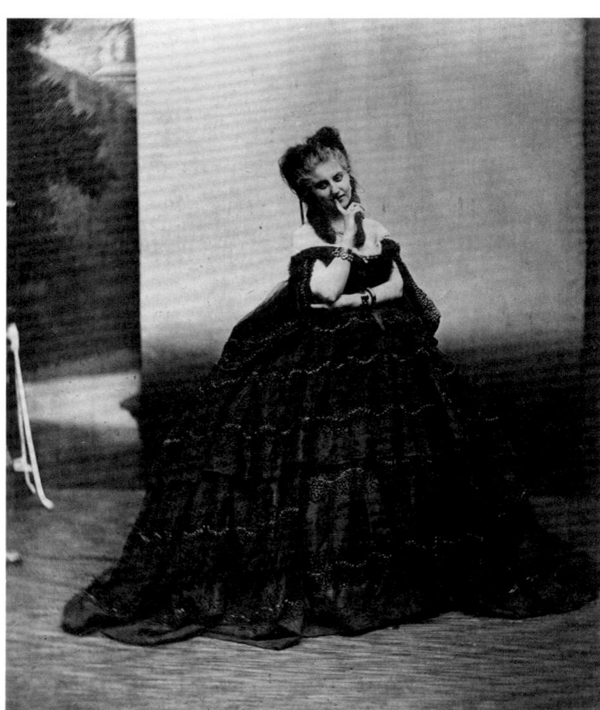
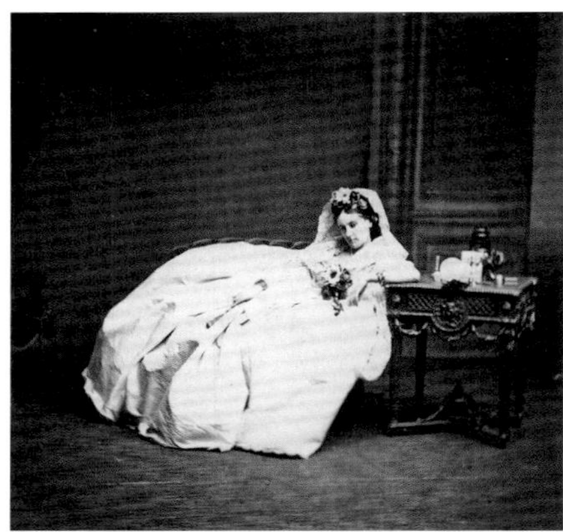
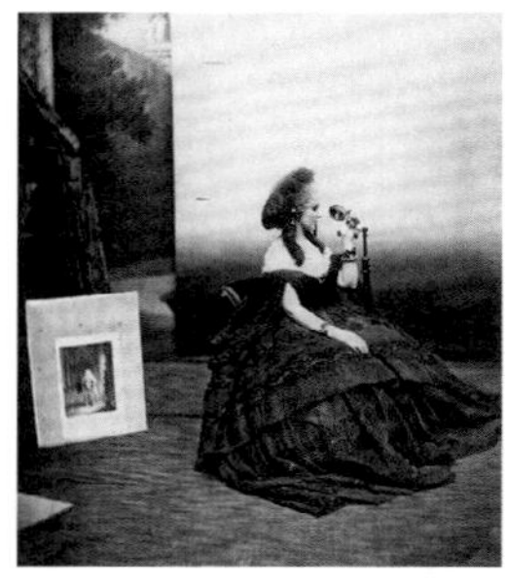
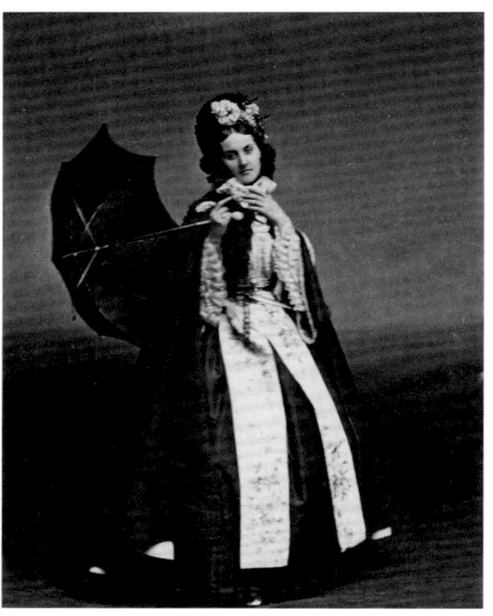

**229**  Pierre-Louis Pierson (1822–1913)
*Comtesse de Castiglione,* 1861–67
Vintage photographs; albumen gelatin silver print,
dimensions variable: 8.8 × 8.8 cm to 46 × 31.5 cm
Martin Kamer

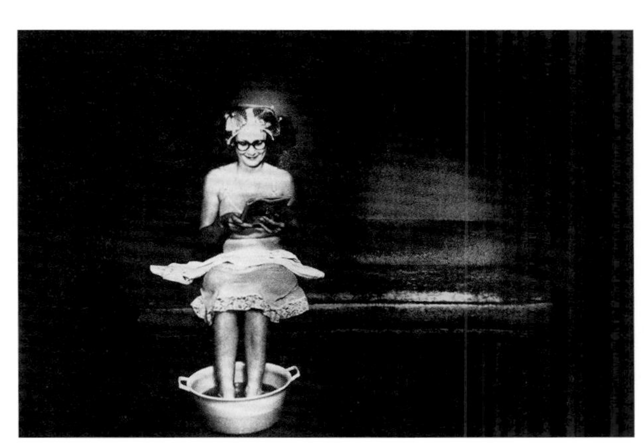
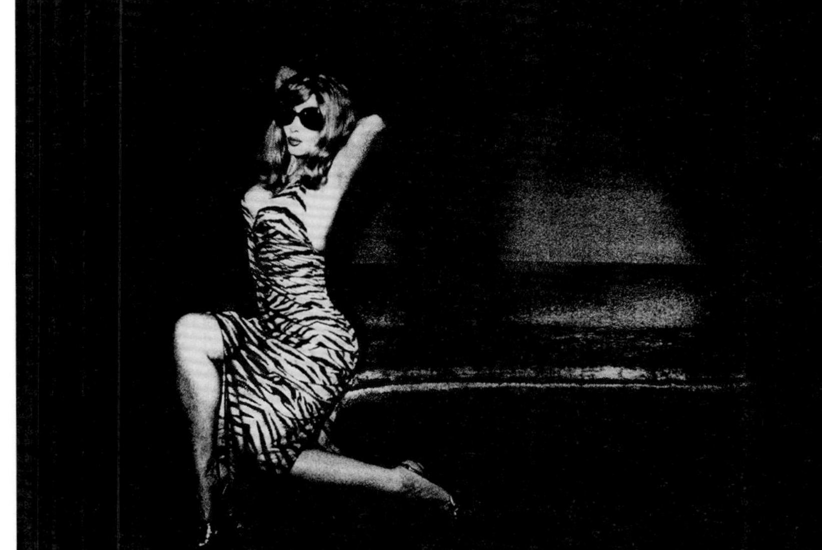
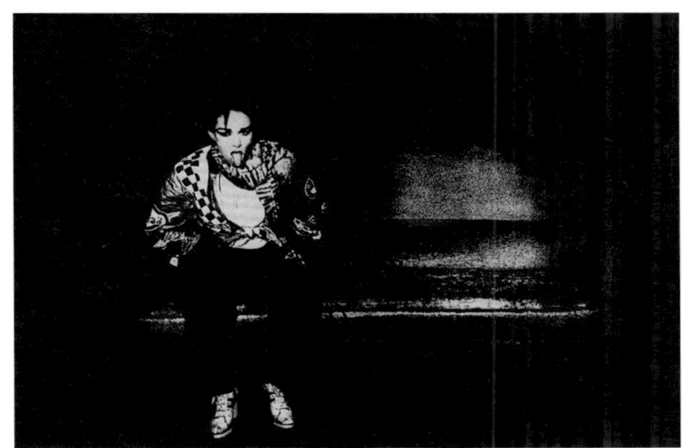
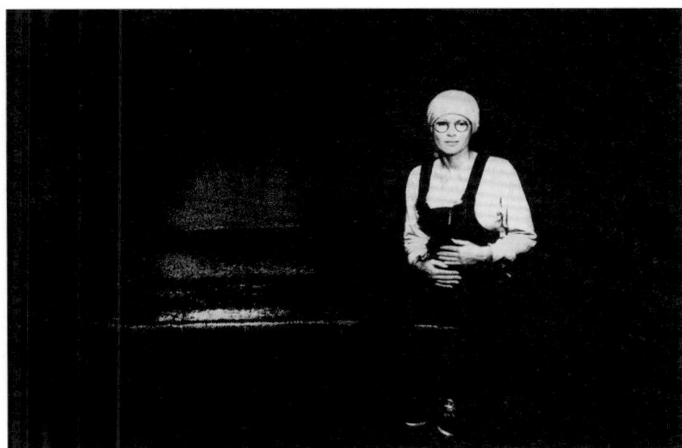

**212**  Manon (b. 1946)
*Ball der Einsamkeiten. 30 Selbstporträts/30 Lebensläufe,* 1980
Gelatin silver prints with artist's montage, 46.3 × 70 cm each
Kunsthaus Zürich, Collection of Photography

# Wear on (Austrian) Righteous

**Elfriede Jelinek**

# Women's and Tear

# Public-Television

So yesterday, no, meanwhile it's become the day before yesterday, no, meanwhile much more time has passed, we've got lost in fashions many times, no wonder, there is no way, you'd think fashion brings forth itself, it's coming back so many times, even though it's never gone; I am curious how long it will take until time has passed altogether, run out on its own runway. So – no, at the time I wrote this, I incidentally saw this program on ORF Austrian TV, it was titled and entitled to command: *Grüss Gott, Österreich* (Greet God, Austria), no, that's not it's title, it was not titled, I think it does not exist anymore. Let's say, it's 2013, the program everyone who's turning it on must accept, is still titled Welcome – no, not well done (and not undone either) – in Austria, and it came on during the so-called Promi-Time (Celebs-Time) show, shortly before six pm when the food starts boiling with rage because no one's around and the *Hausfrau* is sitting in front of the TV. I think that show doesn't exist anymore, time still does, maybe it's time that brings forth fashion, since fashion's still around. Still? Each time brings forth something and then shows it, simply because the new is always shown and with great pride, if sometimes just briefly. So, naturally, I had to take a look, I had to look at the TV, meanwhile at other devices that groan under tons of blogs, but one must always look, looking means determining the named, so then you have to look who belongs to the celebs, luckily not I, for then I'd have to leave myself, after God had left me long ago to my own devices, well no, I sent him away just in time, otherwise he might want to appear with me on TV (it was actually somewhat similar to the derivative of class hatred from which I suffer so much, though less and less so, under the determinant of an alienation ranging from indifferent alienness to actually hostile alienation – as in my case from God, but soon also from the Austrian mass media, tomorrow and tomorrow and tomorrow, no, it's happening now, I didn't even notice since when; thank you for handing me this note or I would have never found out!). Others would not have needed a note, they would have read it off from one of the many displays all around. Soon! In a sec, I'll cut off your airs with a knife, which keep bubbling over from all the air that's constantly pumped in. And already they are off, well not the air, but at least off my radar more or less – of an

Elfriede Jelinek

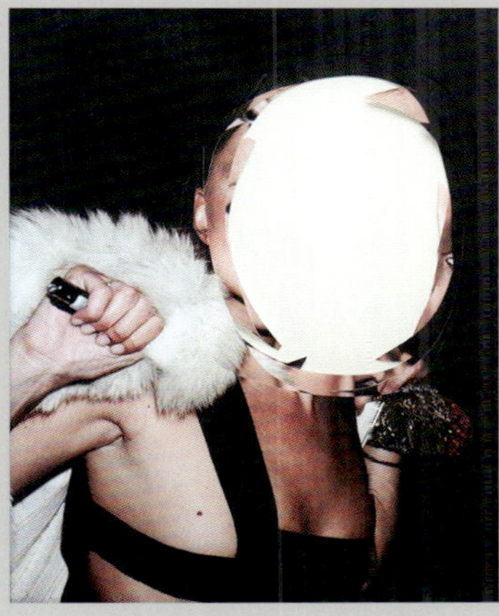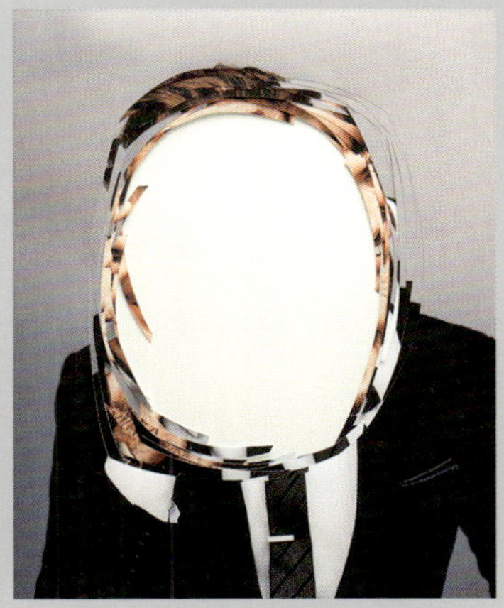

alienation, that is, in this state I must go on and which I must write on, no, off and already they are, well not wrought off but getting more or less unimportant at least. And we are looking what's on and in elsewhere, we can't miss that. Would we be in on it, we'd be on the air ourselves. Only the skinny jeans are allowed to be on to it, which I always missed, but really no one else did but me. Those will go on forever, because a man is allowed to see everything of a woman forever and ever. It is his superordinated right, where was I just now?, at home as always, like the god and his small device he can check anytime to see what on earth he had done now. So then God, I mean our god, whoever it is at the moment and is on duty appears on TV today and looks at his cellphone at what he was doing and its effects on the bodies willed by him (those already desperately wilting at the postulate of what a body must be like so that it can even wear the newest clothes). What did God do wrong that I don't get into this jacket anymore? He's had all options, one could look like this, the other like that. He could have come up with all of it, except that it doesn't always come out the way those having come forward instantly outraged about the bad work imagined it. He has to check himself on the little gorilla glass screen what's coming next, meanwhile no longer by him even though he might still imagine it.

Everything will be shown, because it must be shown. Everything that's done and does us in gets done with craft, diligence and hard work, though the use of materials, the giving it shape is not the decisive factor, but rather the showing. The getting shown. And those who show up because they also want to get their turn and put on quite a show are often rejected by Casting, because everything brought forth for them was not meant for them. Can't make a silk purse out of a sow's ear. They are nothing and must not present themselves or what they've got on them. Well, they could, but no one's interested how it looks underneath, the above is already bad enough.

Okay. So I watched this, back then, on 11.11.03, this Prime-, no Promitime show and there I saw, like a vision of a more beautiful world, a fashion show at the Museums Quartier Vienna, where the work of young designers still gets shown once a year. There was the Chinese awardee for fashion, La Hong (he's still around but not much) who designed beautiful garments which naturally made women more beautiful than they were or highlighted already present beauty in the most natural fashion or rather, beauty as natural, as a matter of fact, which is his job anyway, and then there was another fashion show of Japanese designers, in this case Jun'ya Watanabe pour *Comme des Garçons* and Rei Kawakubo. I was so happy I tuned in on time, because for many years I've been especially interested in Japanese fashion, in the meantime and for the longest time exclusively, I am sure I'll write more about it some time, though it could be that this is it right now, because these Japanese designers sublate in their fashion fashion as such, by preserving everything in it that has ever happened in it (yes, even the Benjaminian tiger leap into the past) so that they can randomly take everything out again. But what did the commentators of the Austrian state television



---

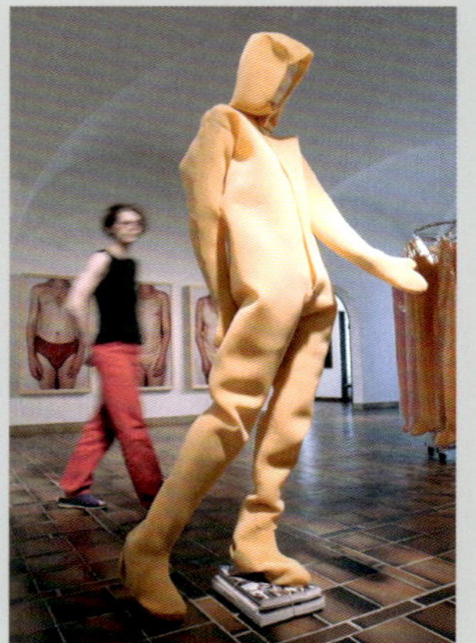

**180** Beat Huber (b. 1956)
*Timepieces (All summer long),* 1997/2002
Installation: mannequin, flexible foam,
stack of fashion magazines, on metal plate
180 × 50 cm
Courtesy the artist
Exhibition view: *Zweite Haut –*
*Kunst und Kleidung,*
Museum Bellerive, Zurich 2002

get out of it? They threw fits fit for a dog raising his hackles – *and perhaps a translator – so then time out for a translator's aside instead of a commercial: In the speaker's Austrian lingo "sie pudelten sich auf" – literally: "They poodled up" translates into "throwing a fit" as well as "dolling up". Now back to the text:* (the Bavarians say, they 'man up', not even that they grant women who've got nothing to look at and who are nothing anyway, no, that's wrong, they are their looks which other people brought out and then corrected). Now they even stand on their hindlegs, digging in their heels, so that one can see their ugly bellies, luckily without any sex, that would really be too much, and their clipped poodle hair down there which has disappeared in the meantime, it's been completely removed. So they really threw some fits, those moderate commentators, that women, instead of panting after their feelings, for which they were originally and exclusively created, let those apparent proponents of the unnatural uglify, distort the most natural thing in the world, their own feminine beauty (a free promotional gift added to the feelings) to run around in rags, actually already shreds, which nonetheless cost a fortune (that's typical, by the way, whenever those philistines attack something that doesn't suit them, they always add how much it cost, no, not how much but that it was a lot, too much for them at any rate. "The artists make plenty of money", that stereotype has been thrown in my face for years. No, we do not make money, I wish I could, yes, we do get money for the crap we make and without giving a crap, we shit all over the State who support it. And that's our doing in any case. It's our doing

that we can do diddleshit. We could have learned something, couldn't we. But the philistines insist it's all our doing, and we shouldn't get money for the Nothing we do, for all that jazz we produce. So they rather pay for our crap to get cleared away again – if they don't simply unload it on the steps of the Vienna Burgtheater, a whole dungheap, the way they did it to the dying Thomas Bernhard in his tight little Nicky sweater with the meticulously pulled out shirt collar he wore for the curtain call at the infamous opening night of his play *Heldenplatz,* which already showed his body's decline, a piece of clothing usually worn by children, and this deteriorating body in its emaciation had turned into a child's body again, yes, that's what they rushed to do to him, so he'd still get it before he died).

So these models are walking around in those wonderful tweed suits by Jun'ya Watanabe, which playfully ironize and parody the (even more expensive) Chanel suits – which in turn more higher-up women personalities carry around on themselves, since those personalities can't walk on their own – by partly ripping them open at the seams, letting them fray, cutting lopsided hems the wrong way, at the same time subverting and ridiculing wealth per se, which encodes itself in such details, no, that's not what rich folk want. After all, they bought these dresses with the sewn-in Chanel or Prada labels so that they – as an event, that blasts any imagination (it's what they want to simulate) and conjures any pleasure – can claim at least some sorts of qualities, gifts and talents, someone's got to do it, after all, and so their dresses do it for their mugs



Elfriede Jelinek

which, mattely tinted, injected, operated, pounded, are jumping up on them like pugs so that it'll show how much one must love them but isn't allowed to because they are so much higher up than we are. Whatever. But the Austrian *Dirndlette* and the Austrian *Lederhosenite* don't like it when the citizens' dress code gets ridiculed, what's a citizen going to look like without wearing the right thing? And we ultimately always recognize the right thing by the right folks wearing it, so then freedom to the right ones according to the times they should also fit in, if it's easy, otherwise they will be made to fit (it was Bruno Walter who described how just one day after the *Anschluss* 1938 urban clothing disappeared from the streets of Vienna and was substituted by the national costume: *Dirndl* everyone! Kneesocks everyone). So now let's sock it to this Jun'ya Watanabe and cut him down to his appropriate size. But real good! Everything else that doesn't fit in with us, cut it off too or tear it out completely. Humans are like grass anyway, like the foliage of a Schönbrunn hedge, I constantly digress, but here I may, or else just throw it out, the entire space belongs to me, you see, well, not this time, but usually it does, it's all for me from it, as much as I want, yes, yes and I belong to me, my heart belongs to Rei Kawakubo. Whatever we've got left afterwards can possibly also be cut to size or cut out entirely right away, okay so, and the people right after that. Take all their clothes before and everything else that can be turned into money. Because we do want to get some of the money back from what the Jews, for example, back then had stolen from our healthy Volkscommunity, when our folks bought something to wear or put gold fillings in their teeth and whatnot. So there they rise on TV, they raise hell (though for the news they remain seated, the same baloney comes out of their mouths, thoroughly processed and in presliced bytes), the Austrian cold cutters and backwater banksters and hinterland rovers, that's not how they want to see a woman, messing with good healthy food, dragging good healthy clean clothing into the mud and tearing down, ripping off healthy, tightly sewn hems and pulling out threads and tying them together and letting them hang down, really now!, why should we have to deal with that at all, we know very well who we are and how we have to dress so we look decent. Something decent

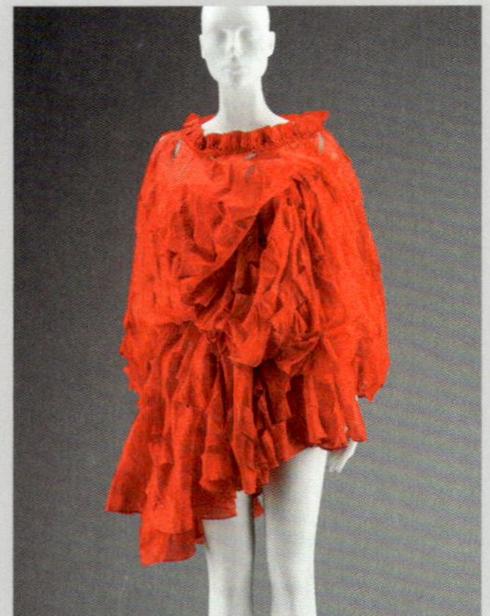



anyway, that's for sure. And for a side dish the cockbiters and sour-pussies on the Austrian Abscess Hollywood version Seitenblicke (Side Eyes) are putting their fattened and toned up and well-stuffed breast buns on stiff supports into the baskets (probably so they won't drop down) for show and tell about this sight, I mean site, like the neighboring women in the socialist housing projects (well, the best-dressed do not live there, no, no! That's out of the question and the question does not come up to begin with) place their front section on the window sills when talking to each other, a genuine female technique, gossiping from window to window. Being a woman means showing oneself as undressed, plungingly necklined, sleekly lacquered as possible and next to a well-heeled gentleman if possible, if such a one could be caught in time.

In his novel *The City Without Jews,* Hugo Bettauer, later murdered (back then when he wrote it he was still able to laugh and one could laugh with him about such a thing) joked how beautiful Vienna would look without Jews: People would walk around in loden and fustian; silk, wit, amusement, beauty would have temporarily disappeared with those people. And by missing these beautiful dresses, one would also realize that some people were missing as well! And get them back in a triumphal procession as quickly as possible! Bettauer actually believed, BEAUTY WOULD BE MISSED BY THE VIENNESE! And they would miss all these people, because they, the dear Viennese ladies and gentlemen could no longer buy beautiful clothes and textiles in their stores. He seriously believed that the Viennese would run screaming from "natural" simplicity and back to luxury, which the "cosmopolitans" (a popular slur for Jews in the Soviet Union) can offer them. He was wrong. While every committed communist in the early days of the communist world movement still believed that the worker's destiny could be expanded for all people, that is, the destiny to simply acquire property through labor, ("the sole purpose of life and existence is direct, physical possession" – a kind of raw-milk communism, which is just a generalization and perfection of private property), that is, the same for everyone, the same amount of it, so that Karl Marx realized, that the suspension of private property is anything but an acquisition, one would

Elfriede Jelinek

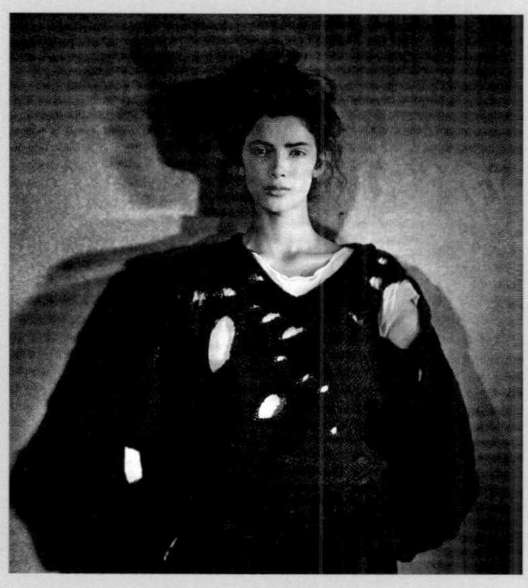





have to negate the whole world, education, civilization (well, that too has already happened! You bet!) and return to the unnatural simplicity of the poor person with few needs, who did not get beyond private property but rather has not even got to it. So there. I have acquired knowledge in the aesthetics of fashion over many years, because it interests me a lot, sure, someone else is interested in something else, I am interested in this, I can decode clothes, so to speak. And while it would be logical to say that this is a bourgeois, elitist stance I am taking here, a snobbish attitude so to speak, there is nothing to learn from me about the bourgeoisie, it's more likely to learn from Watanabe, from Yohji Yamamoto, from Kawakubo, because they consistently undermine its codes, specifically by imitation and simultaneously alterations of these codes (if they weren't imitated, one would not notice the alterations on them), neither would one learn anything by adopting solely the consumers' point of view and, by believing to have the better point of view, even less than nothing. So now, all the more nothing. Maybe it's like that: the Japanese designers imitate a manufacture-like mode of production (Yamamoto's mother was a dressmaker and he says he learned everything from her and wants to help women, yes: help!) And they surely make more by hand than the others, which goes hand in hand with their love and care for the material, mind you, no two frayed jackets and skirts are identical, the threads come out in different places, you understand?, and it's quite possible that by recognizing these things among tons of others I am again catapulting myself out of something

alien, uncanny (something that always stayed alien and uncanny to me), since it is Marx's famous thesis that only on the basis of this very special mode of production, namely the capitalist one, do products adopt the form of goods. Must adopt, as a natural process. I do not acquire anything foreign, nothing that belongs to others, I do not own capital and most certainly I do not embody it (more likely it is embodied by some in our still popular program *Seitenblicke* – yes, it's still running and running and running – with their more or less "discreet" bling blings and their indiscreet silk or pure wooly rags and expensive watches, everything invisibly visible, not visibly invisible, nothing invisible!, everything has to come out, don't anyone steal or tear any of it, because this is, after all, the goal of the uppermost class – most of those who are shown to us here are just their compliant suckers getting their share of the glow, not Rainer Maria Rilke's poverty which is to be a great glow from the inside, great yes, but to hell with the poverty, not here, not now – the goal of this class is pushing their code through as the only possible one and make sure their creatures don't see through it, even though they have to look at them constantly. Their gaze does not cut through. Their gaze did not make the cut with them, at least not inwards). The capitalist functions as personified capital, but not always. In *Seitenblicke,* he is on vacation away from it and thus all the more on duty and on leave, so to speak, from the acquisition and/or control of foreign labor in absentia, of course always only in temporary absentia, but he still personifies it, capital, he embodies not only this control of foreign labor,

---

Women's Wear and Tear on (Austrian) Public-Righteous Television

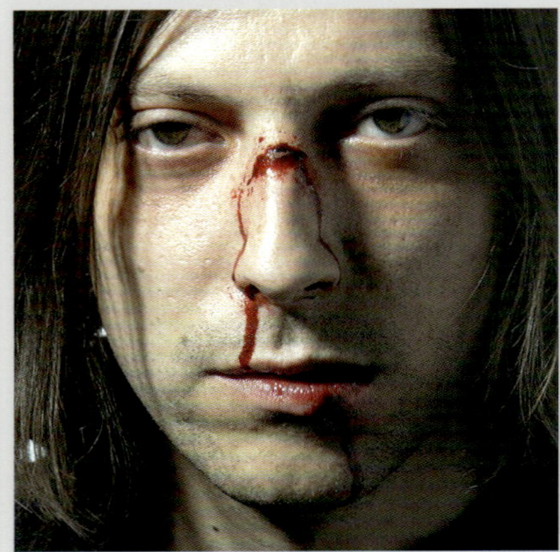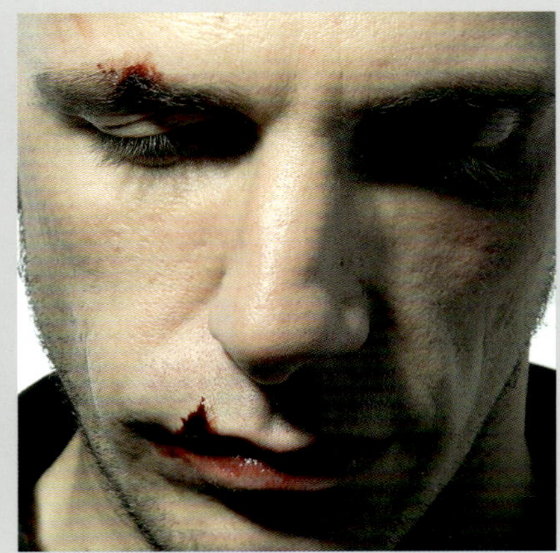

he also personifies the sale of the goods produced by foreign labor. He tells us what and how, he tells it to television and they televisionary kindly pass it on to us, what to wear and what not.

And "torn" dresses by Jun'ya Watanabe, for which he asks horrendous sums of money (even though they are worth nothing, they are kaput, can't you see that?!), is not what we need, we prefer demanding this kind fabulous money for our native clad lads and lasses and their costume-made infamousness, which is a heavy uplift for us whenever we want to lift them out of our blood and our soil with our healthy national attitude (an air cushion! It even heaves whole ships out of the water). It makes us uppity, slowly, but surely. That foreign Japanese stuff is not produced by us, it does not earn us anything and anyway, it is alien to our country-Volk. We have no use for it. And it does cost money, much too much in fact, so get rid of it, because we need that money to produce a concept of ourselves. Running around in such tattered rags won't cut it. Well, today people are allowed to go on living, we don't kill anyone anymore, what's dead here is the economy, so let it fly especially high, because the deader and more content it is with the dead stuff, the better, for in death we are all the same, in death there is only one single concern and one single product made by it; for Rilke it's still the big monasteries that stand like robes around unlived lives, for me it's the clothes I hoarded, I am my own cloister and they also stand on their own, the clothes, they don't need a stand-in either, even though I almost never step forward and show myself, they stand around my unlived life, stupidly, not undamaged, but not unintentionally damaged either. We (I don't move, I just show, but now I say we) also show those pushing them, their economic pushers, okay, yes, we then also show their pushing beyond the 1%, we show it precisely because it is supposed to remain hidden, what everyone sees no one sees. Okay, the economy's object is the commodity. Dead stuff. Death. These Japanese clothes are not a commodity, because they are not really dead. They pull strings like chewing gum, like a living organism, they don't give a shit about the orderliness of the petit-bourgeois alpine festive costume. This year they are making – as mentioned, this year is not now, now is different and something else, but similar, this year, for example, they are making fun of Dior's "New Look", the first distinct post-Nazi-couture in liberated Europe. It seems to be an especially crass misdeed to simply undo such beautiful clothes by parodying what had to first be liberated by a surplus of material. The production process which always has to be driven by others while the side-ogled and the side-flashed one and the super-flasher surely wants to profit from it (by putting on himself what is put down, put up and out at the moment always nicely the same for all, which shows their "eternal" union, until the next separation, when mini is put down, I mean put up there again), in the shown little evening dresses and costumes and pant suits, in that what "normal people" wear while the economy profits from them and shows people what being decently dressed actually means (it means to overdress and draw in the form of money, and if one does not have the same money as the high

Elfriede Jelinek

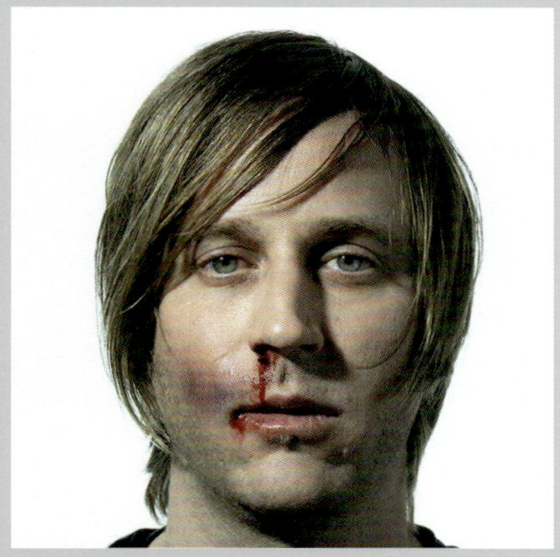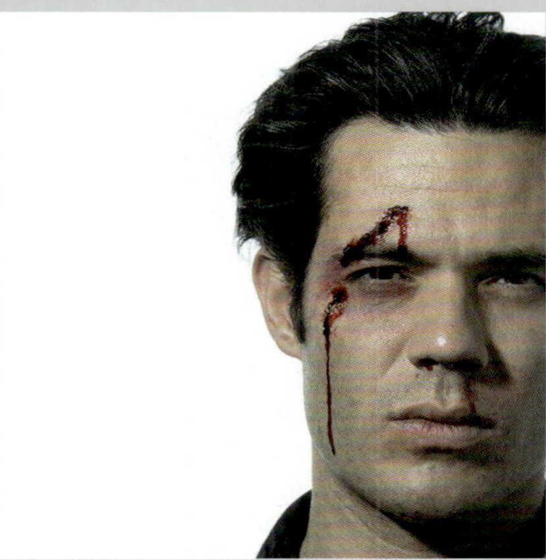

**129** Nik Emch (b. 1967) and Marky Edelmann (b. 1964) *Supreme Psychedelic Underground,* 1998–2004 Sound, 4 records and 2 album covers with portrait shots from Nik Emch, Marky Edelmann, Thomas Ritter and Patrick Owen Meier; photography: FBM Studio; makeup: Giada Venturini; album covers: 31.2 × 31.4 × 0.5 cm each, duration (sound): 60' Courtesy Nik Emch and Marky Edelmann



riders, one still puts on the same things, just that they are cheaper then, anyone who's got a wall in his home, so that's really everyone, recognizes the writing on it), how does the text continue, I always forget it so quickly, though I never forget the current fashion and the shadow it casts into the future, so then: the mode of production, the labor gets thrown into the face of decent products for decent people and because of this draft it goes out in the product with a sigh. The production process comes to a halt, it implodes inside this manufactured ware and disappears like a specter in the woven spin. Which is publicly shown to us. And the *Mensch* should not notice (my God, at that time I still said: *der Mensch!*) that his own ignition spark got put out, what do you want, the vehicle's still running, we do need the spark to go out so that the ware gets value which no longer has anything to do with labor and doesn't even show what's left of it. One should wear clothes that are not worn down by labor, but the poor garment also wants something to put on, otherwise we just might put it down altogether. It would be best for everybody to be dressed the same, same cool, same hot, as shown to us by television and all the other media we've got now, a jumble of pixels, a barbed wire fence marking no borderline and where a cut-in pops up: This moderator, this (female) announcer were outfitted by Tlapa or Fürnkranz (I think both companies are broke now, and I always wondered why these people looked so fitful, I mean fitting, it was their last gasp, before the storm got into their crowns and knocked them down), everything else: get rid of it! The gap between city and country is laboriously bridged by sturdy bridges and now everything is: Country. God's own country. Off with the sinning city, without Jews, of course, or as good as without, yes, much better without! Good. I even know which country. "Ich bin ein Japanese." My sign: work. The sign of my work: what I put myself in. A "screw" ploughing through water. A *Schiffsschraube,* a "ship's screw" in German, a ship's propeller in translation that churns up the sea which yields immediately. Silent owner of something that can't be seen. I, I, I.

2003; revised by the author for this book in 2017.
Translated by Gitta Honegger

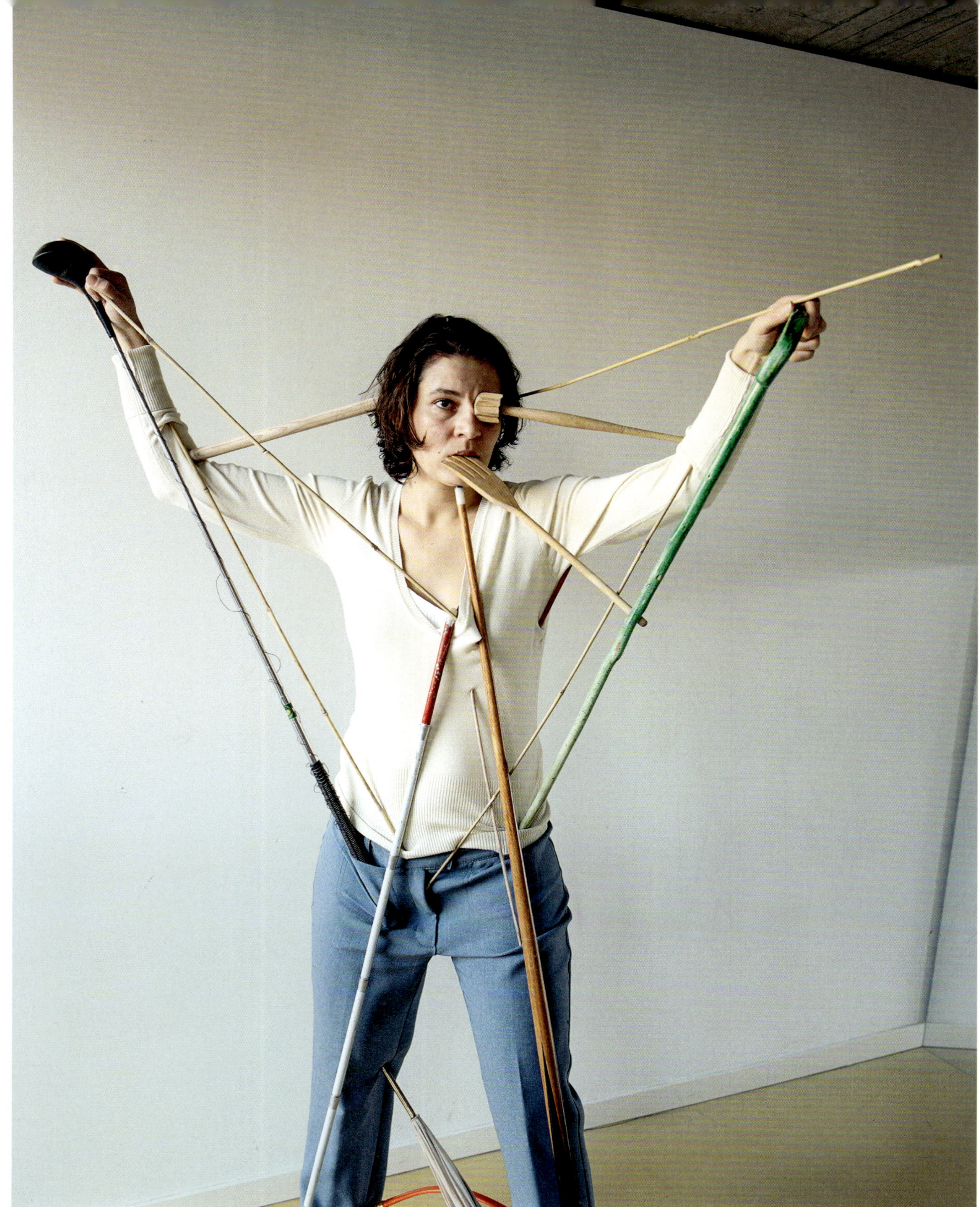

**301** Erwin Wurm (b. 1954)
*Untitled (Cathérine Seifert)*
From the series *Hamlet,* 2007
C-Print, framed, 159.1 × 126.5 cm
Kunsthaus Zürich,
Collection of Photography,
donated by the artist

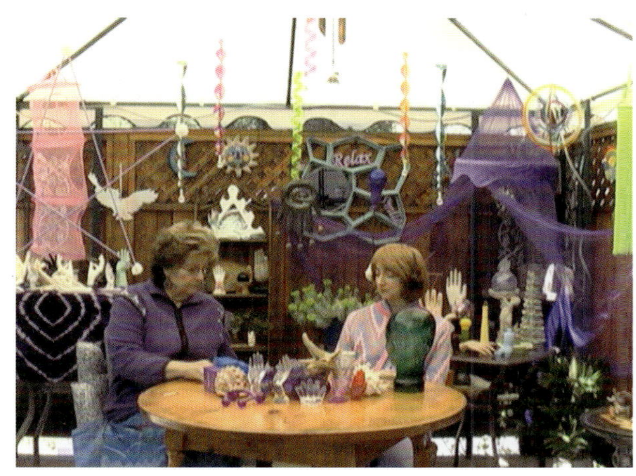
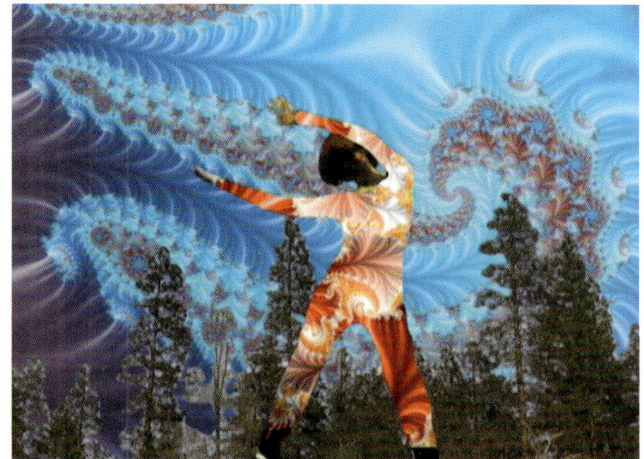
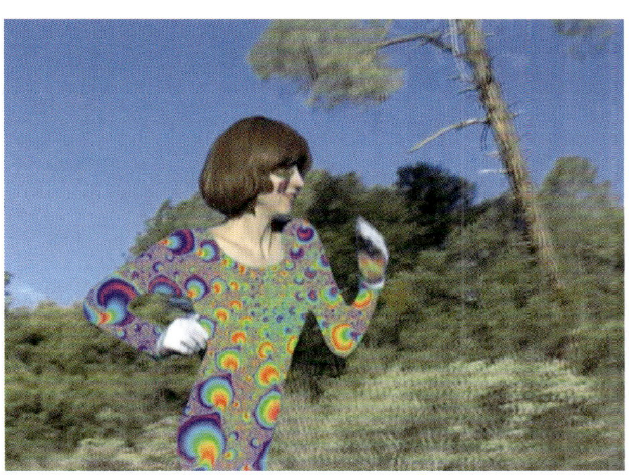
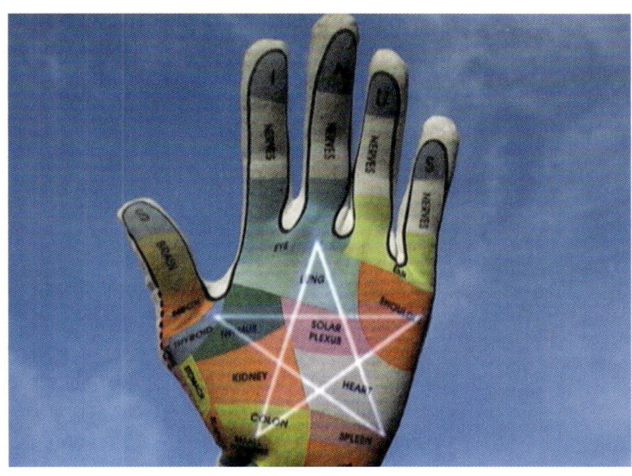



**219** Shana Moulton (b. 1976)
*Whispering Pines #4,* 2007
Video, colour, sound, duration: 10'53"
Courtesy the artist and Galerie
Gregor Staiger, Zurich

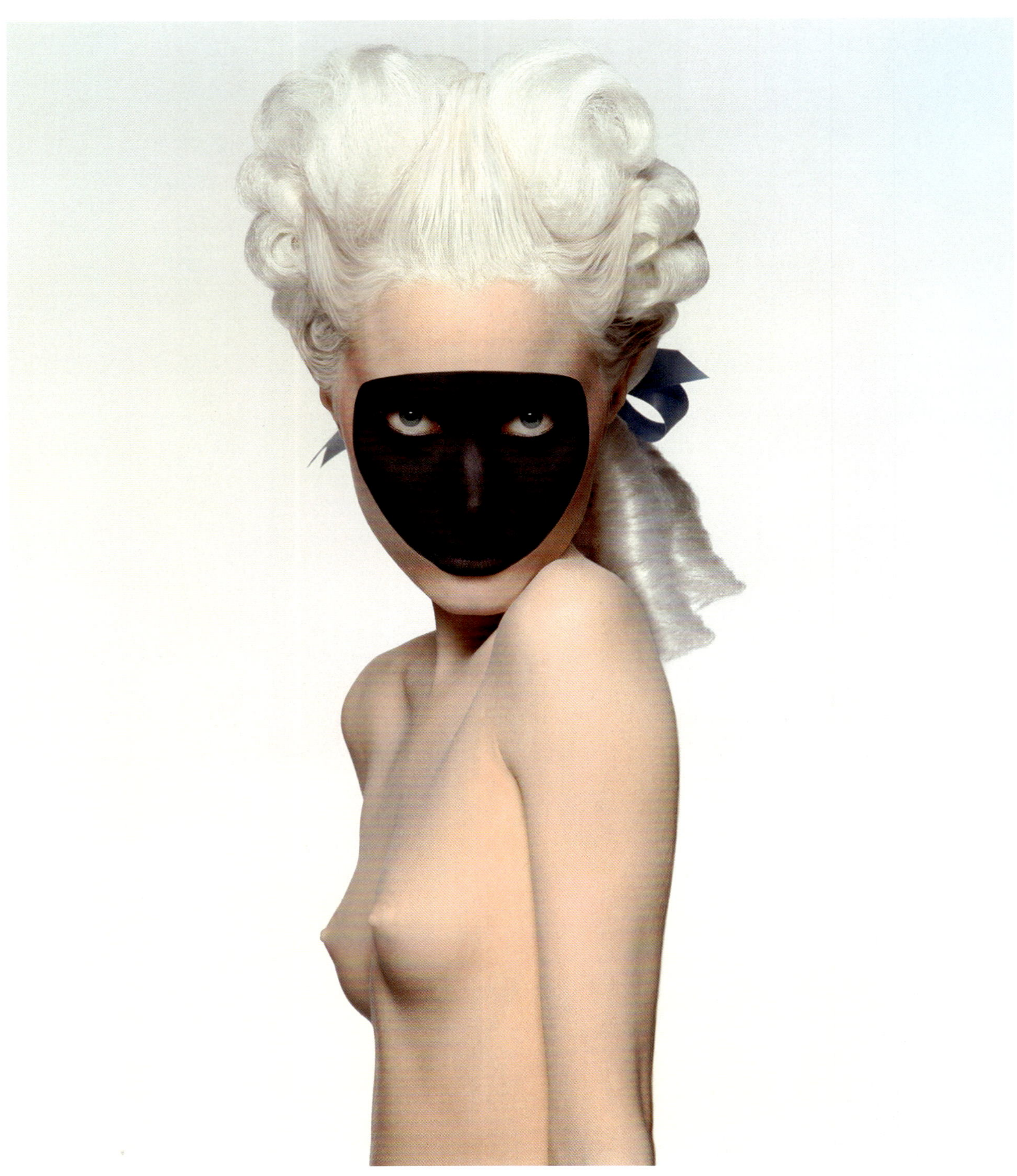

**191** Inez van Lamsweerde (b. 1963)
and Vinoodh Matadin (b. 1961)
*Anastasia,* 2000
C-print in frame of artists, 118 × 104 cm
Private collection
Courtesy of the Gagosian Gallery

# Elfriede Gerstl

*In the middle of despair – this is the place in the fabric, the mesh is missing there, where
a thread does not lie like a leaf of grass, but a blade – there, in the middle of the
publisher's apartment – this is the place where a swastika is carved into the doorframe,
right below the mezuzah, 4<sup>th</sup> ring of the Viennese metropolis –
I met Elfriede Gerstl.*

*I was so young that my words had no importance.
And my corpulence, she found weird, after all she said, what kind of little soul
I seemed to her, like a membrane between always seeing and always blind – said
one who was as tender as a leaf, no, a very sharp blade, on which a hair
almost only splits because of the awe of the possibilities, almost only for fear of torture
by the possibilities.*

*How did she come in? I cannot say.*

*The window was perhaps ajar. This is how the moth
Elfriede Gerstl came into the kitchen like a dream from Escada's great times.
What was spoken? – There, where women once weaved? It was about the flight of
clothes, the book in the making. The publisher, she spoke quickly and
Gerstl looked at me at the same time. We were both silent. After her, no one
has ever told me straight between the eyes that I will play the doll for life.
That was the trick of this poetess.*

*When she died years later, containers were found with Chanel
and dreams of Elfriede Gerstl made of extraordinary fabric.*



---

Nora Gomringer

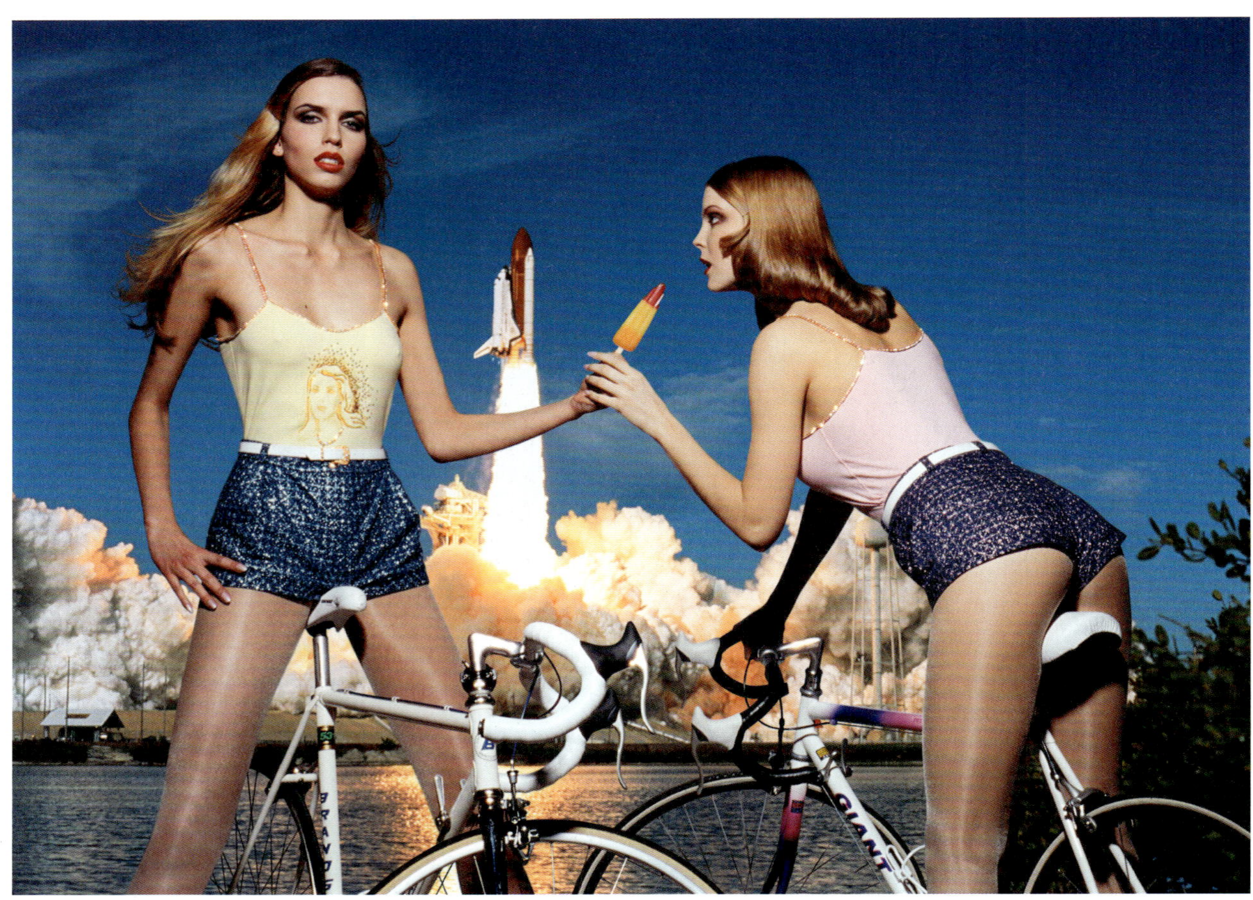

**190** Inez van Lamsweerde (b. 1963) and
Vinoodh Matadin (b. 1961)
*Kym and Zonna. Well, basically basuco
is coke mixed with kerosene,* 1994
Colour photograph, C-print, mounted on
aluminium plate, behind plexiglas, 125 × 183 cm
Collection Nicola von Senger, Switzerland

68  Daniele Buetti (b. 1955)
*A man is his job,* 1993/94
Super-VHS, colour, sound, duration: 4' 24"
Courtesy of the artist

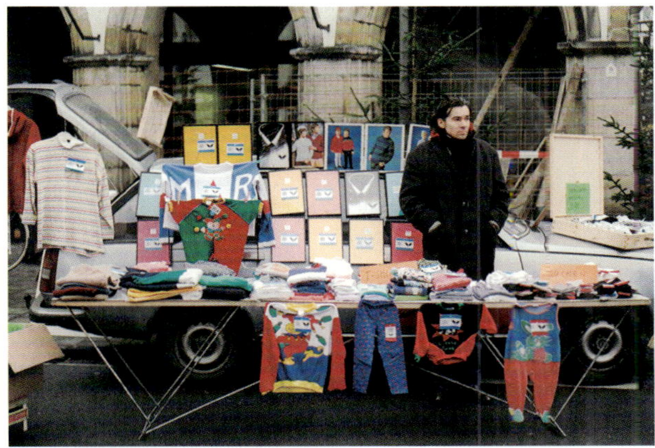

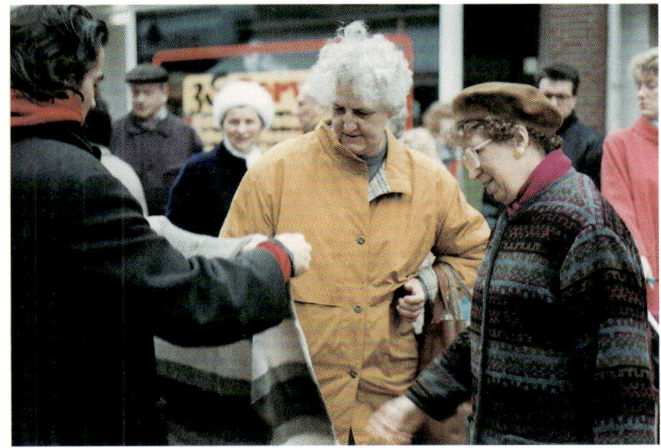

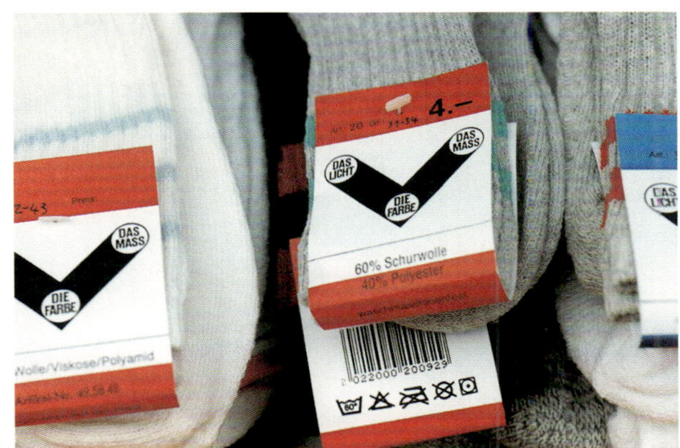

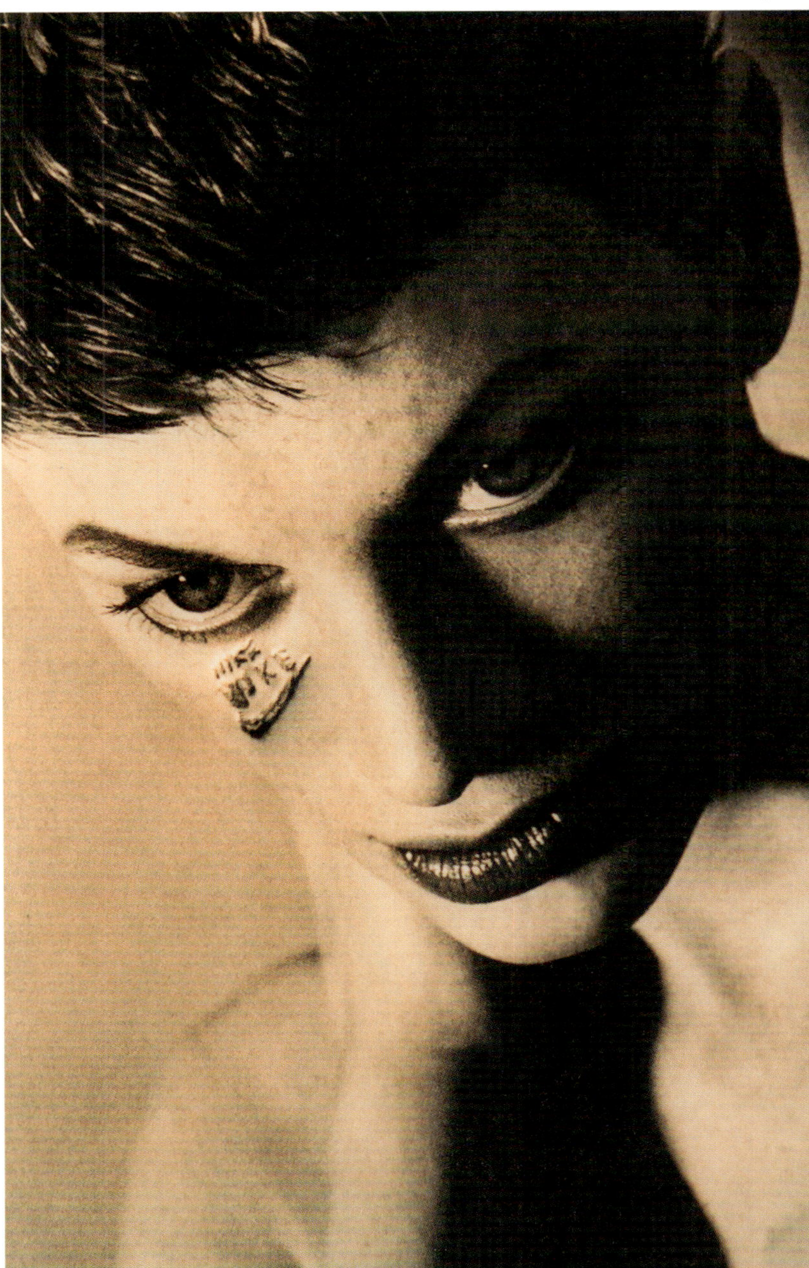

69  Daniele Buetti (b. 1955)
*NIKE,* 1995/2001
C-print, 175 × 123 cm
Kunsthaus Zürich,
Collection of Photography

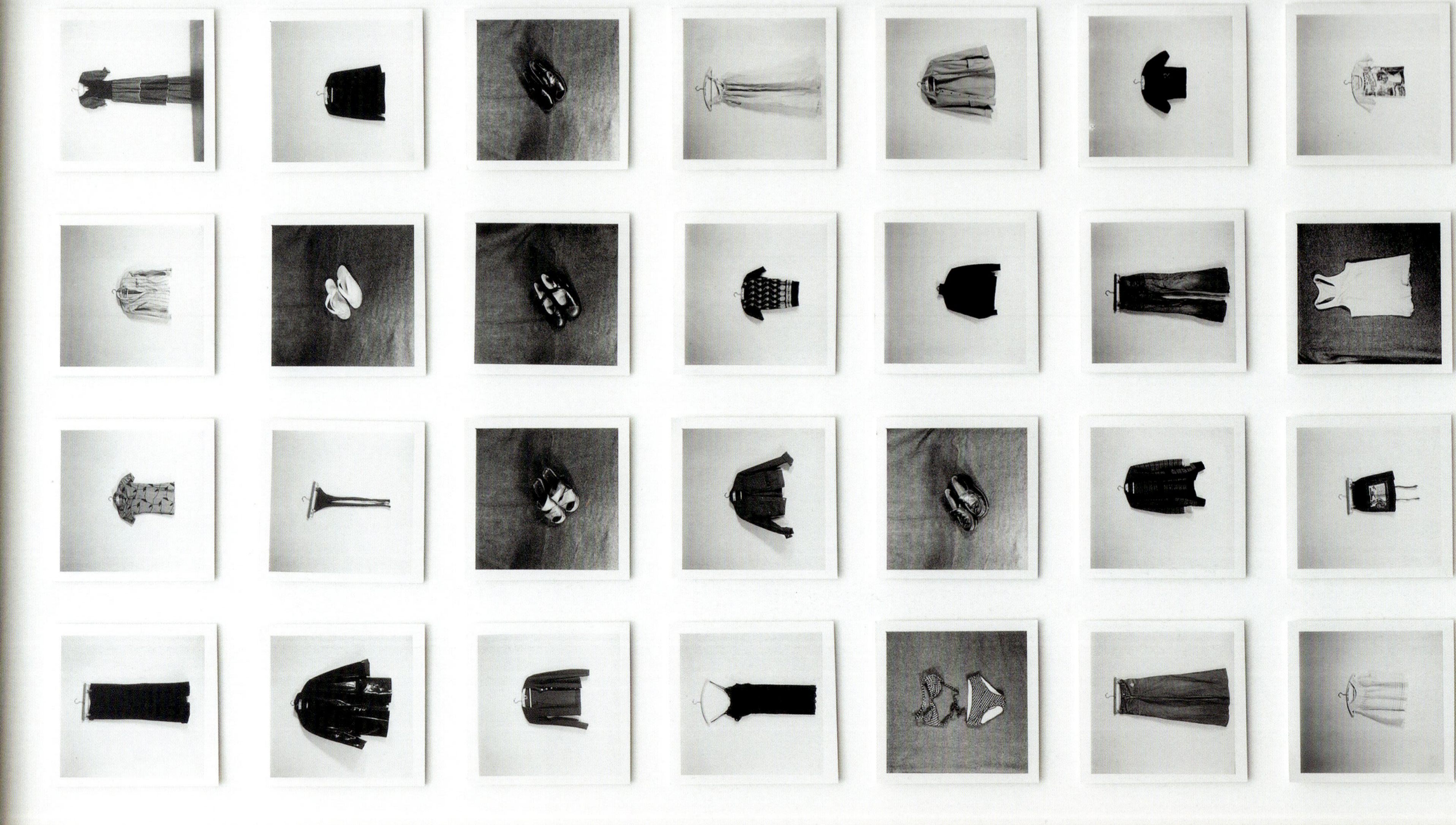

**135**  Hans-Peter Feldmann (b.1941)
*Alle Kleider einer Frau,* 1970
All the clothes of a woman
70 photographs, gelatin silver prints
(individually mounted in object frames)
Images: 10 × 10 cm each
Frame: 78 × 118 cm
Courtesy of the artist and
Galerie Francesca Pia, Zurich

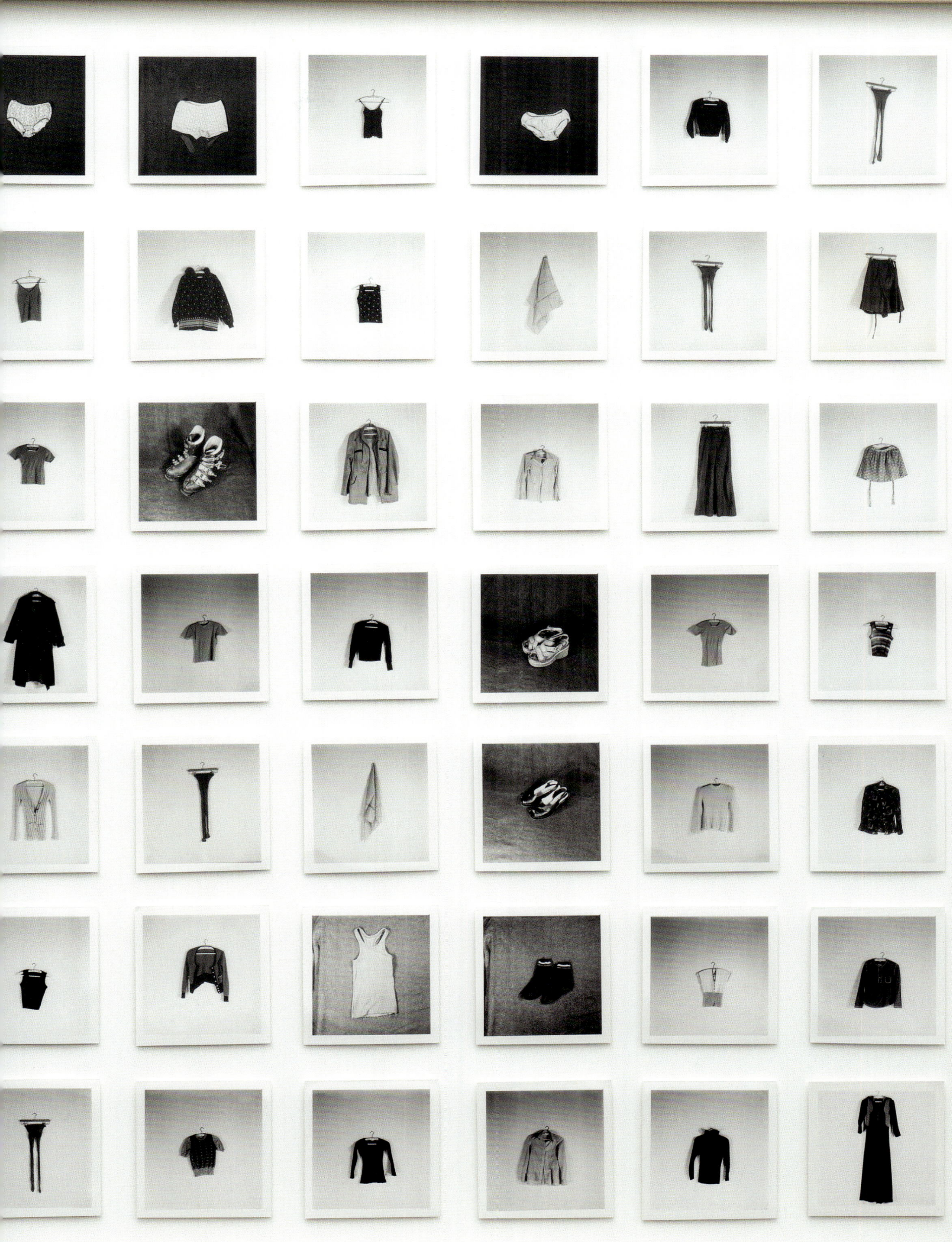

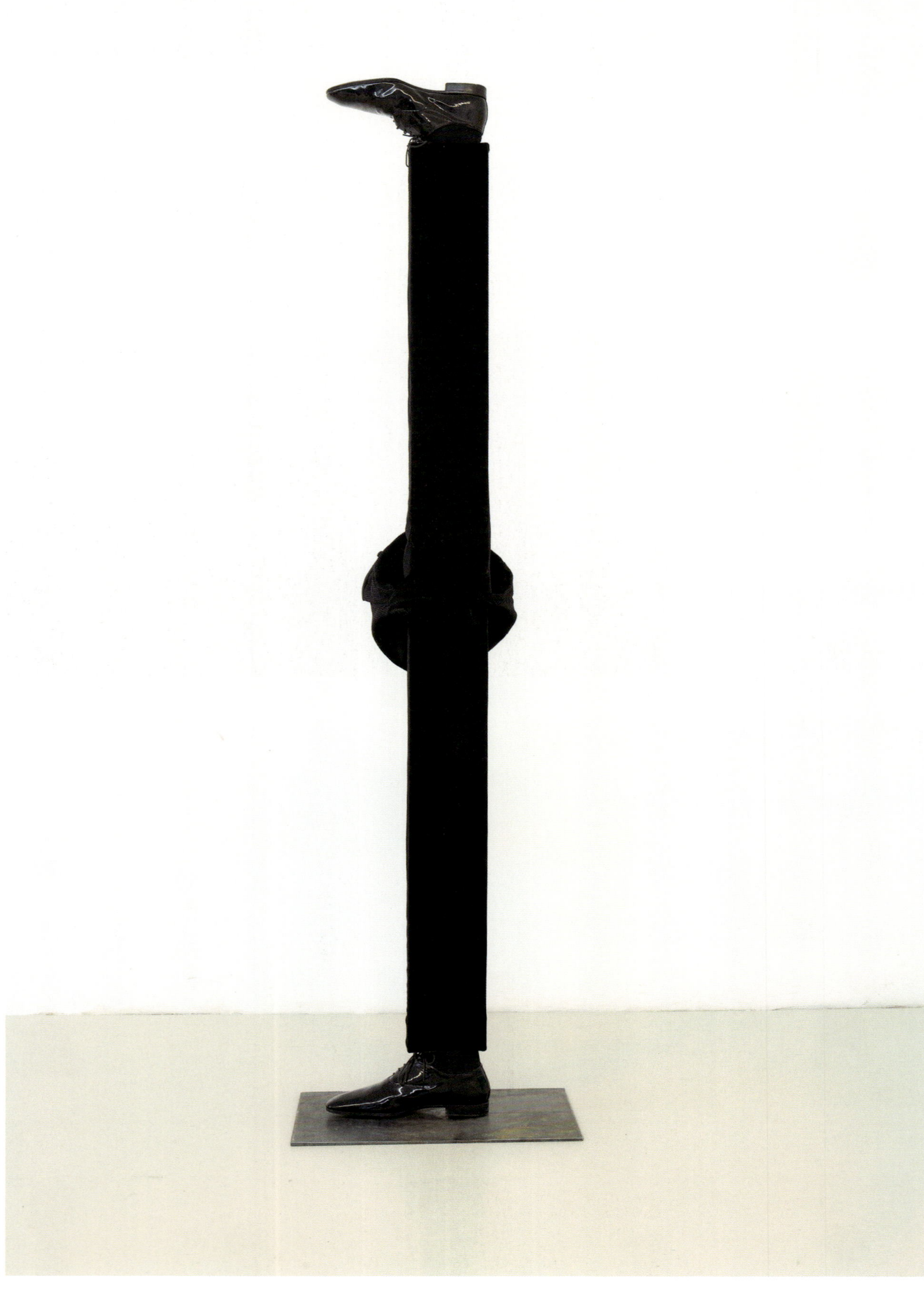

**302** Erwin Wurm (b. 1954)
*Hermès sculpture,* 2008
Wood, resin, clothes, leather,
194 × 33 × 52 cm
Private collection

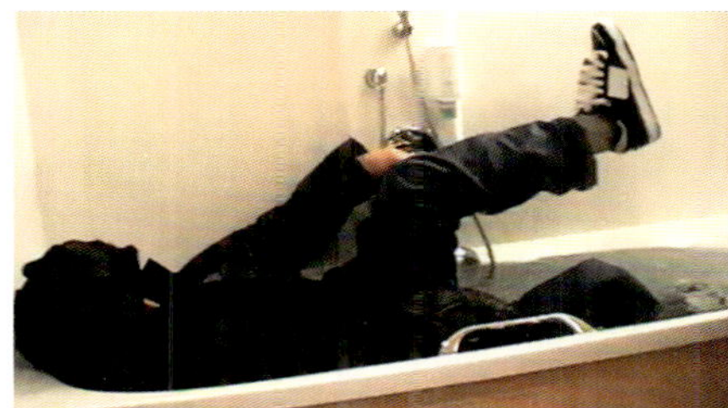

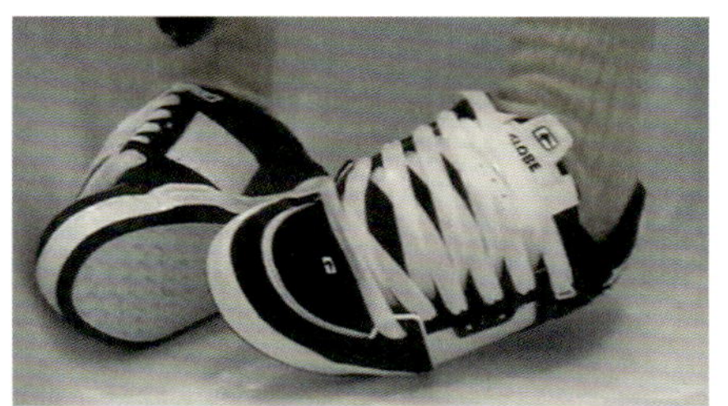

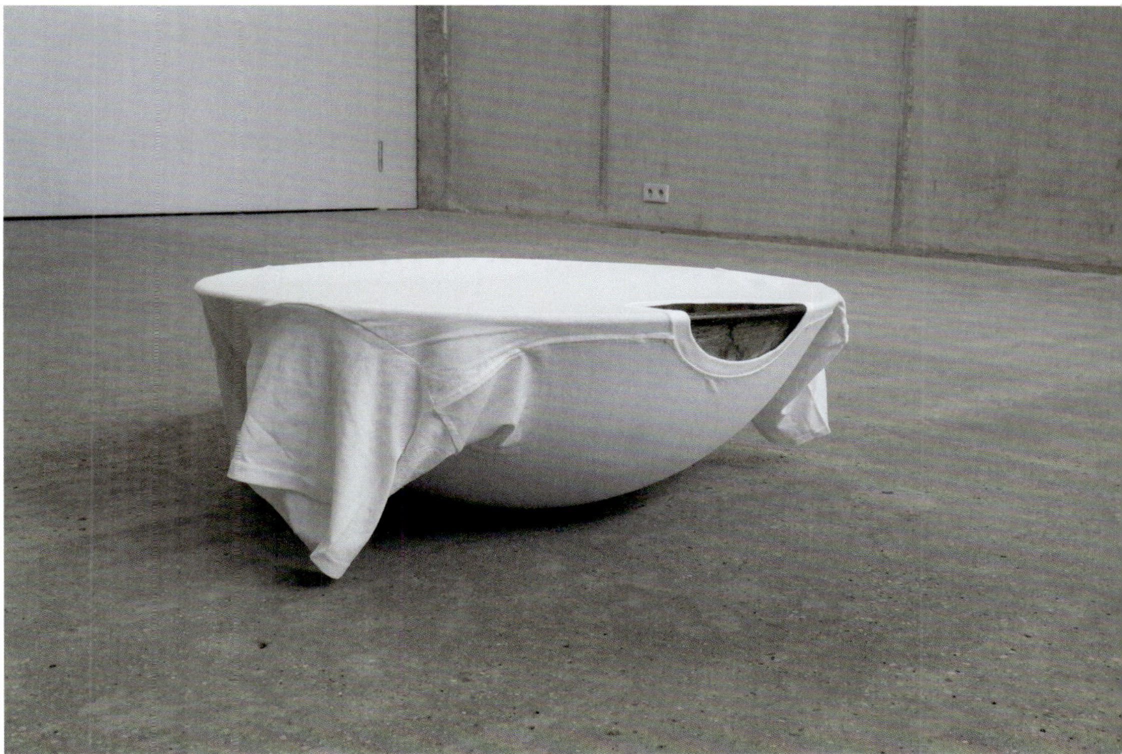

**244** Michael E. Smith (b. 1977)
Stills from *Untitled,* 2015
SD-video, 16:9, found footage,
colour, sound, duration: 9'58"
Courtesy Michael E. Smith and
KOW, Berlin

**243** Michael E. Smith (b. 1977)
*Fat Albert,* 2013
Mixing bowl, T-shirt,
H. 29.5 cm, d. 77 cm
Oehmen Collection

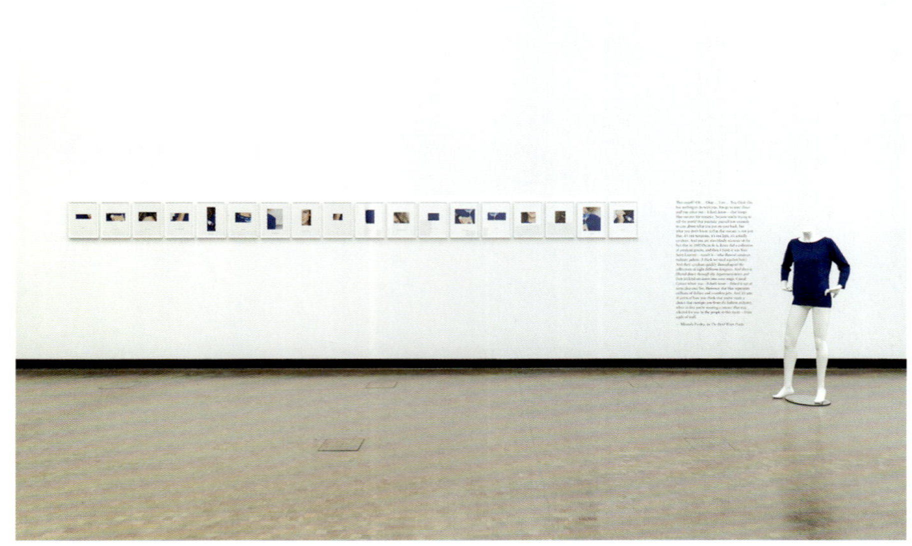

183a  Tobias Kaspar (b. 1984)
*Lumpy blue sweater,* 2010
Installation, consisting of 18 C-prints,
a mannequin with a sweater and booklet,
text layout: Pascal Storz
Frames: 32.5 × 42.5 cm each,
mannequin: 160 × 45 × 60 cm,
text: 120 × 75 cm
Courtesy the artist and
Galerie Peter Kilchmann, Zurich
Exhibition view: *Blue Times,*
Kunsthalle Wien, 2014

183b  Tobias Kaspar (b. 1984)
*The final plot,* part of
*Lumpy blue sweater,* 2010
C-Print, frame: 32.5 × 42.5 cm
Courtesy the artist and
Galerie Peter Kilchmann, Zurich



This ssstuff ? Oh … Okay … I see … You think this
has nothing to do with you. You go to your closet
and you select out—I don't know—that lumpy
blue sweater for instance, because you're trying
to tell the world that you take yourself too seriously
to care about what you put on your back, but
what you don't know is that that sweater is not just
blue, it's not turquoise, it's not lapis, it's actually
cerulean. And you are also blindly unaware of the
fact that in 2002 Oscar de la Renta did a collection
of cerulean gowns, and then I think it was Yves
Saint Laurent—wasn't it—who showed cerulean
military jackets. (I think we need a jacket here.)
And then cerulean quickly showed up in the
collections of eight different designers. And then it
filtered down through the department stores and
then trickled on down into some tragic Casual
Corner where you—I don't know—fished it out of
some clearance bin. However, that blue represents
millions of dollars and countless jobs. And it's sort
of comical how you think that you've made a
choice that exempts you from the fashion industry,
when in fact you're wearing a sweater that was
selected for you by the people in this room—
from a pile of stuff.

— Miranda Presley in the film *The devil wears Prada*
(2006)

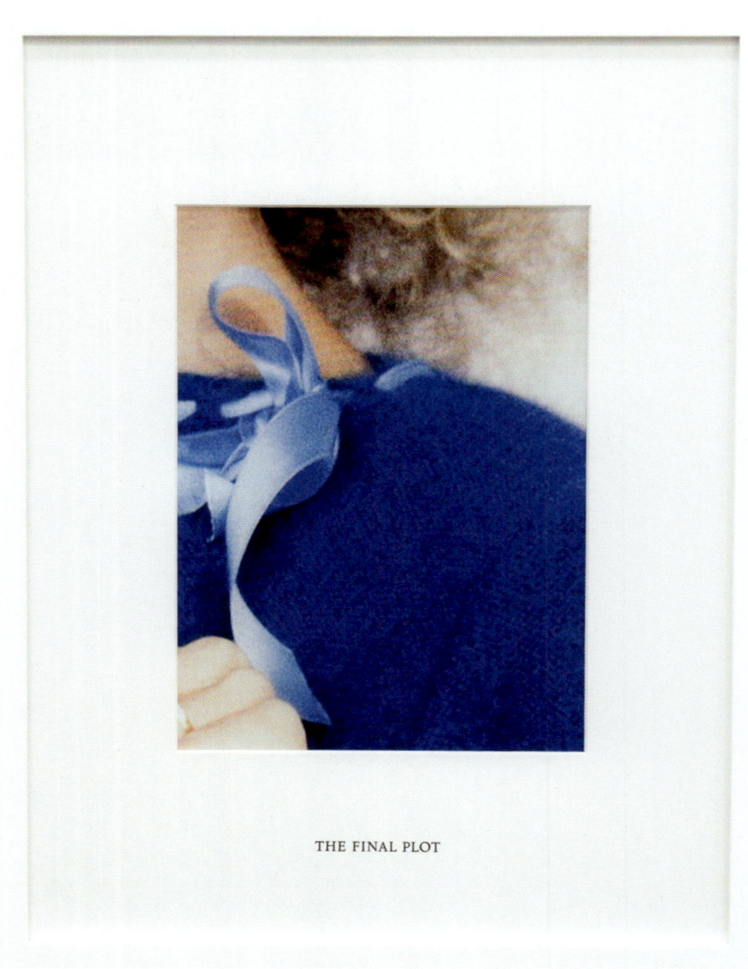

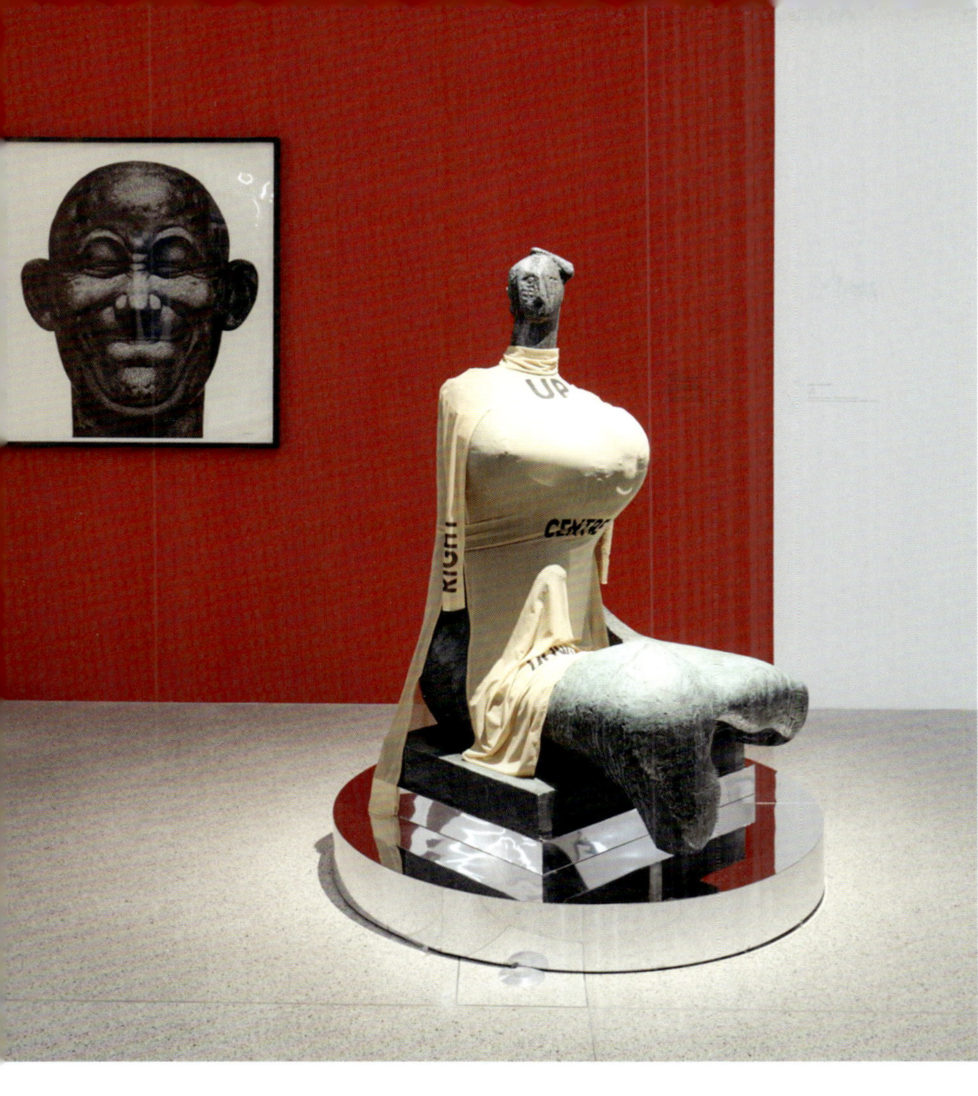

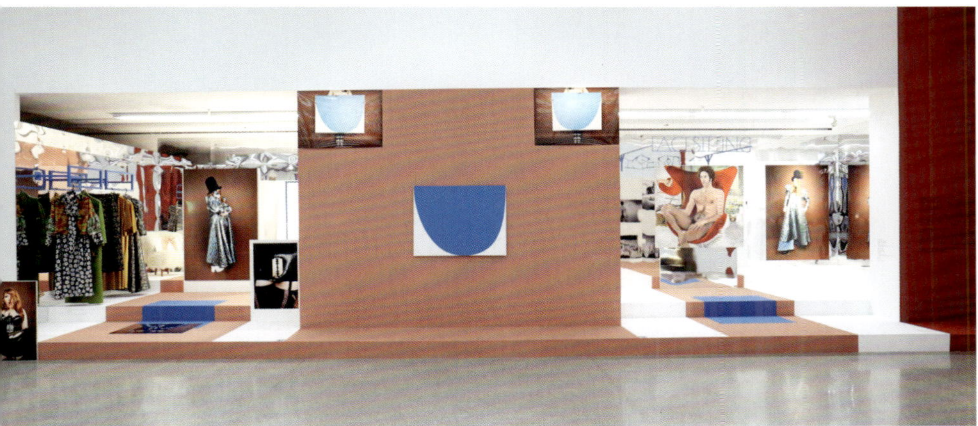

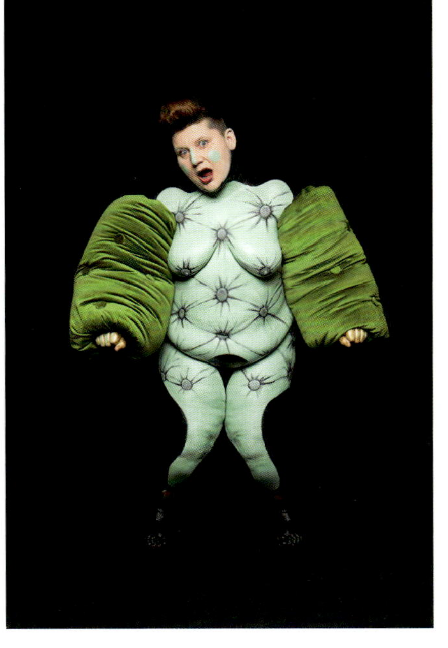



**185** Jakob Lena Knebl (b. 1970)
New work for the exhibition:
*[Space of desire],* 2018
Installation with bronzes from
the Kunsthaus Zürich: Aristide Maillol's
*Vénus au collier* (1918–28), and
Auguste Rodin's *L'âge d'airain* (1875/76)
Courtesy of the artist
Thanks to the generous support of
the Bundeskanzleramt Österreich,
Kunst und Kultur Wien
(no fig.)

**top** Exhibition views:
*Oh … Jakob Lena Knebl and the mumok Collection,*
mumok, Museum moderner Kunst
Stiftung Ludwig Wien, Vienna 2017

Jakob Lena Knebl (*1970)
*Chesterfield,* 2014
Mixed media installation,
dimensions variable
Courtesy Jakob Lena Knebl
Photography: Georg Petermichl

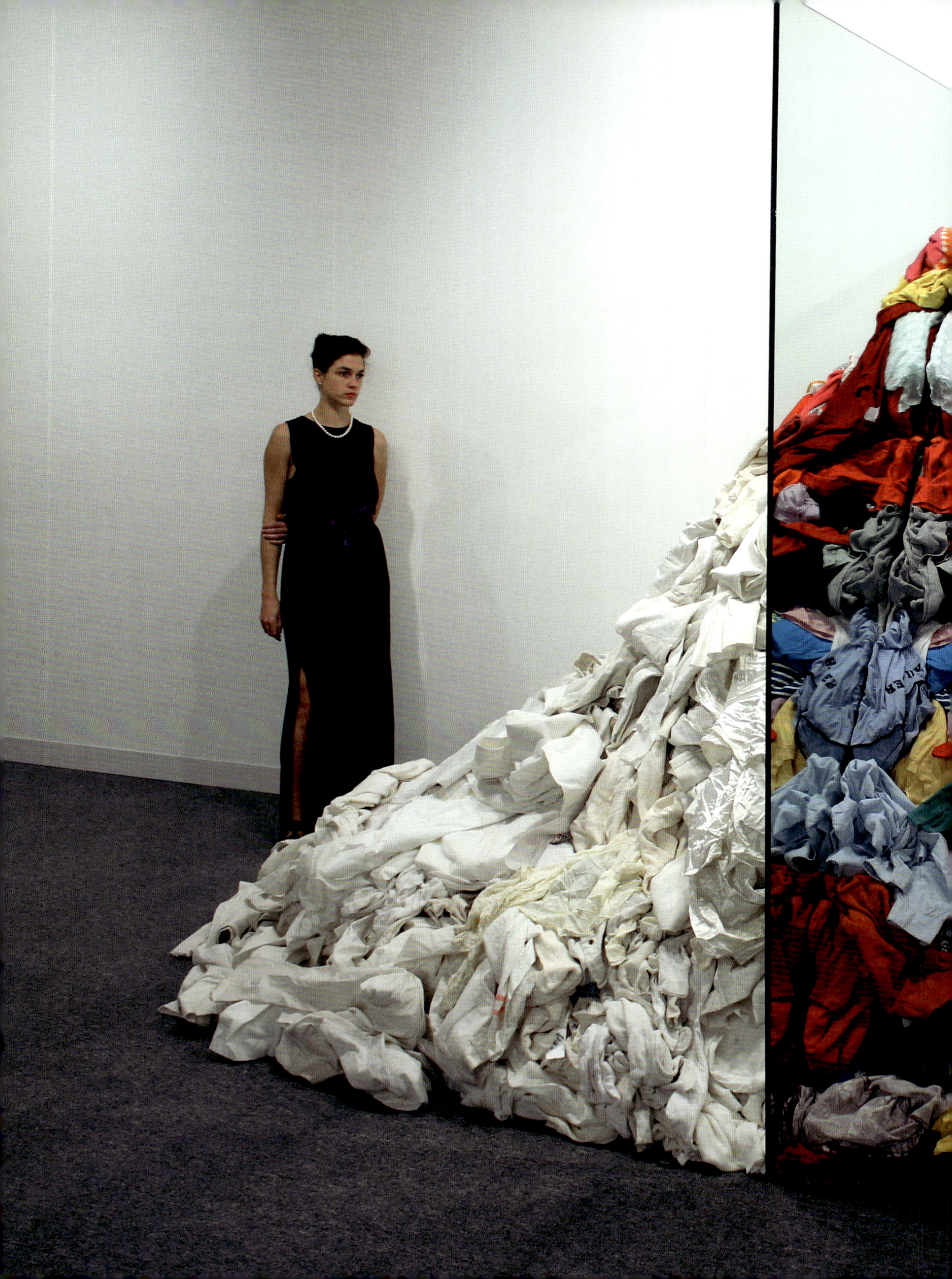

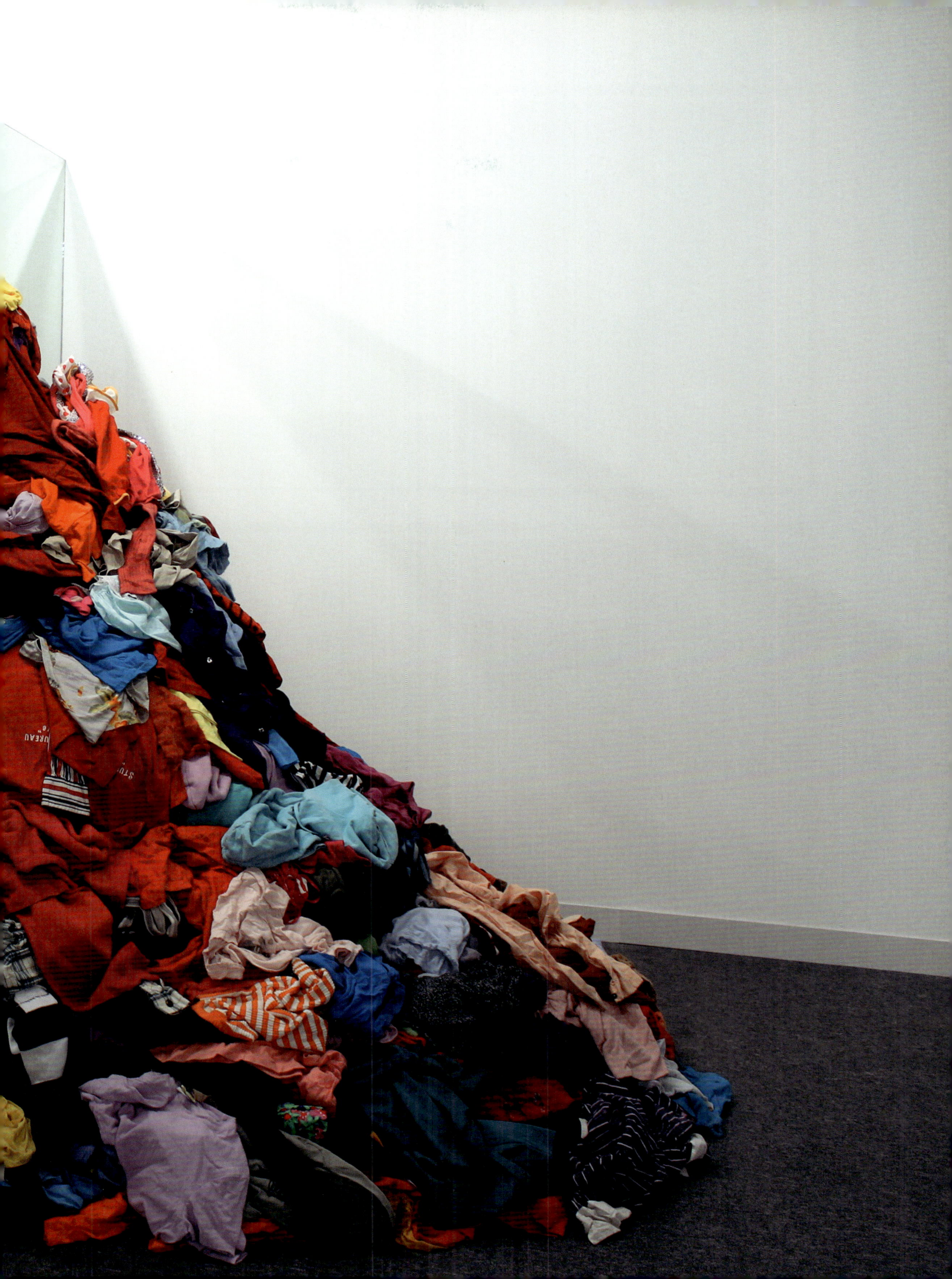

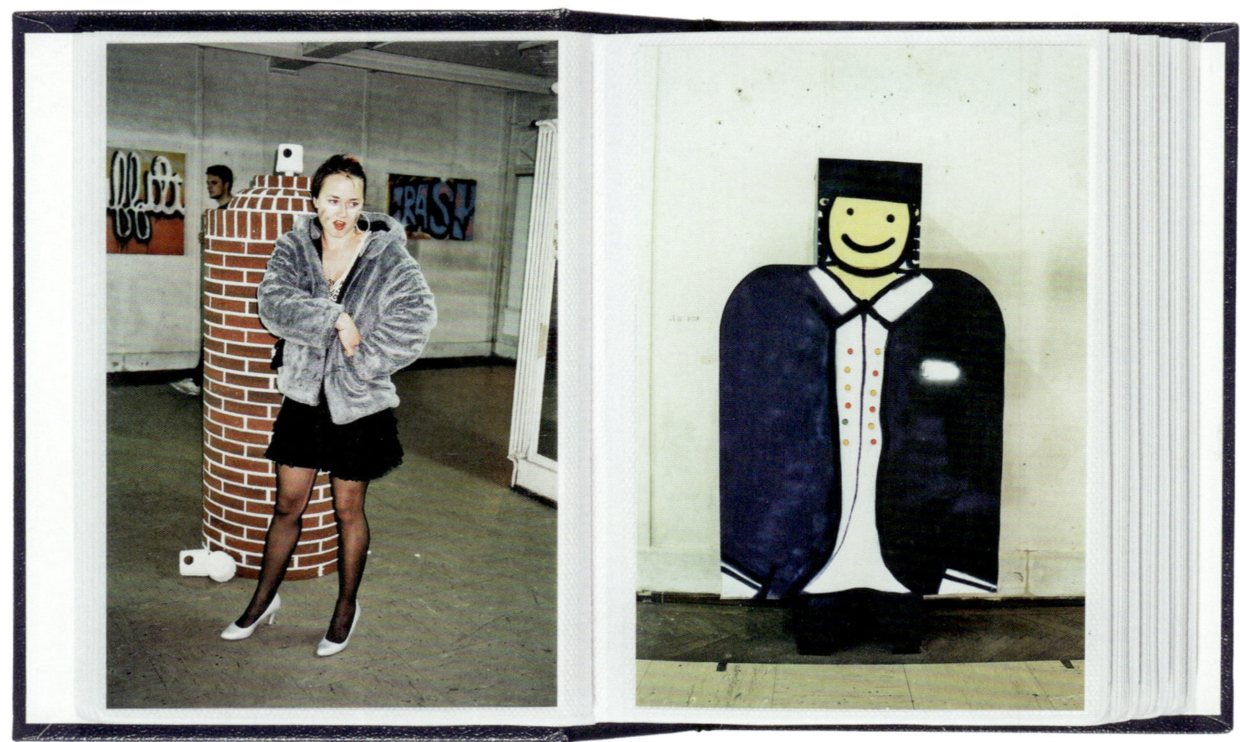

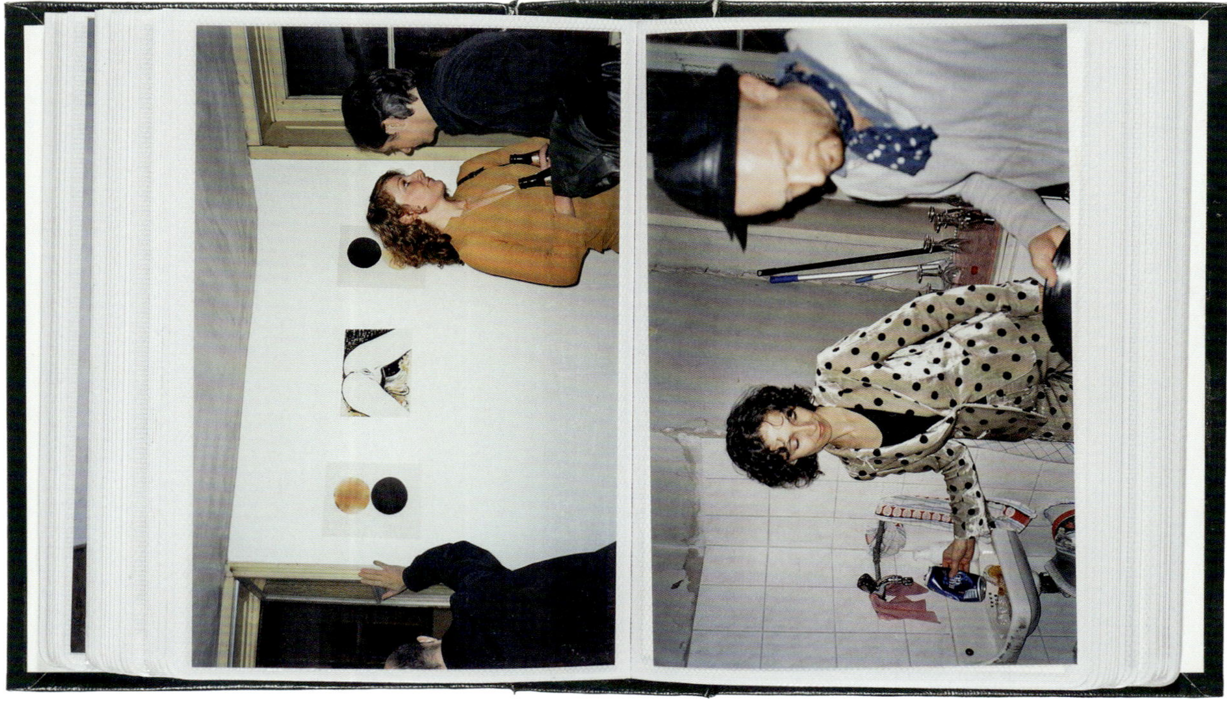





**230** Michelangelo Pistoletto (b. 1933)
*Metamorfosi,* 1976–2016
Mirror, rags, dimensions variable
Courtesy Galleria Continua, San Gimignano/
Beijing/Les Moulins/Habana

**131** Esther Eppstein (b. 1967)
Film stills from *Perla-Mode-Album,* 2016
Message salon chronology September 2006 to December 2013
Video on hard disc of 58 digitalised albums of 100 photographs
each, no sound; repro-photography: Frederic Meyer and
Thomas Züger, video production: Filmerei.ch, duration: c. 300'
Kunsthaus Zürich, Department of Prints and Drawings

*List of
exhibited works*

## Armour

**1**  Page 19
**Kolman Helmschmid (1471–1532),** armourer
Daniel Hopfer (1470–1536), etched decoration
Landsknecht armour of Baron of the Empire
Wilhelm von Rogendorf (1481–1541),
Augsburg 1523
Uncoated iron (with traces of old blueing),
etched ornamentation: filled with black
(traces of former fire gilding), leather
KHM-Museumsverband, Imperial Armoury
Inv. no.: A 374

**2**  Page 25
Armour with pleated skirt of the Margrave
Albrecht von Brandenburg-Ansbach (1490–
1568), Low German (Brunswick) c. 1526
Uncoated iron, partly etched:
with black fillings, leather
KHM-Museumsverband, Imperial Armoury
Inv. no.: A 78

## Historical Costumes, Fashion Photography and Objects

**3**  Page 101
Robe à la française (à grand panier), c. 1765
Brocaded shot silk, with adjustable petticoat,
stomacher recreated
Collection Kamer-Ruf
0380

**4**  Page 100
Habit à la française, c. 1775
Coat and breeches: embroidered uncut velvet,
matching waistcoat: embroidered silk taffeta
Collection Kamer-Ruf
3152

**5**  Page 100
Habit à la française, c. 1775/1780
Probably from the collection of M. Oberkampf,
Jouy-en-Josas
Pink ribbed silk
Collection Kamer-Ruf
3160

**6**  Page 88
Robe à l'anglaise with underskirt, c. 1780
Indienne printed linen
Collection Kamer-Ruf
0530, 0366

**7**  Page 114
'Incroyables' suit, c. 1795
Striped silk coat (steel buttons), breeches,
embroidered waistcoat and under-waistcoat
Collection Kamer-Ruf
3280

**8**  Page 105
**Jacques Grasset de Saint-Saveur
(1757–1810)**
Series of 15 depictions of French municipal
authorities from the time of the Directoire, 1795
Copper engraving on paper, coloured
16.8 × 11.7 cm each
HMB – Historisches Museum Basel
Inv. no.: 2009.629.

**9**  Page 148
Dress coat of the gala uniform of
a Bohemian Landstand, 1800–49
KHM-Museumsverband, Kaiserliche
Wagenburg/Department of Court Uniforms
Inv. no.: MDU 498 1

**10**  Page 149
**Andreas Alkens,** court gold
embroiderer, design
Anton Uzel & Sohn, production
Dress coat of the gala uniform of
an imperial and royal privy councillor
KHM-Museumsverband, Kaiserliche
Wagenburg/Department of Court Uniforms
Inv. no.: MDU 979 1

**11**  Page 149
Bicorn of the gala uniform of
an imperial and royal privy councillor
KHM-Museumsverband, Kaiserliche
Wagenburg/Department of Court Uniforms
Inv. no.: MDU 979 3

**12**  No fig.
Sword of the gala uniform of an imperial
and royal privy councillor
KHM-Museumsverband, Kaiserliche
Wagenburg/Department of Court Uniforms
Inv. no.: MDU 979 4 1

**13**  Page 149
State dress coat, so-called Rococo dress coat,
and Habit à la française, c. 1815
KHM-Museumsverband, Kaiserliche
Wagenburg/Department of Court Uniforms
Inv. no.: MDU 932

**14**  Page 149
Waistcoat for state dress coat, so-called
Rococo dress coat,
and Habit à la française, c. 1815
KHM-Museumsverband, Kaiserliche
Wagenburg/Department of Court Uniforms
Inv. no.: MDU 955

**15**  Page 168
Gentleman's summer top hat,
France c. 1825
Straw
Collection Kamer-Ruf
8467

**16**  Page 182
**Charles Frederick Worth (1825–1895),**
design
Wedding or reception dress, France c. 1878
Labelled: Charles F. Worth
Cream silk faille with silk tassel trim
Collection Kamer-Ruf
1465

**17**  Page 204
Doll's house: gentlemen's outfitters,
France c. 1880
Three-part with round arch joints, papered
floor, patterned in black and brown, light blue
painted walls with sewn-on men's clothing,
two blue wooden counters and two dressed
porcelain dolls, completely furnished
27.5 × 71 × 19.5 cm
Spielzeug Welten Museum Basel

**18**  Page 204
Doll's house: fashion accessories,
Germany c. 1900
37 × 72 × 30 cm
Spielzeug Welten Museum Basel

**19**  Page 207
**A. Bergeret et Cie, Nancy,** publisher
*La Journée de la parisienne,* c. 1900
The day of the parisian woman
10 black-and-white postcards, phototype
14 × 9 cm each
Private collection

**20**  Page 211
**Henry van de Velde (1863–1957) and
Peter Behrens (1868–1940),** design
Photographs of selected clothing designed by
Peter Behrens and Henry van de Velde
In Henry van de Velde, 'Das neue Kunst-Prinzip
in der modernen Frauen-Kleidung',
in *Deutsche Kunst und Dekoration,*
vol. 10, 1902, no. 5, pp. 363–386
Kunsthaus Zürich, Library
Per 38: 106 (1902)

**21**  Page 210
**Anna Muthesius (1870–1961),** design
Photographs of selected clothing designed
by Anna Muthesius
In *Das Eigenkleid der Frau,* Krefeld 1903,
Additionally presented in the exhibition
as a digital image series
Zurich University of the Arts, ZHdK/
Media and Information Centre MIZ
ZHDK-MIZ 9000-585

**22**  Pages 212/213
**Emilie Flöge (1874–1952),** design
Gustav Klimt (1862–1918), photography
Klimt's photographs of reform dresses of his
companion Flöge, Litzlberg am Attersee 1906
In *Deutsche Kunst und Dekoration,* vol. XIX,
1906/07, illustrations from pp. 69/70
Additionally presented in the exhibition as
a digital image series, pp. 62–73
Kunsthaus Zürich, Library
Per 37:19 (1906)

**23**  Page 212
**Unknown photographer**
Photograph of Gustav Klimt and Emilie Flöge
In a passe-partout typical for the current
prevailing taste of 1900
Ferrotype, 9 × 6 cm
Private collection, Vienna

**24**  Page 212
**Unknown designer**
Tunic for Gustav Klimt
Use of probably a North African fabric
From the textile collection of Emilie Flöge,
fashion designer and companion
of Gustav Klimt
Private collection, Vienna

**25**  Page 219
**Madeleine Vionnet (1876–1975),** design
Black tango dress with open back, France 1917
Liquid silk
Martin Kamer

**26**  Page 214
Day dress with belt, Wiener Werkstätte,
Austria c. 1920
Not labelled
Fabric design: *Kanarienvogel*
by Mitzi Vogel, 1915
Printed silk
Collection Kamer-Ruf
2155

**Elsa Schiaparelli (1890–1973)**

**27**  Page 235
Cravat (jumper), 1927
Wool, hand-knitted
V&A, London, Textiles and Fashion Collection
Mus. no.: T.388-1974

**28**  Page 239
Cecil Beaton (1904–1980), photography
Wallis Simpson (later Duchess of Windsor)
wearing the 'Lobster' dress, designed by
Elsa Schiaparelli in collaboration with
Salvador Dalí for the summer collection 1937
In *Vogue,* June–August 1937, pp. 54/55
Gewerbemuseum Basel,
Museum für Gestaltung
W43L5, Inv. no. 4939

**29**  No fig.
**Christian Dior (1905–1957),** design
Sante Forlano (1924–1973), photography
Fashion photograph of a model in the fabric of
the company Abraham AG (1941–2002), Zurich
Dress designed in 1955 by the couturier
Christian Dior. Calf-length, dome-shaped
cocktail dress with rose warp print;
the décolleté is designed similar to a fichu,
the skirt seems to be shaped by a knot at
the hip; in addition, the model wears
a headdress and gloves
Black-and-white photograph,
on photo paper, 37.2 × 27.3 cm
Schweizerisches Nationalmuseum, Zurich
Inv. no.: LM-112085.55

**Abraham AG (1941–2002)**

**30**  Page 216 top
Pattern book with fabrics by the Abraham
company from winter 1953/54, 1955
On each page, a type of fabric in diverse colour
combinations is presented,
including the indication of quality, name,
design number etc.
76 pages with fabric patterns from
embroidered organza, organza with warp
print and taffeta with warp print; hardcover,
binding: linen, book cover: cardboard
50 × 37.2 × 7.6 cm
Schweizerisches Nationalmuseum, Zurich
Inv. no.: LM-114401.1

**31**  Page 216 centre
Scrapbook, 1971/72
Collected press cuttings about topics related
to the Abraham company from summer 1971
to summer 1972
179 pages; paper, hardcover, pasted,
cover: linen
51 × 43.5 × 7 cm
Schweizerisches Nationalmuseum, Zurich
Inv. no.: LM-110496.13

**32**  Pages 12/13
Scrapbook, 1991–96
Collected press cuttings about topics related
to the Abraham company from autumn 1991
to winter 1995/96
231 pages; paper, hardcover, pasted,
binding: linen
51 × 43 × 6.5 cm
Schweizerisches Nationalmuseum, Zurich
Inv. no.: LM-110496.20

**33**  Page 216 bottom
Collection reference book with fabrics
by the Abraham company from
winter 1993/94, 1995
One double page per fabric  Left: folded
repeat pattern of the collection fabric; right:
small design coupons in several colours,
mounted on paper; inscript on: article number,
name of collection. indication of quality,
fabric width, weight
Paper, hardcover, binding: linen,
cover: cardboard
50 × 37 × 7 cm
Schweizerisches Nationalmuseum, Zurich
Inv. no.: LM-115203.1

**Malcolm McLaren (1946–2010) and
Vivienne Westwood (b. 1941)**

**34**  Page 260 upper left
'Venus' T-Shirt, 1975
Labelled: Let It Rock
Black cotton jersey, the armholes edged
with studded rubber tyre bands with
black horsehair fringes, two diagonal zips
placed over the breasts, adorned with chains
and assorted badges, 'Venus' written
in metal studs
Collection of Kim Jones

**35**  Page 260 upper right
Sleeveless, cropped T-Shirt, c. 1976
Labelled: Sex
Collection of Kim Jones

**36**  Page 260 lower left
Short-sleeved T-shirt incorporating a
Jim French illustration from 1969, c. 1976
Labelled: Seditionaries
Collection of Kim Jones

**37**  No fig.
'God Save The Queen' muslin top, 1977
Labelled: Seditionaries
Muslin top featuring Jamie Reid's graphic
and lyrics for the Sex Pistols track
Courtesy Young Kim,
Estate of Malcolm McLaren

**38**  Page 260 lower right
'Witches' sweater and skirt with
Keith Haring print, 1983
Labelled: World's End
Collection of Kim Jones

**39**  No fig.
**Malcolm McLaren (1946–2010) and
Jamie Reid (b. 1947)**
*Anarchy in the U.K. Sex Pistols,* No. 1
(the one and only issue)
Produced for the Pistols' first UK tour,
commencing September 1976
Zine cover featuring Soo Catwoman in
a photograph by Ray Stevenson, 1976
Zine, lithograph, 12 pages
45.1 × 31.8 cm
Courtesy Young Kim,
Estate of Malcolm McLaren

**40**  Page 262
**Malcolm McLaren (1946–2010)**
*Duck Rock,* 2008
A fashion retrospective featuring excerpts
from the catwalk shows of McLaren/Westwood
Worlds End fashion collections: 'Savages' (1981)
and 'Witches' (1983)
Arranged by Malcolm McLaren
Video, colour, Duration: 4'49"
Courtesy Young Kim,
Estate of Malcolm McLaren

**Vivienne Westwood (b. 1941)**

**41**  Page 115
Corset from the 'Portrait Collection',
spring/summer 1990, production 1990
With a depiction of François Boucher's
painting of Daphnis and Chloe printed on front
panel. Shoulder straps feature classical motifs
Polyamide, polyester, Lycra, size 12
V&A, London, Textiles and Fashion Collection;
Purchased with the assistance of The Art Fund,
the Friends of the V&A, the Elsbeth Evans
Trust, and the Dorothy Hughes Bequest
Mus. no.: T.216-2002

**42**  Page 68
Red dress from the
'Cut, Slash & Pull Collection',
spring/summer 1990, production 1991
V&A, London, Textiles and Fashion Collection;
Given by Vivienne Westwood
Mus. no.: T.187:1 to 3-1991

# *Artworks*

**43**   Page 70
**Hans von Aachen (1552–1615)**
*Archduchess Anna (1585–1618), daughter of Archduke Ferdinand II, Territorial Prince of Tyrol, spouse of Emperor Matthias,* 1604
Oil on canvas, 58 × 48 cm
KHM-Museumsverband, Picture Gallery
Inv. no.: GG 4410

**Hans Asper (1499–1571)**

**44**   Page 58
*Portrait of Cleophea Krieg von Bellikon,* 1538
Tempera and oil on wood, 77 × 61 cm
Kunsthaus Zürich, Keller Collection, 1854
158

**45**   Page 58
*Portrait of a Gentleman: Wilhelm Frölich. with the Frölich family's coat of arms and upper coat of arms,* Solothurn 1549
Oil and tempera on wood, 213 × 111 cm
Schweizerisches Nationalmuseum, Zurich
Inv. no.: LM-8622.

**46**   Page 263
**Charles Atlas (b. 1949)**
*The Legend of Leigh Bowery,* 1980s/2002
Video and Super8 on DVD, colour,
sound Duration: 82'
EAI, New York

**47**   Page 190
**John Baldessari (b. 1931)**
*Double Bill: … And Manet,* 2012
Varnished inkjet print on canvas
with acrylic and oil paint, 152.4 × 152.4 cm
Courtesy the artist and
Marian Goodman Gallery, New York
13647

**Giacomo Balla (1871–1958)**

**48**   Page 223
*Studio per motivo di stoffa,* 1913
Study for fabric design
Watercolour on paper
Sheet: 13 × 19 cm
Biagiotti Cigna Foundation
BG/18

**49**   Page 224
*Studio per motivo di stoffa,* 1913
Study for fabric design
Watercolour on paper
Sheet: 13 × 19 cm
Biagiotti Cigna Foundation
BG/19

**50**   Page 224
*Studio per motivo di stoffa,* 1913
Study for fabric design
Watercolour on paper
Sheet: 13 × 19 cm
Biagiotti Cigna Foundation
BG/20

**51**   Page 224
*Bozzetto per vestito da uomo,* 1914
Study for man's suit
Watercolour on paper
Sheet: 29 × 21 cm
Biagiotti Cigna Foundation
BG/21

**52**   Page 224
*Bozzetto per vestito da uomo,* 1914
Study for man's suit
Watercolour on paper
Sheet: 29 × 21 cm
Biagiotti Cigna Foundation
BG/22

**53**   Page 223
*Bozzetto per vestito da uomo,* 1914
Study for man's suit
Watercolour on paper
Sheet: 29 × 21 cm
Biagiotti Cigna Foundation
BG/23

**54**   Page 222
*Le Vêtement masculin futuriste. Manifeste,* Milan 1914
Futurist Men's Apparel. Manifesto
23.3 × 29.4 cm
Kunsthaus Zürich, Library,
Gift of Benedetta Marinetti, Rome 1951
Br 615:20

**55**   Page 225
*Modello di golf motivi prismatici,* 1930
Golf model with prismatic motifs
Tempera, pencil and Chinese ink on paper
Sheet: 22 × 15.5 cm
Biagiotti Cigna Foundation
BG/74

**56**   Page 225
*Modello di golf per tennis,* 1930
Golf model for tennis
Tempera, pencil and Chinese ink on paper
Sheet: 22 × 15.5 cm
Biagiotti Cigna Foundation
BG/79

**57**   Page 225
*Vestito di luce,* 1930
Dress from light
Farbric, clasp from enamelled wood
121 × 141 cm
Biagiotti Cigna Foundation
BG/450

**58**   Page 225
*Modello di golf futurfascista,* 1930
Golf model future fascist
Tempera, pencil and Chinese ink on paper
Sheet: 22 × 15.5 cm
Biagiotti Cigna Foundation
BG/457

**Joseph Beuys (1921–1986)**

**59**   Page 240
*Filzanzug,* 1970
Felt suit
Wool felt, sewn
c. 170 × 60 cm
Collection Ph. Konzett, Vienna

**60**   Page 240
*Das Orwell-Bein. Hose für das 21. Jahrhundert,* 1984
The Orwell leg: Trousers for the 21st century
Jeans with circular holes
Collection Ph. Konzett, Vienna

**61**   Page 171
**Cornelis Bisschop (1630–1674),** attributed
*Interieur mit Jacke auf einem Stuhl,*
undated (c. 1660?)
Interior with jacket on a chair
Oil on canvas
43.5 × 36.5 cm
Staatliche Museen zu Berlin, Gemäldegalerie
Id. no.: 912D

**62**   Page 227
**Erwin Blumenfeld (1897–1969)**
*Bloomfield, President-Dada-Chaplinist,* 1921
Collage with portrait photograph by Blumenfeld, halftone printing and Chinese ink on photograph of a female nude
Sheet: 13.4 × 8.8 cm
Kunsthaus Zürich,
Department of Prints and Drawings
Z.1980/0026

**Giovanni Boldini (1842–1931)**

**63**   Page 206
*A l'opera di Parigi,* 1886
At the Opera in Paris
Oil on canvas, 87.5 × 39 cm
Private collection
Courtesy Jean-Luc Baroni Ltd., London

**64**   Page 176
*Le Comte Robert de Montesquiou (1855–1921),* 1897
The Count Robert de Montesquiou (1855–1921)
Oil on canvas, 115.5 × 82.5 cm
Paris, Musée d'Orsay, don d'Henri Pinard
au nom du comte Robert de Montesquiou, 1922
RF 1977-56

**65**   Page 177
*Portrait de Georges Goursat dit Sem,* 1902
Portrait of Georges Goursat known as Sem
Oil on canvas, 91 × 73 cm
Musée des Arts décoratifs, Paris
37353

**66**   Page 208
**Pierre Bonnard (1867–1947)**
*Panneaux décoratifs – Femmes au jardin,* 1890/91
Decorative panneaux – women in the garden
Distemper on charcoal, pencil and white chalk on paper, mounted on canvas, 154 × 47 cm each
Kunsthaus Zürich,
Vereinigung Zürcher Kunstfreunde,
donated in memory of Ernst Gamper, 1984
1982/24.a–d

**67** Page 108
**Louis-Auguste Brun known as
Brun de Versoix (1758–1815)**
*Portrait équestre de la reine Marie-Antoinette
en costume de chasse montant un cheval
portant le harnachement des Gardes-Nobles
Hongrois à la Cour d'Autriche,* 1783
Equestrian portrait of Queen Marie-
Antoinette in a hunting outfit on a horse with
the harness of the Hungarian Noble Guards at
the Austrian court
Oil on canvas, 59 × 64.5 cm
Musée national des châteaux de Versailles
et de Trianon
MV 5718

**Daniele Buetti (b. 1955)**

**68** Page 295
*A man in his job,* 1993/94
Super-VHS, colour, sound
Duration: 4' 24"
Courtesy the artist

**69** Page 295
*NIKE,* 1995/2001
C-Print, 175 × 123 cm
Kunsthaus Zürich,
Collection of Photography
PH 2001/10

**70** Page 274
*Exercise in futility?,* 2016
Perforated photograph in light box
Photograph: 50 × 40 cm
Light box: 51.5 × 41.5 × 7 cm
Courtesy Feldbusch Wiesner Rudolph Galerie

**71** Page 274
*You are condemned to know me,
motherfucker,* 2016
Perforated photography in light box
Photograph: 50 × 40 cm
Light box: 51.5 × 41.5 × 7 cm
Courtesy Feldbusch Wiesner Rudolph Galerie

**72** Page 283
*No Face. David Beckham,* 2017
Photo collage, 89.5 × 73.5 cm
Courtesy the artist

**73** Page 283
*No Face. Kate Moss,* 2017
Photo collage, 89.5 × 73.5 cm
Courtesy the artist

**74** Page 188
**Joseph Cajetan (1821–1864),** after
Andreas Geiger (1765–1856), engraver
Bureau of the Theaterzeitung,
Vienna, publisher
*Fort mit Schaden!
Gänzlicher Ausverkauf!,* 1842
Away with damage! Total sale!
Copper engraving, coloured with watercolours
Plate: 24.2 × 21 cm
Sheet: 24.5 × 21.4 cm
Staatliche Museen zu Berlin, Kunstbibliothek
Id. no.: 14155279,T,008

**75** Page 237
**Paul Camenisch (1893–1970)**
*Café Commerce Suisse,* 1928
Oil on canvas, 115 × 140 cm
Collection Pictet

**76** Page 50
**Joos van Cleve (1485–1541)**
*Lucretia,* 1515/1518
Oil on oak, 47.7 × 35.3 cm
Kunsthaus Zürich,
The Ruzicka Foundation, 1949
R 6

**77** Page 59
**Alonso Sánchez Coello (1531/32–1588)**
*Infant Don Carlos (1545–1538),* 1564
Oil on canvas, 186 × 82.5 cm
KHM-Museumsverband, Picture Gallery
Inv. no.: GG 3235

**78** Page 173
**John Cook,** engraver
Richard Bentley (1794–1871), publisher
*Beau Brummell,* published in 1844
Stipple and engraving
Sheet: 18.2 × 11.8 cm
Lent by the National Portrait Gallery, London;
Given by Henry Witte Martin, 1861
NPG No D1124

**79** Page 173
**R. H. Cooke,** etcher
*Beau Brummell,* nineteenth century
Etching
Sheet: 21.9 × 13.7 cm
Lent by the National Portrait Gallery, London;
Purchased with help from the Friends of the
National Libraries and the Pilgrim Trust, 1966
NPG No D7812

**80** Page 74
**Gonzales Coques (1614–1684)**
*Charles I of England and Queen Henrietta
Maria,* undated
Oil on oak, c. 45.5 × 78.5 cm
V&A, London, Prints, Drawings & Paintings
Collection; Bequeathed by Rev. Chauncey
Hare Townshend
Mus. no.: 1342-1869

**George Cruikshank (1792–1878)**

**81** Page 127
*Monstrosities of 1816,* 12 March 1816
Etching, coloured
Sheet: 25 × 35.4 cm
Staatliche Museen zu Berlin, Kunstbibliothek
Id. no.: 14155039

**82** Page 127
G. Humphrey, publisher
*Monstrosities of 1821,* 20 May 1821
Etching, hand-coloured with watercolours
Sheet: 25.3 × 35.2 cm
Staatliche Museen zu Berlin, Kunstbibliothek
Id. no.: 14155047

**83** Page 125
G. Humphrey, publisher
*Anglo-Gallic salutations in London,*
6 June 1822
Etching, hand-coloured with watercolours
Sheet: 25.7 × 34.9 cm
Staatliche Museen zu Berlin, Kunstbibliothek
Id. no.: 14155286,T,004

**84** Page 173
Ponthieu, publisher
*Neckclothitania*
Illustration in *Cravatiana Ou Traité
Général Des Cravates: Considérées
Dans Leur Origine, Leur Influence Politique,
Physique Et Morale, Leur Formes,
Leurs Couleurs Et Leurs Espèces,
Ouvrage Traduit Librement De L'Anglais Sur
La Huitième Édition; Orné De Vignettes,
Fleurons, Et D'Un Gravure
En Taille-Douce,* 1823
Book, 84 pages
Staatliche Museen zu Berlin, Kunstbibliothek
R-Lipp Nb 9kl

**85** Page 172
**Isaac Cruikshank (1764–1811)**
Samuel William Fores (1761–1838), publisher
*The dandy lion an exotic lately discover'd
in a stable yard,* 8 December 1818
Etching, hand-coloured with watercolours
Plate: 21.6 × 33 cm
Sheet: 32.9 × 21.6 cm
Staatliche Museen zu Berlin, Kunstbibliothek
Id. no.: 14155034

**86** Page 51
**Salvador Dalí (1904–1989)**
*Transformación de una pintura
de Matthias Gerung,* 1974
Transformation of a Painting
by Matthias Gerung
Oil on wood, 82 × 60 cm
Private collection, Switzerland

**Honoré Daumier (1808–1879)**

**87** No fig.
*Mr. Benjamin Dudessert*
Sheet 287 from the series *Célébrités de
la caricature,* in *La Caricature,* 27 June 1833
Lithograph
Image: 27.2 × 18.4 cm
Sheet: 35.2 × 26 cm
Kunsthaus Zürich,
Department of Prints and Drawings
Delteil/0059

**88** No fig.
*Quel habit Mr. le Président
va-t-il mettre aujourd'hui?*
Which clothes will Mr. President
wear today?
In *Le Charivari,* 30 December 1834
Lithograph
Image: 17.6 × 24.2 cm
Sheet: 23.6 × 30.7 cm
Kunsthaus Zürich,
Department of Prints and Drawings
Delteil/0219

**89** No fig.

*Le Tailleur. Il marche cambré, les épaules
en porte-manteau et les coudes en dehors.
Ses habits, coupés dans le dernier genre,
jurent souvent avec ses bottes et son chapeau,
il a presque toujours un nom très euphonique,
tel que Wahaterkermann ou Pikprunmann*
The tailor. He walks with an arched back,
his shoulders like a coat-hanger and his
elbows out. His clothes are of the latest cut,
but often at odds with his boots and hat. He
nearly always has a very euphoric name such
as Wahaterkermann or Pikprunman.
Sheet 2 from the series *Types Français,*
in *Le Charivari,* 27 September 1835
Lithograph
Image: 24.8 × 15.5 cm
Sheet: 35.2 × 26 cm
Kunsthaus Zürich,
Department of Prints and Drawings
Delteil/0261

**90** Page 189

*O qu'ils sont laids !*
Oh how ugly they are!
Sheet 1 from the series *Les Orang-Outangs 1,*
in *Le Charivari,* 21 September 1836
Lithograph
Image: 26.9 × 21.2 cm
Sheet: 35.2 × 26 cm
Kunsthaus Zürich,
Department of Prints and Drawings
Delteil/0318

**91** Page 189

*Le Narcisse. Le narcisse est une fleur
qui empeste le musc, l'eau de Portugal,
le patchouly, n'importe quelle odeur.
Elle est du reste sans valeur aucune.
Les femmes capricieuses se plaisent quelque-
fois à en orner leurs salons, mais sans les
aimer, par simple coquetterie, et comme elles
ont des tulipes, des perroquets, des chats,
des chiens et de magots de la chine.
On en rencontre beaucoup, sous le nom
plus vulgaire de Dandys ou de fashionables,
à Tortoni, au bois de boulogne, au balcon
de l'opéra & à qui il ne manque, pour
appartenir tout à fait au règne végétal,
que d'être plantés dans un pot de pomade
et arrosés d'huile antique.*
Narcissus. The narcissus is a flower that
stinks of musk, of Portuguese perfume,
of patchouli, of anything. Moreover, it is
absolutely worthless. Capricious women
sometimes enjoy using them as decoration
for their salons, but without really liking
them, just simple coquetry, like having tulips,
parrots, cats, dogs and Chinese porcelain
figures. They can be found often, under the
more vulgar name of dandys or fashionables,
in Tortoni, in the Bois de Boulogne, on the
opera balcony etc. where they are never
missing and where they are part of the floreal
décor, planted in a pot of pomade and watered
with antique oil. (Dejus, *Flore de Paris*)
Sheet 7 from the series *Cours d'histoire
naturelle 7,* in *Le Charivari,* 14 December 1837
Lithograph
Image: 21.3 × 18.7 cm
Sheet: 35.2 × 26 cm
Kunsthaus Zürich,
Department of Prints and Drawings
Delteil/0529

**92** Page 189

*Merci! va dîner en ville mon garçon*
Thank you! Ready to dine out old boy!
Sheet 6 from the series *Émotions Parisiennes,*
in *Le Charivari,* 3 October 1839
Lithograph
Image: 24.7 × 18.1 cm
Sheet: 35.2 × 26 cm
Kunsthaus Zürich,
Department of Prints and Drawings
Delteil/0689

**93** No fig.

*Fashionable,* 1839
Lithograph
Sheet: 10.5 × 8.5 cm
Kunsthaus Zürich,
Department of Prints and Drawings
Gr.1944/2608

**94** No fig.

*C'est singulier comme ce miroir m'aplatit
la taille et me maigrit la poitrine! ...
Que m'importe? ... Mme. de Staël et
Mr. de Buffon l'ont proclamé ...
le génie n'a point de sexe*
Isn't it strange how this mirror flattens my
waist and reduces my bust ... but what does
that matter? ... Mme de Stael and Mr de Buffon
clearly said: genius has no sex.
Sheet 1 from the series *Les Bas-bleus,*
in *Le Charivari,* 30 January 1844
Lithograph
Image: 22.9 × 18 cm
Sheet: 35.2 × 26 cm
Kunsthaus Zürich,
Department of Prints and Drawings
Delteil/1221

**95** Page 189

*Les Étrangers dévisagés par eux mêmes.
La dame de Carpentras. - C'est singulier ...
ces parisiennes ne sont pas si élégantes
qu'on veut bien le dire! ... La dame Quimper-
Corentin. - C'est inoui ... ces habitants
de la capitale, ne sont pas si coquettement
mises qu'on leur en fait la réputation! ...*
Foreigners taking stock of each other. -
The lady from Carpentras: How peculiar,
but Parisian women are not at all as elegant
as one always says. ... The lady from Quimper-
Corentin: It's unheard of ... these women of
the capital are hardly as elegantly dressed
as their reputation has it!
Sheet 15 from the series *Les Etrangers à Paris,*
in *Le Charivari,* 10 August 1844
Lithograph
Image: 21.6 × 17.3 cm
Sheet: 35.2 × 26 cm
Kunsthaus Zürich,
Department of Prints and Drawings
Delteil/1286

**96** No fig.

*Les Magasins de plus en plus monstres -
Pourriez-vous m'indiquer, s'il vous plait,
le comptoir des bonnets de coton? ... -
Au fond de la 9ème galerie à droite,
puis la 4ème à gauche, et une fois arrivé
au 15ème comptoir vous demanderez
les bonnets de coton; là on vous indiquera
parfaitement le chemin que vous devez
prendre pour y arriver ... - Ah! Sapristi ...
je suis bien fâché d'avoir laissé mon cabriolet
à la porte de votre magasin!*
The stores are getting more and more
prodigious. - Would you please be so kind
to indicate to me the counter for cotton night-
caps? ... - At the end of the ninth gallery,
to your right, then the fourth to the left, where
you will see the 15th cashier. There you ask for
the cotton night-caps. From there someone
will indicate to you the way to take in order to
get there ... - Oh Blast! How annoying, I left my
cab waiting for me at the entrance ...
Sheet 17 from the series *Les Etrangers à Paris,*
in *Le Charivari,* 18 August 1844
Lithograph
Image: 23.8 × 19.9 cm
Sheet: 35.2 × 26 cm
Kunsthaus Zürich,
Department of Prints and Drawings
Delteil/1288

**97** No fig.

*Nouveau manteau Talma, ainsi nommé
parce qu'il donne à celui qui le porte un air
complètement comique.*
The new Talma coat. It is named like this be-
cause anyone wearing it will have a comic look.
Sheet 1 from the series *Les Parisiens en 1852,*
in *Le Charivari,* 9 January 1852
Lithograph
Image: 25.6 × 21.9 cm
Sheet: 35.2 × 26 cm
Kunsthaus Zürich,
Department of Prints and Drawings
Delteil/2218

**98** No fig.

*Comment on entrera à l'exposition universelle
et comment on en sortira*
Entering and leaving the World Fair.
Sheet 5 from the series *L'Exposition
universelle,* in *Le Charivari,* 12 May 1855
Lithograph
Image: 21.2 × 25.1 cm
Sheet: 26 × 35.2 cm
Kunsthaus Zürich,
Department of Prints and Drawings
Delteil/2668

**99** No fig.

*Plus que ça d'ballon ... excusez ! ...*
This thing is more like a balloon ... excuse me.
Sheet 199 from the series *Actualités,*
in *Le Charivari,* 13 June 1855?
Lithograph
Image: 20.5 × 24.9 cm
Sheet: 26 × 35.2 cm
Kunsthaus Zürich,
Department of Prints and Drawings
Delteil/2626

**100**  Page 184
*Le Tourniquet. Machine nouvelle inventée
par un ennemi des jupons en crinoline*
The turnstile. A new machine invented
by the enemy of crinoline petticoats.
Sheet 15 from the series *L'Exposition
universelle,* in *Le Charivari,* 26 June 1855
Lithograph
Image: 19.7 × 22.8 cm
Sheet: 26 × 35.2 cm
Kunsthaus Zürich,
Department of Prints and Drawings
Delteil/2678

**101**  No fig.
*Modes nouvelles. Quel est l'homme,
quelle est la femme?… devine si tu peux
et choisis si tu l'oses! …*
The new fashion. Which is the man, which
is the woman?… make your guess if you can
and choose if you dare! …
Sheet 270 from the series *Actualités,*
in *Le Charivari,* 2 February 1856
Lithograph
Image: 21.7 × 25.2 cm
Sheet: 26 × 35.2 cm
Kunsthaus Zürich,
Department of Prints and Drawings
Delteil/2741

**102**  No fig.
*Une Erreur excusable. Poulets croyant
retrouver la cage dans laquelle ils ont passé
leur première jeunesse*
An excusable error. Chickens thinking they
have found the cage where they spent their
early childhood.
Sheet 364 from the series *Actualités,*
in *Le Charivari,* 12 January 1857
Lithograph
Image: 20.2 × 26.2 cm
Sheet: 26 × 35.2 cm
Kunsthaus Zürich,
Department of Prints and Drawings
Delteil/2916

**103**  Page 184
*De l'utilité de la crinoline pour
frauder l'octroi*
The usefulness of the crinoline when
cheating the customs
Sheet 414 from the series *Actualités,*
in *Le Charivari,* 19 June 1857
Lithograph
Image: 20.8 × 26.7 cm
Sheet: 26 × 35.2 cm
Kunsthaus Zürich,
Department of Prints and Drawings
Delteil/2957

**104**  No fig.
*La Crinoline finissant par être soupçonnée*
Crinolines are suddenly getting to be
suspicious
Sheet 419 from the series *Actualités,*
in *Le Charivari,* 4 July 1857
Lithograph
Image: 21.2 × 26.2 cm
Sheet: 26 × 33 cm
Kunsthaus Zürich,
Department of Prints and Drawings
Delteil/2968

**105**  Page 185
*Saprelotte! Si les femmes continuent à porter
des jupons en acier, on fera bien d'inventer,
pour leur donner le bras, des hommes en
caoutchouc. (Réflexion d'un mari qui a toujours
eu un mauvais caractère et qui commence à
prendre en outre, un mauvais pli)*
Damn it! If women continue to wear steel
petticoats one will be forced to invent rubber
men in order to give them an arm.
(Thoughts from a husband who always had
a bad character, and now starts to have
a bad back).
Sheet 437 from the series *Actualités,*
in *Le Charivari,* 9 September 1857
Lithograph
Image: 20.3 × 26 cm
Sheet: 26 × 35.2 cm
Kunsthaus Zürich,
Department of Prints and Drawings
Delteil/2973

**106**  Page 162
**Philip Dawe (1750–1790)**
John Bowles, publisher
*The macaroni. A real character
at the late masquerade,* 3 July 1773
Mezzotint, coloured
Plate: 35 × 25.1 cm
Sheet: 36.5 × 26.2 cm
Staatliche Museen zu Berlin, Kunstbibliothek
Id. no.: 14155026

**107**  Page 136
**Defontaines,** after
Depeuille, Paris, publisher
*Les Suppléans,* 1801
The substitutes
Etching, coloured with watercolour
Sheet: 23.7 × 26.3 cm
Staatliche Museen zu Berlin, Kunstbibliothek
Id. no.: 14155290,-,009

**Sonia Delaunay (1885–1979)**

**108**  Page 236
Librairie des Arts Décoratifs, publisher
Clothing designs, 1915
Plate 4, in *Sonia Delaunay – Ses Peintures,
ses Objets, ses Tissus simultanés,
ses Modes,* 1926
Pochoir print and serigraph on thin board
Sheet: 56.2 × 38 cm
Zurich University of the Arts, ZHdK/
Museum für Gestaltung Zürich,
Graphics Collection
Archiv-Nr.: E DELA 1-4

**109**  Page 236
Librairie des Arts Décoratifs, publisher
Clothing designs, 1919–23
Plate 6, in *Sonia Delaunay – Ses Peintures,
ses Objets, ses Tissus simultanés,
ses Modes,* 1926
Pochoir print and serigraph on thin board
Sheet: 38 × 56 cm
Zurich University of the Arts, ZHdK/
Museum für Gestaltung Zürich,
Graphics Collection
Arch. no.: E DELA 1-6

**110**  Page 236
Librairie des Arts Décoratifs, publisher
Clothing designs, 1923
Plate 1, in *Sonia Delaunay – Ses Peintures,
ses Objets, ses Tissus simultanés,
ses Modes,* 1926
Pochoir print and serigraph on thin board
Sheet: 38 × 55.5 cm
Zurich University of the Arts, ZHdK/
Museum für Gestaltung Zürich,
Graphics Collection
Arch. no.: E DELA 1-1

**111**  Page 236
Librairie des Arts Décoratifs, publisher
Clothing designs, 1923
Plate 5, in *Sonia Delaunay – Ses Peintures,
ses Objets, ses Tissus simultanés,
ses Modes,* 1926
Pochoir print and serigraph on thin board
Sheet: 38 × 55.8 cm
Zurich University of the Arts, ZHdK/
Museum für Gestaltung Zürich,
Graphics Collection
Arch. no.: E DELA 1-5

**112**  Page 236
Librairie des Arts Décoratifs, publisher
Clothing designs, 1923/24
Plate 3, in *Sonia Delaunay – Ses Peintures,
ses Objets, ses Tissus simultanés,
ses Modes,* 1926
Pochoir print and serigraph on thin board
Sheet: 38 × 55.8 cm
Zurich University of the Arts, ZHdK/
Museum für Gestaltung Zürich,
Graphics Collection
Arch. no.: E DELA 1-3

**113**  Page 236
Librairie des Arts Décoratifs, publisher
Clothing designs, 1924
Plate 8, in *Sonia Delaunay – Ses Peintures,
ses Objets, ses Tissus simultanés,
ses Modes,* 1926
Pochoir print and serigraph on thin board
Sheet: 55.7 × 38 cm
Zurich University of the Arts, ZHdK/
Museum für Gestaltung Zürich,
Graphics Collection
Arch. no.: E DELA 1-8

**114**  Page 236
Librairie des Arts Décoratifs, publisher
Clothing designs, 1924
Plate 9, in *Sonia Delaunay – Ses Peintures,
ses Objets, ses Tissus simultanés,
ses Modes,* 1926
Pochoir print and serigraph on thin board
Sheet: 56 × 37.8 cm
Zurich University of the Arts, ZHdK/
Museum für Gestaltung Zürich,
Graphics Collection
Arch. no.: E DELA 1-9

**115**  Page 236
Librairie des Arts Décoratifs, publisher
Clothing designs, 1924/25
Plate 7, in *Sonia Delaunay – Ses Peintures,
ses Objets, ses Tissus simultanés,
ses Modes,* 1926
Pochoir print and serigraph on thin board
Sheet: 38 × 55.5 cm
Zurich University of the Arts, ZHdK/
Museum für Gestaltung Zürich,
Graphics Collection
Arch. no.: E DELA 1-7

List of exhibited works

**135**  Pages 296/297
**Hans-Peter Feldmann (b. 1941)**
*Alle Kleider einer Frau,* 1970
All the clothes of a woman
70 photographs, gelatin silver prints
(individually mounted in object frames)
10 × 10 cm each
Frame: 78 × 118 cm
Courtesy of the artist and
Galerie Francesca Pia, Zurich

**136**  Page 75
**Luca Ferrari (1605–1654),** attributed
**Tiberio Tinelli (1586–1638),** attributed
*Portrait of a lady,* mid-seventeenth century
Oil on canvas
205 × 115 cm
KHM-Museumsverband, Picture Gallery
Inv. no.: 6537

**Sylvie Fleury (b. 1961)**

**137**  Page 235
*Mondrian Dress Rack,* 1993/2016
3 Mondrian dresses, 1 clothes rack, 3 hangers
Courtesy the artist and Karma International,
Zurich and Los Angeles
FLEUR41778

**138**  Page 52
*Concetto Speziale,* 2016
Denim on wooden stretcher
80 × 60 cm
Private collection, Zurich

**139**  Page 218
*Untitled,* 2016
Acrylic on canvas
Frame: 125 × 125 × 10 cm
Courtesy the artist and Karma International,
Zurich and Los Angeles,
and Mehdi Chouakri Berlin
FLEUR41777

**Samuel William Fores (1761–1838),** publisher

**140**  Page 111
*Waggoners frocks or No bodys of 1795,*
4 August 1795
Etching, hand-coloured with watercolours
Sheet: 38 × 28.4 cm
Staatliche Museen zu Berlin, Kunstbibliothek
Id. no.: 14155014

**141**  Page 125
*English and French taste or
A peep into Paris,* 14 April 1818
Etching, hand-coloured with watercolours
Sheet: 24 × 33 cm
Staatliche Museen zu Berlin, Kunstbibliothek
Id. no.: 14155038

**142**  Page 110
**Paul Fürst (1608–1666),** engraver
*Spottstreit der alten und neuen Manns-
und Weibertracht,* c. 1650
Mocking quarrel about the old and
new costumes for men and women
Copper engraving, letterpress
Plate: 13.1 × 25.8 cm
Sheet: 38.8 × 29.9 cm
Staatliche Museen zu Berlin, Kunstbibliothek
Id. no.: 14155121

**143**  Page 86
**Johann Caspar Füssli (1706–1782)**
*Portrait of Anna Ulrich von Orelli (1705–1773)
from Zurich, wife of Johann Caspar Ulrich
(1703–1778), councilman and builder,
daughter of Hans Heinrich Orelli,
merchant prince, and Anna Margaretha
Lavater,* c. 1730–45
Oil on canvas, 87 × 69.3 cm
Private collection, Zurich

**144**  Page 94
**Henry Fuseli (1741–1825)**
*Falstaff in the laundry basket,* 1792
Oil on canvas, 137.5 × 170.5 cm
Kunsthaus Zürich, 1941
2541

**General Idea (Canadian artists' collective:
Felix Partz, Jorge Zontal and AA Bronson,
active 1967–1994)**

**145**  Page 275
*FILE magazine,* IFEL, Special Paris Issue,
vol. 2, no. 3, September 1973
Stampa Galerie, Easel

**146**  Page 275
*FILE magazine,* Glamour Issue,
vol. 3, no. 1, Herbst 1975
Stampa Galerie, Basel

**147**  Page 275
*FILE magazine,* Special People Issue,
vol. 3, no. 3, Sommer 1977
Stampa Galerie, Basel

**148**  Page 275
*FILE magazine,* Punk 'Til You Puke! Issue,
vol. 3, no. 4, Herbst 1977
Stampa Galerie, Basel

**149**  Page 256
**Franz Gertsch (b. 1930)**
*Franz and Luciano,* 1973
Acrylic on cotton, 198 × 298 cm
Kunsthaus Zürich, 1977
1977/9

**James Gillray (1756–1815)**

**150**  Page 137
Hannah Humphrey (1745–1818), publisher
*The fashionable mamma, or The convenience
of modern dress,* 15 February 1797
Etching, hand-coloured with watercolours
Sheet: 34.2 × 24 cm
Staatliche Museen zu Berlin, Kunstbibliothek
Inv. no.: 14156030

**151**  Page 135
Hannah Humphrey (1745–1818), publisher
*The graces in a high wind,* 1797
Etching, coloured
Sheet: 26 × 35.7 cm
Staatliche Museen zu Berlin, Kunstbibliothek
Id. no.: 14156029

**152**  Page 172
*So skiffy-skipt-on, with his wonted grace,* 1800
Etching, hand-coloured with watercolours
Sheet: 24.8 × 17.4 cm
Staatliche Museen zu Berlin, Kunstbibliothek
Id. no.: 14155031

**153**  Pages 14/15
Thomas McLean, publisher
*Monstrosities of 1799*
Plate 159, in *The genuine works of
James Gillray, engraved by himself,* 1830
Etching
Plate: 26.8 × 36.5 cm
Sheet: 58.8 × 42.7 cm
Staatliche Museen zu Berlin, Kunstbibliothek
R-Lipp Xd 5 gr

**Gobert,** lithographer

**154**  Page 138
*Modes de 1830. Encore un degré
de perfection,* 1829
The fashions of 1830:
A further degree of perfection
Lithograph
Sheet: 32.1 × 23.2 cm
Staatliche Museen zu Berlin, Kunstbibliothek
Id. no.: 14155086,T,001

**155**  Page 138
*Modes de 1830. Une Perfection,* 1829
The fashions of 1830: A perfection
Lithograph
Sheet: 31.4 × 22.5 cm
Staatliche Museen zu Berlin, Kunstbibliothek
Id. no.: 14155086,T,003

**Natalja Gontscharowa (1881–1962)**

**156**  Page 233
*Counthe (?)*
Design, 1920s
Mixed media on paper
Frame: 56 × 39.5 cm
Martin Kamer

**157**  Page 233
*Dala*
Design, 1920s
Mixed media on paper
Frame: 56 × 39.5 cm
Martin Kamer

**158**  Page 233
Design, 1920s
Mixed media on paper
Frame: 56 × 39.5 cm
Martin Kamer

**159**  Page 233
Design, 1920s
Mixed media on paper
Frame: 56 × 39.5 cm
Martin Kamer

**160**  Page 233
*Eve*
Design, 1920s
Mixed media on paper
Frame: 56 × 39.5 cm
Martin Kamer

**161**  Page 233
*Lys rouge*
Design, 1920s
Mixed media on paper
Frame: 56 × 39.5 cm
Martin Kamer

**162**   Page 233
*Orchidée*
Orchid
Design, 1920s
Mixed media on paper
Frame: 56 × 39.5 cm
Martin Kamer

**163**   Page 233
*Petroushka*
Design, 1920s
Mixed media on paper
Frame: 64 × 47 cm
Martin Kamer

**164**   Page 233
*Zobeide*
Design, 1920s
Mixed media on paper
Frame: 56 × 39.5 cm
Martin Kamer

**165**   Page 88
**Johann Nikolaus Grooth (1723–1797)**
*Portrait of Valeria Hoffmann-Werthemann
(1741–1819) from Basel, wife of ribbon factory
owner Emanuel Hoffmann (1739–1807),* 1761
Oil on canvas, 82 × 65.5 cm
HMB – Historisches Museum Basel
Inv. no.: 1959.251.

**166**   Page 176
**George Grosz (1893–1959)**
*Dadabild,* c. 1919
Dada picture
Photo and text collage,
Chinese ink and silver gelatin print on paper
Sheet: 37 × 30.3 cm
Kunsthaus Zürich,
Department of Prints and Drawings
Z.1985/0064

**167**   Page 259
**Richard Hamilton (1922–2011)**
*Interior I,* 1964
Oil and collage on wood with
inlaid mirror, 122 × 163 cm
Kunsthaus Zürich, bequest of
Erna and Curt Burgauer, 2002
2002/22

**168**   Page 276
**K8 Hardy (b. 1977)**
*Express Looks (of Outfitumentary),* 2001–2016
HD digital video file, Duration: 16'50"
Courtesy of the artist and Karma International,
Zurich and Los Angeles

**William Heath (1795–1840)**

**169**   Page 158
Samuel William Fores (1761–1838), Verleger
*Poodles preparing for an aquatic excursion,*
27 September 1827
Etching, hand-coloured with watercolours
Sheet: 23.9 × 33.6 cm
Staatliche Museen zu Berlin, Kunstbibliothek
Id. no.: 14155058

**170**   Page 126
Thomas McLean, Verleger
*French salutation, English salutation,* May 1829
Etching, hand-coloured with watercolours
Plate: 26.2 × 37.7 cm
Sheet: 27.4 × 38.7 cm
Staatliche Museen zu Berlin, Kunstbibliothek
Id. no.: 14155065,T

**171**   Page 70
**Joseph Heintz d. Ä. (1564–1609)**
*Archduke Maximilian Ernst (1583–1616)
with hunting dog,* 1604
Oil on canvas, 191.5 × 105 cm
KHM-Museumsverband, Picture Gallery
Inv. no.: GG 9495

**172**   Pages 84/85
**David Herrliberger (1697–1777)**
*Zürcher Kirchenhabit –
Kirchen- und Trauerkleidung,* 1749
Zurich church habit –
church and mourning dress
Sheet IV, in *Zürcherische Kleider-Trachten*
Identification of nos 26 to 28 on the upper
left of each of the three full-figure depictions.
Below the depiction is the description in
German and French: 26. 'Adels-Frau im
Kirchen- und Trauer-Kleid' (Noblewoman
in church and mourning dress), 27. 'Eine vor-
nehme Frau oder Jungfrau im Kirchenkleid'
(An elegant lady or maiden in church dress),
28. 'Eine Bürgersfrau oder Jungfrau im
Kirchen-Kleid' (A bourgeoise or maiden
in church dress)
Copper engraving, coloured
Sheet: 10 × 15.4 cm
Private collection, Zurich

**173**   Page 232
**Hannah Höch (1889–1978)**
*Dompteuse,* c. 1930/1964
Animal trainer
Collage and photo montage; paper on
cardboard, numerous illustrations in
colour and bronze adhesive tape,
mounted on cardboard, with an artist's
frame with suede cover, 35.5 × 26 cm
Kunsthaus Zürich,
Department of Prints and Drawings
Z.1981/0035

**Johann Nepomuk Hoechle (1790–1835)**

**174**   Pages 144/145
*Parade während des Wiener Kongresses,* 1815
Parade during the Congress of Vienna
Pen and ink drawing, watercolours
44.5 × 68.5 cm
Vienna, Österreichische Nationalbibliothek,
Picture Archives and Graphics Department
Pk 270, 11

**175**   Page 140
Franz Wolf (1795–1859), lithographer
*Fest im Prater zum Jahrestag der
Völkerschlacht bei Leipzig 1814,* 1833
Celebration in the Prater on the anniversary
of the Battle of Leipzig
Lithograph
Sheet: 45.9 × 58.9 cm
Vienna, Österreichische Nationalbibliothek,
Picture Archives and Graphics Department
Pk 187, 13

**176**   Page 147
Franz Wolf (1795–1859), lithographer
*Empfang der verbündeten Monarchen in Wien
1814 anlässlich des Wiener Kongresses,* 1833
Reception of the Allied Monarchs in Vienna in
1814 on the occasion of the Congress of Vienna
Lithograph
Sheet: 45.8 × 58.6 cm
Vienna, Österreichische Nationalbibliothek,
Picture Archives and Graphics Department
Pk 187, 12

**177**   Page 78
**Samuel Hofmann (1595–1649)**
*Portrait of Melchior Maag,* 1635
Oil on canvas, 78 × 67 cm
Kunsthaus Zürich, Keller Collection, 1854
182

**178**   Pages 2/3
**William Hogarth (1697–1764)**
*The dance*
Sheet 2 from the series *The Analysis
of Beauty,* March 1753
Etching and copper engraving
Plate: 42.4 × 53 cm
Sheet: 47.9 × 64.4 cm
Kunsthaus Zürich,
Department of Prints and Drawings
Gr.1927/0099

**179**   Page 137
**William Holland (1757–1815)**
*Lath & plaster,* 25 January 1800
Etching, hand-coloured with watercolours
Sheet: 30.2 × 14.8 cm
Staatliche Museen zu Berlin, Kunstbibliothek
Id. no.: 14155018

**180**   Page 284
**Beat Huber (b. 1956)**
*Timepieces (All summer long),* 1997/2002
Installation: mannequin, flexible foam,
stack of fashion magazines, on metal plate
225 × 80 × 45 cm
Courtesy the artist

**181**   Page 109
**Jean-Baptiste Isabey (1767–1855),** after
Eugène Loizelet Beillet (1842–1882),
lithographer
Beillet, publisher
*Le Petit Coblentz,* c. 1875
Lithograph, coloured
Plate: 30.6 × 35.6 cm
Sheet: 38.5 × 50.3 cm
Staatliche Museen zu Berlin, Kunstbibliothek
Id. no.: 14155023

**182**   Page 205
**Arthur Kampf (1864–1950)**
*An den Hallen in Paris,* 1903
At 'Les Halles' in Paris
Oil on canvas, 173 × 235 cm
Kunsthaus Zürich,
bequest of Hildegard Reinelt, 1995
1995/13



List of exhibited works

**183a**  Page 300
**Tobias Kaspar (b. 1984)**
*Lumpy blue sweater,* 2010
Installation, consisting of 18 C-prints,
a mannequin with a sweater and booklet;
text layout: Pascal Storz
Frames: 32,5 × 42,5 cm each
Mannequin: 160 × 45 × 60 cm
Text: 120 × 75 cm
Courtesy the artist and Galerie Peter
Kilchmann, Zurich
KASPA21667

**183b**  Page 300
**Tobias Kaspar (b. 1984)**
*The final plot,* part of *Lumpy blue sweater,*
2010
C-Print, frame: 32,5 × 42,5 cm
Courtesy the artist and
Galerie Peter Kilchmann, Zurich

**184**  Page 87
**Carl Joseph Keiser (1702–1765)**
*Portrait of Maria Anna Barbara Xaveria*
*Zur Gilgen (1730–1793) from Luzern,*
*wife of Johann Jost Mahler (1727–1794),*
*member of the cantonal parliament*
*Lucerne,* 1760
Oil on canvas, 83 × 68 cm
Private collection

**185**  No fig.
**Jakob Lena Knebl (b. 1970)**
New work for the exhibition:
*(Space of desire),* 2018
Installation with Aristide Maillol's *Vénus*
*au collier* (1918–28), Kunsthaus Zürich,
Vereinigung Zürcher Kunstfreunde, 1931,
Inv. no. 2216, and Auguste Rodin's *L'âge d'airain*
(1875/76), Kunsthaus Zürich, 1935, Inv. no. 2380
Mixed media, Dimensions variable
Courtesy the artist
Thanks to the generous support of
the Bundeskanzleramt Österreich,
Kunst und Kultur

**186**  Page 39
**Herlinde Koelbl (b. 1939)**
*Kleider machen Leute,* 2012
Clothes make the man
Projection of a selection of images from
the series of photographs
Courtesy of Herlinde Koelbl

**187**  Page 257
**Eva Kotátková (b. 1982) and**
**Jiří Kovanda (b. 1953)**
*Hanging Sleeves, Hiding Hands,* 2013
Daily performance and two second-hand
trench coats, Dimensions variable
Courtesy the artists

**188**  Page 141
**Franz Krüger (1797–1857)**
*Prinz August von Preussen,* c. 1828
Oil on canvas, 63 × 47 cm
Staatliche Museen zu Berlin, Nationalgalerie
Inv. no.: A I 452

**189**  Page 104
**Johann Kupezky (1666–1740)**
*Portrait of a young artist*
*(Christian Benjamin Müller?),* c. 1705/1710
Oil on canvas, 94 × 74.5 cm
Kunsthaus Zürich, donated by
August Abegg, 1925
1644

**Inez van Lamsweerde (b. 1963) and**
**Vinoodh Matadin (b. 1961)**

**190**  Page 294
*Kym and Zonna. Well, basically basuco*
*is coke mixed with kerosene,* 1994
Colour photograph, C-print,
mounted on aluminium plate,
behind plexiglas, 125 × 183 cm
Collection Nicola von Senger, Switzerland

**191**  Page 292
*Anastasia,* 2000
C-print in frame of artists, 118 × 104 cm
Private collection
Courtesy of the Gagosian Gallery
WV Nr. VANMAT 2000.0005

**William Larkin (1580–1619)**

**192**  Page 54
*Portrait of Diana Cecil,*
*later Countess of Oxford,* c. 1614–18
Oil on canvas, 205.9 × 119.5 cm
English Heritage, The Iveagh Bequest
(Kenwood, London)
Object ID: 88019160

**193**  Page 72
*Unknown lady in a black and*
*white dress,* c. 1615–18
Oil on wood, 57 × 43.2 cm
Private collection
Courtesy The Weiss Gallery, London

**194**  Page 76
**Claude Lefèbvre (1632–1675)**
*Full-length portrait of Louis XIV (1638–1715),*
*King of France and Navarra. Equipped with*
*crown and sceptre on a table in front of*
*a seascape with ship,* c. 1670
Oil on canvas, 196.5 × 159 cm
Musée national des châteaux de Versailles
et de Trianon
MV 8369

**195**  Page 135
**Robert Lefèvre (1755–1830)**
*Half-length portrait of Pauline Bonaparte,*
*Princess Borghese, Duchess of Guastalla*
*(1780–1825),* 1806
Oil on canvas, 65 × 54 cm
Musée national des châteaux de Versailles
et de Trianon
MV 4711

**Nicolas Lejeune (1750–1804)**

**196**  Page 90
*Portrait of Anna Maria von der Mühl-Faesch*
*(1760–1779) from Basel, with lute. A folded back*
*curtain shows a representatively decorated*
*room, in the background a painting with Cupid,*
*who aims an arrow at the female figure,*
dated after source, 1778
Oil-based resin on linen, 63.5 × 50.5 cm
Schweizerisches Nationalmuseum, Zurich
Inv. no.: LM-154456.1-2
(counterpart to 197)

**197**  Page 90
*Portrait of Johannes von der Mühl-Faesch*
*(1754–1815) from Basel sitting at an oval table*
*in front of folded back curtain. Merchant and*
*president of the city council holding a letter in*
*his hand,* dated after source, 1778
Oil-based resin on linen, 63.5 × 50.5 cm
Schweizerisches Nationalmuseum, Zurich
Inv. no.: LM-154457.1-2
(counterpart to 196)

**198**  Page 234
**Tamara de Lempicka (1898–1980)**
*Kizette en rose,* 1927
Oil on canvas, 116 × 73 cm
Musée d'Arts de Nantes
Inv. no.: 928.3.1.P

**Peter Lindbergh (b. 1944)**

**199**  Page 287
*Linda Spierings, Paris,* 1982
Exhibition print; Hahnemühle Photo Rag®
Baryta 315 gr, 60 × 60 cm
Courtesy Peter Lindbergh, Paris
LIND 2701-2

**200**  Page 272
*Lynne Koester, Paris,* 1984
Exhibition print; Hahnemühle Photo Rag®
Baryta 315 gr, 60 × 50 cm
Courtesy Peter Lindbergh, Paris
LIND 2484-12

**201**  Page 273
*Yasmin Le Bon, Paris,* 1985
Exhibition print; Hahnemühle Photo Rag®
Baryta 315 gr, 60 × 50 cm
Courtesy Peter Lindbergh, Paris
LIND 3316-1

**202**  Page 272
*Linda Evangelista, Brooklyn,* 1990
Exhibition print; Hahnemühle Photo Rag®
Baryta 315 gr, 60 × 50 cm
Courtesy Peter Lindbergh, Paris
LIND 15726-13

**203**  Page 272
*Linda Evangelista, Christy Turlington &*
*Naomi Campbell, Brooklyn,* 1990
Exhibition print; Hahnemühle Photo Rag®
Baryta 315 gr, 60 × 50 cm
Courtesy Peter Lindbergh, Paris
LIND POLA-GANGSTER-05

**204**  Page 273
*Models: The Film,* 1991
16-mm and 35-mm film, digitalised,
black-and-white, sound, Duration: 48' 57"
Courtesy Peter Lindbergh

**205**  Page 273
*Kate Moss, Rome,* 1994
Exhibition print; Hahnemühle Photo Rag®
Baryta 315 gr, 60 × 50 cm
Courtesy Peter Lindbergh, Paris
LIND 26481BIS-7

**206**  No fig.
*Keith Richards, New York,* 1999
Exhibition print; Hahnemühle Photo Rag®
Baryta 315 gr, 60 × 50 cm
Courtesy Peter Lindbergh, Paris
LIND 48017-15

**207**  No fig.
*Cate Blanchett, Paris,* 2003
Exhibition print; Hahnemühle Photo Rag®
Baryta 315 gr, 50 × 60 cm
Courtesy Peter Lindbergh, Paris
LIND 62806-34A

**208**  No fig.
*Amber Valletta, Santa Monica,* 2012
Exhibition print; Hahnemühle Photo Rag®
Baryta 315 gr, 60 × 50 cm
Courtesy Peter Lindbergh, Paris
LIND D1408-103-0019

**209**  Pages 220/221
**Lumière Brothers**
**(Auguste Lumière, 1862–1954, and**
**Louis Lumière, 1864–1948)**
*Danse serpentine,* 1897
Choreography: Loïe Fuller,
Dance: Loïe Fuller und Papinta
Digitalised film, no sound, Duration: 59"

**210**  Page 79
**Nicolaes Maes (1634–1693)**
*Portrait of a young boy in*
*Adonis costume,* c. 1670
Oil on canvas, 55.5 × 42 cm
Paintings Gallery,
Academy of Fine Arts Vienna
GG-670

**211**  Page 191
**Édouard Manet (1832–1883)**
*Jeanne Duval, la maîtresse de Baudelaire*
*(La Dame à l'éventail),* 1862
Jeanne Duval, Baudelaire's mistress
(Lady with a fan)
Oil on canvas, 89.5 × 113 cm
Museum of Fine Arts, Budapest
Inv. 368.B

**212**  Page 279
**Manon (b. 1946)**
*Ball der Einsamkeiten. 30 Selbstporträts/*
*30 Lebensläufe,* 1980
Ball of loneliness: 30 self-portraits/30 lives
12 photographs from the series,
gelatin silver prints with artist's montage
46.3 × 70 cm each
Kunsthaus Zürich, Collection of Photography
PH 2004/177; 178; 182–184; 186–188; 193–195;
198

**213**  Page 201
**Johann Adam Meisenbach (1892–1959)**
*Suzanne Perrottet und Tanzende am*
*Lago Maggiore bei Ascona,* 1914
Suzanne Perrottet and dancers at
the Lago Maggiore near Ascona
3 photographs from autochrome plates
Plates: 9 × 12 cm each
Exhibition prints: 18 × 24 cm each
Kunsthaus Zürich, Archive Zürcher
Kunstgesellschaft and Kunsthaus Zürich
SP I 91:112; 114; 116

**Conrad Meyer (1618–1689)**

**214**  Page 83
*Probably portrait of Susanna Meyer Murer*
*(b. 1619) from Zurich, wife of the artist,* 1649
Signed bottom right: 'C. Meyer/Ao/
1649/Forma Habitus ac Mundus Virginis
Thuricensis'. In the background Lake Zurich
and the City of Zurich
Oil on canvas, 85.4 × 56.3 cm
Private collection, Zurich

**215**  No fig.
*Portrait of the court man*
*Heinrich Escher,* 1660
Oil on canvas, 103 × 80 cm
Kunsthaus Zürich, bequest of
Ms Cäcilie Escher von Berg, 1886
454

**216**  No fig.
*Portrait of Heinrich Escher's wife,*
*née von Meiss von Teufen,* 1660
Oil on canvas, 103 × 80 cm
Kunsthaus Zürich, bequest of
Ms Cäcilie Escher von Berg, 1886
455

**217a**  Pages 80/82
**Dietrich Theodor Meyer the Elder**
**(1572–1658),** attributed
*Portrait of Nobleman Hans Caspar Schmid*
*von Goldenberg (1587–1638),* 1622
Representative of the Konstaffel in the Small
Council of Zurich (1621–38); member of
the professional military in French services.
Oil on canvas, 217.5 × 115.8 cm
Private collection
(Counterpart to 217b)

**217b**  Page 82
**Dietrich Theodor Meyer the Elder**
**(1572–1658),** attributed
*Portrait of Barbara Schmid Wydenmann*
*(1587–1624),* 1622
Daughter of a wealthy Catholic business-
man from Constance. Owner of the Zurich
Seidenhöfe, silk industry, through her
first marriage to Hans Rudolf Werdmüller.
Second marriage to Hans Caspar Schmid.
Oil on canvas, 214 × 115.5 cm
Private collection
(Counterpart to 217a)

**218**  Page 56
**Antonis Mor (1516/1521–1576/77)**
*Alessandro Farnese in cape and cap,* c. 1560
Oil on canvas, 174 × 97 cm
Liechtenstein. The Princely Collections,
Vaduz-Vienna
GE 2511

**219**  Page 291
**Shana Moulton (b. 1976)**
*Whispering Pines #4,* 2007
Video, colour, sound, Duration: 10'53"
Courtesy the artist and Galerie
Gregor Staiger, Zurich

**Meret Oppenheim (1913–1985)**

**220**  Page 244
*Designs for cape, cap and*
*varieté lingerie,* c. 1942
Pencil and crayon on paper
Sheet: 29.7 × 20.8 cm
Private collection, Basel

**221**  Page 244
*Robe simple, robe de dîner,* 1942–45
Simple robe, evening robe
Sketches; pencil on paper
Sheet: c. 29.7 × 20.8 cm
Private collection, Basel

**222**  Page 242
*Design for gloves with veins,* 1942–45
The artist had the idea for these gloves
realised for the luxury edition
of *Parkett,* no. 4/1985
Pencil on paper
Sheet: c. 19 × 11 cm
Private collection Basel

**223**  Page 245
*Notes and sketches for paper clothes,* 1967
3 pages from an exercise book,
pencil and Chinese ink on paper
Sheet: 29.7 × 20.8 cm
Private collection, Basel

**224**  Page 242
Claude Lê-Anh (b. 1936), photography
*Meret Oppenheim (1913–1985) with a model*
*of her paper clothes collections and*
*one of her sun protection (half)glasses,*
*designed by herself,* 1967
Plot of the photograph, black-and-white
Courtesy Claude Lê-Anh

**225**  Page 243
*Glove,* 1985
Edition for *Parkett,* no. 4/1985
Gloves made from goat suede, trimmed with
piping by hand and equipped with serigraph
Kunsthaus Zürich,
Department of Prints and Drawings
M.2004/0063

**226**  Page 69
**Robert Peake (1551–1619)**
*Catherine Carey, Countess of*
*Nottingham,* c. 1597
Oil on canvas, 198.1 × 137.2 cm
Private collection
Courtesy The Weiss Gallery, London

**227**  Page 238
**Mai-Thu Perret (b. 1976)**
*Flow My Tears I,* 2011
Mannequin with glass head, copy of
Elsa Schiaparelli's 'Skeleton' dress,
made by Naoyuki Yoneto
175 × 70 × 70 cm
Courtesy of the artist and
Galerie Francesca Pia, Zurich

**228**  Page 188
**Charles Philipon (1800–1862),** lithographer
Genty, publisher
*Le Détalage,* c. 1827
Adversity of trade. Dismantling of
the store display
Lithograph, coloured
Sheet: 32.6 × 24.3 cm
Staatliche Museen zu Berlin, Kunstbibliothek
Id. no.: 14155189

**229**  Page 278
**Pierre-Louis Pierson (1822–1913)**
*Comtesse de Castiglione,* 1861–67
15 vintage photographs;
albumen gelatin silver print
Dimensions variable:
8.8 × 8.8 cm to 46 × 31.5 cm
Martin Kamer

**230**  Pages 302/303
**Michelangelo Pistoletto (b. 1933)**
*Metamorfosi,* 1976–2016
Mirror, rags, Dimensions variable
Courtesy Galleria Continua, San Gimignano/
Beijing/Les Moulins/Habana

---

List of exhibited works

**Victor Ratier (1807–1898)**

**231**  Page 139
Blaisot, publisher (?)
*Merveilleuses*
Plate 1 from *Révolutions cosmopolites,*
after 1829
Lithograph
Sheet: 26 × 32.4 cm
Staatliche Museen zu Berlin, Kunstbibliothek
Id. no.: 14155019,T,001

**232**  Page 139
Blaisot, publisher (?)
*Fashionables*
Plate 2 from *Révolutions cosmopolites,* c. 1830
Lithograph
Sheet: 26 × 32.4 cm
Staatliche Museen zu Berlin, Kunstbibliothek
Id. no.: 14155019,T,002

**233**  Page 226
**Charles Ray (b. 1953)**
*Self-portrait with Homemade Clothes,* 2015
35-mm film, Duration: 3'23"
Courtesy Matthew Marks Gallery

**234**  Page 229
**Man Ray (1890–1976)**
*Portemanteau,* 1920
Clothes rack
Silver gelatin photograph of a collage
of objects (original photograph)
Sheet: 25 × 16.5 cm
Kunsthaus Zürich, Collection of Photography
PH.2004/0132

**Hyacinthe Rigaud (1659–1743)**

**235**  Page 77
*Portrait of Balthasar Keller,*
*brass-founder,* 1685
Oil on canvas, 140 × 107 cm
Kunsthaus Zürich, Keller Collection, 1854
209

**236**  Page 77
*Portrait of Suzanne de Boubers de Bernâtre,*
*wife of Balthasar Keller,* 1686
Oil on canvas, 140 × 107 cm
Kunsthaus Zürich, Keller Collection, 1854
210

**237**  Page 241
**James Rosenquist (1933–2017)**
*Paper suit,* 1998
Paper suit made from Dupont Tyvek,
black, size 52
c. 183 × 86 × 0.5 cm
Kaskanian, Vartanian GbR

**238**  Pages 254/255
**Tula Roy (b. 1934) and**
**Christoph Wirsing (b. 1950)**
*Lady Shiva, oder:*
*'Die bezahlen meine Zeit',* 1974
Lady Shiva, or: 'They pay my time'
With Irene Staub aka Lady Shiva;
script, production, editing: Tula Roy,
cinematography, sound, editing:
Christoph Wirsing,
concept and interview: Sissi Zöbeli
Super-8 blow-up on 16 mm, digitalised,
colour, sound, 4:3 aspect ratio, Duration: 40'
Courtesy Tula Roy and Christoph Wirsing

**239**  Page 53
**Francesco Salviati (1510–1563)**
*Portrait of a young man,* after 1548
Oil on wood, 89 × 69 cm
Liechtenstein. The Princely Collections,
Vaduz-Vienna
GE 848

**240**  Page 175
**John Singer Sargent (1856–1925)**
*W. Graham Robertson,* 1894
Oil on canvas, 230.5 × 118.7 cm
Tate: Presented by W. Graham Robertson 1940
N05066

**241**  No fig.
**Ashley Hans Scheirl (b. 1956)**
New work for the exhibition, 2018
Acrylic on canvas
Courtesy of the artist

**242**  Page 140
**Josef Schütz**
*Ansicht des K.K. Redouten Saales*
*während eines Masquen-Balles,* c. 1815
View of the imperial and royal ballroom
during a masked ball
Etching, coloured
Sheet: 49.5 × 36.5 cm
Vienna, Österreichische Nationalbibliothek,
Map Department and Globe Museum
FKB Vues Wien II, Burg 22

**Michael E. Smith (b. 1977)**

**243**  Page 299
*Fat Albert,* 2013
Mixing bowl, T-shirt
H. 29.5 cm, d. 77 cm
Oehmen Collection

**244**  Page 299
*Untitled,* 2015
SD-video, 16:9, found footage,
colour, sound, Duration: 9'53"
Courtesy Michael E. Smith and KOW, Berlin

**245**  Page 192
**Karl Stauffer-Bern (1857–1891)**
*Portrait of Lydia Welti-Escher,* 1886
Oil on canvas, 150.5 × 100 cm
Kunsthaus Zürich, loan from the
Gottfried Keller Foundation,
Federal Office of Culture, Bern, 1941
2538

**246**  Page 142
**Karl von Steuben (1788–1856),** after
Demanne, lithographer
*Der Hut Napoleons I. in den verschiedenen*
*Lebensphasen des Kaisers,* after 1826
Napoleon I's hat in the various
life stages of the Emperor
Lithograph
Sheet: 25.5 × 37.5 cm
Vienna, Österreichische Nationalbibliothek,
Picture Archives and Graphics Department
Pk 400, 520

**247**  Page 99
**Thomas Stewart (1766–1801)**
after Jean-Laurent Mosnier (1743–1808)
*Chevalier d'Eon,* 1792
Oil on canvas, 76.5 × 64 cm
Lent by the National Portrait Gallery, London;
Primary Collection
NPG No 6937

**248**  Page 199
**John Tenniel (1820–1914)**
*Woman's emancipation (being a letter*
*addressed to Mr. Punch, with a drawing,*
*by a strong-minded American woman)*
In *Punch, or the London Charivari,* London,
vol. 21, July–December 1851, p. 3
Kunsthaus Zürich, Library
D 2017 0171 21-22

**Wolfgang Tillmans (b. 1968)**

**249**  No fig.
*Grey jeans over stair post,* 1991
Colour photograph, 30.5 × 40.6 cm
Kunsthaus Zürich, Collection of Photography
PH 1996/147

**250**  No fig.
*Turnhose (Sandalen),* 1991
Gym shorts (sandals)
Colour photograph, 60.8 × 50.7 cm
Kunsthaus Zürich, Collection of Photography
PH 1996/149

**251**  Page 248
*Christos,* 1992
Colour photograph, 60.8 × 50.7 cm
Kunsthaus Zürich, Collection of Photography
PH 1996/150

**252**  Page 277
*Lutz & Alex, climbing tree,* 1992
Colour photograph, 40.6 × 30.5 cm
Kunsthaus Zürich, Collection of Photography
PH 1996/151

**253**  Page 249
*Travis with tree,* 1994
Colour photograph, 50.8 × 50.7 cm
Kunsthaus Zürich, Collection of Photography
PH 1996/155

**254**  No fig.
*Richie Hawtin, home,* 1994
Colour photograph, 60.8 × 50.7 cm
Kunsthaus Zürich, Collection of Photography
PH 1996/156

**255**  No fig.
*Rachel Auburn, son,* 1995
Colour photograph, 40.6 × 30.5 cm
Kunsthaus Zürich, Collection of Photography
PH 1996/157

**256**  Page 277
*Smokin' Jo,* 1995
Colour photograph
60.8 × 50.7 cm
Kunsthaus Zürich, Collection of Photography
PH 1996/158

**257**  No fig.
*Hole in the Wall,* 1995
Colour photograph, 30.5 × 40.6 cm
Kunsthaus Zürich, Collection of Photography
PH 1996/159

**258**  Page 277
*Michael Bergin & fan,* 1995
Colour photograph, 60.8 × 50.7 cm
Kunsthaus Zürich, Collection of Photography
PH 1996/163

**259**  No fig.
*Frau Pisters,* 1996
Mrs Pisters
Colour photograph, 40.6 × 30.5 cm
Kunsthaus Zürich, Collection of Photography
PH 1996/166

**260**  Page 174
**James Tissot (1836–1902)**
*Baron Aimé de la Seillière,* 1566
Oil on canvas, 128 × 71 cm
Staatliche Kunsthalle Karlsruhe
2826

**261**  Page 228
**Unknown photographer**
*Baroness von Freytag-Loringhoven,*
between 1910–20
Photograph of digital plot from
original glass negative image,
Dimensions variable
Library of Congress, Washington, D.C.,
George Grantham Bain Collection
LC-B2-5677-3 (P&P)

**262**  Page 201
**Unknown photographer**
*Emmy Hennings,* Munich 1912
Black-and-white photograph, 14.5 × 10.5 cm
Kunsthaus Zürich, Archive Zürcher
Kunstgesellschaft and Kunsthaus Zürich
DADA VI:45

**263**  Page 227
**Unknown photographer**
*Verse ohne Worte in kubistischem Kostüm,* 1916
Verses without words in Cubist costume
Hugo Ball in the Cabaret Voltaire,
reciting his sound poems
Photograph, 71.5 × 40 cm
Kunsthaus Zürich, Archive Zürcher
Kunstgesellschaft and Kunsthaus Zürich
DADA VI:5 / B 27 D 4

**264**  No fig.
**Unknown photographer (Hess)**
*Mary Wigman*
Black-and-white postcard, 13.3 × 8.6 cm
Kunsthaus Zürich, Archive Zürcher
Kunstgesellschaft and Kunsthaus Zürich
DADA VI:14

**265**  Page 57
**Unknown artist**
*Portrait of Prince Hartmann
von Liechtenstein (1613–1686),* c.1630
Oil on canvas, 201 × 98 cm
Liechtenstein. The Princely Collections,
Vaduz-Vienna
GE 1255

**266**  Page 84
**Unknown artist**
*Portrait of Elisabeth Gossweiler née Hirzel
(1690–1762) from Zurich, wife of merchant
and guild master Konrad Gossweiler
from Zurich,* c.1715
Damask dress patterned with chinoiseries
and corsage lacing
Oil on canvas, 96.5 × 74 cm
Schweizerisches Nationalmuseum, Zurich
Inv. no.: LM-617.2

**267**  Page 110
**Unknown artist**
*Der weiten Reif-Röck Ehren-Ruhm
muss jetzt in das Exilium,* c.1740
The honorary glory of the wide hoop-skirts
must now go in exile
Etching, letterpress
Plate: 14.5 × 19.7 cm
Sheet: 29.5 × 19.7 cm
Staatliche Museen zu Berlin, Kunstbibliothek
Id. no.: 14155130

**268**  Page 137
**Unknown artist**
*Quel est le plus ridicule?,* 1800/01
Who is the most ridiculous?
Etching, hand-coloured with watercolours,
on light blue paper
Plate: 24.4 × 32.3 cm
Sheet: 25.6 × 33.1 cm
Staatliche Museen zu Berlin, Kunstbibliothek
Id. no.: 14155289,T,022

**269**  Page 137
**Unknown artist**
*Le Coup de vent,* 1802
The gust of wind
Etching, hand-coloured with
watercolours, dotted
Plate: 18.8 × 27.7 cm
Sheet: 24.6 × 31.8 cm
Staatliche Museen zu Berlin, Kunstbibliothek
Id. no.: 14155290,T,012

**270**  Page 112
**Unknown artist**
*Le Suprême Bon Ton no 2,* 1802
Supreme good tone
Etching, hand-coloured with watercolours
Sheet: 19.2 × 25.6 cm
Staatliche Museen zu Berlin, Kunstbibliothek
Id. no.: 14155289,T,001

**271**  Page 112
**Unknown artist**
*Le Suprême Bon Ton no 8,* c.1802
Supreme good tone
Etching, hand-coloured with
watercolours, dotted
Sheet: 19.8 × 27.7 cm
Staatliche Museen zu Berlin, Kunstbibliothek
Id. no.: 14155289,T,006

**272**  Page 112
**Unknown artist**
*Départ des amateurs de l'île St. Ouen,* c.1805
The amateurs' departure from the Ile St. Ouen
Etching, hand-coloured with watercolours
Plate: 21.2 × 26.2 cm
Sheet: 24.3 × 30.5 cm
Staatliche Museen zu Berlin, Kunstbibliothek
Id. no.: 14155289,T,037

**273**  Page 112
**Unknown artist**
*La Galerie du Palais Royal,* 1807–09
Etching, hand-coloured with watercolours
Sheet: 24.6 × 31.7 cm
Staatliche Museen zu Berlin, Kunstbibliothek
Id. no.: 14155290,T,011

**274**  Page 146
**Unknown artist**
*The military festival in the Prater on
18 October 1814,* 1814
Oil on canvas, 102 × 159 cm
Wien Museum
Inv. no.: 102745

**275**  Page 145
**Unknown artist**
*The entry of Empress Maria Feodorovna of
Russia in Vienna 1814,* 1814
Etching, hand-coloured
Image: 15.8 × 24.4 cm
Plate: 18.8 × 26.6 cm
Sheet: 25.9 × 36.8 cm
Wien Museum
Inv. no.: 80966

**276**  Page 145
**Unknown artist**
Anton Leitner, publisher
*Ceremonial entry of Monarchs Alexander I
and Frederick William III on 25 September 1814
in Vienna,* 1814
Copper engraving, coloured
Image: 15.8 × 24.4 cm
Plate: 19 × 26.6 cm
Sheet: 22.8 × 34.6 cm
Wien Museum
Inv. no.: 19972

**277**  Page 159
**Unknown artist**
*Showing the difference between
beasts & babies,* 4 June 1829
Etching, hand-coloured with watercolours
Sheet: 33.8 × 24.2 cm
Staatliche Museen zu Berlin, Kunstbibliothek
Id. no.: 14155059,T,001

**278**  Page 172
**Unknown artist**
*Longchamp,* 1840
Copper engraving, hand-coloured with
watercolours
Sheet: 26.7 × 18.9 cm
Staatliche Museen zu Berlin, Kunstbibliothek
Id. no.: 14155279,T,012

**Félix Vallotton (1865–1925)**

**279**  Page 171
*Le Haut-de-forme, intérieur or La Visite,* 1887
Top hat, interior, or The visit
Oil on canvas, 31.7 × 24.8 cm
Collection Olivier Senn.
Donation Hélène Senn-Foulds, 2004.
Le Havre, Musée d'art moderne André Malraux
Inv. no.: 2004.4.67

**280**  Page 171
*Paul Vallotton avec son chapeau,* 1888
Paul Vallotton with his hat
Oil on canvas, 76 × 61 cm
Private collection

**281**  Page 196
*Le Bon Marché,* 1893
Woodcut on vellum
Image: 20.1 × 25.9 cm
Sheet: 23.6 × 33 cm
Kunsthaus Zürich,
Department of Prints and Drawings
Gr.1946/0030

**282**  Page 196
*La Modiste,* 1894
The milliner
Woodcut
Image: 18 × 22.5 cm
Sheet: 23.6 × 30.7 cm
Kunsthaus Zürich,
Department of Prints and Drawings
Gr.1946/0035

**283** No fig.
*L'Averse*, 1894
The downpour
Woodcut on d'Arches vellum
Image: 18.2 × 22.5 cm
Sheet: 24.5 × 32 cm
Kunsthaus Zürich,
Department of Prints and Drawings
Gr.2003/0128

**284** No fig.
*L'Étranger*, 1894
The stranger
Woodcut
Image: 22.4 × 17.9 cm
Sheet: 32.2 × 24.6 cm
Kunsthaus Zürich,
Department of Prints and Drawings
Gr.1946/0036

**285** Page 208
*Le Coup de vent*, 1894
The gust of wind
Woodcut on Japan paper
Image: 18 × 22,4 cm
Sheet: 25.3 × 31 cm
Kunsthaus Zürich,
Department of Prints and Drawings
Gr.2003/0132

**286** No fig.
*Le Joyeux Quartier Latin*, 1895
The merry Quartier Latin
Woodcut on vellum
Image: 17.8 × 22.3 cm
Sheet: 25.4 × 32.4 cm
Kunsthaus Zürich,
Department of Prints and Drawings
Gr.1946/0041

**287** Page 166
*Le Comte Robert de Montesquiou
(1855–1921)*, 1896
Reproduction of the woodcut,
in *Rémy de Gourmont, Le Livre des masques.
Portraits symbolistes, Gloses et Documents
sur les Ecrivains d'hier et d'aujourd'hui*,
Paris 1896, p. 233
Kunsthaus Zürich, Library

**288** Page 192
*Portrait of Marthe Mellot*, 1898
Oil on canvas, 73 × 60 cm
Kunsthaus Zürich, Vereinigung
Zürcher Kunstfreunde, 1938
2461

**289** Page 193
*Le Chapeau violet*, 1907
The violet hat
Oil on canvas, 81 × 65.5 cm
Dauerleihgabe an die Hahnloser/Jaeggli-
Stiftung, ehemalige Sammlung Arthur
und Hedy Hahnloser-Bühler, Villa Flora,
Winterthur

**290** Page 215
*La Poudreuse*, 1921
Lady powdering herself
Oil on canvas, 82 × 100 cm
Private collection

**291** Page 113
**Carle Vernet (1758–1836)**
*Caricature d'un incroyable*, undated
Caricature of an Incroyable
Black crayon, brown and black
Chinese ink, watercolours
Sheet: 33.7 × 22.1 cm
Paris, Musée du Louvre,
Département des Arts graphiques
RF 3616

**292** Page 103
**Marie Louise Élisabeth Vigée-Lebrun
(1755–1842)**
*Marie-Antoinette en chemise*, 1783
Oil on canvas, 89.8 × 72 cm
Hessische Hausstiftung, Kronberg im Taunus

**293** Page 209
**Édouard Vuillard (1868–1940)**
*Les Bras nus*, undated
Naked arms
Oil on cardboard, 48.5 × 58 cm
Kunsthaus Zürich, Private collection

**294** Page 258
**Andy Warhol (1928–1987)**
*Camouflage. Joseph Beuys*, 1986
Synthetic resin and silk screen colour
on canvas, 254 × 204.3 cm
Udo and Anette Brandhorst Collection
Inv. no.: UAB 594

**Jean-Antoine Watteau (1684–1721)**

**295** No fig.
Jean Adran (1667–1756), etcher
*Femme assise vue de dos*, 1717–26
Seated woman, rear view
Etching and etching needle
Plate: 19 × 13.7 cm
Sheet: 23.9 × 15.7 cm
Ville de Genève, Musées d'art et d'histoire
Inv. no.: E 2012-0454-034

**296** Page 107
Louis Desplaces (1682–1739), etcher
Gabriel Huquier (1695–1772), publisher
*Jeune femme debout avec la tête tournée
vers le spectateur*, 1717–28
Standing young woman, facing the viewer
Etching and etching needle
Sheet: 18.7 × 13.1 cm
Ville de Genève, Musées d'art et d'histoire
Inv. no.: E 2012-0454-018

**297** Page 107
Thomassin (the son), Rue Saint Jacques,
Paris, etcher
*Figures de modes*, first quarter of
the eighteenth century
Series, frontispiece and six of
originally eight plates
Etching and etching needle
Sheet: 11.5 × 7.5 cm each
Rennes, Musée des beaux-arts
Inv. no.: 794.1.4528–4534

**298** Pages 8/9
Pierre-Alexandre Aveline
(1702–1760), etcher
Marguerite Chéreau, publisher
*L'Enseigne*, 1732
Etching and etching needle
Sheet: 57.2 × 84.3 cm
Ville de Genève, Musées d'art et d'histoire
Inv. no.: E 2002-0693

**299** Page 106
Bernard Baron (1696–1762), etcher
*Les deux cousines*, before 1755
The two cousins
Etching and etching needle
Plate: 34 × 38.7 cm
Sheet: 40 × 45.9 cm
Ville de Genève, Musées d'art et d'histoire
Inv. no.: E 2011-0097

**300** Page 71
**Jan Weenix (1642–1719)**
*The white peacock*, 1693
Oil on canvas, 192.5 × 167.5 cm
Paintings Gallery, Academy of Fine Arts Vienna
GG-632

**Erwin Wurm (b. 1954)**

**301** Page 290
*Untitled (Cathérine Seifert)*
From the series *Hamlet*, 2007
C-Print, framed, 159.1 × 126.5 cm
Kunsthaus Zürich, Collection of Photography,
donated by the artist
PH 2007/3

**302** Page 298
*Hermès sculpture*, 2008
Wood, resin, clothes, leather
194 × 33 × 52 cm
Private collection

**303** Pages 254/255
**Andreas Züst (1947–2000)**
*Lady Shiva*
From the series *Menschen, Tiere,
Abendteuer, Lady Shiva*, 1973–83
9 black-and-white photographs on
Baryta paper, 23.7 × 15.8 cm each
Estate of Andreas Züst with
Mara Züst, Zurich
Courtesy Galerie & Edition
Marlene Frei, Zurich

**Christoph Becker (b. 1960)** studied art history and German studies at universities in Stuttgart, Vienna and Munich and wrote his dissertation on the history of the museum in the age of Enlightenment. He worked as an editor at the Gerd Hatje publishing house and also at *documenta 9* and the *Venice Biennale.* Becker was Senior Curator for art of the nineteenth century at the Staatsgalerie Stuttgart with exhibitions on Johann Heinrich Füssli (Henry Fuseli), Paul Gauguin and Camille Pissarro. Since 2000, Christoph Becker has been the Director of the Kunsthaus Zürich and has curated exhibitions on Claude Monet, Félix Vallotton, George Seurat and The Nahmad Collection. He is involved in the planning of the Kunsthaus's expansion by Sir David Chipperfield, which is currently under construction.

**Sonja Eismann (b. 1973)** is a journalist and cultural scientist who lives in Berlin. She studied comparative literature, English and Romance studies at the Universities of Vienna, Mannheim, Dijon and Santa Cruz, California. She is the co-founder of the magazine *nylon. KunstStoff zu Feminismus und Popkultur* 1999 in Vienna. Eismann worked from 2002 to 2007 as an editor at the pop culture magazine *Intro* and published in 2007 the anthology *Hot Topic: Popfeminismus heute.* In 2008, she founded *Missy Magazine* with Chris Köver and Steffi Lohaus. She is a freelance author who has written for *Spex, konkret, Pop-Zeitschrift* and *Deutschlandradio,* and has taught at the Universities of Paderborn, Basel and Salzburg as well as the Academy of Fine Arts Vienna and the University of the Arts Bremen. Sonja Eismann is a member of the Advisory Board of the Music Department of the Goethe Institute as well as the Göttingen Centre for Gender Studies. Research interests include representation of gender in popular culture, current feminist discourses and fashion theory.

**Nora Gomringer (b. 1980)** published her first volume of poetry in 2000, followed by seven others, as well as two volumes of essays, short stories, radio plays, narrative texts and librettos. Her texts have been translated into many languages: Spanish, Belarussian, English and many more. Most recently, she has published the 'Trilogy of Surfaces & Invisibilities': *Monster Poems* (2013), *Morbus* (2015) and *MODEN* (2017), the collection of spoken texts *Achduje* (2015), the *Lockbuch* (2015) that includes her own photographs, and the texts of the Herzau photobook *Bamberg Symphony* (2016). Since 2010, she has been directing the international artist house Villa Concordia in Bamberg, shooting poetry films, participating in exhibitions, and working closely with jazz drummers Philipp Scholz and Günter 'Baby' Sommer. Gomringer has received numerous awards, the Ingeborg Bachmann Prize 2015, the Goethe Institute's residence scholarship in the Villa Kamogawa in Kyoto in 2016 and most recently, with Philipp Scholz, the Honorary Poetry Professorship of the University of Klagenfurt in 2018.
www.nora-gomringer.de

**Cathérine Hug (b. 1976)** graduated with a MA in art history, computer science and journalism from the University of Zurich. Between 2000 and 2007, she was a project-related curatorial assistant at the Kunsthaus Zürich. As a freelance curator she was responsible for the exhibitions: *In The Alps* (2006) with Tobia Bezzola, *Carola Giedion-Welcker and Modernism* (2007) at the Kunsthaus Zürich; *Bunker: Unloaded* (2003) with Giovanni Carmine in bunkers of Oberschan and *Celebrate Life!* (2016) with Robert Menasse at the Kunsthistorisches Museum in Vienna. From 2005 to 2008, she was Assistant Art Unlimited at the *Art Basel,* from 2008 to 2013 curator at the Kunsthalle in Vienna, and curated there, among others, *1989: End of History or Beginning of the Future?* (2009) with Gerald Matt, *Space: About a Dream* (2011), *WWTBD – What Would Thomas Bernhard Do* and *Salon der Angst* (both 2013) with Nicolaus Schafhausen. Since 2013 she has been a curator at the Kunsthaus Zürich, where she worked on, among others, *Europe: The Future of History* (2015) with Robert Menasse, and *Dadaglobe Reconstructed* with Adrian Sudhalter and *Francis Picabia: A Retrospective* with Anne Umland, the latter two exhibitions which were subsequently featured at the MoMA in New York.

**Janine Jakob (b. 1979)** graduated with a MA in journalism and communication sciences, economic and social history and political science with a focus on international relations from the University of Zurich. She also studied economics at the University of St. Gallen. She is currently doing her doctorate at the University of Basel on the subject of women's fashion of the social elite in Zurich, Basel and Lucerne from 1650 to 1789, during which she researches and examines the material culture of clothing and accessories based on urban regulations on fashion, pictorial representations and realia in terms of cultural and social history. In addition to her work as a journalist, on the occasion of the 80th anniversary of the Swiss women's magazine *Annabelle,* she explored its beginnings and first years of 1938 to 1945.

**Elfriede Jelinek (b. 1946)** is a writer who grew up in Vienna and lives in Munich. In addition to plays, poetry, essays, translations, radio plays, scripts and librettos, her work includes the novels *Die Liebhaberinnen* (Women as Lovers, 1975), *Die Ausgesperrten* (Wonderful, Wonderful Times, 1980), *Die Klavierspielerin* (The Piano Teacher, 1983), *Lust* (1989), *Die Kinder der Toten* (The Children of the Dead, 1995) and *Gier* (Greed, 2000). Elfriede Jelinek has been awarded, among others, the Österreichischen Staatsstipendium für Literatur (1973), the Drehbuchpreis des Bundesinnenministeriums der Bundesrepublik Deutschland (1979), the Heinrich-Böll-Preis der Stadt Köln (1986), the Peter-Weiss-Preis der Stadt Bochum and the Walter-Hasenclever-Literaturpreis der Stadt Aachen (both 1994), the Georg Büchner Prize (1998), the Theaterpreis Berlin 2002, the Heine-Preis der Landeshauptstadt Düsseldorf (2002), the Mülheimer Dramatikerpreis (2002, 2004, 2009, 2011), the Stig Dagermann Prize (2004), the Lessing Prize for Criticism (2004) and the Franz Kafka Prize (2004). In 2004, Elfriede Jelinek received the Nobel Prize for Literature.
www.elfriedejelinek.com

**Inessa Kouteinikova (b. 1968)** is an independent art and architecture historian and curator, living between Russia and the Netherlands. She studied in Moscow, New York (Columbia and Cornell Universities), London (Architectural Association), Maastricht and Delft University (PhD). Kouteinikova is currently working on an exhibition on dandyism. Her other scholarly interests include Russian and international orientalism, early colonial photography and the emergence of the photographic industry in Central Asia, focussing on the cultural and artistic life of the region under the Russian rule. Kouteinikova has worked on exhibitions such as *Stroganoff: The Palace and Collections of a Russian Noble Family* (Kimbell Art Museum, Fort Worth, 2000), *Cold War Modern: Design 1945–70* (Victoria and Albert Museum, 2008/09), *Russia's Unknown Orient: Orientalist painting 1850–1920* (Groningen Museum, 2010/11) and most recently, *The Apple: Between Guilt and Innocence* (Museum de Buitenplaats, 2016).

**Monica Kurzel-Runtscheiner (b. 1965)** studied history and art history in Vienna and Rome. She is a member of the Institute for Austrian Historical Research and a lecturer in women's history at the University of Vienna. From 1993 to 2000, she was a curator and since 2001 has been Director at the Kunsthistorisches Museum Wien (Wagenburg and Monturdepot). Since 2001 she has also been head of numerous research projects, and from 2005 consultant for international research institutions. Publications include *Costumes à la Cour de Vienne* (1815–1918), exh. cat. Les Musées de la ville de Paris, Palais Galliera (1995, together with Georg J. Kugler); *Der Kongress fährt: Leihwagen, Lustfahrten und Luxus-Outfits am Wiener Kongress 1814/15,* exh. Kaiserliche Wagenburg Vienna (2014).

**Peter McNeil (b. 1966)** is Distinguished Professor of Design History at the University of Technology Sydney and Distinguished Professor at Aalto University. McNeil trained in History of Art with dissertations on interior design and fashion culture. His many publications include the award-winning *The Fashion History Reader: Global Perspectives* (2010) (with Giorgio Riello); and *Fashion: Critical and Primary Sources, Renaissance to the Present Day,* 4 vols. (2009). McNeil was an Investigator in the *Humanities in the European Research Area* project 'Fashioning the Early Modern: Creativity and Innovation in Europe, 1500–1800' and currently holds a major Academy of Finland research position. As *Membre suppléant,* Comité International d'Histoire de l Art (CIHA), he was Foundation Professor of Fashion Studies at Stockholm University 2008–2017, which did much to establish the dignity of the discipline in the humanities. He is a Fellow of the Australian Academy of the Humanities and its Section Head for 'The Arts'. His monograph *'Pretty Gentlemen': Macaroni Men and the Eighteenth-Century Fashion World* is published by Yale University Press in 2018.

**Aileen Ribeiro (b. 1944)** studied history at King's College, London, followed by postgraduate study (MA and PhD) at the Courtauld Institute of Art, University of London. She was Head of the History of Dress Section at the Courtauld Institute from 1975 to 2009; appointed Professor in the History of Art at the University of London in 2000, she is now Professor Emeritus. Her particular interests lie in the many different ways artists depict clothing in their work, and this is reflected in her many publications including contributions as costume consultant/contributor to major art exhibitions. Among her books are: *The Art of Dress: Fashion in England and France 1750–1820* (1995) *Dress and Morality* (1986, 2003); *Fashion and Fiction. Dress in Art and Literature in Stuart England* (2006); *Facing Beauty. Painted Women and Cosmetic Art* (2011). Her most recent book is *Clothing Art. The Visual Culture of Fashion 1600–1914* (2017), winner of the *Apollo* Book of the Year Award 2017.

**Franz Schuh (b. 1947)** completed his studies of philosophy, history and German in 1975 with a doctoral dissertation entitled *Hegel und die Logik der Praxis.* He is a lecturer at the University of Applied Arts in Vienna and a columnist for magazines and radio stations. His publications include, among others, *Der Krückenkaktus: Erinnerungen an die Liebe, die Kunst und den Tod* (2011), *Sämtliche Leidenschaften* (2014) and recently *Fortuna: Aus dem Magazin des Glücks* (2017). Franz Schuh has been honoured with, among others, the Preis der Stadt Wien für Publizistik (1987), the Jean Améry Prize (2000), the Prize of the Leipzig Book Fair in the category nonfiction/essay writing (2006), the Swiss Media Prize Davos for exceptional achievements in journalism (2003), the Tractatus-Preis des Philosophicum Lech (2009), the Goldenen Ehrenzeichen für Verdienste um das Land Wien (2009), the Österreichischer Kunstpreis für Literatur (2011) and, most recently, the Paul Watzlawick Ehrenring of the Vienna Medical Association (2017).

**Werner Telesko (b. 1965)** studied art history and history at the University of Vienna, where he received his doctorate in 1993 and his habilitation in 2000. Between 1988 and 1990, he worked at the Austrian Historical Institute in Rome, between 1990 and 1993 in the art collections of the Benedictine monastery Göttweig (Lower Austria). Since 1993 he has worked at the Austrian Academy of Sciences, since 2013 as Director of the Institute for Art and Music-Historical Research (IKM). Most of his research has been devoted to the eighteenth and nineteenth centuries, most recently addressing questions of the interrelation between cultural production and identity creation (2006: *Geschichtsraum Österreich;* 2008: *Kulturraum Österreich*). His current research mainly concerns the Habsburg culture of representation in various image and text media as well as the analysis of the reign of Maria Theresa (*Maria Theresia: Ein europäischer Mythos,* 2006).

**Katharina Tietze (b. 1968)** studied clothing design at the College of Fine Arts in Berlin, worked at the Theaterhaus Jena as a costume designer and was a member of the department for fashions and public appearance at the Bauhaus University Weimar. She has been Professor of Design at the Zurich University of the Arts since 2006 and leads the study programme Style & Design. She conducts research on fashion in the context of tension between style and everyday culture. Publications include: *Über Schuhe: Zur Geschichte und Theorie der Fussbekleidung* (2016), ed. with Anna-Brigitte Schlittler; *Mode und Bewegung: Beiträge zur Geschichte und Theorie der Kleidung* (2013), ed. with Anna-Brigitte Schlittler; *Denimpop: Jeansdinge lesen* (2013), ed. with Katharina Hohmann; *Kleider in Räumen* (2009), ed. with Anna-Brigitte Schlittler.

**Barbara Vinken (b. 1960)** has been Professor of Comparative Literature and Romance Philology at the Ludwig-Maximilians-University Munich since 2004 and is an expert in fashion theory. She earned her doctorate in Konstanz in 1989 and at Yale in 1991. In 1996 she completed her habilitation in Jena. Before she moved to the LMU, she was appointed to Romanist chairs in Hamburg and Zurich. As a visiting professor, she has taught, for instance, at Humboldt University Berlin, Freie Universität Berlin, EHESS Paris, NYU, Johns Hopkins University, University of Chicago, the Institute for Advanced Study in Berlin and the ENS Paris. Her bestseller *Angezogen: Das Geheimnis der Mode* (2013) was nominated for the Leipzig Book Fair Prize. In 2016, she published her anthology *Die Blumen der Mode: Klassische und neue Texte zur Philosophie der Mode.* Barbara Vinken writes regularly for *DIE ZEIT* and *NZZ* and is part of the panel discussion in *3sat Buchzeit;* her fashion column *Stilfältig* at Radio Bremen is always broadcasted on Wednesdays.

**Philipp Zitzlsperger (b. 1965)** studied art history, archaeology and modern history in Munich and Rome, and wrote his doctoral thesis on portraits of the Pope and rulers by Gian Lorenzo Bernini (2002). From 2002 to 2010, he was a research associate at the art history department of the Humboldt University in Berlin and conducted research on Roman sepulchral culture. In 2007, he completed his habilitation at Humboldt University in Berlin on the subject *Kleider sprechen Bände: Kostümkunde als Methode der Kunstgeschichte erläutert an Beispielen von Crivelli, Dürer, Giorgione, Tizian, Raffael und Bernini* and presents, above all, vestimentary, art historical research work, which examines the correlation between image and life reality. Since the summer of 2010, Zitzlsperger has been Professor of Image Science at the Hochschule Fresenius, Department of Design (AMD) in Berlin and researches the history of art and design of the early modern and modern period.

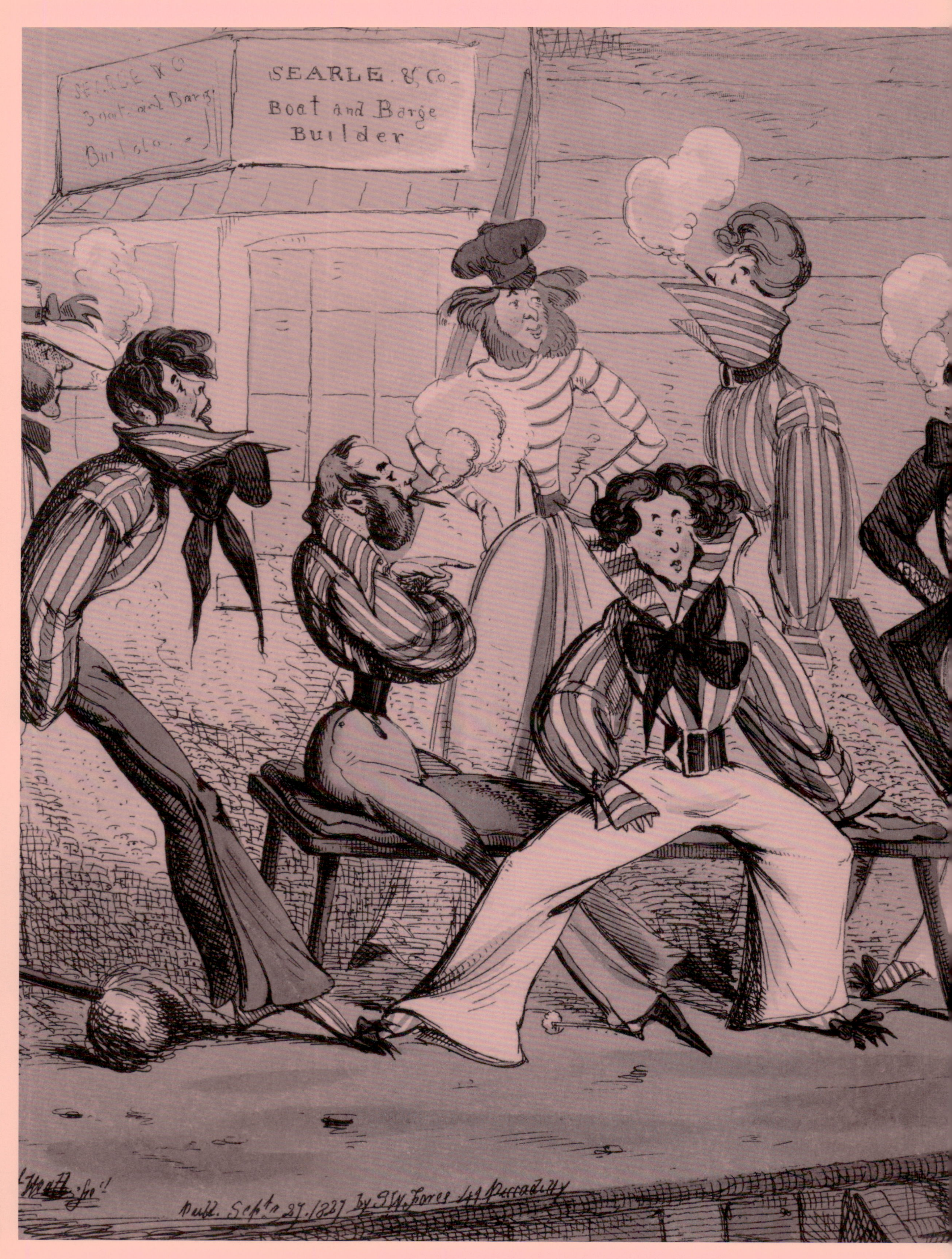

SEARLE & Co
Boat and Barge
Builder
SEARLE & Co
Boat and Barge
Builder
Publd. Septr. 27. 1827 by G.W. Fores 41 Piccadilly

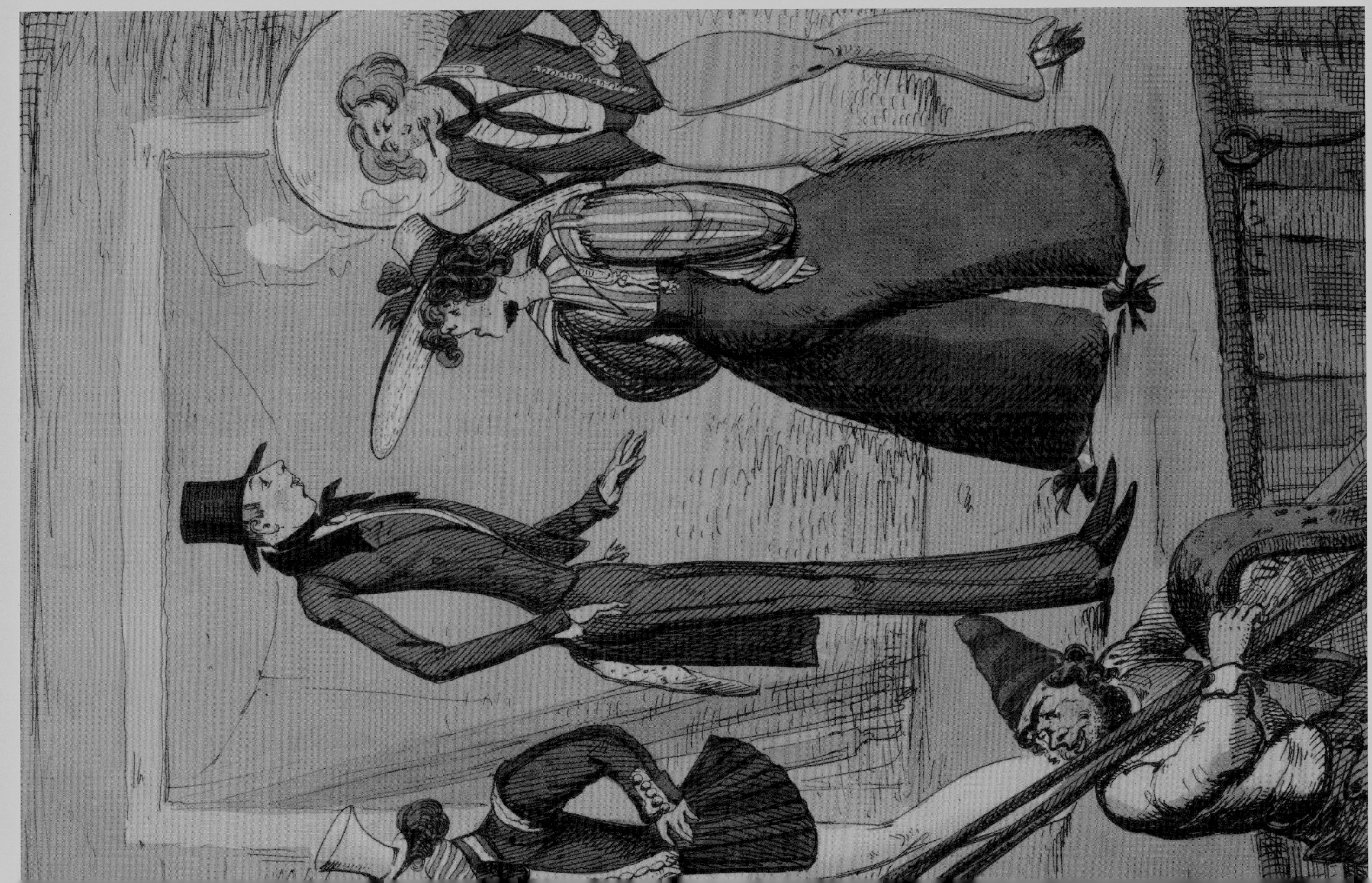

**169** William Heath (1795–1840)
*Poodles preparing for an aquatic excursion,*
27 September 1827
Etching, hand-coloured with watercolours
Sheet: 23.9 × 33.6 cm
Staatliche Museen zu Berlin,
Kunstbibliothek

Gingi Beck berichtet von der Seine:

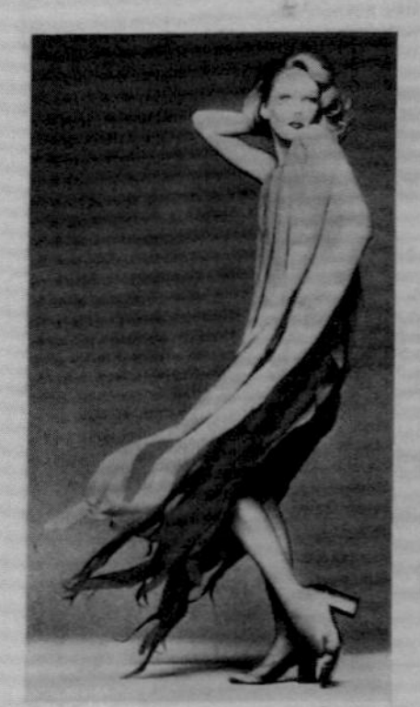

# Ist Paris als Modemetropole noch aktuell?

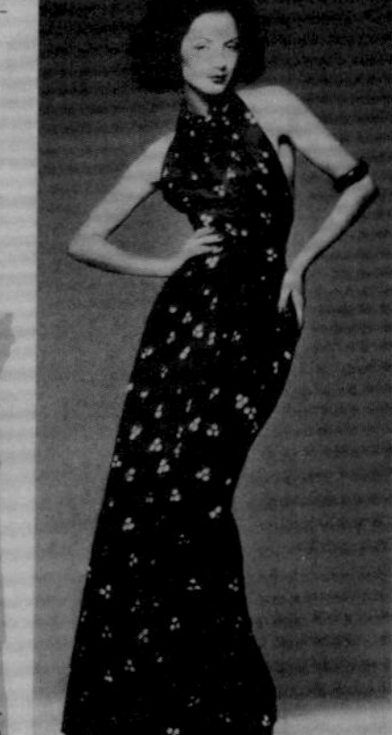

Zu Beginn jeder neuen Saison blickt die Welt nach Paris. Television, Radio, Presse — sowohl Illustrierte als auch alle andern Druckerzeugnisse — vermitteln Männern und Frauen Informationen in Wort und Bild. Im gleichen Masse wie die Informationsflut der Massenmedien, die zu unserem Alltag gehören, angestiegen ist, sinkt die Autorität der Pariser Haute Couture. Ist es ein Zeichen unserer autoritätsfeindlichen Zeit? Dem Widerstand gegen Hierarchien zuzuschreiben? Hat die Pariser Haute Couture ausgespielt? Könnte man sich den zweimal jährlichen, mehrtägigen Modemarathon mit drei bis sechs Kollektionen im Tag nicht sparen? Sollte es zutreffen, dass die Haute Couture seit langem stirbt und Paris als Modemetropole abgedankt hat?

**Die Haute Couture ist eine Institution des 19. Jahrhunderts**

Ihre Blütezeit ist vorüber. Die Haute Couture hat sich während der vergangenen Jahre manchmal aufgeführt wie eine Frau, die es nicht versteht mit Würde älter zu werden. Im Bestreben, möglichst lange jung zu scheinen, ist sozusagen ein Faux-pas nach dem andern unvermeidlich gewesen. Denn bekanntlich gibt es wenig, was lächerlicher und gefährlicher ist, als nicht älter werden zu können. Das gilt für alle Bereiche des Lebens, weil Wandlung nicht unbedingt Anpassung sein muss. Für Paris verdeutlicht: Produktions- und Strukturreformen waren notwendig. Die Frau von 1972 stellt an die Mode andere Ansprüche.

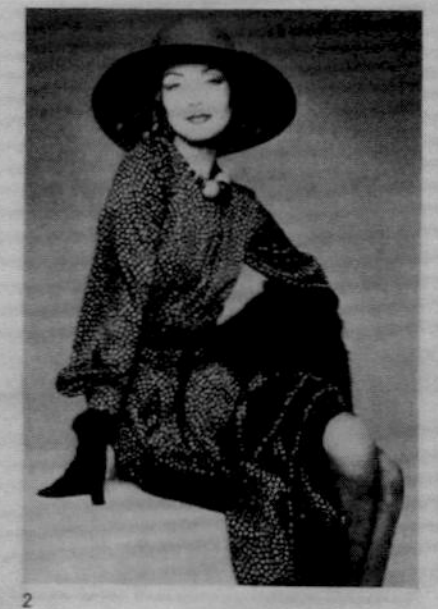

**Mode ist ein Spiegel ihrer Zeit —**

aber sie ist nicht mehr wie früher Zeichen des Standes, der gesellschaftlichen Funktion, kurz, wie wir heute zu sagen pflegen: «Statussymbol». Das Leben der Frauen hat sich — sehr rasch seit dem Zweiten Weltkrieg — verändert. Gewiss, in der Welt draussen, in Paris z. B., wo jede dritte Frau eine alleinstehende, berufstätige Frau ist (ledig, geschieden, verlassen oder verwitwet), sieht es anders aus als bei uns. In Paris ist man mit alleinstehenden Frauen im Restaurant ganz besonders liebenswürdig, bei uns noch meist ungehörig bis arrogant ... Frauen, die arbeiten, haben immer einen sehr anstrengenden Alltag. Denn mit oder ohne Familie wartet auf die Frau noch der Haushalt. Der Arbeitsweg hat sich verlängert, der Horizont erweitert. Hausfrauen kehren in ihren Beruf zurück — Berufstätige kompensieren durch ihre Tätigkeit oftmals andere Lücken in ihrem Leben. Die Frau, während Tausenden von Jahren einer bestimmten [...]

man ebensowenig in den Wind schlagen, wie man Traditionen verdammen sollte!

**Vermännlichung der Frau oder Verzicht auf Mode?**

*Ein Hauch von Star, eine Prise dreissiger Jahre, denn auf den Blick zurück in die Vergangenheit hat Paris nie ganz verzichtet. Auch Marilyn-Monroe-Impressionen, überhaupt Hollywoods untergegangene Starzeit kehrt in diesem rosefarbenen Dégradé-Abendkleid zurück. Sonst ist Cardin einer der zeitgemassen Modeschöpfer von Paris, er fabriziert von der Schokoladenpackung bis zu Herrenmode vieles, subventioniert ein avantgardistisches Theater und stellt Prêt à porter in grossen Mengen für die ganze Welt her.*
Modell Cardin
Tissu Abraham
Foto Barbieri

(2)

*Ein grossartiges schwarz-fuchsia Satin-Imprimékleid. Die Bezeichnung «Nachmittagskleid» allerdings ist überlebt — viel eher eine Robe für festliche Stunden. Der schlichte Chemiseschnitt — Favorit der Saison — steht in raffiniertem Kontrast zum kostbaren, übrigens aus der Schweiz stammenden Seidengewebe. Grosse Hüte sind zwar atemberaubend elegant, doch nicht einmal mehr bei Königin Elisabeth Vorschrift. Im Alltag sind sie fehl am Platz — für gesellschaftliche Ereignisse, wie Hochzeiten usw. richtig.*
Modell Dior, Paris
Stoff Abraham, Zürich-Paris-New York
Foto Barbieri

(3)

*Saint-Laurent beschränkt sich auf Prêt-à-porter-Kollektionen und einige wenige Modelle für seine Privatkundinnen. Dieses, in den Farben Braun Sand besonders raffinierte Imprimé auf weichem reinseiden Crêpe de Chine wäre ohne die Straussenfedergarnitur, die demimondaine wirkt, sehr klassisch. Ob man mit oder ohne Federn auftritt: die einfachen Schnitte dominierten diesmal auch in der Haute Couture — ein teures «understatement» hat um sich gegriffen.*
Modell St Laurent, Paris
Südafrikanische Straussenfedern
Foto JWT Paris

(4)

*Den Zeitgeist erfasst zu haben scheint Michel Goma im Hause Patou. Mit Jersey, Rot und Blau wird dieser praktische und jugendliche Mantel kombiniert. Die Längen spielen ums Knie, auch die vielen Chasublekleider, ärmellos mit schwarzen Blusen getragen, sind eine der Varianten von Goma. So inspiriert Paris noch immer die Mode.*

(5)

*Die langen Abendkleider sind ebenfalls Legion in Paris, und man fragt sich, wo die vielen Bälle überhaupt noch stattfinden werden? Gerade tagsüber sachlich arbeitende Frauen lieben es, sich für einen festlichen Anlass zurückzuverwandeln — und vielleicht ein bisschen davon zu träumen, weniger tüchtig als behütet sein zu dürfen. Das hat die Haute Couture erfasst, auch wenn es vermutlich nicht zum Überleben genügen wird ...*
Modell Dior
Tissu Abraham
Foto Barbieri

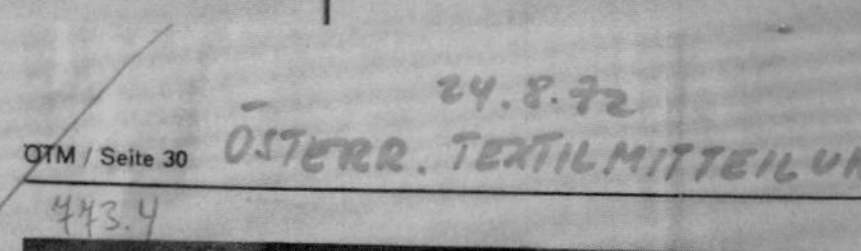

OTM / Seite 30    24.8.72    ÖSTERR. TEXTILMITTEILUN[GEN]    443.4

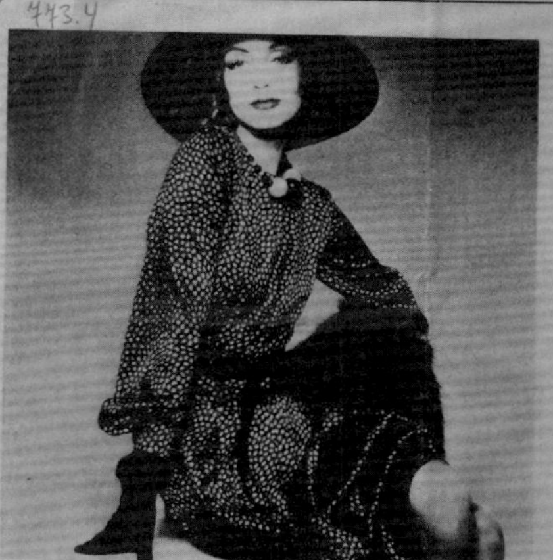

Weichfallendes, elegantes Nachmittagskleid aus Satin Imprimé in den Farben Schwarz/Fuchsie von Dior. Material: Abraham & Co, Seiden AG, Zürich.

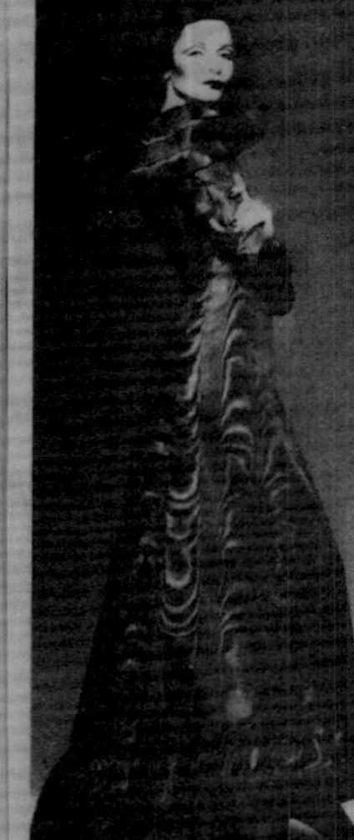

Große Abendrobe mit eleganter Kragenlösung aus Faille Moire von Givenchy. Material: Abraham, Zürich.

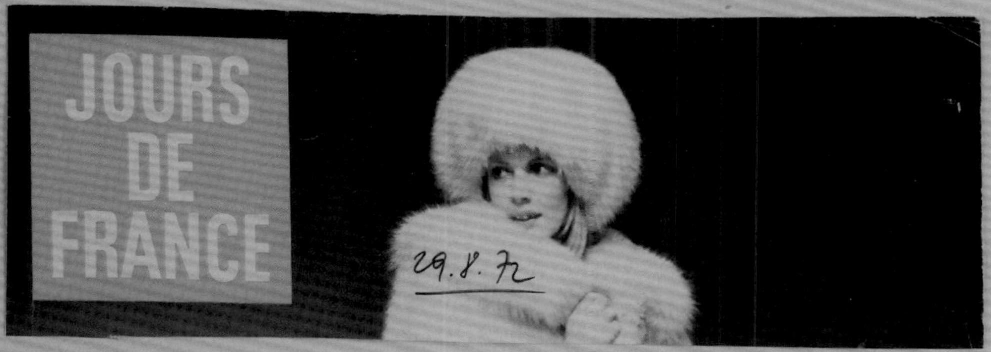


29.8.72

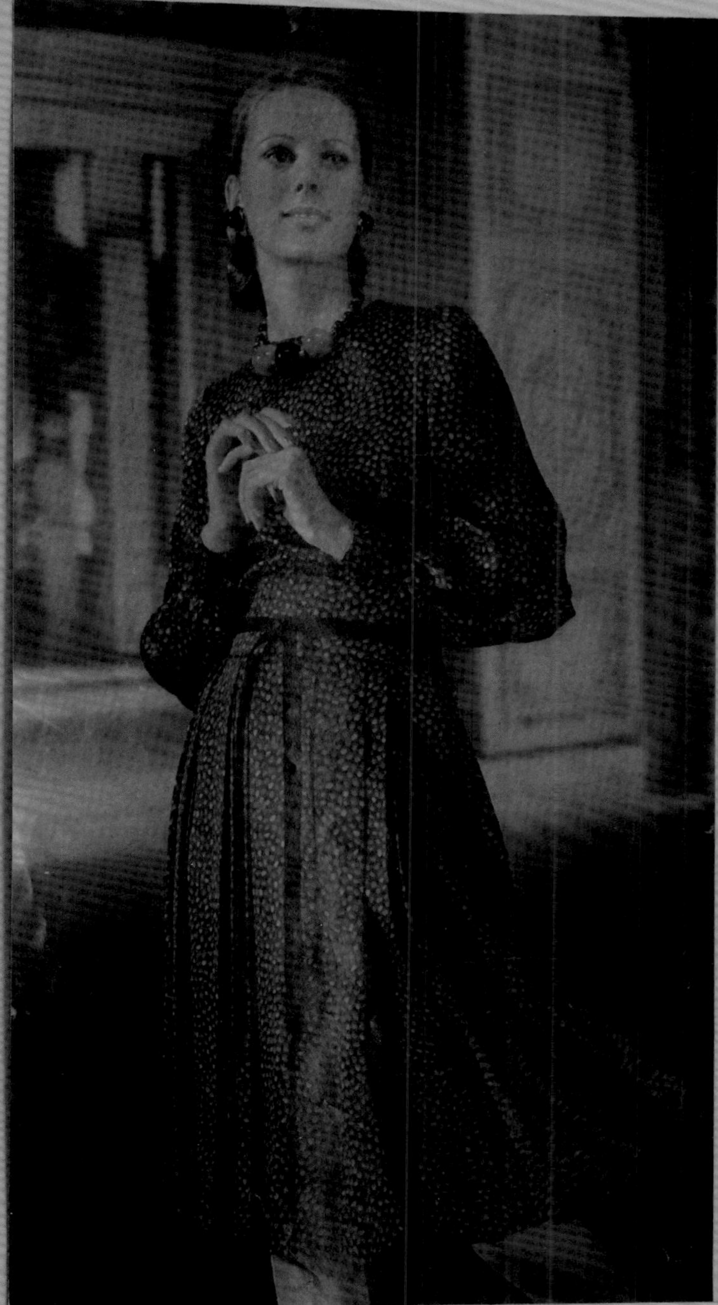

# DIOR

Robe de cocktail en soie
imprimée, la jupe est for-
mée de plis plats. Cor-
sage souple et blousant.
←

Ensemble pantalon en
satin, le chemisier à man-
ches longues est fluide,
le pantalon est évasé.
→

© 2017 LIECHTENSTEIN, The Princely Collections, Vaduz-Vienna/SCALA, Florence: cat. 218; 239; 265

© 2018 Charles Atlas. Courtesy Electronic Arts Intermix (EAI), New York: cat. 46

© Bibliothèque nationale de France: fig. 10, p. 123

© Charles Ray, Courtesy Matthew Marks Gallery: cat. 233

© Château de Versailles, Dist. RMN-Grand Palais / Christophe Fouin: fig. 1, p. 102

© Courtesy Maison Schiaparelli, Paris / Victoria and Albert Museum, London: cat. 27

© Erwin Wurm: cat. 301; 302

© Esther Eppstein, message salon: cat. 131

© Gemäldegalerie, Staatliche Museen zu Berlin, Preussischer Kulturbesitz, photography: Jörg P. Anders: cat. 61

© Hessische Hausstiftung, Kronberg im Taunus: cat. 292

© Historic England Archive: cat. 192

© Inez van Lamsweerde and Vinoodh Matadin, Courtesy Gagosian Gallery: cat. 190; 191; fig. 3, p. 63

© Konzett Gallery: cat. 59; 60

© MBA, Rennes, Dist. RMN-Grand Palais / Jean-Manuel Salingue: cat. 297

© MuMa Le Havre / David Fogel: cat. 279

© Musée d'Orsay, Dist. RMN-Grand Palais / Patrice Schmidt: fig. 2, p. 165

© Musées d'art et d'histoire, Ville de Genève, Cabinet d'arts graphiques / n° inv. E 2012-0454-018: cat. 296 / n° inv. E 2002-0693: cat. 298 / n° inv. E 2011-0097, photography: André Longchamp: cat. 299

© Nachlass Andreas Züst / Graphische Sammlung, Schweizerische Nationalbibliothek: cat. 303

© National Portrait Gallery, London: cat. 78; 79; 247; fig. 1, p. 164

© Paris, Les Arts Décoratifs / Jean Tholance: fig. 5, p. 120

© Peter Lindbergh (Courtesy Peter Lindbergh, Paris): cat. 199–205

© RMN-Grand Palais:

Château de Versailles / droits réservés: cat. 67 / Gérard Blot: cat. 194; fig. 1, p. 89 / Franck Raux: cat. 195 / Daniel Arnaudet / Gérard Blot: fig. 6, p. 121; Musée du Louvre / Thierry Le Mage: cat. 291; Musée d'Orsay / Hervé Lewandowski: cat. 64; fig. 4, p. 2000;

Agence Bulloz: fig. 11, p. 123

© Staatliche Graphische Sammlung München: fig. 1, p. 62

© Staatliche Museen zu Berlin: Kunstbibliothek, photography: Dietmar Katz: cat. 74; 81–85; 106; 107; 117; 140–142; 150-154; 155; 169; 170; 179; 181; 228; 231; 232; 267-269; 270–273; 277; 278; Nationalgalerie, photography: Andres Kilger: cat. 188

© Tamara Art Heritage / ADAGP; RMN-Grand Palais / Gérard Blot: cat. 198

© Tate, London 2017: cat. 240

© The National Gallery, London: cat. 128

© The Trustees of the British Museum: fig. 4, p. 120; fig. 12, p. 124

© Trinity Mirror / Mirrorpix / Alamy Stock Photo: fig. 5, p. 49

© Victoria and Albert Museum, London: cat. 41; 42; 80

© Ville de Liège – Musée des Beaux-Arts de la Boverie: fig. 3, p. 133

© Ville de Perpignan: fig. 3, p. 119

© Wien Museum: cat 274-276

bpk:

fig. 2, p. 44; fig. 2, p. 63; Bayerische Staatsgemäldesammlungen: cat. 294; Bayerische Staatsgemäldesammlungen, Sammlung HypoVereinsbank, Member of UniCredit: fig. 3, p. 199; Deutsches Historisches Museum, Sebastian Ahlers: fig. 5, p. 134; Klassik Stiftung Weimar, Uwe Golle: fig. 1, p. 132;

Museumslandschaft Hessen Kassel: fig. 4, p. 64; Napoleonmuseum, Daniel Steiner: fig. 2, p. 132; Stiftung Preussische Schlösser und Gärten Berlin-Brandenburg, Jörg P. Anders: fig. 4, p. 133

Cecil Beaton/Vogue © Conde Nast: cat. 28

Chris Moore/© Catwalking.com: fig. 4, p. 187

Courtesy Ashley Hans Scheirl: p. 178

Courtesy Barbara Kruger and Sprüth Magers: fig. 2, p. 269

Courtesy Beat Huber: cat. 180

Courtesy Biagiotti Cigna Foundation: cat. 48–53; 55–58

Courtesy Claude Lê-Anh: cat. 224

Courtesy Daniele Buetti: cat. 68–73

Courtesy Diane Simpson and Corbett vs. Dempsey, Chicago, JTT, New York, and Herald St., London, photography: Tom Van Eynde: fig. 2, p. 186

Courtesy Eva Kotátková and Jiří Kovanda: cat. 178

Courtesy Galerie Carzaniga: cat. 75

Courtesy Hahnloser / Jaeggli Foundation: cat. 289

Courtesy Hans-Peter Feldmann and Galerie Francesca Pia, Zurich, photography: Franca Candrian: cat. 135

Courtesy Herlinde Koelbl: cat. 186

Courtesy James Rosenquist Studio / Steve Schapiro: cat. 237

Courtesy John Baldessari and Marian Goodman Gallery, photography: Marc Domage: cat. 47

Courtesy K8 Hardy and Karma International, Zurich and Los Angeles: cat. 168

Courtesy Kim Jones: cat. 34–36; 38

Courtesy Library of Congress Prints and Photographs Division, Washington / Bain News Service, LC-DIG-ggbain-33940: cat 261

Courtesy Mai-Thu Perret and Galerie Francesca Pia, Zurich, photography: Bernhard Schaub: cat. 227

Courtesy Martin Kamer: cat. 25/ photographer: Reto Rodolfo Pedrini, Zürich: cat. 156–164; 229

Courtesy Michael E. Smith and KOW, Berlin: cat. 243; 244

Courtesy Michelangelo Pistoletto and Galleria Continua, San Gimignano / Beijing / Les Moulins / Habana / Installation view: Abu Dhabi Art Fair, 2013, photography: Lorenzo Fiaschi: cat. 230

Courtesy Museum of Fine Arts, Budapest: cat. 211

Courtesy Nik Emch and Marky Edelmann, photography: FBM Studio: cat 129

Courtesy Parkett: cat. 225

Courtesy Private collection Vienna: cat. 23; 24

Courtesy Private collection, Basel: cat. 220-223

Courtesy Private Collection, photography: Janine Jakob: cat. 143; 172; 184; 214; 217a; 217b

Courtesy Private Collection, Switzerland: cat. 86

Courtesy Private collection: cat. 19; fig. 1, p. 197

Courtesy Sammlung Kamer-Ruf: 3–7; 15; 16; 26 / photography: Reto Rodolfo Pedrini, Zürich: fig. 1, p. 183

Courtesy Spielzeug Welten Museum Basel: cat. 17; 18

Courtesy Stampa Galerie, Basel: cat. 145–149

Courtesy Sylvie Fleury and Karma International, Zurich and Los Angeles: cat. 137–139

Courtesy the artist & Galerie Gregor Staiger, Zürich, © Shana Moulton: cat. 219

Courtesy The Lewis Walpole Library, Yale University: fig. 3, p. 46

Courtesy The Paintings Gallery of the Academy of Fine Arts Vienna: cat. 210; 300

Courtesy Tobias Kaspar and Galerie Peter Kilchmann, Zurich: cat. 183 b / Installation view: Blue Times, Kunsthalle Wien 2014 / Georg Petermichl: cat. 183 a

Courtesy Tula Roy and Christoph Wirsing: cat. 238

Courtesy Wolfgang Tillmans and Galerie Buchholz, Berlin: cat. 251–253; 256; 258

Courtesy Yale Center for British Art: fig. 1, p. 118

Courtesy Young Kim, Estate of Malcolm McLaren: cat. 40

Courtesy Zurich University of the Arts, ZHdK / Media and Information Centre MIZ, Zurich: cat. 21

Fondation Félix Vallotton, Lausanne: cat. 280; 290; fig. 1, p. 267

Hikone Castle Museum: fig. 1, p. 42

Historisches Museum Basel, photography: N. Jansen: cat. 165 / photography: P. Portner: cat. 8

Jean-Luc Baroni Ltd.: cat. 63

KHM-Museumsverband: cat. 1; 2: 9–11; 13; 43; 77; 136; 171; fig. 8, p. 122; fig. 1–3, p. 152; fig. 4, p. 153; fig. 6-8, p. 154;

Kunsthaus Zürich: cat. 20; 22; 44; 54; 62; 66; 76; 90–92; 95; 100; 103; 105; 122; 123; 125; 132–134; 144; 149; 166; 167; 173; 177; 178; 182; 189; 212; 213; 234–236; 245; 248; 262; 263; 281; 282; 285; 287; 288; 293; fig. 6, p. 67

mumok, Museum moderner Kunst Stiftung Ludwig Wien: p. 301

Museum für Gestaltung Zürich, Grafiksammlung, ZHdK: cat. 108–116

ÖNB/Wien / FKB Vues Wien II, Burg 22: cat. 242 / Pk 187, 12: cat. 176 / Pk 187, 13: cat. 175 / Pk 270, 11: cat. 174 / Pk 400, 520: cat. 246

Paris, Les Arts Décoratifs / Jean Tholance: cat. 65

Reproduced by courtesy of the Harewood House Trust: fig. 2, p. 119

Royal Collection Trust/ © Her Majesty Queen Elizabeth II 2017: fig. 7, p. 121; fig. 9, p. 122

Royal Museum of Fine Arts Antwerp © www. lukasweb.be – Art in Flanders vzw, photography: Hugo Maertens: fig. 5, p. 65

Schweizerisches Nationalmuseum / DIG-8266: cat. 30 / DIG-8623: cat 31 / DIG-8820: cat. 32 / DIG-8339: cat. 33 / DIG-6143: cat. 45 / DIG-25236: cat. 196 / DIG-25238: cat. 197 / DIG-43194: cat. 266 / DIG-7751: p. 217

St. Pölten, Niederösterreichisches Landesarchiv: fig. 5, p. 153

Textilmuseum Sankt Gallen, Sammlung John Jacoby-Iklé, photography: Jürg Zürcher, 2013: fig. 3, p. 186

The Weiss Gallery, London: cat. 130; 193; 226

© 2018 ProLitteris, Zurich, for the works by

Giacomo Balla, Joseph Beuys, Daniele Buetti, Hugo Erfurth, Max Ernst, Hans-Peter Feldmann, Natalja Gontscharowa, George Grosz, Hannah Höch, Manon, Meret Oppenheim, James Rosenquist, Henry van de Velde, Erwin Wurm

© The Andy Warhol Foundation for the Visual Arts, Inc. / 2018, ProLitteris, Zurich for the works by Andy Warhol

© Man Ray Trust / 2018, ProLitteris, Zurich for the works by Man Ray

© R. Hamilton. All Rights Reserved / 2018, ProLitteris, Zurich for the works by Richard Hamilton

© Salvador Dalí, Fundació Gala-Salvador Dalí / 2018, ProLitteris, Zurich for the works by Salvador Dalí

© 2018 Estate of Sonia Delaunay for the works by Sonia Delaunay

© 2018 for the works by

Paul Camenisch, Hussein Chalayan, Marky Edelmann, Nik Emch, Esther Eppstein, Sylvie Fleury, General Idea, Franz Gertsch, K8 Hardy, Emmy Hennings, Beat Huber, Tobias Kaspar, Jakob Lena Knebl, Herlinde Koelbl, Eva Kotátková, Jiří Kovanda, Barbara Kruger, Inez van Lamsweerde, Peter Lindbergh, Urs Lüthi, Auguste and Louis Lumière, Malcolm McLaren, Vinoodh Matadin, Shana Moulton, Anna Muthesius, Mai-Thu Perret, Michelangelo Pistoletto, Charles Ray, Tula Roy, Yves Saint Laurent, Ashley Hans Scheirl, Diane Simpson, Lady Shiva, Michael E. Smith, Wolfgang Tillmans, Madeleine Vionnet, Vivienne Westwood, Christoph Wirsing

with the artists or their estates

Image credits

**This book
is published in
conjunction with
the exhibition**

**Fashion Drive.
Extreme Clothing
in the Visual Arts**

Kunsthaus Zürich
20 April to 15 July 2018

Front Cover
Peter Lindbergh,
*Linda Evangelista, Christy
Turlington & Naomi Campbell,*
Brooklyn, 1990 (cat. 203)

Back Cover
Carle Vernet,
*Caricature d'un incroyable,*
undated (cat. 291)

## Exhibition

Curators
Cathérine Hug, Christoph Becker

Project Assistance
Carlotta Graedel Matthäi

Coordination
Franziska Lentzsch

Insurance and Transport
Gerda Kram

Restoration Supervision
Eva Glück, Tobias Haupt, Stella Lattanzi

Public Relations
Björn Quellenberg, Kristin Steiner

Sponsoring
Monique Spaeti

Technical Service
Robert Sulzer, Johann-Christoph Knospe,
Phillip Schmocker and Team

Architecture, Scenography
Ulrich Zickler

Graphic Design
Lena Huber

Audioguide
Sonja Eismann and Carin Cornioley

Children's Audioguide
Sibyl Kraft

## Catalogue

Editor
Zürcher Kunstgesellschaft/Kunsthaus Zürich

Idea and Concept
Cathérine Hug, Christoph Becker

Editing
Cathérine Hug, Carlotta Graedel Matthäi,
Franziska Lentzsch

Copyediting
Harold Otto

Translations
Alix Sharma-Weigold and
Bhesham Sharma (German-English)
Gitta Honegger for the text by
Elfriede Jelinek (German-English)
Stephen Sartarelli for *Manifest* by
Giacomo Balla (French-English)
Nelson Wattie for the text by
Meret Oppenheim (German-English)

Graphic Design and Lithography
Lena Huber

Typesetting
Lena Huber und Ralf Klöden,
Etc. pp. – Grafische Gestaltung

Documentation
Cécile Brunner

Project Management Kerber Verlag
Kathleen Herfurth

The Deutsche Nationalbibliothek lists
this publication in the Deutsche
Nationalbibliografie; detailed bibliographic
data are available on the Internet at
http://dnb.dnb.de.

Printed and published by:
Kerber Verlag, Bielefeld
Windelsbleicher Str. 166–170
33659 Bielefeld
Germany
Tel. +49 (0) 5 21/9 50 08-10
Fax +49 (0) 5 21/9 50 08-88
info@kerberverlag.com

ARTBOOK | D.A.P.
75 Broad Street, Suite 630
New York, NY 10004
USA
T: 001/212/6271999
F: 001/212/6279484

Kerber publications are available in
selected bookstores and museum shops
worldwide (distributed in Europe, Asia,
South and North America).

All rights reserved. No part of this publication
may be reproduced, translated, stored in
a retrieval system or transmitted in any form
or by any means, electronic, mechanical,
photocopying or recording or otherwise,
without the prior permission of the publisher.

© 2018 Zürcher Kunstgesellschaft/Kunsthaus
Zürich und Kerber Verlag, Bielefeld/Berlin

© 2018 Texts by the authors or
their legal representatives

© 2018 Illustrations, see picture credits

Museum Edition
978-3-906269-17-7

Trade Edition
978-3-7356-0433-0

www.kerberverlag.com

Printed in Germany

A collaboration with

**FESTSPIELE**ZÜRICH:

Supported by

ZÜRCHERISCHE
SEIDENINDUSTRIE
GESELLSCHAFT

Further sponsors

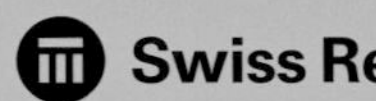

**Swiss Re**

Partner for contemporary art



Colophon